DIVINE TRUTH
OR
HUMAN TRADITION?

DIVINE TRUTH
OR
HUMAN TRADITION?

*A Reconsideration of the Orthodox Doctrine of the
Trinity in Light of the Hebrew and Christian Scriptures*

PATRICK NAVAS

authorHOUSE®

AuthorHouse™
1663 Liberty Drive
Bloomington, IN 47403
www.authorhouse.com
Phone: 1-800-839-8640

© 2011 by Patrick Navas. All rights reserved.

No part of this book may be reproduced, stored in a retrieval system, or transmitted by any means without the written permission of the author.

First published by AuthorHouse   06/28/2011

ISBN: 978-1-4634-1521-1 (sc)
ISBN: 978-1-4634-1520-4 (ebk)

Library of Congress Control Number: 2011909249

Printed in the United States of America

Any people depicted in stock imagery provided by Thinkstock are models, and such images are being used for illustrative purposes only.
Certain stock imagery © Thinkstock.

Because of the dynamic nature of the Internet, any web addresses or links contained in this book may have changed since publication and may no longer be valid. The views expressed in this work are solely those of the author and do not necessarily reflect the views of the publisher, and the publisher hereby disclaims any responsibility for them.

Special thanks to Bonnie Murphy, Scot Han and Danny Dixon for reviewing portions of the manuscript; to Solomon Landers for permission to publish your research on the Coptic translation of John 1:1; and to Mark Rich and Robert Hach for your valuable contributions.

Thank you to my beloved wife Sandy for putting up with many hours of typing.

Divine Truth or Human Tradition?

A Reconsideration of the Orthodox Doctrine of the Trinity in Light of the Hebrew and Christian Scriptures

"The Church's doctrine of the Trinity would seem to be the farthest thing from [the New Testament writers'] minds, and today's reader may well wonder if it is even helpful to refer to such a dogma in order to grasp the theology of the New Testament. When the church speaks of the doctrine of the Trinity, it refers to the specific belief that God exists eternally in three distinct 'persons' who are equal in deity and one in substance. In this form the doctrine is not found anywhere in the New Testament; it was not so clearly articulated until the late fourth century AD."

(Trinitarian) Christopher B. Kaiser, Professor of Historical and Systematic Theology, Western Theological Seminary
— *The Doctrine of God, A Historical Survey*, p. 23 (1982)

~Revised 2011 Edition~ First Published in 2007~

Abbreviations of principal Bible translations referred to throughout:

NAB	*New American Bible*
RSV	*Revised Standard Version*
NRSV	*New Revised Standard Version*
KJV	*King James Version*
ASV	*American Standard Version*
ESV	*English Standard Version*
NET	*New English Translation*
NASB	*New American Standard Bible*
NIV	*New International Version*
NEB	*New English Bible*
JB	*Jerusalem Bible*
NJB	*New Jerusalem Bible*
NWT	*New World Translation*
AT	*An American Translation*
PME	*Phillips Modern English*
TEV	*Today's English Version*
CEV	*Contemporary English Version*
NLT	*New Living Translation*

Table of Contents

Introduction

1 The True God—the "Trinity"
   or *"the Father of our Lord Jesus Christ"*?............12

2 "God the Son" or *"the Son of the Living God"*?............94

3 The Father-Son Relationship............162

4 The "deity" of Jesus Christ............238
   With appending essay by Solomon Landers:
   An Early Coptic Translation and John 1:1c............328

5 The Apostolic Testimony............334
   Philippians, Colossians and the letter to the Hebrews

6 The "I am" Statements of the Gospel of John............414

7 "Trinity" in the Old Testament?............465

8 The Holy Spirit............502

    Appendix (1) Thoughts on the Name "Christian"
                  (2) The Tetragrammaton
                  (3) Donald Macleod on "the form of God"
                  (4) An Alternative View of the Messiah's "preexistence"
                  (5) An Alternative Approach to John 1:1-14
                  (6) Jesus Christ as "the First and the Last"
                  (7) The Contextual Key to John 20:28

"And we also thank God constantly for this, that when you received the word of God which you heard from us, you accepted it not as the word of men [a mere human message, PME] but as what it really is, the word of God, which is at work in you believers."
—The apostle Paul, 1 Thessalonians 2:13, *RSV*

Introduction

My first true introduction to the Christian faith came at a relatively young age through a personal encounter with the holy Scriptures. I still remember, vividly, the experience of being powerfully convinced in mind and profoundly touched at heart by what I read for myself for the very first time in the Bible. It was the message that God, the Creator, was not only true and living, but that he had such an abounding love for the world he created, he was willing to give up the life of his own Son so that sinners could be reconciled to God through their faith in him. Based on but a moment's reflection on such a promise,—that of a God who loved the world, a God who had a Son whom he gave, and the prospect of eternal life—my personal faith was kindled, my heart rejoiced, and the desire to learn more about this message grew strong.[1]

It was not long after this discovery that I began to search and study the Scriptures with great interest. Yet soon after "stumbling" upon this message about God's mercy and loving-kindness expressed in the gift of his dear Son, I began more and more to appreciate the reality of such a tremendously diversified

---

[1] When I was about sixteen I read John 3:16 for the first time from a small pocket New Testament published by the Gideons. The Gideons are the same group whose copies of the Holy Bible can be found in many hospitals, prisons, and in most hotel rooms across the country.

Introduction

world of religious groups and movements that professed faith in Christ and in the Bible, yet whose members were in serious opposition to one another over matters concerning doctrine.

Of course I became aware that the Scriptures wisely instructed believers to assemble together in order to encourage one another as we "see the day drawing near."[2] But naturally,—having no prior spiritual instruction or formal religious affiliation—I became intensely concerned over the question of which religious group was truly following Christ, in the hope that I too could benefit from their spiritual fellowship and from the faith-strengthening, communal experience of worshiping the living God through Jesus Christ, in accordance with the Bible's principles. Although the matter of regular association with a Christian community has always proved to be a special challenge (and somewhat of a spiritual dilemma) for me, and although I have maintained relationships with Christians of diverse backgrounds and affiliations, I came to the conclusion that the genuine Christians of the world are—in the truest and most important sense—recognized by and known to *God* and *Christ*, based on their faithfulness to the message revealed in *Scripture*, not by means of organizational membership or loyalty to a particular creed developed by men. At the same time I came to the realization that one of the primary reasons why so much division exists in the Christian world (the world of those professing the Christian faith) is that so often religious groups and leaders will not only go "beyond the things that are written" in terms of their most distinguishing doctrinal concepts, but they will, in many cases, go as far as to point to their peculiar and often complex belief, interpretation, or set of complex interpretations and beliefs—their "theological system" if you will—as a means or standard by which one should be judged as a true or false Christian.

I have always believed that although the Bible is remarkably and uniquely profound in terms of its divine

---

[2] Hebrews 10:24-25

Introduction

harmony, practical wisdom, and treasure chest of spiritual insights,—its very message about the kingdom of God, and how men may be forgiven of their sins and reconciled to God through the death of his Son—at the same time, its basic message to humanity is actually quite simple and clearly defined, especially so with respect to the issues that *really* matter.

Initially, I did not set out to write a book. Instead, this book came as the result of an accumulation of information and knowledge throughout the years of my personal study of Scripture and from my exposure to the various claims of the various Christian groups and denominations. I certainly do not pretend to have resolved all the "doctrinal" questions Christians have wrestled with throughout the centuries; and although I may have my own opinion on certain matters of faith and scriptural understanding, I do recognize when they are in fact opinions—of course, always endeavoring to form them on the basis of the scriptural harmony and sound reason. However, the teachings that I do hold to with confidence are those which the Scriptures clearly, confidently, and continually present—including the fact that there is one supreme God, *the Father*, that Jesus of Nazareth is God's Son and Messiah (God's anointed one), that God sent him into the world to give his life as a ransom for sinners, that God raised him to life three days after his execution, and that Jesus Christ is Lord by God's own appointment, the possessor of "all authority in heaven and on earth."[3]

To this day, after all my years of research and experience among Christians of diverse religious backgrounds, I still wonder,—in light of what the Scriptures *do* say, and in light of what they do *not* say—who can rightfully claim that it is unchristian or unscriptural to believe that the "one God" of the Bible is "the Father," Jehovah, the God of Israel, the God of all creation, that the man Jesus portrayed in the Gospel accounts is the promised and long-awaited Christ or Messiah, "the Son of the living God," and that the holy Spirit is, in fact, God's Spirit,

---

[3] 1 Corinthians 8:6; 15:3-4; Matthew 16:15-17; 28:19; John 3:16; Mark 10:45; Philippians 2:5-11

Introduction

the Spirit that inspired and empowered the ancient prophets of Israel, the same Spirit that was possessed by the Son of God without measure, that same life-giving and sanctifying Spirit that now dwells in the hearts of the faithful, producing the fruitage of love, joy, peace, patience, kindness, long-suffering, and self-control?[4]

These are, it seems to me, among the teachings that are verified in sacred Scripture with respect to the three subjects traditionally classified by Catholics and Protestants alike under the name and doctrine of the "Holy Trinity." Although the doctrine has long been regarded as an established hallmark of orthodox Christian belief, I was always aware of (and yet seriously perplexed by) what most Trinitarian scholars themselves normally recognize; namely, that the actual doctrine itself—as defined by the historic ecumenical creeds—is not one that is directly or formally taught to us by Jesus or by Scripture. But how could a doctrine as important as this—the very *nature* and *identity* of God—not have been directly taught in the very revelation of himself that God gave to humanity? This is, of course, what ultimately led me into a deeper investigation into the matter, in order that I might "examine everything carefully" and "test the spirits" so to speak, in accordance with the apostles' instructions to the Christians that lived in their own day.[5]

During this period of testing, as I continued to examine literature written in defense of so-called "orthodox" Christian teaching (particularly in reference to the orthodox dogma of the Trinitarian mystery), I frequently came across arguments that at times appeared plausible, sometimes even impressive in their scholarly and confident delivery, but that in every case from my vantage point simply couldn't hold up under close scriptural scrutiny. I found that, with respect to this particular subject, nearly every argument made to advance and uphold an established doctrine always relied on a notably excessive degree of theological inference, an unusual and innovative kind of

---

[4] 2 Peter 1:20-21; John 3:34; Galatians 5:22
[5] 1 Thessalonians 5:21; 1 John 4:1 (*NASB*)

thinking, and even, in certain cases, far-fetched philosophical speculation, based on preconceived notions and already-established theological concepts. None of the meanings assigned to the relevant passages actually gave or expressed the desired, traditionally-accepted meaning by the passage itself in a straightforward way; or, even if the so-called "orthodox" explanation of a certain passage seemed plausible on the surface, there was always another equally if not more plausible and natural alternative that was in perfect harmony with the context and with what the Scriptures teach overall.[6] Yet how could such a definitive and distinctive doctrine (even what is thought to be the 'central' doctrine of Christian faith) be upheld based upon so many questionable interpretations of Scripture, questionable translations of Scripture, and even points that were obviously in clear contradiction to the teachings that were directly presented by Scripture? In fact, one of the most outstanding aspects of my research on the matter revealed that most, if not all, of the most important Scriptures (along with the arguments based on them) generally looked upon as upholding the critical orthodox concepts were not even agreed upon—and, in many cases, essentially refuted—by a number of conservative, orthodox Bible scholars and theologians themselves, most of whom have always been well known and highly regarded within their own respective communities.

Although what I have written is naturally for any and all interested persons, I had specifically in mind those Christians who have professed and practiced their religious convictions under the broader Protestant tradition. Because Protestants have historically professed desire to derive all their beliefs and practices from the Bible itself as the supreme religious authority, my hope was to appeal to open hearts and to clear and conscious minds based on that mutual respect and dedication to the authority and divine inspiration of the Scriptures exclusively. It was rightly observed by one scholar in the Protestant

---

[6] This is not to suggest that my findings were unique or that I did not significantly benefit from the research of many Bible students who had already examined the same issues.

Introduction

community: "The doctrinal matters that have divided evangelical Protestant denominations from one another have almost uniformly been matters on which the Bible places relatively little emphasis, and matters in which our conclusions must be drawn from skillful inference much more than from direct biblical statements…it is ironic and tragic that denominational leaders will so often give much of their lives to defending precisely the minor doctrinal points that make their denominations different from others. Is such effort really motivated by a desire to bring unity of understanding to the church, or might it stem in some measure from human pride, a desire to retain power over others, and an attempt at self justification which is displeasing to God and ultimately unedifying to the church?"[7]

The points made here are true, well said, and much appreciated. I would, however, take the principles expressed therein further and apply them to several of the most prominent doctrines universally maintained within traditional Protestant orthodoxy itself (that is, not simply the doctrines that 'divide,' but certain doctrines that have actually *bound* Protestants together in a historic unity); and the basic concerns expressed, as not only applying to those who identify themselves as "Protestants," but to all individuals within the entire scope of the "Christian" tradition as a whole—including Roman Catholic, Greek Orthodox, Anglican, non-denominational, and even those groups and individuals generally considered to be outside the mainstream by those inside of it.

In a book on a certain Bible topic that I read while in college, one of the book's three coauthors made a statement about what was, in the author's view, the importance of the historic creedal confessions. According to Dr. Kenneth Gentry (professor of systematic theology at Westminster Classical College), who expressed himself along the lines of classical Protestant thinking: "Though subsidiary to the Scripture, creeds play an important role in defining Christian orthodoxy by

---

[7] Wayne Grudem, *Systematic Theology* (Grand Rapids: Zondervan, 1994), pp. 134-135.

Introduction

protecting the church from the corruption of belief within and against the assaults of unbelief from without."[8]

This statement, although general, represents a critical point where I would respectfully disagree, as well as a significant point of departure that accords negatively with the main thrust of what I would ask open-minded Christians to reexamine respecting the traditional doctrine of God specifically. My own conviction is that the authoritative pronouncements of the Scriptures themselves actually—and adequately—*fulfill* the role of defining Christian "orthodoxy,"[9] and that the historic (4th and 5th century) creeds and their dogmatic formulations are ultimately irrelevant and unnecessary, especially so in terms of determining *true* or *original* Christian doctrine. And because the creeds profess to speak authoritatively on certain matters where the Scriptures themselves are well known to be silent (and arguably, there are cases where they are in direct conflict with clear scriptural statements), these "creeds" should be looked upon as suspect and open to reevaluation in light of the purity and divine testimony of the inspired Scriptures.[10] Even if one were to accept, in theory, that the creeds serve as a protection against false teaching, we would still have to keep in mind the existence of the various and conflicting creeds that have come down to us, all of course claiming to reflect true Christian "orthodoxy." But who has the authority to say which creed or confession is the one Christians should look to and why? And why not—as we clearly can—hold exclusively to the "creeds" that already appear in Scripture instead of focusing attention on ones that don't?[11]

I am personally under the conviction that if the biblical message itself is inspired of God (a belief held historically and

---

[8] *Three Views on the Millennium and Beyond*, Blaising, Gentry, Strimple (Grand Rapids: Zondervan, 1999), p. 14.
[9] The term "orthodoxy" simply stands for "right teaching."
[10] Unlike the words and doctrines of imperfect men, "The words of Jehovah are pure words; as silver tried in a furnace on the earth, purified seven times." —Psalm 12:6, *ASV*
[11] John 3:16; 17:3; 20:31; 1 Corinthians 8:4-6; 1 John 4:13-16; 5:1; Romans 10:9-10; 1 Timothy 2:5-7; Matthew 16:13-17; Deuteronomy 6:4; Mark 12:28-34; Ephesians 4:4-5

Introduction

universally among Christians), and if man was intended to live "not by bread alone, but by every word that comes forth from the mouth of God (expressed in Scripture: 'It is written'),"[12] then the very teachings of Scripture constitute a revelation of the mind and will of God himself and must be looked upon as reliable because of their *divine* origin. Human doctrines, philosophies and religious theories, although valuable in many respects and in varying degrees, cannot compare, in my estimation, to the overflowing wealth of the divinely-inspired revelation given by God through the ancient Hebrew prophets and, "in the last of these days," God's very own Son, Jesus Christ.[13] This is why the reader should know that the views expressed and points made in this book were sincerely and, I believe, reasonably made on the basis (and with deep reverence for the sanctity) of the inspired Scriptures, with the ultimate goal of inciting others to the worship of the one God "in spirit and in truth."[14]

What I have expressed throughout this book was written out of a genuine care and concern for those for whom I have deep respect and sincere affection; and my heart goes out to all those seeking to devote themselves in faithful obedience to the one God in accordance with his revealed will—who are, at the same time, seeking to preserve a unity of spirit in the midst of so many conflicting and competing religious claims and traditions. I still look hopefully to a day—or a deeper experience in my own life at least—when Christians will unite around the teaching of our divinely-appointed Lord and Master, when "we all attain to the unity of faith and knowledge of the Son of God, to mature manhood, to the extent of the full stature of Christ."[15]

With these thoughts in mind, my hope for those who read this work is in the same spirit in which the apostle Paul expressed his desire toward the Christians to whom he was

---

[12] Matthew 4:3; compare Deuteronomy 8:3; 2 Timothy 3:14-17
[13] Hebrews 1:1
[14] John 4:23-24
[15] Ephesians 4:13, *NAB*. The Greek word used in this case, *epignosis*, is actually a stronger form of *gnosis* (knowledge). It can be better translated as *"perfect* knowledge" (*NT* by C. B. Williams). *The Amplified Bible* expresses it: "the full and accurate knowledge of the Son of God."

Introduction

writing in the first century:

> "My prayer is that your love for each other may increase more and more and never stop improving your knowledge and deepening your perception so that you can always recognise what is best. This will help you to become pure and blameless, and prepare you for the Day of Christ, when you will reach the perfect goodness Jesus Christ produces in us for the glory and praise of God."[16]
>
> —Philippians 1:8-11, *Jerusalem Bible*

---

[16] The *Revised English Bible* also attempts to express the thoughts of this passage in such a beautiful manner: "And this is my prayer, that your love may grow ever richer in knowledge and insight of every kind, enabling you to learn by experience what things really matter. Then on the day of Christ you will be flawless and without blame, yielding the full harvest of righteousness that comes through Jesus Christ, to the glory and praise of God."

"Where Scripture is silent, it is unwise for us to make definitive pronouncements..." [1]

"The sufficiency of Scripture also tells us that God does not require us to believe anything about himself or his redemptive work that is not found in Scripture." [2]

---

[1] Wayne Grudem, *Systematic Theology, An Introductory to Biblical Doctrine*, p. 500.
[2] Grudem, *Systematic Theology*, p. 131.

1

The True God—"the Trinity" or "the Father of our Lord Jesus Christ"?

> *"But the hour is coming, and is now here, when the true worshipers will worship the Father in spirit and truth, for the Father seeks such as these to worship him. God is a Spirit, and those who worship him must worship in spirit and truth."*
> —Jesus Christ, John 4:23-24

On the night before he died, Jesus prayed for his disciples and in behalf of all those who would put faith in him. He said,

And this is eternal life, that they may know you, the only true God, and Jesus Christ whom you have sent.[1]

As believers, our possession and very hope of eternal life is rooted in our knowing the only true God, and knowing Jesus as the one whom he sent forth. To have knowledge of God and the one he sent is crucial; however, such knowledge is not

---

[1] John 17:3, *NRSV*. Or, as the *New Testament by Kleist & Lily* renders the verse: "And this is the sum of eternal life—their knowing you, the only true God, and your ambassador Jesus Christ."

limited to that of a mere intellectual kind. When we truly come to "know" God, we truly enter into a living fellowship with him as his children; and this has all been made possible by means of our faith in his beloved Son, Jesus Christ, and in everything his Son has done on our behalf. In fact, once we have come to know God and his Son, we may rightfully consider ourselves to be members of a divine family—with God, through Jesus Christ, as our Heavenly Father, and with fellow believers as our dear brothers and sisters.

In addressing the fellow believers of his day, the apostle John—probably near the end of his life—wrote the following inspired words:

> **...that which we have seen and heard we proclaim also to you, so that you too may have fellowship with us; and indeed our fellowship is with the Father and with his Son Jesus Christ. And we are writing these things so that our joy may be complete.**[1]

To think now as Christians, that at one time we did not know the Creator—that we were once disconnected, lost, hopelessly alienated from him due to the contaminating effects of sin and sin's ultimate consequence, death—we can now rejoice in the knowledge that we have been brought near to our Creator through the sacrificial death of his beloved Son, and this we accept truly as "good news."[2] In fact, the apostle Paul undoubtedly viewed this message to be at the very heart of the Christian proclamation of faith.[3] In the last portion of his first letter to the Corinthians, he wrote:

> **And now I want to remind you, my friends, of the Good News which I preached to you, which you received, and on which your faith stands firm. That is the gospel, the message I preached to you. You are saved by the gospel if you hold firmly to it—unless it**

---

[1] 1 John 1:3-4, *ESV*
[2] Romans 5:10; Ephesians 2:13
[3] Compare 1 Corinthians 2:2; Galatians 1:4; 6:14

was for nothing that you believed. I passed on to you what I received, which is of the greatest importance ['among the first,' *Concordant Translation*]: **that Christ died for our sins, as written in the Scriptures; that he was buried and that he was raised to life three days later, as written in the Scriptures.**[4]

A careful look into the rest of the apostle's writings will show that he always held faithfully to the conviction that the sacrificial death of God's Son was essential to the "gospel" or "good news" he proclaimed. He had genuine faith in the fact that Christ not only "died for our sins," but that three days later he was raised to life; and in this, Christ—in behalf of an estranged and dying world—actually achieved victory over the adversarial powers of sin and death themselves. The apostle assured the Christians of Rome:

...if you confess with your mouth that Jesus is Lord and believe in your heart that God raised him from the dead, you will be saved. For one believes with the heart and so is justified, and one confesses with the mouth and so is saved. For the scripture says, 'No one who believes in him will be put to shame.'[5]

Without question, great comfort is to be found in the message of Christ and his chosen apostles throughout the holy Scriptures; for the Scriptures continually make clear, and, in fact, promise, that all who repent of their sins and go on to live by faith in the Son of God will become the inheritors of eternal life in God's coming kingdom.

If we carefully reconsider and take to heart the Lord's prayer at John 17:3 (as well as the aforementioned Scriptures), it will help us to appreciate the great significance of having a true knowledge of God and of Jesus Christ, the one he sent. Unfortunately, in spite of the simple and straightforward declarations of Christ and those of his apostles, many sincere and

---

[4] 1 Corinthians 15:1-4, *Today's English Version* rendering.
[5] Romans 10:7-11, *NAB*

devout persons have misunderstood—or have been led to misunderstand—not only what the Scriptures have revealed about the fundamental identities of God and his Son, but the very content of the faith through which God's promised salvation and gift of eternal life is received.

Given the clarity of the scriptural revelation on these matters, such widespread misunderstanding and confusion may seem unnecessary, but can be easily seen in the wide variety of conflicting doctrines that have developed around the identity and nature of the one God in relation to the Son and holy Spirit.

Countless seekers of truth throughout history, of course, have looked to the Scriptures as a reliable and trustworthy guide for accurate knowledge about the Creator. Multitudes of Bible students throughout the ages have agreed that in the Scriptures we not only receive invaluable knowledge about the Creator—his holy and loving personality, his gracious plan and righteous purposes—but that we also find in them clear direction on how a right standing before him may be realized. Yet, throughout these ages, even careful and committed students of the Bible have engaged in sharp disagreement as to what the Scriptures actually teach regarding the basic identity and defining characteristics of "the only true God," and many groups and individuals alike have divided as a result of this.

Although the Scriptures are essentially clear in defining the relationship that exists between God and Christ, there seems to be a sense in which the existence of all the various and conflicting doctrines (and division that has resulted) is not entirely surprising. If we consider the numerous translations of the Bible that often disagree at critical points, the effects of a nearly two-thousand-year development of church tradition, ecclesiastical creed making, and continuing denominational fragmentation—taking into account the inevitable "falling away" or "apostasy"[6] that was foretold in the Christian Scriptures;[7] at the same time, appreciating the very real influence of hostile

---
[6] "Apostasy" refers more literally to a desertion, abandonment, or state of rebellion.
[7] 2 Thessalonians 2:1-6. Consider also 2 Timothy 4:3-4; Acts 20:29-30

though invisible spiritual powers that surround us,[8] as well as the overall weakness and fallibility intrinsic to the human condition, it becomes, to a certain degree, understandable that devout students of the Bible have gone into different directions on such a crucial matter.

In a book that analyzed some of the most prominent and widely-held theological views among professed Christian groups, it was pointed out:

> Undoubtedly the most popular school of thought in Christendom today attempting to define the Biblical terms 'Father,' 'Son,' and 'Holy Spirit' ('Holy Ghost') is *Trinitarianism*. The concept advanced through this school of thought—the doctrine of the Trinity—is stressed strongly in the Roman Catholic Church, even being described by *The Catholic Encyclopedia* as 'the central doctrine of the Christian religion.'[9]

In the realms of Catholic and Protestant orthodoxy, the doctrine of the Trinity has been—for at least fifteen centuries—regarded as a fixed dogma, an *essential* article of faith, central, and absolutely critical to the true teachings of Christianity.[10] But most historians, New Testament scholars and Bible students in general now agree that the earliest Christian communities of the first century did not know of a "doctrine of the Trinity"—at least, not in any formal sense; that is, in the form of a clearly-thought-out and well-defined doctrine. As an example of one scholarly source, *The New International Dictionary of New Testament Theology* pointed out simply that "primitive Christianity did not have an explicit doctrine of the Trinity such as was subsequently elaborated in the creeds of the early church."[11] It has been likewise noted by respected Bible scholars in the past, as well as in modern times, that neither in the

---

[8] Ephesians 6:12; 1 John 5:19
[9] *Concepts of Father, Son, and Holy Spirit* (Minnesota: Old Theology Book House, 1984), p. 1.
[10] Presbyterian Pastor Philip W. Butin, in agreement with the Roman Catholic view, called the doctrine of the Trinity "the heart and center of Christian faith." —*The Trinity, Foundations of the Christian Faith* (U.S.A: Geneva Press, 2001), p. 13.
[11] Vol. 2, Colin Brown, General Editor (Grand Rapids: Zondervan, 1976), p. 84.

Hebrew nor Christian Scriptures (Old and New Testaments) can there be found any express declaration of the latter ecclesiastical doctrine known respectively as the "Trinity."

In an article in *The International Standard Bible Encyclopedia*, written by the late conservative scholar Benjamin B. Warfield, it was noted: "Certainly we cannot speak broadly of the revelation of the doctrine of the Trinity in the Old Testament. It is a plain matter of fact that none who have depended on the revelation embodied in the Old Testament alone have ever attained to the doctrine of the Trinity."[12] And, as observed by New Testament scholar A. W. Argyle, himself a Trinitarian, in his work *God in the New Testament*: "The fully developed Christian Doctrine that God is three Persons in one Godhead is nowhere explicitly stated in the New Testament."[13]

Although Trinitarian apologists have, at times, attempted to produce evidence for Trinitarian thinking among the earliest "church fathers,"—sometimes referred to as the "apostolic fathers" or the "ante-Nicene fathers" (before the council of Nicea)—Trinitarian scholars Roger E. Olson and Christopher Hall, in their book *"The Trinity,"* had the following to say:

> What do we find in the writings of the Christian leaders during roughly the first sixty years of the second century CE? As we might expect, we do not find the developed Trinitarian language or theology that will blossom from the fourth century on.

A few pages after they state:

> We will be disappointed if we expect to find developed Trinitarian reflection in the early post-apostolic writers. It is simply not there.[14]

Millard J. Erickson (distinguished professor of theology

---

[12] Vol. V, p. 3012.
[13] *God In The New Testament* (New York: Lippincott, 1966), p. 173. Although admitting that the Trinity doctrine is not explicitly taught in the New Testament, professor Argyle believes that "there is to be found in its language concerning the Father, the Son, and the Holy Spirit what may be described as the first germinations of that doctrine."
[14] *The Trinity* (Grand Rapids/Cambridge: Eerdmans, 2002), pp. 16, 20.

at Southwestern Baptist Theological Seminary)—considered by some to be among today's preeminent Trinitarian scholars in the Protestant world—commented on the development of the Trinitarian concept in this way:

> The doctrine of the Trinity as we know it today did not simply spring full blown onto the scene of Christian thought at the beginning of the church's life. It went through a long process in which the church weighed varying interpretations of the biblical data and selected those it judged to be more adequate. At the same time, the church was progressively dealing with different and more refined issues, and in so doing was sharpening the focus of its thinking...We will see the doctrine of the Trinity being developed, layer by layer.[15]

It wasn't until the first half of the fourth century that controversies surrounding the nature of Christ and his relationship to God the Father culminated at what is now considered to be the first ecumenical Council of Nicea (located in modern-day Turkey), convened by the Roman Emperor Constantine in 325 C.E. Although the Council ultimately declared, at the suggestion of the Emperor himself,[16] that Jesus

---

[15] *God in Three Persons, A Contemporary Interpretation of the Trinity* (Grand Rapids: Baker Books, 1995), p. 33. Erickson is "a leading evangelical spokesman with numerous highly regarded volumes to his credit, including the classic text *Christian Theology*."

[16] See: Pelikan, *The Christian Tradition, A History of the Development of Doctrine, The Emergence of the Catholic Tradition 100-600, Volume 1*, p. 209. According to Eusebius of Caesarea (often referred to as the 'Father of Church History'), who wrote in the fourth century, in the end: "The emperor succeeded in bringing [the 300 bishops at the Council of Nicea] into similarity of judgment and conformity of opinion on all controverted points."—Quoted in *McClintock & Strong's Cyclopedia of Biblical, Theological, and Ecclesiastical Literature*, Volume X (Grand Rapids: Baker; originally published 1867-1887, reprinted 1981), p. 642. In summoning the Council, the Emperor Constantine (a professing Christian), whether intentionally or unintentionally, laid the first foundations for the intermixture of Christianity with worldly politics. On this point Philip Schaff observed: "The reign of Constantine the Great marks the transition of the Christian religion from under persecution by the secular government to the union of the same; the beginning of the state-church system...[Constantine] was the first representative of the imposing idea of a Christian theocracy, or of that system of policy which assumes all subjects to be Christians, connects civil and religious rights, and regards church and state as the two arms of one and the same divine government on earth. This idea was more fully developed by his successors, it animated the whole middle age, and is yet working under various forms in these latest times [1800s]...He first introduced the practice of subscription to the articles of a written creed and of the infliction of civil punishment for non-conformity." —*History of the*

Christ was "consubstantial" (Gk: *homoousios*) with God the Father (meaning 'of the same essence/being' as the Father), laying the foundation for the latter Trinitarian creed, the Council did not at that point in time attempt to define the nature of the holy Spirit in relation to the Father and Son.[17]

Eventually, the creed formulated by the Council of Nicea was altered to an extent when it came to be viewed as unsatisfactory. The basic reason was, at the time it was issued, as well as in retrospect, certain aspects of the creed were considered to be ambiguous and, consequently, open to misinterpretation, particularly by those who were holding to dissenting beliefs. In 381 C.E., at the Council of Constantinople, the creed was modified, describing the Holy Ghost as, "The Lord and Giver of life; who proceeded from the Father ['and the Son,'—introduced afterwards]; who with the Father and the Son together is worshipped and glorified."

Significantly, the doctrinal decrees of Constantinople marked an additional step toward the gradual development of what eventually came to be known as the Roman Catholic Church, along with its distinctive ecclesiastical and hierarchical institutions. Nineteenth-century Protestant scholars Dr. John McClintock and Dr. James Strong noted that the Council "confirmed the resolutions of the Council of Nicea," and that it "assigned to the bishop of Constantinople the second rank in the Church, next to the bishop of Rome, and in controversies between the two reserved the decision to the emperor."[18] It was likewise observed by the internationally-known Roman Catholic scholar Hans Küng: "The Christian state religion was crowned

---

Christian Church, Volume 3 (Massachusetts: Hendrickson Publishers, 2002; originally published in 1867), pp. 4, 12, 32.

[17] Originally the creed simply stated, "And I believe in the Holy Ghost."

[18] *Cyclopedia of Biblical, Theological, and Ecclesiastical Literature*, Volume II, p. 491. However, according to another source: "the Chalcedonian council of 451 asserted in its twenty-eighth canon that the bishop of Constantinople had authority equal to that of the Roman bishop. Leo ['the first of the Roman Catholic popes'; 440-461] refused to accept this decision by the ecumenical council, declaring that he would not recognize the bishop of Constantinople as his peer. He preferred to rule alone." —Robert Baker, *A Summary of Christian History* (Nashville: Broadman Press, 1959), p. 77.

by the dogma of the Trinity. Only now can this term be used, since the Second Ecumenical Council, of Constantinople, convened by Theodosius the Great in 381, defined the identity of substance of the Holy Spirit with the Father and Son."[19]

Commenting on the significance of the involvement of the Roman Emperors in the first ecumenical councils, the very significant change this represented in the history of Christianity up to that point, the overall influence of their dogmatic pronouncements (and developing authority structures that empowered them), and the legacy inherited by the Christian/Catholic institutions of the following generations, noted world historian H. G. Wells observed:

> Not only was the council of Nicaea assembled by Constantine the Great, but all the great councils, the two at Constantinople (381 and 553), Ephesus (431) and Chalcedon (451), were called together by the imperial power. And it is very manifest that in much of the history of Christianity at this time the spirit of Constantine the Great is as evident as, or more evident than, the spirit of Jesus...The history of the Church under his influence now becomes, therefore, a history of the violent struggles that were bound to follow upon his sudden and rough summons to unanimity. From him the Church acquired the disposition to be authoritative and unquestioned, to develop a centralized organization and run parallel to the empire.[20]

In a very similar way, Robert Baker, an evangelical scholar, noted that by the close of the period of the first ecumenical councils it would have been "difficult to look at the

---

[19] *The Catholic Church, A Short History* (NY: Modern Library Paperback Edition, 2003), p. 39.
[20] *The Outline of History, The Whole Story of Man* (New York: Garden City Books, 1961), p. 439. The authoritarian disposition spoken of by Wells continued down through the centuries. In reference to the situation in the sixth century, during the reign of the Emperor Justinian, Robert Carden noted: "The Code of Justinian (534 A.D.), the most comprehensive legal code of the ancient world, declared for the trinity and made all other forms of Christian belief illegal, subjecting their adherents to death, imprisonment, confiscation of property and excluding them from public office." —*One God, The Unfinished Reformation*, Third Edition (Naperville: Grace Christian Press, 2005), p. 97.

general state of Christianity and recognize a picture such as the one drawn from the New Testament...No longer were all churches and pastors equal under God and before men. Territorial divisions had been marked off to show the boundaries of the authority of various strong bishops. By 325, then, the very nature of Christianity had become corrupted."[21]

Whether the doctrines of God articulated in the fourth and fifth-century creeds were accurate representations of the Bible's, or whether they were actually human corruptions of the Bible's teaching, has, of course, been disputed among scholars and professors of the faith down through the centuries. The principal dogma itself is found in what is perhaps the earliest known, universally-accepted proclamation of Trinitarian orthodoxy—a proclamation issued well over three hundred years after the last New Testament book was written. The Athanasian Creed (formulated as early as the 5th century C.E., but possibly as late as the 8th), declared in part:

> And the Catholic Faith is this: that we worship one God in Trinity, and Trinity in Unity; neither confounding the Persons nor dividing the substance. For there is one Person of the Father, another of the Son, and another of the Holy Ghost. But the Godhead of the Father, of the Son, and of the Holy Ghost, is all one; the Glory equal, the Majesty co-eternal...So the Father is God, the Son is God, and the Holy Ghost is God; and yet they are not three gods, but one God...And in this Trinity none is afore, or after another: none is greater, or less than another...So that in all things, as aforesaid, the Unity in Trinity, and the Trinity in Unity, is to be worshipped...This is the catholic faith, which except a man believe faithfully he cannot be saved.[22]

The so-called "Athanasian Creed"[23] not only universally

---

[21] Baker, *A Summary of Christian History*, pp. 41-42.
[22] Schaff, *Creeds of Christendom*, Volume II, sixth edition, *The Greek and Latin Creeds* (Grand Rapids: Baker Book House, 1931; 1990 Reprint), pp. 66-68.
[23] Athanasius of Alexandria, known for his theological disputes with Arius, was not the author of this creed, although it bears his name.

established the Trinitarian concept as "orthodox" Christian doctrine, but the creed also officially anathematized, that is, pronounced a curse of condemnation on, those who did not accept the teaching as true and scriptural.

Demonstrating that there has been no essential change in the theological understanding of the Trinity for more than fifteen centuries, Dr. James White, a modern Protestant theologian and apologist, in a fairly well-known work, gives what he describes as a "short, succinct, accurate" definition of the doctrine:

> Within the one Being that is God, there exists eternally three coequal and coeternal persons, namely the Father, the Son and the Holy Spirit.[24]

In agreement, another well-known Protestant scholar offered a concise summary:

> We may define the doctrine of the Trinity as follows: God eternally exists as three persons, Father, Son, and Holy Spirit, and each person is fully God, and [yet] there is one God.[25]

In order to have a truly accurate comprehension, it must be understood, first, that according to the classical doctrine of the Trinity, God the Father, Jesus the Son, and the holy Spirit, are believed to be three distinct "persons." Yet, mysteriously, the three distinct "persons" are nevertheless said to be the same "being" (or 'of the same being'), the same God—*not* three Gods. Ever since it was first articulated in the fourth century, the doctrine of the Trinity has always emphasized that there is *only one God*, and that God is *one* in terms of *being* (or 'essence/substance'), but that God is *three* in terms of *persons*. Hence the theological expressions "three in one," "one God in three persons," "tri-unity," "the triune God," "equal in deity, one

---

[24] *The Forgotten Trinity, Recovering the Heart of Christian Belief* (Minnesota: Bethany House, 1998), p. 26.
[25] Grudem, *Systematic Theology*, p. 226.

in substance," and "the mystery of the holy Trinity."[26]

While Catholics and Protestants have always taught that the doctrine of the Trinity is central to the Christian religion, the concept has at the same time been affirmed by both groups to be an inscrutable mystery, "beyond the comprehension of man." Although ultimately considered to be outside the grasp of human reason, the Trinity is nevertheless regarded by those who defend it as necessary to confess, provided an individual desires approval by, and acceptance into, what is often referred to as the "pale of Christian orthodoxy." As the Athanasian Creed declares: *"he therefore that will be saved, must think thus of the Trinity."* Today the same position is officially maintained by the "orthodox."

In his popular and widely-read work, *The Forgotten Trinity*, James White wrote: *"We hang a person's very salvation upon the acceptance of the doctrine…We must know, understand, and love the Trinity to be fully and completely Christian."*[27]

In agreement, one evangelical reference work made the following claim: "The doctrine of the Trinity is the basis of our Christian faith. Because the doctrine of the Trinity cannot be fully understood, it requires the Holy Spirit of God to direct our minds to believe. '*You cannot be saved if you don't believe in the Trinity.*'"[28]

For good reason, the Trinity has always been held to be a profoundly mysterious doctrine; and it is clear that most advocates regard it as necessary to accept (yet not entirely necessary or even possible to comprehend) in order for one to

---

[26] Or as the well-known author and host of the *Bible Answer Man* radio show and President of the *Christian Research Institute*, Hank Hanegraaff, in attempting to communicate an accurate understanding of the doctrine, often describes the "Triune God" by the phrase, "God is one *What* and three *Who's.*" See: *The Bible Answer Book* (Nashville: J. Countryman, 2004), p. 182.

[27] White, *The Forgotten Trinity*, p. 15 (emphasis added). Perhaps not all Trinitarians would agree that we must "understand" the Trinity to be "completely" Christian. Most Trinitarians agree that the concept cannot be fully understood by the human mind.

[28] Randy Smith, *Theological "isms", A Layman's Reference Guide to Selected Theological Terms* (Southlake: Countryside Institute for Biblical Studies, 1999), p. 90.

qualify as a true Christian and be saved.[29] That is to say, although an individual may express any kind of faith in Scripture, in God, and in Christ, if such an individual were to deny the validity of the doctrine of the Trinity (as defined by the historic creeds), such an individual, in the view of the mainstream, must be regarded as a "heretic," or as a "false" or "incomplete" Christian.

While Trinitarians have traditionally agreed about the centrality and importance of the doctrine, historically, and increasingly in our own time, it seems, Trinitarians have disagreed as to exactly how clear the Bible is in presenting us with such an understanding of God's nature. Some have suggested that the doctrine of the Trinity has been *clearly* revealed by the Bible and through Christ. In *The Forgotten Trinity*, Dr. White expressed the following viewpoint:

> ...upon reflection, we discover that the Trinity is the highest revelation God has made of Himself to His people. It is the capstone, the summit, the brightest star in the firmament of divine truths. As I will assert more than once in this work, God revealed this truth about himself most clearly, and most irrefutably, in the Incarnation itself, when Jesus Christ, the eternal Son of God, took on human flesh and walked among us...God has been pleased to reveal to us that He exists as Father, Son, and Holy Spirit. Since God feels it is important to know, we should likewise. And since God went through a great deal of trouble to make it clear to us, we should see the Trinity as a precious possession, at the very top of the many things God has revealed to us that we otherwise would never have known.[30]

---

[29] This is not necessarily true of all lay Evangelicals and Catholics. It is, however, the official and historic "orthodox" position.

[30] White, *The Forgotten Trinity*, pp. 14-15. By this Dr. White probably does not mean that he believes the Trinity is taught by Scripture in an explicit form, because he acknowledges later on in his book (p. 167) that in Scripture "we don't find a single passage that lays out, in a creedal format, the doctrine of the Trinity." After acknowledging this point, Dr. White goes on to cite the late B. B. Warfield (1851-1921), who attempted to explain why even though the New Testament does not expressly teach the doctrine, it is still to be regarded by Christians as valid and essential. Warfield contended that the Trinity "lies in the New Testament rather in the form of allusions," and that there the doctrine is "everywhere presupposed."

Others, while definitely supporters of the Trinity concept, have expressed less certainty with respect to the degree to which the Scriptures reveal or teach the doctrine with clarity. As one example, Robert Bowman Jr., a well-known advocate and defender of the Trinitarian faith, made the following thought-provoking remarks in a public debate (2003):

> "The doctrine of the Trinity is a post-biblical, human attempt to understand [biblical theology] as best we can, and I do not accord the doctrine of the Trinity the kind of primacy in terms of biblical theology that I do to the deity of Christ—as Jesus being God. [The Trinity] is an inference from a number of biblical statements. I think it's a correct inference, but I'm not going to try to work that out here."[31]

Speaking with an even greater measure of frankness, and in seemingly sharper antithesis to that of Dr. White, A. T. Hanson (professor of theology at the University of Hull), in his work *The Image of the Invisible God*, contended: "No responsible New Testament scholar would claim that the doctrine of the Trinity was taught by Jesus, or preached by the earliest Christians, or consciously held by any writer of the New Testament. It was in fact slowly worked out in the course of the first few centuries in an attempt to give an intelligible doctrine of God."[32]

For additional insight, note the qualifying remarks made with respect to the origin and scriptural basis of the Trinity in the quotations that follow—each quotation coming from learned theologians who hold to the orthodox Trinitarian doctrine:

> The trinity of God is defined by the church as the belief that in God are three persons who subsist in one nature

---

[31] *Is Jesus God?, Examining the Biblical Evidence. A Debate between Robert Bowman and Greg Stafford* (2003). One reference work has a similar observation: "Not only is the word 'Trinity' not in Scripture, but there is no isolated exposition on this attribute of God in either testament. It is an inferred doctrine, gathered eclectically from the entire Canon." —*Today's Dictionary of The Bible* (Minneapolis: Bethany House, 1982), p. 630.
[32] *The Image of the Invisible God* (London: SCM Press Ltd, 1982), p. 87.

[or, 'being']. The belief as so defined was only reached in the 4th and 5th centuries AD and hence is not explicitly and formally a biblical belief...The Trinitarian definitions arose as the result of long controversies...[33]

The doctrine of the Trinity (or triunity of God) refers to the one being of God as Father, Son and Holy Spirit...The concept as such is nowhere explicitly expressed in the scriptures, though such passages as Matthew 28:19 and II Corinthians 13:14 are suggestive. The doctrine itself was thus formulated in the Church, as the community sought to explicate the meaning of the revelation in Jesus Christ.[34]

[The Trinity] presents what seems on the surface to be a self-contradictory doctrine. Furthermore, this doctrine is not overtly or explicitly stated in Scripture...Since the Trinity is not explicitly taught in Scripture, we will have to put together complementary themes, draw inferences from biblical teachings, and decide on a particular type of conceptual vehicle to express our understanding...It will be important to note the type of witness in the Scripture which led the church to formulate and propound this strange doctrine.[35]

The New Testament does not contain the developed doctrine of the Trinity. 'The Bible lacks the express declaration that the Father, the Son, and the Holy Spirit are of equal essence and therefore in an equal sense God himself...the other express declarations are also lacking, that God is God thus and only thus, i.e., as the Father, the Son, and the Holy Spirit. These two express declarations, which go beyond the witness of the Bible, are the twofold content of the Church Doctrine of the Trinity.'...[The Bible] also lacks such terms as trinity (Lat. trinitas which was coined by Tertullian, Against Praxeas, 3; 11; 12 etc.) and *homoousios* which featured in the Creed of Nicea

---

[33] John L. McKenzie, S.J., *Dictionary of the Bible* (New York: Macmillan, 1995), pp. 899-900.
[34] *A Handbook of Christian theology, Definition Essays on Concepts and Movements of Thought in Contemporary Protestantism* (New York: World Publishing, 1958), p. 366.
[35] Erickson, *Christian Theology*, Volume 1 (Grand Rapids: Baker, 1983), pp. 321-322.

(325) to denote that Christ was of the same substance as the Father.[36]

While some theologians in the past, and perhaps a minority in the present, have claimed that the doctrine of the Trinity is *clearly* taught in the Bible, today most Trinitarians acknowledge that the Trinity is actually not a doctrine clearly and directly taught there. Traditionally, defenders of the doctrine have argued that while the actual "doctrine" of the Trinity is not explicitly presented in Scripture, the "concept" is clearly there, underlying the entire revelation, and that the classical Trinitarian formula is the necessary conclusion we must come to with respect to the true nature of God as progressively revealed throughout the Scriptures.

As an example of this type of reasoning, Shirley C. Guthrie (professor of systematic theology at Columbia Theological Seminary) made the following frank admission along with the following claim:

> Although scripture does not teach the doctrine itself, it says some things about God that made the doctrine necessary...The doctrine of the Trinity is not found in the Bible. But the Bible does speak of the one God who is present and at work in three ways.[37]

---

[36] *The New International Dictionary of New Testament Theology*, Vol. 2, p. 84. It is generally acknowledged by Trinitarians that the "church fathers" used and applied Greek philosophical concepts and terminology in order to accurately express the Trinitarian teaching. As mentioned, the Greek term *homoousios*—adopted at the Council of Nicea to describe the Father-Son relationship—means "consubstantial" ('of identical substance/being'). Others at the time of the Council allegedly contended that the Father and Son were not *homoousios* but *homoiusios*, meaning "of like substance." Adolf Harnack, in his *History of Dogma* (Vol. 7, Chapter 4, p. 225), noted that even the celebrated leader of the Protestant Reformation, Martin Luther, "declared such a term as *homoousios* to be unallowable in the strict sense, because it represents a bad state of things when such words are invented in the Christian system of faith:' Luther said, 'we must indulge the Fathers in the use of it...but if my soul hates the word *homoousios* and I prefer not to use it, I shall not be a heretic; for who will compel me to use it, provided that I hold the thing which was defined in the Council by means of the Scriptures? although the Arians had wrong views with regard to the faith, they were nevertheless very right in this...that they required that no profane and novel word should be allowed to be introduced into the rules of faith.'" Additionally, Harnack noted, "In like manner [Luther] objected to and rather avoided the terms 'trinitas' (threefoldness, threeness, oneness, trinity)."

[37] *Christian Doctrine*, Revised Edition (Louisville: John Knox Press, 1994), pp. 77, 80.

A further investigation into the standard scholarly reference works reveals that the viewpoint expressed is typical. Note the similarity of the following quotations. The first is from a Roman Catholic source; the ones following are from Protestant/Evangelical sources:

> The triune mystery of God is the central mystery of Christian faith and life; thus the doctrinal formulation about the nature of this God is the source of all other mysteries of the faith...The doctrine of the Trinity as such is not revealed in either the Old Testament or the New Testament; however, the essential elements of what eventually became the doctrine are contained in Scripture.[38]

> Though 'trinity' is a second-century term found nowhere in the Bible, and the Scriptures present no finished Trinitarian statement, the NT does contain most of the building materials for the later doctrine. In particular, while insisting on one God, it presents Jesus Christ as the divine Son in distinction from God the Father, and probably presents the Holy Spirit or Paraclete as a divine person distinct from both...the doctrine of the trinity does lie in Scripture 'in solution' (B. B. Warfield, *ISBE* [1929], s.v); i.e., the NT presents events, claims, practices and problems from which church fathers crystallized the doctrine in succeeding centuries.[39]

> The word Trinity is not found in the Bible, and though used by Tertullian in the last decade of the 2nd century, it did not find a place formally in the theology of the church till the 4th century. It is, however, the distinctive and all comprehensive doctrine of the Christian faith. Though it is not a Biblical doctrine in the sense that any formulation of it can be found in the Bible, it can be seen to underlie

---

[38] *The Harper Collins Encyclopedia of Catholicism*, p. 1270. On page 1271 it was observed that "Trinitarian doctrine as such emerged in the fourth century, due largely to the efforts of Athanasius and the Cappadocians (Basil, Gregory of Nazianzus, Gregory of Nyssa), who responded to the doctrinal challenges of Arius and Eunomius about the status of Jesus Christ."
[39] *The International Standard Bible Encyclopedia*, Vol. IV, p. 914.

the revelation of God...Although Scripture does not give us a formulated doctrine of the Trinity, it contains all the elements out of which theology has constructed the doctrine...The necessity to formulate the doctrine was thrust upon the church by forces from without, and it was, in particular, its faith in the deity of Christ and the necessity to defend it, that first compelled the church to face the duty of formulating a full doctrine of the Trinity for its rule of faith.[40]

Other scholarly works on the Trinity have made very similar expressions. The general thrust of the argumentation has been that although the Trinity doctrine itself is not explicitly articulated in Scripture, Scripture does provide the "seeds," "elements," "tools" or "building materials" needed for the "construction" of the "latter doctrine." In effect they argue that it was the very information about the Father, Son, and holy Spirit given in the Scriptures that compelled "the church" or "church fathers," or even "theology," to "clarify," "crystallize," "construct," "formulate," "define" or "develop" a doctrine of the Trinity, particularly in response to the rise of certain "heretical" doctrines about the Father and Son that were confronting "the Church" around the time the doctrine was first enunciated.[41]

Essentially, the doctrine of the Trinity represented, in their view, a concerted attempt to preserve an idea or concept of "biblical monotheism"—belief in and worship of only *one* God. It was clear to the early theologians that in the Bible the Father (of Jesus) was presented as God, and likewise clear that the Father and Jesus were presented as two distinct persons—for the Scriptures continually show that Jesus prayed to the Father, and

---

[40] *The New Bible Dictionary* (Wheaton: Tyndale House, 1987), pp. 1221-1222.

[41] One of the views deemed heretical by the Councils was that of Arius, a presbyter (elder) from Alexandria, who evidently taught that Christ was God's first and foremost creation. However, when Constantine finally sided against Arius, he ordered the suppression of all his writings. This is why it is difficult in some respects to ascertain what Arius actually believed and taught on all matters of faith. Another early view held was that of Sabellius (excommunicated in 220), who apparently taught that God was one *person* but manifested himself in different *modes*, hence the term "*modalism*." Today this doctrine is also technically described by theologians as "monarchianism" or "oneness." For those who hold to this view, there is *one* God, *one* person, yet *three manifestations* in Father, Son and Spirit.

The True God—"the Trinity" or "the Father of our Lord Jesus Christ"?

Jesus consistently described himself as one who was "sent" by the Father. In other words, Jesus clearly acted and spoke in such a way as to show that the Father was someone other than himself. But the underlying question was that if Jesus himself was not God (the Almighty, in the flesh), how could he possibly have received the central role and even worship shown to be ascribed to him in the writings of the New Testament? The answer eventually given was that Jesus, although clearly not the same 'person' as his Father, must be—in some mysterious and inexplicable way—the same 'being' or 'God' as his Father—'consubstantial.'[42] Nearly sixty years later, the Council of Constantinople carried this doctrinal development further by defining the Holy Spirit as a third divine 'person' who also shared in the one God's essence or being, and that the Spirit was to be worshipped equally along with the Father and Son as the one God of the catholic or universal Christian religion. This has been the doctrine of orthodox Catholics ever since, and was likewise maintained by the Evangelical-Protestant movement of the sixteenth century. It became, and still remains, a doctrinal standard by which, according to mainstream belief, true Christianity is distinguished from counterfeit expressions of the Christian faith.

The most important questions that need to be asked

Understandably, in light of the various positions that have been expressed on these matters, many Christians have wondered, if the doctrine of the Trinity is in fact central to the faith, and if the true faith held by Christians is communicated accurately and sufficiently in the "God-breathed" Scriptures (which exist so that the man of God may be 'adequate' and 'fully equipped for every good work', 2 Timothy 3:16-17), how could

---

[42] At least this is how the formula is interpreted by modern Trinitarian apologists. Yet the *New Catholic Encyclopedia* states: "Whether the [Nicene] Council intended to affirm the numerical identity of the substance of the Father and Son is doubtful." Even Eusebius, who held views closer to Arius, signed the creed. This is, evidently, one of the reasons why later councils were held in order to clarify earlier dogmatic pronouncements thought to be ambiguous.

it be said, at the same time, that it was "necessary" for the "church fathers" or "church councils" to "develop" or "formulate" a doctrine as significant and as allegedly central as the Trinity, the very definition of who/what God is?[43] Is there any evidence that the formulations of these councils were authorized by God or by Christ? And should Christians, with respect to the essentials of the faith, regard the decisions of the councils as binding and conclusive? Do the Christians who have had little exposure to "creedal Christianity" get the impression from the Bible that post-biblical councils and creeds are needed to clarify its teachings? Do the Scriptures themselves "teach" that salvation depends upon acceptance of the doctrine of the Trinity? Or, should such an ecclesiastical mandate—as long standing and as widely accepted as it has been—be disregarded as an unwarranted human addition to the divinely-inspired revelation of Scripture? And, in light of what we do know about the Scriptures, is it really safe and reasonable to believe that "the Church" really had or has a duty, right, or an authority from God, to "formulate," "develop," or to officially establish essential matters of Christian doctrine? Or, was the entire body of essential Christian doctrine already formally expressed with sufficient clarity by God himself through the inspired Hebrew and Christian writings?

Whether or not the orthodox concept of the "Trinity" is an accurate reflection of God's true nature, when one looks into some of the most popular literature written in defense of the doctrine, it is difficult (if one is reasonably familiar with Scripture) not to notice how they are so often filled with such puzzlingly unqualified and scripturally unsubstantiated statements. For instance, Dr. White asserts: "The church confesses the Trinity to be a mystery beyond the comprehension

---

[43] In a book called "*Why You Should Believe in the Trinity*" (Grand Rapids: Baker, 1989) p. 138. Robert Bowman claimed that the "doctrine of the Trinity was formulated by the followers of Jesus Christ to safeguard the good news that in Jesus Christ we encounter God face to face." But did Jesus Christ leave it up to his "followers" to "formulate" doctrine? Or were the "followers" of Jesus Christ expected to accept and practice the doctrine laid down by him directly and through his chosen apostles?

of man."[44] But one is left wondering: Where does *Scripture* itself make such a confession? Although it is true that the nature and attributes of Almighty God may be beyond the ability of our human minds to fully comprehend, where do the biblical writings themselves speak of God's 'incomprehensibility' or 'mysteriousness' in connection with an alleged 'tri-unity' of divine 'persons' who together constitute the very identity of 'God' in the highest and most distinguishing sense? Or, to ask the question another way: How is it possible that 'the Church' would officially confess that which the very author of its faith has nowhere formally professed?

In another apologetic work, Dr. White says he believes that the Trinity (among other Protestant doctrines mentioned) must be included in "the most basic, fundamental definition of the Christian faith."[45] Again, the natural question arises in the inquirer's mind: If the doctrine of the Trinity should be considered part of the "most basic" and "fundamental definition of the Christian faith," why didn't the apostles and prophets of Scripture ever simply say so, specifically in the way of a clearly-expressed teaching or command to that effect? Why did God and Christ wait to disclose the necessity of accepting such a distinctive doctrinal formulation until the fourth-century creeds of Nicea and Constantinople, particularly through the uncharacteristic method of a humanly (and imperially) initiated council, as opposed to a divinely-inscripturated revelation or prophecy?

In addition to questioning the validity of defining religious dogmas after the Bible itself was completed (and the legitimacy of enforcing doctrines through state-sponsored imperial decrees), many believers find no reason to believe that the founder of their faith left it up to latter councils to decide on matters of faith; but that the founder of their faith simply left the Christian community responsible for bringing itself into conformity with the body of truth already set forth by Christ and

---

[44] White, *The Forgotten Trinity*, p. 173.
[45] *The Roman Catholic Controversy* (Minnesota: Bethany House, 1996), p. 27.

The True God—"the Trinity" or "the Father of our Lord Jesus Christ"?

the traditions delivered through his apostles—as Scripture describes it: *"the faith that was once for all handed down to the holy ones."*[46]

These are at least some of the more obvious questions and concerns that have been expressed by Christians throughout the ages. Trinitarians believe that when the "church fathers" formulated the doctrine of the Trinity they were not in any way changing or adding to what the Scriptures taught. They believe that "the fathers" only systematically defined and expounded upon a concept the Bible had already revealed by necessary implication. Others argue that, in the Bible, no "concept" of a "Trinity" can be found, and that the Bible itself has already *adequately* articulated an "intelligible doctrine of God" with clarity. Many students of the Bible (including some conservative Trinitarians) have, in effect, asked: If God's nature truly is that of a "Trinity," and if our very salvation depends upon acceptance of this fact, why didn't God communicate that to us in such a way that there would be no real possibility of mistaking it?[47] If the Trinity really is to be thought of as "the highest revelation…the brightest star in the firmament of divine truths," why the lack of *one* expression in the Bible clearly stating that "God" is composed of "three" distinct "persons" and that we should express our faith and devotion toward "God" based on such a distinctive doctrinal construction? In addition, if it is true that the Creator communicated his will and the truth about himself in Scripture, how can it be said by one devout Trinitarian: "God revealed this truth about himself most clearly, and most irrefutably," that "God feels it is important to know," that "God went through a great deal of trouble to make it clear to

---

[46] Jude 1:3, *NAB*

[47] Anthony Buzzard, in his book on the Trinity, correctly observed: "There is no passage of Scripture which asserts that God is three. No authentic verse claims that God is three persons…No verse or word in the Bible can be shown to carry the meaning 'God in three Persons.' Any claim that there are three who compose the Deity must be based on inference, rather than plain statements." —*The Doctrine of the Trinity, Christianity's Self Inflicted Wound* (Maryland: International Scholars Publications, 1998), p. 4. It was similarly pointed out by one pastor and critic of Trinitarian doctrine: "the Bible is devoid of any reference to God being made up of three persons." —Carden, *One God*, p. 100.

us," and at the same time be said by another: "The concept as such is nowhere explicitly expressed in the scriptures"?

Professors of theology Roger E. Olson and Christopher Hall, although advocates of the doctrine, have understandably asked a similar question:

> Can it really be so intrinsically connected with the gospel of salvation that denying it (not merely failing fully to understand it) results in loss of salvation or at least loss of status as a Christian? It is understandable that the importance placed on this doctrine is perplexing to many Christians and students. Nowhere is it clearly and unequivocally stated in Scripture...How can it be so important if it is not explicitly stated in Scripture?[48]

Expounding further on the problems and concerns that have been associated with the doctrine historically, professor Millard Erickson made the following critical and perceptive observations:

> [The Trinity] is not clearly or explicitly taught anywhere in Scripture, yet it is widely regarded as a central doctrine, indispensable to the Christian faith.[49] In this regard, it goes contrary to what is virtually an axiom [that is, a given, a self evident truth] of biblical doctrine, namely, that there is a direct correlation between the scriptural clarity of a doctrine and its cruciality to the faith and life of the church. In view of the difficulty of the subject and the great amount of effort expended to maintain this doctrine, we may well ask ourselves what might justify all this trouble.[50]

---

[48] *The Trinity, Guides to Theology*, p. 1.
[49] Compare this with a statement made by another widely-read evangelical author and consider the inconsistency: "*Sola scriptura* means the Bible alone is all we need for our spiritual authority. All the things we need to know, believe and practice are *clearly* stated in the Scriptures..." —Fritz Ridenour, *So What's the Difference? A Look at 20 Worldviews, Faiths and Religions and How They Compare to Christianity* (Ventura: Regal Books, 2001), p. 35 (emphasis added).
[50] In his well-known work, *The Outline of History* (p. 421), H. G. Wells noted in part: "Now, it is a matter of fact that in the Gospels that body of theological assertion which constitutes doctrinal Christianity finds very qualified support. There is, as the reader may see for himself, no sustained and emphatic assertion in these books of several of the doctrines which Christian teachers of all denominations find generally necessary to salvation. The Gospel support for them is often

The True God—"the Trinity" or "the Father of our Lord Jesus Christ"?

On page 21 of his book, Erickson wrote:

> Another difficulty stems from the categories used by those who worked out the doctrine of the Trinity that the church adopted. They used Greek categories such as substance, essence, and person, which had corresponding Latin concepts when translated into forms of thinking that characterized the Eastern church. Over the years, questions have been raised regarding those concepts. One contention is that the Trinity is simply a product of those ancient Greek categories. It is not present in biblical thought, but arose when biblical thought was pressed into this foreign mold. Thus, the doctrine of the Trinity goes beyond and even distorts what the Bible says about God. It is a Greek philosophical, not a Hebraic biblical, concept.[51]

Although in his writings Erickson definitely seeks to defend the validity of the Trinity, on pages 108-109 he wrote the following:

> The question, however, is this. It is claimed that the doctrine of the Trinity is a very important, crucial, and even basic doctrine. If that is indeed the case, should it not be somewhere more clearly, directly, and explicitly stated in the Bible? If this is the doctrine that especially constitutes Christianity's uniqueness, as over against unitarian monotheism on the one hand, and polytheism on the other hand, how can it be only implied in the biblical revelation? In response to the complaint that a number of portions of the Bible are ambiguous or unclear, we often hear a statement something like, 'It is the peripheral matters that are hazy or on which there seem to be conflicting biblical materials. The core beliefs are clearly and unequivocally revealed.' This argument would appear to fail us with respect to the doctrine of the Trinity,

---

allusive and indirect. It has to be hunted for and argued about…We shall see presently how, later on [after the Gospels were written], all Christendom was torn by disputes about the Trinity. There is no clear evidence that the apostles of Jesus entertained that doctrine."
[51] *God in Three Persons*, pp. 11, 21.

however. For here is a seemingly crucial matter where the Scriptures do not speak loudly and clearly.

Little direct response can be made to this charge. It is unlikely that any text of Scripture can be shown to teach the doctrine of the Trinity in a clear, direct, and unmistakable fashion.[52]

In addition, Erickson noted that the concept of the Trinity "in many ways presents strange paradoxes." Yet he went on to observe another significant fact:

> [The Trinity is] a widely disputed doctrine, which has provoked discussion throughout all the centuries of the church's existence. It is held by many with great vehemence and vigor. These [advocates] consider it crucial to the Christian faith. Yet many are unsure of the exact meaning of their belief. It was the very first doctrine dealt with systematically by the church, yet it is still one of the most misunderstood and disputed doctrines.

In a similar way, Dr. White openly discussed some of the perceived deficiencies in the understanding of church members whose denominations consider the Trinity to be a foundational truth:

> Most Christian people, while remembering the term 'Trinity,' have forgotten the central place the doctrine is to hold in the Christian life. It is rarely a topic of sermons and Bible studies, rarely the object of adoration and worship—at least worship in *truth*, which is what the Lord Jesus said the Father desires (John 4:23). Instead, the doctrine is misunderstood as well as ignored. It is so misunderstood that the majority of Christians, when asked, give incorrect and at times downright heretical definitions of the Trinity. For others, it is ignored in such a way that even among those who correctly understand

---

[52] It was contended by one non-Trinitarian source: "One clearly stated Scripture verse would have more weight than a mountain of theology. Until such a verse can be produced, Trinitarians have an impossible burden." —*The Doctrine of Christ, The Key to having "both the Father and the Son"* (Clawson: Associated Bible Students, 1997), p. 29.

the doctrine, it does not hold the place it should in the proclamation of the Gospel message, nor in the life of the individual believer in prayer, worship and service.[53]

In expressing concern about the prominence given to the doctrine by ordinary, contemporary evangelicals, Dr. White laments the fact that the Trinity is rarely a topic of sermons and Bible studies. Along with professor Erickson, there is the belief that many in the Trinitarian community (likely, ordinary church members) do not know exactly what the doctrine is and are consequently unable to give a "correct" definition of it. This is why it is reasonable to ask: How can the average Christian be expected to give *any* sort of definition of the Trinity based on the Bible if the Bible itself never presents us with one? Based on what is generally admitted by some of the most prominent scholars in the Trinitarian community, it would seem likely that even among those who belong to denominations where the Trinity is part of the official creed, that *very few* have actually come to a genuinely personal and inner conviction with regard to its truthfulness based on a careful, individual examination of the scriptural evidence or lack thereof. For many—perhaps the majority—the Trinity remains a tradition gone untested.[54]

Since the Bible itself does not give a definition of the "Trinity," would the position held by the apologists imply that Christians must therefore constantly look to professionally-trained theologians in order to have an accurate concept of God? And in line with a distinctively Christian attitude of reverence toward the ancient scriptural testimony, we can ask ourselves: Was it really proper for the fourth and fifth-century theologians to have *dogmatically defined* what God himself has not expressly defined (scripturally speaking), even having gone so far as to use their definition as a *standard* by which the genuineness of one's

---

[53] *The Forgotten Trinity*, p. 16.
[54] In 1 Thessalonians 5:21, Paul admonished the Christians (as different translations express the thought): "Prove all things" (*KJV*), "try the quality of everything" (*BLE*), "Put all things to the test" (*TEV*), "Test everything" (*NAB*), "Make sure of all things" (*NWT*), "Examine everything carefully" (*NASB*), hold fast to that which is good."

Christianity is to be determined true or false? Can it really be expected that the "Trinity" be a topic of sermons and Bible studies when we are unable to point to a single book, chapter, or verse where there exists any clear mention, any direct presentation, or even one discussion of the doctrine anywhere in Scripture? How can we expect a genuine unity of faith under a doctrine like the Trinity if, in fact, there isn't anything that comes close to even a loose definition of the concept in all of Scripture? Cannot Christians unite under the message that *is* taught directly and under the doctrines that *are* expressly defined in Scripture? If the godly men who wrote the Scriptures felt that the Trinity was a priority for Christians to understand and accept (as do today's 'orthodox Christian' leaders), why did they not devote at least some portion of their writings to the elaboration and exposition of such an important matter of faith—faith in the "only true God"?

The questions that have been asked thus far are by no means unreasonable or unjustified. The most relevant question for Christians was asked by Trinitarian scholar E. Calvin Beisner in his work *God in Three Persons*—the question under consideration: "*Is the doctrine of the Trinity a man-made creed or is it truly a biblical doctrine?*"[55]

In a similar spirit of critical analysis, professor Erickson raises several important issues and questions relating to the traditionally-held concept of God. At the end of the following paragraph, Erickson conveys to his readers a truth that is critical for all those aspiring to be genuine followers of Christ and to be counted among those who worship God "in spirit and truth."

> To those outside the Christian faith, the doctrine of the Trinity seems a very strange teaching indeed. It seems to violate logic, for it claims that God is three and yet that he is one. How can this be? And why would the church propound such a doctrine? It does not appear to be taught in Scripture, which is the Christian's supreme authority in

---
[55] *God In Three Persons* (Illinois: Tyndale House Publishers Inc., 1984), Preface, p. 7.

matters of faith and practice. And it presents an obstacle to faith for those who otherwise might be inclined to accept the Christian faith. Is it a teaching that perhaps was a mistake in the first place, and certainly is a hindrance and an embarrassment to Christianity?...This teaching does not seem to be stated in the Bible. Is it taught there? If not, perhaps the church was mistaken in formulating such a strange teaching. We must look closely at the biblical testimony to determine whether this doctrine is indeed found there...There is no virtue in continuing to hold such a difficult doctrine of the Trinity if it is not actually taught in the Bible.[56]

In this regard, it is worth mentioning that according to traditional Roman Catholic theology, the Bible is viewed and accepted as an inspired revelation from God. But, at the same time, it is held that all established Church traditions are equal to the authority of holy Scripture. For that reason, Roman Catholics do not necessarily feel that they have to prove everything they believe directly from the Bible. If the so-called "teaching magisterium" of the Church holds dogmatically to a certain doctrine, it may be regarded by all members of the Church as being on the same level with the specific teachings of Scripture.

In contrast, ever since the celebrated Protestant Reformation of the sixteenth century, evangelicals have professed to adhere to the honorable principle they refer to as "*sola scriptura* (scripture alone)." Historically speaking, this has always represented an effort, on the part of Protestant denominations, to find solid support for all their beliefs and practices in the Bible (the conviction to follow God and not man); because to them, the Bible is held to be divinely inspired, reliable, sufficient, and authoritative, in all matters of faith and practice.[57]

As demonstrated, most Protestant theologians realize and acknowledge that the doctrine of the Trinity is not set forth by

---

[56] *Making Sense of the Trinity* (Grand Rapids: Baker Books, 2000), pp. 13, 18.
[57] 2 Timothy 3:14-17

Scripture in an explicit form, but that it is nevertheless clearly implied and properly inferred from the biblical testimony overall. As another interesting example of candor, Dr. Shirley C. Guthrie (a Protestant who believes the Trinity is a central feature of the Christian faith), although he seeks to find evidence for the doctrine in the Bible, on pages 92 and 93 of the work already cited, he freely acknowledges: "*The Bible does not teach the doctrine of the Trinity.* Neither the word 'trinity' itself nor such language as 'one-in-three,' 'three-in-one,' one 'essence' (or 'substance'), and three 'persons' is biblical language." And he goes on to correctly note that the "language of the doctrine is the language of the ancient church, taken not from the Bible but from classical Greek philosophy."[58]

What Guthrie points out specifically about the philosophical language associated with the Trinity is at least one reason why many Christians have questioned its scriptural foundation. Those who are familiar with the Bible's contents know that the very terms necessary to define and articulate the doctrine are not found there. That is why many Bible students have concluded that such highly technical, philosophical and sophisticated theological expressions not only move us further away from how the Bible itself presents the truth about the one God, but that such terms and expressions are unnecessary and potentially misleading to those who are trying to conform themselves to the genuinely biblical pattern. There is no doubt that the official theological terms used—terms like "Trinity," "triune God," "Trinity in unity," "one What, three Who's," "coequal," "coeternal," "consubstantial"—regularly used and dogmatically advanced by Trinitarian teachers, are unscriptural terms, and that Christians are therefore under no obligation to recognize, promote, utilize or defer to them—specifically, when endeavoring to communicate to others the truth about the one

---

[58] *Christian Doctrine* (Atlanta: John Knox Press, 1968), pp. 92, 93 (emphasis added). Yet, after, Guthrie claims: "But the church did not simply invent this doctrine. It used the language and concepts available to it to interpret what the Bible itself says about God and his dealings with men in the world."

God, Jesus Christ, and the Gospel message.

Aware of such long-established and widely-used unscriptural expressions, Dr. White counsels fellow Trinitarians:

> When someone says, 'How can you claim to only believe the Bible when you use terms like 'Trinity' that don't appear in the Bible?' we must be quick to point out that we are *forced* to do so by the teaching of the Bible itself on these three points [specifically what Dr. White believes the Bible teaches regarding: (1) Monotheism, (2) the existence of three divine persons, and (3) the coequality and coeternality of the persons]. *Every error and heresy on this doctrine will find its origin in a denial of one or more of these truths.*[59]

However, Dr. White never demonstrates conclusively from Scripture that the three subjects spoken of are in fact "coequal" and "coeternal" persons. Nor would Dr. White be able to cite specific scriptural passages articulating these very significant points, or that his interpretation of "monotheism" accurately reflects that of the Bible's. Whether or not one accepts Dr. White's points and ultimate conclusions as valid, we can know for sure that none of the writers of the Bible and none of the participants in the biblical accounts ever felt "forced" to speak of God in the way that Trinitarians do. We can confirm that the scriptural writers were inspired to speak of the "one God" as "the Father," and they always spoke of the Lord Jesus as God's "Son" and "Messiah"—the one who was "sent" and "exalted" *by* God.[60]

In fact, when we examine the Scriptures closely, we do not find evidence to indicate that Christians would somehow be

---

[59] *The Forgotten Trinity*, p. 28 (emphasis in original). One professor of systematic theology similarly observed: "It was only after the New Testament books and letters had been written that, in the course of debate and controversy, the church introduced new words in the Christian religion: words like Trinity, person, essence, nature and substance. These words do not occur in the New Testament; at least not with the special meanings they bear today. This has created a difficulty for many Christians..." —Donald McLeod, *Shared Life, The Trinity and the Fellowship of God's People* (Christian Focus Publications, 1994), p. 18.

[60] John 17:3; 1 Corinthians 8:6; 1 Thessalonians 1:9-10; Matthew 16:13-17; 1 John 4:14; Acts 2:33; 5:31; Philippians 2:9

"forced" to speak about the one God in a way different than the ancient prophets, first-century apostles, and the promised Messiah himself spoke about him. And yet to note these facts is not to suggest that Christians must hold to an excessively rigid mode of communication in speech or in writing. Nor does calling attention to the fact that such terminology is unbiblical automatically disprove the validity of the Trinitarian theory. There doesn't seem to be anything objectionable about making use of certain terms—though not necessarily or technically scriptural—as long as those terms are relevant, beneficial, and if they accurately describe, reflect, or summarize genuinely biblical principles, teachings, or concepts.

Consider the following point. Without using the word "Trinity," the apostle Paul, in his first letter to the Corinthians, could have said something along these lines:

> "For although there may be so-called gods in heaven or on earth—as indeed there are many 'gods' and many 'lords'—yet for us there is one God: *the Father, the Son, and the Holy Spirit*—three persons, one God."

If the apostle Paul had communicated something like this—which we might have reasonably expected if the Trinity was essential to the true Christian faith and central to his thinking—there wouldn't seem to be a very sound or significant basis for objecting to a term like "Trinity." Because if such was in fact the apostle's teaching, that the "one God" is not simply "the Father," but three persons,—'Father, Son, and Spirit'—then the term "Trinity" or "tri-unity (three-in-one)" would be an appropriate though technically non-biblical term that would accurately reflect and summarize a genuinely biblical concept. Yet we can be sure that the apostle Paul didn't say that, and most Bible students realize that the Scriptures never say anything to that effect. Instead, the apostle wrote:

> **To us there is one God, *the Father*, from whom are all things and for whom we exist, and one Lord, Jesus Christ, through whom are all things and through**

whom we exist.[61]

What Paul tells us in this case should be considered definitional—a genuinely and sufficiently Christian "creed" or "confession of faith." And at this point one should carefully note that the apostle Paul—in perfect harmony with Jesus' words at John 17:3—made a deliberate point to identify the "**one God**" as "**the Father**." No other persons were included in his identification of the "one God." Nor is there an example in the Bible where the "one God" is spoken of as more than one person.[62] In other words, this is one example of how the Bible positively and purposefully presents the identity of the "one God" in plain language, and it is not Trinitarian.

After the apostle officially defined the "one God" as "the Father," he went on to speak of another, Jesus Christ, identifying him as the *one Lord* ('through whom all things are and through whom we exist'); yet this "one Lord," Jesus, is clearly one who is distinct from the "one God." And, with respect to the reference regarding Jesus' "Lordship" in this text (Jesus' status as 'Lord'), it should be kept in mind that the Scriptures continually make clear that the Lordship or ruling authority possessed by Christ was and is a Lordship/authority that was *given* to him by his Father, the "one God."[63] This point was made plain, for example, on the day of Pentecost, when the apostle Peter declared to his countrymen: "Let all Israel then accept as certain that *God has made* this Jesus, whom you crucified, both *Lord* and *Messiah*."[64]

---

[61] 1 Corinthians 8:5-6, *RSV*. Strangely, in his book, *Knowing Christ in the Challenge of Heresy* (p. xxiii), Trinitarian apologist Steven Tsoukalas claimed that "any person's definition of God that excludes the Son (and the Spirit) as God in the biblical sense results in that person's denial of the true and living God." Yet there is not one instance in the Bible where "the true and living God" is identified as anyone else but the Father. This was, in fact, Paul's own definition of God.

[62] The Bible never proposes the equation "God = Trinity (Father, Son and Spirit)," but always "God = Father." For example, in John chapter six, Jesus told his audience: "on [the Son of Man] the Father, God, has set His seal." —John 6:27, *NASB*, Updated Edition.

[63] Matthew 28:18; Philippians 2:6-11.

[64] Acts 2:36, *New English Bible* (emphasis added). Consider the similarity between what God did for Jesus in regard to his Lordship and what God did for Joseph centuries earlier. When Joseph addressed the brothers who had previously sold him into slavery, he said: "Hurry and go up to my father and say to him, 'Thus says your son Joseph, God has made me lord of all Egypt'" (Genesis 45:9). However, unlike Joseph, who was made to be "lord of all Egypt," God made Jesus "Lord of all" (Acts 10:36).

The True God—"the Trinity" or "the Father of our Lord Jesus Christ"?

This is, of course, the true *scriptural* sense in which Jesus should be recognized and understood as "Lord," along with the fact that his Father, God, *gave to him* "all authority in heaven and on earth."[65] That is to say, the Bible itself does not articulate the notion that the Lordship possessed by Jesus is something intrinsic to his "eternal-divine-nature" as "the-second-person-of-the-Trinity." Jesus is "Lord," rather, because God himself has highly honored and exalted him, having gladly endowed him with divine power and authority.[66]

The Scriptures make quite clear that, to the apostles, the "one God" was "the Father"; and for them, Jesus of Nazareth was the one divinely-appointed *Lord* and *Messiah*, **"the one whom the Father consecrated and sent into the world"** (John 10:36). Is it unreasonable to believe that the same is true, or should be true, for all believers in the Messiah today?

Evangelical apologist, Robert Bowman, wrongly claimed that in this text (1 Corinthians 8:6) the terms "God" and "Lord" are 'synonymous.'[67] If that were really the case, we would then have Paul essentially meaning, "to us there is *one God* the Father…and *one God* Jesus Christ," resulting in two apparently equal Gods, and, really, an incoherent statement—and, strangely enough, something that Trinitarianism does not even teach to begin with.

It is really surprising that a Bible scholar would put forward a claim of this sort. The words "God" and "Lord" may be similar but they are definitely not synonymous, especially so in this case.[68] As pointed out, according to the apostolic

---

[65] Matthew 28:18
[66] Philippians 2:9-11; Compare Daniel 7:14.
[67] *The Biblical Basis of the Doctrine of the Trinity: An Outline Study*, p. 10, Apologetics.com.
[68] If Jesus is the "one Lord," does that mean that the Father is not "the Lord"? No. Jesus is the "one Lord" because he is the *one individual* whom God, the Almighty and sovereign Lord, appointed head of all Christians. But this does not compromise the sovereignty or Lordship of God in any way. It is, rather, an expression of God's sovereignty; for God himself was pleased to confer upon his Son authority over all. Such authority belongs to Christ alone based on God's own decision. The Father is the sovereign Lord (Heb. *adonai*) and Almighty God. But, again, the very fact that he is sovereign Lord of the universe affords him the sovereign right to have "made" his Son Lord of all others. And although the Father is the all-powerful, universal Lord, he is *not* the "one Lord" who was "appointed" to that status by another who is "greater" than himself, as

testimony, it was *God* who "made" Jesus *Lord*; and yet God himself has always held the status of supreme and eternally sovereign Lord. That is, no one ever "made" or "gave" the Father his status as sovereign God and Lord.[69] The terms "God" and "Lord" cannot be synonymous in this case. Nor do the terms carry with them an identical degree of status or authority; for the Father—the God described here—is, as Paul describes him elsewhere, "**the *God* of our *Lord* Jesus Christ**" (Ephesians 1:17). Thus, in his scholarly work on *The Theology of Paul the Apostle*, James Dunn observed: "Equally striking is the repeated formula in the Pauline letters in which God is spoken of as 'the God and Father of our Lord Jesus Christ.' The striking feature is that Paul speaks of God not simply as the God of Christ, but as 'the *God*...of our *Lord* Jesus Christ.' Even as Lord, Jesus acknowledges his Father as his God. Here it becomes plain that *kyrios* ['Lord'] is not so much a way of *identifying* Jesus with God, but if anything more a way of *distinguishing* Jesus from God. We may note also 1 Cor. 3.23—'You are Christ's and Christ is God's'; and 11.4—'the head of Christ is God.' And again 1 Cor. 15.24-28: the Lord of all (cf. Rom. 10.12) has been given his lordship by God. It is a lordship which fulfills God's purpose in making humankind (to be responsible in ruling over the rest of creation). And it is a lordship which will in the end be wholly subject to God."[70]

A disappointing pattern of fallacious argumentation

Although there is no text in Scripture that unequivocally identifies the "one God" as a unity of three coequal and coeternal persons, Dr. White, like other evangelical apologists, views the

---

Jesus was (1 Corinthians 8:6; Acts 2:36; John 14:28). Likewise, Jesus is certainly a possessor of Godship according to the Scriptures (John 20:28; Hebrews 1:8), as are the angels and ancient rulers of Israel (Psalm 8:5; John 10:34), but he is not the "one God" who appointed someone else to be the "one Lord."

[69] In another place Paul pointed out that "God *placed* all things under [Christ's] feet and *appointed* him to be head over everything for the church..." (Ephesians 1:22, *NIV*). This confirms that Christ's authority (headship) was given to him at some particular point in time by God.

[70] *The Theology of the Paul the Apostle* (Grand Rapids: Eerdmans, 1998), p. 254.

words of the Lord Jesus at Matthew 28:18-20 (often called 'the great commission') as providing one of the strongest evidences for the doctrine of the Trinity in the New Testament. The noted evangelical pastor and teacher Dr. John MacArthur even referred to the formula given there as "a strong affirmation of trinitarianism."[71]

On page 174 of his book, in a section he titles "The Great Trinitarian Passage," Dr. White wrote: "We close our examination of the wonderful truth of God's triune nature with the single passage of the Bible that comes the closest to providing a 'creedal' statement."

Since this passage is considered by some to be the closest to a formal biblical statement of the Trinity, it will be helpful to examine and discuss it first. According to the *New American Standard Bible*, the text reads:

> **And Jesus came up and spoke to them, saying, 'All authority has been given to Me in heaven and on earth. Go therefore and make disciples of all the nations, baptizing them in the name of the Father and the Son and the Holy Spirit, teaching them to observe all that I commanded you...'**

Arguing in defense of the Trinity, Dr. White makes the point that "the name" believers are baptized into is *singular* ('in the *name* of,' not 'in the *names* of...'), yet it is that of the *three* subjects—Father, Son, and Holy Spirit. Dr. White then quotes the renowned theologian, B. B. Warfield, who made the following claim:

> [Jesus] could not have been understood otherwise than as substituting for the name of Jehovah this name 'of the Father, and of the Son, and of the Holy Ghost'; and this could not possibly have meant to His disciples anything else than that Jehovah was now to be known to them by the new Name, of the Father, and the Son, and the Holy Ghost. The only alternative would have been that, for the

---

[71] *The MacArthur Study Bible* (Nashville: Word Publishing, 1997), p. 1451.

community which He was founding, Jesus was supplanting Jehovah by a new God; and this alternative is no less than monstrous...We are not witnessing here the birth of the doctrine of the Trinity; that is presupposed. What we are witnessing is the authoritative announcement of the Trinity as the God of Christianity by its Founder, in one of the most solemn of His recorded declarations. Israel had worshipped the one and only true God under the Name of Jehovah; Christians are to worship the same one and only and true God under the Name of 'the Father, and the Son, and the Holy Ghost.' This is the distinguishing characteristic of Christians, and that is as much as to say that the doctrine of the Trinity is, according to our Lord's own apprehension of it, the distinctive mark of the religion which He founded.[72]

In this particular quotation, Warfield makes several claims that are very insightful with respect to understanding some common Trinitarian approaches to biblical interpretation. Warfield first insists that the *only* way to understand Jesus' statement is that "the name of the Father, and of the Son and of the Holy Ghost" was actually functioning as a *substitute* for the name *Jehovah* ('Jesus could not have been understood otherwise'). Warfield also argues that we are not witnessing in this passage "the birth" of the doctrine of the Trinity; but, again, claims that the doctrine is already, and simply, "presupposed."

Although Warfield's scholarship and insights into the Bible have much value in many respects, and although Protestants generally regard him as conservative in his appraisal of scriptural teaching, his exposition of this particular text seems to be not only highly speculative, but unnecessarily and unwarrantedly dogmatic. According to Warfield, his explanation is not merely a possibility, or, even, a very likely interpretive option. Rather, Warfield claims, "this could not *possibly* have meant to His disciples anything else..." But do we and can we know for sure that this is how the disciples received and

---

[72] As quoted in White, *The Forgotten Trinity*, pp. 174-175.

understood Jesus' words, in their original setting?

Unfortunately, in attempting to expound upon the implication of Jesus' instructions to his disciples, and in an effort to uphold received tradition, Warfield presents to his readers what may be rightfully characterized as a false dilemma.[73] That is to say—with a strong and confident tone, and with forceful, articulate language—Warfield makes it appear that the *only* choices we have in terms of understanding this text are either "the Father, Son and Holy Spirit" represent the "new name" of God, *or*, Jesus was replacing Jehovah with a new God—*none of which need be true*. Yet Warfield claims: *"The only alternative would have been that, for the community which He was founding, Jesus was supplanting Jehovah by a new God; and this alternative is no less than monstrous..."*

But do the Lord's instructions to his disciples concerning Christian baptism really suggest that Jehovah was to be known by a *new* name, and is this the *only* possible way to understand his words?

As mentioned, Dr. White seeks to attribute special significance to the singular use of the "name" as applying to "Father, Son, and Holy Spirit"—implying that God therefore must have a 'three-in-one' nature. But, in the Hebrew Scriptures, there are similar expressions associated with the concept of a "name" applying to more than one subject that may be expressed in the singular as well. When the patriarch Jacob blessed his son Joseph, he spoke with reference to Joseph's brothers, Ephraim and Manasseh: "in them let my name be carried on, and the *name* of my *fathers* Abraham and Isaac; and let them grow into a multitude in the midst of the earth."[74] Although the patriarch used the *one* "name" as applying to both Abraham and Isaac (his 'fathers'), the expression itself obviously did not imply that Abraham and Isaac were mysteriously two distinct persons in

---

[73] A "false dilemma" is a fallacy of argumentation (sometimes called the 'either-or fallacy'): an argument or "statement that presents two alternatives as if they were jointly exhaustive (as if no third alternative were possible)." —Patrick J. Hurley, *A Concise Introduction to Logic* (Belmont: Wadsworth Publishing Company, 1997), p. 161.
[74] Genesis 48:16, *ESV*, emphasis added.

one entity or being. A reference to Jacob's "fathers" (plural) Abraham and Isaac under the (one) "name" does not cause one to read into the statement any extraordinary, mystical, or theological significance. Nor does it seem likely that such language would raise interpretive difficulties for a careful student of Scripture.

In his scholarly work, *A New Systematic Theology of the Christian Faith*, Dr. Robert L. Reymond attempted to add strength to the Trinitarian position based on this passage as well, saying: "To comprehend fully the import of Jesus' statement, one must appreciate the significance of the term 'the Name' for the Hebrew mind. In the Old Testament, the term does more than serve as the mere external designation of the person. Rather, it refers to the *essence* of the person himself."[75] Dr. Reymond also quotes Warfield who noted that the "Name" of God "was accordingly a most sacred thing, being indeed virtually equivalent to God Himself."

However, when considering both nineteenth and twenty-first-century theologians' claims in light of this particular account, the objective reader may notice first that, in his baptismal commission, Jesus simply did not say anything about the "name" as being a reference to "the name of God" itself; nor does this even appear to be at issue in the context at all. In fact, one might also notice that the most important features of their argumentation in behalf of the Trinity at this point are actually built upon the unfounded premise that the "name" to which Jesus refers to is actually a reference to the name of God specifically. The assertion is simply made but never really proven. Essentially, Dr. Reymond wants the meaning to be that baptism was to be performed in the one "name (of God)," which represents the "essence" of God; and since the "three persons" were coordinated or united under this one "name" or "essence," this should be taken as compelling evidence for the truthfulness of the Trinitarian claim.

---

[75] *A New Systematic Theology of the Christian Faith* (Nashville: Thomas Nelson, 1998), p. 226 (Warfield, *Biblical Doctrine of the Trinity*, 42.) emphasis added.

The True God—"the Trinity" or "the Father of our Lord Jesus Christ"?

Although it is true that in Bible times the particular name of an individual was often rich in meaning, at times symbolizing who a person was, what he or she had done in the past (their reputation), the circumstances associated with their birth,[76] or even the greater role and significance of their overall lives in relation to God's purposes,[77] this did not necessarily mean that the meaning of a certain "name" represented the "essence" of what the person was. Numerous names of persons could be cited to illustrate the point. For example, the Bible name "Jehu" means "Jehovah is he." Yet this obviously did not mean that Jehu was literally, or in "essence," God. The name "Moses" means "'drawn out,' or 'saved out (of water),'"[78] which was probably given to him due to the circumstances surrounding his infancy—the fact that he was "drawn out" of the Nile River by Pharaoh's daughter. In the case of "Moses," the particular "name" given to him was evidently based on the circumstance his adopted mother found him in while he was still an infant, not because it would characterize the very "essence" of his being the rest of his life.

This is one reason why one is able to see that the assertion that the "name" in Matthew 28:19 should be taken (and was intended to be taken by Jesus) as standing for "the name/essence of God" is really a clever and creative technique of argumentation put forward to support an already-established doctrinal concept without a basis in the actual text. Naturally, such crafty and such shrewd though clearly erroneous methods of argumentation could only contribute to further, justified

---

[76] For one example, the firstborn son of Isaac was named "Esau" (meaning 'hairy') because of his unusually hairy appearance at his birth (Genesis 25:25).

[77] God changed Abram's name (meaning 'exalted father') to "Abraham" (meaning 'father of a multitude'). This was so, evidently, because Abraham would ultimately become "the father of all those having faith," and his seed, according to Jehovah's promise, would prove to be as numerous as the sands of the seashore (Genesis 22:17; compare Romans 4:11).

[78] The same point can be made with reference to the name "Immanuel" which was applied to Christ at his birth, meaning "God is with us" (Matthew 1:23, *TEV*). Many apologists have pointed to this name-application to Christ as establishing or confirming the "incarnation of God the Son." They argue, essentially, that since Jesus is called "Immanuel (God is with us)," this means that Jesus *is* God, in the flesh. However, Trinitarian Murray J. Harris noted correctly that by applying this name to Jesus, "Matthew is not saying, 'Someone who is 'God' is now physically with us,' but 'God is acting on our behalf in the person of Jesus.'" —*Jesus As God, The New Testament Use of Theos in Reference to Jesus* (Grand Rapids: Baker Book House, 1992), p. 258.

skepticism with respect to the scriptural foundation of Trinitarian teaching.

In attempting to arrive at a fair and balanced assessment of Jesus' words, however, it is definitely helpful to understand that in the Bible (and even in contemporary English speech), a reference to a "name" does not always have to imply a mere label for identifying a specific person, place, or thing. In fact, the well-known New Testament scholar A.T. Robertson noted that "The use of name (Greek: *onoma*) here is a common one in the Septuagint [the Greek translation of the Hebrew Scriptures] and the papyri for power or authority."[79]

At this point, we can also note that Jesus *did not say* "baptize them in the name (or 'the new name') of *God* or *Jehovah, who is* the Father, Son, and Holy Ghost," nor is it necessary to read an implication like that into his words. Another problem arises in Warfield's reference to the "Lord's own apprehension" of the Trinity, given that there is simply no record in Scripture showing that Jesus or any of his apostles conceived of God in this way.[80] There is, on the other hand, no question that Jesus and the apostles placed great emphasis on the subjects "Father," "Son," and "Holy Spirit," and we see this highlighted particularly in his instructions to the disciples in Matthew 28. Yet the Scripture never speaks of the three subjects as ultimately and collectively constituting the "one God" of the Christian religion. To argue that since Jesus commanded baptism to be performed in the (singular) name of the three subjects, this demands that they now represent a 'substitute' for the name of God (understood as a 'Trinity,' or 'tri-unity' of persons) cannot be proven and seems very unlikely that this is what Jesus himself had in mind—and even less likely that his disciples would have

---

[79] *Word Pictures in the New Testament*, Vol. I (Nashville: Broadman Press, 1932), p. 245. Another source similarly pointed out: "According to Hebrew usage *in the name of* means in the possession and protection of (Ps 124.8)." —*The New Oxford Annotated Bible with Apocrypha, New Revised Standard Version* (New York: Oxford University Pres, 1989), p. 46.

[80] According to Warfield, Christians are "to worship the same one and only and true God under the Name of 'the Father, and the Son, and the Holy Ghost.'" Yet, according to Jesus, true worshipers "must worship *the Father* in spirit and in truth" (John 4:23).

understood him in such a way.[81]

In addition to these points, a cautious and sensitive student of Scripture might also note that what John MacArthur described as "a strong affirmation of trinitarianism," and what Warfield called "an authoritative announcement of the Trinity as the God of Christianity," must constitute more than merely mentioning or coordinating the subjects "Father," "Son," and "Holy Spirit" in a given text, even after an expression like "in the name of..."[82] The claim made by Trinitarian apologists could be effectively substantiated only if the speaker or writer expressly conveyed, or even clearly implied, the idea that the Father, Son, and Holy Spirit are "coequal and coeternal persons," and in an equal sense the "one God." But that is not what is said or necessarily inferred from Jesus' instructions to his disciples; and nothing like this is ever expressly communicated elsewhere in the Hebrew or Greek Scriptures. Although supporters of Trinitarian orthodoxy, respected Bible scholars McClintock and Strong acknowledged that this text, "taken by itself, would not prove decisively either the *personality* of the three subjects mentioned, or their *equality* or *divinity.*"[83] Another writer correctly observed:

> In the New Testament there are some passages which

---

[81] The use of the singular "name" in reference to more than one occurs on other occasions in the Hebrew Scriptures: "But the prophet, who shall speak a word presumptuously in my name, which I have not commanded him to speak, or who shall speak in the *name* of other *gods*, that same prophet shall die" (Deuteronomy 18:20, emphasis added).

[82] It was pointed out by another source: "'Name' can refer to authority by which something is done. That is what we mean by the expression 'in the name of the law,' or 'in the name of the king.' The 'law' has no particular 'name' in the ordinary sense, and it is not a reference to some name such as 'Henry' or 'Louis' or 'Ferdinand' that is meant by 'in the name of the king,' but rather the kingly *authority* and *position* appealed to as basis for the demand made. At Ephesians 1:21, the apostle speaks of government, authority, power and lordship and 'every name named.' This shows clearly that 'name' often represents authority and position." —Raymond Franz, *In Search of Christian Freedom* (Atlanta: Commentary Press, 1991), p. 507.

[83] *Cyclopedia of Biblical, Theological, and Ecclesiastical Literature*, Volume X, p. 552. Another reference work likewise observed: "The baptismal commission in Matt 28:19 and the apostolic benediction in 2 Cor 13:14 are the clearest examples of triadic coordination...Even these texts, however, do not formalize the relationship as that of one in three, but assert somewhat more simply that the work of the three is the same work, whether it is perceived in terms of the creative and ruling power of the universe, the crucified and vindicated messiah, or the religious experience of the community." —*The Anchor Bible Dictionary*, Volume 2, p. 1055.

mention the Father, the Son and the holy spirit, together (For instance, Matthew 28:19; 2 Corinthians 13:14; Galatians 4:4-6), but there is no description of any relationship between the three. The fact, therefore, is that none of the writers of the biblical books saw the need for an ontological identification of the Father, the Son and the holy spirit...They certainly did not formulate a creedal confession expressing faith in an ontological relationship between the three.[84]

Although the above author writes as an opposing critic of Trinitarian doctrine, in his book *The Three Persons in One God*, Roman Catholic Scholar Gerard Sloyan, a Trinitarian, made the same basic point: "We have indicated in the first chapter that the witness of the New Testament is clear on a variety of triadic formulas, none of which is explicitly 'Trinitarian.' In other words, no theology of the trinity of persons in God had been developed by the time the canonical collection of Scriptures was closed."[85]

Respected Anglican scholar, C. F. D. Moule, similarly noted: "There are numerous passages in the New Testament where merely a triple formula, containing words for God, Christ, and the Spirit, appears (1 Cor. 12.4 ff., 2 Cor. 13.13, Eph. 1 ff., 2 Thess. 2.13 f., 1 Pet. 1.2, Rev. 1.4 f.); but these are not in themselves necessarily any indication of an awareness of an eternal and necessary threefoldness in the one Godhead. ...within the New Testament, threefold phrases are not confined to God, Christ and Spirit. There is, for instance, 'God, Christ, and the holy angels' (1 Tim. 5.21)."[86]

Earlier it was noted that Dr. White—in an effort to produce a scriptural case for the fourth-century doctrine of the Trinity—made a reference to "worship in *truth*, which is what the Lord Jesus said the Father desires (John 4:23)." Similarly,

---

[84] Rolf Furuli, *The Role of Theology and Bias in Bible Translation* (Huntington Beach: Elihu Books, 1999), p. 111. "Ontological" is a technical term meaning "having to do with nature or essence of someone or something."
[85] *The Three Persons in One God* (Foundations of Catholic Theology Series, 1964), p. 29.
[86] *The Holy Spirit* (New York: Continuum International Publishing, 2000), p. 25.

Warfield claimed that "Christians are to worship the same one and only and true God ['Jehovah'] under the Name of 'the Father, and the Son, and the Holy Ghost,'" and that such worship is to be regarded as "the distinguishing characteristic of Christians..." Yet if we focus our attention on the account referred to by Dr. White (John 4:19-24), we can easily recognize that Jesus *did* speak about the necessity of worshipping God "in spirit and in truth." But we will also notice that, in this particular case, Jesus did not mention or allude to true worship in connection with a triune-God-concept.[87] Thus, in one of the most well-known scriptural accounts, where the Lord Jesus spoke forthrightly on matters relative to true worship, a concept of a "Trinity" is simply nonexistent. While addressing the Samaritan woman at the well, Jesus—in harmony with the Scriptures—spoke of the importance of worshipping "*the Father* in spirit and in truth, for the Father seeks such as these to worship him." So one is left wondering: If an apologist like James White hopes to provide support for the worship of God as a 'tri-unity' of 'persons,' why would he point to an account (John 4:19-24) that has no relevance?

On the other hand, if Warfield's claim is to be accepted as true, and Trinitarian worship was to be *the distinguishing characteristic* of Jesus' true followers, it would seem that Jesus, in his conversation with the Samaritan woman, either failed, or for some inexplicable reason, did not view it as a priority to inculcate the importance of worshiping the one God under the awareness that God exists as "three persons" (in spite of the fact that it was to be the 'distinguishing characteristic' of his followers), since he only mentioned one, his "Father." What is also not mentioned by Dr. White or Dr. Warfield is that in the

---

[87] With respect to this particular account in John chapter four, F. F. Bruce pointed out: "The important question is not *where* people worship God but *how* they worship him. And part of the 'how' of worshipping him is disclosed in Jesus' language about worshipping him as *the Father*. Jesus habitually spoke of God as his Father—we have seen how spontaneously he referred to the temple as 'my Father's house' (John 2:16)—and addressed him as Father (cf. John 11:41; 12:27 f.; 17:1, etc.); and he taught his followers to do the same." —*The Gospel of John, Introduction, Exposition and Notes* (Grand Rapids: Eerdmans, 1983), p. 109.

The True God—"the Trinity" or "the Father of our Lord Jesus Christ"?

very same account, Jesus himself, as a member of the Jewish nation, told the woman, "*we* worship what *we* know, for salvation is from the Jews,"[88] showing that Jesus Christ himself was a worshiper of God. In view of the overall claim for the centrality of the Trinitarian doctrine of God, it seems exceptionally difficult to explain, in relation to this account, as well as in light of Scripture taken as a whole, why it is that we are unable to find one example of worship or adoration ever expressed toward God in the fullness of who or "what" God is typically claimed to be; namely, a mysterious "tri-unity" of "persons." Not once in the Scriptures do any of the writers ever consolidate or summarize their worshipful attitudes and expressions toward "God" with the thought of an alleged unity of three divine persons in mind or made clear—a common practice among Trinitarians. There is simply no example that can be cited, for none exists in any of the books of the Bible.

To briefly illustrate the point, it is helpful to consider the style of certain hymns and expressions of devotion directed toward the "Trinity" as the ultimate object of Christian worship. In his discussion on Christian worship, professor of systematic theology Donald McLeod speaks of "the most important of all the practical implications of the doctrine of the Trinity." McLeod insists, "we *must* worship God as triune."[89] In harmony with this thought, Dr. White endorses the following hymn with the words:

> *Holy, Holy, Holy, Lord God Almighty!*
> *All thy works shall praise thy Name*
> *In earth and sky and sea;*
> *Holy, Holy, Holy! Merciful and Mighty!*
> *God in three Persons, blessed Trinity!*[90]

Hymns and devotional expressions like these are relatively common among Roman Catholic and Protestant communities. Yet when we carefully consider the actual content

---

[88] John 4:22, *RSV*
[89] McLeod, *Shared Life*, p. 92 (emphasis added).
[90] *The Forgotten Trinity*, p. 175.

of the inspired Scriptures themselves, we are unable to locate a single passage expressing anything that resembles such a form or manner of worship. Nowhere does anyone in the Bible ever demonstrate an awareness of God as a mysterious unity of three divine persons, and there is no suggestion that any man of God in the Scriptures was ever moved or inspired to express any sense of awe or degree of reverence for God's alleged and incomprehensible "triune" nature. Although such expressions of worship are common to orthodox Trinitarian piety, they are nevertheless "far removed from the biblical testimony."[91]

So, if it is true, as claimed, that the doctrine of the Trinity is "the capstone, the summit, the brightest star in the firmament of divine truths," it is certainly remarkable that we are unable to find one example of God's people, particularly in the Christian Scriptures, expressing appreciation for what would have obviously represented to them such a crucial and distinctive conception of the divine nature. And if such a well-read Trinitarian apologist like Dr. White is sensitive to and regretful over the fact that, in most evangelical circles, the Trinity is *"rarely* the object of adoration and worship," it is surprising that he fails to properly discern and to satisfactorily address, as an apologist, the fact that "the Trinity" is *never* presented as an object of adoration or worship in *the Scriptures*.[92] What we *do* find all throughout the sacred record (as alluded to earlier) are expressions like this from the apostles:

For whatever was written in former days was written

---

[91] Compare Dr. White's statements about certain Roman Catholic prayers and forms of worship directed toward the Virgin Mary in his book *The Roman Catholic Controversy*, pp. 198, 211-218.

[92] Dr. White also says that even among those who correctly understand the Trinity, that it "does not hold the place it should in the proclamation of the Gospel message..." However, if we examine the four Gospel accounts and the entire book of Acts, where the gospel is proclaimed in its fullness and in its purest form, we find no instance where the doctrine of the Trinity was a feature of the proclamation, let alone the "central" feature. Pastor Robert Carden made note of a similar point: "Christians often speak of returning to, or maintaining historic Christianity. You cannot get more 'historic' or more 'orthodox' than the Book of Acts...Nowhere in this God inspired history is God called a trinity or three in one...The Book of Acts shows us how the apostles understood and presented Jesus Christ to the world. There is nothing ambiguous about the record of Acts; Jesus of Nazareth was a man approved by God and declared to be lord and Christ. Why is the church today so different?" —*One God, The Unfinished Reformation*, p. 64.

The True God—"the Trinity" or "the Father of our Lord Jesus Christ"?

for our instruction, so that by steadfastness and by the encouragement of the scriptures we might have hope. May the God of steadfastness grant you to live in harmony with one another, in accordance with Christ Jesus, so that together you may with one voice *glorify the God and Father of our Lord Jesus Christ*.[93]

In the opening of his letter to the Ephesians, the apostle abounds with expressions of praise for the Almighty: "**Blessed be the God and Father of our Lord Jesus Christ**, who has blessed us in Christ with every spiritual blessing in the heavenly places..." In his second letter to the Corinthians, Paul again speaks of the "**God and Father of the Lord Jesus**...who is blessed forever."[94]

Do such expressions lead one to believe in the concept of a "Trinity," or that Jesus is the same *being* or *God* as his Father? If so, how and in what way could Paul properly suggest that the Almighty has one who is God and Father to him?[95] In his letter to the Philippians, Paul indicates that because of Christ's obedience, even to the point of death on a cross or stake, God exalted him to the place of highest honor, and has graciously given him the name above every name, so that, at the name of Jesus, every knee will bow and every tongue confess that Jesus is Lord, and that this act of submission and confession of faith would all be "to the glory of God the Father," *not* to the glory of a "triune God."

From this text (which will be examined more closely) it is easy to recognize that even when Christ is honored and exalted by all intelligent beings, the ultimate end of the exaltation is seen in that his Father, God, receives glorification.[96] We do not find that here, or anywhere else in the Scriptures for that matter, that

---

[93] Romans 15:4-6, *NRSV*.
[94] Ephesians 1:3; 2 Corinthians 11:31.
[95] If it is true, as Trinitarians normally argue, that the title "Lord," when applied to Jesus Christ, is an expression of his coequal "deity" with the Father, and that the Father *is* the God of Jesus *only* from the perspective of his "humanity," how then can the "Lord" Jesus Christ have a "God" and "Father"? In Ephesians 1:17, Paul even described the Father directly as "the *God* of our *Lord* Jesus Christ" (emphasis added).
[96] Philippians 2:9-11

the ultimate end of true Christian worship culminates in the glorification of a "triune God." In fact, Jesus Christ, the "pioneer and perfecter" of the Christian faith, never spoke about a "Trinity" in connection with true worship at all. Even in the book of Revelation, in chapters four and five, where God and "the Lamb" (Jesus Christ) are extolled and praised in a heavenly vision, there is no indication or hint of Trinitarian worship, with the Trinity itself as the object of devotion. In view of the dogmatism that so often accompanies Trinitarian teaching, such a concept is notably, and inexplicably, *absent* from the inspired scriptural accounts.

However, what does come across clear enough in Scripture is that Christians worship God the Father through Jesus Christ, and in the power and under the guidance of "the Spirit of truth."[97] But does such a worshipful approach, in and of itself, demand an understanding of the "one God" as a "Trinity"? Worshiping the one God *through* Christ *in* the Spirit, after all (something Scripture clearly advocates), is certainly not the same thing as worshiping the "one God" *as* "Father, Son and Holy Spirit," a difference that many have surprisingly failed to discern. Yet one Trinitarian reference work admits candidly: "Triadic formulas [formulas where the Father, Son and Holy Spirit occur together] in the New Testament are often regarded as implying a developed doctrine of the trinity, but this is to read too much into them."[98] This is, of course, a well-expressed and well-balanced observation.

It was the same lack of ascriptions of praise and devotion directed toward God as a "Trinity" that was noticed by a Bible scholar of the early nineteenth century:

> Look at the devotional character of the New Testament. If the Apostles worshipped God in three persons, it will so appear in their conduct and writings; this circumstance will characterize their devout expressions everywhere. And this the more especially, because they were Jews, a

---

[97] Compare Ephesians 2:18; John 14:17; 15:6
[98] *The Eerdmans Bible Dictionary* (Grand Rapids: Eerdmans Publishing Co., 1987), p. 1020.

people who worshipped God with a strict and most jealous regard to his unity. They could not have changed their practice in this particular without the change being most strikingly observable. Yet we have no intimation of such a change. They appear to have gone on with the worship of the One God of their fathers, without any alteration. Look at this fact. When Paul was converted, he must have passed—supposing the Trinity to be a Christian doctrine—from believing Jesus a blasphemous impostor, to believing him the Lord Jehovah. Is there the least hint of such an amazing change? He speaks with admiration and rapture of the new views and feelings which he enjoyed with his new faith. But all the rest together was not so astonishing and wonderful as this particular change. Yet he nowhere alludes to it. Is it then possible that it could have been so? that so great a revolution of feeling should have taken place, and no intimation of it be found in any act or expression? He speaks frequently of his prayers. And how?...'Blessed be the God and Father of our Lord Jesus Christ.' 'Making mention of you in my prayers, that the God of our Lord Jesus Christ, the Father of glory, may give unto you the spirit of wisdom.' It is plain therefore to whom Paul directed his worship...And not once, either in his epistles, or in any other writing of the Bible, is a doxology to be found, which ascribes praise to Father, Son and Spirit [together as one God], or to the Trinity in any form. This fact is worth remarking. The New Testament contains, I think, twenty-eight ascriptions in various forms; and from not one of them could you learn that the doctrine of the Trinity had been dreamt of in that day...[99]

Even the respected Trinitarian Bible scholar, Emil Brünner, in his book *The Christian Doctrine of God*, was realistic and balanced enough to acknowledge the following:

> It was never the intention of the original witnesses to Christ in the New Testament to set before us an

---

[99] *Testimony of Scripture Against the Trinity*, Printed by I. R. Butts, Boston, 1827.

intellectual problem—that of Three Divine Persons—then to tell us silently to worship this mystery of the 'Three-in-One.' There is no trace of such an idea in the New Testament. This 'mysterium logicum,' the fact that God is Three and yet One, lies wholly outside the message of the Bible. [This mystery has] no connection with the message of Jesus and His Apostles. No Apostle would have dreamt of thinking that there are Three Divine Persons, whose mutual relations and paradoxical unity are beyond our understanding. No 'mysterium logicum,' no intellectual paradox, no antinomy of Trinity in Unity, has any place in their testimony..."[100]

It is true that, in the case of Matthew 28:18-20, James White and B. B. Warfield find in Jesus' words that which conforms to a "presupposed" doctrine, but not one that can be proven to be "presupposed" by Jesus or any of the writers of the New Testament. Contrary to what they propose, the concept of a Trinity is not found in Jesus' instructions to his followers regarding baptism. The concept is only that of their own already-established theological commitment, which must be read into Jesus' words.[101]

In Matthew 28, instead of announcing the Trinity as the God of Christianity, perhaps Jesus was simply emphasizing that believers, upon baptism, were to recognize the respective roles of the Father, the Son, and the holy Spirit, in view of their obedience of faith and commitment to serve God—through Christ, in the Spirit—the rest of their lives. This is appropriate. Because we *are* able to discern the essential roles of God the

---

[100] *The Christian Doctrine of God, Dogmatics*: Vol. I (Philadelphia: Westminster Press, 1949) p. 226. It should be noted that Brünner is Trinitarian and even speaks of "the Lord God" becoming a man for our sakes. However, what he notes about the mystery of the Trinity having no place in the apostolic testimony is undeniable and very telling, especially coming from an "orthodox" scholar who adheres to the traditional Trinitarian teaching.

[101] *The Oxford Companion to the Bible* has the following observation along with an important word of caution: "Because the Trinity is such an important part of later Christian doctrine, it is striking that the term does not appear in the New Testament. Likewise, the developed concept of three coequal partners in the Godhead found in later creedal formulations cannot be clearly detected within the confines of the [Bible] canon...It is important to avoid reading the Trinity into places where it does not appear" (Metzger and Coogan) pp. 782-783.

The True God—"the Trinity" or "the Father of our Lord Jesus Christ"?

Father, his Son Jesus Christ, and God's holy Spirit, continually made clear throughout the rest of the Scriptures. In his second letter to the Corinthians, for example, Paul wrote:

> **And it is *God* who establishes us with you in *Christ*, and has anointed us, and who has also put his seal on us and given us *his Spirit* in our hearts as a guarantee.**[102]

In fact, as Christians, our very access and approach to God is shown to involve his *Son* as mediator, through whom we approach the *Father* in the one *Spirit*, as the apostle wrote in another place:

> **Through [*Christ*], both of us [Jew and Gentile] have in *the one Spirit* our way to come to *the Father*.**[103]

Although Scripture clearly places great emphasis on the roles of God the Father, his Son Jesus Christ, and on God's holy Spirit, promoters of Trinitarian doctrine would benefit from reflecting seriously on the fact that the Bible nowhere instructs Christians to believe in the interpretation of the three as traditionally expressed in the orthodox creedal formulations. It would be difficult for even the most adamant of Trinitarian defenders to deny that the necessity of accepting the doctrine of the Trinity represents a position that goes beyond what is specifically spelled out in Scripture. Looking at it from a scriptural perspective, we can confirm that the only ones who ever told Christians to believe in the doctrine were uninspired humans of post-biblical times. None were divinely directed or divinely commissioned as were Jesus and his apostles.

Of course the necessity of recognizing creedal formulations that present God as a "tri-unity" of "persons" is a distinctive feature of all mainstream church denominations. Yet the Scriptures themselves—carefully considered apart from latter traditions—only reveal the absence of several concepts presented

---

[102] 2 Corinthians 1:21-22, *ESV* (emphasis added).
[103] Ephesians 2:18, *Jerusalem Bible* (emphasis added).

as necessary to accept in the post-biblical creeds; and that the true "capstone" and "brightest star" of divine truth shines forth, not in the recognition of a metaphysical "triune Godhead" proposed by the creeds, but rather, in the predestined exaltation of God's beloved Son, and the recognition of his God-given universal authority—resulting in the everlasting glorification of "the only true" and "living God," "*the Father of our Lord Jesus Christ.*"

In modern times, however, it has been customary for Trinitarian apologists to say, in effect, "It is true that the Bible does not teach the Trinity in an explicit way or in any specific passage, but 'the church' has always accepted the Trinity because we accept *all* of what the Bible teaches about God." For example, on page 86 of his *Systematic Theology*, Robert Reymond admits: "In no single passage of Scripture is the full doctrine of the Trinity set forth." Yet Reymond goes on to qualify his admission by arguing: "But the church has deduced 'by good and necessary consequence,' as the implicate of all the Scripture data, the doctrine of the Trinity..." Similarly, in a sermon given by a popular evangelical teacher, it was argued: "The truth is there is no single passage from which you can exegete the doctrine of the Trinity. That doctrine is the fruit of comparing Scripture with Scripture and understanding *everything* the Bible teaches about the Godhead."[104]

Expounding upon this notion in further detail, James White similarly claims: "Christians believe in the Trinity not because the term itself is given in some creedlike form in the text of Scripture. Instead, they believe in the Trinity because the Bible, taken in its completeness, accepted as a self-consistent revelation of God, teaches that there is one Being of God (Foundation One) that is shared fully (Foundation Two) by three divine persons (Foundation Three) the Father, the Son, and the

---

[104] Phil Johnson, "*A Biblical Appraisal of the Charismatic Movement*," 1 Thessalonians 5:21, Grace Bridge, A ministry of Grace Community Church (1992). "Exegesis" is a technical term referring to the critical interpretation and exposition of the Scriptures. When used in this context it basically means to explain or draw out a correct meaning from the Scriptures.

Holy Spirit. There is, therefore, no contradiction between being a 'Bible believer' and holding to the Trinity. The one leads naturally, and inevitably, to the other."[105]

These are impressive statements. Because what they ultimately imply is that those who subscribe to the doctrine of the Trinity do so, not because of loyalty to a latter theological development, but based on a careful consideration of the totality of the Bible's message (all parts accepted); whereas those who deny the truthfulness of the concept must do so out of a failure to accept the whole of scriptural teaching. And what Christian wants to be guilty of ignoring the fullness of what God has revealed in Scripture—what Paul described as "the whole counsel of God" (Acts 20:27)?

Undoubtedly, the theologians and apologists speak confidently with reference to the notion that "although no one passage teaches the doctrine, the Scripture taken in its entirety does teach it." But if the Bible itself positively and categorically identifies the one God as "the Father" (clearly and consistently placing the Father in a class of his own), and Jesus as the "Christ" or "Messiah" whom the Father "sent," and if the Bible never states that the "one Being of God is shared fully by three divine persons," or that the three divine "persons" are coequal and coeternal, how does the Trinity prove to be a natural and inevitable scriptural doctrine? And as we go on to consider each Scripture generally thought to tie the Trinitarian concept together, one will see that, in the end, such a confident claim amounts to nothing more than a dogmatic assertion without substance, a mere bluff in the context of theological argumentation. Of course, when endeavoring to convince Christians that the concept of the Trinity is biblical, its defenders speak eloquently and with a tone of intellectual and informed confidence, even professing to use the Bible alone to *derive* or *infer* the doctrine. Yet, in the end, we are still left asking: Where does the Bible *teach* the doctrine? Where does the Bible directly

---

[105] Reymond, *A New Systematic Theology of the Christian Faith*, p. 29.

communicate to us that the one "being" of God is "shared" by "three persons"? The truth is, it never does—neither explicitly nor by necessary implication, neither in one text nor in the biblical writings as a whole.

If the doctrine of the Trinity were true, and required to believe upon for salvation itself, it may be pointed out that it is utterly unique in the sense that all other essential Christian doctrines *are* taught to us plainly in the Bible, whereas the truthfulness of the Trinity is somehow derived from "all of what the Bible teaches," without the Bible ever actually saying so. In this regard, the Trinity (and associated concepts) would prove to be the only essential though non-articulated, unannounced doctrine of the Christian faith, scripturally speaking.

As adamant and as forceful as evangelicals have expressed themselves with respect to the centrality of the Trinity and the absolute necessity of its acceptance, it is remarkable that the Bible itself never identifies the one God as "the Trinity," but as "the Father";[106] nor does there exist *one* example in all of Scripture where the term "God" or the name "Jehovah (YHWH)" can be proven to represent all three "persons" of the "Godhead." Any attempt to derive such a meaning would be an exercise in speculation at best. Unfortunately, defenders of Trinitarian dogma have failed to fully come to terms with the implications of these facts. Consider carefully—If the doctrine of the Trinity is true and essential to the Christian religion as is claimed, Scripture itself (the very documents upon which Christianity is based) never defines who or what the one God is in terms of his (or its?) most important and fundamental attribute—the very meaning of "God" in its most distinguishing sense. This is altogether incredible.[107]

As surprising as it might appear, most apologists who profess to follow the Bible alone do not appear to be troubled by

---

[106] This positive identification is made both explicitly as well as implicitly. Consider, for example, John 8:54; 17:3; 1 Thessalonians 1:9-10; 1 Corinthians 8:6; 1 Timothy 2:5.

[107] If Paul claimed that he had "preached the whole counsel of God" (Acts 20:27), how is it that he failed to make mention of the very "heart and center of Christian faith"?

the lack of direct scriptural teaching on a matter thought to be so crucial. Nor do they seem to express any reservation or point out any degree of needed caution when demanding that others accept it. Evidently, they actually do believe, and would ultimately have to defend, the idea that neither Jesus nor his apostles had to be clear in the communication of essential Christian doctrines, in spite of the fact that they always were. But in what way could that *really* be possible?

Although Trinitarian apologists attempt to make light of the fact that the doctrine is not directly taught in the Bible (but somehow deduced from it), notice that in other contexts of biblical discourse, the lack of scriptural clarity or explicitness on certain matters of faith is often pointed to as a serious basis for questioning the soundness of another person's understanding of Christian doctrine. For example, in a recent book that discussed various views relating to the "millennium" (the thousand-year-reign of Christ),[108] Robert Strimple, a professed "amillennialist," objected to his opponent's "postmillennial" doctrine for the simple reason that it is not a teaching explicitly expressed in Scripture.[109] Probably without realizing it, Strimple (a Trinitarian) made a statement that, when taken to its logical conclusion, would have negative implications on other long-held church traditions, even ones that Strimple himself confesses faith in, like the Trinity. In the course of his rebuttal, Strimple wrote:

> This continues to be my most fundamental objection to postmillennialism: that postmillennialism is simply not taught—clearly, explicitly—in any passage of Scripture. It is always presented by way of inference or implication...the reader searches in vain for even *one* biblical text that explicitly sets forth the postmillennial vision of a golden age to come before Christ comes

---

[108] Revelation chapter 20.
[109] An "*a*millennialist" is characterized primarily by the belief that the millennium spoken of in Scripture does not refer to a *literal* thousand year period. A "*post*millennialist" believes that "the present age will develop morally and spiritually until it ushers in the millennial age, with Christ returning to earth at the conclusion of the Millennium" (Smith, p. 66).

again.[110]

Without question, both Roman Catholic and Protestant Christians would likewise search "in vain for even *one* biblical text that explicitly sets forth" several of their most distinctive doctrines, including the orthodox doctrine of the Trinity, the alleged "heart and center of Christian faith." Although Trinitarian, Strimple may not have realized that the very same argument could have been applied with equal force to a doctrine that is—according to church tradition—actually essential to one's very hope of salvation. In fact, the basis for Strimple's objection to "postmillennialism" is *identical* to that which could be applied to the subject of the present inquiry. The point is clearly illustrated if we simply take out the word "postmillennialism" and replace it with the "Trinity." That is, Strimple very well could have said, in the same spirit of reason, and with the same level of propriety:

> This continues to be my most fundamental objection to *the Trinity*: that *the Trinity* is simply not taught—clearly, explicitly—in any passage of Scripture. It is always presented by way of inference or implication...the reader searches in vain for even *one* biblical text that explicitly sets forth the theological vision of a *triune God* to which we must give our devotion.

Consider yet another similar example from evangelical apologist James White. In his work *The Roman Catholic Controversy*, Dr. White argues strongly against the modern-day Roman Catholic concept of the "Papacy"—essentially, the belief that the Catholic Popes were the successors of Peter, the alleged first "Pope" of the Christian Church. Dr. White makes the point, with respect to the writings of the apostle Peter:

> One would expect to find Peter [in his second epistle], writing at the end of his life, directing Christians to follow

---

[110] *Three Views of the Millennium and Beyond*, by Darrell Bock (General Editor), Craig Blaising, Ken Gentry Jr., Robert Strimple (Grand Rapids: Zondervan, 1999), pp. 69, 70.

his successor in the office of Pope, if indeed the Roman position were true. But no such exhortation appears. We have no evidence from Peter's pen that he views himself as a Pope or that he was even the bishop of Rome, for that matter.

In reference to the writings of the apostle Paul and Luke, Dr. White states:

> We hardly need to be reminded that in all of Paul's letters, in which we find discussions of Apostles, bishops, deacons, and all sorts of other positions of ministry in the Church, never is a word said about the most important office of all, the supposed office of the Pope. And the reason is plain: no such office existed…We cannot pass the most crucial evidence with regard to Roman claims: The Book of Acts gives us the clearest insight into the function of the early Church. Here if anywhere we would find clear and unequivocal evidence of Petrine primacy and the function of the Papacy…And so we conclude our initial overview of the New Testament evidence with the plain fact before us that the concept of the Papacy, with Peter as its initial office holder, is nowhere to be found. Not only does the term itself not appear, but the office is not mentioned at all. Instead we find data from the pages of inspired Scripture showing that the early Christians did not look to Peter or to any bishop of Rome as the head of all Christians.
>
> In light of the testimony of the entire New Testament, the Roman apologist must be able to prove beyond a shadow of a doubt that the few passages to which he appeals prove the establishment of the Papacy. We cannot accept the mere *possibility* that the Roman position is correct. Given the absence of the Papacy from all the rest of the New Testament, the few passages cited by Roman apologists such as Matthew 16 and John 21 *must* plainly and unequivocally establish Petrine primacy and

succession in the office of the Pope. But do these passages accomplish this?[111]

Whether or not the historic ecclesiastical concept of the Papacy is a legitimate Christian institution, the answer to the questions from Dr. White's perspective is, obviously, *no*. Yet, once again, the same basic principle could have been applied with respect to the traditional Catholic and Protestant doctrine of God, the same doctrine Dr. White himself zealously defends in other writings. Of course, Dr. White could have put forward the same essential reasoning that follows, nearly, word-for-word:

> One would expect to find Peter, writing at the end of his life, *directing Christians to worship God as a tri-unity of persons, if indeed the traditional, orthodox position were true*. But no such exhortation appears. We have no evidence from Peter's pen that he views himself *as a worshipper of a 'Triune God' or that God was even a being 'shared' by 'three persons,'* for that matter.

And with reference to the writings of Paul and Luke:

> We hardly need to be reminded that in all of Paul's letters, in which we find discussions of *God the Father, Jesus Christ, the Spirit, the resurrection, prayer, worship, and all sorts of other doctrines essential to Christian faith*, never is a word said about the most important *doctrine of all, the supposed true nature of the biblical God as a Trinity*. And the reason is plain: no such doctrine existed…We cannot pass the most crucial evidence with regard to *orthodox claims*: The Book of Acts gives us the clearest insight into *the worship and beliefs* of the early Church. Here if anywhere we would find clear and unequivocal evidence of *the Trinity as 'the brightest star in the firmament of divine truths.'*…And so we conclude our initial overview of the New Testament evidence with the plain fact before us that the concept of *the Trinity, with Jesus as a second, coequal member*, is

---
[111] White, *The Roman Catholic Controversy*, pp. 110-113.

nowhere to be found. Not only does the term itself not appear, but the doctrinal concept is not mentioned at all. Instead we find data from the pages of inspired Scripture showing that the early Christians did not look to *a 'Trinity' or to a figure known as 'God the Son' to be adored by* all Christians.

And the following points are similarly crucial to the remainder of the present investigation:

> In light of the testimony of the entire New Testament, *the Trinitarian apologist* must be able to prove beyond a shadow of a doubt that the few passages to which he appeals prove the establishment of *the Trinity*. We cannot accept the mere *possibility* that the *classical Trinitarian* position is correct. Given the absence of the *'Trinity'* from all the rest of the New Testament, the few passages cited by *Trinitarian apologists such as Matthew 28:19 and John 1:1 (and others) must* plainly and unequivocally establish *the consubstantiality of the Father and Son and the entire concept of a triune God*. But do these passages accomplish this?

Although the answer to this question will be explored throughout the remainder of this work, in the first steps of our attempt to assess the validity of the Trinitarian claim, we can benefit from reflecting on the expressions made by certain Trinitarian reference works already cited. It is noteworthy that the theologians who hold officially to the Trinitarian teaching are unable to say: "the Trinity is defined by Christ and his apostles," or "the Trinity is defined by the Scriptures." Instead they must say, "The Trinity of God is defined *by the Church*," and that the "doctrine itself was thus *formulated in the Church.*" Or it is claimed that, in some way, the Scriptures "led *the church* to *formulate* and propound this strange doctrine." They not only acknowledge that the "doctrine is not overtly or explicitly stated in Scripture" and that "the New Testament does not contain the developed doctrine of the Trinity," but one even frankly admits that the teachings associated with the Trinity are those "which go *beyond* the witness of the Bible." In light of such candid and thought-provoking admissions, it might be asked, at the outset, who will be able to legitimately argue that the Bible "plainly and unequivocally establishes" a doctrine that is "nowhere explicitly expressed in the scriptures"?

The Jews and the Trinity

Another critical and thought-provoking point rarely considered involves the fact that the Jewish nation—uniquely bound to God by way of a special covenant, and exclusively entrusted with God's sacred oracles[112]—had, for over a thousand years, worshipped their God, Jehovah, without any knowledge or consciousness of an alleged "triune" nature (a fact not typically disputed). If in the arrival of the long-awaited Messiah and full disclosure of the Christian gospel (the 'faith which was destined to be revealed')[113] God's people were given a fuller revelation of God's true nature as a mysterious "tri-unity" of persons, why is it that in the Christian Scriptures we are unable to find that either Jesus or his chosen ambassadors ever made it a point (specifically in reference to the Hebrew or Jewish mind) to contend for the notion that their God should no longer be conceived of as one person but somehow three? Such a notion would have, undoubtedly, represented a remarkable change in, or at the least, an extremely significant expansion on the way the one God would be viewed and worshiped by his chosen people. It has been rightly pointed out that such "an innovation would have required the most careful and repeated explanation for men and women who had been steeped from birth in the belief that God was one person only."[114] Yet if we were to carefully investigate the message and overall substance of the New Testament record, we would not find any suggestion that such a significant and distinctive doctrine was ever, in any case,

---

[112] Romans 3:2
[113] Galatians 3:23, *The New Testament, A Translation by* William Barclay
[114] Buzzard & Hunting, *The Doctrine of the Trinity, Christianity's Self-Inflicted Wound*, p. 7.

"taught" to the Jewish people—as either an expansion on their belief in God, or as a further development in the history of divine revelation. Having considered this fact, yet unable to really explain how this could have been the case, one Trinitarian reference work made the following remarks:

> [The Trinity] is not a biblical doctrine in the sense that any formulation of it can be found in the Bible...What is amazing, however, is that this confession of God as One in Three took place without significant struggle and without controversy by a people [the Jews] indoctrinated for centuries in the faith of the one God, and that in entering the Christian church they were not conscious of any break with their ancient faith.[115]

Although the above source expresses awareness of the enigma, there is no consideration given to the more obvious fact that the first Christians (the apostles and disciples of the first century) did not conceive of or ever "confess God as One in Three," as an objective examination of the New Testament writings makes clear.[116] Neither does the writer consider the possibility that the Jews who joined themselves to the earliest Christian communities may not have been conscious of any break with their ancient faith *simply because there was no break with their ancient faith*; but rather, in the man Jesus of Nazareth, there was to be found the fulfillment of their *Messianic* expectations.[117] Yet, ironically, the same source admits of the Trinity, "it did not find a place formally in the theology of the church till the 4th century..."[118]

---

[115] *The Illustrated Bible Dictionary*, Volume 3 (Wheaton: Tyndale House, 1980), pp. 1597-1598.
[116] If so, which passage in the New Testament proves that they did?
[117] It was pointed out correctly by James White: "Nothing in [the apostolic writings] suggests a conscious break with worship of the one true God who revealed Himself to Abraham, Isaac, and Jacob." —*Scripture Alone, Exploring the Bible's Accuracy, Authority, and Authenticity* (Minneapolis: Bethany House, 2004), p. 122.
[118] No doubt the writer of the article keeps in line with what was stated in the Preface by the editors of this work: "We do not apologize for the fact that this book reflects the creedal, confessional and evangelical convictions for which the Tyndale Fellowship stands: *the triunity of God*, the deity, atoning death, and bodily resurrection and approaching return of Jesus Christ" (*The Illustrated Bible Dictionary*, Volume 1, p. vi.). Surprisingly, these kinds of statements are not uncommon among evangelicals. In the Preface to his book on the Trinity, Evangelical

Speaking more candidly in this regard, one Christian writer, after having examined the most problematic scriptural issues relating to the Trinitarian claim, wrote:

> The thoughtful student must ask himself: If it was hard for the Jews in the early church to let go of the Law, wouldn't it have been even harder to get them to change their view of God? Fifteen New Testament chapters are dedicated to changing the Jew's mind on the Law. And if it took that much to deal with the Law, shouldn't we find at least 1 or 2 chapters explaining the change in how God would be viewed from now on? But not a single verse suggests the Jew change his view of God...[In our examination we noted the] lack of a single verse which 'taught' the doctrine. The Bible has many verses which 'teach' justification, 'teach' repentance, 'teach' baptism, 'teach' the resurrection, but not one verse in the entire Bible 'teaches' the doctrine of the Trinity. No verse describes it, explains it, or defines it. And no verse tells us to believe it.

In another place—in light of the facts pointed out, and in light of his own investigation into the Scriptures—the author concluded:

> The more I looked at the Trinity, the more I saw a doctrine rich in tradition, and passionately defended by brilliant and sincere people, but severely weak in reason and badly wanting in Biblical support.[119]

Anglican scholar, Peter Toon, admits, "I am a theologian, who is committed to the Faith expressed in the Nicene Creed from the fourth century. I approach and expound the Scriptures within this creedal and doctrinal framework" (*Our Triune God, A Biblical Portrayal of the Trinity,* 1996 by Victor Books, **p.** 10). The comments made by Geivett/Phillips, in the book *Four Views on Salvation in a Pluralistic World* (Grand Rapids: Zondervan, 1996) are also somewhat strange coming from professed Christians: "Not only do we believe the attribution of divinity to Jesus to be central to the pre-Easter Christology, but *we are hopelessly committed to the Chalcedonian formulation* as well [a reference made to the doctrines of Christ formulated at the Council of Chalcedon, 451 C.E.] (p. 74)." One would think that "evangelical" Christians would prefer something in the neighborhood of: "We are fully committed to the specific scriptural teaching regarding the nature and identity of Jesus Christ and are under the conviction that we must not take away from, alter, or go beyond the original New Testament teaching."

[119] Robert A. Wagoner, *The Great Debate Regarding the Father, Son, & Holy Spirit* (1997-98)

The True God—"the Trinity" or "the Father of our Lord Jesus Christ"?

Similarly, with respect to the reception of the Trinitarian concept in light of the historic Jewish mindset, nineteenth-century Bible scholar Ezra Abbot observed:

> We nowhere find either in the Acts or the Epistles any trace of the controversy and questionings which the direct announcement of such a doctrine must have excited. The one aim of the early apostolic preaching was to convince first the Jews, and then the Gentiles, that Jesus, whose life and teaching were so wonderful, whom God had raised from the dead, was the Messiah, exalted by God to be a Prince and a Saviour. To acknowledge Jesus as the Christ, or Jesus as Lord, which is essentially the same thing, was the one fundamental article of the Christian faith. Much, indeed, was involved in this confession; but it is now, I suppose, fully established and generally admitted that the Jews in the time of Christ had no expectation that the coming Messiah would be an incarnation of Jehovah, and no acquaintance with the mystery of the Trinity.[120]

The same point was made by another nineteenth-century scholar—a point that has never been adequately addressed by Trinitarian apologists:

> Of the same nature is the following argument. There arose several controversies in that age, especially with those Jews who had been converted to Christianity. Some of these are treated of in the Epistles. But it is very observable, that amongst the questions which thus arose and required explanations from the Apostles, there is no record of any question or controversy respecting the Object of worship. And yet, if the new religion was adding two new objects of worship to that of the old, this would have been, to a Jew, by far the most important, most interesting, and most perplexing of all the peculiarities of the gospel. No such doctrine could have been added to the ancient faith of the Jews, with whom the Unity of God was the proud and distinguishing tenet,

---

[120] *On the Construction of Romans IX. 5. From the Journal of the Society of Biblical Literature and Exegesis,* 1881.

without its occasioning some controversy...Yet no such controversy took place; neither is there the slightest appearance in the New Testament, that any objection, difficulty, or doubt arose in any quarter upon this ground. Is it not impossible, then, that any such doctrine should have been taught?[121]

In fact, rather than qualifying, altering, or elaborating upon the central "creed" of the Hebrew faith, Jesus actually affirmed it as part of the greatest of God's commandments, "*Hear, O Israel: Jehovah is our God, Jehovah is one.*"[122] Jesus himself never said that Jehovah, "the LORD," was "one" and yet somehow "three," or that Jehovah was "one" in one sense ('substance') but "three" in another sense ('persons'). Nor did Jesus implicitly teach such a religiously revolutionary concept in any example that can be cited in Scripture. Biblically speaking, the only "numerical formula" revealed in connection with God's identity is that "he" is "one"—without qualification. This has always been, and still remains, the true Christian confession of faith (Deuteronomy 6:4; Zechariah 14:9; Mark 12:28-34; Romans 3:30; Galatians 3:20; James 2:19).

> One of the scribes came near and heard them disputing with one another, and seeing that he answered them well, he asked him, 'Which commandment is the first of all?' Jesus answered, 'The first is, "Hear, O Israel: the Lord our God, the Lord is one; you shall love the Lord your God with all your heart, and with all your soul, and with all your mind, and with all your strength." The second is this, "You shall love your neighbour as yourself." There is no other commandment greater than these.' —Mark 12:28-31, *NRSV*

Trinitarian semantics and equivocations

Before one begins to take a close look at the Bible texts most commonly thought to lend credence to the Trinity, there are some important facts regarding the complexities of Trinitarian doctrine that must be kept in mind. First, from the perspective of

---

[121] *Testimony of Scripture Against the Trinity*, Printed by I. R. Butts, Boston, 1827.
[122] Deuteronomy 6:4, *ASV* (marginal rendering).

Trinitarian theology, there is no problem in saying, "the Father is the only true God," and yet in another place, "the Son is the only true God," and yet in another conversation, "the Holy Spirit is the only true God"—and yet still, "the Trinity is the only true God," and yet, "there is only *one* God." In other words, the concept of the Trinity is of such a nature that it actually allows for *four* distinctive ways to identify the "one" and "only true God." The Bible itself only gives us *one* (John 17:3; 1 Corinthians 8:6). And this is where much of the problem and confusion originates in discussions over the validity of the Trinity doctrine. So, although the Bible itself may positively identify the one God as "the Father" (at the same time depicting the 'one God' as a distinguishable figure from the 'Son'), Trinitarianism reasons that the Father *is* the one God, but so are the Son and Holy Spirit; and yet such notions are advanced despite the fact that the Bible does not identify the Son or holy Spirit as the "one God" or as "the only true God," or all three subjects collectively as constituting the "one" and "only true God."

Secondly, it is important to remember that, according to Trinitarians, the "one God"—*in the ultimate sense of the word*—is the "triune God (Father, Son, and Spirit)." But when Trinitarians say that "the Father *is* God" or "Jesus *is* God," they do not mean to identify either one as the Trinity; but rather, as one member of the Trinity; or, more specifically, as one "person" who eternally shares in the one God's divine "essence." This point is helpful in showing how, in Trinitarianism, the very term "God" must be equivocated, or given different meanings, depending upon what subject the term is being applied to.

Of course, throughout the Bible, particularly in the New Testament, Jesus is always presented as a figure distinct from "God." With respect to one New Testament book in particular, a respected evangelical observed:

> Repeatedly in the Book of Acts Jesus is the person involved in some action of *theos* [God]. He was anointed by God (10:38) and attested by God (2:22). God brought

him to Israel as a Savior (13:23), raised him from the dead (e.g., 2:24, 32), glorified him (3:13), exalted him by his right hand (2:33; 5:31; cf. 2:36), and ordained him to be judge of the living and the dead (10:42; cf. 17:31). Jesus was God's Christ (3:18), God's Son (9:20). The apostolic mission involved preaching the kingdom of God and teaching about the Lord Jesus Christ (28:31; cf. 8:12). But nowhere in Acts is this distinction between Jesus and God more pronounced than in 7:55-56 where at his martyrdom Stephen sees the glory of God and Jesus standing at God's right hand.[123]

In the book of Acts the apostle Peter declared that "*God anointed Jesus* of Nazareth with the holy Spirit and power" and further spoke about how Jesus "went about doing good and healing all those oppressed by the devil, for *God was with him.*"[124] And in his Gospel account, Luke even reports that as a child Jesus "grew and became strong, filled with wisdom; and the favor of God was upon him." After, Luke tells us that "Jesus continued to grow in stature and *in favor with God* and with men."[125]

With texts like these and others in mind, one might immediately wonder, how can the Trinity doctrine be sustained if it teaches that Jesus *is* "God" when the Scriptures so clearly and so consistently distinguish "Jesus" from "God"? The answer is, according to the apologists, "God," in these instances, simply means "Father" (the first 'person' of the Trinity). This is, in fact, the very first step in a Trinitarian's thought process when it comes to understanding or explaining a given text where "God" (even 'the only true God,' John 17:3) is clearly portrayed as a distinct figure from Jesus Christ. This is the same reason why the authors of a book critical toward the Trinity pointed out: "One person cannot be 'God' and 'the *Son* of God' without equivocating the term 'God.' Trinitarians use the term 'God' in

---

[123] Harris, *Jesus as God, The New Testament Use of Theos in Reference to Jesus*, p. 44.
[124] Acts 10:38, *NAB* (emphasis added).
[125] Luke 2:40, 52

the sense of 'the Father' as distinct from 'the Son' and 'the Holy Spirit.' But, in calling Christ 'God,' they use the term 'God' in the sense of 'the second person of the Trinity.' Thus, although the word 'God' is the same, it is given two different meanings."[126]

That is to say, although one could easily point to a multitude of texts that plainly portray "Jesus" and "God" as two distinct entities, for Trinitarian apologists, this does not disprove the notion that Jesus is himself "God," even though common sense would normally lead one to think otherwise. This is so because, in their own minds, and in their own efforts to defend the validity of the doctrine, they take the term "God" (in a given text that distinguishes 'God' from 'Jesus') and simply invest it with the meaning "*the Father*, the first 'person' of the Trinity"— a meaning that actually *harmonizes* with the necessary distinction between the "Father" and "Son" that exists in Trinitarianism, since, in the Trinitarian belief system, the "person" of the "Father" is not the same "person" as the "Son" (and vice-versa), even though they are both equally, and eternally, "God," according to Trinitarians.

So, according to orthodox Trinitarian teaching, the Father (like the Son and Spirit) is, really, a "person" who equally shares in the one "essence/being" of the one God, the Trinity. The problem is, according to the definitive pronouncements of Scripture itself, the Father *is* the "one God."[127]

This also helps to explain why the ability to discern and untangle the fallacies of Trinitarian argumentation does not always come easy. For instance, *it is true* that all scriptural references to "God" (particularly in distinction from the 'Son/Jesus') always constitute references to *the Father*. However, what needs to be appreciated is that when Trinitarian apologists use the word "Father," they are ultimately using the term in a way not used or defined as it is in Scripture. In fact, the very Scriptures Christians accept as authoritative identify the

---

[126] Graeser, Lynn, Schoenheit, *One God One Lord*, Reconsidering *the Cornerstone of the Christian Faith* (Indianapolis: Christian Educational Services, 2000), p. 607.
[127] 1 Corinthians 8:6

The True God—"the Trinity" or "the Father of our Lord Jesus Christ"?

Father as the "one God" or "the only true God" (1 Timothy 2:5; John 17:3). Trinitarianism, on the other hand, defines the Father, ultimately, as "the first person of the Trinity." So in this case, and in this respect, it really comes down to a matter of whether or not one is willing to accept the definition of "God" or "the Father" that the Scripture itself presents (explicitly), or if one decides to accept a definition or sense that was given after the Scriptures were written—a definition derived from highly questionable 'inference' and 'theology.' So, for instance, when the author of Hebrews spoke of "the God (*ho theos*)" who spoke to "our forefathers by means of the prophets"[128] yet who has "in the last of these days spoken by means of a Son," he was speaking unquestionably about God *the Father*. But, *scripturally* speaking, God the Father *is* the "one God," not one "person" who shares in the "essence/being" of the one God with two other "persons." At least we know for sure that the Bible does not articulate meanings of these kinds for references of these kinds. And this is where the arguments in favor of Trinitarianism become verifiably circular. Traditionally, defenders of the doctrine have thought that by changing the meaning/sense from "the God" (a specific being) in a given text to "*the Father*" (first 'person' of the Trinity) that they have now made the distinction between "God/Father" and "Son" allowable within the framework of their own theological system.[129] Unfortunately, the apologists of Trinitarianism have never been able to come to terms with the fact that the Bible itself does not define or articulate the sense of "the-first-person-of-the (essence-sharing)-Trinity" for "God" or "the Father."[130] As mentioned, *the Bible* plainly identifies the Father as "the only true God," the "one

---

[128] Hebrews chapter 1.
[129] See, for example, chapter 6 (*Does the Bible Deny that Jesus is God?*) in Robert Bowman's *Why You Should Believe in the Trinity* (Baker: Grand Rapids, 1989), pp. 71-88.
[130] The Trinitarian use of the term "Father" in the case of Hebrews 1 may be correct *terminologically*, yet its use is shown to be entirely misleading once one begins to break down the essential meaning that is ascribed to it. That is, Trinitarians use the term "Father," the correct referent and a biblical term; however, in the context of Trinitarian theology, the term "Father" takes on a totally distinctive theological meaning; again, a meaning given to us only by Trinitarians, not Scripture.

God"—"the God and Father of our Lord Jesus Christ."

So when Trinitarians suggest that "God" (when distinguished from the 'Son' or 'Jesus') simply means "*the Father*," they unfortunately fail to recognize that "the Father" simply means, or is really a *reference* to, the "one God/the only true God," according to Scripture—a figure consistently presented as someone other than, or distinct from, Jesus Christ. And in these instances it often comes down to a matter of having to identify the theological semantics and equivocations necessary for articulating the Trinitarian doctrinal system. This is also one way in which one can see how many arguments in defense of the Trinity are circular from their inception. That is, during critical instances, Trinitarians will switch from the term "God" to "Father" because Trinitarianism allows for and, in fact, demands a "personal" distinction between "Father" and "Son." Yet they define "Father" in a way that is simply assumed and asserted but not proven, and in such a way that cannot be proven scripturally. *Scripturally*, "Father" does not mean "first-person-of-the-Trinity," and that is undoubtedly the ultimate sense with which Trinitarian apologists invest that term. In fact, that is the reason why, when defending the doctrine, they generally prefer "Father" over the scriptural "God." But the truth is that Trinitarians cannot prove, and certainly cannot show from Scripture, that this is what the apostles or Jesus Christ had in mind. It can, however, be demonstrated—through direct and frequently expressed scriptural language and usage—that they did have in mind a specific being, the one God—"**the God of our Lord Jesus Christ, the Father of glory**..."[131]

The prioritized doctrines of Scripture and the importance of not going "beyond what is written..."

In light of the history and controversy surrounding the Trinity, it is helpful to reflect on another important point. If it is

---

[131] Ephesians 1:17

true that Scripture itself represents the final authority on matters of Christian faith, then, as Christians, we can be certain that in order to worship God and serve the Lord Jesus Christ acceptably, we have no need to look to the theological formulations of "the Church" in the fourth and fifth centuries. According to the apostle Paul, everything we need to know pertaining to right worship and godly living has already been revealed to us in the God-breathed revelation of Scripture. While the proclamations and demands of the "orthodox" certainly represent the majority opinion, and are supported by the weight of long-held—even ancient—tradition, those who are genuinely trying to follow Christ today (and willing to put the doctrine of the Trinity to the scriptural test) can be assured that they have no need to fear adverse judgment for not adhering to doctrines that developed *after* the Scriptures were written.

When Paul wrote his first letter to the Corinthians, he explained that it was a very trivial matter to him whether he was judged by them or by any human tribunal. After, Paul warned them not to judge anything before the appointed time, until the Lord arrives, for "he will bring to light what is hidden in darkness and will manifest the motives of our hearts." Paul went on to say: "I have applied these things to myself and Apollos for your benefit, brothers, so that you may learn from us *not to go beyond what is written*, so that none of you will be inflated with pride in favor of one person over against another."[132]

There is no doubt that the Trinity doctrine is *not* among those things that are "written." Neither the prophets nor apostles (nor Jesus Christ himself) ever called attention to a doctrine like this anywhere in the Hebrew or Christian writings. That is why if Christians were to simply re-tell and reiterate the gospel message as it stands presented in the Bible itself, they would never find it necessary to promote or point to a doctrinal concept known as

---

[132] 1 Corinthians 4:6, *NAB* (emphasis added). According to the footnote in the *New American Bible*, this statement "probably means that the Corinthians should avoid the false wisdom of vain speculation, contenting themselves with Paul's proclamation of the cross, which is the fulfillment of God's promises in the Old Testament (what is written)."

the "Trinity." Thus, we can safely conclude, since the apostles and prophets themselves never called attention to such a doctrine in their writings, neither must we.

While it may prove difficult at times not to be influenced by the pressure of the religious majority, or impressed by the crafty and sophisticated arguments advanced in behalf of the Trinitarian cause, when the Scriptures are studied calmly, soberly, and objectively,—from beginning to end—the notion that the Trinity is presupposed or implicitly revealed by the scriptural writers is exposed as having no sound basis; for all that God's Son said about himself, and all that God said about his Son through the prophets and apostles, shows that the doctrine of the Trinity (as defined by the post-biblical councils and creeds) simply had no place in their thinking. This is probably why even one of the most learned of Trinitarian scholars has acknowledged that, in biblical and in practical terms, such a "great amount of effort" must be expended to maintain the doctrine (Millard J. Erickson).[133]

This is also why, when discussing a matter of one's questioning the scriptural validity of the Trinity, one should recognize that it is not a simple matter of questioning the truthfulness or divine inspiration of the Scriptures themselves, but a question of whether or not we are understanding the Scriptures correctly, in light of a traditionally-proposed theological construct. The doctrine of the Trinity, as already pointed out, and as most Trinitarian theologians and apologists realize, is a doctrine of *inference*, a product of theology—the result of an attempt to synthesize the scriptural data on the Father, Son, and holy Spirit, not a direct scriptural teaching by any means.

In this light, it becomes a little easier to understand and empathize with the reasons why many Christians continue to

---

[133] One evangelical scholar admitted the following: "In honesty and truth, the doctrine of the trinity is difficult to explain or prove conclusively." —Ronald A. Wells (Professor of History at Calvin College, Grand Rapids, Michigan) *History Through the Eyes of Faith, Western Civilization and the Kingdom of God* (New York: HarperSanFransisco, 1989), p. 43.

express reservation about placing confidence in, and unreserved commitment toward, the doctrine—or any other doctrine for that matter—that is, according to the advocates themselves, "not clearly or explicitly taught anywhere in Scripture," or in a "matter where the Scriptures do not speak loudly and clearly," or in that which "the Bible does not teach," even though it is argued that the Scripture itself made the doctrine "necessary."

When one takes the time to carefully scrutinize the teachings of Scripture, however, one will find that there is a definite priority placed on those teachings that *are* essential to salvation and indispensable to living a life that is pleasing to God. Consider the following genuinely scriptural teachings; namely, that Jesus is the promised Messiah; that he died on behalf of sinners; that he was raised to life by God; and that he was exalted to God's right hand. Few believers would object to the statement that these propositions constitute some of Christianity's most critical, most basic, and most distinctive teachings. However, what we find in this case is that not only are each of these propositions taught in a crystal clear way, but that they are *emphasized* and reinforced *repeatedly* throughout the writings of the Bible. Or consider the scriptural testimony to the fact that "God is love" (a 'God of love and of peace,' 2 Corinthians 13:11), and how we are commanded by Christ to "love" God with our whole hearts, with all of our minds, and with all of our strength; and further, that we should love our neighbors as ourselves. Not only was the apostle divinely influenced to declare that "God is love"[134] (a genuine Christian doctrine), everything we are able to gather about the one God from the beginning to the end of Scripture beautifully and definitively establishes the truthfulness of such testimony. This is evident, not only in the profound expressions of love revealed by God in the works of creation and in the history of his people, but particularly through what may be accepted as the supreme and crowning act of God's loving-kindness, in that he "sent forth

---

[134] 1 John 4:8

his only-begotten Son into the world so that we might have life through him."[135] Not only did Moses reveal and Jesus himself affirm that God wills for us to love God and neighbor, when Jesus said, "Do to others whatever you would have them do to you," he went on to say, *"this, in fact, is what the Law and the Prophets mean."*[136] The apostle Paul reaffirmed the same principle when he wrote:

> **Let no debt remain outstanding, except the continuing debt to love one another, for he who loves his fellow man has fulfilled the law. The commandments, 'Do not commit adultery,' 'Do not murder,' 'Do not steal,' 'Do not covet,' and whatever other commandment there may be, are summed up in this one rule: 'Love your neighbor as yourself.' Love does no harm to its neighbor. Therefore love is the fulfillment of the law.**[137]

The point is that these are all truths ('doctrines') that as Christians we can have absolute confidence in based on the clarity and consistency in which they are presented to us in the Bible. When we consider a matter like the Trinity (and other post-biblical doctrinal developments), how can we entertain the same confidence? How can we view a "human attempt to understand biblical theology" and "a doctrine of inference from a number of biblical statements" as being on the same level or in the same category as those teachings that are in fact clearly, continually, and straightforwardly taught to us in sacred Scripture? Scripturally, we can confidently conclude that Jesus is the "Christ" or "Messiah," that he died to save sinners, that he was raised to life by God, that God is his Father, and that we should love God and our neighbor as ourselves. None of these are doctrines that we arrive at by way of inference, or by skillful and carefully-crafted theological argumentation. They are truths that lie on the very face of Scripture, so that anyone, whether they are learned or unlearned, may get the sense of them. Since

---

[135] 1 John 4:9
[136] Matthew 7:12, *NWT*
[137] Romans 13:8-10, *NIV*

the "doctrine of the Trinity is rather a doctrine of inference...than a doctrine directly and explicitly declared," it seems that the way of wisdom and humility would move one to agree that "the doctrine of inference ought never to be placed on a footing of equality with a doctrine of direct and explicit revelation."[138]

In view of the aforementioned facts, it should not be overly difficult to see why the absence of straightforward biblical teaching on a supposedly "essential article of faith" (along with such candid admissions made by Trinitarians themselves) has raised serious questions in the minds of Bible students of many and various backgrounds. The concerns are especially relevant among those earnestly hoping to attain to the salvation promised by the gospel revealed in Scripture, yet who are holding resolutely to the conviction that the plain testimony of Scripture is the most reliable authority we possess with regard to the original Christian faith. These are the Christians who remain convinced that all ecclesiastical dogmas, no matter how long or how widely believed, if not clearly affirmed in the sacred scriptural testimonies, cannot be esteemed among those truly founded on the rock of their divine foundation; but may be disregarded as further manifestations of human tradition, conceived amid the "shifting wind"[139] of human teaching and speculation.

Expressing a very similar conviction, another Bible student of the nineteenth century wrote the following thought-provoking words in light of the traditional Trinitarian claim:

> *It seemed strange to me, that our compassionate Heavenly Father, who so well knew the weakness of human nature, should require us to receive a doctrine, violating the common laws of that very reason which he has given us, without such an explicit statement of it, and*

---

[138] Mr. Carlile, *Jesus Christ the Great God and Saviour*. Quoted in *The Scripture Doctrine of the Father, Son and Holy Ghost. A Course of Lectures by* Frederick A. Farley, D. D., *Pastor of the Church of the Saviour, Brooklyn, N.Y.* (Reprinted by Christian Educational Services), p. 23.
[139] Ephesians 4:14, *TEV*

> *such an authoritative command for its reception, as would leave no possible chance for human reason to gainsay or resist it...I am firmly convinced that no doctrine can be necessary to salvation which is not so plainly revealed that the conscientious inquirer after the truth cannot possibly mistake it. 'Believe on the Lord Jesus Christ, and thou shalt be saved,' 'He that believeth that Jesus is the Christ is born of God,'—about these plain statements there can be no mistake. Here is a glorious platform on which sincere Christians of every name can meet, and exchange the right hand of fellowship.*[140]

The simplicity of truth and the stumbling blocks of "theology"

In the end we have no reason to doubt that whatever our heavenly Father deemed necessary for entrance into his kingdom is that which has been clearly communicated by his servants throughout the Scriptures; and specifically through the message delivered from the mouth of his "own Son." Unquestionably, a treasure chest of spiritual insights into the Father-Son relationship is disclosed to us in Scripture. Yet once we carefully consider the scriptural testimony regarding the nature of that relationship—as defined by the Son of God himself—we will discover that all post-biblical, "systematic," theological definitions are not needed after all.

In harmony with these observations, it was even acknowledged by E. Calvin Beisner, a defender of Trinitarian doctrine: "We must not contend that the Nicene Creed *looks like* the New Testament. The creed is an exercise in *systematic theology*. Although there are portions of the New Testament which are highly theological, the one thing we cannot say is that any of it is systematic theology as it was practiced three hundred years later."[141]

---

[140] Letter from Mary Dana 1845 January 19th (1845)
[141] Beisner, *God In Three Persons*, p. 145 (emphasis added).

The True God—"the Trinity" or "the Father of our Lord Jesus Christ"?

This is a significant and well-stated point that must be kept in mind. However, we should note first that the term "theology" itself is a fine one, meaning, essentially, the study of God and the things related to God.[142] Yet it should be remembered (though it is often forgotten) that there are many aspects of "theology" or "systematic theology" that have unfortunately done a great disservice to the advancement of spiritual light and truth. Generally speaking, in the field of "systematic theology" we find a kind of scientific process or discipline of systematizing and categorizing (theoretical as well as biblical) concepts relating to God, often through the employment of highly sophisticated, technical, and academic language. "Theology" is typically concerned and associated with the official defining and explaining of biblical, or what are perceived to be biblical, teachings, and concepts—in many cases, resulting in the dogmatic formulation of distinctive religious constructs and systems of doctrine. Whether or not any one of the terms and concepts associated with "Trinitarianism" are those which reflect authentic Christian teaching, it is important to distinguish between the various conclusions of "systematic theology" from the spiritual principles and abiding truths essential to the Christian faith and life, as set forth and defined by God himself, in the divinely-inspired Scriptures.

In his widely-read work, *The Christian Doctrine of God*, internationally-known Protestant scholar Emil Brünner, although attempting to elaborate on what he considered to be the valid role of certain forms of theological reflection, still showed himself sensitive to the same principles already expressed with respect to the historic practice of systematic theology, or a concept otherwise known as "dogmatics." Commendably, in the opening chapter of his work, Brünner took note of the same phenomena in a spirit of sympathetic understanding:

---

[142] The word is, technically, derived "from the Greek words *theos*, meaning 'God,' and *logos*, meaning 'word' or 'discourse.' Thus the word theology means 'discourse about God.'" —Smith, *Theological "Ism"s*, p. 88.

A person who has hitherto only encountered the Biblical Gospel in its simplest form, and has been gripped by it in a direct, personal way, must necessarily feel appalled, chilled, or repelled by the sight of massive volumes of dogmatics, and his first acquaintance with the whole apparatus of ideas and of reflection connected with this study of theology as a science. Instinctively the simple Christian murmurs: 'But why this immense apparatus of learning? What is the use of these subtle distinctions and these arid intellectual definitions? What is the use of this process of 'vivisection' of our living faith?' When, further, this 'simple believer' becomes aware of the theological controversies and passionate dogmatic conflicts which seem inevitable, it is easy to understand that the simple Christian man or woman turns away from all this with horror, exclaiming: '*I thank you, Father, Lord of heaven and earth, because you have hidden these things from the wise and the intelligent and have revealed them to infants; yes, Father, for such was your gracious will*' [Jesus: Matt. 11:25]. He sees the contradiction between the simple Gospel of the New Testament and this world of extremely abstract conceptions, between the living concreteness of the speech of Jesus and His Apostles, which speaks straight to the hearts of all who listen aright, and this ruthless analysis, this massive labour of systematic theology, in which only people of high intellectual gifts can share, which seems to be possible only at the cost of losing the freshness and directness of a living experience…From this point of view dogmatics seems to be a perversion of the Gospel…Therefore the introduction of the truth of faith into that intellectual process of reflection, which is so remote from reality, can do faith no good, indeed, it can only do harm, because it diverts the Christian believer from his real duty of active love to God and his neighbour…We must, however, begin at this point: namely, that the Bible itself knows nothing of that process which from time immemorial the Church has known as 'dogmatics.' For more than a thousand years

Israel existed as a religious community without anything like a system of dogma, in the sense, for instance, in which Calvin uses it in his *Institutes*—indeed, the Jewish Church did not even possess a Catechism, and even the Early Christian Church—that is, the Christian Church at the time of its highest vitality and purity, did not produce anything of that kind.[143]

Generally speaking, "systematic theology" is said to be a method of organizing and summarizing what the Bible teaches on a given subject. Unfortunately, the tradition of systematic theology has frequently involved going into the realms of unneeded speculation, complex philosophical enumeration, and in many cases, the issuing of unwarranted and unauthorized dogmatic pronouncements. "Theology," in this sense, as many Christians are aware, is an entirely *human* response to the inspired revelation of Scripture.[144] There even seems to be a sense in which certain expressions of theological thinking are the direct or indirect result of a theologian's lack of contentment with the information that has been given to us in the Scriptures; or, in some cases, it is due simply to the practice and culture of the more academically minded and their fondness of formally categorizing and defining ideas so that all teachings and concepts fit into a definite system, a theological package of dogmatic statements. While not necessarily intending to, however, the practice of theology (or 'theologizing') often clouds the precious and simple truths of Christ's teachings, diminishing and detracting from the power and purity of his original message. This is one of the reasons why, as followers of Christ, we want

---

[143] *The Christian Doctrine of God*, pp. 6-9 (*KJV* changed to *NRSV*). Apparently, Brünner uses the term 'vivisection' metaphorically, which is technically, "The act or practice of cutting into or otherwise injuring living animals, especially for the purpose of scientific research."

[144] Shirley Guthrie similarly observed from his perspective as a "Reformed/Protestant" theologian: "*All* theology, whether that of an individual or of the whole church, is at best an inadequate, fallible, human attempt to understand that truth ['the truth about God, human life, and the world in Jesus Christ as we know him in the Bible']. According to the Reformed churches, therefore, there always has been and always will be the right and responsibility to question any individual's, any denomination's, any creedal document's grasp of the truth—not for the sake of our freedom to think anything we please, but for the sake of the freedom of biblical truth from every human attempt to capture and tame it." —*Christian Doctrine*, pp. 17, 18.

to make sure that we avoid presumptuously defining that which God himself has left undefined, or condemning where God has not condemned, by setting up artificial, man-made boundaries with respect to what makes a genuine Christian and what does not. Such practices have led to a great deal of misunderstanding, confusion and division in the world of those who profess to be followers of Jesus Christ.[145]

This is the reason why—in light of the wide variety of doctrines that have developed through the centuries since the apostolic period—it is crucial to realize the importance of separating out what is truth delivered to us from God from that which had its origin in a human or ecclesiastical tradition. Unfortunately, it has been an all too common practice for theologians and religious leaders to claim to have the ability or authority to distinguish between, and to separate out as, those who are "true" and those who are "false" Christians, based upon a distinctive and highly questionable *interpretation* of Scripture, rather than on that which is *expressly set forth* in Scripture—a humanly-contrived standard rather than a divine one.

> *"When I came to you, my brothers, to preach God's secret truth to you, I did not use long words and great learning [I came to you, without any pretensions to eloquence or wisdom, REB]. For I made up my mind to forget everything while I was with you except Jesus Christ, especially his death on the cross. So when I came to you I was weak and trembled all over with fear, and my teaching and message were not delivered with skillful words of human wisdom, but with convincing proof of the power of God's Spirit, [so that your faith might be built not upon human wisdom but upon the power of God, NEB]."*
> —The apostle Paul, 1 Corinthians 1:1-5, *Today's English Version*

---

[145] This is not said for the purpose of trying to take away from those who are active in the discipline of systematic theology, but to point out a consideration for its dangers and limitations; and to affirm the fact that Christians may function spiritually in the service of God and Christ without using or promoting several of such scripturally-unarticulated, dogmatic propositions and theological formulations commonly advanced.

"...There is nothing wrong with tradition, as long as we do not confuse tradition with truth. As soon as we become more attached to our traditions than we are to truth, we are in very deep trouble...As soon as we make our tradition the test of someone else's standing with God, we have elevated that tradition to a status that is unbiblical..."

—James R. White, *The King James Only Controversy*, p. 17

"There is an epidemic in the world today. People are not open to the possibility of being in error. They hold their beliefs within a clenched fist, unwilling and therefore unable to see possible errors in their respective ideologies. It is not until individuals are willing to place their beliefs on the chopping block of critical scrutiny and rigorous examination that error can be hacked in half and tossed in the fire of falsehood, and truth can be given an opportunity to prove and demonstrate its ability to withstand the fiercest strike. As people of God, we should be the ones who set the bar high for this type of radical intellectual integrity. As genuine truth seekers, we need not be afraid of placing our beliefs to the test or allowing them to be challenged. If our beliefs are well founded, they will be reinforced and strengthened. Conversely, if our beliefs are shown to be weak and faulty, in so far as truth is our objective, we will be thankful to see the errors in our own thinking, thus freeing us to search afresh for what is true, right, and of God. When the world sees a people striving to be responsible thinkers, open to critique, reasonable, reverent, and painfully honest, they will be more willing to lend their ears to consider the kingdom we proclaim and the Messiah we follow…We should be willing to bring our truths under the light of intellectual scrutiny because we are convinced that they will hold strong when not only thoroughly but also fairly evaluated. On the contrary, we must be willing to change our views if they do not withstand meticulous investigation. In the end, this sort of revolutionary intellectual integrity will attract the world's attention. People will be drawn into dialogue concerning the kingdom we eagerly expect and the man from Nazareth whom we follow as the long-awaited Messiah."

— From the Manifesto on *Intellectual Honesty* by Dan Mages

"Who has ascended into heaven, or descended? Who has gathered the wind in His fists? Who has bound the waters in a garment? Who has established all the ends of the earth? What is His name, and what is His Son's name, If you know? Every word of God is pure; He is a shield to those who put their trust in Him. Do not add to His words, lest He rebuke you, and you be found a liar." —Proverbs 30:4-6, *NKJV*

"If God were your Father, you would love me, for I came from God and am here; I did not come on my own, but he sent me. Why do you not understand what I say?"

—Jesus Christ, John 8:42-43

2

Jesus Christ—"God the Son" or "the Son of the living God"?

> *Who (indeed) is the victor over the world but the one who believes that Jesus is the Son of God?*
> —1 John 5:5, NAB

Ever since the days of Jesus of Nazareth, those who were exposed to his unique life and teaching have held widely divergent beliefs about his identity. Some in Jesus' time—because of the miraculous signs he performed, and the great wisdom and authority with which he spoke—took a favorable view toward him, and he was at times described by the people as a good teacher and rabbi. Some described him as a prophet and man of God. On the other hand, there were those among his own people—based on the same miracle working and profession of authority—who derisively called him a "Samaritan." Others said that he was possessed by a demon, that he was a madman, a sinner, and that he was even guilty of blasphemy.[1]

---

[1] Compare John 7:12, *NAB*. The Samaritans were related to the Jews but were generally despised by them because they were racially mixed and held different religious beliefs. According to Albert Barnes, calling Jesus a Samaritan "had the force of charging him with being a heretic or a

"God the Son" or "the Son of the living God"?

Although he was constantly opposed by the Jewish religious leaders (the Pharisees, Scribes and Sadducees), many still believed and followed him. On one occasion, Jesus spoke to those who were believing:

> **If you continue in my word, you are truly my disciples, and you will know the truth, and the truth will make you free.**[2]

To the same who believed but who eventually came to oppose him (apparently),—those who viewed themselves as having a special standing before God based on their physical descent from Abraham—on that same occasion, Jesus said to them:

> **If you were Abraham's children, you would be doing the works of Abraham. But now you are trying to kill me, a man who has told you the truth that I heard from God; Abraham did not do this. You are doing the works of your father!**[3]

Because they had rejected Jesus' teaching and were even intending to kill him, this group of Jews demonstrated that they were really not the children or descendents of Abraham—at least, not in the sense that really mattered to God. Fully aware of their murderous attitudes and intended actions, Jesus told them that they were practicing the deeds of their father; and in the verses following, he declared forthrightly that their father was "the devil" himself, whom Jesus described as "a murderer from the beginning." In response, the Jews proudly contended, "We were not born from fornication. We have one Father, God." But Jesus said to them:

---

schismatic, because the Samaritans were regarded as such…The Samaritans received only the five books of Moses, and rejected the writings of the prophets and all the Jewish traditions. From these causes arose an irreconcilable difference between them, so that the Jews regarded them as the worst of the human race (John 8:48), and had no dealings with them, John 4:9." —*Barnes' Notes on the New Testament, The Gospels* (Grand Rapids: Baker Books: originally published in 1847; reprinted 2005), pp. 274, 109.

[2] John 8:31-32, *RSV.*

[3] John 8:39-40, *NAB.* All Jews trace their lineage to the patriarch Abraham; he is described later by the apostle Paul as "the father of all those having faith" (Romans 4:11).

> **If God were your Father, you would love me, for I came from God and am here; I did not come on my own, but he sent me.**[4]

Through carefully considering the specific content of his teaching in one of the many confrontations he had with the Jews, we can see clearly that Jesus spoke about himself as one who brought the truth from God, and that he was sent by God to fulfill this special purpose. The significance and uniqueness of Jesus' profession is brought into even clearer focus when we consider how, on that same occasion, he said to the Jews, "*I tell you most solemnly, whoever keeps my word will never see death.*"[5]

But rather than responding in faith, the Jews said to Jesus, "Now we are sure that you have a demon. Abraham died, as did the prophets, yet you say, whoever keeps my word will never taste death. Are you greater than our father Abraham, who died? Or the prophets, who died? Who do you make yourself out to be?"

Additionally, in the same account, we see not only that Jesus claimed to bring the truth that he "heard from God," but that the very word he spoke actually had the power to deliver men from death—specifically, men who would *abide* by that word. Given the tremendous and unprecedented nature of such claims, the Jews demanded to know exactly who Jesus professed to be. To this direct and pointed question, Jesus answered:

> **If I glorify myself, my glory is nothing; it is my Father who glorifies me, of whom you say, 'He is our God.' You do not know him, but I know him. And if I should say that I do not know him, I would be a liar like you. But I do know him and I keep his word.**[6]

Although they persisted with their insults and accusations, Jesus went on to claim that he had a relationship

---

[4] John 8:42, *NAB*
[5] John 8:51
[6] John 8:51-55

"God the Son" or "the Son of the living God"?

with God that no man had ever claimed before—at least not with miraculous signs and accompanying deeds of righteousness as compelling evidence. He made the incredibly unique and challenging claim that the very God whom those Jews professed to worship—the God of creation—was his own Father! By the end of this account the Jews had grown even more indignant with Jesus, and they finally picked up stones to hurl at him, "but Jesus hid himself and went out of the temple," the Gospel of John tells us.

Soon after, Jesus is reported to have miraculously opened the eyes of a man who had been blind from birth. But because Jesus performed this deed on the Sabbath, the Pharisees believed he was in violation of prescribed religious law and that therefore he was not of God.[7] According to John's account, some of the Pharisees concluded: "'The man who did this cannot be from God, because he does not obey the Sabbath law.' Others, however, objected, saying, 'How could a man who is a sinner do such mighty works as these?' And there was a division among them."[8]

While various and conflicting opinions began to develop around Jesus and his accompanying supernatural activities, the Jewish leaders began to intimidate anyone who expressed faith in him. John reports that the "Jews had already agreed that if anyone should confess him to be Christ,[9] he was to be put out of the synagogue." Then, after being interrogated by the Pharisees, the man who had been healed told them that he believed Jesus to

---

[7] The Jews are reported to have made this charge against Jesus several times in the Gospel accounts. They often pointed to his alleged violation of the Sabbath law as a proof that he was not a man of God. The Pharisees' rejection of Jesus on this account yields an important insight into their character and general religious attitudes as well. They were so preoccupied with trying to meticulously observe the letters of the law (even adding to the law their own traditions), that they could not accept the fine and miraculous deeds Jesus had performed, because, technically, Jesus did work on the Sabbath, which God intended to be a day of rest (Exodus 20:8-11). But, according to Scripture, unlike any other human that ever lived, Jesus never sinned against God. He said that he—"the Son of Man"—was "Lord even of the Sabbath," and concluded: "it is lawful to do good on the Sabbath" (Matthew 12:12; Mark 2:27; 3:1-6).

[8] John 9:16

[9] That is, the "Messiah," meaning "the anointed one." In the Christian Scriptures, a reference to the *Christ* or *Messiah* is a reference to the long-awaited Deliverer and King of Israel foretold by the prophets in the ancient Hebrew Scriptures.

"God the Son" or "the Son of the living God"?

be a prophet. He said, "Never since the world began has it been heard that anyone opened the eyes of a person born blind. If this man were not from God, he could do nothing."

But instead of rejoicing with the man and expressing sincere gratitude for the miraculous healing that had taken place, the Pharisees followed through on their threat and expelled the man from their synagogue.[10]

When Jesus continued to teach the people, he spoke of himself as "the fine shepherd" who "lays down his life for the sheep," in contrast to "the hired man, who does not care for the sheep." Jesus went on to explain to his listeners that he was loved and approved by his Father, and that he lays down his life voluntarily: "I have power to lay it down, and I have power [lit., 'authority'] to take it up again. This command I have received from my Father." John's Gospel again reports that there arose a "division among the Jews because of these words. Many of them said, 'He has a demon, and he is mad; why listen to him?' Others said, 'These are not the sayings of one who has a demon. Can a demon open the eyes of the blind?'"[11]

Through a careful consideration of these brief accounts, we gain valuable insight into some of the basic issues that surrounded the identity and claims of Jesus of Nazareth in his time. Undoubtedly, Jesus' preaching, teaching, and unique claims about himself resulted in the raising of many questions and in the arousal of a great deal of controversy; and the people continued to dispute about who he was. However, the Gospels clearly testify that Jesus was not only a preacher of righteousness, but that his very appearance onto the scene of history actually proved to be the long-awaited fulfillment of ancient Hebrew prophecy. In addition to the fulfillment of prophecy, the Gospels report that Jesus performed a multitude of good deeds and miraculous signs which, for his true followers, clearly and powerfully established the truthfulness of his Messianic claim. In the end, though, Jesus was officially rejected

---
[10] See John 9:16-34
[11] John 10:18, *NAB*; John 10:19, *RSV*

by the leaders of his own nation and ultimately condemned to a shameful and agonizing death at the hands of the Roman authorities. Yet the New Testament writers (some who were eyewitnesses of these events) report to us that, three days after, Jesus was seen by a multitude of his followers, having been raised to life by God, and, after, exalted to God's right hand—culminating in a decisive vindication of his identity as God's beloved "Son" and "Messiah."[12]

Still, in our own day, even among those who profess to adhere to testimony of the ancient scriptural accounts, people continue to disagree and divide over the fundamental question of who Jesus is. Historically, the interpretation of Jesus' identity has often served as the basis for the formation of distinctive religious factions. It has even been common for those on differing sides to exclude, denounce, and—either directly or indirectly—condemn those who do not conform to their established viewpoint. A consideration of the conflicting doctrines held by the various Christian sects now in existence makes evident that many have added to, or taken away from, what the Scriptures themselves teach about the identity of Jesus. Unfortunately, the leaders of certain movements have not only gone beyond the scriptural teaching (while professing to derive their doctrines exclusively from it), many have expressly declared that those who do not fall in line with their ideology (often defined in an extra-biblical creed, doctrinal statement, or confession of faith) cannot be accepted within their community as true practitioners of the Christian faith. Sadly, because these practices are so widespread and common among Christian denominations, many devout seekers of truth have been presented with a distorted picture of God's Son and the actual faith that was established by him.

Evangelical E. Calvin Beisner made an important observation on this very subject. He began with the question:

What, then, is the dividing line between the Christian

---

[12] Compare 1 Corinthians 15:3-8; Romans 1:1-5

faith and that which is pseudo-Christian or openly non-Christian? *The line must be drawn based on the identity of the person and work of Jesus Christ*, for it is his person on whom the Church is built.[13]

While it is true that today, as in the past, professed followers of Jesus have held vigorously to numerous and contradictory opinions about his true nature and identity, the question of Jesus' identity is not as complicated as it might seem because of this. But in order to be sure that we are holding fast to the truth on such an important matter, it is crucial to recognize that there really is no known, greater, or more trustworthy source to turn to but the very source the Messiah Jesus held as the highest authority—the holy Scriptures, described by the apostle Paul as "inspired of God (literally 'God-breathed')," and by Jesus himself as a standard that could not be "set aside" (*NAB*) or "broken" (*NASB*).[14]

As a study of the apostolic writings shows, there were those in the time of Jesus who described him as a teacher and prophet, which he definitely was. But a consideration of the entirety of the scriptural accounts—including the words of Jesus himself, along with the witness of his closest followers—will show that he was definitely someone and something more than that. As will be seen from an examination of the following accounts, all the books and letters of the Bible are completely harmonious, notably simple in their expression, and remarkably clear in their identification of Jesus of Nazareth—undeniably, the most unique, most influential, and most carefully-studied historical figure who ever lived.

In the very beginning of his Gospel account, Luke relates to his readers the extraordinary and miraculous circumstances that surrounded the pregnancy of the virgin Mary and following

---

[13] Beisner, *God in Three Persons*, p. 19 (emphasis added).

[14] 2 Timothy 3:16; John 10:35. In prayer to God, Jesus declared, "your word is truth" (John 17:7); and in the hour of his temptation, when Satan tempted him to turn stones into bread, Jesus, although hungry from a long period of fasting, pointed to his Father's word (found in sacred Scripture) as final and authoritative: "It is written...'Man does not live on bread alone but on every word that comes from the mouth of God'" (Matthew 4:1-10).

birth of Jesus. When God sent the angel Gabriel to the city of Nazareth, the angel spoke the following words to Mary:

> "'Do not be afraid, for you have found favor with God. Behold you will conceive in your womb and bear a son, and you shall name him Jesus. He will be great and will be called Son of the Most High, and the Lord God will give him the throne of David his father, and he will rule over the house of Jacob forever, and of his kingdom there will be no end.' But Mary said to the angel, 'How can this be, since I have no relations with a man?' And the angel said to her in reply, 'The holy Spirit will come upon you, and the power of the Most High will overshadow you. Therefore the child to be born will be called holy, the Son of God.'"[15]

Here, in the introduction to Luke's Gospel, from the very mouth of the heavenly messenger, we are told that Jesus—who had no human father—would be called "Son of the Most High" and "the Son of God." The disciple Matthew, in his Gospel, also reports on the very same announcement given by the angelic being. In the third chapter of their Gospels, both Matthew and Luke disclose to us a most solemn and most dependable testimony with respect to the identity of Jesus (now a grown man at this point); only in this case, it is a testimony given and confirmed by the Most High himself. Just prior to his temptation in the wilderness, which preceded his public ministry, Jesus went to the Jordan River to be baptized by John the Baptist. Matthew reports:

> ...when Jesus was baptized, he went up immediately from the water, and behold, the heavens were opened and he saw the Spirit of God descending like a dove, and alighting on him; and lo, a voice from heaven, saying, 'This is my beloved Son, with whom I am well

---

[15] Luke 1:30-36, *NAB*. The name "Jesus" (Hebrew: 'Yeshua') was actually a fairly common one in the first century. It appears to be a form or variation of "Joshua" (Hebrew: 'Yehoshua'). The name literally means, "Salvation of Jah (Jehovah)," or "Jah (Jehovah) saves."

"God the Son" or "the Son of the living God"?

pleased ['my favor rests on him,' *Jerusalem Bible*].'[16]

In the seventeenth chapter of Matthew, when Peter, James and John were with Jesus on the mountain (the 'mount of transfiguration'), for the second time the voice of God went forth; this time, out of a bright cloud: *"This is my own dear Son, with whom I am will pleased—listen to him!"*[17]

This could be one of the reasons why Jesus pointed out, in the fifth chapter of John's Gospel, as he was speaking with the Jews who sought to kill him: *"the Father who sent me has himself borne witness to me. His voice you have never heard, his form you have never seen; and you do not have his word abiding in you, for you do not believe in the one he has sent."*[18]

The words of Jesus demonstrate how crucial it is that we, his followers, accept the testimony of his Father. We must believe in the one the Father sent.

Another one of the clearest, most critical and most relevant accounts is found later on in the Gospel of Matthew. Here, on this occasion, Jesus himself directly posed to his disciples the very question regarding his true identity—in the words of E. Calvin Beisner, the very "person on whom the Church is built." The account reads as follows:

> **Now when Jesus came into the district of Caesarea Philippi, he asked his disciples, 'Who do men say that the Son of man is?' And they said, 'Some say John the Baptist, others say Elijah, and others Jeremiah or one of the prophets.' He said to them, 'But who do you say that I am?' Simon Peter replied,**
>
> ***"You are the Christ, the Son of the living God."***

---

[16] Matthew 3:16-17, *RSV*. In *The International Standard Bible Encyclopedia*, Volume III, p. 1411, it was observed: "Jn 3:34 emphasizes the fulness of the bestowal upon Jesus: 'For whom God hath sent speaketh the words of God: for he [gives him the fulness of his Spirit, *TEV*].' In the witness of the Baptist the permanence of the anointing of Jesus is declared: 'Upon whomsoever thou shalt see the Spirit descending, and abiding' (1:33). The gift of the Spirit in fulness to Jesus at His baptism was no doubt His formal and public anointing for His Messianic work (Acts 10:38)."

[17] Matthew 17:5, *TEV*

[18] John 5:37-38, *RSV* (emphasis added).

"God the Son" or "the Son of the living God"?

And Jesus answered him, 'Blessed are you, Simon [son of] Jonah! For flesh and blood has not revealed this to you, but my Father who is in heaven.'[19]

Who is Jesus according to the Scriptures? Jesus is the "Christ" or "Messiah," *the Son of the living God!* This was not something delivered to Peter by any human source; for the Messiah, after having approved of Peter's unambiguous declaration, made clear that it was a truth revealed to him by none other than the heavenly Father himself![20]

In light of such direct and unmistakable scriptural testimony, it may immediately appear difficult to understand how and why there would ever be a dispute among Bible believers over such a fundamental question, and yet such a clearly-given scriptural answer, as to the identity of Jesus, the Christ. A further examination of the scriptural record will show that there was never any doubt or confusion in the minds of the apostles (Jesus' closest associates), particularly once the truth about the Christ was fully made known and confirmed by divine testimony. In fact—according to traditional dating—it was probably about twenty years after the original writing of the Gospel of Matthew, and at least thirty years following the actual event, that the apostle Peter recalled his experience of having beheld Jesus on the mount of transfiguration.[21]

In his second letter, Peter wrote solemnly about the truth

---

[19] Matthew 16:13-17, *RSV*. William Clark, in his essay *"Who is God?"* asked, "Why is it necessary to improve on the foundational Christian confession, 'You are the Christ, the Son of the living God,' and thus alter its clear meaning?...In order to understand God and Jesus and their relationship, we must begin with this confession...The biblical confession of a Christian is simple and clear: 'Jesus is the Messiah, the Son of the living God.' With these words we recognize that: 1. God is living. 2. He is the God who promised to send the Messiah. 3. This God is the Father of Jesus. 4. Jesus is the Messiah. 5. Jesus is the Son of God. This biblical confession of faith represents the central biblical Message." —*Catechism of the Catholic Church*, the German edition, pub. R. Oldenbourg, Munich: Libreria Editrice Vaticana, 1993.

[20] Yet the definiteness and dogmatism with which Trinitarians speak in reference to the identity of Jesus is as if Peter had said in response to Jesus' inquiry, "You are God the Son, the second person of the Trinity, consubstantial with the Father." Such a description/concept, however, is verifiably foreign to the apostolic doctrine.

[21] Some scholars believe that Matthew's Gospel was completed in 41 C.E., possibly in the early part of 50 C.E (covering 2 B.C.E-33 C.E). 2 Peter was probably written around 64 C.E., possibly between 65-68. See: *NIV, Ryrie, and MacArthur* Study Bibles for discussion on these dates.

of Jesus Christ, having emphasized that the very basis of the believers' confidence in that truth rests on the divine testimony of God himself. It was under genuine spiritual inspiration that the apostle wrote the following:

> **We did not follow cleverly devised myths when we made known to you the power and coming of our Lord Jesus Christ, but we had been eyewitnesses of his majesty. For he received honor and glory from God the Father when that unique declaration came to him from the majestic glory, '*This is my beloved Son, with him I am well pleased.*' We ourselves heard this very voice as it came from heaven when we were with him on that holy mountain.**[22]

The readers of the apostle's letter are assured that the power and coming (or 'presence') of the Lord Jesus Christ was not according to any myth or "cleverly invented story" (*NIV*). In fact, Peter was one who actually had the unique privilege of being among the *eyewitnesses* of Jesus' magnificence, when "his face was shown like the sun, and his garments became as white as light."[23] The apostle reminds Christians that it was God the Father himself who spoke out of the bright cloud, purposefully declaring that Jesus was indeed his beloved Son to whom all should listen. Approximately thirty years after Peter wrote his second letter, the elderly apostle John wrote his first. And like Peter, John was one of the select few blessed with the honor of living in close intimacy with Jesus during the final years of his life on earth. In the beginning of his letter, John even speaks of Jesus—"the word of life" manifested—as that which "we have seen with our own eyes" and "have looked upon and touched with our own hands."[24]

Scripturally, we have every reason to accept John as a dependable eyewitness of the life of Jesus Christ. In light of this, yet not in this regard only, Christians can have confidence in the

---

[22] 2 Peter 1:16-18, *NAB* and *The New Testament* by Kleist & Lily (emphasis added).
[23] Matthew 17:2
[24] 1 John 1:1, *NEB*

fact that Jesus truly is God's very own, unique and dearly beloved Son. Here, John may have written some of the most beautiful expressions found in all of Scripture:

> **Beloved, let us love one another, because love is from God; and everyone who loves is born of God and knows God. Whoever is without love does not know God, for God is love. In this way the love of God was revealed to us: God sent his only begotten Son into the world so that we might have life through him. In this is love: not that we have loved God, but that he loved us and sent his Son as propitiation for our sins. Beloved, if God so loved us, we also ought to love one another. No man has ever seen God, but if we love one another, God abides in us and his love is perfected in us…Moreover, we have seen and do testify that the Father sent his Son to be Savior of the world. Whoever acknowledges that Jesus is the Son of God, God abides in him and he in God. And we have come to know and to believe in the love God has for us.**[25]

"In this the love of God was…", as different translations express it, "shown," "revealed," "disclosed," "displayed," "demonstrated," "made manifest toward us…" The expression is reminiscent of one of the most widely-known and well-loved passages of Scripture: *"For God so loved the world, that he gave his only begotten Son, that whoever believes in him should not perish but have everlasting life. For God did not send his Son into the world to condemn the world, but that the world might be saved through him."*[26]

Words do not seem adequate for expressing the gratitude Christians throughout the ages have felt for the way God has demonstrated his great love. In these few passages of Scripture, not only do we receive clear affirmation of Jesus' identity as God's only-begotten (or 'unique') Son, but we are also given the most comforting assurance that we remain in union with God

---

[25] 1 John 4:7-16.
[26] John 3:16-17, *NKJV*.

through our conscientious acknowledgment and confession of this very truth. Accompanied with such knowledge is the fact that we now behold such a beautiful picture, and receive such a heart-warming, joy-inspiring insight, into the kind of person God really is—demonstrated most clearly in this supreme expression of sacrificial love. As we take time to reflect on such an outstanding manifestation of the grace of God, it seems doubtful that we will ever be able to truly fathom the great depth of our heavenly Father's loving-kindness, incomparable generosity, and tender compassion. How can we thank God enough when we discover that his goodness and mercy go to such an extent that he was willing to deliver up the life of his own Son so that sinners could receive life? Our hearts cannot help but to be overwhelmed with joy and our lips cannot but abound with praise for our heavenly Father and his Son for such an undeserved blessing.[27]

The apostle goes on to reason that if God loved us in this way, we ourselves are under obligation to love one another. The apostle makes clear that the love of God means keeping God's commandments; yet, "his commandments are not burdensome, for whatever is born of God overcomes the world, and the victory which overcomes the world is *our faith*." The apostle went on to declare:

> **In fact, this faith of ours is the only way in which the world can be conquered. For who could ever be said to conquer the world but the man who really believes that Jesus is God's Son?**[28]

Most reassuring of all, it seems, is that in the matter of our faith in the Son of God, like Peter, we need not merely rely on human testimony. For John goes on to tell us:

---

[27] In the Genesis chapter 22 account, when God told Abraham to offer his son Isaac on the altar of sacrifice, many Christians believe that there is to be found a picture, a foreshadowing, or a prefiguring, of how God would ultimately sacrifice the life of *his* Son for "the life of the whole world." In this way, and in light of this account, it helps us as humans to better relate to the kind of sacrifice God made in behalf of sinners, in light of the profound love we have for our own children. In this we recognize how much it cost our heavenly Father to make us his children through the sacrifice of Jesus Christ.
[28] 1 John 5:4-5, *Phillips Modern English*

"God the Son" or "the Son of the living God"?

> **If we accept human testimony, the testimony of God is surely greater. Now the testimony of God is this, that he has testified on behalf of his Son. Whoever believes in the Son of God has this testimony within himself. Whoever does not believe God has made him a liar by not believing the testimony God has given about his Son. And this is the testimony: God gave us eternal life, and this life is in his Son. Whoever possesses the Son has life; whoever does not possess the Son of God does not have life. I write these things to you so that you may know that you have eternal life, you who believe in the name of the Son of God.**[29]

In this case John reasons that although we may—as we often and rightly do—accept human testimony, there can surely be no doubt as to the *reliability* and *superiority* of the very testimony of God himself; and we know that God has solemnly testified to the fact that Jesus is his "Son," having been powerfully and decisively demonstrated through the events associated with his baptism, transfiguration, and, as will be shown, by his resurrection from the dead and following exaltation to the right hand of God. Undeniably, the assurance given in John's letter is a cause for great rejoicing; and in light of such assurance, it becomes truly difficult to understand why anyone would have in mind to alter,[30] qualify, or complicate such powerful and convincing testimony as the one laid out before us in sacred Scripture. As God's people, we may finally rest in lasting peace and confidence, for there is nothing confusing

---

[29] 1 John 5:9-13, *NAB*

[30] An example of an alteration commonly advanced is found in Grudem's *Systematic Theology*, page 503: "In light of John's concern in this epistle to combat a heresy that did not confess Jesus as God who came in the flesh (see 1 John 4:2-3), it is likely that this sin 'unto death' is the serious heresy of denying Christ and subsequently failing to obtain salvation through Christ." 1 John 4:2-3, however, has nothing to say about "Jesus as *God* who came in the flesh." It simply says that "Jesus *Christ*" came in the flesh without identifying Jesus as "God." In fact, one can read the entire letter and will find no identification of Jesus as "God who came in flesh." John believed, of course, that Jesus was God's *Son* (1 John 4:15). This is, in fact, one of the more dominant themes to be found in John's letter.

about God's identity,[31] what God has done to reveal who he is, what his will is for our lives, and what our inheritance is as his children; and "if we cannot be condemned by our own conscience, we need not be afraid in God's presence, and whatever we ask him we shall receive, because we keep his commandments and live the kind of life that he wants. *His commandments are these*:

> **That we believe in the name of his Son Jesus Christ and that we love one another as he has told us to. Whoever keeps his commandments lives in God and God lives in him. We know that he lives in us by the Spirit that he has given us.**[32]

Yet, as surprising as it might seem when initially considered, many (and probably the majority) of the organized religious institutions have not been willing, or, for some reason or another, have been unable to reiterate the simple truths concerning the will of God and the critical matters of Christian faith to those looking to them for guidance. For centuries, it has been the common practice of religious leaders to adamantly advance doctrines and theories about God and Christ that do not appear in the scriptural or apostolic testimony; and further, to insist that Christians *must* accept their distinctive theological propositions and doctrinal "deductions" in order to be secure in their standing before God.

In his widely-used work, *Systematic Theology, An Introduction to Biblical Doctrine*,[33] Wayne Grudem, a well-known Protestant theologian, devoted a chapter to the subject of the Trinity and associated doctrines regarding Christ. As the title of his work might suggest, Grudem attempts to "systematically" define and expound upon what many have long considered to be

---

[31] This is not to suggest that we are able to exhaustively comprehend and understand the glorious divine nature and attributes of Almighty God. However, we definitely *can* know, through the revelation of inspired Scripture, who God is and how we can live a life that is pleasing to him; namely, through recognition of, and obedience to, his Son Jesus.

[32] 1 John 3:21-24, *JB*

[33] Wayne Grudem's *Systematic Theology* is used as a standard text book in many private religious colleges and prominent evangelical seminaries.

"God the Son" or "the Son of the living God"?

true "biblical" and true "Christian" doctrine. If examined with care and sensitivity, however, a cautious reader might notice at least one aspect of the chapter that is verifiably not representative of "biblical doctrine."

Throughout the twenty-three page chapter, Grudem—in the course of trying to encourage faith in the doctrine of the Trinity from the Scriptures—makes frequent reference to Jesus by the theological title or description "**God the Son**." In fact, without any qualification, background, or explanatory introduction, Grudem makes use of this particular expression a total of *twenty times* throughout this one section of his book. For instance, in his discussion on Jesus' baptism, Grudem states: "Here at one moment we have three members of the Trinity performing three distinct activities. God the Father is speaking from heaven, *God the Son* is being baptized and is then spoken to from heaven by God the Father; and *God the Holy Spirit* is descending from heaven to rest upon and empower Jesus for his ministry."[34] The passage itself (Matthew 3:16-17), however, says nothing about such figures as "God the Son" or "God the Holy Spirit." But by simply and subtly inserting these phrases, and by superimposing the concept of a "Trinity" onto the subjects appearing in this account, one may see how it can prove difficult for even committed Bible students (especially those already deeply grounded and uncritically accepting of such concepts) to separate out and distinguish what is truly scriptural in this case from that which originated in connection with a post-biblical human tradition.[35]

In his apologetic work, *Knowing Christ in the Challenge of Heresies*, author Steven Tsoukalas likewise made frequent and repetitious use of the same expression. In various though closely

---

[34] Grudem, *Systematic Theology, An Introduction to Biblical Doctrine*, p. 230 (emphasis added).
[35] Protestant scholars McClintock and Strong, although advocates of Trinitarianism, and although viewing all three subjects as "persons," nevertheless pointed out: "Matt. iii, 16, 17 has long been considered a very strong proof-text for the whole doctrine of the Trinity. But though three personal subjects are mentioned, viz. the voice of the Father, the symbol of the Holy Spirit, and Christ, yet nothing is here said respecting their nature." —*McClintock and Strong's Cyclopedia of Biblical, Theological, and Ecclesiastical Literature*, Volume X, p. 552.

related statements made throughout, Tsoukalas speaks of Christ in the ways that follow:

> "It is imperative, therefore, for one to have the *correct view* of Christ in order to have the faith that is able to place one in the Christian camp. A defective view of Christ, a denial of the biblical view of Christ, makes it impossible for one to be a follower of the biblical Christ. Sadly, this is the case with cults, as they make Jesus anything but **God the Son**, second person of the Trinity." (pp. 22, 23) "He is the Son of the Father, and therefore shares the same nature as the Father. 'Son of God' therefore means '**God the Son**.'" (p. 30) "The Christian Church has therefore historically proclaimed Jesus as **God the Son**..." (p. 32) "I have shown that the phrase 'Son of God' means '**God the Son**.'" "As the pre-existent Son of God He was also **God the Son**. At His incarnation He remained fully God, **God the Son**, but added to His person a full human nature. After His bodily resurrection He remained **God the Son**, and since His bodily ascension to the right hand of God the Father He remains **God the Son**. Yet, modern heresies, like their ancient predecessors, deny this essential teaching of Scripture." (pp. 33-34; bold effect added)

Remarkably, in a book of only 224 pages, Tsoukalas ascribes Jesus Christ with the theological title "God the Son" at least *seventy-three times* throughout—even suggesting that the title (and accompanying concept) represents "essential teaching of Scripture."[36]

What arouses concern over such a practice is that if an individual with little familiarity with the Bible were to read through these sections of theological discussion, that individual might be given the impression that the phrase "God the Son" is actually a scriptural description for Jesus Christ, when, in fact, the expression never appears in the Bible. In fact, the "biblical

---

[36] In his book Tsoukalas calls Christ, "Yahweh the Messiah" once, "Jehovah the Son" once, the "God-man" 13 times, and "Yahweh the Son" 30 times—all distinctive theological expressions that do not appear in the Scriptures.

"God the Son" or "the Son of the living God"?

Christ" is never spoken of or described in the Bible as "God the Son, second person of the Trinity." Unfortunately, these kinds of practices do not reflect the professed principle stated in Wayne Grudem's work, a principle that can be safely accepted by all adherents of Scripture:

> *"The sufficiency of Scripture reminds us that in our doctrinal and ethical teaching we should emphasize what Scripture emphasizes and be content with what God has told us in Scripture."*[37]

Taking a similar view regarding the role of Scripture, Tsoukalas states in the introduction to his book: "Jesus also tells us by implication that faith in Him is to involve content, and that content *must* be biblical. One must have a correct definition of who Jesus is. Paul implies the same as he warns the Christians of Corinth: 'For if one comes and preaches another Jesus whom we have not preached...'(2 Cor. 11:4). Paul was aware that there were counterfeit Christs."[38] And, as John Calvin (one of the most respected theologians in the history of Protestant religion) admonished: "let us use great caution that neither our thoughts nor our speech go beyond the limits to which the Word of God itself extends."[39]

In light of the Protestant's given, professed respect for the authority and "sufficiency" of Scripture,—along with the stated goal of holding to a "correct view of Christ...*a correct definition of who Jesus is*," and the avoidance of accepting a "defective" or "counterfeit" one—it comes across as remarkably difficult to reconcile the felt need for such repeated and unreserved emphasis on such an official theological title or definition for Jesus Christ that never appears in the Scripture itself. If checked for verification, any Bible student would see that Jesus is described as the "Son of God" some fifty times

---

[37] Grudem, *Systematic Theology*, p. 134.
[38] Tsoulakas, *Knowing Christ in the Challenge of Heresies*, p. xxi.
[39] John Calvin, *Institutes of the Christian Religion, 1:LXIII:21*; as perplexingly quoted in the opening pages of *The Forgotten Trinity* by James White.

throughout the Scriptures. But we never receive a command from God the Father, Jesus himself, or the apostles, to the effect that Jesus is to be known as, described by, or publicized under, the expression "God the Son." The expression (or 'definition') itself was evidently unknown to the apostles, for it cannot be found in any of their writings.[40]

Yet if we truly respected the sufficiency and accuracy of the inspired scriptural teaching, it would prove difficult for us to accept the propriety of creating official theological titles that do not appear in Scripture, particularly when those official titles and definitions alter or go beyond what the Bible already adequately presents to us concerning the identity of the Messiah. The question may be asked of the theologians: Why, when defending a doctrine they believe to be well founded in Scripture, must they repeatedly and officially promote, even "emphasize," language that is actually foreign to Scripture?[41] If Jesus Christ is already described officially in Scripture as "the Son of God," why is there a need for a "God the Son" figure? And why does "God the Son"—an unscriptural term—frequently prove to be the theological term of choice in reference to Christ if Scripture already gives us clear and adequate terms to describe him?

Again, a careful study of Scripture will assure us that the apostles never taught that it was necessary to confess Jesus as "God the Son." Instead they revealed, on more than one occasion, that we should confess Jesus as the "Son of God." In fact, none of the common theological descriptions—"God the

---

[40] The same point was made by Robert Carden of Grace Christian Fellowship: "In speaking of Jesus Christ, many trinitarians call him 'God the Son.' However, the Scriptures never call him God the son, but rather the son of God. These two phrases are in no way interchangeable. The latter is Biblical truth, while the former is a theological invention." —*One God, The Unfinished Reformation*, p. 115. Yet, according to Trinitarian Dr. Robert Morey, in a chapter in his book titled "*God the Son*": "Any view of Jesus not found in Scripture must be condemned as 'another Jesus.'" —*The Trinity, Evidence and Issues* (Iowa Falls: World Bible, 1996), p. 283.

[41] In light of the basic points that have been brought out thus far, it would be helpful to reflect on what was, on one occasion, even pointed out by a noted Trinitarian apologist, that to truly "learn how to interpret the Bible correctly is to allow God to speak in his own language." —Dr. James White, *The Dividing Line Broadcast*: 5/15/03 (Alpha & Omega Ministries). Yet it was pointed out by Robert Carden: "If you limit your discussion to Biblical terms and phrases, the trinitarian position cannot even be articulated, much less demonstrated or defended." —*One God, The Unfinished Reformation*, p. 77.

Son," "the God-man," "the second person of the Trinity"—are "emphasized" in Scripture. They never actually appear. To neither of these titles and descriptions did the Son of the living God ever give his approval and blessing; to none did Christ, the head of the congregation, ever respond gladly for identifying him as such, "Blessed are you...for flesh and blood did not reveal this to you, but my Father who is in heaven."

If in the midst of all the contradictory doctrinal positions about Jesus of Nazareth it is really our aim to establish his true identity (the attainment of 'the full and accurate knowledge of the Son of God', Ephesians 4:13, *Amplified Bible*), it seems that all Bible-believing Christians can at least agree that we can disregard and abandon all such unscriptural, dogmatic terminology and manner of expression; for they are certainly unnecessary and could potentially lead us outside the realm of divine, scriptural truth, and into the continually resurfacing and ever-threatening presence of humanly-contrived error.[42]

If a question ever arises in our minds, we can recall the teaching of the chosen apostles and see how in addition to God's own testimony at Jesus' baptism, and the express declaration of his closest companions during and after his public ministry, that he was, further, "declared to be [literally 'appointed' or 'marked out as'] the Son of God with power, according to the spirit of holiness by the resurrection from the dead..."[43]

---

[42] Not only is the officially adopted, essentially canonized, term "God the Son" unscriptural and therefore unnecessary to use, one might argue that the very expression doesn't make sense, since "God" is not and could never be the "Son" of anyone. Scripture tells us that Jesus is God's only-begotten/unique Son and Messiah; and as it was pointed out by Wayne Grudem, we should "be content with what God has told us in Scripture."

[43] Romans 1:4, *ASV*. Or as Barclay's translation expresses it; he was "by his resurrection designated *beyond all question* the Son of God." We should note that some have objected, arguing, in effect, "all Christian sects believe Jesus is the 'Son of God.' What matters is how we *define* that expression." In this regard, it is true and necessary to keep in mind that different groups have attached different *meanings* to this scriptural description of Jesus (including Trinitarians). However, it must be pointed out that, with respect to Jesus, "the Son of God" is really a *self-defining* and *self-explanatory* description; particularly in light of Jesus' frequent addressing of God as his own Father. As it was pointed out in one commentary: "Some forty times [in the Gospel of John alone] Jesus speaks to or of God as his Father, thus presenting himself as the Son of God." —Colin G. Kruse, *The Tyndale New Testament Commentaries, The Gospel According to John* (Grand Rapids: Eerdmans, 2003), p. 40. Indicating awareness of the difficulty the expression "Son of God," taken at face value, bears in relation to Trinitarian

"God the Son" or "the Son of the living God"?

In the book *One God & One Lord*, by authors Graeser, Lynn, and Schoenheit, the writers accurately summarized the implications of Christ's resurrection, from a scriptural perspective:

> Indeed, the *historical* validity of Jesus of Nazareth being the promised Messiah is the very core of the Gospel and a necessary element for salvation, because we must have faith in our heart that God has *in actual fact* raised him from the dead. That is, we are asked to believe in the validity of an historical event, because that event, like no other, demonstrated and proved that Jesus of Nazareth was who he said he was: the Son of the living God, Christ the Lord.[44]

Belief in the resurrection of Christ is an essential feature of the Christian faith, spoken of directly and repeatedly throughout the Scriptures. Yet when it comes to the language and concepts promoted by modern-day evangelical theologians, it may be observed how they have so often expressed themselves in such a way as to keep in line with the decrees pronounced by the ecumenical councils of the fourth and fifth centuries, which they evidently view as having been sanctioned by God.

It is well established by secular and religious historians that about sixty years after the Council of Constantinople (the Council that officially defined the orthodox doctrine of the Trinity), the Council of Chalcedon declared for a doctrine of Christ that has been maintained ever since by those who consider themselves "orthodox" with reference to the Christian faith. In 451 C.E, the Council formally established the 'Christological' dogma that says Jesus Christ—from the time of his human/historical conception onward—possesses *two* natures, so that he is "fully God" and "fully man" at the same time. This

---

theology, one Protestant writer made the following remarks: "How can Jesus be the Son of God and also be called 'God' at the same time? I was troubled by the word Son. It suggests that He was born and had a beginning. Since God is eternal and does not have a beginning or end, how could Jesus be God?" —David L. Hocking, *The Nature of God in Plain Language* (Waco: Word Book Publishers, 1984), p. 76.

[44] *One God & One Lord, Reconsidering the Cornerstone of the Christian Faith*, p. 361.

"God the Son" or "the Son of the living God"?

came to be known, theologically, as the "**hypostatic union**" of Christ. In an evangelical handbook on theological terms, a definition is given:

> Concerning the person of Jesus Christ, He is uniquely and completely God while at the same time being uniquely and completely man. He remains forever God-man, with two distinct natures. Though Jesus has two natures, God and man, He does not have two personalities.[45]

The above quotation is a notable example of the sentiment held by contemporary evangelical teachers, representing the doctrine of Christ's two natures as established by religious clergymen of the mid-fifth-century C.E. Well-known evangelical pastor and teacher Dr. John MacArthur, after pointing out what he perceived to be certain defective ideas and doctrines associated with the "Word of Faith" movement, went on to make the following claim:

> "[Kenneth Copeland and those who believe like him] are divesting Jesus of his identity; he is the 'God-man' and to say that he is anything less than the 'God-man' is heresy. And again I mark for you, note carefully, that in cults it is typical to have an aberrant view of Christ."[46]

In a similar and even more extreme way, one evangelical writer wrote the following as a conclusion of an article called *The Deity of Jesus Christ*:

> Those who reject Christ's Divinity [as the second person of the Trinity], in light of the clear, plain, unambiguous teaching of Scripture, will spend eternity in hell, unless they repent and acknowledge that Jesus Christ is who he claimed to be, the God-man.[47]

---

[45] Smith, *Theological "isms"*, p. 42.
[46] Cassette Tape: *Does God Promise Health and Wealth?* Part 2., Grace To You. 1991.
[47] Michael Bremmer, *The Deity of Jesus Christ*, 1|13|03 (From the Website: *Sola Scriptura!* A Reformed Theology Resource, *Dedicated to the Praise of His Glorious Grace!*). Contrary to Bremmer's confident judgment, Jesus never did call himself or claim to be the "God-man" in any known text in Scripture.

"God the Son" or "the Son of the living God"?

This particular expression, the "**God-man**," although never appearing in Scripture (or in the claims of Jesus) as a divinely-approved designation for the Messiah, has, nevertheless, been *regularly* and *aggressively* promoted by evangelical pastors and teachers *as if* the Bible itself commands Christians to confess it. This description, as can be seen, is so highly regarded that it is argued that it would be "heretical" to say that Jesus is anything less than what the term implies. Thus the very term, and accompanying concept, becomes and represents yet another scripturally-unarticulated standard by which one is to be judged—true or false Christian. It should be noted that the position expressed by MacArthur is not simply a unique, personal view, but a *dogmatic* position held universally among evangelicals as constituting the "orthodox" doctrine of Christ, and has been so *for centuries*. Yet, once again, as curious as it may seem, in light of the importance and emphasis attributed to the title by the defenders of "Christological orthodoxy," Jesus is simply never called, described or designated as the "God-man" anywhere in the Bible; nor does the Bible ever actually say or expressly teach that Jesus possesses two natures (that of Almighty God and man) at one time.[48] That is why, from a scriptural perspective, it is difficult to comprehend the entire premise underlying an argument of this kind. Especially problematic—in view of the absence of straightforward apostolic teaching on such an allegedly crucial doctrine—is the notably extreme, unfounded dogmatism and evident lack of modesty that accompanies the position. If it is typical for "cults" to have an "aberrant view of Christ," and the correct view is the one that identifies Jesus as the "God-man" (and this *must* be acknowledged, provided one wishes to avoid spending an 'eternity in hell'), then it is truly remarkable that in their own writings the apostles never made mention of what would have

---

[48] Saying that Jesus is one-hundred-percent God and one-hundred-percent man—as it is often said—is like saying, as Dan Mages has pointed out, that a desk could be one-hundred-percent wood and one-hundred-percent steel at the same time, something we know to be a logical impossibility. But even if one disagrees about the possibility of Jesus' being God and man at the same time, the main point is, the Bible nowhere teaches this.

obviously represented such a distinctively important truth relative to Christ's identity, the very person upon whom "the church" is said to have been built.

Sola Scriptura?

Historically, evangelicals have always professed to believe in what is often referred to as the "sufficiency of Scripture." This expression, of course, reflects the belief that the Scriptures alone are the altogether adequate and all-sufficient source of divinely-revealed truth and authority. Amazingly, however, many who profess belief in such do not seem to realize that many of evangelicalism's most distinctive articles of faith are simply not found or expressly confirmed in any part of Scripture. Remarkably, this has not prevented evangelicals from pointing to these articles of faith as criteria for determining the authenticity of an individual's profession of Christian faith. But the question is, if these kinds of doctrinal concepts ('Trinity,' 'God-man,' etc.) are given such priority and emphasis by the "orthodox" in regard to the essentials of the Christian religion, why do we not find the same spirit of priority given to them in the very Scriptures from which they claim to base them on? It appears that some traditions have been held for so long, and are now so deeply engrained within the collective consciousness of the evangelical communities, that even such non-scriptural expressions and accompanying concepts are reverenced and deferred to as if they were actually scriptural. Official theological phrases like "triune God," "Trinity," "God the Son," "God-man (*theoanthropos*)," and others like it, have apparently been used with such frequency, and have become so familiar to so many, the fact that they are *unbiblical* seems to simply pass by unnoticed. Yet throughout much of "church history," distinctive theological expressions of these kinds have been given such an air of sanctity and appearance of divine authority that many fail to consider the point that the very terms and the doctrines they represent are nowhere purposefully articulated, or in any way prioritized, in the biblical writings. There is, in fact, not *one* Scripture that can be produced that teaches any of the aforementioned doctrines in a straightforward way. They are all argued for on the basis of theological inference, creative, novel reasoning, and, often, sheer sophistry; so that, in the end, every one of these widely-accepted terms amount to theological labels and categories with no corresponding biblical teachings for them to represent.

Although for centuries such official though unscriptural theological expressions have been relentlessly promoted by "orthodox" religious leaders and apologists, the Christians of the apostolic era did not know of or use them. Thus, we can be certain that Christians today are under no obligation to promote, confess, or recognize them, or the concepts that they represent. Thankfully, now that they have become so accessible, those who follow Christ today can appeal to the full body of Hebrew and Christian Scriptures for the original doctrine and truth regarding God and his Son; and because "all Scripture is inspired of God, useful for teaching, correction, and for setting matters straight," having the ability "to make the man of God *complete*," and even "wise unto *salvation*,"[49] it is safe to say that all unscriptural additions, extra-biblical traditions, complex philosophical inferences and theological speculations are not needed, and that they should *never* be put on the same level as the directly-articulated pronouncements of inspired Scripture.

In a recent book, respected Presbyterian pastor and New Testament teacher, Mark D. Roberts, although a believer in the Trinity and in the two-natures-of-Christ-concept, made the following forthright acknowledgement:

> We would be wrong, however, to envision the earliest Christians as somehow thinking in the complex terms of later theology. They did not talk of God as Trinity or refer to Jesus as fully God and fully human.[50]

---

[49] 2 Timothy 3:15-17
[50] *Jesus Revealed* (Colorado Springs: WaterBrook Press, 2002), p. 133. Roberts is pastor of Irvine Presbyterian Church and adjunct NT Professor at Fuller Seminary. He earned degrees in

Other New Testament scholars have likewise expressed awareness that several of the official dogmas held by Catholics and Protestants are simply not presented in the Bible by way of direct teaching. Tom Harpur, an Anglican scholar, in his controversial book, *For Christ's Sake*, made the following candid and revealing observations:

> What is most embarrassing for the Church is the difficulty of proving any of these statements of dogma from the New Testament documents. You simply cannot find the doctrine of the Trinity set out anywhere in the Bible. St. Paul has the highest view of Jesus' role and person, but nowhere does he call him God [although Romans 9:5 and Titus 2:13 are debatable translations]. Nor does Jesus himself explicitly claim to be the second person of the Trinity, wholly equal to his heavenly Father...As early as the 8th century, the theologian St. John of Damascus frankly admitted what every modern critical scholar of the New Testament now realizes; that neither the doctrine of the Trinity nor that of the two natures of Jesus Christ is explicitly set out in Scripture. In fact, if you take the record as it is and avoid reading back into it the dogmatic definitions of a latter age, you cannot find what is traditionally regarded as orthodox Christianity in the Bible at all.[51]

---

philosophy and religion at Harvard University, where he also received a Ph.D. in the New Testament. Again, it should be noted that Roberts is Trinitarian and his observation at this point was not intended to contradict Trinitarian teaching; for after he reasons, "If [Jesus] accomplished that which God alone could do, then the implications are clear: He is the Savior just as God is the Savior. Who else could claim this title, other than a man who was somehow, God?" However, at this point, the professor's logic does not necessarily follow from the premise; for God can, if he decided to, accomplish his will through those whom he has chosen to do so. In Scripture, both God and his Son are described as saviors, but this does not demand that the two are identical, or that Jesus must be "God" in the same sense as his Father. The Scriptures show that God extends salvation to sinners, but that he saves them *through* Jesus, his Son. The apostle John made clear that "the Father *sent* his Son as Savior of the world." And Paul declared: "From the descendants of this man [David], according to promise, God has brought to Israel a Savior, Jesus…" —1 John 4:14; Romans 5:10; Acts 13:23. That is, scripturally, Jesus is the Savior because *God sent him to be the Savior* of mankind, not because he is "God the Son, the second person of the Trinity."

[51] *For Christ's Sake* (McClelland & Stewart Inc., 1993), pp. 11, 104. One scholar likewise observed: "The doctrine of the double nature of Christ, like that of the Trinity, is a doctrine of inference. Neither doctrine is declared in any verse, nor can they be expressed in the language of Scripture. Scattered verses are assembled in quasi-syllogistic form, inferences are drawn from

The rigid disposition of the "orthodox" naturally gives rise to the same thought-provoking questions: If it is *God* who views the doctrines of the Trinity and of Christ's two natures as essential to the kind of faith that would reconcile us to himself, why did he not just tell this to Christians in a crystal clear way, either through the express teachings of Christ, or through the apostolic writings produced after Christ's resurrection and ascension to the Father? How could today's Christian community, realistically, be expected to put confidence in that which its own authoritative writings do not clearly or confidently present?

Without question, Christians who base their beliefs on Scripture *can* rest in full assurance that it *is* essential to acknowledge and confess Jesus as 'the Christ' or 'Messiah, the Son of the living God,' the God-appointed 'Lord' whom they devote their lives in obedience to. Because, when seeking to promote and defend such fundamental biblical truths, we will not find ourselves under any constraint to *prove* these things are so by mere inference, a convoluted process of theological argumentation, or through the intellectual discipline of "systematic theology." Instead, we can simply point to the passages where such fundamental truths are set forth directly by the chosen prophets and apostles. As we would reasonably expect from a genuine, essential point of Christian faith as Jesus' Sonship, Lordship and status as Messiah, we find that these are truths continually presented and emphasized all throughout the Scriptures; whereas, in notable contrast—in the case of the Catholic and Protestant doctrines of the "Trinity" and the "God-man,"—we find that neither the terms nor the explicit teaching on these points are found anywhere in Scripture.

How do "Protestants," specifically, reconcile these facts with their historic and dogmatic position? New Testament

---

newly-created contexts, and it is assumed that the Messiah is both a mortal man and the almighty God...I know of no allusion in the Bible to the doctrine of the Two Natures, either with or without modification..." —Donald R. Snedeker, *The Doctrine of the Double Nature of Christ* (International Scholars Publications, 1998), 6, 7.

scholar Jason BeDuhn has some general though insightful comments concerning historic Protestant belief and practice. In his book on Bible translation, BeDuhn observed:

> You see, Protestant forms of Christianity, following the motto of *sola scriptura*, insist that all legitimate Christian beliefs (and practices) must be found in, or at least based on, the Bible. That's a very clear and admirable principle. The problem is that Protestant Christianity was not born in a historical vacuum, and does not go back directly to the time that the Bible was written. Protestantism was and is a *reformation* of an already fully developed form of Christianity: Catholicism. When the Protestant Reformation occurred just five hundred years ago, it did not reinvent Christianity from scratch, but carried over many of the doctrines that had developed within Catholicism over the course of the previous thousand years and more. In this sense, one might argue that the Reformation is incomplete, that it did not fully realize the high ideals that were set for it...For the doctrines that Protestantism inherited to be considered true, they had to be found in the Bible. And precisely because they were considered true already, there was and is tremendous pressure to read those truths back into the Bible, whether or not they are actually there...Protestant Christians don't like to imagine themselves building too much beyond what the Bible spells out for itself. So even if most if not all of the ideas and concepts held by modern Protestant Christians can be found, at least implied, somewhere in the Bible, there is a pressure (conscious or unconscious) to build up those ideas and concepts within the biblical text, to paraphrase or expand on what the Bible does say in the direction of what modern readers want and need it to say.[52]

Seventh-Day-Adventist Bible scholar Dr. Samuele Bacchiochi had a very similar observation:

---

[52] *Truth in Translation, Accuracy and Bias in English Translations of the New Testament* (New York: University Press of America, 2003), pp. 163, 164.

Evangelicals are conditioned by their denominational traditional teachings, just as much as the Roman Catholics and Eastern Greek Orthodox. In theory, they appeal to Sola Scriptura, but in practice, Evangelicals often interpret Scripture in accordance with their traditional denominational teachings. If new Biblical research challenges traditional doctrines, in most cases, Evangelical churches will choose to stand for tradition rather than for Sola Scriptura…To be an 'Evangelical' means to uphold certain fundamental traditional doctrines without questioning. Anyone who dares to question the Biblical validity of a traditional doctrine can become suspect as a 'heretic.'…Any attempt to modify or reject traditional doctrines is often interpreted as a betrayal of the faith and can cause division and fragmentation. This is a very high price that most churches are not willing to pay.[53]

As already discussed, in the Scriptures, Jesus is never called "God the Son" or the "God-man"; nor is he ever identified as a "member" or "person" of a "Trinity." These traditional, long-standing theological doctrines, regarded by evangelical leaders as "essential" and "foundational" Christian truths, are never expressly set forth in Scripture;[54] they must be *read into* (or, in their view, rightly deduced from) scriptural statements in *every* instance. In light of the absence of express scriptural teaching on these subjects (and corresponding use of language foreign to the biblical documents), however, the leaders and heirs of the Protestant movement are still active in branding as "heretics" those who do not confess faith in either one of them.

---

[53] *Immortality or Resurrection? A Biblical Study on Human Nature and Destiny* (Barrien Springs: Biblical Perspectives, 1997), pp. 28, 30.

[54] It should be noted that the "God-man" dogma is regularly used as a kind of interpretive mechanism used to explain away instances in Scripture where Jesus either explicitly distinguishes himself from "God" or is shown to be a servant of God and under God's authority. So when Jesus referred to the Father as "my God," and when Jesus said that "the Father is greater than I," evangelicals simply contend that since Jesus is the "God-man," he was, on those occasions, speaking from the perspective of his human nature; but at the same time, he is also fully God and therefore equal to the Father. Again, the Bible never says or suggests anything like this.

"God the Son" or "the Son of the living God"?

At this point, and with these facts in mind, the insightful words of a nineteenth-century pastor are submitted for the serious consideration of any and all Bible-believing Christians:

> To justify the epithets which I have applied to the doctrine, let us look at some of the popular statements and expositions to it. I beg especial attention to the fact, not simply how various and often astounding in themselves are these statements and expositions, but how dissimilar to the language of Scripture. That Scripture which those churches and divines who make them, hold to be plenarily inspired; and, so far as they are Protestants, to be the sufficient rule of faith as well as practice. One would think that a scriptural doctrine or truth could be expressed in the language of the Christian Scripture…the most striking acknowledgment upon this point from a learned Protestant, was made in a speech delivered to the Irish House of Lords by Dr. Clayton, Bishop of Clogher, on the second of February 1757. He said: 'The strongest abettors of the Nicene Creed do not so much as pretend that the doctrine of the consubstantiality of the Father and the Son is to be found in the Scriptures, but only in the writings of some of the Primitive Fathers. And I beseech your Lordships to consider whether it is not absolutely contradictory to the fundamental principles on which the Reformation from Popery was built, to have any doctrine established as a rule of faith which is founded barely on Tradition, and is not plainly and clearly revealed in Scriptures?'…Holy Scriptures, then, being our witness—and our appeal lies there,—Holy Scripture nowhere affirms the doctrine…Moreover, I say, nay, I insist, that they have no right in this or in any case to set that up as a fundamental article of Faith, to make that a condition of holding the Christian name, or of Christian fellowship, which is not taught with utmost directness, explicitness, and perspicuity, in the Christian Scriptures. We hold no peculiar or distinguishing doctrine which cannot be stated in the express, unaltered, unqualified words of Holy writ; a thing which our Trinitarian brethren cannot do for

theirs.[55]

As surprising and puzzling as it may seem, those who have historically professed to adhere to the principle of "sola scriptura," to this day, adamantly and passionately insist that Jesus is to be recognized as the "God-man," and as a member of a "tri-personal" God, when the Scriptures themselves do not directly teach this, or anything that *plainly* resembles or reflects such a peculiar and paradoxical concept. If fair and realistic in their appraisal of scriptural teaching, evangelicals must admit, and on occasion *have* admitted, that the notion of Christ simultaneously possessing two natures (that of Almighty God and of man) is another doctrine that is not explicitly set forth by the apostles and prophets of Scripture. Like the Trinity, it must be arrived at through a difficult process of inference and through a very peculiar chain of reasoning, rather than demonstrated through straightforward scriptural instruction. And yet this is not to deny that in our study of the Bible we are called upon to use our God-given powers of reason, and that therefore we will often have to try to interpret the correct meaning of difficult and seemingly unclear passages; and in connection with this, we may arrive at conclusions through considering context, comparing certain portions of Scripture with others, drawing informed and logical inferences, and, at the same time, always keeping in mind the totality of the Bible's basic message. But in no way does this mean that we may presume to officially define, as essential, doctrines that the Scriptures themselves do not officially present to us as essential. We can be sure that whatever is essential to our faith is that which has already been unambiguously taught by Jesus and his apostles in the Bible—as it was once argued by one student of the Bible, "*If it is not articulated in the Bible, then it cannot be dogmatically held up as a Bible teaching.*"[56]

As Christians, and as students of the Bible, we are not

---

[55] *The Scripture Doctrine of the Father, Son and Holy Ghost, A Course of Lectures by* Frederick A. Farley, D. D., pp. 6, 22, 23.
[56] Christians of any background, association or organization would benefit from carefully considering this point, in respect to any given matter of faith.

called upon to demonstrate and express our faith, or manifest our spiritual gifts, or perform a service toward God, by developing and introducing new and novel doctrines into our Christian communities, or by passionately defending traditional though non-scriptural teachings. We can, however, bring glory and honor to our heavenly Father and his Son—in the service our fellow man—by being faithful to, and by simply *reiterating* and *calling attention to* what God, by means of his Son,[57] has already disclosed to us in the inspired biblical writings.

> *"Jesus cried out and said, 'Whoever believes in me believes not in me only, but also in the one who sent me; and whoever sees me sees also the one who sent me. I have come as a light into this world, so that everyone who believes in me might not remain in the darkness. But if anyone hears my words and does not keep them, I do not judge him, for I came, not to judge the world, but to save the world. Whoever rejects me and does not accept my words has one to judge him. The word that I have spoken is what will be his judge on the last day; because I have not spoken on my own initiative, but the Father himself who sent me has commanded me what to say and what to speak. And I know that his commandment means everlasting life. Therefore all that I say, I speak only in accordance with what the Father has told me."*
> —John 12:44-50

God-in-the-flesh?—the Trinitarian doctrine of the "Incarnation"

> *"What I teach is not mine, but belongs to him that sent me. Whoever chooses to do his will shall know whether my teaching is from God or whether I speak on my own. He that speaks on his own is seeking his own glory; but he that seeks the glory of him that sent him, this one is true, and there is no unrighteousness in him."* —Jesus Christ, John 7:16-18

---

[57] Including the Son's authorized representatives, namely, the apostles.

"God the Son" or *"the Son of the living God"?*

The following quotation comes from a learned doctor of Protestant theology. What is claimed here is representative of historic, mainstream Roman Catholic and Protestant belief regarding the identity of Jesus Christ:

> When Jesus of Nazareth was here on earth, He showed that God was willing to come down in human form...As God came down into the world in the person of Jesus of Nazareth, so He wants men to come up to Him through faith in the Lord Jesus Christ...What we mean by the *incarnation* is very nearly the same meaning as in *Jesus*, that God became flesh and took upon Himself the form of man. When the Bible says, 'the Word was made flesh' it means that God Himself took on a human form. This is what is called the *incarnation*.[58]

Is it true that the Bible teaches that "God," the Creator himself, took on human flesh in the person Jesus Christ? If so, why would anyone who professes faith in the Bible's teachings question such a significant doctrine of this sort?

First, it is necessary to understand that whenever Trinitarians speak of the "incarnation,"[59] or the notion that Almighty God himself took on flesh, they do not mean God *the Father*; nor do they believe or teach that "the Father" ever took on flesh. The doctrine of the incarnation teaches, rather, that the "eternal Son, the second member of the Trinity" took on flesh in the man Jesus Christ. Again, according to classical Trinitarian thinking, Jesus Christ *is* "God," but he is *not* "God the Father." He is, according to tradition, "God *the Son*." When we take a careful look at the way the Bible writers communicated their message, however, we will once again find that they never did speak of "God" himself as the one who became a man, whether God *the Father* or "God *the Son*." Nor did they ever even speak of a figure known as "God the Son." If anything—without

---

[58] Gutzke, *Plain Talk About Christian Words* (Grand Rapids: Zondervan, 1964), pp. 99-100.

[59] "Incarnation" is a word that comes from the Latin 'in' (*in*) 'flesh' (*carne*). As a result of the incarnation, Trinitarianism teaches that Christ possesses *two natures* (deity and humanity, each nature possessed by Christ in its fullness) in the *one person* of Christ.

necessarily abandoning faith in Trinitarianism—even those committed to the classical creeds should be able to recognize that the notion of "God becoming a man," or of "God dying on a cross," *is* a significant departure from Scripture at least in terms of *language*. And, much like the entire systematic doctrine of the Trinity, if the "incarnation" (an essential feature of Trinitarian theology) is the true teaching of the Bible, and Jesus was or is literally "God incarnate" or "God in the flesh," it is difficult to comprehend why the apostles did not expend a great deal of energy in an effort to make such a monumental concept completely clear. That is to say, if the apostles believed that Jesus was literally "God," why did they speak about him so often as one who had been *sent by* God, *sanctified by* God, *authorized by* God, *resurrected by* God, and *exalted by* God? In what way would such language move one to believe that Jesus is himself "God"?

To illustrate the difficulty, consider Romans chapter eight, where Paul may have had what one might call a "golden opportunity" to teach the doctrine of the "incarnation." If Paul considered belief in the incarnation of "God" essential to the Christian gospel, and wanted to make this point clear to the people he was writing (and to Christians of all generations), he could have simply said, in the context of his inspired presentation:

"For God has done what the law, weakened by the flesh, could not do: *when God himself* (or when 'God the Son') *took on the likeness of sinful flesh*, and to deal with sin, he condemned sin in the flesh..."

However, when the actual text is examined, along with the whole of Paul's letter to the Romans, one would see that the notion and language of "God" taking on flesh, or becoming a man, was not part of Paul's message. Instead, the apostle, being divinely directed, made clear:

For God has done what the law, weakened by the flesh, could not do: by *sending his own Son* **in the**

"God the Son" or "the Son of the living God"?

likeness of sinful flesh, and to deal with sin, he condemned sin in the flesh, so that the just requirement of the law might be fulfilled in us, who walk not according to the flesh but according to the Spirit.[60]

Again, in the fourth chapter of his letter to the Galatians, Paul wrote:

...when the fullness of time came, *God sent his Son*, born of a woman, born under the Law, that he might redeem those who were under the Law, that we might receive the adoption of sons. And because you are sons, God has sent the Spirit of his Son into our hearts, crying, 'Abba, Father.'[61]

As can be immediately recognized from these two examples (which accurately represent the Bible's normal manner of expression), Paul does not mention an idea of "God" being born of a woman or of "God" coming in the flesh. In keeping with the truth, style, and language of the rest of the apostolic writings, Paul revealed that 'God' actually has a 'Son' and tells his readers plainly that God 'sent' his Son as a redeemer with the goal of making believers his sons through him. Again, one might ask, if Paul *intended* for his audience to understand that "God," the very creator of the universe, was born of a woman, why did he say "God sent his Son, born of a woman"?

An even greater difficulty associated with the idea that God came as a man, in light of the Scripture's own language, is the idea that God himself could actually die. As far as the concept goes, Trinitarians have not always expressed themselves in a uniform manner.

Significantly, in keeping with the concept of Christ's

---

[60] Romans 8:3-4, *NRSV*. A likely response given by Trinitarians in defense of this point would be that when Paul said *God*, he meant *the Father* (a *person* of the Trinity). When *they* say God took on flesh, *they mean* "God the Son," the second person of the Trinity." But the point is, regardless of what Trinitarians may mean when they say *God took on flesh*, the Bible itself never speaks in this way. The Bible teaches that *God gave* and *sent his own Son*. To say that "God" himself took on flesh is misleading and does not accurately reflect the Bible's way of expressing itself.

[61] Galatians 4:4-7, *Douay Version*

identity as the "God-man," based on the incarnation of "God the Son," R. C. Sproul, a well-known Protestant theologian, made the following remarks:

> We must distinguish between the two natures of Jesus without separating them. When Jesus hungers, for example, we see that as a manifestation of the human nature, not the divine. What is said of the divine nature or of the human nature may be affirmed of the person. On the cross for example, Christ, the God-man dies. This, however, is not to say that God perished on the cross.[62]

Accordingly, others have said that when Jesus died, it was, really, only his "humanity," because "deity" cannot die and as "deity" he continued to live. Although some scholars have attempted to clarify themselves theologically on these points, confusion remains. Historically, most apologists have argued that in order for Jesus to have saved the people of the world by his atoning sacrifice, he must have been God because only God himself could possess that saving power.[63] Yet, at the same time, others have made clear that "God" or the divine nature/aspect of Jesus could never have really died. So the question is, in Trinitarian thought, did "God" actually die? If not, why do so many preach that "God" himself died on a cross? The answers that have been given on this matter are varied and unclear. R. C. Sproul emphasizes the fact that "God" did *not* perish on the cross, but that it was the "God-man." Yet these kinds of qualifying remarks not only strike one as confusing and ultimately unintelligible ('God' did not die but the 'God-man' did?), nothing like this is ever indicated or explained to us in the New Testament writings. The Bible simply says *"that Christ died,"*[64] and that three days later he was raised to life by his Father. That is to say, when it comes to the death of Christ, the

---

[62] *Essential Truths of the Christian Faith*, (Wheaton: Tyndale House, 1992), p. 82.
[63] As Fritz Ridenour wrote: "How can Scripture say that Christ's single death is adequate payment for the sins of the entire world? It is adequate because *Christ is God*. No one less than God could make payment for the sins of everyone. God is the one who set the holy standard. Who could fulfill its requirements but God Himself?" —*So What's The Difference*, p. 26.
[64] 1 Corinthians 15:3

Bible itself does not present an intellectual or theological problem of any sort. The problem—and problematic explanation—only surfaces in light of the traditionally advanced Trinitarian doctrine about the "two natures" of Jesus Christ, a doctrine nowhere spoken of in the Scriptures.

In a text that was mentioned in the previous section (Romans 1:4), the apostle Paul wrote about how Jesus was appointed or marked out as "Son of God" in association with his resurrection. A fuller portion of the text shows that Paul spoke of the "gospel of God, which he promised previously through his prophets in the holy scriptures, the gospel about his Son, descended from David according to the flesh, but established [or 'declared,' *NASB*] as Son of God in power according to the spirit of holiness through resurrection from the dead, Jesus Christ our Lord."[65]

Here we have a fairly straightforward scriptural statement about how Jesus was "with power" established as Son of God. In this particular case, however, we can benefit from considering one evangelical scholar's exposition, for it reveals yet another telling insight into the strained and complicated nature of the Trinitarian doctrinal system. Instead of accepting the plain sense of several passage of Scripture or statements made by Jesus, one continually comes across examples where apologists appear forced to expend a great deal of effort elaborating upon scriptural statements in order to have them mean what they want (or what traditionally-accepted doctrine requires) them to mean. This is a practice seen especially with reference to those statements in the Bible that either present difficulty, or that appear to be in direct conflict with, the basic tenets of Trinitarian theology.

In a notably lengthy and detailed discussion on this one text, Dr. Robert Reymond reasoned, essentially, that when Paul said that Jesus was descended from the flesh, he was alluding to the Trinitarian doctrine of Christ possessing two natures. As a descendent of David, Paul was speaking about Jesus in virtue of

---

[65] Romans 1:1-4, *NAB*

"God the Son" or "the Son of the living God"?

his humanity (Jesus was a real *man*). When Paul said that Jesus was designated "*Son of God* according to the spirit of holiness," this means, somehow, that Jesus is *God*. Therefore, Jesus is the "God-man."[66] After a nearly eight-page argument based on this one text, Reymond concludes:

> Thus, Romans 1:3-4, which may well be a portion of an early Christian confession, teaches us that Jesus' resurrection from the dead was both his and his Father's powerful witness to the fact that Jesus of Nazareth is God incarnate and not simply man.[67]

Immediately, one wonders, is there really a need to articulate a conclusion different from that of the apostle's? Jesus is "God incarnate and not simply man"? Is there anything unclear or unsatisfactory about Jesus "designated [or 'appointed/marked out as'] *Son of God* in power according to the spirit of holiness through resurrection from the dead..."?

To understand the basic sense of a passage like this, while at the same time attempting to determine the validity of the Trinitarian explanation, a student of Scripture may simply compare what is asserted by Dr. Reymond with what the Scripture itself actually says, specifically. With this simple comparison in mind, it is interesting to note that, in the same work, Dr. Reymond devotes a significant section to his views relating to the Bible and theories in methods of interpretation. Specifically, in the section titled "The Bible's Perspicuity," which refers to the essential *clarity* of the Bible's overall message, Dr. Reymond quotes approvingly from the *Westminster Confession of Faith* (an important Protestant creed), which says:

> All things in Scripture are not alike plain in themselves, nor alike clear unto all; yet those things which are necessary to be known, believed, and observed, for

---

[66] Trinitarian William Hendriksen similarly claimed: "Paul confesses Jesus to be God's Son. He means that the Savior was God's Son entirely apart from and antecedently to his assumption of the human nature. He is the Son of God from all eternity; hence, he is God." —*Romans* (Grand Rapids: Eerdmans, 1980), p. 42.
[67] *A New Systematic Theology of the Christian Faith*, p. 245.

salvation, are so clearly propounded and opened in some place of Scripture or other, that not only the learned, in a due use of ordinary means, may attain unto a sufficient understanding of them (WCF, I/vii)

Immediately following the citation, Dr. Reymond goes on to say:

> Note that the Confession declares that 'unlearned' men through the utilization of 'ordinary means' may come to a knowledge of the truth of Scripture. What are these 'ordinary means'? Simply the reading, hearing, and study of the Word. For example, one does not need to be 'learned,' when reading the Gospels or hearing them read or proclaimed, to discover that they intend to teach that Jesus was born of a virgin, lived a sinless life, performed mighty miracles, died on the cross 'as a ransom for many,' and rose from the dead on the third day after death. These things are plain, lying on the very face of the Gospels. One does not need to be instructed by a preacher to learn that he must believe on Jesus in order to be saved from the penalty his sins deserve…All one needs to do in order to discover these things, to put it plainly, is to sit down in a fairly comfortable chair, open the Gospels, and with a good reading lamp, read the Gospels like he would read any other book.[68]

In Dr. Reymond's commendable discussion regarding the perspicuity or clarity of the Bible, he acknowledges that it does not require an especially learned person to understand the plain teachings of Scripture, particular those teachings that are necessary for Christians to know and accept unto their own salvation. But is it fair to say that Dr. Reymond's conclusion regarding Romans 1:3-4 fits his characterization of the plain sense of Scripture with respect to necessary Christian doctrine— or, even, as it would relate to the entire systematic doctrine of the Trinity? In attempting to fairly assess the validity of his theological conclusion, it is very difficult to believe that an ordinary, impartial student of Scripture could carefully read this

---

[68] *A New Systematic Theology of the Christian Faith*, pp. 87-88.

text, and, "through the utilization of 'ordinary means," arrive at the same interpretive conclusion advanced by Dr. Reymond. Jesus is "God incarnate"? Is that what Paul said? Or would it be superficial and naive to conclude that Paul actually meant what he did say?

In this particular case, there does not appear to be any reason why the apostle's teaching could not be taken at face value. In verse 4, the apostle simply affirms that Jesus is in fact the *Son* of God, a point powerfully and clearly demonstrated through his resurrection from the dead. Not that this was the only time Jesus was demonstrated to be such, for the Bible shows that he was identified as God's Son prior to the resurrection.[69] While Jesus was a descendant of David physically, and therefore properly considered to be "son of David,"[70] according to the "spirit of holiness," the resurrection itself provided a 'powerful' confirmation of the truth that Jesus Christ was who he claimed to be. There is nothing indicated in Romans 1:3-4 about Jesus being a "God-man" or "God incarnate," either explicitly or by logical and necessary deduction. As a matter of fact, by means of the glorious resurrection, Jesus was, according to the sense of the word, "defined" (*Kingdom Interlinear*), "distinguished" (*Rotherham*), "distinctly set forth" (*Diaglott*), "patently marked out" (*PME*), not as "God incarnate" but as "God's Son."

> *"Brothers, I can tell you confidently that the patriarch David died and was buried, and his tomb is here to this day. But he was a prophet and knew that God had promised him on oath that he would place one of his descendants on his throne. Seeing what was ahead, he spoke of the resurrection of the Christ, that he was not abandoned to the grave,*

---

[69] Matthew 3:17
[70] Matthew 22:41-46

> *nor did his body see decay. God has raised this Jesus to life, and we are all witnesses of the fact. Exalted to the right hand of God, he has received from the Father the promised Holy Spirit and has poured out what you now see and hear.* — Apostle Peter, Acts 2:29-33, *NIV*

It would seem that even in view of such few examples of "orthodox" interpretive proposals, that many of the most learned evangelical scholars—when endeavoring to prove the Trinity and other post-biblical doctrines from the Bible—show that they often excel, not in their skill or willingness to reiterate, expound, or shed light upon what the Bible *does* say, but in the *craft* of making the Bible seem like it says something it does *not* say, in order to uphold and perpetuate acceptance of traditional dogmas. Whether done intentionally or unintentionally, this is the end result, for the Bible simply does not articulate several of these long-held ecclesiastical doctrines as they have come down to us. Dr. Reymond is right for pointing out that in order to learn the essential truths of the Christian faith we may do so through the simple "hearing, and study of the Word." He is right for observing that "one does not need to be 'learned,' when reading the Gospels or hearing them read or proclaimed, to discover that they intend to teach that Jesus was born of a virgin, lived a sinless life, performed mighty miracles, died on the cross 'as a ransom for many,' and rose from the dead on the third day after death." But can one simply study the revealed word of God in Scripture and discover for themselves several key doctrines that evangelicals teach are essential? Do the doctrines of the Trinity and the two natures of Christ "lie on the very face of the Gospels"? Or does the very knowledge of such doctrines require the presence of skilled, strategic and carefully calculated theological argumentation, arrived at through the exposition and "exegesis" of professional doctors of systematic theology? It was observed by one writer: "Incidentally, this is one of the main problems with Trinitarian arguments. Nearly every scripture they lay out as proof is implicit or tacit [meaning 'understood without being openly expressed']. We are required to read *into* the verse a meaning that usually has to be explained to us by Trinitarians."[71]

The source of the Son's authority

> *"All things have been handed over to me by my Father."*
> — Jesus Christ, Luke 10:22, NAB

Another example that sheds light on Trinitarian interpretational methods is found in connection with Matthew chapter nine. This text contains a record of how Jesus once healed a man afflicted with paralysis. Before the man was healed, Jesus said to him, "take courage child, your sins are forgiven." Mark's version of the same account reveals the reaction of those who were critical toward Jesus in this regard: "Now some of the scribes were sitting there, questioning in their hearts, 'Why does this man speak like that? He is blaspheming! Who can forgive sins but God alone?'"[72]

The conclusion typically drawn by evangelical apologists is that since Jesus forgave the man's sins and, as the scribes stated, *only God* can forgive sins, Jesus is therefore God (technically, as a 'member' of a 'triune' being). Dr. Robert Reymond alludes to the same basic argument in his *Systematic Theology*:

> Jesus also claimed as the Son of Man to have the authority to forgive sins (Matt. 9:6; Mark 2:10; Luke 5:24) and to regulate even the observance of the divine ordinance of the Sabbath (Matt. 12:8; Mark 2:28; Luke

---

[71] Brian Holt, *Jesus—God, or the Son of God?* (Mt. Juliet: TellWay Publishing, 2002), p. 63.
[72] Mark 2:7, *ESV*

6:5), clearly prerogative of deity alone.[73]

However, in verse seven, Matthew states by way of explanation: "And [Jesus] rose and went home. When the crowds saw it, they were afraid, and *they glorified God who had given such authority to men.*"

Here the point should be self-evident. In reflecting on these events, Matthew does not suggest that Jesus had authority to forgive sins or to heal people because he was God, but that he did so because God had *given* such authority to him. The remainder of the account reads: "But Jesus, knowing their thoughts, said, 'Why do you think evil in your hearts? For which is easier, to say, 'Your sins are forgiven,' or to say, 'Rise and walk'? *But that you may know that the Son of Man has authority on earth to forgive sins.*"[74]

In reference to the Jews who questioned Jesus' authority to forgive sins, John MacArthur claimed: "they had good theology, they said 'whoa,' only God can forgive sins. That's what Jesus did because that's who he was. They knew exactly what he was claiming; and either he is God or he is a blasphemer."[75]

As pointed out, according to Matthew's account of things, Jesus did what he did based on the authority given to him by God, not because he was actually "God" himself. Yet MacArthur claims that Jesus was "either God or a blasphemer"—another example of a false dilemma; for MacArthur does not, in this case, leave open the possibility that Jesus *truly* could have been God's *Son*.

With the point about Jesus' delegated authority kept in mind, it is also worth mentioning that Jesus himself evidently delegated a similar kind or degree of authority to his disciples, as is recorded in John 20:22-23: "And when he had said this, he breathed on them and said to them, 'Receive the Holy Spirit. *If*

---

[73] *A New Systematic Theology of the Christian Faith*, p. 66.
[74] Matthew 9:4-6
[75] *Audio Tape: Who is This Jesus?*, Grace to You (2004).

you forgive the sins of anyone, they are forgiven; if you withhold forgiveness from anyone, it is withheld.'"

But how could the human disciples possibly forgive sins if none of them were "deity"? Based on the same logic used by Trinitarian apologists, it would be reasonable to conclude that the disciples were themselves members of the "Godhead."

It seems fair enough to say, however, with Dr. Reymond, that the authority to forgive sins is indeed a "prerogative" of the "deity alone." But in our efforts to be responsible and accurate in our handling of the scriptural texts, we should not fail to recognize that *it is the Deity's prerogative to bestow that right on whomever he wishes.* God gave authority to Jesus Christ with respect to the forgiveness of sins. In turn, Jesus delegated a measure of authority in some sense to his closest disciples.[76] This not only makes intelligible sense but is something that is explained to us directly in the Scriptures.[77] Scripturally, we are able to confirm that Jesus received authority from God, and that the disciples themselves received authority from Jesus; but who can *give* authority to the Almighty God?

Further proof of the Son's delegated authority is found throughout the Scriptures in a very specific form. After his resurrection, Jesus declared to his disciples: *"All authority in heaven and on earth has been given to me..."*[78] Even before his death and resurrection, Jesus made a similar statement. He

---

[76] Compare Daniel 4:25; Revelation 2:27. Evidently, in the time of Moses, God gave his angel the "prerogative" to forgive men based on the name/authority God gave him: "Behold, I send an angel before you to guard you on the way and to bring you to the place that I have prepared. Pay careful attention to him and obey his voice; do not rebel against him, for he will not pardon your transgression, for my name is in him." —Exodus 23:20-21, *ESV*. This, of course, is another scriptural example proving that, although God alone may have authority to forgive sins ultimately, God can and does delegate this kind of authority to others who act in his name or as his representatives.

[77] The reason this point is made is that, more often than not, Trinitarian expositors will give more weight to their own theological inferences than to direct scriptural teachings or explanations. In other words, Trinitarians will argue that Jesus had the authority to forgive sins because he was "God in the flesh." But the Bible explicitly tells us that Jesus forgave sins, not because he was God, but based on the authority God gave him. This is not an "inference" but a plain scriptural teaching. This is the way the Bible itself explains how and why Christ has the authority and power that he does.

[78] Matthew 28:19, *ESV* (emphasis added).

prayed to the Father: "glorify your Son that the Son may glorify you, since *you have given him authority over all flesh*, to give eternal life to all whom you have given him."[79] In fact, as Jesus said in another place: *"The Father loves the Son and has placed everything in his hands."*[80] Or, as other translations express it: "[The Father] has put everything in his power" (*TEV*), "has put everything under his control" (*PME*), "has entrusted everything to him" (*JB*), "has entrusted him with all authority" (*NEB*). In his letter to the Ephesians, the apostle Paul confirmed a related truth when he said: "God has placed everything under the power of Christ and has set him up as supreme head to the Church."[81]

In order to correctly understand the true nature and origin of Christ's authority, as presented in Scripture, one must remember that the Father ('the only true God,' John 17:3) "gave" Jesus "authority over all flesh," and that Jesus also possessed, and possesses, the power to give eternal life to all those whom the Father has given him. Undoubtedly, the authority possessed by Jesus would include the authority to forgive sins, to cast out evil spirits, to be "Lord of the Sabbath," and the authority to speak in God's name. *Scripturally*, whatever authority Jesus is shown to have exercised in his earthly and heavenly life is an authority that God has chosen to bestow upon him. On this matter we have direct scriptural verification (Compare Daniel 7:14; Revelation 2:27).

Matthew 24:36

Like Romans 1:3-4, the book of Matthew contains a key insight into the identity and nature of Christ; because in it we find "Jesus' admission of His ignorance of the day and hour of His return in glory."[82] When asked by his disciples for the sign of

---

[79] John 17:2, *ESV* (emphasis added).
[80] John 3:35, *NIV*
[81] Ephesians 1:22, *PME*
[82] Reymond, *Jesus, Divine Messiah, The New Testament Witness* (New Jersey: Presbyterian and Reformed Publishing Company, 1990), p. 77.

"God the Son" or "the Son of the living God"?

his coming/presence and the conclusion of the age, after the end of his discussion on wars, rumors of wars, earthquakes, the coming of false prophets, false Messiahs, and other future events, Jesus said:

> **...concerning that day and hour, no one knows, neither the angels in heaven, nor the Son, but the Father alone.**[83]

For the purpose of this examination, the key phrase is "nor the Son." According to the Gospel of Matthew (and Mark 13:32), even Jesus Christ, the Son of God, does not know (or did not know at that particular time) the day and hour of his future arrival. However, speaking with reference to the Father and Son, Trinitarian and professor of systematic theology Donald Macleod surprisingly claimed: "They share, too, the same *glory*. The Son's glory is a glory *with* the Father (John 17:5). The same is true of divine *knowledge*. Whatever the Father knows, the Spirit and the Son also know."[84]

In light of Jesus' forthright admission that he did not know the day or hour of his return, it is unclear why some theologians feel compelled to propose theological propositions that the Bible does not speak of, and that, in fact, directly contradict what the Bible *does* speak of in a specific way. Of course it is not entirely true that whatever the Father knows the Son knows, as Jesus himself made clear; and yet this is a fact made evident elsewhere in Scripture.

In the opening of the book of Revelation, the apostle John spoke about what he had seen and heard as the "revelation of Jesus Christ, which God gave to him, to show his servants what must happen soon."[85] This shows that the things revealed to John by Jesus Christ were according to the revelation *given* to Jesus Christ *by* God, which must imply—logically speaking— the "revealing" of knowledge that Jesus Christ did not previously

---

[83] Matthew 24:36
[84] MacLeod, *Shared Life*, pp. 74, 75.
[85] Revelation 1:1, *NAB*

possess, or else there would have been no need or occasion for God to have *revealed* it to him.

In another scholarly work, *Jesus, Divine Messiah*, Robert Reymond attempted to explain Jesus' lack of knowledge respecting his future arrival from the Trinitarian perspective. But first Reymond writes: "I believe that one must accept the saying in both Matthew and Mark as authentic (however much we might prefer to have it otherwise because of the doctrinal difficulty it poses for us) and treat it as a further saying that reveals something of Jesus' self understanding of Himself as the Son of the Father."[86]

The obvious question is: If Jesus was really "God in the flesh (fully equal with the Father)" and God "knows" all things exhaustively (including the details of all future events), as traditional theology teaches us, how can this be reconciled with the fact that Jesus said he did not know something that his Father did know?

In attempting to explain what some Trinitarians perceive as a "doctrinal difficulty," Robert Reymond calls upon the doctrines established by historic Trinitarian theology:

> In light of all of the biblical data concerning Christ's person (which we are here reviewing), the church [evidently, the Protestant church] has seen it doctrinally appropriate to affirm that Jesus, 'being the eternal Son of God, became man, and so was, and continueth to be, God and man in two distinct natures, and one person, forever' (*Westminster Shorter Catechism*, Ques. 21). This means that the eternal Son of God, without in any way divesting Himself of His divine attributes (which is to say, His deity), took human nature into union with His divine nature in the one divine person. In sum, He continued to be God when he became a man. But, of course, this means that He possessed two whole and entirely distinct complexes of attributes—the divine and the human. ...because of the union of the two distinct natures in the

---

[86] *Jesus, Divine Messiah*, p. 78.

one person, Christ is sometimes *designated* in terms of what He is by virtue of one of His natures when what is then *predicated* of Him, so designated, is true of Him in virtue of what He is because of His other nature. As the *Westminster Confession of Faith* says...

With respect to the statement made by Jesus specifically (about 'the Son' *not knowing* the day or hour), Reymond went on to say:

I submit that Christ designates Himself as divine ('the Son' of 'the Father'), but then what He predicates of Himself, namely, ignorance as to the day and hour of His return in heavenly splendor, is true of Him as human, though it is not true of Him as divine. As the God-Man, He is simultaneously omniscient as God (in company with the other persons of the Godhead) and ignorant of some things as a man (in company with other persons of the human race). Warfield has quite properly assessed the governing conditions in this present regard when he writes: 'When He speaks of 'the Son' (who is God) as ignorant, we must understand that He is designating Himself as 'the Son' because of His higher nature, and yet has in mind the ignorance of His lower nature; what He means is that the person properly designated 'the Son' is ignorant, that is to say with respect to the human nature which is as intimate an element of his personality as is His deity. (Warfield, *Person and Work of Christ*, p. 63)...' I conclude that in this saying, which brings before us 'the ignorant Son,' Jesus, as 'the Son,' places Himself outside of and above the category even of angels, that is, outside of and above *creatures* of the highest order, and associates Himself as the divine Son with the Father, while testifying at the same time to His full, unabridged humanity.[87]

In case the picture presented is unclear in any sense, Reymond is claiming that since Jesus is the *Son* (God the Son?),

---

[87] *Jesus, Divine Messiah*, 79-81.

and distinguishes himself from the angels ('*creatures* of the highest order'), this means that Jesus is God, in the flesh. When Jesus said that he did not know the day or hour of his future arrival, this shows that Jesus is a man (with accompanying limitations), and thus Jesus is God and man at the same time—one *person*, two *natures*. As God, Jesus knows all things. As man, Jesus does not have knowledge of certain things. In other words, somehow, Jesus *knows* the "day and hour" of his coming and *does not know* the "day and hour" of his coming, simultaneously! Reymond even claims: "Since the phrase 'not even the Son' comes *after* the reference to angels, Jesus places Himself, on an ascending scale of rank, above the angels of heaven, the highest of created beings...Clearly, He classifies Himself with the Father rather than with the angelic class, inasmuch as elsewhere He represents Himself as Lord of the angels, whose commands they obey (Matt. 13:41, 49; 24:31; cf. Heb. 1:4-14)."[88]

By Jesus saying "no one knows the day or hour, not even the angels in heaven, nor the Son, but only the Father," Jesus "clearly" classifies himself with the Father rather than with the angelic class? Is this really a sound and logical conclusion? If the reasoning presented based on such a statement appears strained and unusual, that is because it truly is. Although Jesus, "the Son," clearly distinguishes himself from the angels as well as from the Father in this passage, on the contrary, it would have been more accurate to say that in this particular context, according to the terms relevant, the Son actually placed himself in the same category as the angels; not in the sense that he *is* an angel, or for the purpose of identifying himself *as* an angel, but in the sense that the Son belongs to the class or category of those who—with the exception of the Father alone—do *not* "know the day or hour." Really, in the words spoken by Jesus in reference

---

[88] It is true, as Reymond points out, that Jesus is "Lord of the angels, whose commands they obey." But again, Jesus made clear that he had been *given* all authority, not only on the earth, but in *heaven* as well (Matthew 28:19). Jesus is Lord over all, with the exception of God alone, the one who gave him the authority he now possesses (compare 1 Corinthians 15:27).

"God the Son" or "the Son of the living God"?

to the knowledge of his future advent, a point of emphasis is not on how Jesus is "removed from the category of creatures," but upon the *supremacy* of his Father—"*no one*" knows except for the Father alone. That is, the Father is in a class completely by himself. This is a point that comes across as rather obvious from Jesus' simple statement about the knowledge of his return.

In reality, such complicated apologetic explanations of a rather simple statement do no more than demonstrate the argumentative skill of Trinitarian theologians. Such skillful apologetic methods are highlighted particularly in their ability to extract and present a meaning from the passage which is, when examined closely, seen to be wholly foreign to its true sense; yet which has a certain surface appearance of plausibility, even intellectual profundity, empowered by a calculated process of eloquent expression and sophisticated theological argumentation, thereby deceiving the minds of the careless and undiscerning.

This is one important key in terms of revealing the extraordinary and distinctively abnormal reasoning process necessary to sustain the overall Trinitarian system; for such a characteristic laboring of the text is, as can be clearly seen, quite unnecessary, and what Jesus said in this particular case does not present to Christians a "doctrinal difficulty" of any sort. As one takes the time to reflect on the purpose and implications of Jesus' statement, and, on the other hand, the scholarly arguments employed to arrive at the desired meaning acceptable to the "orthodox," it is helpful to remember, as it was insightfully pointed out by one Bible expositor: "we must never confuse simplicity with superficiality or complexity with profundity."[89]

Simply put, the Bible has nothing to say about the Son simultaneously knowing all things and not knowing all things at the same time, due to his possessing two natures. The Bible simply indicates, in reference to his future return, that "the Son"[90]

---

[89] Robert B. Strimple, *Three Views on the Millennium and Beyond*, p. 101.
[90] In a 2003 sermon, Dr. Philip Johnson claimed that the term "Son of God" is an expression of Christ's "deity." If that is the case, how does "the Son ('deity,' in the coequal/trinitarian sense)" not know something that *was* known by the Father?

did *not* know the day or hour—nothing more, and nothing less.

In the example of Matthew 24:36 (Jesus' admission of his own ignorance), there are, in truth, no complex theological problems to be sifted through. Nor do we require the "exegesis" of professionally-trained theologians to understand and properly interpret the meaning. For here, Jesus simply meant what he said—that "no one knows" the day and hour of his future, glorious advent, including himself. The Father alone is the possessor of such knowledge.[91] If there is any other discernable point that stands out in Jesus' words, it is in reference to the exclusive *supremacy* and over-arching *sovereignty* of his Father, God. The Father "knows" because he is God and it is according to his own province and timing to execute his own purposes in relation to his kingdom under Christ; as Jesus once replied in another place when asked a similar question by his disciples about the establishment of his kingdom: *"It is not for you to know the times or seasons that the Father has established by his own authority"* (Acts 1:7, *NAB*).

Mark 10:18

Mark 10:17-18 in the *New American Bible* reads:

As he was setting out on a journey, a man ran up, knelt down before him, and asked him, 'Good teacher, what must I do to inherit eternal life?' Jesus answered him, 'Why do you call me good? No one is good but God alone.'

In his popular Study Bible, John MacArthur makes the claim that in this statement, "Jesus challenged the young ruler to think through the implications of ascribing to Him the title 'good.' Since only God is intrinsically good, was he prepared to acknowledge His deity? By this query Jesus did not deny His

---

[91] With respect to the statement that only the Father knows the day and hour, however, Gregory Boyd argued: "this can easily be taken as an idiomatic way of saying that it lies in the Father's authority to determine this time. It need not entail that the Father has already set the exact date (See Acts 1:7)."

deity; on the contrary, He affirmed it."[92]

"Why do you call me good? No one is good but God alone"—an affirmation of Christ's "deity"? Was this the true significance of Jesus' words? Does MacArthur's commentary truly embody the spiritual benefit that Bible students can and should derive from Jesus' words today? Or has MacArthur, as a protector of evangelical tradition, creatively endeavored to extract a desired meaning out of Jesus' words in order to somehow accommodate what is said to a preferred theological concept—even going as far as to introduce a notion entirely foreign to what the Lord himself had in mind?

Rather than an affirmation of his "deity," is it possible that Jesus' response to the young ruler could be taken to be an outstanding example of the sincere humility and profound meekness on the part of the Lord Jesus? Could not Jesus' statement, in fact, be looked upon as a perfect reflection of "the humility [or 'modesty,' *NEB*] that is born of true wisdom" spoken of by the disciple James?[93] If that is the case,—which would seem to be most naturally—what appears most compelling and most instructive about Jesus' response is that even though he was in fact the perfect, sinless, Son of God ('a spotless unblemished lamb,' 'the holy one of God,' 'innocent, undefiled' and 'separated from sinners'; 1 Peter 1:19; John 6:69; Hebrews 7:26), he still humbly refused, in response to the young ruler's address, to credit himself with 'goodness.'[94]

If such was in fact the true spirit behind these words, it would be entirely consistent and harmonious with Jesus' continual and unbroken commitment to bringing glory and honor to his Father (the ultimate source and standard of 'goodness') in everything that he said, and in everything that he did. Here we

---

[92] *The MacArthur Study Bible*, p. 1482.
[93] James 3:13, *PME*; Compare Matthew 28:19
[94] Compare with Jesus' words at John 5:41: "I do not accept praise [or 'glory,' *RSV*] from men..." *NIV*. It is as F. F. Bruce pointed out in his commentary on the Gospel of John: "It is his Father's glory that Jesus seeks to promote by obediently delivering his message; he is not concerned for his own reputation. He can trust his Father to take care of that, and in fact he, above all others, receives 'the glory that comes from the only God' (John 5:44)." —*The Gospel of John, Introduction, Exposition and Notes*, p. 203.

would be able to recognize yet another case of Jesus exemplifying the most valuable spiritual principle he repeatedly inculcated to his followers: *"He that exalts himself will be humbled, but he that humbles himself will be exalted."*[95]

As a matter of fact, in Luke's account, it was the very same principle of humility that was emphasized through the parable of the Pharisee and the Tax Collector, along with the lesson of the little children.[96] Incidentally, both appear immediately before Jesus' conversation with the young ruler when he humbly credited goodness to "God alone," in spite of the fact that he was, according to Scripture, "without sin" (Hebrews 4:15; Compare 2 Corinthians 5:21).

Given the clarity present in the context, and the most logical implication of Jesus' words, it is safe to conclude that to argue from the statement in Mark 10:18 that Jesus was somehow affirming his exalted status as "deity incarnate" is, really, an unnecessary and bewildering misrepresentation of its true and seemingly obvious intent. Taken in its most natural sense, in light of the surrounding context, Jesus' statement that "no one is good but God alone" does not appear, or commend itself in any certain or natural way,[97] to be an affirmation of his "deity," but rather, a confirmation of Christ's true wisdom and genuine humility (Compare James 3:13).[98]

> *"I am not seeking glory for myself; but there is One that is seeking and judging... If I glorify myself, my glory is nothing.*

---

[95] See Luke 14:7-11; 18:9-19; compare Philippians 2:5-11.
[96] In Matthew 18:4, Jesus said, "Whoever *humbles* himself like this child is the greatest in the kingdom of heaven."
[97] As strange and perplexing as it may seem, MacArthur's explanation ends up being the complete opposite of what is most clearly and naturally implied by Jesus' statement.
[98] This is not to suggest that the point of Jesus' response was to deny his identity as "God incarnate." Such just happens to be the natural though incidental implication of his statement, when considered in light of the traditional claim. As always, Jesus spoke about the one God as someone *other than himself*. Again, a man calls Jesus "good." Jesus responds by indicating that someone else besides him is good, namely, God. It would seem safe to say that all of Jesus' followers should strive to pattern themselves after the same spirit set forth in this example.

> *"God the Son" or "the Son of the living God"?*
>
> ***It is my Father who glorifies me..."***
>
> —Jesus Christ, John 8:50, 54

Psalm 110:1; Matthew 22:43-44

A Psalm of David: *"A declaration of Jehovah to my Lord: Sit at My right hand, until I place Your enemies as Your footstool."*[99]

When Jesus had taught for several days in the city of Jerusalem, the Gospel of Matthew reports that the following discussion took place between Jesus and the Pharisees:

> **While the Pharisees were gathered, Jesus asked them, saying, What do you think of Christ? Whose son is he? They [said] to Him, David's. He said to them, How then does David by the Spirit call him Lord, saying, 'the LORD said to my Lord, Sit on My right until I make Your enemies Your footstool for Your feet?' If David then calls Him Lord, how is He his son? And no one was able to answer Him a word, nor did anyone dare from that day to question Him any more.**[100]

Here Jesus posed a question to the Pharisees based on Psalm 110:1 which they were unable to give an answer to. In his popular *Systematic Theology*, Wayne Grudem made the following claim respecting this account:

> Jesus...identifies himself as the sovereign Lord of the Old Testament when he asks the Pharisees about Psalm 110:1, 'The Lord said to *my Lord*, sit at my right hand, till I put your enemies under your feet' (Matt. 22:44). The force of this statement is that 'God the Father said to God the Son [David's Lord], 'Sit at my right hand...' The Pharisees know he is talking about himself and identifying himself as one worthy of the Old Testament title *kyrios*, 'Lord.'[101]

---

[99] Psalm 110:1, *Literal Translation of the Holy Bible* translated by Jay P. Green Sr.
[100] Matthew 22:41-45, *Modern King James Version of the Holy Bible* by Jay P. Green Sr.
[101] *Systematic Theology*, p. 545.

"God the Son" or "the Son of the living God"?

The viewpoint expressed is common among evangelical teachers. Of the original Psalm that Jesus made reference to, John MacArthur claimed: "God the Father invited *God the Son* in His ascension to sit at the place of honor in the heavenly throne room..."[102] With regard to Jesus' actual use of the Psalm in his conversation with the Pharisees, MacArthur similarly claimed: "The inescapable implication is that Jesus was declaring His deity."[103]

Aside from the fact that there is no such figure in the Bible known as "God the Son," Wayne Grudem errs when he claims that Jesus—based on Psalm 110—identified himself as "the sovereign Lord of the Old Testament." As with so many expositions of Scripture designed to uphold traditional doctrine, and in light of the abundant resources now available to us as Bible students, it is surprising that this kind of claim is made regarding such a text.

In Psalm 110:1 the speaker is King David. An accurate representation of the Hebrew original reads: "A declaration of Jehovah to my Lord: Sit at my right hand, until I place your enemies as a stool for your feet." Here it is *Jehovah God* who speaks to David's *Lord* (a scripturally verifiable reference to the Messiah).[104] The name translated "Jehovah" is the English form of the divine name of God (where most English translations have the substitute-title 'LORD'). Jehovah, God, gives utterance to David's "Lord," the English translation of the Hebrew *adoni*, meaning "my lord" or "my master." Yet God is not speaking to someone called "*adonai*" ('sovereign/supreme Lord') as Wayne Grudem seems to wrongly suggest; for "*adonai*" is a description applied exclusively to the one God of Israel in the Hebrew Scriptures.[105]

---

[102] *MacArthur Study Bible*, p. 843 (emphasis added).

[103] *MacArthur Study Bible*, p. 1436.

[104] The Reverend J.R. Dummelow observed in his commentary: "The Jews fully accepted the Messianic interpretation of this Psalm. Rabbi Joden said, 'In the time to come the Holy and Blessed God will place King Messiah at His right hand, according to Ps 110.'" —*The One Volume Bible Commentary*, p. 699.

[105] However, the second form of '*adonai*' is used in the plural, of men, on occasion.

"God the Son" or "the Son of the living God"?

In a recent work called *"The Messiah,"* Dr. William Varner (professor of Biblical Studies at the Masters College) likewise made the following unfortunate statements with respect to the Messianic Psalm:

> The psalmist David, in verse one, records a conversation between two members of the Godhead...A literal translation of the first phrase is: 'Yahweh said to my Adonai....' Yahweh (sometimes pronounced as Jehovah) and Adonai are two names for God in the Old Testament. The only adequate explanation for this conversation between two persons with Divine names is that there must be a plurality of personalities within the Godhead—a concept consistent with many other passages (Gen. 1:1, 26; 3:22; 11:7; Dt. 6:4; Isa. 48:16-17).[106]

Is it really fair to say, with Varner, that the *"only* adequate explanation" for this conversation is "that there *must* be a plurality of personalities within the Godhead"? Do we find any indication in the original Psalm that the two figures mentioned were in fact members of the same "Godhead"? Or is this yet another example of an educated Bible expositor importing an unrelated meaning onto a scriptural statement from without, with view to upholding the foundations of a traditional theological framework?

The first problem is, strictly speaking, "Yahweh" and *"adonai"* are not two "names" for God in the Old Testament. "Yahweh" (or 'Jehovah') is God's proper name alone; whereas *"adonai"* is an exalted, descriptive title meaning "sovereign (or supreme) Lord."[107] Of course, Yahweh is in fact the "sovereign/supreme Lord," but his proper and unique name is *Yahweh/Jehovah*, not "sovereign Lord."[108]

---

[106] *The Messiah, Revealed, Rejected, Received* (Bloomington: Author House, 2004), p. 68. The passages Dr. Varner refers to are examined in the chapter "'Trinity' in the Old Testament?"

[107] In the same way that the terms "God," "Almighty," "Most High," and "God the Father" are all descriptions and titles for the Father of Jesus Christ, whose *one* name is Jehovah or Yahweh.

[108] Similarly, Barack Obama is the "President" of the United States; although his title or position is that of "President," his personal and proper name is "Barack Obama."

"God the Son" or "the Son of the living God"?

    The second problem with the proposed interpretation is that, in the original Psalm, the writer was, in all likelihood, not intending to express the specific connotation of *"adonai"* (sovereign Lord) of the one Jehovah was addressing; but, rather, the more general concept of *"adoni"*;[109] again, a respectful form of address meaning "my lord" or "my master." In fact, we know for certain that *adoni* is not a term that connotes the idea of "Godhead" or "Deity" (nor does it ever carry the sense 'God the Son' or 'second member of the Godhead'), for the term is used in reference to humans all throughout the Hebrew Scriptures. With reference to the occurrence of the word "Lord" in Matthew 22:44—in light of Jesus' reference to Psalm 110:1—the noted Bible expositor Albert Barnes correctly observed: "A *lord* or master is a superior. The word here does not necessarily imply Divinity, but only superiority. David calls him his superior, his Lord, his Master, his Lawgiver; and expresses his willingness to obey him."[110]

    In his commentary on the original Psalm in the Hebrew Scriptures, Barnes also correctly noted that the word translated *Lord* "means one who has rule or authority; one of high rank; one who has dominion; one who is the owner or possessor, etc. This word is applied frequently to a creature. It is applied to kings, princes, rulers, masters. The phrase '*my* Lord' refers to someone who was superior in rank to the author of the psalm; one whom he could address as his superior. The psalm, therefore, cannot refer to David himself, as if Jehovah had said to *him*, 'Sit thou at my right hand.' Nor was there any one on earth in the time of David to whom it could be applicable; any one whom *he* would call *his* 'Lord' or superior. If, therefore, the psalm was written by David, it must have reference to the Messiah—to one whom he owned as *his* superior—*his* Lord—*his* sovereign. It cannot refer to God as if *he* were to have this rule over David, since God himself is referred to *as speaking* to him whom David called his Lord:—'Jehovah said unto my

---

[109] Pronounced: 'adonee.'
[110] *Barne's Notes, Notes on the New Testament, Matthew and Mark*, p. 238.

Lord.' ...*Sit at my right hand*...The phrase is properly applicable to the Messiah as exalted to the highest place in the universe—the right hand of God."[111]

On this point it was even noted in a periodical for Bible students: "The Bible in Psalm 110:1 actually gives the Messiah the title that *never* describes God. The word is *adoni* and in all of its 195 occurrences in the Old Testament it means a superior who is human (or occasionally angelic)..."[112]

Roman Catholic scholar John L. McKenzie likewise pointed out in his *Bible Dictionary*: "In most of the instances where the title [*adon*] belongs to Yahweh it appears in the unique and grammatically anomalous form of Adonai...this is probably a vocalization of uncertain date and origin to distinguish the divine title from the usual *adoni*, 'my lord,' addressed to human beings."[113]

In an article in *The International Standard Bible Encyclopedia*, it was noted specifically: "The form *adoni* ('my lord') (pl. *adonay*), a royal title (1 Sam. 29:8), is to be carefully distinguished from the divine title *adonay* ('my Lord,' 'Lord,' or 'O Lord') used over 130 times of Yahweh especially in the Psalms and Isaiah."[114]

The point is clearly illustrated by Genesis 24:12, when Abraham's servant said, "Yahweh, God of my master (*adoni*) Abraham, be with me today, and show your kindness to my master (*adoni*) Abraham."[115] In this case, the same expression "my lord/master" (*adoni*) is used of Abraham. It is not a word that implies a reference to God. However, in Genesis 15:2, Abram (before his name was changed to 'Abraham') called God "Sovereign Lord (*adonai*) Jehovah." In a solemn prayer of thanksgiving, David likewise exclaimed, "you are indeed great, O Sovereign Lord (*adonai*) Jehovah; for there is no other like

---

[111] *Barne's Notes, Notes on the Old Testament, Psalms Volume 1*, pp. 136, 137.
[112] *Focus On the Kingdom Magazine*, emphasis added.
[113] *Dictionary of the Bible*, John L. McKenzie, S.J., p. 516.
[114] *The International Standard Bible Encyclopedia*, Vol. 3, p. 157.
[115] *Jerusalem Bible* rendering

you, and there is no God except you among all of whom we have heard with our ears."[116]

It should be pointed out that the words *adonai* and *adoni* in the Hebrew text are actually identical with the exception of the differing vowel points, as explained by British Bible scholar Allon Maxwell:

> The main form of '*Adonai*' has a different vowel point under the '*n*' to distinguish it from the second much less common form of the word. (The second form of '*Adonai*' is used in the plural, of men, very occasionally.)...The Hebrew text identifies vowels by a system of vowel points (which, to the untrained eye, look like random 'dots' and 'squiggles') placed above, below, or alongside the appropriate consonant. This vowel pointing system was developed by the Masoretes. As mentioned above, the two words '*adonai*' and '*adoni*' are both formed from the root word '*adon*.' The difference is in the vowel pointing: '*adonai*' is formed by placing the points 'quamets' under *nun*. '*adoni*' is formed by placing the point '*hireq*' under *nun*. (Just one tiny letter different, but an enormous difference in meaning!)

Maxwell goes on to observe:

> The Masoretes were Hebrew scholars who, over several centuries, established a system of vowel markings to indicate the traditional pronunciation and intonation. We call these the 'vowel points.' This work was not completed until several centuries after the beginning of the Christian era. One sometimes encounters people whose determination to retain Psalm 110:1 as a Trinitarian 'proof text' leads them to (selectively) discount the reliability of the Massoretic vowel pointing system, in favour of some other personal preference,

---

[116] 2 Samuel 7:22, *NWT*. Regarding the Hebrew word *adonai*, form of the word *adon*, it was observed by one source: "The ending *ai* added to the Hebrew word '*adohn* is a different form of the plural of excellence. When *Adhonai* appears without an additional suffix in Hebrew, it is used exclusively of Jehovah and indicates that he is the Sovereign Lord." —*Insight on the Scriptures*, Volume 2, p. 267.

especially when it suits their particular theological bias. However unless there is compelling documented evidence for changes of this kind, they are seldom helpful. We must be very cautious about introducing arbitrary changes of this kind, lest we leave ourselves open to accusations of 'intellectual dishonesty.'[117]

In his book on the Trinity, Anthony Buzzard discussed the import of Psalm 110:1 in detail. In a footnote, the following observation was made:

> It is amazing that a number of commentaries wrongly assert that the second lord [of Psalm 110:1] is *adonai*. See, for example, *The Bible Knowledge Commentary* (ed. Walvoord and Zuck, representing Dallas Theological Seminary faculty, Victor Books, 1987) which states mistakenly that 'my lord' in Ps. 110:1 'translates the Hebrew *adonay*, used only of God' (73). Unfortunately this comment suggests that the Messiah is God Himself. In fact the Hebrew for 'my lord' is not *adonai* but *adoni*, which is *never* used of God but often of the king of Israel and other human superiors.[118] This surprising error of fact is symptomatic of widespread confusion of God with the Messiah. 1 Sam. 24:6 is typical of the Hebrew manner of distinguishing 'my lord, the king' from the Lord God. No one reading Ps. 110:1 could imagine that the Messiah was the Lord God. The Messiah is the Lord's anointed…The same error about the word 'lord' in Psalm 110:1 appears frequently in evangelical literature. See, for example, Hebert Lockyer, *All the Divine Names and Titles in the*

---

[117] *Sit Thou at my right hand (Psalm 110:1)*, Bible Digest, Number 86, September 1998. It was pointed out by one Bible scholar: "Occasionally, it will be objected that this distinction between Adonai and adoni was a late addition to the Hebrew text by the Masoretes around 600-700 AD and therefore is not reliable. This objection needs to be considered in light of the fact that the Hebrew translators of the Septuagint (the LXX) around 250 BC recognized and carefully maintained this Hebrew distinction in their work. They never translated the second 'lord' of Psalm 110:1 ('my lord,' *kyrios mou*) to mean the Deity. The first LORD of Psalm 110:1 (the LORD, *Ho Kyrios*) they always reserved for the one God, Jehovah." —Greg S. Deuble, *They never told me this in church!* (Atlanta: Restoration Fellowship, 2006), pp. 119, 120

[118] Buzzard noted that in the Hebrew Scriptures there are almost 200 occurrences of *adoni* ('my lord') referring to mostly humans (and on occasion, angels), and nearly 450 occurences of *adonai* ('Sovereign Lord') referring to the one God of Israel.

Bible (Zondervan: 1975): 'Here, Jehovah speaks to Adonai words that are properly applied to Christ' (15). The Lockman Foundation NASB marginal note on Acts 2:36 likewise reports the Hebrew word as *Adonai*. They happily agreed to correct the mistake in future printings.[119]

The force of the statement in Psalm 110:1 is not "God the Father said to *God the Son*," an alleged "conversation between two members of the Godhead"; but rather, "Jehovah (God) said to David's (messianic) Lord (master/superior), sit at my right hand until I place your enemies as a stool for your feet."

It should be noted that these are not merely speculative inferences based on preconceived doctrinal viewpoints; nor are they arguments designed for "apologetic" purposes; but facts based on the specific language used and overall harmony of the Hebrew and Christian Scriptures. As it was noted by Anthony Buzzard and Charles Hunting: "Neither the Jews nor Jesus misunderstood their own language on this critical matter of defining God and His Son. They never thought that Psalm 110:1 had introduced distinctions in the Godhead...Traditional orthodoxy has substituted its own definition of Lord, as it applies to Jesus, and advanced the extraordinary and very un-Hebrew idea that God is more than a single person, in opposition to the definitive oracular utterance of Psalm 110:1...The whole Trinitarian argument from this Psalm fails because the facts of the language are wrongly reported."[120]

Commenting on the apostle Peter's reference to the same Scripture on the day of Pentecost (Acts 2:34), Professor I. Howard Marshall (Senior Lecturer in New Testament Exegesis) pointed out in the conservative *Tyndale New Testament Commentaries*:

> We may note that there is an ambiguity in the English use of the word 'Lord' which is not present in the Hebrew Psalm where the first word translated 'Lord' is YHWH,

---

[119] Buzzard & Hunting, *The Doctrine of the Trinity*, footnotes: pp. 48-49.
[120] Buzzard & Hunting, *The Doctrine of the Trinity*, pp. 52, 56, 57.

"God the Son" or "the Son of the living God"?

the name of God, and the second word is *'adon* which can be used of lords and masters. In both cases the Greek text has *kyrios*, and this facilitated the transfer to Jesus of other Old Testament texts which referred to Yahweh. Here, however, it is simply the attribute of lordship which is given to Jesus; he is not equated with Yahweh.[121]

So what we find in this example, unfortunately, is how an otherwise careful, capable and dedicated Bible scholar[122] can overlook a fairly basic point with respect to the language and context, and thus proceed to color a scriptural statement with an idea wholly foreign to the scripture's original intent; not because the sense is necessary or even plausible, but due to being under the constraint of having to conform key scriptural statements to a long-held theological "orthodoxy."

Instead of viewing passages like these in light of their historical context and specific language used, the thinking and exposition is governed by a doctrinal framework already considered to be true. When there exists a certain pressure to uphold and perpetuate doctrines held by the traditional religious establishment, the evidence shows that apologists often attempt to conform biblical statements to a presupposed yet *unscriptural* doctrinal system; perhaps, in many cases, not even realizing that this is the case. They are, in effect, held captive to a theological concept, resulting in a nearly unconscious loyalty to a traditional though unbiblical creed—which, in turn, negatively affects their otherwise sound exposition of scriptural teaching, whether considering certain passages independently, or when considering the Bible's essential message and basic themes as a whole.

Jehovah telling David's Lord (*adoni*)—the Messiah—to sit at his right hand actually had its true fulfillment in a future

---

[121] *The Acts of the Apostles, An Introduction and Commentary*, Tyndale New Testament Commentaries (Grand Rapids, Michigan, 1980), pp. 79-80.

[122] Dr. Varner's book on the Messiah has many beneficial aspects, especially so in the tracing of those OT prophecies relating to the advent of the Messiah, from the book of Genesis onward; demonstrating clearly from the Hebrew Scriptures that Jesus was in fact the one who would "bruise [the serpent's] head" (Gen. 3:15) and "bear the sins of many" (Isaiah 53:12).

time from David's perspective, and in the past from our own.[123] According to the apostolic testimony, after Jesus had lived in unfailing obedience to God to the point of death (in fulfillment of the Law, Psalms and Prophets), three days later God raised him from death to life and exalted him to his right hand, having given Jesus "all authority in heaven and on earth." That is another reason why we know that, in the case of Psalm 110:1, the Messiah is not called "Lord" for the purpose of identifying him as a member of a "triune Godhead," but based, prophetically, on his Father having gladly conferred upon him such a unique and lofty position. As the apostle Peter gave assurance, we can know and *"accept as certain"* that Jesus is Lord (David's 'Lord') because *"God has made* this Jesus, whom [the Jews] crucified, both *Lord* and *Messiah."*[124]

The producers of the Translation Handbook for the *Today's English Version* of the Bible were correct in their observation:

> *The Lord* of Psalm 110.1 is understood absolutely of God, while *my Lord* is used of the Promised Messiah. If David then refers to the Messiah (who is also his 'son') as *my Lord*, this automatically reveals that the Messiah is superior to David. Matthew is not so much concerned to prove the Davidic origin of Jesus (this is assumed in the structure of his Gospel), but rather to demonstrate that Jesus, who is both descendant of David and Messiah, is superior to David.[125]

The scholars involved in the production of the *New English Translation* were also correct when they called attention to a similar point: "Jesus was pressing the language here to get his opponents to reflect on how great Messiah is."

---

[123] Respecting Jesus' question to the Pharisees in verse 45, "If David then calls him 'Lord,' how can he be his son?" *The Interpreter's Bible* (Volume 7, p. 527) noted: "This is not an absolute statement that the Messiah cannot be David's Son; the point is that he cannot be thought of *merely* in these terms."

[124] Acts 2:36, *NEB*

[125] *A Handbook On The Gospel of Matthew*, by Barclay M. Newman and Philip C. Stine (New York: United Bible Societies, 1988), p. 699.

"God the Son" or "the Son of the living God"?

The Messiah is David's *Son* because he was David's descendent according to the flesh (Romans 1:3). The Messiah is called David's *Lord*, evidently, because when God's kingdom is fully and finally established under the reign of his anointed one, all people, of all nations, tribes and tongues—including David—will recognize him as their divinely-appointed Lord and King, to the glory of God (compare Philippians 2:11).

The observation made in the *Translator's Handbook* may also help to better understand the practice of those translators who, in the interests of clarity, have placed the divine name Jehovah/Yahweh (although the Greek text has 'Lord'—*kyrios*) whenever the New Testament writers made clear quotations or allusions to Old Testament texts where the divine name appeared:

> If at all possible, translators should retain the expressions of the text, *the Lord* and *my Lord*. However, if the resulting translation is extremely confusing, they may say 'The Lord God said to my Lord' or 'God, who is the Lord, said to my Lord.' A footnote could indicate that *my Lord* referred to the Messiah, although occasionally translators have felt they had to say 'my Lord, the Messiah.'[126]

Some New Testament translations have simply, "The *Lord* said to my *Lord*..." (*RSV*, emphasis added). This may be confusing because it doesn't help most readers in terms of understanding the important difference found in the original reference. Matthew 22:44 in the *King James Version* is a slight improvement, for it has, "The LORD (all capitals, signaling a reference to the divine name, Jehovah) said unto my Lord..." Matthew 22:44 in *The Restoration of the Original Sacred Name Bible* reflects even more accurately the sense of the original Psalm in Hebrew from which Jesus quotes, "*YAHVAH hath said*

---

[126] *A Handbook On The Gospel of Matthew*, p. 699 (words in italics originally in bold-underlined). It was also pointed out: *"How is he his son?"* is a literal representation of the Greek and is translated *'how can the Messiah be David's descendant?'* by TEV. This requires no more than identifying *he* as 'the Messiah,' and *his son* as '*David's descendant.*'"

"God the Son" or "the Son of the living God"?

unto my *Master*..."[127]

If a Bible reader does not fully appreciate the distinction that comes through in the original Hebrew reference of Psalm 110:1, the translation "The Lord said to my Lord" (a rendering with no distinction) can result in an unfortunate impairment in the understanding of the sacred oracle. This is one of the reasons why Bible readers can benefit from studying from a Bible version that faithfully translates the divine name (either as 'Yahweh' or 'Jehovah') where it originally appeared in the Hebrew Scriptures, as opposed to those that follow the latter Jewish tradition of substituting God's proper name with the title "Lord." Whether or not the divine name actually occurred in the original writings of the New Testament is a subject of controversy.[128] But whatever the case may be,—with respect to the appearance of the divine name in the Greek text—far from being a Scripture that in some way lends credence to traditional Trinitarian conceptions of the "Godhead," Psalm 110:1 is actually one of the numerous and harmonious examples in Scripture where, although the Messiah is undoubtedly presented as a highly honored and highly exalted being, he is, nevertheless, revealed to be one who is distinct from Jehovah God—being as he is, the very one to whom Jehovah himself said, "sit at my right hand until I place your enemies as a stool for your feet."[129]

---

[127] The autographs or original writings of the NT are no longer in existence or in our possession. All translations are based on copies (most likely, copies of copies of copies...). Some Christians believe that the original NT writings actually contained the name of God; especially in cases where the NT writers quoted from OT texts where the name occurred. Although there are several reasonable points that can be given in support of the belief that the divine name occurred in the original NT Scriptures (actually, an abbreviated form of the name *does* appear 4 times in the book of Revelation: 19:1-6), this cannot be proven with certainty. There is, however, no question that in many instances where the Greek NT has *kyrios* ('Lord') that it is representative of the proper name of God, Jehovah. This is an obvious point in Jesus' reference to Psalm 110:1 during his conversation with the Pharisees in Matthew 22:44.

[128] However, the abbreviated form of the divine name, "Jah" (Gk. *ia*), does appear in the book of Revelation (chapter 19:1-6) four times in the expression "hallelujah" (Gk. *allelouia*).

[129] It was correctly observed in the *International Critical Commentary* on Peter: "We are not to suppose that the apostles identified Christ with Jehovah; there were passages which made this impossible, for instance, Psalm 110." (T&T Clark, 1910), p. 99.

> *"Be therefore cautioned, reader, not to embrace the determination of prejudiced councils for evangelical doctrine; which the Scriptures bear no certain testimony to, neither was believed by the primitive saints..."*
> —William Penn, *The Sandy Foundation Shaken*, 1668.

"Perhaps the councils did not come to correct and final conclusions. Since some councils overruled and contradicted other ones, in principle not all of them could have been correct. It therefore becomes incumbent on us to scrutinize carefully the creeds formulated by the councils, to make certain they embody most fully the truth about the deity...We must look closely at the biblical testimony to determine whether this doctrine is indeed found there...There is no virtue in continuing to hold such a difficult doctrine of the Trinity if it is not actually taught in the Bible..."
— Millard J. Erickson, *God In Three Persons*

> *"We deny that any creed, council or individual may bind a Christian's conscience..."*
> —James R. White, *Scripture Alone*, p. 42

"The determinative elements of the Christology of the Fourth Gospel are those that present Jesus as the one who carries out the functions of God and embodies the activity of God because he is identified with God in the way that a Son is identified with a Father...In every possible formulation, Jesus is portrayed as one whose identity and actions originate with God, and whose ministry points and leads to God. Jesus is a prophet, the Son of Man to whom judgment has been entrusted, the Messiah, the Son of God, the one who does the work of God and who speaks the words of God, and the one who has seen God and so makes him known. He comes from God, the Father who sent him. As the one who has seen God, Jesus reveals God; as the one who hears from God, Jesus speaks words of life. Jesus embodies God's glory in the flesh."

—Thompson, *The God of the Gospel of John*, pp. 232, 233

"And He ordered us to preach to the people, and solemnly to testify that this [Jesus] is the One who has been appointed by God as Judge of the living and the dead."

—The apostle Peter, Acts 10:42, *NASB*

"Believe in God; believe also in me."
—Jesus Christ, John 14:1, *ESV*

"…they said to him, 'What can we do to accomplish the works of God?' Jesus answered and said to them, 'This is the work of God, that you believe in the one he sent.'"
—John 6:28-29, *NAB*

3

The Father-Son Relationship

> *"Those who love me will keep my word, and my Father will love them, and we will come to them and make our home with them. Whoever does not love me does not keep my words; and the word that you hear is not mine, but is from the Father who sent me."*
> —Jesus Christ, John 14:23-24, NRSV

John chapter seventeen provides a record of the Son's solemn prayer to his Father on the night before his execution, when he sacrificially laid down his perfect life as a "ransom for all." In addition to the overall simplicity, beauty, and faith-strengthening power of his message that night, his words also prove significant in view of assessing the alleged validity, centrality, and biblical status of the Trinity.

In the beginning of his prayer, Jesus made clear that eternal life means "knowing" the only true God and Jesus

The Father-Son Relationship

Christ, the one whom the only true God sent forth.[1] Although these words are clear enough, in and of themselves, it must be respectfully pointed out (in light of the historic conflicts regarding Jesus' identity) that Jesus did not identify himself as "the only true God." As any student of Scripture can easily see, Jesus made a very careful and transparent distinction between God and himself—even doing so in connection with the knowledge that represents "eternal life."

When it comes to the biblical revelation regarding the "Father-Son" relationship, there is nothing dishonorable or unscriptural in calling attention to the truth that Jesus clearly presented "the only true God" as a distinct figure from himself, and that he identified himself, not as "the only true God," but as one who had been "sent" by "the only true God." In fact, the making of a point such as this would not even be called for if it were not for the long history and prevalence of extra-biblical teachings regarding the identity of "Jesus Christ" and his relationship to his "Father."

What we have here in John 17:3 is paramount, a true and *definitional* statement of genuine Christian faith. In other words, *this* is the manner in which the Bible presents the truth about the identity of the true God and his Son, the one he sent forth. Jesus himself revealed that he was the one "sent" by the only true God, making plain—as he did in so many other instances—that he conceived of God as a figure distinguishable from himself. Clearly, "the only true God" is a definite reference to a specific being (the Almighty one), not to an alleged "first person" who "shares" in the only true God's being with two other "persons," as Trinitarianism tells us. John 17:3 is, in fact, a defining example of Jesus himself presenting the truth about his and his Father's identities. It is a presentation of original Christian doctrine in its *purest* and *fullest* and *clearest* form of expression—from the mouth of the very Lord and founder of the Christian faith. If it is true that our very salvation is tied to our

---

[1] The term "everlasting life" might be more literally rendered "life of the age (to come)."

knowing "the only true God" as "Father, Son, and Spirit (the incomprehensible Trinity)," it is reasonable to ask why Jesus did not make mention of this concept at this point, particularly in light of the concern he went on to express for the security and well-being of his true followers, and the importance of their abiding in, and being sanctified by, his Father's "word" of "truth" (John 17:9-19).

This is also why it is appropriate to ask: Why is it that whenever there was an occasion for discussing the identity of the true God, the authors and participants of Scripture *always* spoke of him as "the Father" and never as the "triune God" or the like? Why is it that every positively and deliberately-set-forth scriptural presentation of God's identity is always *different* from Trinitarianism's? Perhaps these facts do not decisively affect the validity of Trinitarian teaching (what Trinitarian apologists would ultimately have to contend), but who could rightfully deny the reasonableness and significance of such questions?

If we assume the Trinity to be biblical, in a considerable number of cases it can be pointed out that whenever opportunities arose to introduce or defend the Trinitarian concept (an entirely distinctive and revolutionary one from the biblical and Jewish perspective), not one of God's faithful servants in Scripture, including Jesus himself, ever made it a point to speak a word on its behalf. Instead, they always made expressions that, when considered in hindsight, leave one with the impression that the notion of a Deity whose most distinguishing characteristic involved the idea of one "being" or "essence" shared by three distinct "persons" had no place in their understanding of God's nature and identity after all.

In this most solemn and insightful prayer, we not only see exhibited Jesus' real dependence upon God,—marked by a pure, profound and loving loyalty toward him as his Father—but we can also clearly discern the priority given by Jesus with respect to the spiritual well-being of his followers. To the only true God, his Father, Jesus prayed: "**Sanctify them in the truth; your word is truth**" (John 17:17).

The Father-Son Relationship

Undoubtedly, it was out of such a deeply felt and abiding concern that Jesus made such a request, not only for his inner and immediate circle of disciples, but also, as Jesus said, for all "those who will believe in me through *their* word, so that they may all be one, as you, Father, are in me and I in you, that they also may be in us, in order that the world may believe that you sent me."[2]

If we go on to consider what is said in the fifth verse, we will find that Jesus made another revealing statement tied to his identity and status in relation to God, evidently, before the world (as we know it) existed. Yet in a brief article written in 2004, James White suggested that Jesus' statement to his Father indicated, as Trinitarian teaching would hold, that Jesus was "sharing the essential glory of the godhead before time itself began."[3] Yet once again, as in other examples already mentioned, a simple reading of Jesus' statement will give another clue into how common it is that Trinitarian apologists will read an idea or concept into a text that is simply not discernable in the words or contexts themselves. What Jesus actually said, specifically, was:

Now glorify me, Father, with you, with the glory I had with you before the world began.[4]

From this expression it is clear that Jesus spoke of himself as one who had glory *with* (Gk: *para*; literally 'beside' or 'alongside') the Father "before the world was." But does such an expression really carry with it the idea that Jesus shared "the *essential* glory of the *godhead* before time itself began"? The obvious fact is that *none of these ideas are present* in Jesus' words.

Not only did Jesus distinguish himself from "the only true God" as the one "sent" by God in verse three, but in verse five, he revealed more specifically that, before the world began,

---

[2] John 17:17-21 (emphasis added).
[3] *Apologetics Blog Archives, Alpha &Omega Ministries, Christian Apologetics and Theology*, March, 2, 2004.
[4] John 17:5, *NAB*.

he existed—whether *ideally*, in the *plan* and *purpose* of God, as some believe, or *literally*, as the Son, as others believe—and had glory "with" or "alongside" the "only true God," not that he *was* "the only true God," or that he was somehow a coeternal divine "person" who "shared" in the one "being" or "substance" of "the only true God."

Unlike Dr. White's unproven conjecture, overconfidently put forward as the definite sense of Jesus' words, Jesus did not say or suggest that he was a member of a "Godhead." Rather, *the most* this verse could suggest is that the Son of God evidently did not begin his life on earth as a man.[5] Yet it is still not entirely clear why some Trinitarian apologists consider it reasonable, or think it permissible, to impose ideas onto scriptural statements that are not directly presented or necessarily implied; in this case, reading a very specific concept into words that they do not carry in and of themselves. In spite of the prevailing disagreements over the question of Jesus' identity and relationship to God (and the tradition of pointing to the ecumenical creeds of the 'historic faith' for definitive answers), there doesn't seem to be any convincing reason why Christians cannot derive an accurate understanding from the clearly-set-forth teachings already given to us by Jesus and his apostles in the Scriptures.

In addition to the point concerning John 17:5, Trinitarians have often argued that since Jesus spoke of himself as one who had "glory" with the Father before the world was, and in the book of Isaiah God said, *"my glory will I not give to another,"*[6] the only sound conclusion that one can deduce is that Jesus must therefore be a second "person" who shares in the one God's being, or else he could not have had glory from or with the Father. Yet in the very same prayer in John chapter seventeen, Jesus said to God: *"The glory that you have given me*

---

[5] However, for an alternative consideration of the texts that appear to support the concept of Christ's *pre-human* existence, see: *The Trinity, Christianity's Self-Inflicted Wound*: Ch. VII., The Nature of Preexistence in the New Testament, and Ch. VIII., John, Preexistence and the Trinity (Buzzard and Hunting).

[6] Isaiah 42:8

I have given to them..."—a reference to Jesus' disciples. The reason being, as Jesus went on to explain, "that they may be one even as we are one, I in them and you in me, that they may become perfectly one, so that the world may know that you sent me and loved them even as you loved me" (John 17:20-23).

In this example even *the disciples* are "given" the "glory" that God had "given" to the Son. According to Jesus, they can even participate in the unity or 'oneness' characterized by the Father-Son relationship ('that they [the disciples] may be one *even as we* [Father and Son] *are one*'; John 17:20). None of this, of course, makes the disciples "coeternal with the Father" as members of a so-called "Godhead," and neither does the "glory" possessed by the disciples make them part of a "Godhead" either, even though God explicitly declared that he would not share his glory with another (Isaiah 42:8).[7]

God's unwillingness to share his glory with others, in the context of Isaiah, clearly speaks to how God will not share glory with a rival or competing god, particularly a man-made "idol." From a biblical perspective, however, God gladly confers "glory" upon those who serve him and carry out his will and purpose, as in the case of his "beloved Son" and all of God's faithful "children" (Compare Psalm 8:5; Luke 2:32; Acts 3:13[8]; Romans 8:17, 21, 30; 9:4; Hebrews 2:10; 1 Peter 5:1, 4, 10).

Earlier, in the fourteenth chapter of John's Gospel, Jesus told his disciples, in light of his then soon-to-come departure:

---

[7] John 17:22-24, *ESV*. This is another example revealing the common type of flawed and superficial reasoning used by Trinitarian apologists. Many have in fact argued, in effect: "The Son had glory with the Father, but God does not give his glory to another, says Isaiah; therefore the Son is also God." Yet they overlook that the disciples themselves received the glory that the Father had given to the Son. The entire verse from Isaiah reads: "I am Jehovah, that is my name; and my glory will I not give to another, neither my praise unto graven images." —Isaiah 42:8, *ASV*. This shows from the context that Jehovah was excluding the gods of the nations in the form of "carved idols" (*ESV*) at the time of the prophet; certainly not his "only-begotten Son" whom he would later glorify and exalt, the beloved one with whom God is "well-pleased." Compare Isaiah 52:13; Matthew 3:17; Philippians 2:8-11.

[8] That is why Peter could say to his fellow Israelites: "The God of Abraham, the God of Isaac, and the God of Jacob, the God of our fathers, *glorified his servant Jesus*" (Acts 3:13). This text clearly shows that God willingly glorifies (gives 'glory' to) those who serve him, as in the case of his Son Jesus, whom Peter—in his proclamation of the Christian message—portrays as God's "servant," not as "God" himself.

The Father-Son Relationship

Do not let your hearts be troubled, have faith in God, have faith also in me.[9]

Then, as the Gospel reports, Jesus explained to his disciples that he was about to go to his Father's house in order to prepare a place for them, and that he would come again so that they could be with him and that they would know the way. But the disciple Thomas said, "Lord, we do not know where you are going. How can we know the way?" To this, Jesus answered:

I am the way, the truth and the life, no one comes to the Father but by me.[10]

These words are also among the most well known and often quoted by Christian believers. Jesus is the only way to the Father—a saying that is trustworthy, a genuine scriptural teaching that as Christians we can have confidence in. This is not the only place where such an essential article of Christian doctrine was expressed or alluded to; for in his first letter to the disciple Timothy, the apostle Paul reiterated the very same truth first announced by Christ in relation to his being the one approved means by which men and women may have access to the heavenly Father. Paul wrote:

For there is one God and one mediator between God and men, the man Christ Jesus, who gave himself as a ransom for all, the testimony to which was borne at the proper time. For this I was appointed a preacher and apostle (I am telling the truth, I am not lying), a teacher of the Gentiles in faith and truth.[11]

Given the nature and clarity of these texts and others like them, it would seem that in the absence of theological

---

[9] John 14:1. Although Jesus plainly presents a distinction between himself and "God," Trinitarians would generally reason that since the Son too presents himself as an object of belief or faith, this implies that Jesus is also God. However, the book of Exodus shows that the people of Israel had faith in God *and* in Moses, without, obviously, resulting in the meaning that Moses was himself God—"Israel saw the great power that Jehovah used against the Egyptians, so the people feared Jehovah, and they believed in Jehovah and in his servant Moses" (Exodus 14:31).
[10] John 14:6
[11] 1 Timothy 2:5-7

disputation surrounding the essential natures and respective identities of God and Christ, there would be no necessary thought given in terms of clarifying such straightforward scriptural teaching; for the apostle's teaching speaks clear enough on its own, quite free of ambiguity. But because of the prevailing doctrinal viewpoints and variety of theological paradigms widely and historically advanced, we should note that Paul *did* declare that there is "one God," but he did not speak of the one God as "three persons,"—either in this text or in any other—nor did he identify Christ as the "one God." To Paul the "one God" was *the Father* (the undeniable referent in this verse), whereas Jesus Christ was, to him, the "one mediator *between*" the one God and men.

It was earlier noted that ever since the historic ecumenical councils, Jesus, the Son, was declared to be "coequal" with the Father, an equal partaker in the Father's eternal "essence." The doctrine of Christ's "coequality" with God the Father is considered by most to be a fixed religious tenet, fundamental to the "historic Christian faith." Yet in the course of his parting words to his inner group of disciples, Jesus said (as the *New English Bible* renders his words):

> **Peace is my parting gift to you, my own peace, such as the world cannot give. Set your troubled hearts at rest, and banish your fears. You heard me say, 'I am going away, and coming back to you.' If you loved me you would have been glad to hear that I was going to the Father; for the Father is greater than I. I have told you now, before hand, so that when it happens you may have faith.**[12]

---

[12] John 14:27-29. According to one source: "Neither [Jesus] nor his disciples, give the slightest reason to suppose that he or they meant anything but what their words obviously mean...Unless some part of speech requires an unusual interpretation, such as an idiom, we ought to interpret the words according to their normal meanings. But exceptions to this must constantly be made for one to accept Trinitarian doctrines as true. Jesus said such things as *My Father is greater than I*. The obvious meaning must be circumvented in order to sustain the notion that he is co-equal with God. The notion of a double nature in Christ was invented to do exactly this. It makes it possible, even *acceptable*, to cast our Lord's words in an entirely different sense than they were meant

The Father-Son Relationship

Here is a case where we are confronted with the direct, unmistakable, and defining testimony of Christ himself concerning his relationship to God the Father. Instead of teaching his disciples, in harmony with a fourth-century creed that says the Son is "coequal" to the Father, Jesus clearly and humbly acknowledges to his disciples that the Father is "greater than" he is.[13] Yet as clear as these words may be, from the very mouth of the Lord Jesus Christ, Trinitarian apologists insist that all believers must confess that Christ is "equal" to his Father in order to be considered Christ's true followers. However, the Scriptures even confirm for us elsewhere:

> **When *God* made the promise to Abraham, since he had *no one greater* by whom to swear, he swore by himself...**[14]

This clearly demonstrates that, according to the biblical teaching, "no one" is or could be "greater" than God. In perfect harmony, God's Son plainly stated that his Father, "the only true God," is "greater" than himself. The Almighty God, of course, could never truthfully say such of anyone, as Hebrews 6:13 makes evident.

In responding to Jesus' own revelation of himself and his relationship to the Father, evangelicals have traditionally argued that when Jesus said the Father was "greater" than himself, in this case, he was not speaking with reference to his "nature" or "essence" but to his *functional role* as a servant, or to the *position* or *rank* that Christ voluntarily took on as a man (or as the 'God-man') in the "incarnation"; and it is only in this particular sense that Jesus could have properly said that the Father was "greater." However, it may be pointed out simply, in this case, that Jesus did not speak of or suggest any such idea;

---

when they were originally spoken." —Snedeker, *The Doctrine of the Double Nature of Christ*, pp. 9, 10.
[13] A similar point was elaborated by Jesus in the previous chapter of the Gospel of John, when Jesus said, "Truly, truly, I say to you, a servant is not greater than his master; nor is he who is sent greater than he who sent him" (John 13:16).
[14] Hebrews 6:13, emphasis added.

nor is there anything in the words or overall context that would move or require one to speculate about whether Jesus meant "position" or "nature" or "function," or whether he was speaking from the perspective of his "human nature" as the alleged "God-man."

While it is true that there are cases in Scripture where a speaker or writer makes use of poetic, figurative, metaphoric, parabolic, and, even, hyperbolic language, there are also cases in Scripture where the writer or speaker simply meant what was said and that may be understood in all the simplicity and clarity that language allows for.[15] The statement ('the Father is greater than I') requires no complex theological qualification. One person is not *equal* to the other person. One person is *greater* than the other person—"The **Father** is greater than **I**." It is safe an honorable to conclude: The Father is "**greater**" than Jesus, the Father's Son.

So, when attempting to accurately describe and define the relationship of the heavenly Father and Son, we can be certain that the Father (the 'one God,' 1 Corinthians 8:6) is "greater" than the Son without further qualification or elaboration, as Jesus himself made certain. At the same time, a careful examination of the Scriptures will make evident the sense in which the Father is "greater" than the Son. However, when considering the history and controversies involved, it must be emphasized that in referencing a statement such as this made by Jesus, it is in no way an attempt to portray the Father and Son as somehow having competing roles or attributes, or that in our faith and practice we are to exalt the Father at the exclusion of the Son.

---

[15] Why did Jesus say that his disciples should *be glad* that he was going to the Father "because the Father is greater than I"? Perhaps, because already knowing, by experience, what a great and powerful person Jesus was, as well as the great comfort they felt while in his presence, they should have been grateful that he was about to be in the presence of one who was even greater than himself, a definite cause for rejoicing, for Jesus' sake. Or, perhaps, as Albert Barnes paraphrases, "[You] would rejoice that I am to leave this state of suffering and humiliation, and resume that glory which I had with the Father before the world was" (*Barnes' Notes, The Gospels*, p. 334). Since the Son was evidently well acquainted with living in the blessed presence of God (if one takes the Son's statement in 17:5 *literally* as opposed to *prophetically*), the fact that he was then on his way to God made it appropriate for him to suggest to the disciples that they should have been happy for him.

The Father-Son Relationship

Scripturally, there is no conflict or dilemma in acknowledging the truth that Jesus has one (and *only* one) who is greater than he is. Nor would the pointing out of such a fact represent an attempt to denigrate or dishonor Christ, for he is—in addition to obedience to his commands—honored only when we speak of him in truth and in line with what he himself taught. Furthermore, it might be worthwhile to ask ourselves: If Jesus thought it critical for his followers to believe that he was "coequal" with the Father,—as the orthodox, Trinitarian formula implies—why, at such a critical point in his loving oversight of his disciples, did he impress upon their minds *another concept?* And if neither Jesus nor his apostles dictated to us in Scripture that the Son is "coequal" with the Father, why would there even be a concern about whether or not one's faith is in line with the dictates of such a doctrine? It seems wiser for us to acknowledge, as one Bible student reminds us: "It is only by clinging closely to the exact language of Holy Writ that we may hope to gain a clear conception of the relation of the Father to the Son."[16]

For those who accept the unique authority and supreme value of the inspired scriptural accounts, there should be no problem or reluctance in disregarding and abandoning any and all post-biblical doctrinal developments, or any kind of official, essentially canonized, expressions, theological terms, formulas and mantras that do not appear in the Bible or on the lips of the founder of our faith. We can accept that the Bible itself presents a satisfactory account of the identity of God and Jesus Christ, even in terms of the language it uses.

Although Jesus himself declared forthrightly that the Father was greater than himself, Trinitarian teachers have appealed to another passage as a "proof text" for the substantial

---

[16] A. E. Knoch, *Christ and Deity*, (Canyon County, CA: Concordant Publishing Concern), p. 45. With respect to the Father-Son relationship as presented throughout the Gospel of John specifically, Professor Marriane Thompson correctly noted: "Rather than predicating the virtual equality of the one who is sent with the one who sends, John tends to stress that the one who sends is greater than the one who is sent." —*The God of the Gospel of John* (Grand Rapids: Eerdmans, 2001), p. 94.

"coequality" tradition teaches is shared by God the Father and "God the Son." In the fifth chapter of the same Gospel account, Jesus is reported to have healed a sick man on the Sabbath day. In response, the Jews began to persecute Jesus. But Jesus himself responded: "My Father is working until now, and I also am working." Then, the apostle reports: "For this reason the Jews were seeking all the more to kill him, *because he was not only breaking the Sabbath, but was also calling God his own Father, thereby making himself equal to God"* (John 5:18).

From this particular verse it is generally concluded by Trinitarian apologists that by calling God "his own Father," Jesus intended to assert his "coequality" with the Father in terms of his consubstantial "deity." But note carefully Jesus' following response to the Jewish leaders. Some Bible versions even say, "To this charge Jesus replied..." (*NEB*); "To this accusation Jesus replied..." (*JB*); or "Jesus gave them this answer..." (*NIV*):

> **Truly, truly, I say to you, the Son can do nothing of his own accord, but only what he sees the Father doing; for whatever he does, that the Son does likewise.**

Significantly, Jesus went on to say,

> **For the Father loves the Son, and shows him all that he himself is doing; and greater works than these will he show him, that you may marvel. For as the Father raises the dead and gives them life, so also the Son gives life to whom he will. The Father judges no one, but has given all judgment to the Son, that all may honor the Son, even as they honor the Father who sent him. Truly, truly, I say to you, he who hears my word and believes him who sent me, has eternal life; he does not come into judgment, but has passed from death to life.**[17]

While considering the verse in question (John 5:18), it is important to keep at least two important facts in mind. One, by

---

[17] John 5:20-24

The Father-Son Relationship

healing a man on the Sabbath—contrary to the view of the Jews at that time—Jesus was *not* in violation of God's law. This was a *mistaken* view on the part of the Jewish leadership. And, two, given the fact of such a false accusation, it would be difficult to sustain the idea that the Jews were correct in their other accusation that Jesus was "making himself equal to God," particularly when we keep in mind Jesus' specific answer to the charge. If Jesus had really thought of himself as equal to God (particularly in the sense defined by Trinitarian doctrine), and that he himself *was* "God," one wonders why he said in response, as another translation expresses it, "**In all truth I tell you, *by himself, the Son can do nothing*; he can do only what he sees the Father doing.**"[18] Do these words reflect the attitude of one who viewed himself as "God," or as "coequal" with God?

Even if one were to accept that Jesus was in fact making himself equal to God on some level,[19] it would still be plain that Jesus is not the one ('God') he is equal to. It would remain clear that Jesus is a figure who is distinguishable from "God," given the obvious point that the notion of "equality" with another is entirely different from the notion of "identity" with another.

In commenting on this verse, under the premise that Jesus *did* make himself equal to God by calling God "his own Father," one source pointed out: "It accurately records that Jesus was saying that God was his father, not that he was himself God, or that he was 'God the Son.' It is clear that Jesus' authority came from the fact that he was the Son of God, not God Himself."[20]

---

[18] *New Jerusalem Bible* (emphasis added).

[19] See John 17:2; compare Matthew 28:18. Because Jesus possesses such an all-encompassing authority given to him by his Father (and because Jesus is God's Son in a way that sets him apart from all others), it is quite reasonable to accept that Jesus *is* equal to God in terms of his function and in the exercise of his authority. Or, it could be, as it was pointed out by F. F. Bruce in reference to John 5:18 specifically: "...the manner of his reference to God as 'my Father' was more offensive still: it suggested rather pointedly that he was putting himself on a level with God. In their synagogue services of prayer and thanksgiving the Jews were accustomed to address God as 'our Father'; but Jesus appeared to be claiming God as 'his own Father' in an exceptional, if not exclusive, sense." —*The Gospel of John, Introduction, Exposition and Notes*, p. 127. William Barclay translated the last portion of the verse: "...he also kept speaking of God as his own father, thus *putting himself on an equality with God*, that the Jews tried all the harder to kill him."

[20] Graeser, Lynn, Schoenheit, *One God & One Lord*, p. 477.

The Father-Son Relationship

However, in responding to the traditional Trinitarian interpretation of this passage, one writer made the following observation:

> Almost every book the author has read on the Trinity makes a statement similar to 'The religious leaders correctly understood Jesus as claiming to be equal to God.' However, is it safe to assume the religious leaders were correct?...Consider the verse in question. The Jews are *already* losing credibility by their first charge, claiming Jesus broke the Sabbath since he did a good work on the Sabbath. Do those who say the religious leaders were correct want to claim they were correct on this charge? Probably not, since Jesus said, '*It is lawful to do good on the Sabbath.*' (Matthew 12:10-12) So let us stop right here. We have already seen they were wrong on their first accusation. Is it possible they could have been wrong on the other one as well? Yes, as Jesus shows by his response in the next verse...Jesus realizes they drew the wrong conclusion from his saying God is his Father so he *immediately* sets them straight.[21]

Although the comments made above were from a non-Trinitarian source, note the following acknowledgment made by Roman Catholic scholar, John L. McKenzie, a Trinitarian:

> The relation of Father and Son as set forth in this passage is the foundation of later developments in Trinitarian and Christological belief and theology; it is not identical with these later developments. Much of the discourse seems to be a refutation of the charge that Jesus claimed to be equal with God (v. 18). This is met by affirming that the Son can do nothing independently of the Father. Later theology found it necessary to refine this statement by distinction between person and nature [or 'being'] which John did not know.[22]

In *The New Clarendon Bible* with commentary, J. C.

---

[21] Holt, *Jesus—God or the Son of God?*, pp. 62, 63.
[22] *Light on the Gospels* (Chicago, Illinois: The Thomas More Press, 1975), p. 187.

Fenton commented on this passage, making a very similar observation: "...*making himself equal with God*: this is what the Jews wrongly supposed, not what John believes, as the speech follows shows. '*Truly, truly: ...the Son can do nothing of his own accord*: i.e the Son is not 'equal with God' in the sense that he can act independently; all initiative is with the Father, and the Son is wholly his imitator."[23]

Marianne Thompson (professor of New Testament interpretation at Fuller Theological Seminary) highlighted a similar point:

> In the Gospel the charge is twice raised against Jesus that 'he makes himself equal to God' (5:18; 10:33). It is a charge that Jesus does not flatly deny, but rather interprets in two ways. In the first instance, the charge that Jesus makes himself 'equal to God' is countered by showing that the Son does all that he does through his dependence on the Father (5:19). Hence, the Son is not independent of, but rather dependent on, the Father in all things. The Father has *authorized* the Son precisely to exercise divine activities and prerogatives, including the giving of life, passing judgment, and working on the Sabbath.[24]

Additionally, after speaking about his Father giving him authority to judge, Jesus went on to say again:

> ***I can do nothing on my own authority*; as I hear, I judge; and my judgment is just, because I seek not my**

---

[23] *The New Clarendon Bible (New Testament), The Gospel According to John, With introduction and commentary* (Durham: Oxford at the Clarendon Press, 1970), p. 71.

[24] Thompson, *The God of the Gospel of John*, p. 234 (emphasis added). In another place (pp. 52-53) Thompson wrote: "When Jesus' adversaries accuse him of 'making himself equal to God' (5:18), they charge him with usurping the divine prerogatives of working on the Sabbath. Jesus not only admits to the offense but heightens it by claiming to exercise the distinctive divine functions of judgment and giving life, activities that God does on the Sabbath. In defense of his action, Jesus responds that 'the Son can do nothing on his own' and repeatedly asserts that he does only what the Father tells him to do and shows him to do. In other words, he argues for his dependence on God. Because the Son depends upon the Father for all he does, he does not engage in an independent or separate work but carries out the work of the one God. Hence, arguments for the Son's dependence on the Father are ultimately arguments for the unity of the Son with the Father."

The Father-Son Relationship

own will but the will of him who sent me.[25]

Continuing on in the same context, we receive added insight into the Son's relationship to God, according to Jesus' own teaching. But, first, we will take note of a view advanced by a Trinitarian apologist so that we can demonstrate the contrast between the theological conjectures often associated with Trinitarian theology with the simple, straightforward teachings of God's Son in Scripture. In attempting to expound upon the idea of God's alleged triune nature, Millard Erickson speculated:

> Each [person of the Trinity] is essential to the life of the whole. God could not exist simply as Father, or as Son, or as Holy Spirit. Nor could he exist as Father and Son, as Father and Spirit, or as Son and Spirit, without the third of these persons in that given case. Further, none of these could exist without being part of the Trinity. There would be no basis of life, apart from this union.

Then, perhaps unwittingly, Erickson went on to literally contradict what Jesus himself said with respect to the Father having "life in himself":

> Each [Father, Son and Holy Spirit] is dependent for his life on each of the others. *None has the power of life within itself alone. Each can only exist as part of the Triune God.* This means that each of the persons of the Trinity is essential to the whole. Beyond that, *each is essential to each of the others*...Another way of putting it is that God could not be and not be triune. The triune nature of God is essential to his very being...While the Father may be the cause of the existence of the Son and the Spirit, they are also mutually the cause of his existence and the existence of one another. There is an eternal symmetry of all three persons.[26]

In keeping with the traditional speculative nature of Trinitarian dogma, Erickson (without any reference to Scripture)

---

[25] John 5:30, *RSV* (emphasis added).
[26] Erickson, *God in Three Persons*, pp. 1, 310.

asserts that God could not exist apart from the union of the "three persons" and that no "member of the Trinity" has the power of life within itself alone. Yet in the course of his interchange with the Jews—specifically, those Jews who were making accusations against him and seeking to kill him—Jesus declared:

> **I most solemnly say to you, whoever listens to me and believes Him who sent me possesses eternal life, and will never come under condemnation, but has already passed out of death into life. I most solemnly say to you, a time is coming—indeed, it is already here—when the dead will listen to the voice of the Son of God, and those who listen to it will live.** *For just as the Father has life in Himself, so He has granted to the Son to have life in Himself.* **He has also granted to Him authority to act as Judge, because He is the Son of Man.**[27]

In this one simple yet illuminating statement, Jesus discloses a very significant fact that helps to increase and deepen our understanding of the Father-Son relationship; and he does so in a way far clearer—certainly more trustworthy—and more meaningful than the claim or conjecture of any theologian or decree of any Church council. Unlike the speculative and unscriptural assertion made by Millard Erickson, Jesus not only pointed out candidly that the Father is one who "has life in himself," but that the Father has "granted" to the Son to have the same. Again, it should be noted that Jesus *does* say that he has "life in himself," yet, as professor Thompson points out, "the statement does not stand on its own. Precisely in holding together the affirmation that the Son has 'life in himself' with the affirmation that he has 'been *given*' such life by the Father, we find the uniquely Johannine characterization of the relationship of the Father and the Son."[28]

---

[27] John 5:24-27, *The New Testament, by C. B. Williams*
[28] *The God of the Gospel of John*, p. 79. Thompson also writes: "Unless Jesus' life were granted to him from the Father, he would have no life; unless he came from the 'living Father,' he would

The Father-Son Relationship

This is a difficult fact to reconcile with the idea that Jesus is eternally equal to, or eternally the same being as, his Father. From Jesus' own words, it is made clear that nothing is "essential" to the Father; for the Father (contrary to Erickson's theological speculation) is not dependent on anyone to "grant" him the possession of life within himself, for this is something possessed by the Father alone; and he alone is the one who confers this blessing upon others—at least, verifiably, in the case of his own Son.

In a brief chapter on the subject of the "Self-Existence of God," the distinguished evangelical teacher R. C. Sproul wrote what follows in his book *Essential Truths of the Christian Faith*:

> Every *effect* must have a *cause*. That is true by definition. But God is not an effect. He has no beginning and therefore no antecedent cause. He is eternal. He always was or is. He has, within Himself, the power of being. He requires no assistance from outside sources to continue to exist. This is what is meant by the idea of *self existence*...God, like us, cannot be self-created. But God, unlike us, can be self-existent. Indeed, this is the very essence of the difference between the Creator and creation. This is what makes Him the Supreme Being and *source* of all other beings...God exists in Himself eternally. He is the source and fountainhead of all being. He alone has, within Himself, the power of being. Paul declares our dependence upon the power of God's being for our own existence when he says: 'In Him we live and move and have our being' (Acts 17:29).[29]

---

be unable to confer life. The two assertions of this verse offer analogous, although not parallel, affirmations about the way in which Jesus and the believer receive life. Just as the Father has life and gives life to the Son, so the Son has life and gives life to those who have faith." Thompson (p. 175) also observes: "According to the assertions found in John 5:21-27, the Father has given two other powers into the hands of the Son: First, the Father has given the Son the power to give life...Second, the Father has granted the Son the power of judgment...(5:22, 27; cf. 10:29-30)...Crucial to the interpretation of these texts are the twin affirmations that (1) the Son exercises certain divine prerogatives, and (2) the Son exercises them even as God does, because God has *given* him those prerogatives. Jesus exercises judgment and confers life because God has *conferred* these powers upon him, and this implies that Jesus exercises these powers as no other figure—save God—can or does" (emphasis added).

[29] *Essential Truths of the Christian Faith*, pp. 37-38.

The Father-Son Relationship

As Sproul notes, "God has no beginning and therefore no antecedent cause" and "requires no assistance from outside sources to continue to exist." That is, God alone, the Supreme Being, is not dependent on any other being or source of power for his life and existence. Few would deny that God is the source and creator of all life, and that all life is *dependent* on him, according to the Scriptures. In fact, even the Lord Jesus Christ himself, who *always* spoke the truth, affirmed his very own dependence upon the Father for his own life. In the sixth chapter of John's Gospel, Jesus spoke of himself as "the bread of life" and "the living bread that came down from heaven." He went on to say, "if anyone eats of this bread he will live forever; for the bread that I shall give is my flesh in behalf of the life of the world."[30] And, near the end of his discourse, Jesus told his listeners:

Just as the living Father sent me, and *I have life because of the Father*, so also the one who feeds on me will have life because of me.[31]

As one reflects on such a significant and revealing insight into the Father-Son relationship, it is worth remembering the fact that the Most High God, "the creator of heaven and earth," does not live *because* of anyone or anything, for he himself is the very source of creation and the sustainer of all living things.[32] Just as the apostle Paul, as expressed by R. C. Sproul, "declares our dependence upon the power of God's being for our own existence when he says: 'In Him we live and move and have our being,'" so the Son of God declared *his* dependence upon his Father for his own existence—he lives *because of the Father*. Just as God's Son possesses life *because* of his Father, so too may men and women have life *because* of God's Son;

---

[30] John 6:48, 51, *RSV*
[31] John 6:57, *NAB*
[32] In another place (p. 79), Sproul claimed: "All three members [of the Trinity] are equal in nature, in honor, and in glory. All three members are eternal, self-existent; they partake of all aspects and attributes of deity." In light of this claim we may ask, is there anything in the words spoken by the Son, "I live *because* of the Father" that would lead one to believe and embrace a doctrine that says that the Son is "*self*-existent"?

specifically, by their union with God secured through faith in him—**"in the same way, the person who feeds on me will live because of me."**[33]

Respected Bible scholar F. F. Bruce's observations are worth considering at this point:

> The Son's dependence on the Father for 'life in himself,' as well as for every function which he exercises, has been emphasized in John 5:19-30, especially in 5:26. Here it is stated briefly. The Son who derives his own life from the Father has authority to impart that life to those who believe in him, with this distinction: what he receives is 'life in himself'; what they receive is life in him.[34]

With respect to the Father-Son relationship as presented in the Gospel of John particularly, it was pointed out by Professor Thompson:

> Of all the functions and activities of God, the one that defines God as Father is that of giving life. God is the one who, as Father, gives life to and through the Son. Or, put differently, the designation of God as Father indicates that God is the source and origin of the life of the one who is designated as Son (e.g., 5:25-26). Because God is 'Father' in relationship to the Son, that relationship constitutes God's very identity as Father in the Gospel of John. God is known as Father through the Son, and God is known as the Father of the Son…The Father-Son relationship underscores the fundamental portrayal of God in the Gospel of John as the living God and creator of all life (1:1-3; 6:57)…God is the living God and source of life and is known through the life-giving work of the Son, who himself has life from the Father (5:25-26).[35]

---

[33] *The Simple English Bible* rendering

[34] *The Gospel of John, Introduction, Exposition and Notes*, p. 161. In another place Bruce correctly noted: "All immortality except God's is derived. The Father, who has life in Himself, has shared with the Son this privilege of having life in Himself. All others receive life in the Son." —Bruce in his *Foreword* to Edward Fudge's *The Fire That Consumes* (Lincoln: An Authors Guild Backinprint.com Edition, 2001), p. vii.

[35] *The God of the Gospel of John*.

Thompson also goes on to point out the following:

> The conviction that God is uniquely and distinctly the Father of Jesus undergirds the predications in the Gospel that link Father and Son together. Their 'kinship' as Father and Son becomes the basis for a number of claims made for Jesus, including his authority to judge, to give life, to mediate knowledge of the Father and to reveal him, to do the works and will of the Father, and therefore to receive honor, as even the Father does…it is not a particular characteristic of God that shapes understanding of God as Father, but rather the fundamental reality that a father's relationship to his children consists first in terms of simply giving them life. What it means to be a father is to be the origin or source of the life of one's children. For John, this pertains particularly to the way in which the Father has given life to the Son, and through the Son has mediated life to others, who become 'children of God.' (1:12; 11:52; see 1 John 3:1-2)…When Jesus calls God 'Father,' he points first to the Father as the source or origin of life, and to the relationship established through the life-giving activity of the Father. Yet once again these terms apply differently to those 'born of God,' and to Jesus as the only Son of God. Since he is the Son, Jesus' very life and being are to be found within the Father. He has life because 'the living Father' (6:57) gives it to him; in fact, he has 'life in himself' just as the 'Father has life in himself' (5:26), a remarkable statement that simultaneously affirms that the Son derives his life from the Father and yet has life in a distinct way, as the Father has it. [These points] are essential to understanding John's delineation of God as Father and Jesus as Son…In coining the phrase 'the living Father' John actually joins two very similar ideas into one: as the living one, the Father is the source of the life of his Son.[36]

In the context of human conceptualization, even when spoken of figuratively, we would generally and rightly associate

---

[36] Thompson, *The God of the Gospel of John*, pp. 71, 72.

The Father-Son Relationship

the concept of "Father" itself with one who is "senior," "originator," "maker," "creator," "author," "founder," "beginner," "sustainer," "progenitor" and "life-giver." It seems only natural that God's "Son" spoke about his "Father" in a way that would convey notions like these; and in speaking in this way, Jesus immediately communicated an idea that his human followers could readily identify with and relate to. Commenting further on Jesus' statement about the Father as the origin of his own life, Thompson noted: "Taken together, the ideas of God as 'Father,' and hence the source of life, and of God as the living God, the creator of all that is, account for the belief that God gives *life* through the Son who, by definition, derives his life from the Father. A father gives life to his son; *indeed, a son by definition is one who has life from his father*. So also, the Father gives life to his Son...Therefore, through him life can be given to others as well."[37]

Just as none of Christ's true followers could deny (scripturally speaking) that Christ lives "because" of his Father, so none could deny that the Christian's very life depends upon a continual feeding upon, exercising of faith in, and remaining in union with, Christ. He is, without question, the Christian's life-giver. All believers, in fact, depend upon Christ ('the living bread that came down from heaven') for life itself; so too, Christ clearly reveals his own reliance upon his Father for *his* life, for he himself made the clear analogy; and in this we receive yet further defining insight into the Father-Son relationship as presented by Jesus himself in the sacred scriptural accounts.

It is not only from the Gospels that we can derive reliable insight into Jesus' special and unique relationship to God as God's unique Son, but we also discover a great deal of valuable knowledge in the epistles written to the earliest Christian congregations. In writing his first letter to the Corinthians, Paul commended the Corinthians for remembering him in everything,

---

[37] Thompson, *The God of the Gospel of John*, p. 77 (emphasis added).

The Father-Son Relationship

and for maintaining the traditions *"just as I passed them on to you."* He went on to say:

> **Now I want you to realize that the head of every man is Christ, and the head of the woman is man, and the head of Christ is God.**[38]

When this letter was written it was well after Christ had ascended into heaven to be with God. It is especially important to note that, in this instance, we are privileged to be in possession of the original, authoritative, *apostolic* tradition as passed on to the first Christians with respect to how woman relates to man, how man relates to Christ, and, most significantly—as it relates to the subject under consideration—how Christ himself relates to God. In light of the case made for the Trinitarian tradition, we should observe that Christ (just as clearly as Christ is distinguished from every man) is once again clearly distinguished from, and subordinated to, "God." Secondly, we can observe that Christ is specifically said to have God as his head, whereas we can be sure that God does not look to or have anyone who is head to (or authority above) him. He is supreme above everyone and everything that exists.

In an attempt to reconcile the plain sense of the apostolic tradition with that of the Trinitarian, Trinitarian apologists typically argue as follows:

> This statement concerning the man and woman does not teach that the man is a being superior to the woman. Therefore, we should not conclude that this verse teaches that God the Father is a being superior to Christ. This verse is describing people under authority. The wife is under the husband's authority just as Christ is under God the Father's authority.[39]

Although it seems quite clear that Paul was speaking about "authority" in this context, it should be noted that Paul

---

[38] 1 Corinthians 11:2-3, *NIV*
[39] Pool, *God in Three Persons, Biblical Testimony to the Trinity*, (P& R Publishing, 2001), p. 50.

The Father-Son Relationship

simply said that "the head of Christ is **God**." In spite of the fact that Jesus already made it clear that the Father is "greater" than he is, Pool argues that, since a woman is not a being inferior to man, we must not conclude that God the Father is a being superior to Christ—an argument that almost seems to be valid. However, what is overlooked by Pool is the simple fact that a woman is not a man. The man is the head of the woman and they would obviously constitute two distinct human beings. Likewise, a Christian man is obviously not the Christ, for the Christ is the head of every believing man; they are also distinguishable as two beings. In turn, if the apostle teaches that the head of Christ is "God," how and why would we conclude that God and Christ are the same being or the same "God," or that Christ *is* "God"? If Jesus Christ is "God" ('the Most High'), how could he be spoken of as having another with greater authority above him? Or, does such a teaching—as Trinitarian theology tells us—only have reference to Christ in his "human" nature as opposed to his "divine"? Or when Paul used the term "God," did he really have in mind, and would his original readers have taken him to mean, "*the Father*, the first *person* of the Trinity," as opposed to "God"?

Actually, what Paul stated in this case is remarkably simple and straightforward, as it was probably intended to be. God is supreme, exercising headship (or authority) over and above *all*, including Jesus Christ. This is a basic truth regarding the Father-Son relationship that is specifically stated and continually alluded to all throughout the Christian Scriptures, including the passage that will be considered next.

1 Corinthians 15:28

"No doubt much of what passes for Christian theology is merely the theologian's attempt to justify his own belief." —R. C. Sproul

"Without diligent study, it is easy to wrongly divide the word; to believe and to teach error. The main way this takes place is because we draw illegitimate inferences from the text—when we read into

The Father-Son Relationship

the text things that are not actually said by the text, and draw out of the text things that are actually not there (known as eisegesis). Sadly, this happens all too frequently."
— Dr. James R. White, A Thirst for Hermeneutics (07/28/2005, Alpha & Omega Ministries, Christian Apologetics and Theology)

In the same letter to the Christians of Corinth, the apostle Paul wrote about the details of a future resurrection of the dead and the consummation of all things in relation to God's kingdom under Christ. Evidently, the idea that there was no such thing as a resurrection was taking hold among some within the Corinthian assembly. This is why Paul reasoned out the matter to the Corinthians in this way:

Now if Christ is preached as raised from the dead, how can some of you say that there is no resurrection of the dead? If the dead are not raised, then Christ has not been raised, and if Christ has not been raised, your faith is futile and you are still in your sins.[40]

Paul went on to make the point that if it is only for this life that we have hoped in Christ, then believers or apostles, out of all men, are the most to be pitied. However, the apostle went further in proclaiming with confidence a truth that was a cause for great rejoicing in his day as well as in our own: *"But the fact is that Christ has been raised from the dead. He has become the first of a great harvest of those who will be raised to life again* (lit., 'the first fruits of those who have fallen asleep')."[41] Since death came by a man (Adam), the resurrection of the dead also comes by a man (Jesus, described by Paul after as 'the last Adam,' v. 45). Just as in connection with Adam all die, so in connection with Christ all will be made alive. Then the apostle pointed out, as the *New Living Translation* renders this portion of his letter (1 Corinthians 15:23-28):

---

[40] 1 Corinthians 15:12-14
[41] 1 Corinthians 15:20, *NLT*

The Father-Son Relationship

> But there is an order to this resurrection: Christ was raised first; then when Christ comes back, all his people will be raised. After that the end will come, when he will turn the Kingdom over to God the Father, having put down all enemies of every kind. For Christ must reign until he humbles all his enemies beneath his feet. And the last enemy to be destroyed is death. For the Scriptures say, 'God has given him authority over all things.' (Of course, when it says 'authority over all things,' it does not include God himself, who gave Christ his authority.) Then, when he has conquered all things, the Son will present himself to God, so that God, who gave his Son authority over all things, will be utterly supreme over everything everywhere [more literally, 'When everything is subjected to him, then the Son himself will (also) be subjected to the one who subjected everything to him, so that God may be all in all' *NAB*].

According to the apostle's teaching, here and elsewhere, it was God who subjected all things under Christ's feet. In fact, "In putting everything under him, God left *nothing* that is not subject to him" (Hebrews 2:8, *NIV*).[42] In other words, the authority possessed by the Lord Jesus Christ to rule as King is an authority that has been delegated to, or conferred upon, Christ by his Father. That is why Paul makes the specific point that when the Scripture (apparently) says that "all things have been subjected (under Christ's feet)" it is evident that the one who put all things under his feet—God—is the one exception.[43] On this point it was even observed in the *Anchor Bible* commentary, that the "emphasis on the messianic victory leads Paul to emphasize

---

[42] Emphasis added.
[43] It was observed in one commentary: "Here Paul offers the fascinating tangential remark that 'all things' of course does not include God himself... It is impossible to avoid the impression that Paul is operating with what would later come to be called a subordinationist christology. The doctrine of the Trinity was not yet formulated in Paul's day, and his reasoning is based solely on the scriptural texts themselves, read in light of his Jewish monotheistic convictions and his simultaneous conviction that Jesus is proclaimed 'Lord' by virtue of his resurrection." —Richard B. Hays, *First Corinthians, Interpretation, A Bible Commentary for Teaching and Preaching* (Louisville: John Knox Press, 1989), p. 266.

The Father-Son Relationship

that God himself remains exempt from the subjection under which all things are placed by Christ. This careful statement seems so obvious that it may perhaps hint at some confusion in Corinth that Paul perceives as a dangerous misunderstanding of the relation of Christ to God." It is also pointed out that in this case, "Paul has not developed a Trinitarian doctrine, but his christology is nonetheless a remarkable achievement."[44]

So it turns out that one of the benefits we derive from considering this section of Paul's writings is a very specific and revealing description of Christ's role as the ruler of God's kingdom, and what God will ultimately accomplish through him by that rulership. Christ will reign as King until all enemies have been subjected beneath his feet—the last enemy to be destroyed is "death." Finally, when all things have been subjected, or put under the ruling authority of God's Son, then the Son too will subject himself to God, as the apostle says, "so that God may be all in all"—or as some translations express it: "so that God may be all things to everyone."[45]

On a radio show called "The Dividing Line (11/03/01)," hosted by Dr. James White, a caller phoned in regarding the difficulty he was having making sense of this passage in terms of reconciling what it says with Trinitarian doctrine. Below are some of the basic points made by Dr. White in response, who speaks as a committed apologist of Trinitarianism:

> "I would note that the last phrase of 1 Corinthians 15:28 is not 'so that *the Father* may be all in all.' That would be a very difficult thing to explain, if it said 'so that *the*

---

[44] *The Anchor Bible, 1 Corinthians, A New Translation, Introduction with a Study of the Life of Paul, Notes, and Commentary* by William F. Orr and James Arthur Walther (New York: Doubleday, 1976) p. 334. Another evangelical commentary correctly pointed out: "All things have been placed in subjection to Christ, but that does not include God. It refers only to creation and the hostile powers that have provoked and abetted creation's fall, not to the Creator. The ultimate power belongs to God at the beginning and at the end. [Paul] explains, 'When it says, 'All things have been made subject' [by God], clearly that excludes the one [God] who made all things subject to him [Christ].'" —David E. Garland, *1 Corinthians, Baker Exegetical Commentary on the New Testament* (Grand Rapids: Baker Academic, 2003), p. 713 (words in brackets in original, except for 'Paul').

[45] *An American Translation* (Goodspeed). *Revised Standard Version* is similar.

Father might be all in all.' It does not say that. It says so that '*theos*' might be all in all...the final phrase of 1 Corinthians 15:28 is 'that *God* may be all in all,' not 'the *Father* may be all in all,' or 'the *Son* may be all in all,' or 'the *Spirit* may be all in all.' In eternity to come the focus of our worship will not be divided between the divine persons so that one person is more of the object of our attention and our adoration than another person, but instead, because the work is really that of the Triune God Himself...what Paul's saying is, but when everything is subjected, when death has been banished, then those distinctions that we make, they're not going to cease. It's not that we're not going to know who the Father is or who the Son is or who the Spirit is. But the object of our worship will be one, there will be a unity of that, [be]cause we will be able to fully understand how each of the divine persons was fully involved in the work of salvation itself. So, Paul is not subjecting Jesus in the sense of making Him a part of the created order. But he is saying that a time will come when the Son, notice, the Son Himself will also will be subjected to the one who subjected all things to Him; that would be the Father, so that, and then he uses the term *theos*; he doesn't say *pater*; he doesn't say so that 'the *Father* will be all in all,' but so that *God* will be all in all. *God* alone will be the object of our worship in His fullness. And the final wrapping up of all things will allow us to have that kind of unified worship."

His caller then asks, "So this is one of the few passages where/when Paul uses the Greek word '*theos*' he's not referring to the Father specifically?" To which Dr. White responds:

"Well, see, I don't think that there is any reason for him to refer, when he uses *theos* in/at the end of 1 Corinthians 15:28, solely to the Father. He had just, in the previous phrase, referred to the Son Himself also will be subjected to the one who subjected all things to Him. He's already just identified the Father. He could just simply use that as the reference; he doesn't. Instead he goes back and

The Father-Son Relationship

specifically, he doesn't say 'God the Father,' which he had used only back in verse 24. If he wanted to distinguish the Father from the Son he could have, he specifically does not. And so, I think that does tell us that, in this light, since he's just been talking about the Father and the Son, and then he uses just the generic *theos*. To try to say, 'well, this just simply means the Father will be all in all' just throws a monkey wrench in what he's trying to say…the issue is that last verse in verse 28. Is that last phrase supposed to be taken to mean, that once the Son has subjected Himself to the Father, that the Son for example is no longer the object of worship? We're told the Son is worshipped in Revelation chapter five. What happens to where the Son is no longer worthy of worship? Is there ever anyone who is worthy of true divine worship that ceases being worthy of true divine worship?, well, of course not. So, no, I think there's many reasons to/that would militate against taking *theos* in 1 Corinthians 15:28 as being solely the Father and not including the Son and the Spirit."

In case the points made above are not entirely clear,[46] Dr. White is arguing that in the concluding phrase ('so that **God** may be all in all') the word "**God**" means or represents God as "**the Trinity**." For example—without specifically saying it at that point—when Dr. White says that "*God alone* will be the object of our worship in His fullness," he means "God (as the entire *tri-unity* of persons) alone will be the object of our worship…"[47]

The claim advanced by Dr. White respecting 1

---

[46] At first, Dr. White almost seems to avoid directly saying that the word "God" in the last line means "the triune God," which is what he ultimately wants his listeners to accept.

[47] It is confusing when Dr. White says that "*God* alone will be the object of our worship in all *His* fullness," and when he speaks of "the Triune God *Himself.*" Because by saying "God/His/Himself" he is talking about God as the *Trinity*. Yet, according to popular Trinitarian belief, the Trinity is not a "who" but a "what" ('one *what* three who's'; see *The Forgotten Trinity*, p. 27). Evangelical apologists Norman Geisler and Ron Rhodes also affirm the same doctrine: "there is only one *What* in God, but there are three *Who's*, there is one *It*, but three *Is*." — *Correcting the Cults, Expert Responses To Their Scripture Twisting* (Grand Rapids: Baker Books, 1997) p.130. Dr. White says himself: "We dare not mix up the *what's* and the *who's* regarding the Trinity." But here Dr. White speaks of "His" glory, referring to the glory of the Trinity (and 'the triune God *Himself*'). How can a *what* or *it* be spoken of as a *who*?

Corinthians 15:28 is in line with what he argues in his book *The Forgotten Trinity*. In the fifth chapter of his book Dr. White claims that the term "'God' can refer either to the person of the Father, or can be used more generically of the godhead *en toto*."[48] By the godhead "en toto," Dr. White means that there are certain occasions in the Bible (at least in the New Testament) where the term "God" refers to *all three* "persons" of the Trinity—the "triune" God. Unfortunately, in this instance, Dr. White simply makes this assertion without providing any proof or citing any specific scriptural examples. In fact, it is critical to keep in mind, before one even considers the implications of White's "exegesis" of 1 Corinthians 15:28, that White would be unable to produce **one** occurrence in all of Scripture where the term "God" (*el*, *elohim*, or *ho theos*) refers, or can be proven to refer, to the "godhead *en toto*"—that is, to all three persons of the "Trinity."

When Dr. White's explanation of 1 Corinthians 15:28 is considered carefully, one will find that the problem is, simply, that such a distinctive meaning—'God in three persons'—is attached to the phrase—"so that *God* may be all in all"—without *any* basis in the context. But the reason why Dr. White must introduce the concept of the Trinity onto this passage is because if the last verse is in fact a reference to God the Father, as Dr. White says, this "would be a very difficult thing to explain"— that is to say, a very difficult thing to explain if one supposes the doctrine of the Trinity to be true and scriptural. So the question is, if the reference in verse 28 ('that God may be all in all') is to God *the Father*, is it really true that this would "throw a monkey wrench in what [Paul is] trying to say"? Or, would it actually throw a "monkey wrench" in what Dr. White is trying to convince his audience of?[49] It would be helpful at this point to

---

[48] White, *The Forgotten Trinity*, p. 90.
[49] Note how White states: "If [Paul] wanted to distinguish the Father from the Son he could have; he specifically does not." The distinction Paul could theoretically have made between the Father and Son, however, is entirely irrelevant in terms of supporting the argument White tries to advance. Yet White makes this statement as if it somehow helped establish his ultimate conclusion regarding verse 28. This is a clear example of a "red herring," a type of logical fallacy in which one purports to prove one's point by means of irrelevant arguments. In doing so the

reconsider the passage in light of its fuller context.

Here, the translation of the Greek text is from the *New American Bible*, and the words in parenthesis will be added in order to clarify the references, but will in no way alter Paul's clear meaning.

After describing the order and facts related to the resurrection, Paul writes: "then comes the end, when he (that is, 'Christ' v. 23) hands over the kingdom to his God and Father, when he has destroyed every sovereignty and every authority and power. For (Christ) must reign until he has put all his enemies under his feet. The last enemy to be destroyed is death, for 'he (that is, 'God the Father') subjected everything under (Christ's) feet.'[50] But when it says that everything has been subjected, it is clear that it excludes the one (that is, 'God the Father') who subjected everything to him. When everything is subjected to him (the Son), then the Son himself will (also) be subjected to the one ('God the Father') who subjected everything to him, so that God **(Gk: *ho theos* = 'the triune God' or 'God the Father'?)** may be all in all."[51]

In our attempt to appraise the soundness of the Trinitarian explanation of this text, we need to ask ourselves first, is there any mention of a "Trinity" concept in the context of Paul's discussion? Are there any references in the entire chapter to a third "divine person"? How is it that the Son having subjected himself to God the Father results in "the Trinity" becoming "all in all," and how would such a meaning be legitimately derived from the passage or language itself? Additionally, is it not true that *ho theos* (lit., 'the God')—in the overwhelming majority of occurrences—is a reference to *the Father* in the New Testament,[52] and that there is not one instance

---

point advanced only serves to divert the listener's attention from the weakness of their own argument.

[50] Compare Ephesians 1:15-23, specifically verse 22, which states: "And he ['the God of our Lord Jesus Christ, the Father of glory,' v. 17] put all things beneath his [that is, Christ's] feet..."

[51] *New American Bible* rendering. The word "also" in parenthesis is in the original translation.

[52] Evangelical Murray J. Harris—based on a careful study of New Testament usage—agreed that there is "little difficulty in demonstrating that *ho theos* nearly always refers exclusively to the Father...When (*ho*) *theos* is used, we are to assume that the NT writers have *ho pater* [the Father]

The Father-Son Relationship

where *ho theos* refers to "the Trinity"? If so, can this be *proven*? Or would any attempt to make that application result from mere speculative or even wishful thinking? Would Trinitarians themselves even agree about where *ho theos* or "God" would refer to "the triune God" in the New Testament writings?[53]

Dr. White points out that the apostle "doesn't say so that '*the Father* will be all in all,' but so that '*God* will be all in all.'" But isn't God *the Father*?—"the God and Father of our Lord Jesus Christ"? And, if the entire context and conclusion revolves around Christ ultimately handing the kingdom over to the Father (Christ reigns 'until' all enemies have been subdued), and subjecting himself to the Father, so that the Father's supremacy above all is made clear through such emphasis, would it not perfectly fit the flow, overall content and immediate issues presented that in the expression "so that God may be all in all" that "God" would naturally be understood as a reference to the Father? Actually, a close consideration of the surrounding context will show that there is no other reference to which we could apply the statement to.

Although Paul uses the term "God the Father" in the first part of his discussion, and then simply "God" in the last, there is no contextual reason to believe that this somehow signals a change in any essential meaning or reference; nor is this manner of expression entirely unusual in the Scriptures. It has already been noted that, in John chapter four, Jesus spoke of a time "when the true worshipers shall worship *the Father* in spirit and

---

in mind unless of course the context makes this sense of (*ho*) *theos* impossible." —*Jesus as God, The New Testament Use of Theos in Reference to Jesus*, pp. 42, 47.

[53] Roman Catholic scholar, Karl Rahner, after having examined the New Testament witness concerning the use of the term God (*ho theos*), concluded: "Nowhere in the New Testament is there to be found a text with *ho theos* which has unquestionably to be referred to the Trinitarian God as a whole existing in three Persons." —*Theological Investigations, Volume 1, Theos in the New Testament* (Baltimore: Halicon Press, 1961), p. 143. If there is not one text in the New Testament where the occurrence of "God" represents—'unquestionably'—the entire "triune" Godhead, how is it even possible (scripturally speaking) to suggest that *ho theos* in 1 Cor. 15:28 is a reference to the Trinity—aside from the fact that nothing in the context points to such a concept? If a reader or student were to consider the entire chapter carefully, it would become clear that the concept of a "Trinity" is entirely absent. But because Paul uses the term "God" and not "God the Father" in verse 28, this should lead one to believe that the "God" he speaks of in this case is the Trinity? Is this truly a reasonable and even-handed "exegetical" conclusion?

truth, for *the Father* seeks such to worship Him." Immediately after Jesus said, "*God* is a spirit, and they who worship Him must worship in spirit and in truth."[54] In this case, Jesus first uses the term "the Father ('the true worshippers shall worship *the Father*')," then, at the end, he uses the term "God ('*God* is a spirit,' to be worshipped 'in spirit and in truth')." Does this mean that all of the sudden—without any explanation, qualification, or signal of change—Jesus switched from the meaning "(God) the Father" to "God" in the sense of "(the triune) God"? No; for the logical and natural continuity of thought makes self-evident that the reference in both cases is the same. The focus on "the Father" as the subject and object of true worship makes clear and obvious that in the subsequent mention of "God" (though not the specific language 'Father') Jesus has *not* introduced an entirely unprecedented and theologically distinctive meaning onto the term "God" like "the triune God"—a concept nowhere mentioned by Jesus or his apostles. There is simply no valid reason—either here, for the term "God" to stand for "the *triune* God," or in the context of 1 Corinthians chapter fifteen, the *entire* letter to the Corinthians,[55] or from the Bible as a whole—to introduce into the phrase, "so that *God* may be all in all," the idea "so that the *Trinity* may be all in all."[56]

Actually, the attempt on Dr. White's part to point out some special significance about the fact that in verse 28 Paul uses the expression "God" and not "God *the Father*" specifically, as he does in verse 24, is found to be even weaker when one considers the usage of the term "God (*ho theos*)" in the

---

[54] John 4:23-24, *MKJV* translated by Jay P. Green Sr. (Sovereign Grace Publishers, 1962-1998)
[55] Again, it should be carefully noted that Paul's first letter to the Corinthians contains in it no reference to a concept of the "one God" as a "Trinity." In chapter eight, Paul identified the "one God" as "the Father, from whom all things are and for whom we exist." It should be pointed out that, in addition to the use of the term 'God' in the phrase 'so that *God* may be all in all' (1 Cor. 15:28), there is a total of about 100 references to 'God' (54 specific uses of *ho theos* in its various forms) in Paul's first letter to the Corinthians. *Every single occurrence* is almost certainly a reference to *the Father*.
[56] In 1 John 3:1 the apostle wrote: "See what love the Father has given us, that we should be called children of God…" (*RSV*). Since John used the term "Father" first and then "God," does that mean that John had in mind: "…that we should be called children of (the triune) God…"? Is there anything in the context that would point to such a conclusion?

earlier portion of the very same chapter.

Before Paul spoke about the future resurrection and ultimate subjection of Jesus Christ to God, Paul said that he had "persecuted the church **of God** (*tou theou*; lit., 'of the God')," (v. 9); "by **God's** grace (*chariti de theou*) I am what I am"; "not I but the grace **of God** (*tou theou*) that is with me" (v. 10); and, "we are even found to be false witnesses **of God** (*tou theou*)" (v. 15). Since in these instances Paul uses the term "God" and not "God *the Father*" specifically, are we to view all such occurrences of "God" as a reference that should include all "three divine persons" of the Trinity? The context once again confirms that this is not the case. We can be assured in this case that Paul's use of the word "God" denotes a reference to the Father based not only on the apostle's explicit identification of the "one God (*eis theos*)" as "the Father" in 8:6, but in the second part of verse 15, Paul goes on to point out the fact that if Christ was not raised from the dead, then "we have testified against **God** (*tou theou*, lit., 'the God') that he raised up Christ..." This is, unquestionably, a reference to the Father (*not* the 'Trinity'), and shows that the four previous occurrences of "God" were all references to God the Father as well. This also demonstrates—from the immediate and surrounding context itself—what was, in Paul's mind, the *interchangeability* of the term/concept "God" and the term/concept "God the Father" (within the same discussion that extends to verse 28). These points are, in fact, quite decisive in highlighting the futility in the attempt to draw out and establish special significance in the apostle's use of the term "God (*ho theos*)" as opposed to God "the Father (*ho pater*)" specifically—as if this was somehow intended to alert readers that "the God" who would become "all in all" should be viewed as a concept or reference denoting the same "triune God" of Nicene and post-Nicene theology.[57]

---

[57] Additionally it may be asked (as it concerns a sound 'hermeneutical' approach to the issue), how is it that those who read this verse in the first century (the original audience, in its original setting) were supposed to understand "God" to refer to "the triune God" if there is no instance in the Hebrew or Christian Scriptures where the term "God" stands for the Trinity (or is explained to

The Father-Son Relationship

It is really strange that Dr. White characterizes a viewpoint that would identify the God in verse 28 as "God the Father" as one that is trying to say, "well, this *just* simply means the Father will be all in all," and that such would "throw a monkey wrench in what [Paul is] trying to say..." How could the idea that the Father—identified in Scripture as the "one God" (1 Cor. 8:6) and "the only true God" (John 17:3)—ultimately becoming "all things to everyone" result in any other significance than that which is in perfect harmony with Paul's discussion and with the rest of the inspired Scriptures? Even when considered independently of these factors, it becomes quite clear that any attempt to impose the idea of "all three persons of the Trinity" onto the word "God" in verse 28 would entirely disrupt the logical outcome of the apostle's inspired presentation. Again, how does it *logically* follow that the Son would hand over the kingdom to his Father, and *subject* himself to the Father, so that the "three persons of the Trinity" would become all in all? Where is the connection? And yet how reasonable, how natural, and how logical would it be to accept Paul as meaning that the Son would deliver the kingdom to the Father in the end, putting himself in subjection to the Father, so that the Father (the 'only true God') would be the one who would ultimately become all things to everyone? In what way would that "throw a monkey wrench" in what the apostle is trying to say?

Although a defender of Trinitarian orthodoxy, well-known Bible scholar Arthur W. Wainwright (associate professor of New Testament at Candler School of Theology) nevertheless contradicted the common attempt to read the doctrine of the Trinity into verse 28, by observing:

> When all the enemies of God have been overthrown, the Lord Christ will hand over his kingdom to the Father. Here Paul seems to be teaching a subordinationism which is not limited to the earthly life of Christ but which is ultimate and absolute. The final status of the Son is one of

---

be a reference to the Trinity); when, on the other hand, there exists such a great multitude of cases where "God" undoubtedly refers to the Father of Jesus Christ?

subjection to God. And in this passage God is *not* Father, Son, and Holy Spirit, *but Father only*.[58]

In the *New International Commentary on the New Testament*, New Testament professor Gordon Fee (coauthor of the book '*How to Read the Bible for All Its Worth*'), similarly wrote:

> The key for Paul lies in the fact that an external subject is responsible for the act of subjecting all things to Christ. Thus, 'When it says that 'everything has been subjected,' it is clear that 'everything' excludes the one (i.e., God) who did the subjecting to him (i.e., Christ).' As the next verse makes clear, this has to be explained because in Paul's view a twofold act in subjecting is going on in the raising of the dead. On the one hand, death itself will thereby finally have been subjected to Christ (v. 24c); on the other hand, with that final subduing of death the time of Christ's reign comes to its end, so that he may hand over the 'rule' *to the Father (v. 24b) who thus becomes 'all in all' (v. 28)*...Paul's point is that in raising Christ from the dead God has set in motion a chain of events that must culminate in the final destruction of death and thus of God's being once again, as in eternity past, 'all in all.'[59]

The respected nineteenth-century Bible commentator, Dr. Heinrich Meyer, likewise observed:

> The object aimed at in the Son's becoming subject under God is the absolute sovereignty of God: '*in order that God may be the all in them all*,' i.e. in order that *God* may be the only and the immediate all-determining principle in the inner life of all the members of the kingdom hitherto reigned over by Christ. Not as though the hitherto continued rule of Christ had *hindered* the attainment of this end (as Hofmann objects), but it has *served* this end

---

[58] *The Trinity In The New Testament* (London: S.P.C.K., 1962), p. 187 (emphasis added).
[59] *The New International Commentary on the New Testament, The First Epistle to the Corinthians* (Grand Rapids: Eerdmans, 1987), p. 759 (emphasis added).

as its final destination, the complete fulfillment of which is the complete 'glory of God the Father' (Phil. ii. 11) to eternity...up to this last consummation the Son is the regulating governing principle in all, but now gives over His kingdom to the Father, and becomes Himself subject to the Father, so that then the *latter* [the Father] is the all-ruling One in *all*, and no one apart from Him in *any*.[60]

The well-known British Bible scholar and translator, William Barclay, also accurately summarized several implications connected to the apostle's teaching. Barclay noted that "here Paul clearly and deliberately subordinates the Son to the Father. What he is thinking of is this. We can use only human terms and analogies. God gave to Jesus a task to do, to defeat sin and death and to liberate man. The day will come when that task will be fully and finally accomplished, and then, to put it in pictorial terms, the Son will return to the Father like a victor coming home and the triumph of God will be complete...It is a case of one who, having accomplished the work that was given him to do, returns with the glory of complete obedience as his crown. As God sent forth his Son to redeem the world, so in the end he will receive back a world redeemed..."[61]

It is interesting to take note of the fact that Dr. White is an active Protestant apologist, well known for his polemical works and numerous public, theological debates. He is even known to regularly lecture on the importance of discovering the true meaning and intent of Scripture through the principles of "consistent exegesis" and "sound hermeneutics." In a 2003 radio broadcast, where he is alleged to have taught a lesson in the practice of "exegesis," Dr. White even said:

> "I want to encourage our listeners today to become equipped to engage in the task of exegesis; learn the

---

[60] Heinrich Meyer, TH.D., *Critical and Exegetical Hand-Book to the Epistles to the Corinthians* (Peabody: Hendrickson Publishers, Inc., first published 1884; reprinted 1983), pp. 362-363.
[61] *The Letters to the Corinthians, Revised Edition, The Daily Bible Series* (Philadelphia: The Westminster Press, 1975), pp. 151-152.

The Father-Son Relationship

> canons and rules of sound hermeneutics; understand that *truly* to learn how to interpret the Bible correctly is to allow God to speak in his own language. That is, when we do not self-consciously submit ourselves to the proper means of hermeneutics, then the normal reason we do so, other than ignorance, is because the application of sound principles of hermeneutics would result in the destruction of our own traditions and our own positions which are actually *not* biblical. In other words, when you do not practice sound hermeneutics, you are not allowing the text to speak for itself. You are determining that *God* must speak in the way that *you* want him to speak."

Then, Dr. White went on to criticize those individuals whom he believed were,

> "not applying consistent hermeneutics so that they are approaching each passage to hear it in its own context. Instead they have their own overriding traditions, and they have their own perspectives that they are attempting to defend, and they then force these upon the text of Scripture itself. And as a result, God's word is muted for them; instead what you get is man's tradition masquerading as if it is the word of God."[62]

It is remarkable that in light of such a professed respect for and commitment to the principles of sound biblical interpretation, we find that Dr. White's very own "exegesis" of 1 Corinthians 15:28 qualifies as an outstanding example of what Dr. White himself outspokenly criticizes others of practicing, and of which he strongly warns his listeners to avoid.[63] While the conclusion advanced by Trinitarian apologists like Dr. White is perfectly understandable in light of the requirements of Trinitarian thinking and tradition, when one calmly and soberly examines the context and specific point of the apostle's

---

[62] Dr. James R. White, *The Dividing Line Broadcast*, 5/15/03 (Alpha & Omega Ministries)
[63] In the Dividing Line Archive on the AO Ministries website, the writer of the caption claimed that "James gives a lesson in exegesis using Colossians chapter 2 as his text," and also indicated belief that Dr. White shows how certain religious groups "miss the clear teaching of the deity of Jesus Christ in this passage due to their lack of exegetical abilities."

The Father-Son Relationship

presentation (from beginning to end), one will be able to see that no such conclusion can be legitimately or "exegetically" derived, according to what the apologists profess to so highly value as "the sound principles of hermeneutics." "Instead what you get is man's tradition masquerading as if it is the word of God."

In light of the fact that in the Christian Scriptures the supreme God is never identified as a "tri-unity" of persons, that *ho theos* ('God') never represents (or can be proven to represent) the "Trinity," and that there is no idea or suggested concept of a Trinity anywhere in Paul's discussion, it becomes truly difficult to follow the reasoning of those who would suggest that the term "God" in verse 28 stands for a "triune godhead," or even how such a meaning could be looked upon as among the possibilities of sound interpretation. For from any perspective it is argued for (whether contextually, in the immediate sense, or when the Bible is viewed in its totality—or *logically* speaking), such a desired theological meaning is found to be wholly untenable. Yet if one were to examine a number of evangelical commentaries, one would find that this is one of the most common proposals given for the meaning of this particular text.[64]

Really, the fact that no instance in all of Scripture can be established where the term "God" represents a "triune God," and such an obvious and abundant use of the term "God" as a reference to "God the Father," shows that one cannot

---

[64] The interpretation goes back at least as far as Augustine (354-430 C.E.): "Augustine's treatise *On the Trinity* ends with the acclamation of 'the one God, the Trinity,' as He who remains 'all in all.'" —*The First Epistle to the Corinthians, A Commentary on the Greek Texts*, by Anthony C. Thiselton, p. 1238. The *MacArthur Study Bible* footnote on vs. 28 states: "Christ will continue to rule because His reign is eternal (Rev. 11:15), but He will reign in His former, full, and glorious place within the Trinity, subject to God (v. 28) in the way eternally designed for Him in full Trinitarian glory." Another evangelical source writes: "Once that has been finally achieved by Jesus...he will submit himself in his obedient manhood to God the Father. Thus God, in the eternal perfection of the Trinity, will *be everything to everyone* (28)." —David Prior, *The Message of 1 Corinthians, Life in the Local Church* (Downers Grove, U.S.S: Inter-Varsity Press, 1985) p. 268. It was similarly said in another evangelical commentary: "All this is to be done so that God will be recognized by all as sovereign, and he—the triune God—will be supreme (cf. Rev 22:3-5)." —*The Expositor's Bible Commentary, Volume 10 (Romans-Galatians)* (Grand Rapids: Zondervan, 1976), p. 286. Note, however, in Revelation 22:3-5 there is no mention or allusion to a concept of a "triune God." It is unclear why the writer points to this passage in an attempt to establish such a viewpoint.

The Father-Son Relationship

legitimately appeal to the overall biblical context (in terms of the usage and significance of the term 'God'); nor can one appeal to any particular element within the immediate context of 1 Corinthians 15 for such a meaning.[65] This is, unfortunately, a classic case in point of a professionally trained and experienced Trinitarian apologist tactfully *reading into* (or superimposing and forcing a meaning onto) a text an idea that is simply not there.[66]

In this regard, and in light of this example, it is helpful to keep in mind that the Bible as a whole—including the four Gospels and apostolic epistles—constitutes a *revelation*. That is to say, the intended purpose of Scripture is to *reveal* the truth about God, his identity and personality, and his purposes toward humanity—especially toward those who believe. It is true that any kind of in-depth and specialized study of the Bible may not only require intense effort, accompanied by both *intellectual* and *spiritual* discipline, but will very often involve a committed, patient-minded and *long-term* reflection—sometimes even knowledge of, and a degree of competence in, the original Bible languages (something that requires special training). But this does not mean that the Bible is a collection of books that in some way conceals knowledge (so that its real messages and most

---

[65] In addition to the use of the term "God" in the phrase "so that *God* may be all in all" (1 Cor. 15:28), there are a total of about **100** (97, according to my count) references to "God" (**54** specific uses of ***ho theos*** in its various forms) in Paul's first letter to the Corinthians. *Every single occurrence* is certainly a reference to *the Father* (made clear by Paul's use of the term 'God' in the introductory chapter, by the individual contexts, and by 1 Cor. 8:6 where Paul explicitly identifies the 'one God' as 'the Father'—*not* as 'the Trinity'). There is not *one* case where "God" means, or can be fairly argued to mean, "the triune God" in 1 Corinthians (and no place known in all 66 books of the Bible for that matter). The claim that in the phrase, "so that God may be all in all," Paul had in mind 'the *triune* God,' along with any suggestion that Paul's original audience would have understood him in this way—particularly in light of the fact that *God the Father* is the only one in view in 1 Cor. 15:28—cannot be sustained from a scriptural perspective.

[66] 'Hermeneutics' is a technical term which the dictionary defines as "the theory and methodology of interpretation, especially of scriptural text." According to White: "Exegesis can be defined with reference to its opposite: *eisegesis*. To exegete a passage is to *lead the native meaning out from the words*; to eisegete a passage is to *insert a foreign meaning into the words*. You are exegeting a passage when you are allowing it to say *what its original author intended*; you are eisegeting a passage when you are forcing the author to say *what you want the author to say*." —*Scripture Alone. Exploring the Bible's Accuracy, Authority, and Authenticity* (Minnesota: Bethany House Publishers, 2004), p. 81.

important concepts need to be 'decoded,' so to speak, by a special class of learned scholars), or that it presents its teachings in such a way that would require one to be a professionally-trained theologian in order to discover and disclose its true meaning and most essential teachings.

If it truly was in the apostle's mind to persuade his readers to believe and understand that in the end a "triune God" would be "all in all," he certainly did not make that clear to those on the receiving end of his divinely-inspired letter. In fact, the apostle speaks with such an obvious sense of finality and ultimacy of purpose (in terms of outlining the final consummation of the Son's divinely-appointed rulership: In the end, the Son 'hands over the kingdom to his God and Father' and 'the Son himself' ends up 'subjected to the one who subjected everything to him'), what comes across as most remarkable—in light of the common claims of Trinitarian theology—is the *absence* of anything that reflects the notion of a "triune God" in the apostle's thinking. There is nothing in this section of Paul's writings consistent with, reflective of, or any element remotely resembling what one would expect from traditional, so-called "orthodox" teaching on the Trinity; for here, in this chapter, Paul not only expressly distinguishes the Son from "God" (*God* is the one who 'raised up' Christ, v. 15), but also speaks of the ultimate and final *subjection* of the Son to God, demonstrating the ultimate supremacy of the Son's God and Father above all. Thus it was observed in *The Pulpit Commentary*, with respect to the Son's final "subjection" to the Father: "The words can only be taken as they stand. The attempts to explain them have usually been nothing but ingenious methods of explaining them away."[67]

In this light, it is also instructive to note how numerous other evangelical commentaries have expressed awareness of the problem the apostle's statements present toward traditional evangelical dogma, and how accurate the comments made in the Pulpit Commentary prove to be.

---

[67] *The Pulpit Commentary. 1 Corinthians*, Exposition by the Very Rev. F. W. Farrar, D. D. (New York and London: Funk & Wagnalls Company, n.d.), p. 487.

The Father-Son Relationship

In his comments on verse 28, for example, evangelical Leon Morris writes: "The climax of this process of 'putting under' comes when *the Son* (the one occurrence of this designation of Jesus in Paul) is 'put under' the Father. This presents difficulty, for it appears to some that one member of the Trinity is seen as inferior to another."[68] Gordon Clark also perceives a problem in that, "one is again confronted with something that could be taken as a denial or a weakening of the full Deity of the Son..." Clark also notes that "Augustine tried to explain it as the subjection of the *human nature* of Christ." But Clark writes: "At best, this is inadequate. Some Nicene expositors, in their anxiety to defend the hardly yet established doctrine of the Trinity, resorted to the desperate expedient of interpreting 'the Son' as the Church, His body, as in 12:12, where the word *Christ* means the Church."[69]

Another Trinitarian source recognized a similar problem associated with the apostle's teaching: "We here come on one of the most important and difficult conceptions of our Epistle, and of St. Paul's Epistle in general. It is difficult to harmonize this idea of the subjection of the Son with the ordinary conception of the Trinity, according to which the Son is eternally equal with the Father."[70]

However, such attempts to bring the apostle's teaching into conformity with latter Trinitarian concepts are discussed by the same source:

> The subjection of the Son, according to Chrysostom, denotes his full agreement with the Father. According to Augustine, it is the act whereby the Son will guide the elect to the contemplation of the Father; according to Beza, the presentation of the elect to the Father; according to others, the manifestation by means of which the Son will make the Father fully known to the whole

---

[68] *Tyndale New Testament Commentaries, 1 Corinthians, Revised Edition* (Grand Rapids: Eerdmans, 1999), p. 213

[69] *First Corinthians, A Contemporary Commentary* (Jefferson: Trinity Foundation, 1975), p. 268.

[70] *Commentary on the First Epistle of St. Paul to the Corinthians, Volume II*, F. Godet, Th.d. (Grand Rapids: Zondervan, 1957), p. 368.

world (Theodoret): meanings which are all utterly insufficient to render the force of the expression used by the apostle. It has also been attempted to understand by the Son; here the mystical body of Christ, the Church (Ambrose); and this is perhaps why the words *ho huios, the Son*, are omitted by some of the Fathers.—A larger number distinguish between the Divine and the human nature of Christ, and ascribe what is here said of Him only to the latter. This attempt to divide the Lord's person into two natures, one of them subject, while the other remains free and self-sufficient, is the more unfortunate in this passage, as the word used to designate Christ is precisely that which most forcibly characterizes His Divine being., *ho huios, The Son*, absolutely speaking.[71]

It should be noted at this point as well that there are no elements present within the immediate context of 1 Corinthians 15 (and nothing in the Scriptures when considered as a whole) suggesting that Jesus Christ is a possessor of two natures, so that one could attempt to limit Christ's subjection to the Father to the terms of his *human* as opposed to his *divine* nature. Nor is there any indication that, in the end, when the Son delivers the kingdom to his God and Father, that the alleged "Trinitarian God" will reign supreme. Although these are among the most common expositions of 1 Corinthians 15:24-28 put forward by orthodox interpreters, there is simply no evidence suggesting that the apostle had any of these concepts in mind.

Paul's description, however, does suggest that the kingdom of God involves a long-term process whereby Jesus Christ, God's Son and anointed executioner of God's will, undoes all the effects that the original transgression of God's commandment resulted in. The Messiah—sent forth first to lay down his life in order to reconcile sinners to the Father—will reign as King (for a 'thousand years' according to Revelation 20), eventually bringing to nothing all that is in opposition to God's sovereignty and righteousness; including sin, unrepentant

---

[71] *Commentary on the First Epistle of St Paul*, p. 369.

sinners, Satan ('the one having the means to cause death,' Hebrews 2:14) and, ultimately, death itself ('the last enemy'). When all has been accomplished by means of the Son, and all enemies have been subdued by the Son's power, then the Son himself will subject himself to God, his Father, which can only result in a final demonstration of the Father's supremacy and glorification above all.[72] Evangelical scholar C. K. Barrett summarized the events described in this way:

> The Son has been entrusted with a mission on behalf of his Father, whose sovereignty has been challenged, and at least to some extent usurped by rebellious powers. It is for him to reclaim this sovereignty by overcoming the powers, overthrowing his enemies, and recovering the submission of creation as a whole. The mission he will in due course execute, death being the last adversary to hold out, and when it is completed he will hand the government of the universe back to his Father.[73]

F. F. Bruce's comments are also insightful and worthy of consideration at this point:

> When this subjection is completed and the last enemy destroyed, Christ has fully accomplished his mediatorial ministry. He has brought the whole estranged creation back into harmony with God; now he 'delivers the kingdom to God the Father' that God may be everything to everyone, or more literally, and more accurately, 'that God may be all in all' (cf. Rom. 11:36). The kingdom of Christ comes to an end in its present phase,[74] but only to merge in the eternal kingdom of God, so there is no failure of the prophetic promise that Messiah's kingdom will know no end (Isa. 9:7; Lk. 1:33). His mediatorial kingship is the means for the consummation of the

---

[72] Compare Philippians 2:11.
[73] *A Commentary on the First Epistle to the Corinthians*, p. 360.
[74] In Meyer's commentary, it was argued that "a great deal of dogmatic theology has been imported, in order to make the apostle teach—what, in truth, he does teach with the greatest distinctness—that there is a cessation of the rule of Christ." —*Critical and Exegetical Hand-Book to the Epistles to the Corinthians*, p. 362.

kingdom of God, which was inaugurated by his work on earth. The humble submissiveness to his Fathers' will which characterized him then will continue to characterize him to the consummation, when the Son himself will also be subjected (or 'will subject himself') to him who put all things under him.[75]

A further reflection on the whole of scriptural teaching reveals that one of its most consistent themes is found in the goal of the ultimate glorification of, and final reconciliation of creatures to, God *the Father*. In his letter to the Romans, for example, the wish of the apostle was expressed that, harmoniously, in accord with Christ Jesus, all Christians would together "with one voice glorify the God and Father of our Lord Jesus Christ."[76] Jesus Christ himself indicated that through him men and women would be able to "come to the Father," and that people should worship "the Father" in spirit and in truth.[77] Similarly, the apostle Paul made clear that there was "one mediator *between God* [an unquestionable reference to the Father] *and men*." John indicated that, in reference to believers, "we have an advocate *with the Father*…"[78] Paul even seemed to indicate that the very heart of his divinely-directed ministry involved the proclamation that through Christ men and women could be reconciled to "God," namely, the Father.[79] And, most significantly, the apostle likewise indicated that the end of God the Father's purpose in the exaltation of his Son would be that he, the Father, would receive glorification.[80] On the other hand we find, biblically, no indication that in the goal of our reading Scripture, or in the expression of our Christian unity, or in the final consummation of all things, would there be an outcome

---

[75] *New Century Bible, Based on the Revised Standard Version, 1 and 2 Corinthians*, Edited by F. F. Bruce (London: Marshall, Morgan and Scott Publications, 1971), p. 148.
[76] Romans 15:5, *NAB*
[77] John 14:6; 4:23-24
[78] 1 John 2:1
[79] 2 Corinthians 5:18-20
[80] Philippians 2:11

The Father-Son Relationship

involving the glorification of a "triune" God;[81] nor do we ever find that a mediation would occur between men and a "triune" God, or that a reconciliation would take place between men and the "Trinity."

The truth is, the idea of an entity that is "trinitarian" in nature being the ultimate object of reconciliation, true worship, glorification, or the one that would ultimately become "all things to everyone," does not appear in the Scriptures. All is ultimately to the glory of the one God, the Father. How difficult is it to believe, then, in light of these facts, that Christ will eventually hand over his kingdom to the Father, so that his Father ('the only true God,' John 17:3), the one who entrusted to him that kingdom and authority to rule over it, would, in the end, become "all things to everyone." As the Scripture continually makes clear, one of the ultimate designs of Christ's consecrated role and ministry is to *reconcile* all things back to his Father and to bring glory to the Father's name: "For the universe owes its origin to Him, was created by Him, and has its aim and purpose in Him. To Him be the glory throughout the Ages! Amen."[82]

"The Kingdom of Christ is a thousand times called eternal. Yet in the consummation of the ages He shall restore it to God. Not that the glory of Christ is thereby diminished, for it is His highest glory to have ruled all things well, even to the end, and to have subjected them all as He intended to the Father. Thus it is to deliver up the Kingdom of God, just as the general of the universal army renders up the palm of victory to the emperor."[83] — Michael Servetus (16th century)

---

[81] Even throughout all of the vivid prophetic imagery set forth in the books of Isaiah, Ezekiel, Daniel, and—perhaps most significantly—the book of Revelation, there is not one case where the author reveals or presents a vision of a "triune" God that is worshiped by the inhabitants of heaven and earth. No recognition of the concept is given in any of their writings.

[82] Romans 11:36, *The New Testament by the Late Richard Francis Weymouth*

[83] Quoted in *Hunted Heretic, The Life and Death of Michael Servetus* (Boston: The Beacon Press, 1952), by Roland H. Bainton, p. 51. Before the book was published, a pre-edited copy of this discussion was sent to several respected Bible scholars from prominent theological Seminaries, including Princeton, Denver and Southeastern Baptist Theological Seminaries. Four evangelical scholars (and one Greek Orthodox scholar) agreed that 1 Cor. 15:28 refers to the Father, not the Trinity. Dr. Craig Blomberg, a respected Bible Professor, wrote: "I think I would agree with you, Fee and Garland (both evangelicals). Many commentaries I've looked at don't take a clear stand, so I don't know whether the Trinitarian view really is the common evangelical one or not" (Correspondence: 3/14/06). Denver's New Testament Professor, Dr. Bill Klein, also expressed agreement: "Ultimately, Jesus is the Father's son, and it is the Father who receives ultimate honor and glory. All submit to the Father who is all in all" (Correspondence: 4/20/06).

"And it shall come to pass in that day, that living waters shall go out from Jerusalem; half of them toward the eastern sea, and half of them toward the western sea: in summer and in winter shall it be. And Jehovah shall be King over all the earth: in that day shall Jehovah be one, and his name one." — Zechariah 14:8-9, *ASV*

Jesus Christ—The Creator, or the one *through* whom God created?

> *The Logos is John's explanation of the creation of the universe. The author of Hebrews (Hebrews 1:2) names God's Son as the one 'through whom [God] made the ages.' Paul pointedly asserts that 'the all things were created in him" (Christ) and 'the all things stand created through him and unto him' (Colossians 1:16). Hence it is not a peculiar doctrine that John [1:10] here enunciates. In 1 Corinthians 8:6, Paul distinguishes between the Father as the primary source (ex ou) of the all things and the Son as the intermediate agent as here (dia ou).* —A.T. Robertson, *Word Pictures in the New Testament*

Most evangelical apologists—based on New Testament texts like Colossians 1:16 and others—believe and argue that Jesus Christ is the Creator of "all things" and that therefore he is to be thought of as the Most High God, just like the Father.[84] They suggest that the Son is spoken of in certain sections of Scripture as the very one who created the universe. On one level this is understandable, for the *NIV* and other translations render the verse in Colossians: "For *by* him all things were created: things in heaven and on earth, visible and invisible, whether thrones or powers or rulers or authorities; all things were created *by* him and for him" (*NASB* is similar). What the text actually states specifically, however, is that the "all things" in this context were created not "by" but "in" or "by means of" the "beloved Son" (v. 13).[85] That is, in agreement with the first chapter of Hebrews, God is really understood and presented as the Creator and source of what is in view, whereas the "Son" is spoken of as

---

[84] See White, *Scripture Alone* (Minnesota: Bethany House, 2004), p. 151.
[85] More literally, "the Son of [God's] love."

The Father-Son Relationship

the one *through* whom God brought the creation in view into existence.

What is presented by Paul in his letter to the Colossians appears to be perfect in harmony with other portions of Scripture that speak about God's creative activities; for in Genesis we are told that God *spoke* or *commanded* what came to be into existence—**"God *said*, 'let there be light,' and there was light."** Yet on the earth, long after the creation, Jesus Christ was God's very word (*logos*) "made flesh" (John 1:14, *KJV*). The "beloved Son" is "before all things (*pro panton*)," evidently, because the "all things" (*ta panta*) were created *through* him (*di autou*) and *for* him (*eis auton*). Logically, one would rightly think, the Son had to be "before" the "all things" in order for him to be the one "in" and "through" whom they were created. But this does not logically mean that he has to be "before" all things because he is "eternal/without beginning," as Trinitarians often claim. He can be described as "before all things" because, out of "all creation" (whatever 'creation' is in view), he is "firstborn" (Colossians 1:15).

But the expression "before all things (Gk. *pro panton*)" does not necessarily have to mean "before" in the sense of "before (in time)." Contextually speaking, the statement can very well mean that the Son *is* (not *was*) "before all things" in the sense that he is *preeminent* above all, in harmony with the thought articulated in verse 18 which says "[the Son] might have first *place* [or 'preeminence'] in everything." The Greek *pro* can bear the sense of "before (in time)" or "superior" in rank or importance. We know this because the identical expression is used this way in 1 Peter 4:8 where the apostle wrote, "above all things (Gk. *pro panton*) have fervent love for one another" (*NKJV*)—meaning, evidently, that "love" among Christians should be 'preeminent' or the 'most important,' above all other virtues.[86] In the same way, the statement that the Son is "before all things (*pro panton*)" could simply mean that the Son is *above*

---

[86] This was pointed out to me by Greg Deuble (Correspondence: Monday, 22 June, 2009). See *They Never Told Me This in Church*, pages 227-232.

The Father-Son Relationship

or that he has 'first place' in all things, a meaning that would fit the context perfectly.

This is entirely fitting; for Jesus is God's own Son, the one who would, in God's design, be appointed heir of all (Hebrews 1:2). It is even possible, as some argue, that the "all things" said to be created in the Son are not a reference to the original Genesis creation, but to the "all things" in the realm or domain of "the kingdom" believers have been transferred into (v. 13), the new order of things effected by God through Christ and all of its associated blessings (vs. 15-21). This view is likewise in harmony with the Scriptures and derived from the context.

The main point, however, is that in Colossians 1:16 Paul is not altering or deviating from what is taught elsewhere in Scripture; namely, that God's Son was the one *"through* [lit., 'in'] whom God created the ages" (Hebrews 1:2). The New Testament writers are actually quite clear in disclosing the facts related to the Son's involvement in the creation of "the ages" and "all things," whatever "the ages" and "all things" are taken to have reference to (John 1:10). They are careful to express in harmonious agreement that it was "God" who created "all things," yet that he did so through the agency of the word (*ho logos*)—the same "word" that appeared embodied in the flesh and blood man, Jesus Christ. As it was correctly noted at this point in the *Tyndale Commentaries*:

> All that God made, he made by means of him. Paul actually says 'in him,' and, though the word *en* can mean 'by' as well as 'in,' it is better to retain the literal translation than to paraphrase as NIV has done. Not only is there an intended parallel with verse 19, which would otherwise be lost: the passive 'were created' indicates, in a typically Jewish fashion, the activity of God the Father, working *in* the Son. To say 'by', here and at the end of verse 16, could imply, not that Christ is the Father's agent, but that he was alone responsible for creation.[87]

---

[87] *The Epistles of Paul to the Colossians and to Philemon, An Introduction and Commentary*, N. T. Wright (Grand Rapids: Eerdmans, 1986), p. 71. With respect to John 1:3, a very similar text,

The Father-Son Relationship

These observations are correct. The *NIV's* translation "by him" could not only imply that the Son alone was responsible for the creation in view, but that the Son himself was the ultimate source or power behind the creation, when in fact, he is, according to one interpretive rendering, "*the one through whom God created the universe*" (Hebrews 1:2, *TEV*).[88] *The Bible in Living English* expresses the thought accurately in John 1:3: "Everything was made by his agency." This is why it was observed by Bible scholar Ezra Abbot in the late 1800s:

> We find a still more remarkable passage in the Epistle to the Colossians, 1:15-20, where it is affirmed concerning the Son that 'he is the image of the invisible God, the first-born of all creation; for in him were all things created, things visible and invisible...all things have been created through him and unto him...In this passage, and in Col. 2:9, 10, where the Apostle says of Christ 'in him dwelleth all the fulness of the Godhead bodily, and in him ye are made full, who is the head of all principality and power,' we find, I believe, the strongest language which Paul has anywhere used concerning Christ's position in the universe and his relation to the Church...Here, certainly, if anywhere, we might expect that he would call him God; but he has not only not done so, but has carefully distinguished him from the being for whom he seems to reserve that name. He does not call him God, but 'the image of the invisible God' (Comp. 2 Cor. 4:4, and 1 Cor. 9:7). His agency in the work of creation is also restricted and made secondary by the use of the prepositions *en* and *dia*, clearly indicating that the conception in the mind of the Apostle is the same which

---

evangelical Gary F. Zeolla, translator of the *Analytical-Literal Translation of the New Testament*, noted, "other passages clearly show Jesus was the 'intermediate agent' in creation. Hence, 'by' would not be correct as it would make Jesus, not the Father, the 'primary agent' in creation. So 'through' or 'by means of' would be the most correct translation." —*Differences Between Bible Versions* (1st Books Library, 2001), p. 211.

[88] With regard to Colossians 1:16, A. T. Robertson noted that the word *created* "is the connotative aorist passive indicative of *ektisthe* (from *ktizo*, old verb, to found, to create (Rom. 1:25)...'*Have been created* (*ektistai*). Perfect passive indicative of *ktizo*, 'stand created,' 'remain created.' ...*Through him* (*di' auto*). As the intermediate and sustaining agent." —*Word Pictures in the New Testament, Volume IV, The Epistles of Paul*, p. 478.

The Father-Son Relationship

appears in the Epistle to the Hebrews, 1:2; that he is not the primary source of the power exerted in creation, but the being 'through whom God made the worlds, '*di ou epoiesen tous aionas*; comp. also 1 Cor. 8:6...Neither Paul nor any other New Testament writer uses the preposition *hupo*, 'by,' in speaking of the agency of the Son or Logos in creation. The designation 'first-born of all creation' seems also a very strange one to be applied to Christ conceived of as God. Some of the most orthodox Fathers of the fourth and fifth centuries, as Athanasius, Gregory of Nyssa, Cyril of Alexandria, Theodore of Mopsuestia, and Augustine, were so perplexed by it that they understood the Apostle to be speaking here of the new spiritual creation...[89]

Similar points were highlighted as far back as the third century C.E. by the well-known Bible scholar, Origen, in his commentary on the Bible:

And the apostle Paul says in his epistle to the Hebrews: 'At the end of the days He spoke to us in his Son, whom He made heir of all things, 'through whom' also He made the ages,' showing us that God made the ages through His Son, the 'through whom' belonging, when the ages were made to the Only-begotten. Thus if all things were made, as in this passage also, *through* the Logos, then they were not made *by* the Logos, but by a stronger and greater than He. And who else could this be but the Father?[90]

F. F. Bruce translated John 1:3: "All things came into being through him, and apart from him not even one thing that has come into being came into being." On this point, Bruce commented:

This rendering is somewhat clumsy because it is excessively literal, but the excessively literal rendering is designed to make the Evangelist's point clear. *God is the*

---

[89] Ezra Abbot, *Romans 9:5*.
[90] *Origen's Commentary on John, The Ante-Nicene Fathers*, Volume X, Book 2, chap. 6 (Grand Rapids: Eerdmans, 1969), p. 328.

Creator; his Word is the agent. The two parts of the verse say the same thing, first positively ('through him everything came into being'), and then negatively ('apart from him nothing that exists came into being'). This twofold affirmation sums up the teaching of Gen. 1, where the record of each creative day is introduced by the clause, 'And God said'. In Ps. 33:6 this is interpreted as meaning that 'by the word of the LORD' the heavens (and everything else) came into being; in the Wisdom literature it is similarly interpreted to mean that all things exist by his wisdom (cf. Prov. 3:19; 8:30; also Ps. 104:24). The Johannine prologue is not the only place in the NT where this creative agency is ascribed...In Col. 1:16 f. Paul states that 'in [Christ] (and 'through him') all things were created...and in him all things cohere', while Heb. 1:2 speaks of the Son of God as the one 'through whom he ['God'] made the worlds', and in Rev. 3:14 he introduces himself as 'the Amen...the beginning of God's creation' (where 'Amen' may be a variant on Heb. *amon*, 'master workman,' of Prov. 8:30).[91] (Emphasis added)

    The points are confirmed by the preaching of the apostles in the book of Acts as well. In raising "their voices to God with one accord," Peter and John indicated that Jesus is the 'maker of heaven and earth's' "holy servant whom ['the maker of heaven and earth'] anointed..." (Acts 4:24-30, *NAB*). In chapter seventeen, the apostle Paul revealed that the "God who made the world and all that is in it, the Lord of heaven and earth" is the one who "will 'judge the world with justice' through a man he has appointed, and he has provided confirmation for all by raising him from the dead" (Acts 17:24-31, *NAB*). In both cases, the apostles carefully differentiate between the one who created the world from his "holy servant," the one whom the Creator

---

[91] *The Gospel of John, Introduction, Exposition and Notes*, p. 32. Commenting also on the *KJV*'s rendering "by," one source pointed out: "Our common version, however, misleads us on this matter. In the first chapter of John's account we read that 'All things were made *by* him' (John 1:3), and again, 'the world was made *by* him' (John 1:10). In both cases it should be *through*. The Logos, or Word, of God was the *means* of making all, not the efficient first Cause of all. Christ is never set forth as the absolute Source." —*Christ and Deity*, A. E. Knoch, p. 45.

The Father-Son Relationship

"anointed" and "appointed" and "raised him from the dead."

The Scriptures do not teach that the Son of God was the primary, direct cause, or chief initiator of the creation he is associated with; but rather, that he was the very one *through* whom *God* performed these creative works. This is something the Bible teaches in a very straightforward way, and this is why it is surprising that so many evangelical apologists have failed to fully appreciate the significance of such a basic and oft-repeated scriptural point.[92] As pointed out by the internationally-respected Protestant theologian Emil Brünner: "God alone is the Creator, ...the Son is called simply and solely the mediator of the Creation. In the New Testament the Son, or Jesus Christ, is never called the Creator. The title is given to the Father alone."[93]

All of the above texts mentioned—Colossians 1:16, John 1:10, Hebrews 1:2 and 1 Corinthians 8:6—appear to communicate the same fundamental concept;[94] namely that "the world came into existence through him" (not *by* him), "for *in* (or, '*by means of*,' the beloved Son) all things were created, in heaven and on earth, visible and invisible, whether thrones or dominions or principalities or authorities—all things were created *through* him and *for* him"; and that "he is before all things, and in him all things hold together." And although "God spoke of old to our fathers by the prophets...in these last days he has spoken to us by a Son, whom he appointed heir of all things, *through* whom also [God] made the ages." In fact, to us (to Christians), "there is one God, the Father, from (lit., 'out of') whom are all things and for whom we exist, and one Lord, Jesus Christ, *through* whom are all things and *through* whom we

---

[92] Or, perhaps the work of creation, as in the case of the powerful signs performed by the Son while on earth, which are spoken of as those "which *God worked through him*" (Acts 2:22) can/should be viewed in the same way. So if it is ever said that the Son created the world (Hebrews 1:10), it was, in reality, *God* working through him; or that God endowed the Son with the power of creation. In either case, God the Father is ultimately and rightfully credited with creating what is in view, but he did so *through* the Son.

[93] *The Christian Doctrine of God, Dogmatics*: Vol. I (Philadelphia: The Westminster Press, 1949), p. 232.

[94] In fact, *none* of theses passages teach that the "ages/all things" were created "by" Christ.

214

exist."[95]

> *"By the word of Jehovah were the heavens made, And all the host of them by the breath of his mouth."* —Psalm 33:6, ASV

Colossians 1:15-19

In the beginning portion of his letter to the Colossians, Paul says of the Father:

> **He delivered us from the power of darkness and transferred us to the kingdom of his beloved Son, in whom we have redemption, the forgiveness of sins.**

Then, Paul spoke with reference to the Son:

> **He is the image of the invisible God, the firstborn of all creation. For in him were created all things in heaven and on earth, the visible and the invisible, whether thrones or dominions or principalities or powers; all things were created through him and for him. He is before all things, and in him all things hold together.**[96]

Incredibly, professor of systematic theology Dr. Robert Reymond argued "there can be little doubt that Paul, with the New Testament writers in general, intended to assert that Jesus Christ is the invisible God made visible" and "as the image of the invisible God, that is God himself, by his incarnation made the invisible God visible to men."[97]

---

[95] It was observed in one source: "We have here a marvelously exact and concise definition of the relationship which we sustain to God and to the Lord, which in turn, throws much light on their respective relationship with each other. Briefly put, God is the *Source* and *Object* of all; Christ is the *Channel* of all; Thus it is always found. We are never said to come *out of* Christ, but *out of* God. Indeed, Christ asserts that He Himself came out of God. (John 8:42)." —Knoch, *Christ and Deity*, p. 1.
[96] Colossians 1:13-17, *NAB*
[97] *A New Systematic Theology of the Christian Faith*, pp. 251, 252.

The Father-Son Relationship

It is not too difficult, however, to discern the subtle and peculiar way Dr. Reymond adds a strange sort of twist to Paul's own description of Christ. Jesus Christ *is* "the invisible God made visible"? Is that what Paul really means? Is that what he says?

No doubt Paul's description of the Son harmonizes well with what John wrote in the prologue of his Gospel, concerning the fact that "no man has seen God at any time" (a clear reference to 'the invisible God' mentioned by Paul); and that the Son is, according to the most ancient manuscript readings, "an only-begotten/unique god (Gk: *monogenes theos*)," the one who has made the invisible God known. In perfect agreement, and in the very same Gospel account, Jesus himself said: "Everyone who listens to my Father and learns from him comes to me. Not that anyone has seen the Father except the one who is from God; he has seen the Father" (John 6:45-46, *NAB*).

Neither the apostle John nor any other New Testament writer indicates that Jesus was or is "the invisible God made visible." Rather, they make clear that Jesus is the very one who has "revealed" or "explained" the invisible God (he 'has told us all about him,' *The Living Bible*).[98] The statements in Colossians 1:15 and John 6:46 make equally clear that *the Father* is "the invisible God," not Jesus Christ. Yet only Jesus Christ has "seen" the Father, is "without sin," and is therefore uniquely qualified to "make him known" to others.

What John wrote is not only related to what Paul meant when he described Jesus as "the image of the invisible God," but also likely related to what Paul said in another place, how "the light of the knowledge of God's glory shines in the face of Christ,"[99] or when Christ himself said, "he that has seen me has seen the Father."[100] It is not that Christ *is himself* the invisible God (the Father), but that *in, through,* or *by means of* Christ, the invisible God, the Father, is 'seen' or 'made known.' Note also

---

[98] John 1:18
[99] 2 Corinthians 4:6
[100] John 14:9

The Father-Son Relationship

that Paul does not identify Jesus Christ as "God himself" or as "the invisible God," but as "the *image* of the invisible God"[101] (or, as Weymouth translates, 'the *visible representation* of the invisible God'[102]). With respect to the word "image" (Gk: *eikon*) used in this verse, it was observed by one scholar and translator:

> In order to clarify our thoughts, let us study a few occurrences of the word 'image' in the Scriptures. He Who is God's Image, and Who spoke as no man ever spoke, used it in contending with the Jews. Taking a minted piece of money, a denarius, He asked, 'Whose is this image and the inscription?' Their reply was, 'Caesar's.' He responded, 'Be paying, then, Caesar's to Caesar, and God's to God' (Matt. 22:21). The image was probably like that on modern coins, possibly an embossing, which suggested the emperor to the mind. …The fact that they were using money minted by Rome indicated their subjection to Rome. They were under obligations to the one whose image appeared on their coins. This image was only a partial likeness. It was made of metal, not flesh and blood. It was only a miniature of the original. It probably depicted only a part of his body, and that in hardly more than two dimensions. Yet it symbolized all that he was, especially what he was to those who used the coin. From this illustration, supplied by the divine Image Himself, we may readily deduce that, as the Image of God, He need *not* be of the 'same substance,' as the theologians assert, He need *not* reveal every phase of God's existence, but He *must* be a symbol of God's relationship to mankind—His love, His power, His wisdom, and His grace. A sight of Him should impress us with all that we could get by a vision of God. While seeking thus to define and limit the exact thought which lies in the term *image*, let no one imagine that Christ is not more than this. He is the Effulgence of

---

[101] Genesis 1:27 tells us that man was made in the image of God. At this point it is not unreasonable to suggest that Jesus Christ is the *perfect* image ('the exact representation' Hebrews 1:3) of God, not *literally* God himself.
[102] Richard Francis Weymouth, *New Testament in Modern Speech* (1978).

The Father-Son Relationship

God's glory. Indeed the effigy of Caesar on the coin of the realm probably was not much to look at, much less to admire. But Christ is not a lifeless representation but a life-giving illumination...He is the Effulgence of the radiant glory of the invisible Deity (Heb. 1:3). He is all that an image ought to be, the ideal representation of the most marvelous Original. Seeing Christ, we see Him Whom no man has seen or can see. Instead of being stricken to death by the sight, as we surely would were it the absolute Deity, we are given life, and the power to look upon His glory, yea, we ourselves partake of it and become like Him...Let it suffice to say, so perfect is His presentation of the Father, that our eyes are satisfied with seeing God in Him. There are innumerable idols in the world. Each one successfully conceals Him. The Son alone reveals Him.[103]

The next expression Paul makes about the Son represents another scriptural example that has provoked controversial discussion relevant to the doctrine of the Trinity; when Paul describes the Son by the much debated phrase: "the firstborn of all creation" (*NASB*), or "the first born of every creature" (*KJV*). The word translated "firstborn" is *prototokos*, which, lexically, of course, not only implies *birth*, but being born *first*. Although Jesus is identified by Paul as "the firstborn *of* all creation" (*prototokos pases ktiseos*), a few Trinitarian Bible translators have actually attempted to change the translation to "firstborn *over* all creation" (*NIV* and *NKJV*); but that is not a literally accurate or necessary translation. In a typical effort to defend Trinitarian concepts, John MacArthur advanced two interpretive ideas in his commentary on this verse. He said that, one, Paul "refers to Christ as *the creator* of everything that exists" and two, that "the genitive *ktiseos* is better translated 'over' than 'of'," thereby interpreting "firstborn of all creation" to mean "the preeminent *inheritor* over all creation."[104]

---

[103] *Christ and Deity*, A. E. Knoch (Canyon County, Concordant Publishing Concern), pp. 6-8.
[104] *The MacArthur New Testament Commentary, Colossians & Philemon* (Chicago: Moody Press, 1992), p. 47.

The Father-Son Relationship

Beyond the fact that Paul nowhere "refers to Christ as the creator of everything that exists," it was pointed out by Greek scholar Jason BeDuhn that, in terms of translation, the word 'over' actually "qualifies as an addition because 'over' *in no way* can be derived from the Greek genitive article meaning 'of.' The NIV translators make this addition on the basis of doctrine rather than language."[105] The correct translation is the one found in most literal Bible versions—"the firstborn *of* all creation." Literally, the word must be rendered not "over" but "of," a necessary element, part of the word *pases*, the genitive form of the word "all." The word *ktiseos* is likewise a genitive form of the Greek word for "creature" or "creation."[106]

However, it may be of significance to note that, in the Colossians letter, the Son is not merely referred to by Paul as the "firstborn," so that the expression stands alone. He is, rather, "the firstborn of all creation." This could simply mean (based on the language itself), and would seem to mean most naturally, that out of all of creation (whatever creation is in view[107]), the Son was the one born or conceived first, with his exalted position emphasized and the connotation of preeminence naturally retained.[108] Even if one accepts that firstborn means "preeminent" or "foremost" in this case, it would only then strike one as meaning that the Son is "the preeminent (one) *of all creation*" or "the foremost *of all creation* (or 'of every creature')." Yet there is nothing unreasonable (or outside the language or in violation of the context) to prevent the word "firstborn" from meaning "one who was born first," in relation to the rest of "creation." In fact,

---

[105] Beduhn, *Truth in Translation*, p. 81 (emphasis added).

[106] The "genitive" is the grammatical case conveying possession, ownership, origin, or derivation. Greek does not have a preposition "of"; it is part of the genitival form of a word/phrase as in *huios tou theou* ('Son of God') The sense of "of" is in the phrase *tou theou* (genitival form of *ho theos*) and must be rendered "Son *of* God," not "Son *over* God."

[107] The context, as some have argued, may be more supportive of understanding "the first born of all creation" as a reference to the new order of things as opposed to the original Genesis creation.

[108] "Conceived" in the sense of "began, originated, or founded (something) in a particular way..." —*Random House Webster's College Dictionary*. In the footnotes to his New Testament translation, Weymouth has, "Or, 'of earlier birth than any created being,'" and "'born before anything was created.'" Although not a literal translation, this may in fact accurately convey the sense that Paul intended, if Paul is in fact referring to the original Genesis creation.

that is what the word actually means—granted, on certain occasions, the word is used in a figurative sense and is not to be taken literally.

The Septuagint rendering of Genesis 4:4 reads: "And Abel also brought of *the first born of his sheep*"—clearly referring to the "firstborn" as a *member* of Abel's sheep. Since this is the same grammatical construction found in Colossians 1:15, it demonstrates that it certainly is possible, grammatically, to view Christ as a part of the "creation" in this text—"the firstborn of all creation."[109]

In the book of Romans, Paul said: "For those [God] foreknew he also predestined to be conformed to the image of his Son, so that he might be the *firstborn among many brothers.*"[110] Here, Christ is portrayed as the firstborn "among" or as a part of a group of "brothers." In verse 18 of Colossians, Paul said that Christ is "the beginning, the *firstborn from the dead...*"—likely, a parallel reference to Christ as "the first fruits of those who have fallen asleep," i.e., asleep in death.[111] In terms of time and sequence, Christ was the first among many who would ultimately be raised to immortal life. Logically, one *could* (and likely would) apply the same principle with respect to the phrase, "the firstborn of all creation." That is, out of all the creation in view, the "beloved Son" was the first one born, the first to come into existence.[112]

Although Trinitarian apologists strongly argue against understanding Paul's expression as meaning that God's Son was the literal "firstborn of all creation," it is certainly a valid possibility based not only on the language and grammar, but on

---

[109] Trinitarian Gordon H. Clark writes: "So is [Christ] not the first member or part of a group that was created? Grammatically, therefore, 'of all creation' would be a partitive genitive. Doubtless this is possible, but it is not necessary, even grammatically." —*Colossians, Another Commentary on an Inexhaustible Message* (The Trinity Foundation, Jefferson Maryland, 1979), p. 50.

[110] Romans 8:29, *NAB* (emphasis added).

[111] 1 Corinthians 15:20

[112] However, for a cogent and compelling argument for understanding the Son as, essentially, "the firstborn [of the new] creation," and that the descriptions in Colossians 1:15-17 do not demand the notion of a "pre-human" Son, see: *They never told me this in church!, A Call to read the Bible with new eyes,* by Greg S. Deuble (Atlanta: Restoration Fellowship, 2006), Ch. 5., pp. 132-246.

the very concept of *sonship* itself. Jesus is, of course, as Scripture describes him elsewhere, God's "firstborn" Son, the very "Son of the Father."[113] That is to say, we have no valid (logical or biblical) basis for ignoring the fact that the very notion of a "Father" in relation to a "Son"—whether used literally or figuratively—suggests the idea of one, a Father, who brought into existence or gave life to another, a son ('A father gives life to his son; indeed, a son by definition is one who has life from his father'; Thompson, *The God of the Gospel of John*, p. 77).[114] With this in mind, is it unreasonable to believe that God would have taken terms from human relationships—in light of a most common, most natural, and easy-to-understand human idea—and use them to communicate concepts that human beings would readily comprehend and appreciate?

This may relate to the point some have made that if Paul had intended to communicate the idea that Christ was the first of God's creations, he could have used the word *protoktizo*—"first created." That is, Paul's use of "firstborn" as opposed to "first created" has led some to suggest that Jesus Christ was not "created" in the same sense that all other living and non-living things came into existence; but that as God's Son—based on the language used here and in other texts—he was truly "born/begotten," spiritually "produced" or "generated" of God at one particular point before the creation of which he is the "firstborn."[115] In that case, some believe that Jesus Christ would not be properly described as God's first "creation," but as God's *firstborn son*, his literal offspring—spiritually speaking. Others, however, would argue that, scripturally, there is no substantial

---

[113] See 2 John, verse 3 (emphasis added). Compare Hebrews 1:6.
[114] Of course, one may also become a "son" by *adoption*.
[115] In fact, Hebrews 1:3 actually describes God's Son as a "reproduction" or "copy" (*charakter*)" of God's own "being." William Barclay observed: "*charakter* comes very easily to mean 'an exact replica,' copy or reproduction. This meaning was extended so that, for instance, a man could speak of a statue as *character tes emes morphes*, an exact reproduction of my shape. So then to say that Jesus is the *charakter* of God is to say, as it were, that Jesus is the exact reproduction of God, that in Jesus there is a clear and accurate picture of what God is." —*Jesus As They Saw Him* (Grand Rapids: Eerdmans, 1962), p. 319.

difference between creation and "birth" (or 'begettal').[116]

Even if the traditional translation is accepted as correct ('firstborn of all creation'), evangelicals Robert Bowman and Ed Komoszewski make a compelling point against a "literal" interpretation of 'firstborn' in this phrase:

> ...the description 'firstborn of all creation' is best understood to mean that the Son is the principal heir of all creation. Notice how this interpretation makes perfect sense in the immediate context: the Son is the principal heir of all creation (v. 15) because everything was created in, through, and for him (v. 16). The Son's inheritance, which the Father has graciously qualified us to share, is the subject in the broader context of the passage (vv. 12-14). The Old Testament background for this use of the term *firstborn* is found in a messianic passage describing David, the royal figure who anticipates the coming Messiah, as 'the firstborn, the highest of the kings of the earth' (Ps. 89:27). This statement did not mean, of course, that David (or Christ) was the first one born among all the kings of the earth. Rather, it refers to David (as a type of the Messiah) as the preeminent ruler, God's heir, the one who rules as his son in his stead (see also Ps. 2:2, 6-8). Paul's description of the Son as 'firstborn of all creation' is thus equivalent to the description in Hebrews of the Son as 'heir of all things' (Heb. 1:2; cf. Heb. 1:6).[117]

If the understanding of the early and earliest church fathers was correct, however, and Proverbs 8:22-31 is applicable to Christ, this would appear to harmonize with Paul's description of the Son in the Colossians letter quite well.[118] What is described

---

[116] For example, Psalm 90:2 (*NASB*) reads, "Before the mountains were born, Or You gave birth to the earth and the world, Even from everlasting to everlasting, You are God." Here references to the mountains being "born" and the earth coming to existence through "birth" are figurative or poetic ways of saying that they were *created* by God. But does this rule out the possibility that Christ was "born" as opposed to "created"?

[117] Robert M. Bowman Jr., J. Ed Komoszewski, *Putting Jesus in His Place, The Case for the Deity of Christ* (Grand Rapids: Kregel, 2007), pp. 105-106.

[118] Justin Martyr, Clement of Alexandria, Origen, Eusebius of Caesarea, Cyril of Jerusalem, Ambrose, Cyril of Alexandria, John of Damascus, as well as Arius and Athanasius, all believed that the "wisdom" of Proverbs 8:22 was the *logos* of John 1:1—which became embodied in the

The Father-Son Relationship

there would also seem to square away with the fact that, as John said, the *"logos"* was "with/toward" God in the beginning, and, when on earth, how Jesus prayed that he would be glorified with God, his Father, with the glory he had "beside" or "alongside" God "before the world began." With respect to the figure/concept of "wisdom" (*sophia*) itself (a concept closely related to *logos*), the writer of Proverbs wrote (according to *RSV* translation):

> **The LORD created me at the beginning of his work, the first of his acts of old** [compare the description of God's Son as *'the firstborn of all creation'*, Colossians 1:15]. **Ages ago I was set up, at the first, before the beginning of the earth.**

The Hebrew word *'qanah,'* translated in *RSV* as "created," "made" (*TEV*), "framed" (*Byington*), is translated "possessed" in some translations (*KJV*, *NASB*), carrying a different idea altogether.[119] Thus the observation was made in *The Daily Study Bible*, "There are three ways of taking the first phrase of verse 22: (1) 'The Lord possessed me' (AV, NIV), (2) 'The Lord created me' (RSV, NEB), or (3) 'The Lord brought me forth' (*ie* 'begot', NIV footnote). The problematic word is *quanah*. Basically it means to 'acquire', and so to 'possess'. It is often used of acquiring through purchasing (Gen. 47:20), but can also be used of acquiring through creating (Gen. 14:19) or begetting (cf. Gen. 4:1). All three translations are therefore possible."[120] However, the section of Proverbs goes on to say:

---

man Jesus Christ. Thus in the Roman Catholic *Jerusalem Bible* it was noted that "Christian tradition from St. Justin onwards sees in the Wisdom of the O.T. the person of Christ himself." Also, "the Greek [Septuagint], Syriac Peshitta., Aramaic Targums, cf Si 1:4,9; 24:8,9, translate the Hebrew verb (*qanani*) ['Yahweh *created* me']. The translation 'acquired me' or 'possessed me' (Aquila, Symmachus, Theodotion) was adopted by St Jerome (Vulgate), doubtless with an eye to the heritc Arius who maintained that the Word (= Wisdom) was a created being." (New York: Doubleday, 1966), p. 943.

[119] The Septuagint also has 'created' (Gk: *ektise*). *Strong's Dictionary* gives both meanings as possible: "primitive roots to erect, i.e. create; by extension, to procure, especially by purchase (causatively, sell); by implication own." Commenting on the statement in Proverbs, *The New Bible Dictionary* (a work of Protestant scholarship) observes: "wisdom claims to be the first creation of God and, perhaps, an assistant in the work of creation..." (p. 1256).

[120] *The Daily Study Bible (Old Testament)* (Philadelphia: The Westminster Press, 1986), p. 82.

The Father-Son Relationship

When there were no depths I was brought forth ['I was born,' *NJB*]**, when there were no springs abounding with water. Before the mountains had been shaped, before the hills, I was brought forth ['I came to birth,'** *NJB*]**; before he had made the earth with its fields, or the first of the dust of the world. When he established the heavens, I was there, when he drew a circle on the face of the deep, when he made firm the skies above, when he established the fountains of the deep, when he assigned to the sea its limit, so that the waters might not transgress his command, when he marked out the foundations of the earth, then I was beside him** [compare John 17:5], **like a master workman; and I was daily his delight, rejoicing before him always, rejoicing in his inhabited world and delighting in the sons of men.**[121]

As mentioned, there is disagreement among Bible scholars about how we should understand the Hebrew word as either "possessed/acquired" or "created." But the footnotes in the *New English Translation* have the following observation:

> There are two roots (*qanah*) in Hebrew, one meaning 'to possess,' and the other meaning 'to create.' The older translations did not know of the second root, but suspected in certain places that a meaning like that was necessary (e.g., Gen 4:1; 14:19; Deut 32:6). Ugaritic confirmed that it was indeed another root. The older versions have the translation 'possess' because otherwise it sounds like God lacked wisdom and therefore created it at the beginning. They wanted to avoid saying that wisdom was not eternal. Arius liked the idea of Christ as the wisdom of God and so chose the translation 'create.' Athanasius translated it, 'constituted me as the head of creation.' The verb occurs twelve times in Proverbs with the meaning of 'to acquire'; but the Greek and the Syriac versions have the meaning 'create.' Although the idea is that wisdom existed before creation, the parallel ideas in

---

[121] Proverbs 8:22-31, *RSV*.

these verses ('appointed,' 'given birth') argue for the translation of 'create' or 'establish' The third parallel verb is (*kholalti*) [v. 24], 'I was given birth.' Some translate it 'brought forth'—not in the sense of being presented, but in being 'begotten, given birth to.' Here is the strongest support for the translation of (*qanah*) as 'created' in v. 22.[122]

The Interpreters' Bible is also in agreement on this point: "The verb *qanah* may be translated either way [*possessed me* or *created me* (with LXX)]. In view of the statements made in the following verses concerning wisdom, it would seem that the RSV ['created'] translates correctly."[123]

Similarly, according to the notes in the *Anchor Bible* commentary: "The words' *lexical* meaning, the semantic content it brings to context, is 'acquire,' no more than that. But one way something can be acquired is by creation. English 'acquire' implies that the object was already in existence, but this is not the case with *qanah*. To avoid misunderstanding, the better translation in context is 'created.' While both 'created' and 'acquired' are legitimate contextual translations of this verb, 'possessed' (Vul[gate], KJV) is not."[124]

Instead of "created," other prominent English translations have "fathered" (*ESV*mgn.), "produced" (*NWT*), "formed" (*AT*), "begot" (*NAB*), "constituted" (*Rotherham*), "brought forth" (*NIV*). If such is the intended meaning, and Proverbs 8:22-33 is

---

[122] Another commentary made the same point: "The verb *qanah* can mean either 'possess' or 'create.'...Although the idea is that wisdom existed before creation, the parallel ideas in these verses (*qanani* ['brought me forth,' v. 22]; *nissakti* ['I was appointed,' v. 23]; and *kholalti* ['I was given birth,' v. 24] argue for the idea of 'create/establish.'" —*The Expositor's Bible Commentary* (Grand Rapids: Zondervan, 1991), p. 946. According to another source, "In view of the following verb ('I was brought forth,' vv 24-24), 'beget' seems preferable (cf. also Gen 4:1)..." —Murphy, *Word Biblical Commentary, Proverbs*, Volume 22 (Nashville: Thomas Nelson, p. 1998), p. 48.
[123] *The Interpreter's Bible, Volume IV, The Book of Psalms, The Book of Proverbs* (Nashville: Abingdon Press, 1980), p. 830.
[124] *The Anchor Bible, Proverbs 1-9, A New Translation with Introduction and Commentary*, by Michael V. Fox (New York: Doubleday, 2000), p. 279. On page 280, it was observed, "*Qanah* is used of human acquisition of wisdom in Prov 4:7a: 'The beginning of wisdom is: get (*qeneh*) wisdom!; also 1:5; 4:5; 15:32; 16:16; 17:16; 18:15; 19:8; 23:23. At the same time, since *qanah* can refer to the parent's role in procreation, this verb introduces the theme of *begetting* as the governing metaphor in describing this act of creation."

The Father-Son Relationship

attributable to Christ, understanding the term in any one of these ways could also support the notion that God's Son ('the word' and 'wisdom of God,' Revelation 19:13; 1 Corinthians 1:24) came into existence before the creation of the world, not as a "creation" *per se*, but through having been "born" or "begotten" of God as his first and foremost spiritual offspring (the 'exact reproduction of God's very being' Hebrews 1:3)—God's *firstborn* Son, "the *firstborn* of all creation."[125] The interpretation can only be established, of course, if one can, at the same time, clearly demonstrate that the "wisdom" of Proverbs 8 can be equated with a "pre-human-Son-of-God" concept, another point that continues to be debated among students of the Bible.

Justin Martyr (100-150 C.E.) appeared to hold to the "pre-human-Son-of-God" concept when he wrote in the second century: "But this Offspring which was truly brought forth from the Father, was with the Father before all the creatures, and the Father communed with Him; even as the Scripture by Solomon [Pr 8:22-31] has made clear, that He whom Solomon calls Wisdom, was begotten as a Beginning before all His creatures and as Offspring by God…"[126] In his well-known Dialogue with Trypho, Justin also said of the Son: "He was *begotten* of the Father by an act of will…", and later that "the Scripture has declared that this Offspring was begotten by the Father before all things created; and that that which is begotten is numerically distinct from that which begets, any one will admit." He also said, with respect to the *logos*: "God begat before all creatures a Beginning, [who was] a certain rational power [proceeding] from himself…"[127] Of God the Father, Tertullian (ca. 190-220 C.E.) believed, "He has

---

[125] However, it was pointed out by one commentary: "We should notice that the ideas of creation and birth are not nearly so diametrically opposed in Old Testament thought as we might suppose—and as they later became in the Christological controversies of the early Church, as indicated in the phrasing of the Nicene creed 'begotten, not made'. In the Old Testament, birth can happily be described as an act of creation (Ps. 139:13; cf Deut. 32:36), and an act of creation just as happily as a birth (Ps. 90:2). The language is in any case poetical and metaphorical, and the choice between created and born is not of terribly great importance." —*The Daily Study Bible*, pp. 82, 83.
[126] *Ante-Nicene Fathers*, Vol. 1, chap. 62, (Grand Rapids: Eerdmans, 1973), p. 228.
[127] *Ante-Nicene Fathers*, Vol. 1, pp. 227, 264.

The Father-Son Relationship

not always been Father and Judge, merely on the ground of His having always been God. For He could not have been the Father previous to the Son, nor a Judge previous to sin. There was, however, a time when neither sin existed with Him, nor the Son."[128]

There is another text that has been interpreted to mean that Jesus Christ was God's first "creation." In the book of Revelation, Jesus Christ is called "the Amen, the faithful and true witness, the beginning of the creation of God." (Revelation 3:14, *KJV*)—"the beginning of the creatures of God" (*Tyndale*, 1525). But even the precise nuance of this text is open to question. The Greek word *arche* is correctly translated "beginning" but can also mean "ruler," so that Christ could be described here as "the ruler of God's creation," as in *NIV*. Although this particular meaning for Revelation 3:14 is less likely,[129] it would still harmonize with the rest of the Scriptures which teach that God appointed Jesus to be "Lord of all," granting him "all authority in heaven and on earth," so that he would indeed be fittingly described as the one who rules over all that God has created (Compare Acts 2:36; 10:36; Matthew 28:18).

It is worth noting at this point how several of the Ante-Nicene Christians believed, evidently, that "the word" or *logos* itself was *eternally* within the mind or heart of the Father,[130] but,

---

[128] *Ante-Nicene Fathers*, Vol. 3, Chap. III (Hendrickson Publishers, 2004), p. 478. Although Tertullian is often pointed to as among the first to use the word "trinity," his statements clearly demonstrate that he did not have in mind the same meaning/doctrine of the "Trinity" that the modern-day orthodox do. According to mainstream Trinitarianism, Jesus, as *a Son*, is "coeternal" with the Father. In the fourth century, Athanasius, considered by many to be one of the first champions of christological orthodoxy, claimed that: "Those who maintain 'There was a time when the Son was not' rob God of his Word, like plunderers." On this point, Athanasius was in direct conflict with the fathers who preceded him.

[129] Mark 1:1 speaks of "The beginning (*arche*) of the gospel of Jesus Christ, the Son of God." Here *arche* (beginning) is obviously part of "the gospel of Jesus Christ." In the same way, "the beginning of the creation of God" could easily and, again, most naturally, be taken to mean that the *arche* is part (although the first) of "the creation of God."

[130] Theophilus wrote, "God, then, having His own Word internal within His own bowels begat him, emitting him along with His own Wisdom before all things. He had this Word as a helper in the things that were created by Him, and by him He created all things." (To Autoclychus, Chap. 10) —*Ante Nicene Fathers*, Volume 2, p. 98.

at a certain point, perhaps when the Father issued forth his first utterance, "the word" had independent existence as God's "first-begotten." Today, some even believe that "the word"—whether eternal or not—was not necessarily a personal being, but that the Son, as a person, came into existence when Jesus Christ was born as a man on earth and that this is where the actual birth or begettal of "the Son" took place—the point when "the word became flesh" (John 1:14). There is, however, what most view as a considerable number of passages that seem to suggest that Jesus Christ did have a real, personal, pre-human existence as God's Son prior to his coming to the earth, making it difficult for many to see, at least on the surface, how such a view could be maintained. For the most part, controversies regarding the so-called "pre-human" existence of Christ have revolved around the question of whether or not certain expressions made by Christ and others in Scripture should be taken *literally* or in a kind of *metaphorical* sense; or, in some cases, what some interpreters have described as the "prophetic past tense."[131]

There are other expressions found in Scripture that seem to point in this direction (that the Son came into existence through begettal) as well. 1 John 5:18 in the *NIV* reads: "We know that anyone born of God does not continue to sin; *the one who was born of God* keeps him safe, and the evil one does not touch him." Some translations attempt to make explicit in this case what they believe to be the implicit meaning (see, for example, *JB* and *PME* translations). If the understanding

---

[131] See: John 3:13; 6:32, 33, 38, 50, 51, 62; 8:14, 23, 42, 58 (*Living Bible*); 16:28; 17:5, 24. An argument can be made, however, that none of these texts need to be taken *literally*. The difficulty seems to lie in whether or not we can make that determination with certainty. The "prophetic past tense," otherwise known as "prolepsis," is a scriptural reference to a future, destined event spoken of as if it has already taken place. This occurs, for example, in Isaiah 53, which speaks of the one who "*was wounded* for our transgressions" and "*bruised* for our iniquities..." Here the prophet speaks of a future event (from the prophet's time and perspective) as if it had occurred in the past. Evidently, this means that Christ's atoning death was so certain in the mind, purpose, and plan of God that it could be spoken of *as if* it already occurred, although it would *really* take place in the future. This is essentially how some interpreters view Jesus' statement at John 17:5 and other expressions that seem to suggest that he existed before his physical birth and before the world was created.

The Father-Son Relationship

expressed by these translations is correct, Jesus is once again described as one who *was* "born" or "begotten" of God.[132]

The producers of the *New English Translation* reject this interpretation in their footnotes, arguing that for Christ to be the subject here comes across as "sudden." But the context appears to support the meaning that "the one born from God" is Jesus Christ (who is, in fact, God's *Son*); for in verse 20 John goes on to say that "the Son of God has come and has given us discernment to know the one who is true" (*NAB*). This is consistent in terms of the continuity of thought with respect to the Son of God's active involvement in watching over and protecting God's people so that "the evil one" would not be able to overcome and destroy them.[133] The footnote in the *NIV Study Bible* agrees: "*The one who was born of God.* Jesus, the Son of God." *The Interpreters' Bible* is also in agreement on this point: "He who was born of God [i.e., Christ] keeps him." A. T. Robertson observed:

> *He that was begotten of God* (*ho gennetheis ek tou theou*). First aorist passive articular participle referring to Christ, if the reading of A B [the Alexandrine and Vatican Codices] is correct (*terei auton*, not *terei heauton*). It is Christ who keeps the one begotten of God (*gegennemenos ek tou theou* as in 3:9 and so different from *ho gennetheis* here). It is a difficult phrase, but this is probably the idea. Jesus (John 18:37) uses *gegennemai* of himself and uses also *tereo* of keeping the disciples (John 17:12, 15; Revelation 3:10).[134]

According to the popular *New Testament Commentary* by William Hendriksen & Simon J. Kistemaker:

In the next clause, John presents a message that appears

---

[132] *RSV, LB, TEV, NEB* (apparently *NASB, ESV*) are in agreement with this understanding (that the subject is the Son of God)

[133] Compare John 10:27-28: "My sheep hear my voice, and I know them, and they follow me; and I give them eternal life, and they shall never perish, and no one shall snatch them out of my hand."

[134] *Word Pictures in the New Testament, Volume VI*, p. 244.

The Father-Son Relationship

to be vague. What does he mean by the words 'The one who was born of God keeps him safe'?... If God keeps the believer safe, the phrase 'the one who was born of God' must refer to Jesus Christ...Because both Jesus and the believers are called 'born of God,' John differentiates by using the past tense 'was born' for Jesus and the phrase *born of God* for the believer. Furthermore, John places Jesus 'who was born of God' over against 'the evil one.' Jesus keeps the believers safe and asks God to protect them from the evil one (John 17:12, 15).[135]

The observation in the *Tyndale Commentaries* is helpful at this point as well:

> The AV, following the Codex Sinaiticus and most of the Greek manuscripts, reads 'he that is begotten of God keepeth himself'. For the concept of 'keeping oneself' see 1 Timothy 5:22; James 1:37; Jude 21, and also 3:3. The very important Alexandrine and Vatican Codices, however, which are followed by the Vulgate, have not *himself* (*heauton*) but him (*auton*). So the NIV. If, as seems probable, the latter is the correct reading, then the subject of the verb (*viz.* 'he that is begotten of God' or *the one who was born of God*) is Christ, not the Christian, and the truth here taught is not that the Christian keeps himself but that Christ keeps him. In adopting this interpretation, the RSV eliminates ambiguity by printing 'He' with a capital letter: 'but He who was born of God keeps him'. So the NEB 'it is the Son of God who keeps him safe'. If this is correct, we need to note that John deliberately uses almost identical expressions to portray Christ and the Christian, at the beginning and end of verse 18. Both are said to be *born of God*; only the tense of the verb is different. It is appropriate that *the one who was born of God* should keep safe *anyone born of God*.[136]

---

[135] *New Testament Commentary, Exposition of James, Epistles of John, Peter, and Jude* (Grand Rapids: Baker Books, 1996), pp. 365, 366. Footnote: "*auton*—manuscript evidence for the reflexive pronoun *eauton* (himself) is strong. However, internal evidence together with varied textual witnesses favors the personal pronoun *auton* (him)."

[136] *Tyndale New Testament Commentaries, The Letters of John, An Introduction and Commentary*, by John R. W. Stott, (Grand Rapids: Baker Books, 1990), pp. 194-195. According

The Father-Son Relationship

If the reading of the Alexandrine and Vatican Codices is accepted, then the idea that the Son *was* "born of God" (past tense) would weigh heavily against the notion typically associated with Trinitarian doctrine called the "eternal generation of Christ." This is a difficult concept to grasp. For some of the defenders of the doctrine advanced by Athanasius in the fourth century would have agreed that Christ *is* "begotten" of God—even professing that the Son was "begotten" and not "made." But instead of meaning "begotten" or "born" in the sense that we would normally understand it (coming into being or existence, i.e., born into the world), it meant, to them, somehow, "eternally" born (an *eternal* generation—no beginning or end). Unfortunately, for those who hold to this view, nowhere does the Bible teach that Jesus was somehow "eternally begotten" of God. But the Bible *does* (if the translation and understanding of 1 John 5:18 is correct; *NASB*) indicate that Jesus "was" born of God, clearly indicating that this was an event that actually took place at some point in the past.

J.O. Buswell, a Trinitarian and former Dean of Covenant College, concluded as the result of his scriptural investigation:

> The notion that the Son was begotten by the Father in eternity past, not as an event, but as an inexplicable relationship, has been accepted and carried along in Christian theology since the fourth century...We have examined all the instances in which 'begotten' or 'born' or related words are applied to Christ, and we can say with confidence that the Bible has nothing whatsoever to say about 'begetting' as an eternal relationship between the Father and the Son.[137]

---

to another respected source: "In 1 John most references to being born of God relate to believers...However, the reference here in 5:18 to 'the one born of God' is best interpreted as a reference to Jesus himself. That this is an appropriate interpretation is supported by the fact that in the Fourth Gospel Jesus is portrayed as the one who keeps his disciples safe. In Jesus' prayer in John 17 he speaks of having kept safe all those whom God had given him (except Judas, who was doomed to destruction), and prays, not that God will take them out of the world, but that he will 'protect them from the evil one (John 17:12-15).'" —*The Pillar New Testament Commentary*, General Editor D. A. Carson, *The Letters of John*, (Grand Rapids: Baker, 2000), p. 195.

[137] *A Systematic Theology of the Christian Religion* (Grand Rapids: Zondervan, 1962), p. 110.

The Father-Son Relationship

So, whatever the case may be in the end, whether the Son of God was "created," "begotten," "generated" or "produced" by God before God brought "the all things" into existence through him (Compare: John 1:3; Colossians 1:16), there can be no doubt in terms of what the Scriptures teach about his essential identity, ultimate origin, and dependence upon his Father for life; for Jesus himself made clear to his followers, not that he *was* "God," but that he "proceeded and came forth *from* God," indeed that he "*came out* from God."[138] He did not teach that the life he had was originally based on his own internal, self-sufficient or self-generating power, but that the life he had within himself was that which was "granted" to him and that he himself "lives *because* of the Father."[139]

Even if, in the course of study, one remains uncertain as to whether or not God's Son was born of God at some point before the creation of the world, or if his only real birth took place in Bethlehem, we can know scripturally that his true "origins are in the distant past, from the days of age-past time,"[140] that he lived as a flesh-and-blood man approximately two-thousand-years ago (a fact attested by the Gospel accounts and independent secular writings)—that although he was put do death through the instigation of his religious contemporaries, three days after, God raised him to immortal life and exalted him to the highest place of honor; that he is the God-appointed righteous ruler of the coming age, that he *lives now* and will *always live*, and that he gives life to all those exercising faith in his name.

In reference to the same issues that have been discussed, one Bible student made the following comments that may help to put the issues into a healthy and balanced perspective—if not accurate in every detail, at least beneficial in terms of the overall

---

[138] John 8:42; 16:28; "out of God I came forth…", *RSV, Concordant Literal New Testament*
[139] John 5:26; 6:57
[140] Micah 5:2, *New English Translation, Rotherham's Emphasized Bible*. Micah 5:2 could mean that the origin of the Messiah's life extended even further back in time than his birth in Bethlehem (referring to a 'pre-human existence'). But some argue that this could simply be a reference to the Messiah's ancestral roots (David, Abraham, etc.).

approach and spirit that comes through:

> Something we need to keep in mind when considering this matter is that time is a human measure. There was no such thing as time in the sense that we think of time before the creation of the heavens and the earth. It was first, then, when the 'lights in the expanse of the sky' appeared to 'mark the seasons and days and years.' (Gen. 1:14) When we get to talking about things that took place before creation—before time—we get into a sphere of reality we know absolutely nothing about. We run into the same trouble when we start talking about God's form or substance...When we start talking about what 'stuff' God is composed of we are talking out of profound ignorance. Men may invent words to describe what we cannot know and attach their own meanings to these words, but that doesn't change the reality that we simply do not know. Similarly, we cannot know when the one called the 'Word' (*logos*) appeared or how he [it?] came to be, or if there was a time when he [it?] was not. In the unmeasured epoch which preceded creation, we are not told what happened or how it happened. Whether we place the pre-existent Word within creation or set [the Word] apart from it doesn't change the fact that [the Word] became flesh. We know we must look to Christ for all things at this time because it has pleased the Father to submit all things and all creatures to him. He died for us and he now lives for us. He will judge us, he will resurrect us, he will give us immortal life, he is the head of his body, the church, and we gladly bow down before him as our Lord and King. In doing this we know we please the Father who has ordained it to be so. In time, Christ's rule will accomplish the complete will of the Father. In time all of the unknowns will be made known. Until then we must be content with what God has been pleased to give us—and what a wonderfully full and enriching storehouse that is! We are fully informed about ourselves and our condition, our needs and what God has done to satisfy those needs. We are fully informed as to what lies ahead—beyond the horizon of this present age.

The Father-Son Relationship

I'm convinced that what we must know and believe is fully and completely presented to us in the Scripture. The real challenge, as I see it, is not knowing what to believe or what God asks of us, but the spiritual strength to faithfully live out those things from moment-to-moment and from day-to-day; Jesus tells us, 'Now that you know these things, you will be blessed if you do them.' (John 13:17) That is our challenge.[141]

As we continue exploring the rich treasure of God's revealed word of truth, we should always remember that the Scripture itself—along with the Spirit that would guide the disciples "into all the truth" (John 16:13)—continues to abide as the most reliable resource for the understanding and application of true Christian faith.[142] Yet the Scriptures—inspired by God through that same Spirit—do not characterize the relationship Jesus has to God in the theological or metaphysical terms of "coequal," "coeternal" or "consubstantial," but in the simple, filial and familiar terms of a "Father" and a "Son." These are in fact the terms that satisfactorily define and inform us regarding the true nature of Christ's relationship to God and God's relationship to Christ.[143] These are the terms presented to us in the Bible. In spite of the confusion and differences of opinion that still exist, a careful study of the Gospels reveal that the Son was very careful about the way he spoke about his relationship to God, his Father. The Father has life in himself but "granted" the Son to have the same. The Father is "greater" than the Son,

---

[141] Ron Frye, *The Father/Son Relationship* (Published by Christian Correspondent, Inc. 1999. Available at Commentary Press, pp. 86, 87 (words in brackets added).

[142] 2 Timothy 3:16-17

[143] "The consistent repetition of the designation of God as 'the Father who sent me' not only underscores the identity of Jesus in terms of his relationship to God but also the reverse—God is most characteristically identified and named in relationship to Jesus. Furthermore, when Jesus and God are defined in mutual relationship, the terms used to designate their relationship are 'Son' and 'Father.' While the term 'Father' for God has a history of usage independent of the Gospel, the virtual limitation of 'Father' to the relationship of God to Jesus as Son moves toward a reshaping of the content of the word 'God.' What it means to know God is to know God as the Father of the Son, and this inevitably implies a reconceptualization of the identity of God. Hence, the Father-Son language of the Gospel of John is a prime example of the point that NT Christology is formulated primarily in relational terms, and that it articulates the relationship of God and God to Jesus." —Thompson, *The God of the Gospel of John*, p. 51.

The Father-Son Relationship

but—according to the Son's apostles—has, due to the Son's perfect life of obedience, "exalted" the Son to his right hand, having fittingly appointed the Son to be the inheritor of all things.

The Bible itself does not identify Jesus as "God the Son," but it does tell us that he is God's "beloved Son," "the apostle and high priest of our confession."[144] The Scriptures do not teach that it is obligatory to believe or confess that the Son is "of one substance/being" with God. But the Scriptures *do* teach that the Son is the very "image of the invisible God," "the reflection (or outshining) of God's glory, and the exact representation of God's very being."[145] *These* are the terms of the Father-Son relationship, presented to us in a very direct way by God's Son himself, and of course, by his carefully-selected and divinely-authorized representatives.

As imperfect human beings, we may never be able to fully understand the intricacies and depths of the intimate relationship and special bond of union that exists between God and his Son. But this is what the Father has been pleased to reveal about the nature of his Son and their relationship to one another, according to the language that the Father himself has chosen to use, the language of the Bible. Christians are simply not required to accept or confess faith in that which exceeds what has been revealed by Christ and subsequently preserved in the Scriptures.

Contrary to the official proclamations of Evangelical-Protestant and Roman Catholic leaders, post-biblical, "creedal" definitions and formulas are not needed to safeguard or protect

---

[144] The word "apostle" (Gk: *apostolos*) simply denotes 'one commissioned/sent forth.' However, it was observed by New Testament Professor D.A. Carson: "It is arguable that although *apostolos* is cognate with *apostello* ['I send'], New Testament use of the noun does not center on the meaning *the one sent*; but on 'messenger.' Now a messenger is usually sent; but the word *messenger* also calls to mind the message the person carries, and suggests he represents the one who sent him. In other words, actual usage in the New Testament suggests that *apostolos* commonly bears the meaning of a *special representative* or a *special messenger* rather than 'someone sent out.'" —*Exegetical Fallacies* (Grand Rapids: Baker Books, 1996), p. 30. If Jesus literally is or was "God in the flesh," why did he always speak about himself (and why does the Bible always speak of him) as one who was sent as a *representative* of another?

[145] Hebrews 1:3; 3:1; Colossians 1:15

against false teaching; for this is one of the principal ends for which Scripture itself was intended.[146] Although the fourth-century doctrine of the Trinity claims ability to give a true and authoritative definition of Christ's relationship to the Father, the Bible already accurately and satisfactorily defined that relationship. Although the Father is God and Jesus is the Son "born" from him, our fixing attention and directing our devotion to God's Son in no way interferes with, detracts, compromises, or takes away from, the glory of the one God; instead, it magnifies that glory. According to the Scriptures, it is God's will that we recognize Jesus as our Lord, by God's own appointment. Because of this, we can always be sure that God is pleased when we honor, exalt and glorify his Son, recognizing him as our head, our King, and as our blessed savior—something we can fully accomplish without reference to the post-biblical creeds.

---

[146] 2 Timothy 3:14-17

"Reason directs those who are truly pious and philosophical [those who love wisdom] to honour and love only what is true, declining to follow traditional opinions [lit., 'the opinions of the ancients'], if these be worthless. For not only does sound reason direct us to refuse the guidance of those who did or taught anything wrong, but it is incumbent on the lover of truth, by all means, and if death be threatened, even before his own life, to choose to do and say what is right."
—Justin Martyr (110-165 C.E) *The First Apology of Justin, Ante Nicene Fathers*, Vol. 1, p. 163.

>"Once a belief has been accepted both intellectually and emotionally as truth, any challenge to that cherished tenet is liable to almost automatic rejection. The very human desire of all of us to conform to the group which has nourished us and the lifetime of patterns of thought learned from sincere teachers we trusted and respected tends to create barriers which secure us against all objections and can blind us to the most obvious truths. When those deeply held beliefs are challenged, we naturally feel threatened and defensive....Few Christians can conceive the possibility that they may have embraced long-standing error."
>—Anthony F. Buzzard and Charles F. Hunting, *The Doctrine of the Trinity, Christianity's Self-Inflicted Wound*

4

The "deity" of Jesus Christ

> "...confusion regarding 'meaning of god' and 'concepts about God' can be illustrated by the question of identity most frequently asked about Jesus: Does the NT call Jesus God? Once an affirmative answer is received, the inquirer then assumes that we understand who Jesus is: Jesus is God. However, the crucial question here is, What does the NT *mean* when it calls Jesus God?" —Marianne Thompson, *The God of the Gospel of John*, p. 19 (emphasis added).

For the most part, arguments in favor of the Trinity have focused primarily on proving from the Scriptures that Jesus is called "God," or that he has the same attributes as God, or that he was worshiped by the apostles and Christians of the first century.[1] Although several passages often said to call Jesus "God" are debatable as far as translation is concerned, there *are*

---

[1] It is worthy to note that although Trinitarians profess that the "three persons" of the Trinity are worthy of equal worship, they do not generally give equal treatment or attention in trying to prove from Scripture that the holy Spirit is identical with God as the third member of the Trinity. In his *New Systematic Theology of the Christian Faith*, described by one evangelical pastor as "an excellent biblical defense of the doctrine of the trinity," Robert Reymond devotes 107 pages trying to prove from Scripture that Jesus is God in the Trinitarian sense; but only spends 4 pages on the "deity" and "personhood" of the holy Spirit.

in fact a few occasions where the writers of Scripture undoubtedly applied the Hebrew or Greek words for "God" (or 'god') to the Messiah.[1] However, in an inquiry of this kind, the principal question of concern is not really whether or not the Messiah is described by the writers of Scripture as *el* (Hebrew for 'god') or *theos* (Greek for 'god'), for the writers of Scripture ascribe the term to others as well. The question is: What was the true significance of describing the Messiah in this way? And, in the context of that period of time, what did the writers of Scripture have in mind? This is the main question that will be explored and focused upon throughout the foregoing discussion.

Since in the New Testament the term *theos* (or *ho theos*) almost always refers to God the Father, when the New Testament writers called Jesus *theos* did they mean that Jesus Christ *was* God the Father, the "one God" (1 Corinthians 8:6)? Or, did they think—as Trinitarianism teaches—that Jesus was distinct from the Father "personally" but that he was, nevertheless, somehow, the same *God* as the Father; and did they understand this to mean that Jesus was one divine "person" within a Deity composed of two other persons, resulting in a total of three? Or, is it possible that the scriptural writers thought of Jesus as God's perfect representative, and did they mean, in certain instances, that Jesus himself was a unique, exalted being (or a human endowed with divine power) distinguishable from, though in close union, complete harmony with, and in the service of, the "one God"? These are, it seems, among the most basic questions that may be asked in light of the biblical application of the term "God" to Jesus Christ.

In order to accurately understand what the Bible writers meant when they applied the term God to Jesus Christ, it will not

---

[1] Isaiah 9:6 gives the Messiah the name "Mighty God" (Hebrew: *el gibbhor*). The Greek word for god (*theos*) is applied to "the word (*ho logos*)" in the NT without a doubt at John 1:1 ('and the word became flesh' in the man Jesus; v. 14), more than likely to Christ in v. 18 and in Hebrews 1:8, and to the risen Christ by Thomas at John 20:28. Romans 9:5, Titus 2:13 and 2 Peter 1:1 may or may not call Christ God. These last three texts involve questions of how to accurately translate the sense of the verse from Greek into English. Some scholars argue in favor of Jesus being called God in these texts; others argue that the term applies to the Father. Technically, both translations are grammatically possible.

The "deity" of Jesus Christ

be necessary to refer to the theological formulations of early Church councils; nor will we benefit from attempting to apply and integrate the categories of ancient Greek philosophy. In this case, the principal thing to do is to take into consideration how the term "god" was used and understood in the Bible, throughout both the Hebrew and Greek Scriptures. That is, only when we take into account the *biblical* usage of the term will an accurate picture begin to unfold. In this regard it is crucial to appreciate the fact that in the Scriptures the term "god" actually has a much broader application than many are sometimes inclined to think. Naturally, the word (*elohim* or *theos*) is, in its highest sense, used as a title or descriptive term for Jehovah, the Most High God.[2] Yet not many are fully aware that the term is also used to describe angels (God's celestial messengers), certain humans (particularly the kings and judges of ancient Israel), the various so-called "gods" of the nations that once surrounded Israel, and, evidently, to Satan himself—"the god of this age."[3]

In his scholarly work, *Jesus as God* (an in-depth evaluation of the term 'God' as it refers to Jesus in the NT), evangelical biblical scholar Murray J. Harris documents how others in addition to the Almighty One are appropriately called "gods" in Scripture. As mentioned, these include:

> Human rulers or judges, regarded as divine representatives or as bearers of divine authority and majesty (Exod. 21:6; 22:8 [cf. 1 Sam. 2:25]; Judg. 5:8; Psalm 82:1, 6) b. Spiritual or heavenly beings, including God (Gen. 1:27) and angels (Psalm 8:6 [Engl. V. 5]) c. Angels (Ps. 97:7; 138: 1) d. Heathen gods with their images (Exod. 20:23; Jer. 16:20) …both *el*, [meaning 'god'] and *elohim* [meaning 'gods'], have extended or 'irregular' applications to angels or to persons who represent on earth divine power, judgment, or majesty.[4]

---

[2] Scholars generally agree that the Hebrew word *el* carries with it the idea of strength, power, or might, so that the term "God" would essentially mean *Mighty* or *Powerful One*.

[3] 2 Corinthians 4:4

[4] *Jesus as God, the New Testament Use of Theos in Reference to Jesus*, pp. 24, 26. Professor Thompson similarly pointed out: "human judges are called *elohim* [gods], even as they are called

The "deity" of Jesus Christ

As Harris points out, in the Bible the term "god(s)" may in fact apply to angels or persons on earth who *represent* divine power and majesty. A brief consideration of some specific examples will be helpful at this point.

According to the book of Exodus, one of the oldest books of the Bible, Jehovah said that Moses would serve as "God" to his brother Aaron:

> **You are to speak to him and put the words in his mouth; and I, even I, will be with your mouth and his mouth, and I will teach you what you are to do. Moreover, he shall speak for you to the people; and he will be as a mouth for you and you will be as God to him.**[5]

In the seventh chapter of Exodus, Moses was made "God" to another:

> **And Jehovah said to Moses, See, I have made thee God to Pharaoh; and Aaron thy brother shall be thy prophet.**[6]

In the time of God's ancient people, during the period before kings Saul, David and Solomon, magistrates, or "judges" as they were called, were appointed by God to "judge" (to direct and administer justice) or rule over the people of Israel. Because these judges were of a high rank and possessed judicial authority delegated to them by God, they were appropriately designated "gods" by God himself, as in the case of Psalm 82:6. In Psalm 45—a Scripture quoted later in the New Testament—the king of Israel was likewise honored with the title "God." The *NIV Study Bible* gives insight into why this was the case:

---

theoi [gods] in the Septuagint translation of the Hebrew (...Exod.22:27). In the Dead Sea Scrolls one finds angels spoken of as *elim* or *beney elim* [sons of God]...the latter in keeping with Psalms 29:1 and 89:7. Other passages from the Scrolls attest to the use of *elohim* [gods] for the angels, as is found in Psalms 8:6; 82:1, 6; 97:7; 138:1, and so on." —*The God of the Gospel of John*, p. 21.

[5] Exodus 4:15-16, *NASB*. Commenting on this verse, Bible scholar F. C. Cook likewise noted: "The word 'God' is used of persons who represent the Deity, as kings or judges, and it is understood in this sense here: 'Thou shalt be to him a master.' —*Barnes' Notes, The Bible Commentary, Exodus to Ruth*, p. 15.

[6] Exodus 7:1, *A New Translation from the Original Languages* by J. N. Darby.

In the language of the OT—and in accordance with the conceptual world of the ancient Near East—rulers and judges, as deputies of the heavenly King, could be given the honorific title 'god' (see note on 45:6; see also NIV text notes on Ex 21:6; 22:8) or be called 'son of God'...[7]

According to the *NRSV* translation, Psalm 82:1 reads: "God has taken his place in the divine council; in the midst of the gods he holds judgment." The "gods" mentioned in this particular case could represent either heavenly, angelic beings, or earthly, human magistrates. Nineteenth-century Bible scholar Albert Barnes, who believed the "divine council" or "congregation of the mighty" (*KJV*) applied to human magistrates, gave added insight into the reason why certain human beings could be called "gods," in reference to Psalm 82:1. He argued that the reference was

> undoubtedly to magistrates, and the idea is, that they were to be regarded as representatives of God; as acting in his name; and as those, therefore, to whom, in a subordinate sense, the name gods might be given. Compare Psalm 82:6. In Ex 21:6; 22:8-9, 28, also, the same word in the plural is applied to magistrates, and is properly translated *judges* in our common version…The idea is, that they were the representatives of the divine sovereignty in the administration of justice. Compare Rom 13:1-2, 6. They were, in a sense, *gods* to other people; but they were not to forget that God stood among them as their God; that if they were exalted to a high rank in respect to their fellow men, they were, nevertheless, subject to the One to whom the name of God belonged in the highest sense.[8]

---

[7] *The NIV Study Bible* (Grand Rapids: Zondervan, 1995), p. 866.

[8] *Barnes' Notes on the Old Testament, Psalms, Volume 1*, p. 328. However, there is some uncertainty respecting the reference. "The Septuagint renders it, *In the synagogue of the gods.* So also the Latin Vulgate." *NIV* translates: "the great assembly." J. P. Green has "assembly of the mighty." Whatever one determines as the reference (angels or judges; or even God, *Darby*) in this case, Barnes's comments are still valuable in terms of explaining why individuals beside God can be called gods in Scripture. Commenting on the statement, "in the midst of the gods he holds judgment," *The MacArthur Study Bible* (p. 815) says: "Some have taken this psalm to be about demons or false pagan gods. The best interpretation is that these 'gods' are human leaders, such

The "deity" of Jesus Christ

In Psalm 8:5 angels are likewise referred to as *elohim*—"gods":

You (that is, God) **have made him** ('the son of man') **a little lower than the** *elohim* (lit., 'gods'; 'heavenly beings' *ESV*; 'divine beings or angels.' *NRSV* footnote).[9]

Although some apologists have denied that *elohim* is a reference to the angels in this verse, not only does the Septuagint (Greek translation of the Hebrew Bible) translate *elohim* as angels (Gk: *angelous*), but we receive an important confirmation that such is the correct meaning when the author of Hebrews quotes from the Septuagint rendition, which, again, uses "angels" where the original Hebrew had "gods."[10] As Murray Harris suggested, the angels were referred to as "gods" probably because they represented God and were the possessors of god-like qualities (representing 'divine power' and 'majesty'). They are powerful, divine, spiritual beings who dwell with and serve God in the heavenly realm; often, acting as messengers to, and protectors of, God's people on earth; and even, at times, as bearers of divine judgment.[11]

With respect to the application of the term to certain humans, in John chapter ten, Jesus actually made the point that certain men of ancient Israel were properly called "gods," again, by God himself. In answer to the Jewish accusation of blasphemy, Jesus referred specifically to Psalm 82 where, as noted, the ancient rulers of Israel were referred to by the Hebrew

---

as judges, kings, legislators, and presidents (cf. Ex. 22:8, 9, 28; Judg.5:8, 9). God the Great Judge, presides over these lesser gods."

[9] *The Modern Language Bible* footnote states: "Angels=gods: Psalm 8:5, 'Yet Thou hast made him little less than heavenly beings [Heb: *elohim*] *and* Thou hast crowned him with glory and honor.'" The *NAB* footnote: "Hebrew *elohim*, the ordinary word for 'God' or 'the gods' or members of the heavenly court." *The NIV Study Bible*: "*heavenly beings*. The exalted angelic creatures that surround God in his heavenly realm (as, e.g., in Isa 6:2)." The *NASB* (Updated edition) translates the verse: "You have made him a little lower than *God.*" But the *Interpreter's Bible* rightly points out: "Obviously the psalmist would not say *than God.* The word *elohim* is capable of these three interpretations, since it means either a divine being (god) or divine beings (angels) or the divine being par excellence (God). The context must be our guide to its sense (cf. 97:7; 138:1)."

[10] Hebrews 2:7

[11] Compare Psalm 103:20; Genesis 19:13, 24; 2 Kings 19:35

elohim (Gk. *theoi*).[12] John MacArthur's commentary on this account is correct and helpful for the present investigation: "Jesus' argument is that this psalm *proves* that the word 'god' can be legitimately used to refer to others than God Himself. His reasoning is that if there are others whom God can address as 'god' or 'sons of the Most High,' why then should the Jews object to Jesus' statement that He is 'the Son of God' (v.36)?"[13]

Yet one might understandably ask: How do all these scriptural references to other "gods" square away with the scriptural teaching that there is *only one true* God? For example, in Isaiah 43:10, Jehovah explicitly said: "Before me there was no god formed, and after me there shall be none" (*NAB*). And in chapter 45, verse 5, God said, "I am Jehovah, and there is none else; besides me there is no God" (*ASV*).

Simply put, the writers of Scripture often used the term "God" with different senses. Although it is true that with the exception of Jehovah there is no God, there are still other individuals that can properly bear the description God/god, only in a different sense. Satan is described as "the god of this age" likely, because, as the apostle John tells us in his first letter, "the whole world lies in the power of the wicked one."[14] Expressing himself along very similar lines in the Gospel of John, Jesus himself called Satan "the ruler of this world."[15] Because Satan yields so much power and influence over the inhabited world, he is, according to Paul, "the god (*ho theos*)" of this present world system.[16]

---

[12] Some scholars identify the gods of Psalm 82:6 as angels.
[13] *MacArthur Study Bible*, p. 1605 (emphasis added).
[14] 1 John 5:19. A very small minority of Trinitarians dispute that "the god of this age" refers to Satan, suggesting that the phrase actually refers to God himself.
[15] John 12:31. This is probably another or similar way of calling Satan "the god of this age." It also suggests a close relationship between the idea of godship and the capacity to *rule* over others.
[16] The Greek word Paul used is *aion* and conveys the idea of 'age,' 'order' or 'system.' Unlike *kosmos* ('world') *aion* includes an aspect or element of time. MacArthur notes that *aion* refers to "an order or system, and in particular to the current world system ruled by Satan." —*MacArthur Study Bible*, p. 1788. According to another reference work, the word "as used of the *world*, presents it, in distinction from *kosmos*, in its temporal aspect, 'this present state of things." —S. D. F. Salmond, *The Expositor's Greek Testament*, Volume 3, p. 279.

Although it is true that Jehovah declared that he is the only God, the most outstanding point to keep in mind is that it was *Jehovah himself* who designated the ancient rulers of Israel with the honorific title "gods." Yet this never represented a contradiction, nor did it somehow imply that these "gods" must have been "of the same essence" or "being" as God; neither did the Bible writers intend for them to be thought of as "false gods." They were properly called gods because they had authority delegated to them by the Almighty God. That is why we benefit from remembering, as the Psalmist declared, "Jehovah is a great King over all other gods."[17] He is "the God of gods."[18] That is why the angels are commanded to worship Jehovah: "Worship him all ye gods...For thou, Jehovah art the Most High above all the earth; thou art exalted above all gods."[19]

With regard to such references, Marianne Thompson offers an insightful observation:

> Calling Israel's God the 'God of gods' raises the question of the status or existence of these other 'gods.' They may have been conceived of as divine or supernatural beings, whether beneficent or demonic. Clearly Jews and Christians alike believed in the existence of such entities. What is at issue in describing more precisely the nature or identity of these beings is their relationship to the Most High God. As Shaye Cohen notes, it is not belief in multiple heavenly beings that compromises monotheism, but rather the attribution of independence to them.[20]

In Isaiah, the historical context is key to understanding what Jehovah specifically meant when he said, "beside me there is no God." In reference to Isaiah 43:10, one author pointed out: "Jehovah was talking about how there were no *man-made* gods that could rival Him or equal His power. The Israelites often

---

[17] Psalm 95:3
[18] Psalm 136:2
[19] Psalm 97:9, Darby's translation. The Septuagint and the Vulgate render this as "all his angels."
[20] Thompson, *The God of the Gospel of John*, p. 28. Thompson refers to *From the Maccabees to the Mishnah, Library of Early Christianity* (Philadelphia: Westminster, 1987), p. 84.

looked to other gods for help and Jehovah was letting them know there were not other gods that could help them. They were figments of their imagination, manifested in man-made idols."[21]

In discussing the different kinds of applications and varying degrees of usage for the term "God" in Scripture, one student of Scripture observed:

> That the God of Israel is identified as 'Most High' (God), and 'Almighty' (God), should make it plain that the generic word for 'God,' either in the singular or plural form, does not carry a fixed value. The same word or words can be used to identify other gods or deities...If we keep in mind that the root from which the Hebrew El is derived indicates 'strength or might' we will not be aghast to see it sometimes used of men in the Old Testament. After all, there is the element of strength and might associated with human authority. The context in which either El or Elohim are used determines the value to be attached to those words. We make a mistake if we attach a fixed value to those words when the very source of our inquiry does not.[22]

Appreciating the well-established biblical tradition that there are beings beside God Almighty (particularly angels and human rulers) that can properly be called "god" or "gods" in a *positive* scriptural affirmation—without in any way compromising the biblical truth that there is only *one* Most High God—may in fact be the essential key to understanding those few texts, both in the Old and New Testaments, that do in fact apply the term "God" to God's Son, Jesus Christ. As pointed out, in the Old Testament, the term God was applied to Moses (Exodus 4:16; 7:1), to the king of Israel (possibly king Solomon; Psalm 45:6), to the pre-monarchical judges of Israel (Psalm 82:6), as well as to the angelic hosts of heaven (Psalm 8:5). They were all honored with the title, evidently, based on their

---

[21] Brian Holt, *Jesus—God or the Son of God?*, p. 53.
[22] Frye, *The Father/Son Relationship*, pp. 25, 26.

The "deity" of Jesus Christ

representative role (or function) and exalted position given to them *by* God.

In this light, and with these facts in mind, it is not difficult to see that if Moses and the king of Israel were considered "God" in some sense, and if angels and Israelite rulers were scripturally called "gods," how it would have been entirely fitting and, in fact, expected that the Lord Jesus himself, the long-awaited *Messiah*, would be spoken of in the same or similar way based on the unique honor that he rightfully deserves and which Scripture rightfully ascribes to him. Just as Moses served as God to Aaron and was God to Pharaoh, in a similar sense, it is not unreasonable that Jesus too would be recognized as "God" to his followers, as well as in the terms of his representation of God before the world in general. Thus it stands to reason, if the angelic beings of heaven are fittingly called "gods" in Scripture, how much more can the one who is "far superior to the angels" be honored with the same kind of exalted description (Hebrews 1:4, *NAB*)?

As God's Son, appointed King and exalted Messiah, Jesus is one who faithfully reflects the will, and perfectly represents the authority of, his Father, Jehovah God. It was observed by one source:

> The closest analogy to the use of the word (or title) 'god' for Jesus, however, is the use of such a term for Moses. Already Ex. 7.1 says that God makes Moses god to Pharaoh; and even before that Ex. 4:16 makes nearly the same claim (*le lohim,* 'as god') of Moses in his relation to Aaron. Consequently, Philo [1st century Jewish philosopher from Alexandria] does not hesitate to call Moses god, and in quite an unrestricted sense: 'for [Moses] was called god and king of the whole people, for he was said to enter the dark cloud wherein was God' (*Life Mos.* 1.158)…it is clear that by calling Moses god, Philo does not actually equate Moses with the supreme God, just as it is clear that the Johannine Christians, by calling Jesus god, do not actually equate him with the supreme God, inasmuch as Jesus is in Johannine tradition

The "deity" of Jesus Christ

otherwise Son of God and the revealer sent from heaven. Beyond Philo, the divine appellation adheres to Moses when Josephus calls him a *theios aner* ('divine man', *AF* 3.180). One may suspect, on the basis of this evidence, that there was some connection between the equation of Jesus with God in the Fourth Gospel and the comparison of Jesus to Moses."[23]

If we can verify from Scripture that mere men with a measure of authority from God can appropriately be called "gods" without calling into question the principle of "biblical monotheism," it is easy to see how fitting it was for Scripture to have called God's very own Son "God," the one who was given not merely a *measure* of authority but "*all authority*" in heaven and on earth,"[24] without representing a negation of that principle in any way. Actually, in light of the fact that other beings in addition to the Father are rightfully called "God" (Psalm 8:5; 45:6) or "gods" (based on the authority delegated to them; and with angels, perhaps because of their divine nature as powerful celestial beings), it would have really been inconsistent, even surprising, for the Bible *not* to have described God's Son by that very same kind of description; he is, clearly, far more worthy of that special dignity.

The similarities between the angels and judges as "gods" (including the King as 'God,' Psalm 45:6) and Jesus Christ as "God" cannot be neglected; for as Murray Harris noted, with respect to the judges, that, as "gods," they were "regarded as divine representatives or as bearers of divine authority and majesty..."

Is not Jesus, the Messiah, the ultimate "divine representative" and "bearer of divine authority and majesty" (compare Hebrews 1:1-8; John 17:2)?

Albert Barnes similarly noted, with respect to the Israelite judges as well, that "they were to be regarded as

---

[23] Jack T. Sanders, *Schismatics, Sectarians, Dissisdents, Deviants: The First One Hundred Years of Jewish-Christian Relations* (Trinity Press International, 1993), pp. 93, 94.
[24] Matthew 28:18; John 17:2

representatives of God; as acting in his name; as those, therefore, to whom, in a subordinate sense, the name gods might be given. The idea is, that they were the representatives of the divine sovereignty in the administration of justice...They were, in a sense, *gods* to other people; but they were not to forget that God stood among them as their God; that if they were exalted to a high rank in respect to their fellow men, they were, nevertheless, subject to the One to whom the name of God belonged in the highest sense..."

Was and is not the Messiah God's *perfect* "representative," one who acted "in God's name" as God's chosen messenger and ultimate spokesman (compare Hebrews 1:1-3; Matthew 21:9; John 5:43)? Could we not—in light of such clear scriptural precedents and principles—say the same with respect to the Christ in the terms of his own Godship? Namely, "The idea [in Scripture] is, that Christ was the representative of the divine sovereignty in the administration of justice...(Hebrews 1:3, 8; Matthew 28:18; compare Daniel 7:13-14; Isaiah 11:1-6) He was, in a sense, 'God' to other people (John 20:28); but he was not to forget that God stood among him as his God (John 20:17; Hebrews 1:8, 9); that if he was exalted to a high rank in respect to his fellow men (Philippians 2:9-11), he was, nevertheless, subject to the One to whom the name of God belonged in the highest sense (1 Corinthians 11:3; 15:26-28; compare Revelation 3:2, 12)."

Professor Thompson's comments will help to further illuminate some of the points made thus far in light of the picture presented in the Gospel of John particularly:

> ...when the word 'god' is used with reference to some figure other than the Most High God, it is typically because of the powers and authority delegated to that individual. The argument of the Fourth Gospel is that the distinctive divine prerogatives of creation and sovereignty have been delegated and are being exercised by Jesus, that the conferring of these prerogatives upon Jesus rests on the relationship of the Father and the Son, and that

therefore the Son may be known as 'God.' John makes his argument for the identity of Jesus, and simultaneously for the identity of God, by attributing to Jesus alone powers that are not routinely granted to any other agent or mediator figure. By concentrating these functions uniquely in Jesus, John thus denies the exercise of these prerogatives to other mediator figures. By making Jesus not only the one who exercises these prerogatives, such as the power to give life and to judge, but who also *has them 'in himself'* (5:25-26), John places Jesus in a different category from all other figures who might be thought worthy or capable of exercising similar prerogatives. Consequently, John also maintains the imperative of honoring the Son even as one honors the Father (5:23).[25]

The points that have been made are also well illustrated in the scriptural use of a similar or associated term, "savior." In the same passage in Isaiah already mentioned, Jehovah declared himself to be the *only* Savior (Isaiah 43:11), a statement that may be confidently accepted. Specifically, Jehovah said, "*beside me there is no savior.*" However, it is also true that Jehovah himself raises up others to be saviors:

> **And when the children of Israel cried unto Jehovah, Jehovah raised up a saviour to the children of Israel, who saved them, even Othniel the son of Kenaz, Caleb's younger brother...But when the children of Israel cried unto Jehovah, Jehovah raised them up a savior, Ehud, the son of Gera...**[26]

One could theoretically put forth the argument that since Jehovah said that there is *no other* savior but him, then no one else could properly be described as a savior in any sense without contradicting Jehovah's express declaration. Or, if another figure

---

[25] Thompson, *The God of the Gospel of John*, p. 52. In another place (p. 47), Thompson also observed: "As we have seen, *theos* may refer to the one true God, and most typically does so, but it may also be used of other individuals. Yet it refers to other figures, human or heavenly, only when they are understood to exercise some sort of office or function on God's behalf and when assigned that office or function by God."

[26] Judges 3:9, 15, *ASV*. Compare Obadiah 1:21.

The "deity" of Jesus Christ

is called "savior" in the Scriptures, then that figure must actually *be* Jehovah because Jehovah is the only savior. When examined carefully, however, one will see that such would amount to a very flawed and superficial kind of reasoning. No doubt God is the only true savior; but, at the same time, the Scriptures show, without doubt, that there were men in Old Testament times who were also described by God as "saviors" (or 'deliverers') because God raised them up in order to perform the act of saving (or delivering) on his behalf or as his representatives—the very *instruments* of his saving acts. Yet this does not make void Jehovah's words: "beside me there is no savior."

When the totality of the Scripture's testimony is considered, we will find that because of laying down his perfect life as a ransom for the world's sinners, Christ Jesus is fittingly described as "the savior of the world." But the fact that the Scriptures describe the Messiah in this way does not necessarily demand that the Messiah is God Almighty, the "second member of the Trinity." God is the Savior because he is the ultimate origin and chief initiator of man's salvation. He saved sinners by "sending" his Son who, in turn, gave up his life in sacrifice in order to accomplish the intended salvation of the ungodly. Therefore, God's Son, Christ Jesus, is the means by, or the chosen one through whom, God saves sinners, and is himself a savior.[27] Indeed, as the apostle John rightfully declared: "...*the Father has sent his Son to be the Savior of the world*" (1 John 4:14, emphasis added).

In Old Testament times, God raised up saviors for the

---

[27] Typical is the kind of argumentation advanced by Dr. Robert Morey: "[Jesus] is the Savior of the world (John 4:42; 1 John 4:14) and our Redeemer (Gal. 3:13; Tit. 2:14). Such titles as 'Savior' are clear indications of deity because Yahweh stated that He was the ONLY Savior..." —*The Trinity, Evidence and Issues*, p. 375. But, as shown, others beside Jehovah are appropriately designated by the same title; yet this is not, in any way, an indication of "deity." Trinitarians have also argued that Jesus cannot be properly described as a god, because then he would have to be a false god, because Jehovah is the only true God. This is, again, an example of erroneous argumentation, a false dilemma. The angels and rulers of Israel were called gods but they were neither the true God nor false gods. God is a relative term. It is not relegated or limited to the simple categories of 'true' and 'false'; at least, not in the Scriptures.

The "deity" of Jesus Christ

people of Israel according to their given need.[28] In these final days God has raised up the ultimate Savior. In his proclamation of the good news, the apostle Paul declared to his people:

> **"Of this man's** [King David's] **posterity *God has brought to Israel a Savior*, Jesus, as he promised"**[29]

In the time of Israel God raised up those who might be considered "saviors" in a *temporary* sense (courageous men who delivered the people from surrounding enemies). But, "when the fullness of time had come, God sent his Son" as a Savior in the ultimate and *everlasting* sense—becoming, as Scripture states: "the source of *eternal salvation* for all who obey him…"[30] Through Christ's "being born in the likeness of men" (Philippians 2:7, *ESV*), and by means of his foreordained sacrificial death and following resurrection, God mercifully provides deliverance from humanity's enemies—namely, sin, death, and "the evil one" who introduced these into the world. As the author of Hebrews reminds us: "so that by going through death as a man he might destroy him who had the power of death, that is, the devil; and might also set free those who lived their whole lives a prey to the fear of death."[31]

The Scriptures make clear that God is the Savior in the highest and most vital sense. He is the ultimate initiator of human salvation. But there are still others whom God himself describes as saviors—those whom God is pleased to use as the agents of his salvation. In the same way that Jehovah is the *only* "Savior," yet others are still called "saviors," Jehovah is still, at the same time, the *only* "God," yet others are nevertheless appropriately called "gods"—based, most significantly, on Jehovah's own decision to call them such. This is at least one of

---

[28] In fact a group of Levites once cried with a loud voice to Jehovah: "in the time of [the forefather's] suffering they cried out to you and you heard them from heaven, and according to your great mercies you gave them *saviors* who saved them from the hand of their enemies." — Nehemiah 9:27, *ESV* (emphasis added).
[29] Acts 13:23, *NRSV*
[30] Galatians 4:4; Hebrews 5:9, *NAB*
[31] Hebrews 2:14-15, *PME*

the reasons why Bible students would benefit from reevaluating long-held theological concepts and from carefully considering if the same proves to be true with respect to the term "God" when it is applied to Christ by the writers of Scripture. Jesus is definitely called "God" in the Scriptures. But in order for us to properly understand the quality and degree of Godship possessed by him, we must never forget that there is also one who is, and always remains, God to him—his Father, Jehovah the Most High. The Scriptures, and Jesus himself, communicate this fact with plainness.[32] Which is all to say that the Scriptures certainly reveal Jesus Christ to be a possessor of "Godship" (or 'Godhood'); only, his is the *kind* of Godship that allows for him to have one who is God *to* or *above* him (Compare Hebrews 1:8-9; John 20:28, 17). The Father's Godship, however, is unqualified and absolute. That is why he is called the "Most High" God, or God in the 'absolute' sense (Psalm 7:17; 9:2; Acts 16:17)—given the fact that he does not have one who is "God" to or above him, as the Lord Jesus clearly does (Matthew 27:46; Ephesians 1:17; Revelation 3:12).

So before one makes a decision about what the Bible means when it calls Jesus "God," it is helpful to remember that the term itself has a broad application in the original languages and within the ancient cultural context in which the Scriptures were written. The Scriptures themselves prove that the term "God"—both in Hebrew and in Greek—is not exclusively confined to references to the Almighty; it properly applies to other individuals as well, only in what might be appropriately described as a *secondary, representative,* or *derivative* sense. But this does not, in any way, take away from the fact that there is only one true and Almighty God, according to Scripture. Again, as it was observed by Marianne Thompson, in her book *The God of the Gospel of John*:

> Ancient Israelite and Jewish monotheism clearly did not preclude belief in other heavenly beings, such as angels

---

[32] John 20:17; Ephesians 1:17; Revelation 3:12

The "deity" of Jesus Christ

and spirits, but there is no contradiction between a plethora of supernatural beings and the unity of God so long as these beings are understood to be dependent upon and answerable to God. It is not their mere existence, but rather the suggestion of their autonomy, that threatens monotheism.[33]

Jesus Christ has been appropriately honored with the title "God" in Scripture, and Christians may rightfully consider Jesus to be their "Lord" and their "God," as the disciple evidently Thomas did at John 20:28. Yet regardless of how many times Jesus is ascribed with the title "God" in the Bible (a debated point among Bible scholars), the truth that there is one who is God above him always remains.[34] This is, in fact, *the* unalterable, defining point of truth that cannot be set aside when one considers what the Bible means whenever it may be said to ascribe the term "God" to Jesus Christ.

With respect to the famous declaration made by Thomas to the risen Lord Jesus ('My Lord and my God'), Marianne Thompson made the following remarks:

> Because [Jesus] is the one who embodies the very Word and glory of God, and who now lives with the Father, the Son may be honored and confessed as 'my Lord' and 'my God.' He does not 'take the place of God' but comprehensively and fully manifests the Word, presence, glory, and life of God. As the Son of the Father, Jesus has and brings the very life of God and fully reveals the

---

[33] Thompson, *The God of the Gospel of John*, p. 53.
[34] John 20:17. In light of the broader scriptural use of the term God and the fact that Thomas addressed the resurrected Lord Jesus as "my Lord and my God" (John 20:28), Ron Frye reminds us: "the term 'God' does not have a rigidly fixed degree of power. The title is not limited in its biblical application to the *Almighty* God. We must keep this perspective in mind when making a judgment about what Thomas meant by what he said...Naturally, we invest the fullest dignity and power in the word 'God' when we see it in the Bible, but we must remind ourselves that it doesn't always carry the same sense. The *degree* of power, honor and dignity assigned to it is relative and its sense must be determined by the way in which it is used, and against the context of the Scriptures as a whole. Because the Son of God is sometimes called God, does not prove he is God in the same sense as his Father who is presented to us in Scripture as the Almighty God. We must think of Jesus as God in the sense that it is presented to us in the Scriptures." —*The Father/Son Relationship*, pp. 38, 39.

> Father...John thus presents Jesus as the one *through* whom worship is directed to God. In so doing, John also speaks of the Son not just in terms that assign to him a prominent, distinct, or exalted role of agency but that predicate an inseparable unity with God. As noted in an earlier chapter, terms such as Wisdom, Word, and Glory are the best explications of the sort of relationship and unity that already exist between the Father and Son by virtue of that Father-Son relationship. To confess the risen Jesus as 'my Lord' and 'my God' always takes into account the character of this relationship...To honor the Son as one honors the Father pays equal honor to both but also recognizes that the Son is who he is precisely because he is the Son of the Father.[35]

Thompson also goes on to observe:

> In light of the rest of the Gospel of John, Thomas's confession cannot mean that the risen Jesus is the only God. That epithet has already been used by Jesus himself in a context that clearly distinguishes the Father and the Son (17:3). Moreover, in a resurrection appearance to Mary Magdalene, Jesus had commanded her to go tell his disciples that he was 'ascending to my Father and your Father, to my God and to your God' (20:17). It is highly unlikely that John intends the reader to understand that at some point the Father and Son are simply 'collapsed' into one, or that the one identified by Jesus as 'my God' somehow has become the risen Lord himself.[36]

As a concluding point of clarification, it should be pointed out how Trinitarianism reasons, essentially, that since

---

[35] Thompson, *The God of the Gospel of John*, p. 225.
[36] *The God of the Gospel of John*, p. 235. William Barclay observed: "It is extremely significant that on the one occasion when there is no argument [about whether or not the NT calls Jesus 'God'], in the case of Thomas, the statement is not a theological proposition but a lover's cry; it is not the product of intellectual reasoning but of intense personal emotion" (*Jesus As They Saw Him*, p. 33). Thompson also points out (p. 55): "When, in the climactic confession of the Gospel, Thomas addresses the risen Jesus as 'My Lord and my God!' this formulation stands as the summary and elaboration of the work and person of Jesus through the Gospel. The direct confession of the risen Lord as God stands alongside and interprets, but does not eclipse, the narrative that points to his dependence upon and authorization by the Father."

Jesus is called "God" in certain places, and the Scriptures clearly teach that there is only *one* God ('monotheism,' Isaiah 43:10), Jesus must be—in some mysterious sense—the same God as his Father, yet distinct from the Father *personally* (multiple 'persons' that share the same 'being').[37] But such an extraordinary, peculiar and, arguably, hasty line of reasoning simply ignores or overlooks the way the word "God" (both in Hebrew and in Greek) is used throughout the Bible; and, at the same time, represents a failure to properly take into account the clear and continually expressed scriptural teaching that the authority, power, status, godship, and highly exalted name possessed by the Lord Jesus Christ is that which his Father has been pleased to confer upon him.[38]

John 1:1
"...and the Word was with God..."

Perhaps one of the most controversial passages relating to the question of Christ's deity and Trinitarian doctrine is the one found in the beginning verse of the Gospel of John. Issues revolving around the translation and interpretation of this unique text have provoked a great deal of scholarly discussion and debate. Although the holy Spirit is not specifically mentioned, the text has been regularly appealed to by evangelicals as establishing an important foundation for Trinitarian teaching.

---

[37] Since Trinitarians teach that Jesus is the very same God as his Father, *yet not the Father*, we might ask: How could Jesus be *"the God* of our Lord Jesus Christ" as the apostle describes the Father at Ephesians 1:17 (which he *must* be if he is—as Trinitarians say he is—the *same* God)? One of the more obvious difficulties in accepting the belief that Jesus is the same God as his Father is found in Colossians 1:15 where the Son is described, not as "the invisible God," but as the invisible God's "image" or "visible representation." Jesus is obviously not "the invisible God," but the *image* or *representation* of him. This is in perfect agreement with Hebrews 1:3 which describes the Son as "the exact representation of [God's] being." Simply put, the Scriptures do not teach that the Son is "the invisible God" (Colossians 1:15); nor do they teach that the Father is the "only-begotten/one of a kind god" (John 1:18). The Father is "the Most High God," "the invisible God," while Jesus Christ is the "only-begotten/unique god," the one who has made "the invisible God" known.

[38] Colossians 1:19, 2:9; John 17:2; Matthew 28:18; Philippians 2:9-11; Hebrews 1:2, 4.

The traditional translation—found in all mainstream Bibles[39]—reads as follows:

In the beginning was the Word,
and the Word was with God,
and the Word *was God*.

Soon after, in verse 14, John says that "the Word was made flesh, and dwelt among us, (and we beheld his glory, the glory as of the only begotten of the Father,) full of grace and truth" (*KJV* rendering).

Many Bible students have pointed out that the opening of John's Gospel coincides well with the first verse of the book of Genesis: "*In the beginning* God created the heavens and the earth." Like the Septuagint's rendering of the opening verse of Genesis, John's prologue also reads "*en arche*" ('in the beginning'). However, Trinitarians typically argue that when John said "in the beginning was the word (understood as 'the Son')," he was implying that "the word" was eternal in nature; or that "the word," like the one God, *always* existed. Yet all that John reveals explicitly in this verse is, simply, that "the word (*ho logos*)" was (or was in existence) with God *in the beginning*. Whether "the word (or Word)" should be thought of as eternal (without beginning) or not, contrary to what Trinitarian apologists have traditionally argued, a concept of eternal existence is not articulated or necessarily demanded here. We can, however, know with certainty that, in the mind of the author, the *logos* clearly did exist before God brought the world into existence through the *logos*, and that, in fact, apart from the *logos* "not even one thing came into existence" (v. 3).

The nature of the word's existence (considered with the Genesis account in mind) was discussed by Jaroslav Pelikan, respected author of the five-volume *The Christian Tradition: A History of the Development of Doctrine*:

---

[39] These include the *KJV*, *NKJV*, *NIV*, *NASB*, and the relatively new *ESV* (2001).

The vocable 'word' here translates the Greek noun *logos*, which comes from the verb *legein*, 'to say' or 'to speak.' *Logos* can also mean 'reason' or 'mind,'...But whatever other meanings it may or may not be said to have, 'In the beginning the Word already was' may be read as a summary and paraphrase of the repetition of the elevenfold 'In the beginning God said' from the first chapter of Genesis. Before there was light and order, before there were stars or animals, before there was a human race, 'God said'; and therefore 'In the beginning the Word already was.' That declaration of the common Jewish and Christian faith in the God who speaks then also provides the framework to 'define'—which means 'to draw the boundary lines'—the distinctive creed of Christianity that the speaking of God had 'become flesh' and taken human form in Jesus and had 'made his home among us.'[40]

The "Word" (*KJV*), after being spoken of as having become flesh, is, as commonly known, identified by the apostle John in his Gospel as Jesus Christ. Traditionally, Trinitarians have argued—according to the traditional translation—that since "the Word" is said to have become flesh in the person of Jesus (v. 14), and the last line of the first verse says that the Word "was God," Jesus *is* God, in the flesh—yet not God *the Father*, the one "the Word" was clearly "with."

Does the traditional view truly reflect the meaning John intended to communicate to his readers? Can such a concept be supported by the original language used by the apostle? Or is it possible that the common translation/interpretation of John 1:1 is inaccurate and, consequently, misrepresentative of what the apostle was actually trying to get across? On what basis do we rightfully interpret the term *logos*—which can mean and be translated "word," "speech," "utterance," "message," "saying"—as a reference to a "person," the Son of God?

---

[40] *Whose Bible Is It? A Short History of the Scriptures* (London: Penguin Books, 2005), p. 25.

The "deity" of Jesus Christ

First, it is helpful to simply note the reasonableness of the questions in light of the fact that not all English Bible translations have rendered this verse in exactly the same way. As one might expect, different understandings have resulted. For example, instead of translating the last line as "the Word was God," Goodspeed's *American Translation* (1923) has "the Word was *divine*." In the late 1800's, Dr. Robert Young, Bible scholar and translator of *Young's Literal Translation of the Holy Bible*, wrote in his commentary: "AND THE WORD WAS GOD,] more *lit.* 'and a God (i.e. a Divine Being) was the Word.'"[41]

Although the translation of this verse into English may be said to come across as relatively quite basic in terms of grammar, it is worth considering some of the history behind the grammatical and interpretive issues that have surrounded it.

As many Bible students are aware, a considerable degree of controversy arose when the Watchtower Bible & Tract Society (the publishing corporation of Jehovah's Witnesses) published their own translation of the New Testament in 1950 called *The New World Translation of the Christian Greek Scriptures*. Scholars in the evangelical community strongly objected to their translation of this particular verse, because, similar to that of Robert Young's suggested translation, it read:

> **Originally the Word was,**
> **and the Word was with God,**
> **and the Word was a god.**

Jehovah's Witnesses were definitely not the first to publish or suggest an English translation of John 1:1 in the above manner.[42] But because their Bible translation was disseminated so widely, and because of their world-wide, door-to-door public outreach, their rendition of John 1:1 inevitably came to the attention of scholars in the Evangelical-Trinitarian community. Dr. Bruce Metzger—highly respected and well-known Greek

---

[41] *Concise Critical Comments on the New Testament* (Grand Rapids: Baker, n.d.), p. 54.
[42] The *Emphatic Diaglott*, by Benjamin Wilson, in the interlinear rendering had, "and a god was the word" (1796-1806 edition).

scholar and textual critic—suggested that the *New World Translation* of John 1:1 represented a flagrant violation of Greek grammar: "It must be stated quite frankly that, if the Jehovah's Witnesses take this translation seriously, they are polytheists...such a rendering is a frightful mistranslation."[43] About forty years later, in 1994, Donald MacLeod similarly remarked that the translation was a reflection of "bad grammar and even worse theology..."[44]

Although the translation was negatively criticized by Metzger and other scholars, the justification presented by the translators of the *NWT* was not only based on an appeal to a relatively basic point of Greek grammar, but also on a consideration of the immediate context. The basic reasons given for the translation are found in the Appendix to the *NWT 1984 Reference Edition*. It is observed that:

> Translations use such words as 'a god,' 'divine' or 'godlike' because the Greek word θεος (*theos*) is a singular predicate noun occurring before the verb and is not preceded by a definite article. This is an anarthrous *theos*. The God with whom the word, or *logos*, was originally is designated here by the Greek expression *ho theos*, that is, *theos* preceded by the definite article *ho*. This is an articular *theos*. Careful translators recognize that the articular construction of the noun points to an identity, a personality, whereas a singular amorphous predicate noun preceding the verb points to a quality about someone. Therefore, John's statement that the Word or Logos was 'a god' or 'divine' or 'godlike' does not mean that he was the God with whom he was. It merely expresses a certain quality about the Word, or Logos, but it does not identify him as one and the same God himself.[45]

Still, for many years, prominent evangelicals disputed the

---

[43] "The Jehovah's Witnesses and Jesus Christ," *Theology Today* (April 1953): 75.
[44] From the book *Shared Life, The Trinity*
[45] *New World Translation Reference Edition* 1981, p. 1579.

validity of the translation primarily on 'theological' (and what they also believed were legitimate grammatical) grounds. Well-known critics like Bruce Metzger, Walter Martin and Robert Countess, regularly appealed to what came to be known as "Colwell's Rule." The purpose of appealing to the said rule was to prove that in a construction like John 1:1, where the predicate noun comes before the verb (*theos en ho logos*; word-for-word: *god was the word*), the noun does not require the definite article (*ho*) in order for the noun to express definiteness (that is, for the noun to mean *God*, capital 'G'). In referring to "Colwell's rule" the apologists were hoping to demonstrate that the traditional translation—"the Word was God"—was valid, and that the *NWT* rendition—"the Word was a god"—was conclusively wrong. The proposed rule said that a "definite predicate nominative has the article when it follows the verb; it does not have the article when it precedes the verb,"[46] as in the case of John 1:1.

However, Colwell himself found fifteen exceptions to the said rule, showing that it really was not a strict or absolute "rule" of Greek grammar after all. Yet, unfortunately, Dr. Metzger argued strongly that in translating the last part of the verse "the Word was a god," the translators overlooked entirely *"an established rule* of Greek grammar which *necessitates* the rendering, '…and the Word was God.'"[47]

Similarly, the late Dr. Walter Martin—regarded by some evangelicals as "the leading American authority on American cults" and "the Father of cult apologetics"—in his famous and widely-read work, *Kingdom of the Cults*, wrote the following:

> …the Greek grammatical construction *leaves no doubt whatsoever* that ['the Word was God.'] is the *only possible rendering* of the text…In fact, the late New

---

[46] As quoted on page 49 of *The Jehovah's Witness' New Testament, A Critical Analysis of the New World Translation of the Christian Greek Scriptures* (New Jersey: Presbyterian and Reformed Publishing Co., 1982). Colwell outlined his study in the *Journal of Biblical Literature* entitled "A Definite Rule for the Use of the Article in the Greek New Testament," *Journal of Biblical Literature* LII (1933), pp. 12-21.

[47] Bruce M. Metzger, *"The Jehovah's Witnesses and Jesus Christ," Theology Today*, pp. 65-85. As quoted in Countess, p. 53 (emphasis added).

Testament Greek scholar Dr. E. C. Colwell formulated a rule that clearly states that a definite predicate nominative (in this case, *theos*—God) *never* takes an article when it precedes the verb (was), as we find in John 1:1. It is therefore easy to see that no article is needed for *theos* (God), and to translate it 'a god' is both incorrect grammar and poor Greek...Christ, if He is the Word 'made flesh' (John 1:14), can be no one else except God unless the Greek text and consequently God's word be denied.[48]

For decades prominent evangelical leaders argued forcefully for the accuracy of the definite translation "the Word was God." And in an effort to add strength to their position, they frequently appealed to the rule proposed by Colwell, even referring to it—mistakenly, as it turned out—as an *established* rule of Greek grammar. Yet in his widely-read *Kingdom of the Cults*, not only did Walter Martin accuse the *NWT* translators of effecting "a show of pseudo scholarship," in the foreword to another apologetic work on the same subject (a book that criticized the *NWT* rendition of John 1:1 and 8:58), Martin suggested that the Witnesses had been guilty of "mishandling biblical texts" and of having engaged in "consistent abuse of the rules of grammar and context..." Yet, amazingly, in the very same work (authored by Robert Bowman Jr.), Walter Martin was shown to have erred in his dogmatic argument based on Colwell's rule, which was used to cast favorable light on the traditional definite translation, "the Word was God."

According to Martin, "there was no doubt whatsoever" that this was the "only possible rendering." Yet in his work *Jehovah's Witness, Jesus Christ and the Gospel of John* (the same work endorsed by Martin), Robert Bowman showed that "[Colwells' rule] is not an absolute rule but a useful generalization that holds in the vast majority of cases. It is thus a mistake to argue that Colwell's rule proves that *theos* in John 1:1

---

[48] Page 138 (Expanded Anniversary Edition, 1997; Emphasis added).

is definite..."⁴⁹ Significantly, Bowman went on to acknowledge: "Where Colwell's rule can and has been severely abused is in the popular evangelical apologetic argument that the rule alone refutes the JW rendering 'a god.' Such an argument goes far beyond what Colwell himself, a careful scholar that he was, said..."⁵⁰

It is noteworthy that in the very same work in which Walter Martin gave an endorsement in the preface—where he charged the *NWT* translators of "consistent abuse" in this same area—Martin's "popular evangelical apologetic argument" was the one that was actually exposed as an abuse of Colwell's study. Not only was Colwell's rule shown to have no bearing on the translation and understanding of John 1:1 (in terms of decisively proving that the last clause should be translated definitely), the problem of the traditional definite translation itself was realized by more careful Trinitarian scholars and clarified by apologists like Robert Bowman.

The problem was that all the attempted scholarly argumentation for the defense of the definite translation ('the Word was God') was not only erroneous, but the translation itself—when taken at face value, along with the assumption that 'the word' of John 1:1 is a reference to a 'person'—actually proves unfavorable and even contradictory to Trinitarian doctrine.

The first difficulty is that the more common translation—"the Word was **with God**, and the Word **was God**"—really communicates to the reader the mentally-perplexing notion that "the Word" (if conceived as a 'person') was the exact same one "the Word" was said to be *with*, which, logically, does not make sense and which, in reality, proves incomprehensible. How can someone be *with* someone else and at the same time *be* that someone else?[51] Secondly, if the Word was *with* God, and if

---

[49] Bowman, *Jesus Christ and the Gospel of John*, p. 67.
[50] Bowman, *Jesus Christ and the Gospel of John*, p. 69.
[51] The only alternative would seem to be that "the word *was God*," not in the sense of being a "person" who "shares the substance" of God, but in the sense that God's word (his literal utterance) is the expression of his inner mind and personality; and, in that sense, God's word can

"God" is taken as a reference to God the Father, and the Word *was* God, this would result in the meaning that, somehow, the Word *was* God the Father. If the "God" whom the Word was "with" is taken to be a reference to the "Triune God," then to say that the Word *was God* would mean that the Word was the Trinity—implications that are irreconcilable with and unacceptable to Trinitarian teaching. As Robert Bowman correctly pointed out in his book, the translation found in most Bibles can actually be viewed as more conducive to a type of "modalistic" view, the view that says Jesus Christ *is* God the Father—a concept that neither the Bible nor Trinitarianism teaches.[52]

Bowman writes: "The significance of *theon* [God] being definite in Clause B, then, is to identify the One spoken of there as a specific person—God the Father. If, then, *theos* in Clause C were to be 'definite' in the same way that *theon* is in Clause B, it would then be saying that the Word was God the Father. Such a statement would contradict Clause B and imply some sort of modalistic view of God, which of course Trinitarians oppose..."[53] Bowman also states, "the point that is being made here is that for *theos* to be definite *in this context*—after just using the definite *ton theon* to refer specifically to the person of the Father—would be modalistic." And on page 42: "Therefore, those who have argued that in John 1:1 *theos* is definite [Metzger, Countess, Grudem,[54] Martin and others] were in error...As surprising as it may seem, arguing that *theos* is definite in this context actually is

---

be said to be equivalent to God himself, and, hence, truly "God," in so far as God's word reveals and expresses him. This is, in fact, what some Christians understand John 1:1 to mean.

[52] Although many sincere people have contended for the doctrine that says Jesus Christ *is* God the Father, the apostles nowhere testify that the Father *was* or *became* the Son, or that he *took on a role* as the Son. Instead, John wrote, "we have seen for ourselves, and we *testify* that the Father *sent* the Son to be the savior of the world" (1 John 4:14). In another place, Jesus clearly spoke of himself and the Father as constituting *two* distinct witnesses (John 8:17-18. Compare Deuteronomy 17:6; 19:15), and that the Father was greater than himself (John 14:28). In John 5:31, 2, Jesus said, "If I testify on my own behalf, my testimony cannot be verified. But there is *another* [evidently, the Father] who testifies on my behalf, and I know that the testimony he gives on my behalf is true."

[53] Bowman, *Jesus Christ and the Gospel of John*, p. 40.

[54] See: *Systematic Theology*, page 234.

The "deity" of Jesus Christ

inconsistent with the Trinitarian distinction between the Father and the Son."[55]

As already mentioned, most translations read, "the Word was *with* God, and the Word *was God*." But what is conveyed by this translation is that the word or *logos* is the same exact one that John had in the previous line just said the word was *with*.[56] But that is definitely *not* what Trinitarians themselves actually believe. So it follows that the traditional translation—which was defended for decades in response to the alternative 'a god' rendering—is really unsupportive of, and even *contradictory* to, the interests of Trinitarian theology.[57]

While advocates of Trinitarian doctrine typically refer to the traditional translation of John 1:1 as a "proof-text" for identifying Jesus as "God the Son, the second person of the Trinity" (a concept articulated nowhere Scripture), today, even respected Trinitarian scholars admit that "the-Word-was-God" may not be the most accurate way of translating the apostle's words into English. Commenting on the translational issues of John 1:1 already considered, one evangelical source remarked:

> ...another reason to omit the article is if the noun is functioning as a predicate adjective, giving a quality of the subject. That is probably John's main reason for not including it here...That is John is quite aware that the Word was not all of God. The Father still existed separately after the Word became flesh (Jn 1:14). *Thus, 'The Word was God' could be misleading*: it could imply

---

[55] Bowman (p. 26) writes: "The Word certainly cannot be with 'God' and be 'God' unless the term *God* somehow changes significance from the first to the second usage. The question is what sort of shift in nuance is inferred."

[56] Again, unless we say that the word *was God*, not in the sense that the word was *literally* God the Father, but in the sense that, since "the word" of God is the expression of God's inner-self, and because "the word" reveals/mediates God's presence and purpose in the world, the word therefore *is* "God" in that sense. Which is to say, the word is "God" *expressed*, "God" *in communication* with others, the very vehicle of expressing God's mind, will and purpose.

[57] Murray Harris states: "'the Word was God' suggests that 'the Word' and 'God' are convertible terms, that the proposition is reciprocating. But the Word is neither the Father nor the Trinity. Therefore few will doubt that this time-honored translation needs careful exegesis, since it places a distinctive sense upon a common English word. The rendering cannot stand without explanation." —Harris, *Jesus as God*, p. 69.

The "deity" of Jesus Christ

that all of God had become incarnate in Jesus. The omission of the article makes this verse mean 'The Word was divine' or 'What God was the Word was.' In other words, the text is indicating that the Word had all of the qualities of God. But this text is also indicating that not all of God was in the Word.[58]

It is also worth noting how Walter Martin criticized the argument made by the *NWT* translators in this way: "according to [the *NWT* translators] it is 'unreasonable' that the Word (Christ) should be the God with whom He was (John 1:1). Their own manifestly erring reason is made the criterion for determining scriptural truth."[59] Yet a similar and actually quite sensible line of reasoning was made by the respected evangelical scholar F. F. Bruce: "Had *theos* as well as *logos* been preceded by the article the meaning would have been that the Word was completely identical with God, which is *impossible* if the Word was also 'with God.'"[60] Again, Robert Bowman makes the same essential point: "the usual translation of John 1:1 can be misunderstood to imply that the Word was the same person as the person with whom he existed in the beginning, which would of course be nonsense."[61]

In principle, the point made by Bruce, Bowman, and the *NWT* committee, is the same. The only difference is that the *NWT* committee argued that the Word cannot be the same "God" John said the Word was *with* (simply because the Word was '*with* the God'); while the evangelicals stress that the Word cannot be the same "person" that John said the Word was with. This is so because Trinitarian theology demands that the distinction be made in terms of "person." That is, the "Father" must be distinguished from the "Word" or "Son," even though

---

[58] *Hard Sayings of the Bible*, Walter C. Keiser Jr., Peter H. Davids, F. F. Bruce, Manfred T. Brauch (Illinois: InterVarsity Press, 1996), p. 491.
[59] Martin, *Kingdom of the Cults*, p. 140.
[60] *The Gospel of John, Introduction, Exposition and Notes*, by F. F. Bruce (Grand Rapids, Michigan, 1983), p. 31 (emphasis added).
[61] Bowman, *Jesus Christ and the Gospel of John*, p. 27. Similarly, Professor MacLeod noted: "The Word could not be the One that he himself was *with*." —*Shared Life, The Trinity and the Fellowship of God's People*, p. 24.

they are both "God" according to Trinitarian belief. This is the reason why, in the case of John 1:1, Trinitarians are forced to say that *ho theos* ('the God') means "the Father" (the first person of the Trinity), and that "the Word" must mean "the Son" (the second person of the Trinity).[62] This is where the argumentation gets notably complicated, for several reasons.

It is true, as Trinitarians point out, that in John 1:1 *ho theos* is a *reference* to the Father. But we should be careful to note that John specifically said, meant, and wrote, *God (ton theon)*. The point is that the purposefully selected terms (or category) in which John himself makes the distinction between the God and the *logos* that was with God are, in fact, in the terms of "*theos.*" That is to say, there is one subject called *theos* "with" another one who is *ho theos*. However, in order to preserve the established doctrine of God at this point, Trinitarian apologists are essentially forced to *change* the very terms of distinction from "God *(ton theon)*" and "god *(theos)*" to that of "Father" and "Son."[63] Of course it is legitimate to say or point out that the term "God *(ton theon)*" is a reference to the Father, but there exists no proof in Scripture that the word "God" or even "Father" ever means "the-first-person-of-the-essence-sharing-Trinity," and that is in fact what Trinitarians really mean when they make this unscriptural or, at least, scripturally unverifiable, qualification. In other words, in John 1:1, the first occurrence of "God" is identified by Trinitarians as the Father, which is correct; but a *meaning* that is not given to the term "Father" in the Bible is poured into the term in order to preserve the Trinitarian distinction; and thus the text is interpreted through a theological framework that the Bible itself does not present or articulate. So the problem is, instead of drawing conclusions based on what is

---

[62] "[John] adds that 'the Word was *with* God.' In this particular statement, God means *God the Father.*" —MacLeod, *The Trinity and the Fellowship of God's People*, p. 23.

[63] The fact that Trinitarian apologists must change the *specific terms* used shows that they do not accept the text *as is*. John said, "In the beginning was the word, and the word was *with* God, and the word was god/a god," yet this becomes, for Trinitarians: "In the beginning the Word (or pre-incarnate 'Son') was *eternally existing*, and the Word was with the *person of the Father* (the first member of the Trinity), and the Word (or pre-incarnate 'Son') shared the being/essence of God."

specifically written, unbiblical meanings are poured into certain words, and distinctions are made in terms that are not actually present. Nor are they articulated elsewhere in the scriptural accounts as we possess them.

Essentially, most Trinitarians interpret this verse as if it had said: "In the beginning was (eternally existing) the Word/Pre-Incarnate Son, and the Word/Pre-Incarnate Son was (eternally) with God (the *person* of the *Father*, first member of the Trinity) and the Word/Pre-Incarnate Son was God (as to his 'essence'; not the *person* of the Father, but still *God*, the second member of the *Trinity*).

The question that needs to be asked is this: Where does one find a warrant for such a meaning in the language of the text itself, the overall context, or from the Bible as a whole? Is there any Scripture in the Bible where these concepts are actually taught so that we can properly interpret the apostle's teaching in light of such? Or, is this merely another case of a committed community of apologists seeking to impose a preconceived theological concept onto a biblical text?

Regardless of whether or not one accepts the modern Trinitarian explanation of this text (or the alternatives), it is helpful to note that most Trinitarian scholars now recognize that there *is* significance to the distinction between the first occurrence of *theos* (with the definite article) and the second occurrence of *theos* (without the article), which is *concealed* in the translation "the Word was God." Yet, inexplicably, in a 2003 public debate, Robert Bowman said,

> "One thing that many of you may be familiar with in the annals of the debate over this subject that has been going on for some time is the fuss and feathers over the fact that there is no article, the word 'the' before God in the Greek text of John 1:1 part C, 'the Word was God' or 'the Logos was God.' One of the things that you'll see on this handout that's been made available to you is what's really surprising in John 1 is that the article is *ever* used in front of the name God...If you look at that table I think you

can see that there's probably no significance to the omission of the article whatsoever."[64]

However, in his work on the Trinity, James White quoted Daniel Wallace approvingly where he said: "In the least, we cannot treat [the article] lightly, for its presence or absence is the crucial element to unlocking the meaning of scores of passages in the NT."[65] White was also correct when he went on to say: "The writers of Scripture used the article to convey meaning, and we need to be careful not to overlook the information they provide to us through the use, or nonuse, of the article."[66]

In a discussion revolving around the significance of the definite article in Greek, a consideration of the study notes on 1 Corinthians 14:2 in the *MacArthur Study Bible* also proves instructive to an extent. *The New King James Version* translates the verse: "For he who speaks in a tongue does not speak to men but to God, for no one understands *him*; however, in the spirit he speaks mysteries." Yet in an effort to defend his well-known viewpoints regarding "spiritual gifts" (specifically, the gift of tongues), MacArthur argues: "This is better translated, 'to a god.' The Gr. text has no definite article (see similar translation in Acts 17:23, 'an unknown god.'). Their gibberish was worship of pagan deities."[67]

In this instance, MacArthur is attempting to discourage Bible readers from seeking to practice the gift of tongues (MacArthur himself holding to the view that says the gift of

---

[64] These comments are strange because Bowman's 1989 work shows that he fully understood and appreciated the fact that the absence of the article in John 1:1 *is* significant for understanding John's meaning. This is why he recommends (in an effort to preserve Trinitarian doctrine) the alternative translation, "the Word was Deity." His comments were made 13 years later in 2003. (*Is Jesus God? A Debate Between Robert Bowman and Greg Stafford*)

[65] Author of *Greek Grammar Beyond the Basics: An Exegetical Syntax of the New Testament* (Grand Rapids: Zondervan, 1996). It should not be difficult to see the significance of the lack of the article in John 1:1c, even for those unfamiliar with Greek. After *en arche* (in [the] beginning) there are a total of 5 nouns in the verse (6 including verse 4); 5 nouns are definite/articular; 1 noun is article-less/anarthrous. Again, John said that in the beginning "was *the* word and *the* word was with *the* god and *the* word was *god* (no article; lit., 'god was the word'). This (one) was in the beginning with *the* god." To translate "*a* god" is quite natural and in perfect accordance with the grammar and normal translational procedure.

[66] White, *The Forgotten Trinity*, p. 53.

[67] *The MacArthur Study Bible*, p. 1751.

tongues ceased after the time of the apostles). Here, Paul speaks about tongues in a manner that seems to suggest that certain Christians would be gifted with the ability to speak to God in such a way that only God would understand, while others would not be able to comprehend the language. However, for the specific purpose of discrediting the legitimacy of speaking in tongues after this particular manner (and in post-apostolic times), MacArthur prefers to view Paul's statement as meaning that some would misuse or pervert the practice of speaking in tongues; in effect, speaking "gibberish" to a "pagan deity" or "to a god," *not* to the true God himself. And in this case, MacArthur calls attention to the lack of the definite article in the Greek to support his argument. According to MacArthur, since there is no definite article present, the phrase should be rendered and understood not as "to God" but "to *a* god." Whether or not MacArthur's viewpoint is correct on this particular matter, these comments help to further support the reasonableness (given that in John 1:1 the first occurrence of *theos* has the article but the second occurrence does not) of translating the verse "the word was a god," or, possibly, "a divine being," "a divine one," or "a deity."[68]

Although Bible students may continue to wrestle with the understanding and *interpretation* of this text, recognition of what the apostle said in the original language, and the possibilities of what the language can allow for, must be given adequate consideration. Arguably, a more accurate translation would reflect the seemingly clear *distinction* that the apostle makes between the first occurrence of 'God' (*ton theon*, with the article) and the second occurrence of 'god' (*theos*, without the article). The traditional translation does not bring out the careful distinction that the apostle made and has consequently led many to a misuse, misunderstanding and misapplication of this

---

[68] Actually, when occurring in the dative case ('to God') as in 1 Cor. 14:2, the lack of the definite article does not demand that the phrase mean "to a god." However, in the nominative case (as in John 1:1c) the lack of the article *would* normally indicate an indefinite sense for a predicate noun such as *theos*.

important text. But the distinction has been pointed out by numerous Bible scholars and commentaries—albeit, with varying implications. The footnote in the Catholic *New American Bible* pointed out: "*Was God*: lack of article with 'God' in Greek signifies predication rather than identification."[69] It was noted in the *Anchor Bible*: "To preserve in English the different nuance of *theos* with and without the article, some would translate 'the Word was divine.'" The translational notes in the *Translators New Testament* state: "There is a distinction in the Greek here between 'with God' and 'God.' In the first instance the article is used and this makes the reference specific. In the second instance there is no article and it is difficult to believe that the omission is not significant. In effect it gives an adjectival quality to the second use of *Theos* (God) so that the phrase means 'The Word was divine.'"[70] And perhaps even more accurate to the sense, Jesuit scholar John L. McKenzie observed in his *Dictionary of the Bible*, "Jn 1:1 should rigorously be translated 'the word was with the God [= the Father], and the word was a divine being.'"[71] Bible scholar William Loader also made the following remarks:

> It is true, on the most natural reading of the text, that there are two beings here: God and a second who was *theos* but this second is related to God in a manner which shows that God is the absolute over against which the second is defined. They are not presented as two equal gods.[72]

Bible scholar and professor of systematic theology at Western Theological Seminary, Dr. Christopher B. Kaiser, in his book *The Doctrine of God* similarly stated:

> The reference to the Word as 'God' in John 1:1f. could be taken as a technical way of distinguishing Christ from the Father as a subordinate 'deity' (*theos* as opposed to *ho*

---

[69] *Saint Joseph Edition of the New American Bible*, p. 145.
[70] *The Translator's New Testament*, London (British and Foreign Bible Society, 1973), p. 451.
[71] *McKenzie Dictionary of the Bible*, p. 317.
[72] William Loader, Ph.D, *The Christology of the Fourth Gospel-Structures and Issues*, p. 155.

theos) in view of the absence of the definite article. Such a distinction would be consistent with John 14:28 ('the Father is greater than I')...[73]

In a correspondence regarding the same text, Jason BeDuhn made a helpful observation that may put the issues into clearer focus:

> The phrase is *theos en ho logos*, which translated word for word is 'a god was the word.'...Now in English we simply say 'God'; we do not say 'The God.' But in Greek, when you mean to refer to the one supreme God, instead of one of the many other beings that were called 'gods,' you would have to say 'The God': *ho theos*. Even a monotheistic Christian, who believes there is only one God and no others, would be forced to say in Greek 'The God,' as John and Paul and the other writers of the New Testament normally do. If you leave off the article in a phrase like John 1:1, then you are saying 'a god.' (There are some exceptions to this rule: Greek has what are called noun cases, which means the nouns change form depending on how they are used in a sentence. So, if you want to say 'of God,' which is *theou*, you don't need the article. But in the nominative case, which is the one in John 1:1, you have to have the article...So what does John mean by saying 'the word was a god'? He is classifying Jesus [more accurately, 'the word'] in a specific category of beings. There are plants and animals and humans and gods, and so on. By calling the Word 'a god,' John wants to tell his readers that the Word (which becomes Jesus when it takes flesh) belongs to the divine class of things. Notice the word order: 'a god was the word.' We can't say it like this in English, but you can in Greek. The subject can be after the verb and the object before the verb, the opposite of how we do it in English (subject-verb-object). Research has shown that when ancient Greek writers put a object-noun first in a sentence

---

[73] *The Doctrine of God, A Historical Survey—Foundations For Faith* (Westchester: Crossway Books, 1982), p. 31. However, Kaiser ultimately disagrees with what he acknowledges as a possibility based on the absence of the article.

like John 1:1 (a be-verb sentence: x is y), without the definite article, they are telling us that the subject belongs to the class represented by the object-noun: 'The car is a Volkswagen.' In English we would accomplish the same thing by using what we call predicate adjectives. 'John is a smart person' = 'John is smart.' So we would tend to say 'The word was divine,' rather than 'The word was a god.'

Professor BeDuhn went on to observe:

> No one in John's day would have understood the phrase to mean 'The word was God'—the language does not convey that sense, and conceptually it is difficult to grasp such an idea, especially since that author has just said that the word was *with* God. Someone is not with himself, he is with some other. John clearly differentiates between God from the Word. The latter becomes flesh and is seen; the former cannot be seen. What is the Word? John says it was the agent through whom God made the world. He starts his gospel 'In the beginning...' to remind us of Genesis 1. How does God create in Genesis? He speaks words that make things come into existence. So the Word is God's creative power and plan and activity. It is not God himself, but it is not really totally separate from God either. It occupies a kind of ambiguous status. That is why a monotheist like John can get away with calling it 'a god' or 'divine' without becoming a polytheist. This divine being does not act on its own, however, does take on a kind of distinct identity, and in becoming flesh brings God's will and plan right down face to face with humans."[74]

In his book on Bible translation, BeDuhn also remarked: "If John had wanted to say 'the Word was God,' as so many English translations have it, he could have very easily done so by simply adding the definite article 'the' (*ho*) to the word 'god' (*theos*), making it 'the god' and therefore 'God.' He could have

---

[74] Jason BeDuhn, Northern Arizona University, Department of Humanities Arts and Religion. (*Wed: Jul 30 22:10:49 EDT 2003*)

The "deity" of Jesus Christ

simply written *ho logos en ho theos* (word-for-word: 'the word was the god'), or *ho logos ho theos en* (word-for-word: 'the word the god was'). But he didn't...Others have argued that *theos* does not require the definite article to be definite, and that there are examples of article-less ('anarthrous') *theos* used definitely in the New Testament. While this may be true of anarthrous *theos* in the genitive or dative case, two forms that freely dispense with the article in a number of uses, it is not the case for anarthrous *theos* in the nominative case, the form used in John 1:1c. The nominative case is much more dependent than other Greek cases on the definite article to mark definiteness."[75]

According to the more refined argument put forward by Trinitarian apologists, John is not trying to say that the Word was God (*ho theos* = the Father), but rather *God* (as to his 'substance/essence'); or that the Word was *theos* in the exact same sense as the Father (but still not the same 'person'). As Dr. White puts it: "The person of Christ as presented in John's Gospel is indeed of an exceptionally high character—John asserts that Jesus is 'the Word become flesh' (John 1:14). He says that this Word is eternal, has always been 'with' God (*pros ton theon*) and indeed shares the very being of God (John 1:1)."[76]

However, a simple reading of the text will reveal that John neither says nor "asserts" that the Word is "eternal (without beginning)" nor that the Word "shares the very being of God." Strangely, in this case, Dr. White simply claims that the apostle says something that he does not actually say.[77] In his book, *God In Three Persons*, E. Calvin Beisner claims:

> It need hardly be noted that the most obvious statement of the deity of Christ is John 1:1...The phrase *theos en ho*

---

[75] BeDuhn, *Truth in Translation*, pp. 115-117.
[76] *Purpose and Meaning of "Ego Eimi" in the Gospel of John in Reference to the Deity of Christ*, by James White; 2005 Alpha Omega Ministries.
[77] Dr. White would probably have been better off saying that this is what he *believes* the text *means* or that this is how he *interprets* the text; for John certainly did not *say* what Dr. White claims that he said. Again, it should be emphasized that God is correctly identified by Dr. White as "the Father." Ultimately, however, a definition for the Father not given in the Scriptures is given to the term; namely, the first person of the Trinity. The Bible itself defines the Father as the "one God," or "the only true God," *not* "the first person of the Trinity."

logos has been the object of innumerable studies, and it can confidently be said that it ascribes absolute deity to the Word. The translation 'the Word was deity' is advocated by many scholars and seems to be the best phrase to bring forth the meaning of the Greek. The predicate nominative, *theos*, preceding the verb, is clearly qualitative (though in no sense can it be said to be indefinite), and hence bears the meaning of 'that quality which to have is to be God,' or simply 'the state of being God.' It is useless to attempt any other understanding of this phrase than that John intended for us to recognize that the Word himself was God.[78]

The difficulty in the position now taken by Trinitarian apologists is that the suggested translation (and associated interpretation) is that, for the specific and calculated purpose of upholding an established theological teaching (Trinitarianism), an attempt is made to *change* a predicate nominative, or singular noun (*theos* = 'god'), into a kind of abstract noun (similar to *theotetos*, Col. 2:9) denoting "quality," or, more specifically, "substance." Yet it is clear that any attempt to derive such a meaning from the term would go against the point made by R. C. Sproul with respect to what he characterizes as "literal interpretation" of the Bible:

> Literal interpretation, strictly speaking, means that we are to interpret the Bible *as it is written*. A noun is treated as a noun and a verb as a verb. It means that all the forms that are used in the writing of the Bible are to be interpreted according to the normal rules governing those forms. Poetry is to be treated as poetry. Historical accounts are to be treated as history. Parables as parables, hyperbole as hyperbole, and so on...The Bible is not to be interpreted according to our own desire and prejudices. We must seek to understand what it actually says and guard against forcing our own views upon it.[79]

---

[78] Beisner, *God In Three Persons*, pp. 31-32.
[79] *Essential Truths of the Christian Faith* (Wheaton: Tyndale House Publishers, 1992) pp. 25, 26.

What Beisner previously said about the noun being "qualitative" is sound, acceptable, and may even allow for a range of possible meanings. In order to uphold the orthodox viewpoint based on this verse, however, the singular noun (predicate nominative *theos*) is not and cannot be "treated as a noun," but, rather, as a very specific theologically-loaded term connoting the idea of "substance" or "essence." Yet it really goes without saying that the actual word *theos* is a noun (like 'angel,' 'demon,' 'prophet,' 'priest,' etc.) referring to a specific type of being or status, not an abstract term used for denoting a certain kind of substance like "gold" or "silver" or the like. And if it really was in fact John's intention to express the idea of "quality" at this point, the translation "the-word-was-a-god" is quite effective in terms of communicating the qualitative connotation.[80]

New Testament professor Marianne Thompson makes a helpful point relevant to the same issue at hand:

> 'God' does not connote a 'divine essence' that can be shared by a number of beings, even though there may be a number of beings who are called 'god.' In this sense, *theos* functions slightly differently than does the English term 'deity.' Although we use 'deity' to refer both to God ('the Deity') and to a property (as in the 'deity of Christ'), 'god' does not refer to a characteristic or property the possession of which renders one 'divine.' Rather, 'God' in biblical texts and Jewish thought either refers to the one and only God or, when use of a human figure, relates

---

[80] In a written debate on the same subject with an evangelical scholar, Jason BeDuhn said: "...if I go along, and say, 'okay, let's call [*theos* in John 1:1c] qualitative,' then our next joint task is to look at how English conveys qualitative relative to how Greek conveys it. Some examples from sentences using the same grammatical construct as John 1:1c: John 4:19 'You are *a* prophet' not 'You are prophet.' John 8:34 'Everyone who does sin is *a* slave of sin' not '...is slave of sin.' John 8:48 'You are *a* Samaritan' not 'You are Samaritan.' John 9:24 'This man is *a* sinner' not 'This man is sinner.' John 9:28 'You are *a* disciple of that man' not 'You are disciple of that man.' John 10:1 'This one is *a* thief' not 'This one is thief.' John 12:6 'He was *a* thief' not 'He was thief.' —Dr.J.Beduhn and R.Hommel: *A Discussion upon the translation of John 1:1c*. (Christian Apologetics Research Ministry Jan/Feb, 2002). According to another source: "Often, the only way to effectively communicate a qualitative noun in the English idiom is by prefacing the noun with 'a.'" —Paul Stephen Dixon, *The Significance of the Anarthrous Predicate Nominative in John* (Th.M. thesis, Dallas Theological Seminary, 1975), p. 47.

The "deity" of Jesus Christ

that figure to God by the exercise of some divine prerogative that is further exercised by God's authority.[81]

Unfortunately, Trinitarian apologists either ignore or try to explain away by way of a doctrine not found in the Bible the fact that the *logos* was "with" God, which, automatically, demonstrates that the *logos* was a distinct entity or concept from "God." If "the Word" or "word" was *theos*, it follows logically that the word was *divine*; but the language itself does not carry the notion of "deity" in the same exact sense as God the Father; nor would it have carried the anachronistic, theologically-loaded meaning "sharing-the-same-substance-as..." This is an example of another concept that must be read into a verse, one that the words contained in the verse itself do not naturally or normally express. Trinitarian apologists want the phrase to mean that the *logos* had all the qualities of God Almighty, so that the *logos* (conceived as a 'person') was just as much the one God as the Father. For example, earlier it was noted how one Trinitarian source claimed that "the Word had all of the qualities of God." But if by this statement the authors meant that "the Word had all the qualities of *ho theos*," they are mistaken; for the only thing that can be legitimately said, based on the language itself, is that the *logos* possessed all the qualities that make one *theos*, not *ho theos*.

Although most informed Trinitarians now realize that the "a god" translation is grammatically justifiable, it is nevertheless contended that John's "monotheism" (his devotion to *one* God) would not have allowed for such a meaning. For example, Robert Bowman contends: "The point is that for JWs to translate 'a god' is in one sense grammatically possible, but *only if they are willing to adopt a pagan interpretation of this verse.*"[82] Similarly, in a 1977 periodical sent to Bible scholars, C. H. Dodd argued: "*As a word-for-word translation ['the Word was a god'] cannot be faulted,* and to pagan Greeks who heard early

---
[81] Thompson, *The God of the Gospel of John*, p. 46.
[82] Bowman, *Jesus Christ and the Gospel of John*, p. 62.

The "deity" of Jesus Christ

Christian language, *theos en ho logos*, might have seemed a perfectly sensible statement...the reason why it is unacceptable is that it *runs counter to the current of Johannine thought, and indeed Christian through as a whole.*"[83] Murray J. Harris's work, *Jesus as God*—described by one source as "the most extensive exegetical treatment ever published dealing with New Testament passages that refer to Jesus as 'God'"[84]—conceded to the same point with respect to the *grammar* while maintaining the same position with respect to the *theology*:

> Accordingly, from the point of view of grammar alone, *theos en ho logos* could be rendered 'the Word was a god,'...But the theological context, viz., John's monotheism, makes this rendering of 1:1c impossible, for if a monotheist were speaking of the Deity he himself reverenced the singular *theos* could be applied only to the Supreme Being, not to an inferior divine being or emanation as if *theos* were simply generic. That is, in reference to his *own* beliefs, a monotheist could not speak of *theoi* [gods] nor could he use *theos* in the singular (when giving any type of personal description) to any being other than the one true God whom he worshiped."[85]

In *The Forgotten Trinity*, Dr. White advances the same kind of reasoning: "In reference to the [translation, 'the word was a god'], we can dismiss it almost immediately. The reasons are as follows: *Monotheism in the Bible*—certainly it cannot be argued that John would use the very word he always uses of the one true God, *theos*, of one who is simply a 'godlike' one or a lesser 'god.' The Scriptures do not teach that there exists a whole host of intermediate beings that can truly be called 'gods.' That is gnosticism."[86]

Unfortunately, such objections are both superficial and misleading. Surprisingly, Harris claims that "a monotheist [like

---

[83] *The Bible Translator*, Vol. 28, No. 1, Jan. 1977 (emphasis added).
[84] Grudem, *Systematic Theology*, p. 544.
[85] Harris, *Jesus As God*, p. 60.
[86] White, *The Forgotten Trinity*, pp. 55, 56.

John] could not speak of *theoi* ('gods') nor could he use *theos* in the singular (when giving any type of personal description) to any being other than the one true God whom he worshiped." But in the very same Gospel account, Jesus himself spoke of "gods" (*theoi*) as a term applying to the ancient human rulers of Israel.[87] Other Scriptures *truly* call the angels "gods" (*elohim*, Psalm 8:5); and in Psalm 45:6 the king of Israel was truly called "God" (*elohim*, which is plural in form but *singular* in meaning). Thus, the arguments of James White and Murray Harris simply contradict the information given to us in the Scriptures.[88]

In light of the issues that have been raised surrounding the accurate translation and meaning of John 1:1, one would benefit from considering the question: If there *is* scriptural precedent for angels and even human rulers to be called "gods"[89] (something perfectly acceptable within the framework of 'biblical monotheism'), why, then, is it problematic for the one that was "with God in the beginning" to be called "a god" or "a divine being" when that one is obviously so much closer to God and hence more deserving than them?[90] The question is critical. Because although it is vigorously contended that John could not have said that there was another god or divine being (*theos*) alongside the one God (*ho theos*) in the beginning, defenders of

---

[87] Or perhaps the angels of God as some Bible expositors believe.

[88] Harris also appears to contradict himself on this point. As mentioned, in the same book (p. 26), Harris noted that "both *el*, [god] and *elohim* [gods], have extended or 'irregular' applications to angels or to persons who represent on earth divine power, judgment, or majesty." And in a footnote on page 44, Harris quotes another scholar who noted, in light of John 10:34-35, that there is in fact, "scriptural precedent for the use of *theoi* [gods] in reference to mere mortals who received God's word..." Additionally, it should be noted that the Scriptures *do* indicate that the angels are *elohim* ('mighty/divine beings' or 'gods'), and that there is, in fact, a whole host of such beings in heaven, and who, in many cases, *do* act as intermediaries or messengers. In his revelation, John wrote: "I heard the voice of many angels around the throne...and the number of them was myriads of myriads, and thousands of thousands..." (Revelation 5:11, *NASB*)

[89] Psalm 8:5; Hebrews 2:7; Psalm 45:6, 7; Psalm 82:6

[90] Marianne Thompson makes a helpful observation relevant to the Gospel of John and the Jewish-Christian mindset as a whole: "John is working within the same constraints that bind Jewish authors such as Philo and the translators of the Targums: namely, the biblical affirmation that there is one God and the scriptural warrant for referring to individuals as 'god' or 'gods.' As we saw...Jewish authors interpret the attribution of 'god' to individuals because they either have attained a particularly intimate status with God or have been assigned a particular function or status by God." —*The God of the Gospel of John* (Grand Rapids: Eerdmans, 2001), p. 234.

The "deity" of Jesus Christ

Trinitarian orthodoxy never explain how and why it is that Israelite rulers and angels (God's *messengers*)[91] can rightfully be called "gods" ('and the scripture cannot be broken'),[92] yet God's very own word or *logos* (which ultimately became flesh in the man Jesus), the supreme revealer of God's will and purpose, could not be described in a similar way. Trinitarian apologists endeavor, unsuccessfully, to give the impression that the alternative translation is "impossible" because no one else beside God can properly be termed "god"—in spite of the fact that the Scriptures themselves already verify that others can rightfully bear that description. So, in reality, it turns out that the meaning "a god" for John 1:1 is not only grammatically legitimate in terms of translation, as well as contextually and logically coherent (remembering that 'the word' was 'with' God), but reconcilable and harmonious in terms of the overall biblical worldview.

Interestingly, the point about the use and nonuse of the article in John 1:1 was made as early as the third century C. E. In his scholarly work, *The Orthodox Corruption of Scripture*, Bart Ehrman commented: "it is worth pointing out that Origen already used the *absence* of the article in John 1:1 to demonstrate Christ's subordination to God (*Jn.* Com 2.2.17-18)."[93] Origen, probably the most learned Bible scholar of the third century, wrote under the (modern editor's) subtitle *"In what way the Logos is God. Errors to be avoided on this question"*:

> We notice John's use of the article in three instances. He does not write without care and respect, nor is he unfamiliar with the niceties of the Greek tongue. In some cases he uses the article, and in some he omits it. He adds the article to the Logos, but to the name of God he adds it sometimes only. He uses the article, when the name of

---

[91] As it was noted by one source: "The Bible shows that Yahweh is thought of as supreme in a heavenly assembly of divine beings. (cf. note on [Ps]82)" —*Peake's Commentary on the Bible* (Thomas Nelson, May 1962), p. 442.
[92] See John 10:35
[93] *The Orthodox Corruption of Scripture, The Effect of Early Christological Controversies on the Text of the New Testament* (New York: Oxford University Press, 1993), p. 179.

The "deity" of Jesus Christ

God refers to the uncreated cause of all things, and omits it when the Logos is named God...God on the one hand is Very God (Autotheos, God of Himself); and so the Savior says in His prayer to the Father, 'That they may know Thee the only true God;' but that all beyond the Very God is made God by participation in His divinity, and is not to be called simply God (with the article), but rather God (without article). And thus the first-born of all creation, who is the first to be with God, and to attract to Himself divinity, is a being of more exalted rank than the other gods beside Him, of whom God is the God, as it is written, 'The God of gods, the Lord, hath spoken and called the earth.' The true God, then, is 'The God,' and those who are formed after Him are gods, images, as it were of Him the prototype. But the archetypal image, again, of all these images is the Word of God, who was in the beginning, and who by being with God is at all times God, not possessing that of Himself, but by His being with the Father...[94]

Ultimately, however, there is a point where debate around this one phrase reaches a kind of impasse or standstill regarding its true significance. Defenders of a particular viewpoint on the translation have argued their points in debate form through literally hundreds of pages of exchange. Did the apostle mean that the *logos* was "*a* god," or "deity (*God* as to his substance," or did he mean something else?

Whether one comes to a settled conviction on the matter or not, it is good that at least we are now able to clear away many of the popular and widespread misconceptions that have surrounded this text. The fact is, not only is the meaning "the-word-was-a-god" in the realm of legitimate (and even most natural of) possibilities,—in terms of language, grammar, and

---

[94] Origen's *Commentary on John, Book II, Ant-Nicene Fathers,* Volume 9 (Peabody: Hendrickson Publishers, 1994), p. 365. Justin Martyr, an early Christian writer, wrote in reference to Christ: "There is, and there is said to be, *another God* and Lord subject to the Maker of all things; who is also called an Angel, because He announces to men whatsoever the Maker of all things—above whom there is no other God—wishes to announce to them." —*Dialogue With Trypho, Ante Nicene Fathers,* Volume 1, p. 223 (emphasis added).

translation into English—the meaning is also appropriate in terms of the Bible's overall presentation concerning the recognition of one supreme God, while, at the same time, allowing for the existence of others who are rightfully called "gods," "God," or "a god," in another sense. In addition to the grammatical issue, this is a point confirming that there are no significant obstacles in the way of the proposed indefinite translation, although it is true that such a meaning may be contrary to popular and traditional perceptions.

Although in English it may come across as unconventional and unfamiliar, even awkward[95],—especially if one is accustomed to the traditional "Word was God" reading—an English translation true to the sense that can be derived from the grammar would be: "the word was a god" (or 'the word was a deity' or 'a divinity'); or even, as suggested by Protestant Bible translator Dr. Robert Young and Roman Catholic scholar John L. McKenzie: "the Word was a divine being/a Divine being was the Word."[96] However, in the interest of modern sensibilities, perhaps the verse could satisfactorily be rendered (as it already has been rendered by some translators) "the word was divine" in the main text, with a marginal footnote that reads "literally: '*a god was the word*' or 'the word was *a* god.'"

Traditional aversions to the "a god" translation have probably stemmed from a combination of factors. Generally, they have had to do with long-time familiarity with, and uncritical acceptance of, the traditional "Word was God" rendition. Objections may also involve a conditioned, negative reaction toward the possibility that another divine being could have existed alongside the one God before the creation of the

---

[95] In order to avoid awkwardness, one might translate: "In the beginning was the word, and the word was with God, and the word [itself] was a god [or, the word himself was a god]."

[96] It should be noted that if the suggested translation/sense is correct, it would seem difficult to reconcile such with the idea that the *logos* of John 1 is not a reference to a personal being. In this way the *logos* might have been thought of as God's principal, divine messenger or spokesperson who, later, *gave up* his divine existence in order to become a man. But perhaps it is possible—if "the-word-was-a-god" is the sense John intended—that this was John's rhetorical or poetic way of *personifying* the *logos*—the wisdom, promise and purpose of God—*which became a literal person when* "the word became flesh (v. 14)."

world;[97] and even, reluctance to accept what has now come to be almost exclusively associated with a religious group considered by many to be outside of the "mainstream"—a group often negatively described as a "cult"—so that it is perceived to be an aberrant translation designed to further the sectarian interests of a "heretical" religious body. This has often been accompanied by a *mistaken* impression that the "a god" translation is unique to, and had its origin with, the *New World Translation*. But however one views a particular religious group, in the end, such should not decisively influence or interfere with the Christian's goal of rooting out and abandoning all unscriptural traditions, with view to the discovery and exclusive attainment of divinely-revealed truth—which, for most of us, depends largely upon accuracy of Bible translation.[98]

The corresponding significance of John 1:18

In the same chapter discussed—according to the most ancient papyrus manuscripts—John went on to link the term *theos* to Jesus Christ for the second time.[99] In verse 18, John wrote: "No one has seen God at any time; an only-begotten god [or, 'a unique' or 'uniquely-derived god'; Gk: *monogenes theos*], the one existing in the bosom of the Father, he has explained him."[100]

---

[97] Additionally, to speak of the *logos* (which became the man Jesus Christ) as "a god" might be perceived as meaning that the *logos* is not special or unique, but merely one god out of numerous gods without any distinction. However, the *logos* is spoken of specifically as "a god" only once in the Scriptures (assuming the translation is correct), and it should be remembered that the *logos* is not merely some strange, ordinary, arbitrary or rival god. In reference to *the Son*, at least, the apostle John speaks of him as the "unique" or "only-begotten" god who dwells in "the bosom of the Father" (John 1:18).

[98] Quite a few translations depart from the traditional *KJV* rendition: "The Logos existed in the very beginning, the Logos was with God, the Logos was divine" (*A New Translation, by James Moffatt*); "In the Beginning was the Word. *And the Word was with God.* So the Word was divine" (*The Original New Testament, Schonfield*). If John had used the Greek word *theios*, the translation "divine" would then be a literal or formally equivalent translation.

[99] Or at the least we could say that, with respect to John 1:1, the term *theos* is applied to the subject/figure that would *become* Jesus Christ.

[100] John 1:18 (*NASB* similar). *Weymouth's New Testament in Modern Speech* renders the phrase: "only-born God" in a footnote. The main text of the *Bible in Living English* has "an Only Born

The meaning of the word *monogenes*, however, is disputed, and almost every English Bible version renders the expression contained there in a different way.[101] The expression itself is a combination of two words—the word *mono*, meaning "only," and the word *genes*, which was, at one time, generally thought to come from the word *gennao* (to 'give birth' to); hence the translation "only-begotten (or 'only-born/generated') god." But many scholars have appealed to evidence indicating that *genes* is actually derived from *genos*, a different word, meaning "kind" or "type." If that is the case, the phrase may then mean and be translated "unique" or "one-of-a-kind," a rendering preferred by some Trinitarian scholars. Murray Harris, however, questioned the exclusive notion of "uniqueness," saying that *monogenes* really means "'of sole descent,' referring to the only child in a family, a meaning attested in secular Greek literature, and the LXX and other Jewish literature, and the NT.'"[102]

Some evangelical scholars have thought that since *monogenes theos* might mean "one-of-a-kind-god" (rather than 'only-begotten-god'), that this somehow lends credence to the Trinitarian doctrine on the nature of Jesus Christ. However, what the apologists have failed to recognize in this regard is that even

---

God." J.B. Rotherham translated it: "No one, hath seen, God, at any time: An Only Begotten God, The One existing within the bosom of the Father, He, hath interpreted him."

[101] Some translations, like *KJV*, have "the only begotten Son" (*monogenes huios*). But this is a rendering generally agreed to be based on an inferior tradition of manuscripts. According to F. F. Bruce, the reading *monogenes theos* is "attested by early authorities, including the two earliest known (the Bodemer papyri 66 and 75)..." —*The Gospel of John*, p. 44. Another source likewise points out: "The manuscript evidence for the first reading, *an only-begotten, God* (*monogenes theos*) is decidedly superior to the evidence for the second reading, *the only-begotten Son* (*monogenes huios*). The papyrus MSS [manuscripts] (P66 P75), the earliest and best uncial MSS ([Aleph]* B C* L) and some good early versions (Coptic and Syriac) support the first reading...The fact that P66 [A.D. 150-175] and P75 [A.D. 200], two of the earliest extant MSS, read—*God* has firmly secured this reading a place in the text of John." —*Guide to the Ancient Manuscripts, A Guide to Understanding Marginal Notes on Differences in the New Testament Manuscripts*, Philip W. Comfort (Wheaton: Tyndale House, 1974), p. 2004.

[102] Harris, *Jesus as God*, p. 84. "That *monogenes* may bear the meaning 'unique' when applied to nonpersonal objects is beyond dispute. But it is less clear that this is the predominant or primary sense of the word...Certainly in Johannine usage the conjunction of *monogenes* and *huios* shows that it is not the personal uniqueness of Jesus in itself that John is emphasizing but his being 'of sole descent' as the Son of God." Some Trinitarians have pushed for the translation "God the only Son," but Harris notes, "John did not write *theos monogenes*, which makes it doubtful that the popular translation 'God the only Son' is the most accurate." —Harris, *Jesus as God*, pp. 85, 91.

if we were to take the expression to mean "unique" or "one-of-a kind-G/god," we still have the Scripture revealing to us that the Son is *a certain kind* of god, whether "only-begotten" or "one-of-a-kind."

But why, one might understandably ask, was the Son described as a "unique" or "one-of-a-kind" god? Likely, because—as certain translations render the verse—he is "the only God" that dwells in "closest intimacy with the Father," the Most High God (*ESV*, *PME*). This one alone, as a god (or in the form of 'the word'), was "with God" in the beginning. These are, it seems, at least some of the reasons that may constitute the Son as "unique."

So, regardless of what the term *monogenes* means (whether 'only-begotten' or 'unique'), if *monogenes theos* represents the original reading, the description itself would only seem to confirm that the Son was regarded by John as "a god" of a specific type (not a 'person' *of* God, but himself a unique and distinguishable *theos*), and that the indefinite sense for John 1:1 ('a divine being' or 'a god') is correct. If the Son is an "only-begotten-god," this may be so because he was, according to one possible way of looking at it, *uniquely* and *directly* generated by his Father; all others were created *by* God *through* him. If the Son is a "unique/one-of-a-kind-god," this is so, likely, because he is the only one that dwells in "the bosom of the Father." In either case, the doctrine of the Trinity is clearly at odds with this text, for the Almighty God could never have been described as "an-only-begotten/unique-god" who dwells in someone else's bosom. And since Trinitarianism teaches that the members of the "Godhead" can be "with," or in relation to one another, as "persons" (and *only* as 'persons,' not as 'beings'), how can a certain kind of "G/god"—a specific kind of *being*—be in the bosom of the "person" of the Father?

In view of the controversial issues of translation discussed here and in the rest of this chapter, it should be remembered that whenever one come across aspects of Scripture that appear to be open to more than one possible

The "deity" of Jesus Christ

understanding,—in terms of the meaning of the original language, or in terms of the understanding of a particular expression that comes across as ambiguous, or even in the case of a controversial textual variation—it is not advisable to approach the texts in the spirit of trying to produce evidence for a preferred or already-established doctrinal concept. There are many aspects of the Bible that are straightforward and clearly stated; there are other aspects, however, that are not so clear. Or, at least, there often proves to be, from the human perspective, several legitimate possibilities open to us, when it comes to certain matters of Bible teaching and interpretation. In whatever parts of Scripture that may present a degree of ambiguity, we can only examine what the language allows for, what seems to make the most logical sense, and what harmonizes with the Bible's teaching as a whole. In these areas, however, hasty interpretation, dogmatism and intolerance are not only unwise but unnecessary.[103] This is so particularly when the issues under consideration do not negatively alter or affect the way we live or the way we treat others. The teachings that *are* essential *are* clear and unchangeable. Among them is the fact that there is one true God (Jehovah), the Father, creator of all; that Jesus of Nazareth is God's beloved Son and Messiah; that God sent his Son into the world to rescue sinners from condemnation; that God raised him from the dead, exalted him to his right hand as Lord, and that Jesus—the "one mediator between God and men"—has "the only name under heaven given among men by which we must be

---

[103] It was pointed out by one Bible student: "Many times it is not tenable to speak in terms of certainties, but rather probabilities and possibilities. The best Bible commentaries provide multiple translation and interpretation options and then give reasons why one particular understanding may be more viable than others. When legitimate alternative understandings of a given text are slighted, overlooked, or simply ignored, the impression is given to the learner that there is only one interpretation and understanding...When a modern reader looks at a text written 2000-3500 years earlier, there are many gaps that need to be bridged in order to comprehend the intended meaning. Many times, even after attempting to bridge each gap of language, culture, geography, and presuppositions, the interpretation of a text still remains in the realm of possibility rather than certainty." —*A Humble Plea for Intellectual Honesty and Authenticity among the People of God* by Dan Mages

saved."[104]

In whatever way a Christian understands certain portions of Scripture that may be ambiguous to some degree, such will not change the fact that the Christian life should be characterized first and foremost by loving God with all of our strength, and by loving our neighbors as ourselves, in imitation of the way God loved us, manifested in the sacrifice of his Son for our sake.

In reference to whatever measure of uncertainty we might face in our continuing pursuit of knowledge, the countless questions we may ask, ponder over, and explore along our spiritual path, the comforting words of the apostle will always prove worthy of reflection in their light:

> **At present we are men looking at puzzling reflections in a mirror. The time will come when we shall see reality whole and face to face! At present all I know is a little fraction of the truth ['the knowledge I have now is imperfect,' *JB*], but the time will come when I shall know it as fully as God has known me! In this life we have three lasting qualities—faith, hope and love, But the greatest of them is love.**[105]

John 10:30

In terms of shedding light on the true identity of Jesus Christ, the account in John chapter ten is very significant. In fact, in this particular account, Jesus expresses himself quite plainly about who he is in relation to God (vs. 30, 36); at the same time, further enlightening us with respect to the broader scriptural application of the term "god(s)" (vs. 34, 35). For the sake of clarity and full comprehension, the entire account is reproduced according to the *New Revised Standard Version* (10:22-38):

> **At that time the festival of the Dedication took place in Jerusalem. It was winter, and Jesus was walking in**

---

[104] Jeremiah 10:10; Matthew 16:16; John 3:16; 14: 6; 17:3; Colossians 1:16; Philippians 2:5-11; 1 Timothy 2:5; Acts 4:12
[105] 1 Corinthians 13:12-13, *Philip's Modern English*

the temple, in the portico of Solomon. So the Jews gathered around him and said to him, 'How long will you keep us in suspense? If you are the Messiah, tell us plainly.' Jesus answered, 'I have told you, and you do not believe. The works that I do in my Father's name testify to me; but you do not believe, because you do not belong to my sheep. My sheep hear my voice. I know them, and they follow me. I give them eternal life, and they will never perish. No one will snatch them out of my hand. My Father who has given them to me is greater than all, and no one can snatch them out of the Father's hand. The Father and I are one.' The Jews took up stones again to stone him. Jesus replied, 'I have shown you many good works from the Father. For which of these are you going to stone me?' The Jews answered, 'It is not for a good work that we are going to stone you, but for blasphemy, because you, though only a human being, are making yourself God [or, 'You, a mere man, claim to be a god,' *New English Bible*].' Jesus answered, 'Is it not written in your law, 'I said, you are gods'? If those to whom the word of God came were called 'gods'— and the scripture cannot be annulled ['and Scripture cannot be set aside,' *New English Bible*]—can you say that the one whom the Father has sanctified and sent into the world is blaspheming because I said, 'I am God's Son'? If I am not doing the works of my Father, then do not believe me. But if I do them, even though you do not believe me, believe the works, so that you may know and understand that the Father is in me and I am in the Father.

As is evident from the above account, during the course of Jesus' confrontation with the Jews, we receive additional confirmation regarding his identity and deeper insight into his unique relationship to God the Father. Because Jesus said that he and the Father are "one," many Trinitarians have argued that Jesus had in mind, "I and the Father are one in *essence* (or

The "deity" of Jesus Christ

being)."[106] One Trinitarian apologist even said that here, "Jesus asserts His *ontological* oneness with the Father...Both the Father and the Son are one substance, God." The apologist concluded: "we should view 'I and the Father are one' as a *metaphysical* statement, a statement that Christ and the Father are of the same nature. Hence, Jesus in His incarnate state is God the Son."[107] Evangelical author Dr. Robert Morey likewise claimed: "When Jesus said in verse 30, 'I and the Father, we are One,' the Jews rightly understood that He was saying that He and the Father were one in nature and essence."[108]

Although many Trinitarian apologists have pushed for a similar interpretation, others have expressed open disagreement. John Calvin (1509-1564), one of Protestantism's most respected and celebrated Bible scholars (described by Morey as the 'greatest of the Reformers,' *The Trinity, Evidence and Issues*, p. 294), directly contradicted the common Trinitarian exposition in his commentary on the Gospel of John:

> *I and the Father are one.* [Christ] intended to meet the jeers of the wicked; for they might allege that the power of God did not belong to him, so that he could promise to his disciples that it would assuredly protect them. He therefore testifies that his affairs are so closely united to those of the Father, that the Father's assistance will never be withheld from himself and his *sheep*. The ancients made a wrong use of this passage to prove that Christ is (*homoousios*) of the same essence with the Father. For Christ does not argue about the unity of substance, but about the agreement which he has with the Father, so that whatever is done by Christ will be confirmed by the power of his Father.[109]

It was similarly observed in the modern and conservative *Tyndale Commentaries*:

---

[106] Other groups have even taken this expression to mean, in effect, "I am God the Father" (or 'I and the Father are one and the same person').
[107] Tsoukalas, *Knowing Christ and the Challenge of Heresy*, pp. 77, 78 (emphasis added).
[108] Morey, *The Trinity, Evidence and Issues*, p. 327.
[109] *Calvin's Commentaries* (Delaware: Associated Publishers and Authors, n.d.), p. 780.

One translates the Greek neuter *hen*. This verse was much quoted in the Arian controversy by the orthodox in support of the doctrine that Christ was of one substance with the Father. The expression seems however mainly to imply that the Father and the Son are united in will and purpose. Jesus prays in [John 17:11] that His followers may all be one (*hen*), i.e. united in purpose, as He and His Father are united.[110]

As perceptively pointed out by the above commentary, the Lord's prayer for his disciples in John chapter seventeen really does help to clarify the sense in which Jesus meant that he and his Father are one. Speaking with reference to his followers, Jesus prayed:

> **Holy Father, protect them by the power of your name—the name you gave me—so that they may be one (*hen*) as we are one...My prayer is not for them alone. I pray also for those who will believe in me through their message, that all of them may be one, Father, just as you are in me and I am in you. May they also be in us so that the world may believe that you have sent me. I have given them the glory that you gave me, that they may be one as we are one: I in them and you in me. May they be brought to complete unity ['that they may be made perfect in one (*hen*),' *KJV*] to let the world know that you sent me and have loved them even as you have loved me.**[111]

When Jesus prayed for his disciples to be "one," he did not mean that he wanted them to constitute "one metaphysical substance" or "one being," but that they would be *united* as one, just as he and his Father are. It seems reasonably clear that in John chapter ten, when Jesus spoke to his Jewish opponents

---

[110] *The Gospel According to St John*, Tyndale New Testament Commentaries, p. 136. It was further pointed out by F. F. Bruce: "So responsive is the Son to the Father that he is one in mind, one in purpose, one in action with him. Where the eternal wellbeing of true believers is concerned, the Son's determination and pledge to guard them from harm is endorsed by the Father's all-powerful act." —*The Gospel of John, Introduction, Exposition and Notes*, p. 283.
[111] John 17:10-11; 20-23, *NIV*

about his "oneness" with the Father, that he was speaking primarily about the fact that he was perfectly united—in complete agreement and harmony—with his Father, particularly with regard to the *one purpose* or *commitment* they held to in safeguarding the sheep (disciples) by keeping them within the safety of their respective fold. Such appears likely when we consider how Jesus first said, "no one will snatch them out of *my* hand," then, "no one will snatch them out of *the Father's* hand," and then, "*I and the Father are one*."[112]

At the same time, the statement may also include reference to the Son's special and intimate bond of union that he has with the Father as God's unique Son; the one whom John had earlier described as being "in the bosom of the Father"; or that he was the one who is, as the *New English Bible* expresses it, "nearest to the Father's heart."[113] But whether or not Jesus intended to emphasize this fact—the very quality of his relationship with the Father—in this case may be difficult to determine with certainty.[114]

It is also helpful to note that the apostle Paul made use of a similar expression in his first letter to the Corinthians: "I planted, Apollos watered, but God gave the growth. So neither he who plants nor he who waters is anything, but only God who gives the growth. He who plants and he who waters are *one* (*hen*), and each will receive his wages according to his labor. For we are God's fellow workers."[115]

In this instance, the one who plants and the one who

---

[112] In her work *The God of the Gospel of John* (p. 78), Mariane Thompson points out that "throughout the Gospel, there is a concerted effort to argue that the work of the Son is indeed the very work of the Father, and that the Father does his work through the Son. Hence the most famous of all the Johannine assertions regarding the unity of the Father and Son, namely, 'I and the Father are one' (10:30), actually refers in context to Jesus' promise that the Father and Son are one in the work of preserving the sheep of the fold from loss or harm."

[113] John 1:18

[114] According to one student of Scripture: "The glory of Christ's relationship to God as Son is very much obscured by the claims of Trinitarian teaching. The unity of Father and Son cannot lie in oneness of 'Substance' or 'Essence' but in the Son's loving obedience to the Father's will. 'Lo! I am arriving—in the summary of the scroll it is written concerning me—to do Thy will, O God' (Heb. 10:7)." —*Christ and Deity*, A. E. Knoch, p. 31.

[115] 1 Corinthians 3:6-9, *ESV*

waters are not *metaphysically* "one (as to their essence)" but functionally "one (united)" in their cooperation, agreement, or aim to cause the plant—evidently, the believer—to grow, with the aim of bearing fruit spiritually—or as the *NIV* paraphrases: "The man who plants and the man who waters *have one purpose*..."

In all likelihood, Jesus was expressing a very similar thought in John chapter ten with respect to the "oneness" he had with his Father, particularly in view of their promised provision of security for Jesus' true followers—"In the work of salvation the Father and the Son are completely at one."[116] There is no evidence that such was to be taken as an "ontological" or "metaphysical" statement. And, although, as John Calvin rightly stated, "the ancients made a wrong use of this passage to prove that Christ is of the same essence with the Father," there still remain many among our own contemporaries who, unfortunately, wrongly use the passage for the same purpose.

The next part of the passage that must be considered is the one describing the way in which the Jews reacted to Jesus' claim, along with Jesus' answer to their accusation of blasphemy. When the Jews picked up stones to stone him, Jesus asked them (rhetorically) to identify which one of the fine deeds he performed was the cause for their desire to stone him. The Jews in turn indicated that they were not attempting to stone Jesus for any fine deed, but for blasphemy, because although he was a mere man, he was making himself out to be a god.[117] The point that Jesus made, in answer to the Jewish charge of blasphemy, was that according to the very Law or Scripture that the Jews themselves professed belief in, "I," that is, God, "called

---

[116] F. F. Bruce, *The Gospel of John*, p. 153.

[117] In terms of grammar, the verse may be legitimately rendered "God" or "a god." However, Jesus responded by citing an OT text where others were called "gods," suggesting on what level the charge was being made. If the Jews accused Jesus of making himself out to be God himself, and he really was "God-in-the-flesh," why did he quote from a text where others are called "gods" as an answer to their accusation? Yet even if the Jews *did* accuse Jesus of making himself out to be "God," notice what would then be rightfully considered to be a *correction* or *clarification* in Jesus response: "can you say that the one whom the Father has consecrated and sent into the world blasphemes because I said, 'I am *the Son* of God'" (v. 36)?

The "deity" of Jesus Christ

them (the judges of Israel) 'gods,'"[118] *and the Scripture cannot be broken*; and if this is a fact established by Scripture itself, how is it that the Jews are now accusing Jesus (in reality, the very one whom the Father 'consecrated' and 'sent forth' into the world) of blasphemy because he said that he was God's *Son*? And although it really goes without saying, it should be pointed out respectfully in regard to this particular account that Jesus never did claim to be God but, rather, God's "Son"—did he not?[119]

The only aspect requiring closer attention is the background and context of the Old Testament quotation. In this respect, most commentators actually agree as to the basic point Jesus' was intending to get across. Indeed the point is quite clear and, if we are careful, difficult to miss. Charles Ryrie correctly noted: "Christ's point is that if the O.T. uses the word 'God' (Elohim) of men who were representative of God, then the Jews should not oppose Him for calling Himself the Son of God."[120] J. C. Fenton observed: "The quotation is from Ps. 82:6, in which the rulers and judges of Israel are addressed as *gods*. The argument is *a fortiori* [meaning, 'for a still stronger, more certain reason']: if those who received the Law (= *the word of God*) are called *gods*, how much more is it right that the unique agent of God (called 'the Word' in 1:1; 14) should speak of himself as *the Son of God?*[121] *The Interpreter's Bible* similarly states: "He quoted Ps. 82:6, where God says to the judges of Israel, 'I said

---

[118] "In Ps. 81 (82):6, rulers are called 'gods,' because they represent God." —*The New Testament by Kleist and Lily*, p. 263. Yet it was observed by F. F. Bruce: "Jewish interpreters were divided (as other interpreters have been divided since then) on the question whether those addressed in these terms by God are celestial beings or human judges. For our present purpose this question is not of the first relevance: what is relevant is that they are manifestly inferior beings to the supreme God, and yet he calls them 'gods' (verse 6)—*theoi* in Greek. If God himself calls them 'gods' (and 'sons of the Most High' at that), why should it be counted a capital offense in the sent one of the Father if he calls himself the Son of God." —*The Gospel of John, Introduction, Exposition and Notes*, p. 235

[119] Again, even if the translation "you make yourself out to be *God*" is the correct sense, part of Jesus' point in his response would have been to prove that they were *mistaken* in this conclusion. But F. F. Bruce was right in his commentary: "He is not 'making himself God'; he is not 'making himself' anything, but in word and work he is showing himself to be what he truly is—the Son sent by the Father to bring light and life to mankind." —*The Gospel of John, Introduction, Exposition and Notes*, p. 234.

[120] *The Ryrie Study Bible, New American Standard Version New Testament*, p. 183.

[121] *The New Clarendon Bible, The Gospel According to John*, p. 117.

Ye are gods, and all of you sons of the Most High.' If an inspired scripture allowed that title to mere men to whom God entrusted a message, how much more can he, whom the Father consecrated and sent into the world, claim to say I am the Son of God (vs. 36), without incurring the reproach of blasphemy?"[122] John Calvin further elaborated on the point:

> Scripture gives the name of gods to those on whom God has conferred an honourable office. He whom God has separated, to be distinguished above all others [His Son] is far more worthy of this honourable title...The passage which Christ quotes is in Psalm 82:6...where God expostulates with the kings and judges of the earth, who tyrannically abuse the authority and power for their own sinful passions, for oppressing the poor, and for every evil action...Christ applies this to the case in hand, that they receive the name of gods, because they are God's ministers for governing the world. For the same reason Scripture calls the angels gods, because by them the glory of God beams forth on the world...In short, let us know that magistrates are called gods, because God has given them authority.[123]

Not only do we find in the Bible examples of other individuals legitimately called "gods" (by God himself), Jesus Christ, God's own Son, was the very one who made this point in his own defense against the Jewish charge of blasphemy; even noting—as a reinforcing principle—that the very Scriptures that establish this point cannot be "set aside" (*NEB*) or "broken" (*NASB*).[124] When Trinitarian apologists argue, in essence, that

---

[122] *The Interpreter's Bible*, p. 634.

[123] John Calvin, *Commentary on the Gospel According to John*, p. 419, 20. The point can be made that since, as Calvin pointed out, Scripture calls angels gods "because by them the glory of God beams forth in the world," how much more appropriate would it be for the Scriptures to apply the title 'God' or 'a god' to Christ, when the author of Hebrews said that he in fact "radiates God's glory" (*The Translator's New Testament*). Or, as rendered in other versions: "He reflects the brightness of God's glory and is the exact likeness of God's own being" (*TEV*). He is, "the outshining of His glory and [the] exact expression of His essence" (*Analytical-Literal Translation*), or "the beam of his glory and imprint of his essence" (*The Bible in Living English*).

[124] "The parenthetical note *And the scripture cannot be broken* belongs to Jesus' words rather than the author's. Not only does Jesus appeal to the OT to defend himself against the charge of

The "deity" of Jesus Christ

Jesus cannot be called "God" without him being "of-the-same substance-as-the-Father," or "a god" without jeopardizing the truth of biblical "monotheism," they are, in effect, 'setting aside' the very Scriptures that already establish that this is not the case. They are, at the same time, simply forgetting the fact that, as Calvin says, "Scripture gives the name of gods to those on whom God has conferred an honorable office." And who could deny from Scripture that God has conferred upon his Son a most honorable office? God has not only "highly exalted him" and given him a "seat at the right hand of the Majesty on high," where he acts as "high priest" and "mediator" of a "new" and "better covenant," but has even gone as far as to confer upon him "all authority in heaven and on earth" and "the name that is above every name."[125] Clearly, Christ has received the most "honorable office" of all.

In light of Jesus' reference to other individuals called "gods" by God in this account,[126] the producers of the *New English Translation* go a step further, yet correctly infer the following point—striking at the very heart of the issues discussed in relation to an accurate understanding of the Godship possessed by Christ: "The reason the OT judges could be called

---

blasphemy, but he also adds that the scripture cannot be 'broken.' In this context he does not explain precisely what is meant by 'broken,' but it is not too hard to determine. Jesus' argument depended on the exact word used in the context of Ps 82:6. If any other word for 'judge' had been used in the psalm, his argument would have been meaningless. Since the scriptures do use this word in Ps 82:6, the argument is binding, because they cannot be 'broken' in the sense of being shown to be in error." —*New English Translation* footnote.

[125] Philippians 2:5-11; Hebrews 1:3; 8; 9:15; 12:12:24; Matthew 28:18.

[126] Yet it is true that one "should not rashly exaggerate the number of instances in which 'god' is used of human beings or other figures in Jewish tradition, which acknowledged multiple 'heavenly' beings, such as angels and spirits. Nor should one ignore the conditions, including the existence of biblical precedent and the focus on the exercise of specific functions, that attend the application of the term 'god' to such figures. Whether or not one ought to apply the label 'divine' to such beings depends entirely on how one construes the meaning of that term. Yet however many 'heavenly beings' there might be, and whether they ought to be called 'divine,' what ultimately discloses their identity is not whether they are called 'god' but what sort of honors or veneration they merit, what functions they exercise, and, perhaps most importantly, how they came to exercise those functions. Thus, when human beings or angels overstep their limits, demanding worship or exercising their authority by virtue of claims to divinity or kinship with the divine, the charges leveled against them typically do not refute their claims to metaphysical status of divinity but rather rebuke them for their failure to keep their own place." —Thompson, *The God of the Gospel of John*, p. 45.

gods is because they were vehicles of the word of God (cf. 10:35). But granting that premise, Jesus deserves much more than they to be called God. He is the Word incarnate ['the word became flesh,' John 1:14], whom the Father sanctified and sent into the world to save the world...If it is permissible to call men 'gods' because they were the vehicles of the word of God, how much more permissible is it to use the word 'God' of him who is the Word of God?"[127]

Acts 20:28

> "But we shall find that on almost every occasion in the New Testament on which Jesus seems to be called God there is a problem either of textual criticism or of translation. In almost every case we have to discuss which of two readings is to be accepted or which of two possible translations is to be accepted."
>
> —William Barclay, *Jesus As They Saw Him, New Testament Interpretations of Jesus*, p. 21

"Therefore take heed to yourselves and to all the flock, among which the Holy Spirit has made you overseers, to shepherd the church of God which He purchased with His own blood." —Acts 20:28, NKJV

The statement that "God" purchased the church with "his own blood" is found in several English Bible translations, including *KJV* and *NASB*. Some Trinitarians view this as a "proof-text" establishing the "absolute deity" of Christ as traditionally understood in Catholic and Protestant theology.

---

[127] *New English Translation*, p. 321. A close look at the original Psalm from which Jesus quotes shows that although these individuals were called "gods" by virtue of the office given them, they were actually denounced in judgment by God because of their wickedness and failure to execute justice. How much more worthy is God's own Son, the one who was "consecrated and sent into the world" (the righteous 'one who has been appointed by God as Judge of the living and the dead' Acts 10:42) to be considered and accepted as "God" or "a god" in such a positive light?

Other Trinitarians are more reluctant to find proof of such in this passage.[128] Additionally, this is not only another example in Scripture where one must consider the factor of a textual variant, but one must also face the challenge of how to accurate translate the verse into the receptor language.

Other translations, instead of saying that God purchased the church "with his own blood," state that God purchased the church with "the blood of his own" (with the 'Son' being the implied subject). Grammatically, both translations are possible. In addition, there are some manuscripts that do not read "God" but "Lord (Gk: *kyrios*)," so the latter part of the verse would read: "*the church of the Lord which he purchased with his own blood.*"

Most New Testament scholars agree, however, that the best manuscripts read "the church of **God**"; and as it was observed by evangelical Bible scholar William MacDonald: "Perhaps J. N. Darby comes closest to the correct sense of the passage in his New Translation: '*The assembly of God which He purchased with the blood of His own.*' Here God is the One who purchased the Church, but He did it with the blood of His own Son, the blessed Lord Jesus."[129] In the *New English Translation* the verse is rendered:

> **Watch out for yourselves and for all the flock of which the Holy Spirit has made you overseers, to shepherd the church of God that he obtained with the blood of**

---

[128] According to one scholar: "The language here seems to mean that God purchased the Church with his own blood, which is certainly a strange and startling phrase; and in many MSS we find 'the Lord' instead of 'God'. But the Greek (*dia tou hamatos tou idiou*) may mean 'by the blood which is His own' i.e. that of His Son..." —A.W.F. Blunt, *The Acts of the Apostles, The Clarendon Bible, Introduction and Commentary*, p. 232. Another Trinitarian source remarked: "Nowhere does the Bible speak of the blood of God the Father. The Greek here can read 'by the blood of His own,' that is, His own Son.' —*The Bible Knowledge Commentary, New Testament Edition*, p. 414.

[129] *Believers Bible Commentary, New Testament*, p. 465 (emphasis added). In the footnote to his translation, Darby writes: "I am fully satisfied that this is the right translation of ver. 28. To make it a question of the divinity of Christ (which I behold to be the foundation of Christianity) is absurd. It has been questioned whether 'of his own' can be used thus absolutely in the singular. But we have it in John 15.19, and in the neuter singular for material things, Acts 4.32..." —*The Holy Scriptures, A New Translation from the Original Languages* (Illinois: Bible Truth Publishers, 1991), p. 1334.

his own Son.

In their footnotes, the translators point out that the literal Greek translation is: "with the blood of his own." And they go on to observe: "The genitive construction could be taken in two ways: (1) as an attributive genitive (second attributive position) meaning 'his own blood'; or (2) as a possessive genitive, 'with the blood of his own.' In this case the referent is the Son, and the referent has been specified in the translation for clarity..."[130]

It was pointed out in the respected *Tyndale Commentaries*: "The cost of redemption was (literally) his own blood (RSV mg.). It is, however, unlikely that an early Christian would have spoken of *God* shedding his own blood, and therefore we must either assume that Jesus is the subject of the clause (which is just possible, but unlikely) or that the phrase means 'the blood of his Own' (RSV mg.), which is grammatically possible and fits in with the use of the phrase *his own Son* (Rom. 8:31)."[131]

The late F. F. Bruce—considered by many to be among the foremost Bible scholars of the Protestant world—said similarly, though with respect to the Christian elders of Ephesus to whom Paul was addressing: "Their responsibility was the greater in that the flock which they were commissioned to tend was no other than the church of God which he had purchased for himself (an echo here of Old Testament language)—and the purchase price was nothing less than the life-blood of his beloved Son."[132] In another esteemed work by Bruce, *Paul, Apostle of the Heart Set Free*, he stated that "here only in Acts [20:28] is explicit mention made of the saving efficacy of the *death* of Christ. 'Feed the church of God', says Paul, 'which he purchased with the blood of his beloved one' (Acts 20:28)." And in a corresponding footnote Bruce explains: "Literally, 'his own

---

[130] *New English Translation Bible, New Testament*, p. 475.
[131] *The Acts of the Apostles, An Introduction and Commentary* by I. Howard Marshall (Grand Rapids: Eerdmans, 1980), p. 334.
[132] *The New International Commentary on the New Testament, The Book of Acts*, pp. 392, 393.

one': Gk. *dia tou haimatos ton idiou*, where *ton idiou* is better construed as possessive genitive governed by *tou haimatos* than as being in attributive concord with it."[133]

The *NIV Study Bible* says of "*his own blood*. Lit. 'the blood of his own one,'" that it can properly be identified as "a term of endearment (such as 'his own dear one,' referring to his own Son)."[134] The *Interpreter's Bible* explains: "...the last clause should probably be translated 'with the blood of his Own.' It is quite possible that 'his Own', with the omission of the word 'Son,' was an early title of Jesus comparable with 'the Beloved,' 'the Only-begotten.' In Rom. 8:32 we have the words, 'he who did not spare his own Son' in a verse which is obviously an echo of Gen. 22:16, where LXX has 'beloved son.'"[135]

In a *Translator's Handbook* on the *Today's English Version* of the Bible, all of the relevant issues were summarized:

> There is a textual problem as to whether the reading should be *the church of God* or 'the church of the Lord.' The choice of the reading at this place depends in large measure upon the choice one makes regarding the phrase rendered by the TEV *through the death of his own Son*. The text followed by the TEV at this point literally reads 'through the blood of his own.'...Moreover, those who accept this reading understand 'his own' to mean *his own Son*, and so the TEV has made this explicit. The alternative reading at this point is literally 'through his own blood,' which also must be understood in the sense of 'through his own death.' However, if this second reading is followed, then it would go much easier with 'the church of the Lord' then it would with *the church of God*. Since the textual evidence more strongly favors the

---

[133] Bruce, *Paul, Apostle of the Hear Set Free* (Cambridge: Paternoster Press, 1977), p. 342.
[134] *The NIV Study Bible*, p. 1689. See also footnotes to Acts 20:28 in the *Ryrie Study Bible* and *English Standard Version*.
[135] *The Interpreter's Bible*, p. 273. It was remarked in another source: "Before leaving [*idious*] something should be said about the use of [*ho idios*] without a noun expressed. This occurs in Jn 1.11; 13.1; Ac 4.23; 24.23. In the papyri we find the singular used thus as a term of endearment to near relations: eg. [*ho deina to idio khairein*.] In [The] Expositor, vi.iii. 277. I ventured to cite this as a possible encouragement to those (including B.Weiss) who would translate Ac 20.28 'the blood of one who was his own.' —J. H. Moulton, *Grammar of New Testament Greek*, p. 90.

reading which the TEV has in the text, *through the death of his own Son*, it would seem better to follow the text which reads *the church of God* rather than 'the church of the Lord.' On the other hand, if one feels bound to follow the text 'through his own death,' this would refer to 'the church of the Lord' (that is, the Lord Jesus). *Through the death of his own Son* specifies the means by which God made the church his own, but in many languages it is not easy to introduce an event such as death as an instrument. The closest equivalent may be 'the fact that his own Son died made this possible,' 'by dying his own Son caused this to be,' or 'his own Son died, and this made the church belong to God.'[136]

Below are various examples of translations that have rendered the verse in accord with what has been discussed above:

> **...care for the flock in which the Holy Spirit has appointed you as guardians. Make it your aim to be the shepherds of the Church of God, which he has bought for himself with the blood of his own One.**
> —*The New Testament, by William Barclay*
> **Keep watch over yourselves and over all the flock, of which the Holy Spirit has made you overseers, to shepherd the church of God that he obtained with the blood of his own Son. [Gk *with the blood of his Own*]**
> —*New Revised Standard Version*
> **Look to yourselves and to the whole flock, of which the Holy Spirit has made you overseers, to guard the church of God, which he won for himself by the blood of his own (Son).** —*The Anchor Bible*
> **Be on your guard for yourselves and for all the flock of which the Holy Spirit has made you the guardians, to feed the Church of God which he bought with the**

---

[136] *A Translator's Handbook on the Acts of the Apostles*, by Barclay M. Newman and Eugene A. Nida (United Bible Societies, 1972), pp. 394-395 (underlining in original changed to *italics*).

The "deity" of Jesus Christ

blood of his own Son. —*New Jerusalem Bible*

Romans 9:5

> "Belief in the deity of Christ has traditionally been the keystone of the doctrine of the Trinity, yet explicit references to Jesus as 'God' (*theos*) in the New Testament are very few, and even those few are generally plagued with uncertainties of either text or interpretation." —Christopher B. Kaiser,
> *The Doctrine of God, A Historical Survey*, p. 29

"Christ, who is God over all, forever praised! Amen." (NIV)

A footnote to Romans 9:5 in the *New Oxford Annotated Bible* points out: "Whether Christ is called God here depends on the punctuations inserted." Similarly, the following observation is found in *The Interpreter's Bible*: "The issue appears from a comparison of our two English texts. Is God over all, blessed forever (or the one who is over all, God blessed forever)...The question cannot be answered on the basis of the Greek since it is a matter almost entirely of punctuation, and Greek MSS in the early period were not punctuated. There is even another possibility, viz., '...flesh, who is over all. God be blessed forever'..."[137]

The translators of the *New American Bible* viewed the last part of verse five as an independent expression of praise directed not to Christ but toward God. In context, the passage would read:

> **...my conscience joins with the holy Spirit in bearing me witness that I have great sorrow and constant anguish in my heart. For I could wish that I myself were accursed and separated from Christ for the sake**

---

[137] *The Interpreters' Bible*, Volume 9, p. 540.

> of my brothers, my kin according to the flesh. They are Israelites; theirs the adoption, the glory, the covenants, the giving of the law, the worship, and the promises; theirs the patriarchs, and from them, according to the flesh, is the Messiah. God who is over all be blessed forever. Amen.

The footnote in the *NAB* states: "Some editors punctuate this verse differently and prefer the translation, 'of whom is Christ according to the flesh, who is God over all.' However, Paul's point is that God who is over all aimed to use Israel, which had been entrusted with every privilege, in outreach to the entire world through the Messiah."

The *Translator's Handbook* observes:

> Since the earliest New Testament manuscripts were without any systematic punctuation, it is necessary for scholars to punctuate the text according to what seems appropriate to syntax and the meaning. Basically, the question is whether the doxology has reference to God (TEV *May God, who rules over all, be praised forever!*), or to Christ (TEV alternative rendering 'And may he, who is God ruling over all, be praised forever!'). Although there are strong grammatical arguments to the contrary, the UBS textual committee prefers the reading represented in the TEV (so RSV, NEB, NAB, Goodspeed, Moffatt), but some do prefer the rendering represented in the alternative rendering of the TEV (so JB and Phillips).[138]

The *Interpreter's Bible* states: "the choice is probably to be made between the KJV and the RSV translations. The majority of modern commentators favor the latter because of the unlikelihood of Paul's having here referred to Christ as 'God'..."[139]

---

[138] *Helps For Translators, A Translators on Paul's Letter to the Romans*, by Barclay M. Newman and Eugene A. Nida (United Bible Societies, 1973) p. 180 (words in italics originally underlined). A "doxology" is an ascription of praise normally directed toward God.
[139] *The Interpreters' Bible*, Volume 9, p. 540.

The "deity" of Jesus Christ

It would be difficult for one to raise a convincing objection to what is observed here, concerning the "unlikelihood" of Paul referring to Christ as "God." This is so because in the book of Romans Paul *always* distinguishes between "Jesus Christ" and "God." It is not *impossible* that Christ is called God here; it is, however, *unlikely* in light of Paul's regular manner of expression found throughout the whole of his writings.

For the same essential reasons, Anthony Buzzard (a non-Trinitarian) believed it was more likely that the words were an independent ascription of praise directed toward God the Father. He notes: "Paul uniformly makes a distinction between God and the Lord Jesus. In the same book Paul blesses the Creator and there is no reason to doubt that the Father is meant (Rom. 1:25). In another passage he speaks of 'God our Father, to whom be the glory forever more. Amen.' (Gal. 1:4, 5). Romans 9:5 is an obvious parallel. It should not be forgotten that the word *theos*, God, occurs more than 500 times in Paul's letters and there is not a single unambiguous instance in which it applies to Christ."[140]

F. F. Bruce, although preferring the translation that applies *theos* to Christ, nevertheless pointed out:

> It is, on the other hand, impermissible to charge those who prefer to treat the words as an independent doxology with Christological unorthodoxy. *The words can indeed be so treated*, and the decision about their construction involves a delicate assessment of the balance of probability this way and that.[141]

---

[140] Buzzard, Hunting, *The Doctrine of the Trinity*, pp. 281-283.

[141] *Romans, Tyndale New Testament Commentaries*, pp. 176, 177 (emphasis added). Greg Stafford observed: "there is nothing unusual about taking the words following 'according to the flesh' as a doxology to the One responsible for the coming of Christ, as a self contained expression of thanks and praise to the One who is frequently referred to and distinguished from Christ in the preceding eight chapters of Romans...The grammar of Romans 9:5 will admit of either a rendering that predicates *theos* of Christ, or one that recognizes a doxology to the God and Father of Jesus Christ. In view of Paul's use of *theos* throughout this letter to the Romans and in the rest of his writings, as well as his consistent use of *eulogetos* ['blessed'] for occasions of praise to God in distinction to Christ, it is best to accept the translation which renders this passage as a doxology to God the Father. The grammatical arguments given in support of the translation which makes *theos* predicate for Christ are relevant, but they are certainly not incontrovertible."

The "deity" of Jesus Christ

Although the *New International Version* (1984) translates the verse so that Christ is called God in the main text, in the footnote attention is called to an alternative rendering:

Or, Christ, who is over all. God be forever praised!

Translations that also view the last part of the verse as an independent expression of praise directed toward God the Father have rendered the verse in the following ways. It is worth noting that all of the translators below were Trinitarian in their background—so that it cannot be claimed that the kind of translation given was motivated out of a desire to deny the 'deity' of Christ:

> **To them belong the patriarchs, and of their race, according to the flesh, is the Christ. God who is over all be blessed forever. Amen.** —*Revised Standard Version*
>
> **Theirs are the patriarchs, and from them, in natural descent, sprang the Messiah. May God, supreme over all, be blessed forever! Amen.** —*New English Bible*
>
> **The patriarchs are theirs, and from them by natural descent came the Messiah. May God, supreme above all, be blessed for ever! Amen.** —*Revised English Bible*
>
> **...they are descended from the patriarchs, and Christ, as a human being, belongs to their race. May God, who rules over all, be praised forever! Amen.**
> —*Today's English Version*
>
> **They have those famous ancestors, who were also the ancestors of Jesus Christ. I pray that God, who rules over all, will be praised forever! Amen.**
> —*Contemporary English Version*
>
> **Theirs are the fathers, and in human descent it is from them that the Messiah comes. God who is over all be blessed forever! Amen.** —*The New Testament, by William Barclay*
>
> **...the patriarchs are theirs, and theirs too (so far as**

—"God over All" in Romans 9:5, *Translation Issues and Theological Import* (July 5, 2000 Edition)

natural descent goes) is the Christ. (Blessed for evermore be the God who is over all! Amen.)
—*The Bible, A New Translation by James Moffatt*
...the patriarchs, and from them physically Christ came—God who is over all be blessed forever! Amen.
—*The Bible, An American Translation*
The patriarchs are theirs, and so too, as far as human descent goes, is Christ himself, Christ who is over all. May God be blessed forever. Amen. —*Phillip's Modern English*
Great men of God were your fathers, and Christ himself was one of you, a Jew so far as his human nature was concerned, he who now rules over all things. Praise God forever! —*The Living Bible* (paraphrased)
...theirs are the fathers and of their race is Christ in his human nature. (Blessed be God who is over all for ever, Amen.) —*The New Testament in Plain English, Charles Kingsley Williams*[142]

Ultimately, this is a text that will probably always be debated among Bible scholars regarding whether or not *theos* applies to the Father or to Christ. In support of a translation like the ones cited above, however, consider the insightful points made by Ezra Abbot based on the larger, surrounding context of Romans 9:5. The discussion appeared in the *Journal of the Society of Biblical Literature and Exegesis* for 1881. Selected parts are submitted for consideration:

[The Apostle Paul] delights to enumerate the magnificent privileges by which God had distinguished [the Jews] from all other nations,—'the adoption, and the glory, and the giving of the Law, the covenants, the temple service, and the promises.' Theirs were the fathers; and, from among them, as the crowning distinction of all, the Messiah was born, the supreme gift of

---

[142] For in-depth, scholarly and technical discussions on the translation of this verse, see Murray J. Harris, *Jesus As God*, who favors the translation that calls Christ "God over all."; and Ezra Abbot, in the *Journal of the Society of Biblical Literature and Exegesis* (1881), who argues that the phrase "God over all" refers to the Father.

God's love and mercy not to the Jews alone, but to all mankind. All God's dealings with his chosen people were designed to prepare the way, and had prepared the way, for this grand consummation. How natural that, when, in his rapid recital of their historic glories, the Apostle reaches this highest distinction of the Jews and greatest blessing of God's mercy to men, he should express his overflowing gratitude to God as the Ruler over all; that he should 'thank God for his unspeakable gift'!...The doxology springs from the same feeling and the same view of the gracious providence of God which prompted the fuller outburst at the end of the eleventh chapter, where, on completing the treatment of the subject which he here introduces, the Apostle exclaims: 'O the depth of the riches and wisdom and knowledge of God! How unsearchable are his judgments and untraceable his ways!...For from him, and through him, and to him, are all things: to him be (or is) the glory forever. Amen.'...It is objected that a doxology here is wholly out of place; that the Apostle is overwhelmed with grief at the Jewish rejection of the Messiah and its consequences, and 'an elegy or funeral discourse cannot be changed abruptly into a hymn.' He is, indeed, deeply grieved at the unbelief and blindness of the great majority of his countrymen; but his sorrow is not hopeless. He knows all the while that 'the word of God hath not failed,' that 'God hath not cast off his people whom he foreknew,' that at last 'all Israel shall be saved'; and nothing seems to me more natural than the play of mingled feelings which the passage presents,—grief for the present temporary alienation of his countrymen from Christ, joy and thanksgiving at the thought of the priceless blessings of which Christ was the minister to man and in which his countrymen should ultimately share...Can we, then, reasonably say that, when, in his grand historic survey and enumeration of the distinctive privileges of the Jews, the Apostle reaches the culminating point in the advent of the Messiah, sprung from that race, a devout thanksgiving to God as the beneficent ruler over all is wholly out of place? Might we not rather ask, How could it be repressed?...It is very strange that it should be urged as an argument against the doxology that God is not mentioned in the preceding context. The name does not occur, but almost every word in verses 4 and 5 suggest the thought of God. So, to a Jew, the very name 'Israelites'; so 'the adoption and the glory and the giving of the Law and the covenants and the service and the promises'; and so, above all *ho cristos*, the Anointed of God, the Messiah: as to the flesh, sprung from the Jews; but, as to his holy spirit, the Son of God, the messenger of God's love and mercy, not to the Jews alone, but to all the nations of the earth...On the other hand, as we have seen above, the enumeration of blessings which of the advent of Christ, naturally suggests an ascription or praise and thanksgiving to God as the Being who rules over all; while a doxology is also suggested by the *amen* at the end of the sentence...I waive here all considerations of doctrine and call attention only to the use of language. When we observe that everywhere else in this Epistle the Apostle has used the word *theos* of the Father in distinction from Christ, so that it is virtually a proper name, that this is also true of the Epistles previously written—those to the Thessalonians, Galatians, Corinthians, how can we reasonably doubt that, if the verbal ambiguity here occasioned a momentary hesitation as to the meaning, a primitive reader of the Epistle would naturally suppose that the word *theos* designated the being everywhere else denoted by this name in the Apostle's writings, and would give the passage the construction thus suggested?...Let us now look for a moment at the connection of thought in the passage before us, and we shall see this distinction is important. The Apostle is speaking of the favored nation to which it is his pride to belong. Its grand religious history of some two thousand years passes rapidly before his mind, as in a panorama. Their ancestors were the patriarchs,— Abraham, Isaac, and Jacob. Theirs were 'the adoption, and the glory, and the covenants, and the giving of the Law, and the temple service, and the promises.' But God's choice and training his 'peculiar people,' and the privileges conferred upon them, were all a providential preparation for the advent of the Messiah, whose birth from among the Jews was their highest national distinction and glory; while his mission as the founder of a spiritual and universal religion was the crowning manifestation of God's love and mercy to mankind. How could this survey of the ages of promise and preparation, and the great fulfillment in Christ, fail to bring vividly before the mind of the Apostle the thought of God as the Being who presides over all things, who cares for all men and controls all events? 1. The use of the word *eulogetos*, 'blessed,' which never occurs in the New Testament in reference to Christ. If we refer *eulogetos* to God, our passage accords with the doxologies Rom. i. 25; 2 Cor. i.3; xi. 31; and Eph. i.3. In Rom. i.25, we have *eulogetos heis tous aionas*, as here; and 2 Cor. xi. 31, 'The God and Father (or God, the Father) of the Lord Jesus knows—he who is blessed for ever!—that I lie not,' strongly favors the reference of the *eulogetos* to God. The Apostle's use of the word *theos*, 'God,' throughout his Epistles. This word occurs in the Pauline Epistles, not including that to the Hebrews, more than five hundred times; and there is not a single clear instance in which it is applied to Christ. Alford, and many other Trinitarian commentators of the highest character, find no instance except the present. Now, in a case of ambiguous construction, ought not this uniform usage of the Apostle in respect to one of the most common words to have great weight? To me it is absolutely decisive...I do not see how any one can read the Epistles of Paul without perceiving that, in speaking of the objects of Christian faith, he constantly uses *theos* as a proper name, as the designation of the Father in distinction from Christ...Can we believe that he who has throughout his writings placed Christ in such a relation of subordination to the Father, and has habitually used the name GOD as the peculiar designation of the Father in distinction from Christ, who also calls the Father the one God, the only wise God (Rom. xvi. 27), the only God (1 Tim. i. 17), and the God of Christ, has here, in opposition to the usage elsewhere uniform of a word occurring five hundred times, suddenly designated Christ as 'over all, God blessed for ever'? At least, should not the great improbability of this turn the scale, in a passage of doubtful construction?...Beyond a doubt, all the writers of the New Testament and the early preachers of Christianity believed that God was *united with* the man Jesus Christ in a way unique and peculiar, distinguishing him from all other beings; that his teaching and works and character were divine; that God had raised him from the dead, and exalted him to be a Prince and a

Saviour; that he came, as the messenger of God' love and mercy, to redeem men from sin, and make them truly sons of God; that 'God was in Christ reconciling the world unto himself.' But no New Testament writer has *defined the mode* of this union with God. How much light has been thrown upon the subject by the councils of Nicaea and Constantinople, Ephesus and Chalcedon, and the so-called Athanasian creed, is a question on which there may be differences of opinion. The *authority* of councils is another question. But it has been no part of my object, in discussing the construction of the passage before us, to argue against the doctrine of the Nicene Creed. My point is simply the *use of language* at the time when this Epistle was written.[143]

Titus 2:13

"...looking for the blessed hope and glorious appearing of our great God and Savior Jesus Christ." —Titus 2:13, NKJV

Paul's statement in Titus 2:13 is another one of the few examples in the New Testament where the term *theos* may or may not apply to Jesus Christ. Much like Romans 9:5 and 2 Peter 1:1, the grammar of this verse legitimately allows for Christ or the Father to be described as *theos*. This is why if one were to check several English Bible translations, it would be found that some call Christ "our great God and Savior" (*NASB, NIV, ESV*), while others translate in such a way that two subjects are spoken of, God and Christ (*NAB, ASV*). Some translations may even lean toward one view, thus translating one way in the main text, while relegating the alternative rendering to a marginal footnote, informing the reader that such is also a valid translational possibility (*RSV, JB*).

With respect to Titus 2:13, scholars—including conservative Trinitarians—have always been divided on whether the Father and Christ are both meant, or only Christ. James

---

[143] *On the Construction of Romans IX. 5. by Ezra Abbott. From the Journal of the Society of Biblical Literature and Exegesis for* 1881.

The "deity" of Jesus Christ

White exaggerates when he claims that those who have rendered the verse in a way so that both God and Christ are in view have "mistranslated" the verse.[144] Murray J. Harris—credited with having performed the most detailed analysis of New Testament references to Christ as *theos*—expressed himself more moderately. Although Harris believed that the entire description refers to Christ alone, he was not absolute, but concluded as the results of his analysis: "*it seems highly probable* that in Titus 2:13 Jesus is called "our great God and Savior…"[145]

However, in *The Forgotten Trinity*, White argued: "the context gives us *no reason whatsoever* to think that two persons are in view here. Only Christ is under discussion. One must wonder, then, why anyone would *wish* to find a second person, since the context does not push us in that direction."[146] White also states: "I add that there is simply no reason, outside of theological reasons (which should not drive our translations in the first place), to avoid the proper rendering of either Titus 2:13 or 2 Peter 1:1. Both testify to the deity of Jesus Christ."[147]

It is true that often times the personal beliefs or "theology" of a translator influences their decision in a case where a certain reading is ambiguous (as in Titus 2:13), but not necessarily in every case. For example, the *Emphatic Diaglott*, although produced by a non-Trinitarian scholar, translates the verse so that Jesus is called *God*: "the glory of our great God and Savior Jesus Christ." When Dr. White suggests that "there is simply no reason, outside of theological reasons" to translate the verse so that two figures are in view, he is wrong. The Roman Catholic *New American Bible* and *Philip's Modern English*

---

[144] *The King James Only Controversy* (Minnesota: Bethany House Publishers, 1995), p. 219.
[145] *Jesus as God*, p. 185. On page 176 Harris notes: "No one will doubt that if these two verses [Titus 2:13 and 2 Peter 1:1] afford instances of a christological use of *theos*, such usage is exceptional in the New Testament." And on page 177: "Any NT use of *theos* as a Christological title will produce certain linguistic anomalies and ambiguities, for in all strands of the NT *theos* generally signifies the Father." Yet Harris also points out: "But there is an ever-present danger in literary research of making the writer's 'habitual usage' so normative that he is disallowed the privilege of creating the exception that proves the rule."
[146] *The Forgotten Trinity*, p. 77 (emphasis added).
[147] *The Forgotten Trinity*, p. 79.

translation, both produced by Trinitarians,[148] render the verse so that both God and Christ are the subjects: *PME*: "the glorious dénouement of the Great God and of Christ Jesus our saviour." *NAB*: "the glory of the great God and of our savior Jesus Christ."[149]

Here the translators were not driven by their "wish" or biased, theological desire to deny the divinity of Christ, but by what is allowable grammatically and what probably made sense to them contextually (in the immediate sense, or in the larger, overall, biblical sense). In fact, because both translations (*NASB* and *NAB*) are grammatically justifiable, no one should dogmatically claim that the other is "mistranslating" the verse.

In his discussion, Dr. White attempts to put forward the argument that the context is decidedly in favor of a rendering that calls Jesus Christ "*our great God* and Savior." In the verse immediately after (v. 14), Paul speaks about how Christ gave himself to "redeem us" and to "purify himself a people for his own possession, zealous for good deeds." Since Paul speaks of Christ as a redeemer in possession of a certain people, and the Old Testament shows that the redeemed persons are *God's* possession,[150] we should conclude that Jesus must be God in the same sense as his Father, and this should move one to accept a translation that calls Jesus "our great God..." According to Dr. White: "To the person whose ear is attuned to the words of the Old Testament, this is a phrase that would bring to mind none other than Yahweh himself...The context, then, is one that

---

[148] *The New American Bible* was produced by a team of mostly Catholic scholars and a few Protestant scholars. *Philip's Modern English* was the work of one Protestant scholar, J. B. Phillips. Although an Evangelical like Dr. White might attempt to dismiss the *NAB* as a "liberal" Catholic translation, it should be pointed out that the same translation renders 2 Peter 1:1 in a manner that he and other Trinitarians would likely advocate—renderings seen as supporting the "deity" of Christ as defined in Trinitarian theology. Certain statements in the Gospel of John (8:24; 8:58; 13:19; 18:5, 6, 8) are even rendered in all capitals—'I AM'—which represents an attempt on the part of the translators to equate Christ with God. In those cases, the *NAB* translators actually go further than most Trinitarian translations in trying to give the impression that Jesus was "God incarnate."

[149] The footnote in the Catholic *Jerusalem Bible* likewise states: "This verse is regularly accepted by the Fathers as a statement of the divinity of Christ...but possibly translate '...God, and of our saviour Christ Jesus'. For Christ as 'the brightness of the glory of the Father'. cf. Heb 1:3."

[150] Exodus 19:5

would find no problem at all in calling Jesus 'God and Savior,' since it has freely applied to Him words that had been used by God's people for centuries to describe Yahweh, their Savior."[151]

Interestingly, a similar argument was put forward back in the late 1880's, to which Ezra Abbot responded:

> The case seems to me to present no difficulty, and to afford no ground for such an inference. The relation of Christians to God and Christ is such that, from its very nature, the servants of Christ are and are called the servants of God, the church of Christ the church of God, the kingdom of Christ the kingdom of God. So Christians are and are represented as the peculiar people and possession of Christ, and at the same time the peculiar people and possession of God (1 Pet. 2: 9, 10). If Christians belong to Christ, they must belong also to God, the Father, to whom Christ himself belongs (1 Cor. 3:23, 'ye are Christ's, and Christ is God's'). To infer, then, that because in ver. 14 Christians are spoken of as Christ's peculiar people, the title 'great God' must necessarily be understood as applied to him in ver. 13, is a very extraordinary kind of reasoning.[152]

It is not necessary, as Dr. White suggests, to equate Jesus with the *Most High* God because God's people are also considered Christ's people; nor does such an argument add support to the translation Dr. White seeks to defend. Such a common leap in logic on the part of Trinitarian apologists simply disregards the manner in which the Bible presents the relationship of God the Father and Jesus Christ to Christians.

In the Gospel of John, Jesus himself said that the people belonging to him were *given* to him by God, his Father. In fact, it may be properly said that all that belongs to the Son belongs to God and vice-versa; for in prayer to his Father, Jesus spoke in behalf of God's people in this way:

---

[151] *The Forgotten Trinity*, pp. 76, 77.
[152] *Construction of Titus II. 13, from the Journal of the Society of Biblical Literature and Exegesis*, 1881, p. 9.

> "Father...I revealed your name to those whom you gave me out of the world. *They belonged to you, and you gave them to me*, and they have kept your word. Now they know that everything you gave me is from you, because the words you gave to me I have given to them, and they accepted them and truly understood that I came from you, and they have believed that you sent me. I pray for them. I do not pray for the world but for *the ones you have given me, because they are yours, and everything of mine is yours and everything of yours is mine*, and I have been glorified in them."[153]

If Paul did have in mind two persons—"the glory of the great God and of Christ Jesus our savior"—such would harmonize well with the Gospel teaching that Jesus would one day appear in the glory of his Father: "For the Son of Man will come with his angels in his Father's glory, and then he will repay everyone according to his conduct."[154] In another place, Mark reports that Jesus said: "Whoever is ashamed of me and of my words in this faithless and sinful generation, the Son of Man will be ashamed of when he comes in his Father's glory with the holy angels."[155] According to his promise, when Jesus is revealed from heaven, he will appear in his Father's glory; hence, "we await our blessed hope, the appearing of the glory of the great God and of our Savior Christ Jesus."[156] It was observed by Abbot:

> ...when we consider that in the *concomitants* [the accompaniments] of the second advent, the resurrection of the dead, and the judgment of men, in which the glory of Christ will be displayed, he is everywhere represented as acting, not independently of God, the Father, but in union with him, as his agent, so that 'the Father is glorified in the Son,' can we find the slightest difficulty in

---

[153] John 17:6-10, *NAB* (emphasis added).
[154] Matthew 16:27, *NAB*. In his scholarly *Greek Testament*, Henry Alford notes that the sense of this passage is an "exact parallel" to Titus 2:13. *The Greek Testament, Volume III Galatians–Philemon* (Chicago: Moody Press, 1958), p. 419.
[155] Mark 8:38, *NAB*. Luke 9:26 says that the Son of man will come "in his glory and in the glory of the Father and of the holy angels."
[156] *New American Bible*, 1970.

supposing that Paul here describes the second advent as an 'appearing of the *glory* of the great God, and our Saviour Jesus Christ'?[157]

This was written in the late 1880's when Abbot discussed the translation of Titus 2:13 in a detailed essay in the *Journal of the Society of Biblical Literature and Exegesis*. Abbot concluded that both God the Father and Jesus Christ were referred to by the apostle in this verse, having observed:

> In the case of a grammatical ambiguity of this kind in any classical author, the first inquiry would be, What is the usage of the writer respecting the application of the title in question? Now this consideration, which certainly is a most reasonable one, seems to me here absolutely decisive. *While the word theos occurs more than five hundred times in the Epistles of Paul, not including the Epistle to the Hebrews, there is not a single instance in which it is clearly applied to Christ*...An examination of the context will confirm the conclusion at which we have arrived. I have already shown that the title 'God our Saviour' in the Pastoral Epistles belongs exclusively to the Father. This is generally admitted; for example by Bloomfield, Alford and Ellicott. Now the connection of ver. 10 in which this expression occurs, with ver. 11 is obviously such, that if *theou* denotes the Father in the former it must in the latter. Regarding it then as settled that *theou* in ver. 11 denotes the Father (and I am not aware that it has ever been disputed), is it not harsh to suppose that the *theou* in ver. 13, in the latter part of the sentence denotes a different subject from the *theou* in ver. 11 at the beginning of the same sentence?...To sum up: the reasons for which are urged for giving this verbally ambiguous passage the construction which makes 'the great God' a designation of Christ, are seen, when examined, to have little or no weight; on the other hand, the construction adopted in the common English version, and preferred by the American Revisers, is favored, if not

---

[157] Abbot, *Construction of Titus II. 13*, p. 6,

required, by the context (comparing ver. 13 with ver. 11); it perfectly suits the references to the second advent in other parts of the New Testament; and it is imperatively demanded by a regard to Paul's *use of language*, unless we arbitrarily assume here a single exception to a usage of which we have more than five hundred examples. I might add, though I would not lay much stress on the fact, that the principal ancient versions, the Old Latin, the Vulgate, the Peshito and Harclean Syriac, the Coptic, and the Arabic, appear to have given the passage the construction which makes God and Christ distinct subjects. The Aethiopic seems to be the only exception. Perhaps, however, the construction in the Latin versions should be regarded as somewhat ambiguous.[158]

If it is true, however, that Paul did have in mind to call Jesus "our great God and Savior," this definitely would constitute a testimony to "the deity [or godship] of Jesus Christ." But it would not automatically mean that such should be understood through the framework of Trinitarian thinking—unless, of course, Scripture said otherwise. It has, in fact, been a repeated oversight on the part of Trinitarian apologists to think that if they can establish that the Scriptures call Jesus "God" in a given verse, that this somehow establishes the biblical case for the post-biblical Trinitarian concept of Christ's deity. That is why it is critical to understand that when Trinitarian theologians call Jesus "God," the meaning is not as simple as it might appear on the surface. Most Trinitarians recognize that the Bible reserves the title "God" primarily for the Father. But when they call Jesus "God," they don't mean to identify Jesus as the Father. And although Trinitarians believe that the one God of the Bible is the Trinity (the 'triune God'), when they say that "Jesus *is* God," they do not mean to identify Jesus as the Trinity. By calling Jesus "God," what they really mean is that Jesus is one divine "person" who shares in the one "being" that is God. Unfortunately, for this view, there is no scriptural evidence or

---

[158] Abbot, *Construction of Titus II. 13* (emphasis added).

The "deity" of Jesus Christ

direct scriptural teaching that this is what the application would signify. There is simply no substantial way to verify that this is the case because the Bible does not articulate such a concept, in any place. In other words, the Scriptures themselves nowhere indicate that Jesus was ever thought of as "God" in the sense of being "one person (out of three)" who holds a "coequal" position within a Trinitarian "Godhead." That is why, in whatever case that the Bible may be said to call Jesus "God," we must interpret such through the framework the Bible itself gives to us, not through the framework of a theological system that was developed and defined centuries after the Bible was written. If we consider Jesus "God" in light of the entirety of the biblical presentation, we *are* able to confirm the fact that, although undoubtedly in a category of his own,[159] he still remains the kind that has a God above him (the God who is 'greater than *all*,' John 10:29), and that he always remains subject (and/or ultimately will subject himself; 1 Cor. 15:26-28) to the one he looks to as *his* God and Father, the Most High.[160]

A translation that calls Jesus "our great God and savior" is justified grammatically—which is even conceived of as 'natural' by many, primarily Trinitarian, scholars—accompanied by the fact that, in the Pauline writings, the "appearing" or "manifestation" (*epiphaneia*) is always associated with Jesus Christ;[161] and these are all points that may be said to speak in favor of such a translation. A translation that does not apply the term "God" to Jesus is likewise justified, grammatically speaking. The fact that the Old Testament refers to the Father as the "great God,"[162] and that Jesus said he would arrive in "the

---

[159] John 1:18

[160] Romans 15:6; Ephesians 1:17; Hebrews 1:8, 9; Revelation 3:12; Compare 1 Corinthians 11:3.

[161] However, although the word "manifestation" is always associated with Christ in the Pauline writings, Christ himself said that he would arrive in the glory of his Father. Paul did not simply speak of the appearing/manifestation (*epipheneia*) of the great God, but of the appearing/manifestation *of the glory* of the great God..." See: Matthew 16:27; Mark 8:38. This would seem to lessen the force of an argument for calling Christ "the great God" based simply on the use of *epiphaneia*.

[162] LXX, Psalm 85:10. Abbot notes: "The expression 'the great God' does not occur elsewhere in the New Testament, but it is not uncommon in the Old Testament and later Jewish writings as a designation for Jehovah." —*Construction of Titus II. 13*, p. 7.

glory of his Father"—accompanied by the fact that in the writings of Paul there is not *one* unambiguous example where Christ is called "God" and an abundance of examples where Christ is *distinguished* from "God"—are all points that would weigh in favor of the translation where both God and Christ are in view. In this case, where the grammatical construction can be interpreted either way, Paul's clear presentation of the identity of God in relation to Christ, and his consistently discernable mode of expression and use of language, are very significant factors that cannot be casually set aside. Whatever the case may be, the observation made by professor BeDuhn should be kept in mind: "We have no way to judge which translations correctly understand the verse and which does not…This is a case where grammar alone will not settle the matter. All we can do is suggest, by analysis of context and comparable passages, the 'more likely' and 'less likely' translations, and leave the question open to further light."[163]

Because the verse is ambiguous in terms of translation, several Bible versions place what might be called a "one person" rendering in the main text, while, at the same time, alerting readers to the fact that the verse may be legitimately translated in a way so that two subjects are present:

Or 'Appearing of the glory of the great God and our Saviour.' —*The New Testament in Modern Speech*, R. F. Weymouth
Or 'our great God and our savior, Christ Jesus.'

---

[163] *Truth in Translation*, p. 94. Trinitarians who argue that "Sharps' Rule," formulated by Granville Sharp (1735-1835), is decisive in settling the translational question have also overstated their case. Sharp's rule said that when two singular nouns of the same form or grammatical case are joined by the Greek conjunction *kai* (and),—as in Titus 2:13; 2 Peter 1:1—if the first noun has the article and the second one does not, then both are referring to the same subject. However, Sharp noted several exceptions to this rule, including proper names and plurals. BeDuhn writes: "it should be pointed out that *ho theos* ('the God') functions as a proper name ('God') in the New Testament. So by a strict reading of 'Sharp's Rule,' it wouldn't even apply to the verses Sharp hoped to interpret." Murray Harris, who favored a translation that calls Jesus "God," acknowledged: "No one will deny that the repetition of the article is not essential to ensure that two items be considered separately, but it is difficult to prove what an author was or was not assuming." —*Jesus as God*, p. 181 (Matt. 16:21; 20:18; 27:3 and Acts 15:22 are cited as examples).

—*Jerusalem Bible*
Or *of the great God and our Savior*.
—*Revised Standard Version*
Or, *of the great God and our Saviour*
—*Revised Version*
Or *of the great God and our Savior*
—*New Revised Standard Version*
***Or* of the great God and our Saviour…**
—*New English Bible*

Other translators, who were evidently persuaded that both God and Jesus Christ are in view, place the "two person" rendering in the main text:

> **Looking for that blessed hope, and the glorious appearing of the great God and our Saviour Jesus Christ.** —*King James Version*[164]
> **…looking for the blessed hope and appearing of the glory of the great God and our Saviour Jesus Christ.**
> —*American Standard Version*
> **…expecting the blessed hope; namely, the appearing of the glory of the great God, and of our Saviour Jesus Christ.** —*Douay-Rheims*
> **…as we await our blessed hope, the appearing of the glory of the great God and of our Savior Christ Jesus.**
> —*New American Bible* (1970)
> **…as we await the blessed hope, the appearance of the glory of the great God and our savior Jesus Christ.**
> —*New American Bible* (1991)
> **Looking for that blessed hope, and the glorious appearing of the great God and our Saviour Jesus Christ** —*The Webster Bible*
> **And while we live this life we hope and wait for the glorious dénouement of the Great God and of Christ Jesus our saviour.** —*Phillip's Modern English*
> **Looking for that blessed hope and the glorious appearing of the great God and our Saviour Jesus Christ.** —*Holy Bible, From Ancient Eastern Manuscripts*

---

[164] Considered ambiguous by some.

> **Prepared to welcome the happy hope and forth shining of the glory of the great God and our Saviour Christ Jesus** —*Rotherham's Emphasized Bible*
> **…looking forward to the blessed hope and the appearing of the glory of the great God and our savior Christ Jesus** —*Acts and Letters of the Apostles, Newly translated from the Greek by Richard Lattimore*
> **Anticipating that happy expectation, even the advent of the glory of the great God and our Saviour, Jesus Christ** —*Concordant Literal New Testament*
> **…waiting for the blessed hope, the glorious appearing of the great God and of our Savior Christ Jesus** —*The Riverside New Testament*
> **…while we await for the blessed thing we hope for, the appearing of the glory of the great God and of our Saviour Jesus Christ** —*The New Testament in Plain English*

2 Peter 1:1

> *"To those who have obtained like precious faith with us by the righteousness of our God and Savior Jesus Christ."*
> —2 Peter 1:1, NKJV

The grammatical structure of 2 Peter 1:1 is similar to Titus 2:13. The *MacArthur Study Bible* states: "The Gr. construction has only one article before this phrase, making the entire phrase refer to the same person. Thus, Peter is identifying Jesus as both Savior and God."[165] However, it was observed by Dr. Nigel Turner in *A Grammar of New Testament Greek* (Moulton-Turner, 1963): "The repetition of the article was not strictly necessary to ensure that the items be considered separately." And in another place: "Unfortunately, at this period of Greek we cannot be sure that such a rule [regarding the article] is really decisive. Sometimes the definite article is not repeated even where there is clearly a separation in idea."[166]

---

[165] *The MacArthur Study Bible*, p. 1952.
[166] Moulton-Howard-Turner, *Grammar*, Vol. III, p. 181.

The "deity" of Jesus Christ

Many other translations (as in the case of Titus 2:13) render the verse so that both God the Father and Jesus Christ are in view. Not only is this way of translating the verse grammatically legitimate, but the very next verse distinguishes between the two so that, contextually, one finds added reason for doing so. Verse two reads: "**Grace and peace be multiplied to you in the knowledge of God and of Jesus our Lord**" (*NASB*).[167] Although arguably not decisive (when the grammar is considered independently), such a fact cannot by any means be set aside as irrelevant. This may be why the footnote on 2 Peter 1:1 in the Catholic *New American Bible* acknowledges: "The words translated *our God and Savior Jesus Christ* could also be rendered 'Our God and the savior Jesus Christ.'" Several other translations also call Jesus God in this instance but are careful to inform their readers about the alternative rendering:

Or: 'and [our] Saviour.'
—*Rotherham's Emphasized Bible*
Or, *our God and* **the Saviour**
—*Revised Version*
Or *of our God and the Savior Jesus Christ.*
—*Revised Standard Version*
Or *of our God and the Savior Jesus Christ.*
—*New Revised Standard Version*
Or 'of our God and of the saviour Jesus Christ'.
—*Jerusalem Bible*

The following versions translate the verse a similar way in the main text:

---

[167] One scholar wrote: "Next, in the words, of our God and [our] Saviour Jesus Christ, I would interpret, as in Titus ii. 13 [where see note] our God of *the Father*, and [our] Saviour Jesus Christ of *the Son*. Here, there is the additional consideration in favour of this view, that the Two are distinguished most plainly in the next verse):...of God, and of Jesus our Lord." —Alford, *The New Testament for English Readers*, pp. 1671-72. Another commentator said, "Gerlach and Dietlein maintain that 'our God and Saviour Jesus Christ' are here intimately connected, so that Jesus is called God. But seeing that the Petrine doctrine calls Jesus Lord, but in no other place except this, God, the former is more correctly applied to the Father." —*Lange's Commentary on the Holy Scriptures*, Vol. 12, p. 10.

The "deity" of Jesus Christ

...to them that have obtained like precious faith with us through the righteousness of God and our Saviour Jesus Christ —*King James Version*

...to them that have obtained a like precious faith with us in the righteousness of our God and *the* Saviour Jesus Christ. —*American Standard Version*

...to those who are chancing upon an equally precious faith with us, in the righteousness of our God, and the Saviour, Jesus Christ —*Concordant Literal New Testament*

To the people who have received a faith which is like our precious faith. *It came* through the righteousness of our God and of our Savior, Jesus Christ.
—*The Simple English Bible, New Testament*

To: those who, through the righteousness of our God and of our Deliverer Yeshua the Messiah
—*Jewish New Testament, Translation by David A. Stern*

To those who by the beneficence of our God and of our Saviour Jesus Christ have obtained a faith equal in privilege to ours. —*The Original New Testament, Schonfield*

To the people who have received a faith which is like our precious faith. *It came* through the righteousness of our God and of our Savior, Jesus Christ.
—*The International English Bible translation*

To those to whom there has been allotted a faith of equal privilege with ours through the righteousness of our God and of our Saviour Jesus Christ —*New Testament in Modern Speech, Weymouth*

...to those who have obtained a precious faith with us in the righteousness of our God, and our Savior Jesus Christ[168] —*The New Simplified Bible*

---

[168] The presentation of these translations (Romans 9:5; Titus 2:13; 2 Peter 1:1) is not intended to suggest that the more translations that can be produced the more likely it is that they are correct in their rendering. They are presented to demonstrate how numerous and how wide a variety of translators from different backgrounds have independently arrived at the same conclusions (most are actually Trinitarian in their background). Additionally, this provides helpful information for those who may not normally have ready access to such sources. The majority of Protestants use *KJV, NKJV, NASB, ESV, NIV*. These are all versions produced by Trinitarian scholars and tend to prefer translations thought to be harmonious with Trinitarian theology.

The "deity" of Jesus Christ

In favor of a rendering that calls Jesus "God" is the fact that it is supported by what the grammar allows for along with the fact that 2 Peter 1:11 has the same construction where there is clearly one person ('our Lord and Savior Jesus Christ') in view.[169] In favor of the translation that refers to two figures (God and Jesus Christ) is the fact that such is also correct grammatically, along with the fact that Jesus is clearly distinguished from "God" in all of the writings of Peter, in the rest of the Christian Scriptures, and, most significantly, in the *very next verse* (which also has an identical grammatical construction).[170]

But if it is in fact true that Jesus Christ was described by the apostles as "God over all" (Rom. 9:5), "our great God and Savior" (Titus 2:13), and "our God and Savior" (2 Peter 1:1), it should be kept in mind that although these kinds of descriptions are more often applied to the Father,[171] the Lord Jesus would be fully deserving of such descriptions based upon the exalted position that was given to him by that same God and Father.

With respect to the texts that have been mentioned, the error is not in arguing for a particular translation, for one may put forward valid arguments in favor of either rendering. But a real problem does exist in attempting to lead others into believing that the case for a particular translation can be proven with absolute certainty—at least at this point with what is known about the Greek language and rules of Greek grammar.

If Paul and Peter did intend to call Jesus "God" in any one of these verses, this must be understood in light of the biblical revelation as a whole, not through an extra-biblical

---

[169] 2 Peter 2:20 and 3:18 also have the same constructions. Speaking from the perspective of an orthodox Trinitarian, Albert Barnes wrote: "Erasmus [16th century Roman Catholic scholar] supposes that [the verse] may be taken in either sense. The construction ['our God and Savior Jesus Christ'], though certainly not a violation of the laws of the Greek language, is not so free from all doubt as to make it proper to use the passage as a proof-text in an argument for the divinity of the Saviour." Barnes then claimed: "It is easier to prove the doctrine [of Christ's divinity as understood in Trinitarianism] from other texts that are plain, than to show that this *must* be the meaning here." —*Barnes' Notes, Hebrews to Jude*, p. 218.

[170] John 3:16; 17:3

[171] More specifically, "God," or "our great God." Both the Father and Son are described as "savior" in the Bible.

theological system.

1 John 5:20

"And we know that the Son of God has come, and has given us understanding so that we may know Him who is true; and we are in Him who is true, in His Son Jesus Christ. This is the true God and eternal life." —1 John 5:20, NASB

Many leading evangelical apologists have cited 1 John 5:20 as solid support for the belief that Jesus is the second member of a triune Deity.[172] They believe that in this passage Jesus is, like the Father, called "the true God," hence part of a 'multi-personal' divine entity. But the footnote to this verse in the *Knox Bible* states: "It is not certain whether the word 'he' [lit. 'this (one)'] refers to the word 'God' ['him who is true'] or to the word 'Son.'" *The Interpreter's Bible* commentary also has the following observation: "Theological controversy has long raged about this passage. But the natural sense of the passage and the characteristic thought of the epistle and the Gospel preclude this interpretation [that Christ is called 'the true God' here]. It is through Christ that we are in God. This God so known is **the true God**. The thought centers in God from vs. 18 on, and the contrast with idols in the last verse confirms it. This God so known also means **eternal life**."[173]

The principal reason why the verse is thought to call Jesus Christ "the true God" is because the previous phrase—"His Son Jesus Christ"—contains in it the nearest antecedent noun. But it should be carefully noted that the nearest noun does not always indicate the author's intended referent. An obvious case is found in the very same letter, where John wrote: "Who is the liar but the one who denies that Jesus is the Christ? *This is the*

---

[172] See notes on this verse in *The MacArthur Study Bible* and Robert Reymond's *Jesus, Divine Messiah, The New Testament Witness*, pp. 310-312.
[173] *The Interpreter's Bible*, p. 301. The footnote in *The Harper Collins Study Bible, NRSV*, p. 2299, states, "*know him who is true...the true God and eternal life*. This probably means the Father rather than Jesus (see Jn 17.3, but note that Jesus is identified with life in Jn 1.2; Jn 1.3-4; 11.25; 14.6)."

antichrist, the one who denies the Father and the Son."[174] It is clear from this example that "This" does not refer back to the closest noun, "Christ," but to "the one *who denies* that Jesus is the Christ...the one who denies the Father and the Son." Similarly, a text in the book of Acts states: "[Jesus of Nazareth] went about doing good and healing all those oppressed by the devil, for God was with him."[175] In this case, "God" was clearly with "Jesus of Nazareth" not "the devil," even though "the devil" is the nearest antecedent noun. In the same way, "*This* is the true God and eternal life" need not refer to "His Son Jesus Christ." Instead, the phrase more likely refers to "Him who is true," the Father of Jesus Christ (Compare John 17:3).[176] This is why another respected evangelical commentary made the remarks that follow:

> The final sentence of verse 20 runs: *This is the true God, and eternal life*. To whom does *this* refer? Grammatically speaking, it would normally refer to the nearest preceding subject, namely *his Son Jesus Christ*. If so, this would be the most unequivocal statement of the deity of Jesus Christ in the New Testament, which the champions of orthodoxy were quick to exploit against the heresy of Arius. Luther and Calvin adopted this view. Certainly it is by no means an impossible interpretation. Nevertheless, 'the most natural reference' (Westcott) is to *him that is true*. In this way the three references to 'the true' are to the same Person, the Father, and the additional points made in the apparent final repetition are that is *this* One, namely the God made known by Jesus Christ, who is *the*

---

[174] 1 John 2:22, *NASB*
[175] Acts 10:38, *ESV*
[176] Nineteenth-century Bible scholar B. F. Westcott's observation was: "As far as the grammatical construction of the sentence is concerned the pronoun [*houtos*, 'this one'] may refer to 'Him that is true' or to 'Jesus Christ'. The most natural reference however is to the subject not locally nearest but dominant in the mind of the apostle (comp.) c[hapter]. ii.22; 2 John 7; Acts iv.1; vii.19). This is obviously 'He that is true' further described by the addition of 'His Son.' Thus the pronoun gathers up the revelation indicated in the words which precede…This being—**the One who is true who is revealed through and in His Son,** with whom we are united by His Son—is the true God and life eternal." —Brooke Foss Westcott, *The Epistles Of St. John: The Greek Text With Notes And Essays* (London, Macmillian And Co., 1883), p. 187.

true God, and that, besides this, He is *eternal life*...[177]

Roman Catholic John L. McKenzie made comments on 1 John 5:20 and some of the disputed texts that have been discussed. Although officially Trinitarian, McKenzie states the following:

> In the words of Jesus and in much of the rest of the New Testament the God of Israel (Gk *ho theos*) is the Father of Jesus Christ. It is for this reason that the title *ho theos*, which now designates the Father as a personal reality, is not applied in the New Testament to Jesus Himself; Jesus is the Son of God (of *ho theos*). This is a matter of usage and not of rule, and the noun is applied to Jesus a few times...The application of the noun [*theos*] is less certain in Romans 9:5: Paul's normal usage is to restrict the noun to designate the Father (cf 1 C 8:6), and in Romans 9:5 it is very probable that the concluding words are a doxology. 'Blessed is the God who is above all.' 2 Peter 1:1 is slightly more ambiguous than Titus 2:13, to which it is not strictly parallel; it may be rendered 'our God and Jesus Christ savior.' The pronoun 'this' in 1 John 5:20 is easily referred to God, who is implicit in Jn 5:19, although 'Jesus Christ' is the nearest noun.[178]

Although some evangelicals—in an effort to uphold Trinitarian doctrine—argue that Christ is called "the true God" in this verse, some of the most qualified, well-known and respected scholars in the Trinitarian community acknowledge the greater probability, based on the context, that the reference applies to God the Father. The respected Greek grammarian and Baptist A. T. Robertson wrote: "Grammatically *houtos* ['this'] may refer to Jesus Christ or to 'the True One.' It is a bit tautological to refer it to God, but that is probably correct, God in Christ, at any rate. God is eternal life (John 5:26) and he gives

---

[177] *The Epistles of John, An Introduction and Commentary by* The Rev. J. R. W. Scott, *Tyndale New Testament Commentaries* (London: Tyndale Press, 1st edition, July 1964), pp. 195, 196.
[178] *Dictionary of the Bible*, pp. 317, 318.

it to us through Christ."[179]

In his scholarly and detailed work dedicated exclusively to the issue of calling Jesus "God," Murray Harris concluded: "Although it is certainly possible that *houtos* refers back to Jesus Christ, several converging lines of evidence point to 'the true one,' God the Father, as the probable antecedent. This position, *houtos* = God, is held by many commentators, authors of general studies, and, significantly, by those grammarians who express an opinion on the matter."[180]

Similarly, in the *Epworth Commentary* series, William Loader summarized the points accurately:

> The Greek of 5:20 has only the true (one) and reads literally: *we know that the Son of God has come and has given us understanding* 'so that we know *the true (one)* and we are in the true (one)', *in his Son Jesus Christ.* 'This (one) is the true God and eternal life.' It is clear from this that 'the true (one)' is God throughout. Christ is *his Son*. In the final sentence *this* (one) most naturally refers still to God, not to Christ, as some have suggested. It is not unknown for Christ to be given God's name (Phil. 2:9-11) or even to be called 'God' (Heb. 1:8-9; John 1:1), but that would run contrary to the theme here, which is contrasting true and false understandings of God for which Christ's revelation is the criterion. 5:20 reminds us of Jesus' prayer according to John 17:3: 'This is eternal life: to know you the only true God and Jesus Christ whom you have sent.'[181]

In conclusion, it may be said that the term *theos* probably applies to Jesus Christ directly in the New Testament three

---

[179] *Word Pictures in the New Testament, Volume VI, The General Epistles and The Revelation of John*, p. 245. However, with respect to what Robertson referred to as "a bit tautological," Henry Alford answered, "this charge is altogether inaccurate. As referred to the Father, there is in it no tautology [useless repetition] and no aimlessness. It serves to identify the *ho alethinos* ['the true one'] mentioned before, in a solemn manner, and leads on to the concluding warning against false gods." —*The Greek Testament*, p. 515.
[180] Harris, *Jesus as God*, p. 253.
[181] *The Johannine Epistles, Epworth Commentaries* (Epworth Press, 1992), p.79.

The "deity" of Jesus Christ

times,[182] verifying the fact of his genuine Godship, divinity or divine authority; yet he is never described unequivocally as *the* God (*ho theos*). In John 1:1, "the word" (*ho logos*)—before becoming flesh—is described as *theos* without the definite article, suggesting that "the word" cannot be literally, directly, or personally, equated with "*the* God." John 1:18 evidently calls Christ an "only born/one of a kind god."[183] Hebrews 1:8 calls Jesus Christ "O God," and the risen Christ is addressed by the disciple Thomas as "my Lord and my God" (John 20:28).[184] Romans 9:5, Titus 2:13 and 2 Peter 1:1 are grammatically ambiguous and may or may not call Jesus "God"; and whether or not he is called God in a given English translation of these texts depends largely upon the translator's preference. The Scriptures definitely teach that Jesus is *the Son* of God. Since, in the Scriptures, other beings are called "gods" based on the authority given to them *by* God, and because of their roles as God's representatives, it is entirely fitting that God's Son, the possessor of "all authority in heaven and on earth" and "the exact representation of [God's] very being,"[185] is also called "G/god," since he always exercises that Godship in perfect harmony with the will of the Most High God, his Father.

---

[182] John 1:18; 20:28; Hebrews 1:8 (possibly at Rom. 9:5; Titus 2:13; 2 Peter 1:1). John 1:1 is normally thought to apply to Christ. Yet many reasonably dispute that in this case the *logos* is a reference to an actual 'person' (or could be directly equated with 'Christ' at this point) and that John 1:18 even uses the term *theos* of the Son (preferring the reading of other ancient manuscripts). In reference to another disputed text, Richard Longenecker (PhD) observed: "The appeal to 1 Tim. 3:16 is undoubtedly illegitimate, for the reading 'who (*hos*) was manifested in the flesh' has much stronger textual support than 'God (*theos*) was manifested in the flesh'."
—*The Christology of Early Jewish Christianity* (Vancouver: Regent College, 1970), p. 139.

[183] According to Murray Harris: "Whether one considers external evidence or transcriptional probabilities, *monogenes theos* ['only begotten god'] has a considerably stronger claim to originality than *ho monogenes huios* ['the only begotten son'], the other principal variant. External attestation for *monogenes theos* is admittedly restricted in extent, representing, as it does, mainly the Alexandrian textual tradition, but it is not uncommon for this text type alone to have preserved the original reading." —*Jesus as God*, p. 82.

[184] Although Thomas called Jesus "my Lord and my God" (lit., *the* god of me), *ho theos* (with the article) is the necessary part of that particular grammatical structure and form of address and does not reveal anything in terms of proving that Jesus should be identified as the Most High God, "the God and Father of our Lord Jesus Christ" (Ephesians 1:3). Paul described Satan as "the god (*ho theos*) of this age" (2 Corinthians 4:4). But he is not *the god* (*ho theos*) in an unequivocal sense.

[185] Matthew 28:18; Hebrews 1:3.

The "deity" of Jesus Christ

An Early Coptic Translation and John 1:1c

Prepared by Solomon Landers (Revised November, 2010)

ἐν ἀρχῇ ἦν ὁ λόγος
καὶ ὁ λόγος ἦν πρὸς τὸν θεόν
καὶ θεὸς ἦν ὁ λόγος

Transliteration of Greek Text, John 1:1:

1:1a: *en arche en ho logos*
1:1b: *kai ho logos en pros ton theon*
1:1c: *kai theos en ho logos*

ϨΝ ΤΕϨΟΥΕΙΤΕ ΝΕϤϢΟΟΠ ΝϬΙ ΠϢΑϪΕ
ΑΥⲰ ΠϢΑϪΕ ΝΕϤϢΟΟΠ ΝΝΑϨΡΜ ΠΝΟΥΤΕ
ΑΥⲰ ΝΕΥΝΟΥΤΕ ΠΕ ΠϢΑϪΕ

Transliteration of Coptic, John 1:1:

1:1a: *Hn tehoueite nefshoop nci pshaje*
1:1b: *Auw pshaje nefshoop nnahrm pnoute*
1:1c: *Auw neunoute pe pshaje*

In harmony with Jesus' command to them, the early Christians eagerly spread the message of the good news of God's Kingdom far and wide. They made translations of the Koine Greek Gospels into several languages. By about the year 200, the earliest of these were found in Syriac, Coptic, and Latin.[i] Coptic (from the Greek word for 'Egyptian') was the language spoken by professed Christians in Egypt, in the Sahidic dialect. That dialect was eclipsed by use of the Bohairic dialect by the 6th century and in Coptic church liturgy by the 11th century C.E.

Coptic was the last stage of the hieroglyphic Egyptian language used since the time of the Pharaohs. Under the influence of the widespread use of Koine Greek, the Coptic language came to be written, not in hieroglyphs or the cursive Egyptian script called Demotic, but in Greek letters, supplemented by seven characters derived from hieroglyphs. Coptic is a Hamito-Semitic language, meaning that it shares elements of both Hamitic (North African) languages and Semitic languages like Hebrew, Aramaic, and Arabic.

---

[i] Aland, p. 68.

Much was made of it in the scholarly world when an apocryphal "gospel" written in Sahidic Coptic, titled the "Gospel of Thomas," was discovered in Egypt near Nag Hammadi in December 1945. Yet, after an initial welcome, the scholarly world has been strangely silent about an earlier and more significant work, the English translation of the Sahidic Coptic canonical Gospel of John. This Sahidic version may date from about the late 2nd century C.E.[ii] This version was introduced to the English-speaking world in 1911 through the work of [Reverend] George William Horner. Today, it is difficult even to find copies of Horner's translation of the Coptic canonical Gospel of John. Apparently, it has been largely relegated to dusty library shelves. But copies of the "Gospel of Thomas" (in English, some with Coptic text) line the lighted shelves of popular bookstores.

In the book, *The Text of the New Testament* (Eerdmans, 1987), Kurt and Barbara Aland, editors of critical Greek New Testament texts, state:

> "The Coptic New Testament is among the **primary** resources for the history of the New Testament text. Important as the Latin and Syriac versions may be, it is of **far greater importance** to know precisely how the text developed in Egypt." (Page 200, emphasis added)

The Sahidic Coptic text of the Gospel of John has been found to be in the Alexandrian text tradition of the well-regarded Codex Vaticanus (**B**) (Vatican 1209), one of the best of the early extant Greek New Testament manuscripts. Coptic John also shows affinities to the Greek Papyrus Bodmer XIV (**p75**) of the late 2nd/3rd century.[iii] Concerning the Alexandrian text tradition,

---

[ii] George William Horner, *The Coptic version of the New Testament in the southern dialect, otherwise called Sahidic and Thebaic*, 1911, pp. 398, 399.
[iii] Aland, p. 91

The "deity" of Jesus Christ

Dr. Bruce Metzger states that it "is usually considered to be the best text and the most faithful in preserving the original."[iv]

Therefore, it is all the more strange that insights of the Sahidic Coptic text of John 1:1 are largely ignored by popular Bible translators. Might that be because the Sahidic Coptic Gospel of John translates John 1:1c in a way that is unpopular to many? The Sahidic text renders John 1:1c as **auw neunoute pe pshaje**, clearly meaning literally "and *a* god was the Word." Unlike Koine Greek, Sahidic Coptic has both the definite article, **p**, and the indefinite article, **ou**, which may contract to **u** following the joined verbal prefix **ne** (i.e., **ne ou noute** becomes **neunoute**.) The Coptic text of John 1:1b identifies the first mention of **noute** as **pnoute**, "the god," i.e., God. This corresponds to the Koine Greek text, wherein *theos*, "god," has the definite article *ho* at John 1:1b, i.e., "the Word was with [the] God."

The Koine Greek text indicates the indefiniteness of the word *theos* in its second mention (John 1:1c) of "god," by omitting the definite article before it, because Koine Greek had no indefinite article. *But Coptic does have an indefinite article*, and the text employs the indefinite article at John 1:1c. This makes it clear that in reading the original Greek text, the ancient Coptic translators understood it to say specifically that "the Word was *a* god." The early Coptic Christians had a good understanding of both Greek and their own language, and their translation of John's Koine Greek here is very precise and accurate. Because they actually employed the indefinite article before the Sahidic word "god," **noute**, the Sahidic Coptic translation of John 1:1c is more precise than the translation found in the Latin Vulgate, since Latin has neither a definite nor an indefinite article. The 6th century Coptic Bohairic version also employs the indefinite article before the Coptic word for "god.": **ne ounouti** in the full form **ou**, because the verbal particle **ne** is

---

[iv] Bruce M. Metzger, *A Textual Commentary on the Greek New Testament*, 2nd edition, United Bible Societies, 1994, page 5.

not joined to it, reading: ***ne ounouti pe picaji***, "a god was the Word."

The Sahidic Coptic word ***neunoute*** (***ne-u-noute***) is made up of three parts: ***ne***, a verbal particle denoting imperfect (past) tense, i.e., "was [being]..."; ***(o)u***, the Coptic indefinite article, denoting "a,"; and ***noute***, the Sahidic word for "god." Grammarians state that the word ***noute*** "god," takes the definite article when it refers to the One God, whereas without the definite article it refers to other gods. But in Sahidic John 1:1c the word ***noute*** is not simply anarthrous, lacking any article at all. *Here the indefinite article is specifically employed.* Thus, whereas some scholars impute ambiguity to the Greek of John 1:1c, this early Coptic translation can be rendered accurately as "the Word was a god." This is the careful way those 2nd century Coptic translators understood the Koine Greek text of John 1:1c.

According to Coptic grammarian J. Martin Plumley, the Coptic indefinite article is translated simply as "a", as in ***ourwme*** "a man", ***ouchime*** "a woman." When used with abstract nouns, such as ***ourase*** "joy", ***oume*** "truth," it may be left untranslated. The same is true when the indefinite article is used with nouns indicating substance or material, e.g., ***ounoub mn-oulibanoc mn-ousal*** "gold and frankincense and myrrh." (Matt. 2.11)v

However, the Coptic word ***noute***, "god," is neither an abstract noun, nor a substance, nor a material. John 1:1b has already identified God with the ***definite*** article, ***p-noute***. Therefore, at John 1:1c, the ***indefinite*** article ***(o)u*** before ***noute*** should be fully translated: "the Word was **a** god," just as ***ourwme*** would be translated "**a** man." Additionally, the Sahidic Coptic expression for "was *a* god," ***ne-u-noute pe*** at John 1:1c, is of the same construction as found at John 18:40, where it says of Barabbas that he ***ne-u-soone pe***, "was *a* robber," accurately rendering the Greek original, ***en de ho barabbas lestes***. Here the Greek word for "robber" or "thief," ***lestes***, is anarthrous, without the definite article: "**a** robber." No English version renders this,

---

[vi] J. Martin Plumley, *Introductory Coptic Grammar*, London: Home & Van Thal, 1948, sections 85-87.

"Barabbas was Robber," nor "Barabbas was robber-like." Every single one renders: "Barabbas was **a** robber," or "**a** thief," and correctly so. Likewise, John 1:1c should not be rendered to say, "the Word was God," whether the text is English or Coptic. There is no grammatical justification for rendering it that way.

In George Horner's 1910 English translation of the Sahidic text he gives this translation: "In the beginning was being the word, and the word was being with God, and [a] God was the word." (It may be noted that while Horner puts the indefinite article in brackets at John 1:1c, he does not do so consistently. For example, at John 18:40, where the exact same Coptic grammatical construction appears, Horner translates, "Barabbas was a robber," without putting the indefinite article in brackets. There is no need to do so at John 1:1c.) In another translation made from the Coptic text in 2003 by Lance Jenott we read: "In the beginning existed the Word, and the Word existed with God, and the Word was a God."[vi]

It may be noted that the earliest Coptic translation, the Sahidic, was likely made before Trinitarianism gained a foothold in the churches of the 4th century. That may be one reason why the Coptic translators saw no reason to violate the sense of John's Greek by translating it "the Word was God." By rendering the verse to read, "the Word was a god," the ancient Sahidic Coptic translation of John 1:1c faithfully and accurately translated the Greek text. But since this conflicts with the traditional and popular English translation, it may be why the ancient Sahidic Coptic version of John 1:1c is largely kept under wraps in academic religious circles today. Bible translators make some note of the Coptic readings for certain other verses, but not this one. And most new English Bible translations continue to translate this verse to say "the Word was God." But the Coptic text provides clear evidence—from about 1700 years ago—that the most accurate English rendering of John 1:1c is "the Word was a god."

auw ne-u-noute pe pshaje,

diagrammed:*auw* = "and";

ne = verbal prefix denoting past tense, i.e., "was (being)";
u = Coptic indefinite article, "a," contracted from *ou* following joined verbal prefix *ne*
noute = god

pe = Coptic particle meaning "is" or "this one is."

p = Coptic definite article, "the"

shaje = "word"

Literally the Coptic says, "and - was being- a god - (is)- the -Word."
Or more smoothly in literal English, "and the Word was a god."
The Coptic Bohairic version also has the indefinite article, written in full form, *ou* before the word for "god," at John 1:1c, i.e., "a god." This is basically the Bible in use by the modern Coptic church, reading in Coptic: *ouoh ne ounoute pe Picaji*, literally, "and was a god the Word." However, certain *English* translations of the Coptic Bible ignore this fact. The modern Coptic church, following Orthodox tradition since the 4th century C.E, rather than its Bible, ignores this reading to teach Trinitarianism. Similarly, the modern Greek Orthodox church tradition, holding to the same doctrine, "invalidates" the reading of the Koine Greek text. (Compare Matthew 15:6; Mark 7:13) Sahidic: **neunoute** literally, "was a god," Bohairic: **ne ounouti** literally, "was a god."

5

The Apostolic Testimony

> *"If there is any encouragement in Christ, any solace in love, any participation in the Spirit, any compassion and mercy, complete my joy by being of the same mind, with the same love, united in heart, thinking one thing. Do nothing out of selfishness or out of vainglory; rather, humbly regard others as more important than yourselves, each looking out not for his own interests, but (also) everyone for those of others. Have among yourselves the same attitude that is also yours in Christ Jesus, Who, though he was in the form of God, did not regard equality with God something to be grasped. Rather, he emptied himself, taking the form of a slave, coming in human likeness; and found human in appearance, he humbled himself, becoming obedient to death, even death on a cross. Because of this, God greatly exalted him and bestowed on him the name that is above every name, that at the name of Jesus every knee should bend, of those in heaven and on earth and under the earth, and every tongue confess that Jesus Christ is Lord, to the glory of God the Father."*
> —Philippians 2:1-11, *New American Bible*

What the apostle Paul said about Jesus Christ in his letter to the Philippians is another example where issues of translation and the understanding of certain terms have proved controversial among students of the Bible. In fact, due to several uncertainties present in terms of the original language used, nearly every aspect of this one passage has yielded diverse and conflicting interpretations relative to the nature and identity of Christ.

During the course of his letter Paul encouraged the Christians to whom he was writing not to do anything out of selfish ambition or conceit; that, in humility, they should regard others as better than themselves; and further, that they should not merely look out for their own interests, but for the interests of others as well. Then, the apostle urged the Christians to have the same mentality that was in Christ Jesus, pointing out that although Christ was existing in the "form" of God, "he did not think to snatch at equality with God" (*New English Bible*). Or, as *The Interpreter' Bible* renders it: "he did not consider equality with God a thing to be seized."[1]

The word normally rendered "form" in the English Bible is a translation of the Greek word *morphē*. Most—though not all—Bible students have taken the expression "form of God" (*morphē theou*) to be a description of Christ in a pre-human state when he is thought to have been in the presence of the Father "before the world began" (John 17:5). In support of their viewpoint, however, many Trinitarians have contended that the word usually translated "form" really means "essence," so that Paul was actually intending to communicate the notion that Christ was "in essence" God, or that he was of the same "substance" as the Father.

Unfortunately, one Trinitarian source made the following argument: "R.C. Trench shows that the deity of Christ is affirmed by the phrase 'in the form of God': The *morphē* then, it may be assumed, is of the *essence* of a thing. We cannot conceive the thing as apart from its formality, to use 'formality' in the old logical sense."[2] Similarly, according to the footnote in the *New English Translation*, "The Greek term translated *form* indicates correspondence with reality. Thus the meaning of the phrase is that Christ was truly God."[3] In basic agreement, the

---

[1] *The Interpreter's Bible* rendering, Vol. 11, p. 48. It was noted by the authors that this is the reading of the verse if "literally translated."
[2] Beisner, *God In Three Persons*, pp. 30, 31.
[3] *New English Translation Bible, New Testament*, p. 621.

MacArthur Study Bible footnote states: "The usual Gr. Word for 'being' is not used here. Instead, Paul chose another term that stresses the *essence* of a person's nature—his continuous state or condition."[4] And, lastly, in his book *Knowing Christ and the Challenge of Heresy*, Trinitarian Steven Tsoukalas takes a non-traditional approach; arguing that Paul was speaking about Christ in his "incarnate" (in-the-flesh) state, as opposed to his alleged "pre-incarnate" state. However, Tsoukalas maintains the same argument for the meaning of the term *morphē*. He writes: "What does 'form of God' mean? It refers to the very *essence* of nature of the God-man Jesus. He is in His very nature God. This is an explicit affirmation of the full deity of the Son."[5]

So the first question revolves around the meaning of this one Greek word, in view of the common argument advanced by the orthodox. Is it true, as the orthodox have claimed, that the word *morphē* actually means "essence"? If so, why do most English Bibles translate it as "form," and what do the lexical sources tell us? Are there any clues within the context itself that can shed light on its meaning? Furthermore, how was the word used and understood elsewhere in the New Testament, in the Greek Septuagint, and in the non-biblical Greek literature of the same period?

First, it should be noted that in *Bullinger's Critical Lexicon* there is no mention of the term carrying the idea of "essence." In fact, the *only* definition given for *morphē* is "form." The scholarly lexicon by Walter Bauer (translated and revised by Arndt and Gingrich) also has "form," along with "outward appearance, shape." According to *Kittel's Theological Dictionary*, another standard lexical source, the word means: "form," "external appearance." According to *Thayer's Greek-English Lexicon, morphē* means, "(1) the form by which a person or thing strikes a vision" and '(2) external appearance.'" Likewise, the well-known lexicon by *Liddell & Scott* defines *morphē* as, "form, shape, fine, beautiful form or shape, figure,

---

[4] *MacArthur Study Bible*, p. 1822 (emphasis added).
[5] *Knowing Christ in the Challenge of Heresy*, pp. 101, 102. The idea that the "form of God" is a description of Christ while he was a man on earth is a minority view among Trinitarians. On this view Tsoukalas was apparently influenced by Dr. Robert Reymond (footnote, p. 99). See Reymond's *Jesus, Divine Messiah* (pages 251-266), and his *A New Systematic Theology of the Christian Faith* (pages 259-264).

The Apostolic Testimony

fashion, appearance, outward form or semblance."

In his book on the Trinity, Dr. White proposes a twofold definition for *morphē* that apparently seeks to accord with its true lexical meaning while at the same time retaining the desired meaning often advanced by Trinitarian apologists. According to White: "The Greek term 'form' means the 'outward display of the inner reality or substance.'[6] However, Dr. White's proposal of this exclusive sense for *morphē* is shown to be highly improbable, not only when we consult the definition given in the standard dictionaries, but also when we take into account how a word derived from *morphē* is used by Paul and in other places throughout the New Testament.

In his second letter to Timothy (Ch. 3:1-5), the apostle spoke about those who, in the last days, would be "lovers of self, lovers of money, boastful, arrogant, revilers, disobedient to parents, ungrateful, unholy…lovers of pleasure rather than lovers of God, holding to a form (*morphosis*)[7] of godliness, although they have denied its power…"

Here the point made is clear. There would be those in the last days who would hold to a *form* or *outward appearance* of godliness but who were in reality ungodly. If one were to accept Dr. White's definition of *morphē*, this would mean, in effect, that such people would hold to an "outward display" of godliness which would reflect the "inner-reality" or "substance" within, yet that they still somehow denied the power of godliness.[8] It is evident, however, that the apostle was making the opposite point. The people in view would *outwardly appear* to be religious, but the inner-reality was that of ungodliness. In this case, the context

---

[6] White, *The Forgotten Trinity*, p. 123.

[7] The basic meaning is confirmed by the way other translations have rendered this verse. Many translations properly use the simple "form" to convey the sense; but some have: "*outward form* of godliness" (*NRSV*), "the *appearance* of godliness" (*ESV*), "*outward appearance* of religion" (*JB*). It is also interesting how MacArthur claims that "form (*morphē*)" refers to "essence" in Philippians chapter 2, yet he acknowledges the sense of the word *morphosis* (an essentially synonymous term) in his study notes on the verse in 2 Timothy: "'Form' refers to outward shape or appearance. Like the unbelieving scribes and Pharisees, false teachers and their followers are concerned with mere external appearances…Their outward form of Christianity and virtue makes them all the more dangerous." —*MacArthur Study Bible*, p. 1879. However, it also seems possible to understand *morphosis* here to carry the idea of "formation," so that the people of the last days would have a "formation" (as in the beginning traces or qualities) of godliness, yet who ultimately denied its power.

[8] The concept of "essence" would not fit here either. Paul is not saying that such people would hold to an "essence of godliness."

The Apostolic Testimony

of the passage itself provides added confirmation that the term normally denotes the basic idea of "external appearance."[9]

It should be carefully noted that *morphē* also occurs at Mark 16:12 (Luke 24:13-35 is Luke's account of the same occurrence) where, following his resurrection, Jesus is said to have appeared in another "form," so that the disciples did not immediately recognize him. Yet this clearly did not refer to a change in "essential nature" or "inner-essential-being." Rather, there is a reference to a change in Jesus' external appearance. Albert Barnes observed:

> The word rendered 'form'—(*morphe*), occurs only in three places in the New Testament, and in each place is rendered 'form.' Mark 16:12; Phil 2:6-7. In Mark it is applied to the form which Jesus assumed after his resurrection, and in which he appeared to two of his disciples on his way to Emmaus...*The word properly means, form, shape, bodily shape, especially a beautiful form, a beautiful bodily appearance*...In Phil 2:7, it is applied to the appearance of a servant...The word 'form' is often applied to the gods by the classic writers, denoting their *aspect* or *appearance* when they became visible to people.[10]

The authors of one book on the Trinity also contradicted the notion that "form" carries the meaning often advanced by evangelical teachers:

> Trinitarians insist that *form* conveys the idea of 'essential nature'. The NIV translates the phrase as 'being in very nature God', and relegates 'in the form of God' to a footnote. The word Paul used was *morphe*, a Greek word that basically means 'form, fashion, appearance, external shape,[11] sort'. The idea is of an external shape that can make identification possible. It has been transferred into

---

[9] The same point was made in the *Concordant Commentary on the New Testament* by A. E. Knoch: "*Form* denotes outward appearance, as is shown by Paul's use of it in the contrast, 'having a *form* of devoutness, yet denying its power' (2Tim.3:5). We have found it impossible to sustain the idea that it refers to intrinsic essence. *Figure* or *fashion* denotes the form prevailing at any time. Christ was the Image of God, the visible representation of the Deity" (Concordant Publishing Concern: Santa Clarita, 1968) p. 298.
[10] Barnes' *Notes on the New Testament, Ephesians to Philemon*, p. 169 (emphasis added).
[11] William Tyndale (1494-1536) translated the phrase "being in the *shape* of God..."

English in such words as *morphology*, the study of shape or appearance, and *metamorphosis*, as a change of shape. Despite many claims to the contrary, the internal nature or [intrinsic] condition of that which is being described does not seem to be implied in the word *morphe*, particularly in every day speech (the so-called *koine* or 'common' Greek)...it is the Scriptural use of *morphe* and related words that should be our best guide to their meaning.[12]

And, after having investigated the use of the word in the New Testament and in other types of Greek literature, another source pointed out:

> ...the real definition of *morphe* should become apparent as we check the sources available at the time of the New Testament. After all, the word was a common one in the Greek world...the actual evidence clearly reveals that *morphe* does not refer to Christ's essential being, but rather to an outward appearance...The Jews translating the Septuagint used *morphe* several times, and it always referred to an outward appearance. Job says, 'A spirit glided past my face, and the hair on my body stood on end. It stopped, but I could not tell what it was. A form (*morphe*) stood before my eyes, and I heard a hushed voice' (Job 4:15, 16). There is no question here that *morphe* refers to the outward appearance. Isaiah has the word *morphe* in reference to man-made idols: 'The carpenter measures with a line and makes an outline with a marker; he roughs it out with chisels and marks it with compasses. He shapes it in the form (*morphe*) of man, of man in all his glory, that it may dwell in a shrine' (Isa. 44:13). It would be absurd to assert that *morphe* referred to 'the essential nature' in this verse, as if a wooden carving could have the 'essential nature' of a man...*Schema*, as Kittel points out, can be synonymous with *morphe*, but it has more of an emphasis on outward trappings rather than outward appearance, and often points to that which is more transitory in nature, like the clothing we wear or an appearance we have for just a

---

[12] *The Trinity, True or False?* 2nd edition, Broughton and Southgate (The Dawn Book Supply: Nottingham, 2002), pp. 208-211.

short time.[13]

Another basic point to keep in mind, in addition to the linguistic evidence, is that the apostle did *not* say that Jesus "*was God,*" or "*was in essence God,*" as some have taken the phrase to mean. Rather, Paul said that Jesus was in the "*form of God*" (*NASB*), or in "*God's form*" (*Diaglott*), and it is helpful to recognize the important distinction. This is why Ezra Abbot observed:

> Without entering into any detailed discussion of this passage, it may be enough to remark that being in the form of God, as Paul uses the expression here, is a very different thing from being God; that the *morphe* cannot denote the nature or essence of Christ, because it is something of which he is represented as emptying or divesting himself. The same is true of the *to einai isa theo*, 'the being on an equality with God,' or 'like God,' which is spoken of as something which he was not eager to seize, according to one way of understanding *harpagmon*, or not eager to retain, according to another interpretation.[14]

If one were to investigate the matter further, it would be found that a few translations, including *Today's English Version*, attempt to communicate the idea by saying that Christ "always had the *nature* of God," or something similar. But in a corresponding handbook on the translation, the point was made:

> To say *he always had the nature of God* is not equivalent to saying that 'Christ is God' or that 'Christ is of one substance with God.'...In a number of languages there is no abstract term such as *nature*. The closest equivalent would be an expression of 'likeness,' and therefore the first line of this hymn may be rendered as 'He has always

---

[13] Graeser, Lynn, Schoenheit, *One God & One Lord*, pp. 505-507.
[14] *On the Construction of Romans IX. 5. From the Journal of the Society of Biblical Literature and Exegesis for* 1881. The point about the "form of God" is confirmed by Donald Macleod ('recognized as a leading contemporary systematic theologian'): "In Philippians 2:6 Paul refers to Christ in a way which falls little short of calling him *God*. He speaks of him as being 'in the *form* of God (*en morphē theou*)." —*Jesus is Lord, Christology Yesterday and Today* (Great Britain: Christian Focus Pub., 2000) p. 22 (emphasis added). Macleod also goes into some detail contradicting the common Trinitarian argument that *morphe* refers to "essence." See Appendix for his entire discussion on this point.

been just like God.' One must obviously avoid an expression which would be equivalent to saying 'He has always been God himself.'[15]

Additionally, quite a few New Testament scholars have pointed out that in Greek the words "form" (*morphē*) and "image" (*eikōn*) are closely related. R. P. Martin argued that "*morphe* and *eikon* are equivalent terms that are used interchangeably in the LXX [*Septuagint*]."[16] James Dunn states in *Christology in the Making*: "It has long been recognized that *morphe* and *eikon* are near synonyms and that in Hebrew thought the visible 'form of God' *is* his glory."[17] Similarly, *Kittel's Theological Dictionary* states: "[Christ] is in the form of God, i.e., he bears the *image* of the divine majesty."[18] Paul Zeisler noted: "Christ like Adam was in the image ('form': the words in Greek can be synonymous) of God, unlike Adam he did not regard equality with God (i.e. being like God, see Gen. 3: 5) a matter of grabbing (or perhaps a prize to be snatched). Indeed unlike Adam (v. 7) he voluntarily accepted servanthood and mortality even to the point of a humiliating death on the cross (v. 8). He obeyed God, in contrast to Adam who vaingloriously disobeyed…"[19] This is probably the reason why Daniel Mace, in his 1729 New Testament Translation, rendered the verse:

> **…for the same temper of mind ought to be in you as was in Christ Jesus: who tho'** *he was the image of God*, **did not affect to appear with divine majesty…**

However, the fact that the words *eikōn* and *morphē* appear to be related does not imply that the translation "form" is inaccurate. It is, in fact, the best-known English representation of the Greek *morphē*.

The meaning of the following part of verse six has likewise been translated and understood in a variety of ways. According to the renderings of a few English translations, Paul said:

---

[15] *A Handbook on Paul's Letter to the Philippians*, by I-Jin Loh and Eugene A. Nida (United Bible Societies, 1977), pp. 56, 57 (words in italics were underlined in the original).
[16] *Morphe* in Phillipians 2:6, *Expository Times*, Vol. 70, no. 6, March 1959, 183-184.
[17] *Christology in the Making*, 2nd edition (Grand Rapids: Eerdmans, 1989), p. 115.
[18] *Kittel's Theological Dictionary of the New Testament* (Grand Rapids: Eerdmans, 1985), p. 609.
[19] *Pauline Christianity*, revised edition (Oxford University Press, 1990), p.45.

The Apostolic Testimony

Let this mind be in you, which was also in Christ Jesus: Who, being in the form of God, thought it not *robbery* (Gk: *harpagmos*) *to be equal with God...*

According to the way the text is translated in the *King James Version*, Jesus did not think that it was wrong ('robbery') to be equal with God. But it was correctly observed in the *Westminster Version of the New Testament* that the expression is literally translated, "'did not think [it] a thing to be snatched at': the Latin version has suggested the common translation 'thought it not robbery' [same as *KJV*]: a sense the words in themselves might bear, but which does not convey the lesson of humility on which St. Paul is insisting."[20]

The reason the point is made about the "common translation" not conveying the lesson of humility Paul intended should be clear. It simply would not make sense for Paul to have urged Christians to have the same mind as Christ, and in the next line, to have said that Christ did not think it was wrong—a crime like 'robbery'—to be equal with God. When the surrounding context is carefully considered, it becomes clear that the apostle's point was to induce Christians to imitate the lowliness of mind exemplified by their Master Jesus; and, in doing so, for Paul to have pointed out that Christ, as an example, saw nothing wrong with being equal with God, would have been entirely contradictory to the overall spirit and thrust of the apostle's inspired instruction. This is why many modern translations—in accord with the meaning of the language—convey a totally different, even opposite, sense with regard to Jesus' being "equal" with God.

Paul's admonition regarding humility to the early Christians has always been clear. According to Paul, Christians should "have the same attitude which was also in Christ Jesus." Then, the example given by Christ Jesus is described: "although he was existing in God's form," as the *Revised English Bible* expresses it: "**he laid no claim to equality with God.**" Or, more literally, as the *New American Bible* (1970) reads: "**he did not**

---

[20] *The Westminster Version of the Sacred Scriptures, The New Testament, Volume III, St. Paul's Epistles to the Churches* (Third Edition, Revised: London, New York, Toronto, 1939), p. 213.

The Apostolic Testimony

deem equality with God something to be grasped at."[21]

In light of the traditional viewpoints surrounding this controversial text, and when considering the multiple ways in which it has been rendered by modern translators (not to mention the fact that there is more than one possible meaning in terms of the Greek language), the following will be helpful in terms of offering some insight into the challenges of interpretation faced by modern readers. According to one respected commentary:

> *Thought it not robbery* is one translation of the key-word *harpagmos* which may be taken actively as in [*KJV*] or passively as in [*RV*]: 'counted it not a prize to be on an equality with God'. Both versions are linguistically possible. The real difficulty is encountered in the question: Does it mean that Christ enjoyed equality with God but surrendered it by becoming man, or that He could have grasped at equality with God by self-assertion, but declined to do so…?[22]

This appears to be the principal question of interpretive concern, and, naturally, has a critical bearing on how it should be translated. Additionally, it should be noted that according to some translations and paraphrased versions, including *Philips Modern English*, Jesus "did not cling to his privileges as God's equal." This is a translation that, from one point of view, reflects the doctrine of many Trinitarian teachers. It implies that Jesus was "equal" with God but that he did not hold on or "cling" to the rights associated with the equality with the Father he already possessed.[23] However, with respect to the Greek word underlying the translation, Ralph P. Martin observed: "We cannot find any passage where [*har-pa'zo*] or any of its derivatives [including *har-pag-mon'*] has the sense of 'holding in possession,' 'retaining'. It seems invariably to mean 'seize,' 'snatch violently'. Thus it is not permissible to glide from the true sense

---

[21] Or, as *Today's English Version* puts it, "he did not think that by force he should try to become equal with God." With regard to a translation like this that says, "Christ did not "grasp for" or attempt to obtain "by force" equality with God, Dr. White concedes that "in all fairness, the Greek term translated 'to grasp' *can* be translated in this way." —*The Forgotten Trinity*, p. 124.

[22] *The Epistle of Paul to the Philippians: An Introduction and Commentary*, pp. 97, 98.

[23] Trinitarian scholars maintain that Christ never actually relinquished his 'coequality' with the Father, but that he simply chose not to *take advantage* of his prerogatives as the Father's consubstantial equal.

'grasp at' into one which is totally different, 'hold fast'." Martin goes on to say: "However, what if the word *harpagmos* is in the active rather than the passive sense? This would mean that this double accusative is different from those where *hegomai* is stative. The above examination of this word and its derivatives strongly gives the case that *harpagmos* is to be taken in the active rather than the passive sense. This would mean that rather than just mean 'to think' or 'to regard' *'hegomai'* would be, here, 'to make plans for,' 'contemplate' or 'deliberate.' So that Jesus did not just 'consider' in the sense to not to 'think' or not to 'believe' but not to *'make plans for'* or did not *'contemplate'* a snatching.'"[24]

In the *Tyndale Commentaries*, Martin elaborated further on the possible meaning of the word *harpagmos*, again saying:

> It is questionable, however, whether the sense of the verb can glide from its real meaning of 'to seize', 'to snatch violently' to that of 'to hold fast'; and the second interpretation hardly does justice to the structure of the whole sentence as well as to the force of 'exalted to the highest place' in verse 9. Attempting a different approach, Kennedy and those who see as a background here the Genesis story and the temptation presented to Adam to 'be like God' (Gn. 3:5) draw the parallel between the first and the last Adam. The former senselessly sought to grasp at equality with God, and through pride and disobedience lost the glorious image of his maker; the latter chose to tread the pathway of lowly obedience in order to be exalted by God as Lord (v. 9-10), *i.e.* to be placed on an equality which he did not have previously, because it is only by 'the suffering of death' that he is 'crowned with glory and honour' (Heb. 2:9,

---

[24] *The Expositor's Greek Testament*, W. Robertson Nicoll, Vol. III, pp. 436, 437. In their handbook on Bible translation, I-Jin Loh and Eugene A. Nida note, among other interpretive explanations: "It can mean 'a prize to be seized.' This is the meaning adopted by the TEV (so also RSV 'did not count equality with God a thing to be grasped,' NEB 'he did not think to snatch at equality with God, NAB 'he did not deem equality with God something to be grasped at'). On this understanding, 'equality with God' is not something already possessed by Christ. He declined to do what he could have done." —*A Handbook on Paul's Letter to the Philippians*, pp. 56-57. The *KJV* is justified in rendering the word 'robbery' but *incorrect* when it says that Christ did not think it was robbery to be equal with God. It is much more likely, given the exhortation to humility, that Paul was saying that Christ did not think or give consideration to performing the act of robbery (or seizure), namely, that of trying to be equal with God.

RSV)...Here once more, if the key to the text lies in the intended parallel between the first Adam and the second Adam, one of the latter options is to be preferred; and this is the generally prevailing modern view which Stauffer believes has been definitely settled: 'So the old contention about *harpagmos* is over: equality with God is not a *res rapta*...a position which the pre-existent Christ had and gave up, but it is a *res rapienda*, a possibility of advancement which he declined.'[25]

It is critical to note that the same root word appearing in *harpagmos* (*harpazo*) appears in other places in the Christian Scriptures, and all of them carry the sense of *seizing* something not previously possessed. Here are three examples of statements made by Jesus (and one by the apostle Paul) where a form of the word is used:

> **...how can anyone enter the strong man's house and *carry off* [*harpazo*] his property, unless he first binds the strong man?** —Matthew 12:29, *NASB*.

> **When any one hears the word of the kingdom and does not understand it, the evil one comes and *snatches away* [*harpazo*] what is sown in his heart...** —Matthew 13:19, *RSV*

> **I give them eternal life, and they shall never perish, and no one shall *snatch* [*harpazo*] them out of my hand.** —John 10:28, *RSV*

> **Then we who are alive and remain will be *caught up* ('*snatched up*,' Unvarnished New Testament) [*harpazo*] together with them in the clouds to meet the Lord in the air...** —1 Thessalonians 4:17, *NASB*

The account reported in John 6:15 says: "When Jesus therefore perceived that they [those who 'had seen the miracle that Jesus did'] would come and **take him by force** [*harpazo*], to make him a king, he departed again into a mountain himself alone" (*KJV* rendering). The Greek *harpazeizn auton* indicates that the people tried to "seize him" in order to make him king.

---

[25] *The Tyndale New Testament Commentaries, The Epistle of Paul to the Philippians, An Introduction and Commentary*, pp. 101, 102 (word in brackets added for clarification).

That is why some translations have: "they meant to come and seize him" (*NEB*), "come and snatch Him" (*Concordant*), "seize him by force" (*NET*), "carry Him off by force" (*Williams*).

This helps to explain the *Today's English Version's* choice of words for Philippians 2:6: "he did not think *that by force he should try* to become equal with God." And this is why it was observed in *The Interpreter's Bible*, in part: "Since [the Son] had this affinity with God, he might have aspired to 'equality' with him; he might have claimed an equal share in all the powers which God exercises and in all the honors which are rendered to him by his creatures. Standing so near to God, he might have resented his inferior place and thrown off his obedience...Yet he never attempted the robbery which might have raised him higher...[in] the Greek, and in English, the word [*harpagmos*] involved the idea of violent seizure, and what Christ resisted was not merely the prize but the means of obtaining it. He refused to seize for his own the glory which belonged to God."[26]

According to James Broughton and Peter Southgate,—who also see in this passage an allusion to Adam and Eve partaking of the prohibited fruit in the Garden of Eden—the passage should be understood in the following way:

> Paul is continuing this theme of contrasting Adam with Christ. Thus, in the passage still under consideration, seeking 'equality with God' is a reference to the subtle temptation by which the serpent in Eden induced Eve to eat the forbidden fruit: 'For God knows that when you eat of it your eyes will be opened, and *you will become like God,* knowing good and evil' (Genesis 3:5). It was this desire to be equal with God that was the alluring prospect, and so Eve reached out and *grasped* the fruit, with disastrous results. The relevance to Paul's theme of humility is clear. Adam through pride grasped at the opportunity for equality with God, but Jesus, the second Adam, although a perfect manifestation of the attributes and character of God, did not seek to grasp a shortcut to divine equality. Clearly this was the message Paul wanted to get across. Christ, unlike Adam, did not count equality

---

[26] *The Interpreter's Bible*, Vol. 11, p. 48.

The Apostolic Testimony

with God a thing to be grasped, or snatched.[27]

Unlike the rendering of the verse in certain translations (*KJV, NKJV, PME*), many translators who have evaluated the language do not express the idea that Jesus was equal to God; but rather, that even though he was existing in God's form (or 'external appearance')—being as he is described in other places, 'the image of the invisible God' (Col. 1:15), 'the beloved Son,' (Matt. 3:17) 'the radiance of God's glory' and the 'exact representation of God's being' (Heb. 1:3)—he never attempted to 'seize' or 'grasp at' equality with God. Which is to say that Jesus, unlike Satan and Adam, *never considered* committing such an act. And in light of Paul's exhortation to humility and selfless service toward others, he is set forth as an example to us.

Remarkably, there is yet another way this passage has been translated that may also be said to legitimately accord with the language, grammar, and general thrust of the apostle's spiritual exhortation. Some translations and commentators believe the sense is that Jesus, before he came to earth (some, while he was on earth), gave up an equality/likeness or similarity of form (or nature) with God, instead of attempting to exploit it for his own advantage, as Satan evidently did. This understanding also appears to be reflected in Ralph Martin's discussion in the *Tyndale Commentaries*:

> There is, however, another possibility which may be briefly stated as follows. *Harpagmos* can have the meaning of 'a piece of good fortune, a lucky find'. Bonnard takes the illustration of a spring-board (*tremplin*) with the same essential thought of an opportunity which the pre-existent Christ had before him. He existed in the divine 'condition' or 'rank' as the unique image and glory of God, but refused to utilize this favored position to exploit his privileges and assert himself in opposition to the Father.[28]

Some, who have adopted a similar understanding of the text, even take the rendering of the Greek word *theou* (the genitive form of the Greek word for 'god') as indefinite,

---

[27] Broughton & Southgate, *The Trinity, True or False?*
[28] *The Tyndale New Testament Commentaries, Philippians*, p. 103.

resulting in the translation, "the form of a god"[29] or "in divine form"[30] or similar.[31] The following are examples of suggested translations appearing to fall into the same or similar category:

> **Adopt the same attitude as Messiah Jesus: Who, though having divine status, did not consider his equality with God something to be exploited for his own advantage (*NRSV* is similar).**[32]
>
> **...continue to have this mind that was also in Christ Jesus, who though existing in a god's form, did not consider retaining things equal to divinity.**[33]
>
> **Who, even though he was existing in the form of a god [or 'a divine form,' or 'God's form'], did not consider being on an equality with [or, 'existing in a likeness to'] God as something to exploit.**[34]

As one takes the time to reflect on some of the potential meanings for this particular verse, it should be remembered that, in either case of translation, Jesus is shown to be an example of humility to us; namely, in what he gave up or "emptied himself" of (as indicated by the following verse), taking on the form of a slave, and becoming obedient to God even to the point of death on a cross or stake. As it was observed by one source: "About the Apostle Paul's general intention in this passage there can be

---

[29] Grammatically, the phrase can be taken either way: definitely, "the form *of God*," or indefinitely, "the form of *a god*." The expression "form of *a* god" (*morphe theou*) has a parallel construction in the following verse, the "form of *a slave*" (*morphen doulou*).

[30] See footnote to Philippians 2:6 in *Rotherham's Emphasized Bible* (Grand Rapids: Kregel Publications, 1994), p. 202.

[31] It is possible, based on the language, to understand the *morphe theou* as the "form of God," and to mean that Christ subsisted in God's form in the sense that he, at one time, existed in the same form/likeness in which God exists, namely, a divine, spiritual, glorious, celestial form of existence. It may also be possible to interpret the *morphe theou* as meaning "the form of a god," in the sense that, before appearing "in the likeness of men," the Son's very mode of existence (or external likeness) was that of a god, a divine being (compare John 1:1, 18). Yet it was also observed in the footnotes of the *New American Bible*: "While it is common to take Philippians 2:6, 7 as dealing with Christ's preexistence and Philippians 2:8 with his incarnate life, so that lines Philippians 2:7b, 7c are parallel, it is also possible to interpret so as to exclude any reference to preexistence...and to take Philippians 2:6-8 as presenting two parallel stanzas about Jesus' human state (Philippians 2:6-7b; 7cd-8); in the latter alternative, coming in human likeness begins the second stanza and parallels 6a to some extent."

[32] Buzzard, *The Doctrine of the Trinity, Christianity's Self Inflicted Wound*, p. 104. However, Buzzard does not take the rendition "divine status" as a reference to a "pre-existent Christ."

[33] *The Nazarene Commentary 2000*

[34] Greg Stafford, *Three Dissertations on the Teachings of Jehovah's Witnesses* (Huntington Beach: Elihu Books, 2002), pp. 213-216.

The Apostolic Testimony

no doubt: the followers of Christ must show the same humility of mind as did their Master."[35] Another source similarly argued: "The supreme example that should ever be before the eyes of all Christians is that of Christ himself, who did not hesitate to shed his divine status, not only becoming a man, but making himself the Servant, of whom Isaiah had spoken, living and dying in perfect obedience to God, and enduring the last humiliation of a Cross."[36]

The next expression made by the apostle is likewise disputed by Bible interpreters of varying backgrounds. Paul went on to say that Christ "emptied himself (*heauton ekenosen*), having taken the form of a slave." Yet one Trinitarian apologist attempted to extract the following meaning out of the text:

> As if the fact that Paul called Christ *theos* is not enough, we have even in the very passage in which Paul speaks of the *kenosis* of Christ, the 'emptying' which Christ effected in being incarnated, a statement of Christ's abiding deity.[37]

Another Trinitarian source made these remarks:

> The description of the 'self-emptying' of Jesus in Philippians 2:5-11 gives us a clue to follow. When he became a Man, Christ still remained 'in the form of God': that is to say, he retained the essential attributes of God. It was not these of which he divested himself.[38]

After Christ was described as existing in the divine form, Paul said that "he emptied/divested himself," or, as some translations express it, "he made himself nothing" (*NIV*), "he gave it all up" (*TEV*). Yet Trinitarians attempt to convince others that this is somehow "a statement of Christ's abiding deity"? Given the force and clarity of such language, it is not unfair or unreasonable to wonder: What about the expression "he emptied/divested himself" carries with it the idea of "abiding" or

---

[35] Fred Parce, *Jesus: God the Son or Son of God? New Edition* (United Kingdom: Christadelphian Publishing Office, 1998), p. 19.
[36] *Harper's Bible Commentary* (Harper & Row Publishers: New York, 1962), p. 479.
[37] Beisner, *God In Three Persons*, p.30.
[38] *Hard Questions*, edited by Frank Colquhoun, answered by Michel Green, J. I. Packer & John R. W. Stott, (Illinois: InerVarsity Press, 1977), p. 31.

The Apostolic Testimony

"remaining" in a certain condition? A simple reading of the passage will show that, unlike the argument put forward by the writers previously cited, nothing is said about Christ "remaining" God or "retaining the essential attributes of God (or 'the form of God')," or that Christ "abided in his deity." Yet, remarkably, this is one of the most common arguments put forward by evangelical expositors. So, once again, as surprising as it may seem in light of the common arguments put forth, nothing in the words themselves suggest that Christ "retained" anything central or related to the points brought out in the context of the apostle's letter—only, rather, that Christ truly "emptied himself."

At this point, a comparison of what Trinitarians have traditionally claimed the passage as a whole *means* with what Paul actually *wrote* will be helpful, for it will demonstrate the level and degree of theological speculation that must be superimposed onto Paul's words in order to arrive at the desired meaning. If one were to examine the most popular evangelical literature on the subject, one would find that, essentially, Trinitarians want Philippians 2:5-11 to mean:

> *"Have the same mind that was also in Christ Jesus; although he was eternally of the same essence as the Father, he did not think to take advantage of his status as God [or, 'he did not think to take advantage of his prerogatives as the Father's equal'], but made himself of no reputation, combining the essence of God with the nature of a man (thereby veiling his deity with flesh), combining the two natures into one person, so that he would be the 'God-man'..."*

It should be noted that the above paragraph is not a misrepresentation or exaggeration, for this is *precisely* how the passage is "exegeted" by most Trinitarian teachers.[39] For example, one Trinitarian apologist made the following claim:

---

[39] After a reading through Philippians 2:6-11, the noted Calvinist preacher John Piper said: "That is a very amazing passage of Scripture. [Christ] *is* equal with God. He *is* God. He became a human being without ceasing to be God." —*All Things Subject to the Risen Christ* (Audio Sermon), Date Recorded: 03-27-05. Yet nowhere does the passage say that Christ *is* God (how could he be *equal* to or *like* 'God' if he *was* 'God'?) or that Christ became a human being without ceasing to be God.

350

God the Son divested Himself of certain divine prerogatives and, veiled in flesh, He voluntarily positioned himself in submission to God the Father. The Father and the Son were still partaking of the same divine essence; Jesus was still God, but He had taken on human flesh and, as is eloquently testified to in Philippians 2:8, He humbled Himself and became obedient even unto death.[40]

If what is expressed by the apologist above is a genuine reflection of the Bible's teaching about the nature of Jesus Christ, such a concept is by no means articulated or "eloquently testified" in the Philippians passage. First, it should be noted that in the previous verses there is no mention of Christ as "God the Son" having "divested himself of certain divine prerogatives." Nor does there appear in verse 8 any testimony of Christ "still partaking of the same divine essence" as the Father, and of Jesus remaining or *ever being* "God." Once again, what Paul really said in verse 6 is that Christ was "existing in God's form (or, in a god's form)," and in verse 7, that he "emptied himself"[41] and took on "a slave's form." Additionally, a simple and objective reading of the text will show that Christ is distinguished from "God" throughout: Christ was in God's *form* (v. 6); Christ did not consider seizing equality with another, namely, God (v. 6); and in the verses that follow: "God" *exalted* Christ, and "God" *gave* Christ the name that is above every name (v. 9), with a view to his own glory.[42]

Before the remainder of the passage is examined, it should be pointed out that Trinitarian apologists normally point to their unique conception of Philippians 2:5-11 as a kind of 'exegetical grid' or 'interpretive mechanism' which, from their

---

[40] *A Response to an Article Critiquing the Dividing Line Broadcast of Saturday*, June 24, 2000, by Colin Smith (This article can be read on the Alpha & Omega Ministries website).

[41] Daniel Mace attempted to make explicit in his translation what he evidently believed to be the implicit meaning: "tho' he was the image of God, [he] did not affect to appear with divine majesty, but *divested himself thereof*, by assuming the form of a servant."

[42] Some Trinitarian apologists believe that when others point out that Jesus is distinguished from "God" in a given passage that this represents a misunderstanding of Trinitarian doctrine. Because in Trinitarianism, God means "the Father"; so, for that reason, and with that understanding in mind, it is acceptable to distinguish between "God" and "the Son." But again, although it is true that "God" is normally a *reference* to "the Father," neither the word "God" nor "Father" ever means (or is defined as) "the first person of the Trinity" in the Bible; which is what Trinitarians really mean when they say "God" means "the Father."

The Apostolic Testimony

point of view, satisfactorily explains all the cases in Scripture where Christ is spoken of as distinct from "God" and under God's authority, or subordinate to him. In other words, Christ may have said that the Father was "greater" than he was and that the Father was his God (John 14:28; John 20:17), but, in Philippians chapter 2:5-11—according to Trinitarians—Paul reveals to us that Christ, the Father's essential equal, voluntarily took on a *functional* role of inferiority and submission to the Father (combining 'deity' with 'humanity'), so that the Father *is* greater, as well as his God, but *only* in the terms of Christ's *position* as a servant or *nature* as a human being; but as to the *essence* of his "deity" Christ always remained "coequal." Yet, as noted, in order to arrive at such a conclusion based on this particular Scripture, not only must certain words be redefined and other expressions essentially ignored, several foreign and creative elements must be imported onto the passage from an outside source.

In his exposition of this passage—which seeks to conform what is said to the traditional Trinitarian concept—James White argues that Christ's glory as God was *hidden* in flesh while he was a man. As evidence, White claims: "When the Lord walked this earth, men did not see Him as a glorious heavenly being, for His glory was hidden, veiled. With the single exception of the Mount of Transfiguration, where a chosen few saw Him in His true glory..."[43] However, Matthew chapter seventeen, where the account spoken of by Dr. White occurs, the author actually reports that Jesus was "transfigured" or "transformed," showing that, on that occasion, Jesus underwent a *change* in form or appearance ('His form underwent a change.' *Weymouth*). In fact, in reference to the same incident, Luke specifically states: "While he was praying *his face changed in appearance* and his clothing became dazzling white."[44]

Contrary to the argument Dr. White seeks to advance, there is actually nothing in the text suggesting that Christ "unveiled" himself as God, the glory of which was previously hidden or veiled in the flesh. Essentially, Dr. White wants to

---

[43] White, *The Forgotten Trinity*, p. 125.
[44] Luke 9:29, *NAB*

persuade his readers to view the occurrence that took place on the mountain primarily as an "unveiling (of his deity as a member of a triune being)." But the text actually reveals that Christ, as brief of a time as it was, underwent a real *change*,[45] an authentic "transformation."[46]

Without question, in order to maintain the classical Trinitarian formula based on this text, one must disregard Paul's statement that Christ was existing in one form ('God's form'), that he "emptied himself" and took on the form of another ('the form of a slave').[47] Nothing in the epistle says or suggests that Christ ever *was* God, *remained* "God," or *combined the essence of God with the nature of a man* so that he ultimately came to exist as a "God-man." If such a concept is indeed representative of divine, biblical truth, it cannot be found here. Even if the expression "he emptied himself" is taken *metaphorically*—as suggested by some—resulting in the sense appearing in the *Authorized Version* ('he made himself of no reputation'), it would still not change the fact that Christ is depicted as having been in one form at one time but took on another form at another time.[48] The authors of the *Interpreter's Bible* commentary were more critical of the *Authorized Version* on this point:

> ...the KJV rendering **made himself of no reputation** is only an attempt, and not a very intelligent one, to explain what [Paul] means. The translators, no doubt, were influenced by the theological debate of their time, which

---

[45] Of "form/external appearance" that is.
[46] The term translated "transfigured" (Matthew 17:2, *NASB*) is *metamorphothe* (*metamorphosis*) which denotes a *change* in form or appearance, thus a *transfiguration* or *transformation*. This is not to suggest that *metamorphosis* can only refer to a change in *outward* appearance. The significance of the change may vary depending on the context and according to what the change specifically applies to (Compare Romans 12:2). A. E. Knoch observed that despite his "supernatural dignities, the disposition of Christ was one of love and compassion, and utterly lacking in selfishness and pride, is shown by his self-abasement. He *empties* Himself. What this means is clearly indicated by the change in *form*. He was not God and He did not become a slave. But He had God's *form*, yet He took a slave's *form*. He did not carry with Him any of the former into the latter. This is clearly shown by the word *empties*. Only when He was trans*formed*, as on the holy mount (Matt.17:2), then His face shone as the sun and His garments became white as the light. In this vision He anticipates the form which He will have in the kingdom, after His exaltation. But it was not a permanent form, only a vision. When He descended the glory was gone." —*Studies in Philippians (Part Four of Eight) The Example of Christ, Philippians 2:1-8*
[47] Compare: "the word was a god/a divine being (*theos en ho logos*)," yet "the word *became flesh* (*ho logos sarx egeneto*)" (John 1:1c; 14).
[48] That is, Paul did not say or suggest that Christ combined both forms into one, or that he simply veiled one form with that of another.

The Apostolic Testimony

turned largely on the question of how far Christ ceased to be God when he became man. Did he strip himself entirely of the divine nature, or merely forgo certain attributes of majesty? But Paul is here not primarily concerned with any theological problem. He says only that Christ **emptied himself**; instead of aspiring to a higher status he gave up that which he had. He abdicated his divine rank and assumed **the form of a servant** (literally 'a slave').[49]

Most significantly, in another place, the apostle Paul said by way of reminder: "For you know how generous our Lord Jesus Christ has been: *he was rich, yet for your sake he became poor*, so that through his poverty you might become rich."[50]

This statement seems to be an allusion to, or another way of describing, what Christ did in Philippians chapter two; once again, suggesting that, at a certain point, Christ was subsisting in one state or condition, but that, "for our sake," he voluntarily took on that of another. That is, Christ willingly went from 'wealth' to 'poverty'—the "form/likeness of God" to the "form/likeness of a slave."[51]

Strangely, in an effort to sustain the classical Trinitarian concept (the concept that says Christ was God and 'remained' God when he became a man), Robert Morey translated the verse: "For you know the grace of our Lord Jesus Christ, that for you He became poor while *being and remaining to be rich*, that you through His poverty might become rich." Not only is such a novel and creative "translation" one that cannot be legitimately supported by the original language it professes to represent, it completely distorts the critical point the apostle Paul was really attempting to get across. Unfortunately, such a strange and obvious manipulation of Scripture is a common approach among evangelical apologists in these kinds of instances.[52]

---

[49] *The Interpreter's Bible*, Vol. 11 (Nashville: Abingdon Press, 1955), p. 49.

[50] 2 Corinthians 8:9, *New English Bible* (emphasis added).

[51] The principal reason why Trinitarians argue that Christ was God and man at the same time is based on a mistaken and forced interpretation of the "form of God." Since Trinitarians argue that this means "in nature/essence God," they reason that God, by nature, can never cease being God; therefore, he must have combined both natures into one. However, as noted, saying that Christ was in God's *form* is not the same as saying that Christ was *God* or in *essence God*.

[52] *The Trinity, Evidence and Issues*, p. 340. This is often done with texts such as John 1:1 and Hebrews 1:1-3. Trinitarian apologists frequently attempt to exploit the significance of a verb like

In a very significant discussion on this disputed passage, Robert Reymond departs from the traditional Trinitarian view (the view that understands the beginning of the passage as referring to a 'pre-human Christ') exactly because he doesn't see how Paul could have said that Christ "emptied himself" and this *not* refer to a total relinquishing of the divine form previously mentioned. This is why Reymond takes the beginning of the passage (Christ 'in the form of God') as a reference to Christ while he was a man (or 'God-man') on earth. Reymond explains:

> The first difficulty is this: If we understand the beginning point of the 'flow' of the passage, as the classical view does, as the preexistent state of the Son of God ('in the form of God being') and take the phrase 'Himself He emptied, taking the form of a 'servant' as the metaphorical allusion to the 'downward' event of the incarnation, it is only with the greatest difficulty, because of the intervening clause, that we can avoid the conclusion that the 'emptying' involved His surrendering the 'form' ('very nature'—NIV) of God...One has only to peruse the evangelical literature on these verses to discover the 'hermeneutical gymnastics' that are resorted to to affirm, on the one hand, that the Son did not regard equality with God ('the form of God') a thing to be held onto, and that He accordingly 'emptied Himself' (or, 'made Himself nothing') by becoming a man, and yet, on the other hand, that He still retained all that He essentially is and was from the beginning.[53]

"is" or "was" or "being/existing," suggesting that since these kinds of verbs express a state of continuous existence (no reference to a beginning or end) that this then demands or implies a concept of eternality. This is like saying that in the expression "Paul is an apostle," the verb "is," in and of itself, conveys continuous existence (no beginning and no end), so this means that Paul has *eternally* been an apostle.

[53] *Jesus, Divine Messiah, The New Testament Witness*, pp. 259, 260. By "hermeneutical gymnastics," Reymond basically means that evangelicals must go through a great deal of unnatural twisting, turning and effort to arrive at the meaning they want, because the desired sense is so far from what the text says here—that is, if the "form of God" is in fact a reference to a pre-human Son. On page 261, Reymond says that he appreciates "the fearless willingness" on the part of those who take the beginning of the passage as referring to a pre-human Son; and that when taking the passage "at face value" conclude that in "some essential way" the Son "divested Himself of His 'form of God' in the course of His taking the 'form of servant.'"

Although some (mostly Socinians/Biblical Unitarians,[54] and a very small minority of Trinitarians) believe that the statement in Philippians 2:6 is a reference to God's Son in his *human* state, most interpreters find it difficult to sustain the interpretation that verse 6 does not represent a description of Christ in a pre-human, heavenly condition. This is so because Paul said that Christ was "existing in God's form," that he "emptied himself," that he "*came to be* in the likeness of men," and that he was "found in human fashion/appearance." That is to say, if the text presents a description of Christ's decisions and actions in chronological order (an ordered sequence of events), then his being in the form of God and his resistance of the temptation to be equal with (or refusal to exploit equality with/likeness to) God occurred *prior to* his "coming into the likeness of humanity" (*Bible in Living English*). If the *morphē theou* ('god-form') is a description of Christ when he was already in his human existence, one wonders, how could Paul then say *after* that he "came to be in the likeness of men"? This would seem to imply, quite naturally, that before Christ *came to be* in the likeness of men, he was in some other state of existence or likeness. The statement that follows—"**when he was found in fashion as a man**"—likewise seems to be suggestive of pre-human existence. After all, one might understandably ask, *what was so significant about one who had never been anything but a man being "found in fashion as a man"*? It almost seems as if this statement would be robbed of its relevance if Christ did not enjoy another kind of existence at some point before he was "found in appearance as a man" (*NASB*). For many interpreters, it seems to make more sense that the one who once existed as a divine spirit, in a "divine form (the form of God or a god)," was, at another point in his existence, "found in fashion as a man." And, when this was so, he further humbled himself in obedience to the extent of dying a criminal's death. That is, he gave up what he once had (the wealth and riches of his glorious heavenly existence), took on the lowly appearance of a slave, lived in obedience to God when *found in fashion as a man*, and did so to

---

[54] "Socinians," sometimes called "Biblical Unitarians," deny the classical doctrine of the Trinity but they deny that Christ had a real, personal, pre-human existence, emphasizing the virgin birth as Christ's true origin.

the extent of sacrificing his own life for the benefit of others, to the glory of God.

In corroboration with this view is the existence of several expressions made by Jesus, particularly in the Gospel of John, interpreted by many Bible students to mean that the Son of God was one who previously dwelt in the heavenly realm prior to coming to the lower realms of the earth. For example, on one occasion, Jesus told his Jewish persecutors: "You are from below, *I am from above*; you are of this world, I am not of this world" (John 8:23, *RSV*). On another occasion Jesus likewise declared to his listeners: "*I have come down from heaven*, not to do my own will, but the will of him who sent me" (John 6:32, 38, *RSV*).[55]

In fact, Paul's words in 2 Corinthians 8:9 may very well correspond to the second chapter of Philippians (and other scriptural points) in the following ways: "For you know the grace of our Lord Jesus Christ, that though he was rich ('though he was in the form of God,' Phil. 2:6; and had 'glory with [the Father] before the world was,' John 17:5), yet for your sake he became poor ('he emptied himself, taking the form of a slave,' humbling 'himself, becoming obedient to death,' Phil. 2:7, 8; coming down 'from heaven, not to do [his] own will, but the will of him who sent [him],' John 6:38), so that by his poverty you might become rich (so that you 'were reconciled to God through the death of his Son, how much more, once reconciled, will [you] be saved by his life.' Romans 5:10)." At least, that is how

---

[55] Some have argued that the "came-down-from-heaven" language is simply a reference to how God brought the man Jesus into existence through the virgin birth (a heavenly/miraculous birth as opposed to an exclusively earthly/human one) and subsequently sent him forth into the world (Matthew 1:18; Luke 1:35), and that the language need not demand a literal notion of a personal, pre-human, heavenly existence. This may be true. However, according to John 3:13, Jesus similarly said, "**No one has ascended into heaven except he who descended from heaven** [*ek tou ouranou katabas*], the Son of Man." Essentially, the same language is used of the "angel of the Lord" in Matthew 28:2 *whom we know did actually live in the heavenly* realm before coming to the earth: "**And behold, there was a great earthquake, for an angel of the Lord descended from heaven** [*aggelos gar kuriou katabas ex ouranou*] **and came and rolled back the stone and sat on it**" (Matthew 28:2) It seems clear that the angel dwelled in the realm called "heaven" (with God or where God dwells) and left this realm ('wherever' that is) to come to the earth. The language Jesus used of himself is essentially identical. Thus it would only seem natural to conclude that the Son of God lived in the heavenly dimension—like the 'angel of the Lord' clearly did—before he was born in the earth as a human being.

many interpreters have understood these texts in conjunction with one another.[56]

What follows are several examples of different ways in which translators have attempted to convey the sense of the apostle's words. Partial quotations of this verse have already been noted in some translations but are here reproduced again:

> **The same thing esteem in yourselves which also in Christ Jesus [ye esteem],—Who in form of God [ftnt: Or: 'divine form'] subsisting Not a thing to be seized accounted the being equal with God. But himself emptied...** —*Rotherham's Emphasized Bible*
>
> **Let your disposition, indeed, be that of Christ Jesus, who though he had godlike form, did not regard it as a prize to be equal to God, but divested himself...**
> —*The Original New Testament, Schonfield*
>
> **The attitude you should have is the one that Christ Jesus had: He always had the nature of God, but he did not think that by force he should try to become equal with God. Instead of this, of his own free will he gave up all he had...** —*Today's English Version*
>
> **Keep on fostering the same disposition that Christ Jesus had. Though He was existing in the nature of God, He did not think His being on an equality with God a thing to be selfishly grasped, but He laid it aside...** —*The New Testament in the Language of the People, Williams*
>
> **Let the very spirit which was in Christ Jesus be in you also. From the beginning He had the nature of God. Yet He did not regard equality with God as something at which He should grasp. Nay, He stripped Himself of His glory...** —*New Testament in Modern Speech,*

---

[56] However, if the passage can be interpreted apart from notions of 'pre-existence,' it might be understood along the following lines: "Let the same mind be in you that was in Christ Jesus, who, though he was in the form of God (like Moses, who evidently had the status of 'God' in terms of his representation of God before the people: Compare Exodus 7:1), did not regard equality with God as something to be exploited (that is, he did not regard the functionally equal status he had with God as something to be used for his own gain or advantage), but emptied himself (that is, he humbled himself, pouring out his life in the service of God and fellow man, to the point of death: Compare Isaiah 53:12), taking the form of a slave (taking on the role/function of a slave), being born in human likeness (he appeared to be born into the world like an ordinary man). And being found in human form (he appeared like an average human, not like a king), he humbled himself and became obedient to the point of death, even death on a cross."

Weymouth
Let what was seen in Christ Jesus be seen in you: Though being divine in nature, he did not claim in fact equality with God, but emptied himself... —*Christian Community Bible, Catholic Pastoral Edition*

The points that have been made thus far are further magnified when we consider what Paul went on to say about Christ (in association with his 'exaltation' by God) being *given* the name above every name. In the *Tyndale Commentaries* it was correctly noted: "The honour which [Christ] refused to arrogate to himself is now conferred upon him by the Father's good pleasure: *gave him* (*echarisato*) bears the sense of 'granted by the exercise of a favour' (*charis*)."[57] This is the reason why careful translators have rendered the verse, not simply "given him," but "graces him" (*Concordant*), "favoured him" (*Rotherham*), "freely granted him" (*Diaglott*), "kindly gave him" (*NWT*) the name that is above every other name." But what name was "kindly given" to Christ by God? It appears reasonable, given the context, that it refers to the name "Jesus" itself; for the apostle goes on to say, "so that at the *name of Jesus*, every knee should bow and every tongue confess..."[58] This could mean that since God the Father exalted Jesus to such a high status and invested the name (and hence the *person* of) "Jesus" with all power and authority in heaven and on earth, that his is indeed the name above every name, with the name of his Father, the one who *gave* Christ his name and exalted position, being the only exception.[59] Or, it is even possible, as some think, that "the name" given to the Son is actually the divine name of the Most High itself. If that is the case, this would mean that God's Son, *by inheritance*, is the rightful and deserving bearer of his

---
[57] Martin, *The Tyndale New Testament Commentaries, Philippians*, p. 109.
[58] A. T. Robertson wrote: "The name which is above every name (*to onoma to huper pan onoma*). What name is that? Apparently and naturally the name Jesus, which is given in verse 10." —*Word Pictures in the New Testament, Volume IV, The Epistles of Paul* (Broadman Press: Nashville, 1931), p. 445. It should be kept in mind that not all Trinitarians agree on this point. Some believe the name given to Christ was *Jehovah*; others believe that it was the name *Jesus*.
[59] A truth that harmonizes perfectly with this possibility is found at 1 Corinthians 15, where Paul spoke of a time when "all things" would be subjected to Christ (or put under Christ's authority). But Paul goes on to qualify his statement by saying: "Of course, when it says 'authority over all things,' it does not include God himself, who gave Christ his authority..." (*NLT*). Paul goes on to conclude, at the end: "When everything is subjected to him, then the Son himself will (also) be subjected to the one who subjected everything to him, so that God may be all in all."

Father's name, as his Father's representative—in harmony with the spirit of Hebrews 1:3-4: "When he had accomplished purification from sins, he took his seat at the right hand of the Majesty on high, having become as much superior to the angels as *the name he has inherited* is more excellent than theirs."[60]

In his work, *Pauline Christianity*, Paul Zeisler reflects on the meaning of Paul's message. Although each detail of his assessment may be open to other possibilities of interpretation, the overall points made are scripturally based and worthy of consideration:

> The second stanza shows that in God's purpose the way of humiliation is the way of exaltation. God freely gives Christ what Adam had tried to grab, and bestows on him 'the name above every name', the title of 'Lord' (v.9). This Lordship is universal and total. The quotation from Isaiah 45.23, 25 that at his name 'every knee should bow...' is another instance where a passage that in the Old Testament refers to Yahweh is by Paul referred instead to Christ, and where the divine honours that are appropriate to Yahweh are rendered to Christ. To make the point absolutely clear the quotation is expanded by the words 'in heaven and on earth and under the earth', so that nothing at all is excluded from his Lordship. The ruling function that belongs properly to Yahweh alone is now Christ's also; he is cosmic Lord and as such receives the honour that hitherto has been given only to Yahweh. Yet before we rashly conclude that the two have simply become identified, we must note that the element of subordination remains. It all happens, even the exaltation of Christ, 'to the glory of God the Father' (v.11), and Christ does not exalt himself but is exalted by God and is given the title 'Lord' by him (v.11). Christ has become the bearer of the powers of God and the recipient of divine homage (v.10), but is still distinct from him and subject to him.[61]

We can also perceive throughout the entire course of Paul's teaching (as alluded to above by Zeisler) the principle

---

[60] Hebrews 1:3-4
[61] Zeisler, *Pauline Christianity*, pp.45-46.

originally taught by Jesus to his disciples fulfilled in the most outstanding and most exemplary sense, as his entire life-course made clear—"**everyone that exalts himself will be humbled, but he that humbles himself will be exalted.**"[62] In this case, Christ's humility, expressed in unfailing love and obedience to God,—even to the extent of dying a criminal's death 'for our sake'—resulted in God "highly" exalting him and kindly bestowing upon him the name and superior position as 'Lord of all,' with its true and final aim in the magnification of "**the glory of God the Father.**"[63]

"Worshiping" God through Jesus Christ

> "...to the only wise God be glory forevermore through Jesus Christ! Amen."
>
> —The apostle Paul, Romans 16:27, *ESV*

When Jesus Christ was on earth, he always directed worship (and prayer) to his Father, the Most High. In John chapter four, Jesus did not speak of worshiping God as a "Trinity," but spoke about the necessity of worshiping "the Father" in spirit and truth—at the same time, revealing that he himself was a worshiper of God (John 4:22; compare Matthew 4:10). Just after his baptism by John in the Jordan River, Jesus faced temptation in the wilderness. There Satan offered Jesus all the kingdoms of the world and their glory if he would only perform an act of worship toward him. Yet Jesus refused the temptation, having said, "Go, Satan! For it is written, 'YOU SHALL WORSHIP THE LORD YOUR GOD, AND SERVE HIM ONLY.'"[64]

In harmony with most Trinitarians, Wayne Grudem points out that there are certain cases in the Bible where Jesus

---

[62] Luke 18:14
[63] "This pattern of exaltation following humiliation is thoroughly biblical, and especially evident in the teaching of Jesus (see Mt. 18:4; 23:12; Lk. 14:11; 18:14; *cf.* 2 Cor. 11:7; Phil. 4:12)." — Martin, *The Tyndale New Testament Commentaries*, p. 108.
[64] Matthew 4:10, *NASB*. Here, Jesus referred to Deuteronomy 6:13: "Yahweh thy God, shalt thou revere And him, shalt thou serve, And by his name, shalt thou swear." (*Rotherham's Emphasized Bible*). Unlike the word *proskuneo* (worship/homage), the Greek word for "serve" (*latreuo*) used by Jesus is purely religious in character. This is why some translate it as "divine/sacred service" (See: *Concordant Literal NT, Rotherham,* and *NWT*).

Christ himself is shown to have received worship, and that, therefore, he must be God—ultimately, in the sense of being one "person" out of three who shares in the *one being* that is "God."

In the Scriptures the term normally rendered "worship" when Christ is the object is *proskuneo*. Although the word may be used and understood in varying senses, depending upon the context, the term itself normally carried with it the idea of physically "bowing before" one who is recognized as a superior, or anyone who was worthy of a special honor or some form of submission.[65]

In an argument for understanding the "deity" of, and "worship" given to, Christ in the classical Trinitarian sense, Grudem writes:

> Another clear attestation to the deity of Christ is the fact that he is counted *worthy to be worshipped*, something that is true of no other creature, including angels (see Rev. 19:10), but only God alone. Yet Scripture says of Christ that 'God has highly exalted him and bestowed on him the name which is above every name, that at the name of Jesus every knee would bow, in heaven and on earth and under the earth, and every tongue confess that Jesus Christ is Lord, to the glory of God the Father' (Phil. 2:9-11). Similarly, God commands the angels to worship Christ, for we read, 'When he brings the first-born into the world, he says, 'Let all God's angels worship him' (Heb. 1:6)[66]

The point Grudem is making—a point repeatedly put forward by Trinitarian apologists—is that since Jesus Christ is given worship in the Scriptures, and God alone should be worshiped,[67] Jesus must *be* God (in the fourth-century Trinitarian sense).

So, in the view of Trinitarianism, although Jesus Christ is *not* God the Father, he—like the Father—is one divine "person" who shares equally in the one "being" of "God," and is,

---

[65] Under *proskuneo*, *Vines Expository Dictionary* (p. 686) states: "'to make obeisance, do reverence to' (from *pros*, 'towards,' and *kuneo*, 'to kiss')' noting that it "is the most frequent word rendered 'to worship.'"
[66] Grudem, *Systematic Theology*, p. 549.
[67] Exodus 20:3-5

The Apostolic Testimony

therefore, fittingly worshiped as Almighty God along with the Father and Holy Spirit. If Jesus is not "God," Trinitarians reason, then to "worship" him would constitute an act of idolatry; that is, an unjustified reverence given to a "*mere* creature." Since the Scripture condemns every form of idolatrous practice, anyone who would promote the worship of Christ, with the exception of those who believe he is God (in the Trinitarian sense), would, in the view of Trinitarians, ultimately find themselves at odds with Scripture.[68] The question that may be asked in this regard, then, is: How is it possible that Christ could appropriately receive "worship" if he is not "God" in the sense of being a "person" who shares in the one "essence" of Almighty God? Does the explanation given by Trinitarians harmonize with the Scriptures? Does the Trinitarian explanation have any scriptural basis at all?

It may seem surprising to some, but the most appropriate answer really lies within the very statement made by Wayne Grudem, as well as within the very texts from which he quotes. How and why could Jesus Christ be worshipped? It is as Grudem says, specifically, because "*God commands* the angels to worship Christ." Is the Lord Jesus Christ worshipped *as* or *because* he is "God the Son, second member of the Trinity," "coequal" and "consubstantial" with the Father? Or is Jesus given worship *as* "the Christ" and *because* God himself declared, "*Let* all God's angels worship him"? Do all intelligent creatures in heaven and on earth and under the earth bow down and confess Jesus Christ as "Lord" because he is "God," or, because "*God has highly exalted him* and kindly given him the name that is above every name"? Notice, also, that the submission and confession is all "**to the glory of God the Father**." In fact, it would be fair to say—in perfect harmony with Scripture—that the worship, honor, glory and respect attributed to Christ is something that God not only allows but commands, is pleasing to him, and God himself is glorified in this. According to the sacred text, God said "Let" all of the angels worship Christ, showing that such is God's will, an *authorized* worship.

---

[68] For example, the well-known evangelical John R. W. Stott claimed: "Nobody can call himself a Christian who does not worship Jesus. To worship him, if he is not God, is idolatry; to withhold worship from him, if he is, is apostasy." —*The Authentic Jesus* (1985), p. 34; Quoted in Bowman & Komoszewski, *Putting Jesus in His Place, The Case for the Deity of Christ*, p. 42.

The Apostolic Testimony

We gain greater insight into the "reverence" and "homage" given to Christ as we consider the use of the Greek word often translated "worship" in the Scriptures. An occurrence of a form of the word *proskuneo* in the book of Revelation is one example that clearly demonstrates how the word can and is used with varying degrees of intensity. According to the *King James Version* rendering, Jesus said, "I will make them [of the synagogue of Satan] to come and *worship* [*proskuneo*] before thy [the early Christian's] feet" (Rev. 3:9). Of course Jesus was not in any way promoting an act of idolatry when he said that he would make certain people "worship" (*proskuneo*) before the feet of the apostles or early Christians. Nor did the advocating of such an act represent a contradiction of his citation of Deuteronomy 6:13 in the wilderness before Satan ('You shall worship the LORD/Jehovah your God, and serve him only'). At the time the *KJV* was translated, the term "worship," like the underlying Greek word it represents, was capable of being used in different ways—from *worship* in the highest possible sense, directed toward God—to the respect, honor, and submission that could be rightfully given to a king or an individual with authority. Again, the same was true with the word *proskuneo* in the time it was used in the Christian Scriptures. Like so many other words and terms used in the Bible (and in other forms of literature), the *context* is really the key to understanding what degree and in what specific sense a particular word is being used. To translate the word as "worship" in Revelation 3:9 is proper. But today most people normally associate the concept of "worship" with the adoration or cultic devotion given to a deity. That may be why other translations properly render the verse: "I will make them come and *bow down* ['*fall prostrate*,' *NAB*] at your feet, and make them know that I have loved you" (*NASB*).

If people were, at the command of the Lord Jesus Christ, made to "worship/fall prostrate" at the feet of men, and this is definitely *not* an act or endorsement of idolatry, then surely, it is entirely appropriate for angelic and human beings alike ('those in heaven and on earth' Philippians 2:10), to "worship/fall prostrate" at the feet of Christ, at the very command of God himself—especially so in light of Christ's honor and uniqueness as God's very own beloved Son, and in light of the fact that

The Apostolic Testimony

Christ laid down his life as a sacrifice to save sinners; that he rose from the grave never to die again, and that he now rules as King over the realms God created through him.[69]

Many Bible translations correctly render the Greek *proskuneo*—when applying to Christ—with the English "worship." But The *New English Bible* and other translations also properly render the verse: "Again, when he presents the first-born to the world, he says, 'Let all the angels of God pay him homage,'"[70] "let all God's angels bow before him" (*American Translation*), "bow down before him" (*Twentieth Century New Testament*), "prostrate themselves before him" (*Anchor Bible*), "honour him" (*Holy Bible in Modern English*), "adore him" (*Douay Rheims*).

The angels of God "bow down" to or "worship" God's Son based on the supremely-elevated position, authority, honor and power *given* to him by his Father: "For he has now entered Heaven and sits at God's right hand, with all angels, authorities and powers made subject to him."[71] When the book of Revelation (Ch. 5:12) speaks about Jesus ('the Lamb') receiving "power and riches and wisdom and honor and glory and blessing and dominion," it is because Jesus—as the Son of God and as the Savior of the world—is completely *worthy* of such blessing and honor.[72] As noted, because God's Son lived a life of perfect obedience to his Father, even to the point of death, God exalted him to the highest place of honor possible—God's right hand. According to Scripture, he has been *"crowned with glory and*

---

[69] This is not to suggest that the "worship" (*proskuneo*) commanded to be given to the Christians was on the same level as the worship that God commands Christians to give to Christ. He is clearly worthy of a much higher form of worship. He is God's very own Son.

[70] The *NJB* and *REB* translations render this verse the same way. Deut 32:43. (LXX); Ps. 96:7.

[71] 1 Peter 3:22, *PME*

[72] Some apologists have argued that since the Father and Son are worshiped together in Revelation chapter 5, both are therefore equally (and 'ontologically') God in the Trinitarian sense. But notice that in 1 Chronicles 29:11 very similar expressions of adoration are made toward God in the same context where "worship" is given not only to God but to his earthly representative, the King of Israel: "Yours, O Jehovah, is the greatness, and the power, and the glory, and the victory, and the majesty: for all that is in the heavens and in the earth *is yours*; yours is the kingdom, O Jehovah, and you are exalted as head above all. Both riches and honor come from you, and you rule over all..." And in verse 20 it says: "David said to all the assembly, Now bless Jehovah your God. And all the assembly blessed Jehovah, the God of their fathers, and bowed down their heads, and worshipped Jehovah, *and the king*." (*ASV*) The assembly of Israelites "worshipped" Jehovah *and the king*, yet they were clearly not committing "idolatry" or worshiping the king as a member of the "Godhead."

honor because of the suffering of death, so that by the grace of God he might taste death for everyone."[73] However, the "glory" Christ receives in harmony with the Scriptures is not the glory of "God-the-Son, the-second-person-of-the-Trinity," but *"the glory as of the only begotten of the Father, full of grace and truth"* (John 1:14, *KJV*).

That is to say, Jesus Christ *is* in fact worthy of "worship" relative to his unique identity as God's "beloved Son" and in light of the "highly exalted" status given to him by his Father, based on his obedient life and sacrifice. The Scriptures make clear that it is *God's will* that all intelligent creatures everywhere should submit themselves and openly acknowledge the authority and power of his Christ, for the Father himself is glorified in this. In other words, the Bible does not indicate that Christians are to worship and exalt Jesus as "Lord" based on his alleged eternal position and nature within a Trinitarian "Godhead," but because by doing so we bring glory and honor to his Father, "the only true God."

Based on the commands and principles set forth in Scripture, Christians continue to exalt God as the Creator and Ruler of all things; but Christians also glorify and exalt God's *Son* because God himself takes delight in us doing so. The Scriptures are entirely clear on the point that the Creator gave his Son all authority, and that the Creator's Son now rules over the entire created order because the Creator exalted him to that lofty position; and what Trinitarians unfortunately fail to recognize is that, what this really amounts to, in the end, is a profound demonstration of, and resulting testimony to, the loving-kindness, generosity, good nature and *wisdom* of Almighty God. Of course it remains true that Jehovah is completely deserving of our *exclusive* worship because he is God and Creator of all. But because he is God, he possesses the right to decree that all intelligent creatures ('in heaven and on earth, and under the earth') should bow down and openly confess the Lordship of his

---

[73] Hebrews 2:9, *RSV*. "We see him crowned with glory and honor now because of the death he suffered" (*TEV* rendering).

Son Jesus; for he has *gladly* endowed his Son with such an honorable and all-encompassing divine authority.[74]

Yet still, it has been contended that if Jesus Christ is not God—in the sense ascribed to him by Trinitarianism—then there would be no "meaningful mechanism" whereby one could distinguish true worship from idolatry, and that Christians would have no substantial or scriptural basis for worshiping Christ. However, such arguments simply fail to take into consideration the fact that one *can* differentiate idolatry from true worship only when it is understood that if whatever one is devoting himself to *takes attention away*, or *detracts from*, or *takes the place of*, the glory of the only true God, then one would in fact be committing idolatry in the *biblical* sense of the word. However, in the case of God's Son, the "worship," "homage," "reverence"[75] and "adoration" he is commanded to receive—and of which he is fully deserving—not only brings the Son glory, but furthers the glory of the one who gave him authority over all things; and this is pleasing to God, for Jesus himself said:

My Father will honor the one who serves me.[76]

And in his letter to the Romans, Paul gives added insight into the relationship of worshipful service to Christ in connection with the will of God. When he admonished his brothers not to "pass judgment on one another" and to "never put a stumbling block or hindrance in the way of a brother," he went on to say that:

Whoever thus serves Christ is acceptable to God and approved by men.[77]

The whole of the Christian life, in fact, is to be characterized by an honoring of the Son just as we "honor the Father." For, as Jesus made clear, whoever "does not honor the

---

[74] With the sole and obvious exception of God himself, the one who gave Christ this authority (See: 1 Corinthians 15:27).

[75] In the second century, Justin Martyr wrote in his well-known dialogue with Trypho: "For the man who loves God with all the heart, and with all the strength, being filled with a God-fearing mind, will reverence no other god; and since God wishes it, he would reverence that messenger [Gk: *angelos*] who is beloved by the same Lord and God."

[76] John 12:26

[77] Romans 14:18, *ESV*

The Apostolic Testimony

Son does not honor the Father who sent him."[78] Yet the honor and adoration given to Christ is, in the ultimate sense, an honor and adoration given through Christ to *the Father*, the ultimate source of every blessing in Christ. This is why the apostle Peter could say to his fellow Christians: "Whoever preaches, let it be with the words of God; whoever serves, let it be with the strength that God supplies, *so that in all things God may be glorified through Jesus Christ*, to whom belong glory and dominion forever and ever. Amen."[79]

Trinitarians have often quoted John 5:23 (about 'honoring' the Son as we would the Father) as if it somehow represented a dilemma for those who do not adhere to their teaching. They reason, if we honor the Father by "worshiping" him as God, then we must do the same toward the Son, and the Son is therefore God. This is strange reasoning. The fact that Jesus is God's *own Son* whom the Father "consecrated and sent forth into the world" as God's emissary and as the one whom God has committed all judgment to (John 10:36; 5:22), automatically explains why God is pleased that we honor his Son just as we would honor him. It makes perfect sense that we should revere the one who came in God's name and with God's authority just as we would revere the God who sent him; since the one "whom God has sent utters the words of God" (John 3:34). In the same way, with reference to the Messiah spoken of in the book of Deuteronomy, God said: "I will raise up for them a prophet like you from among their brothers. And *I will put my words in his mouth*, and he shall speak to them all that I command him. And whoever will not listen to my words that he shall speak in my name, I myself will require it of him" (Deuteronomy 18:18-19). Since the Messiah, God's Son, faithfully speaks the words God gave to him, how could we disagree that all should honor the Son—God's ultimate prophet

---

[78] John 5:23, *NAB*. F. F. Bruce was right for pointing out: "...when Christ receives such honours, the glory of God is not diminished or given to 'another'; it is rather enhanced, for Christ receives these honours 'to the glory of God the Father' (Phil. 2:11). When the Son is exalted, the Father is glorified. So here the honouring of the Son is the Father's good pleasure." —*The Gospel of John, Introduction, Exposition and Notes*, p. 130.

[79] 1 Peter 4:11, *NAB*. The worship and glorification of God *through* the Son are common themes in New Testament doxologies. In the conclusion of his letter, Jude similarly wrote: "...to the only God our Savior be glory, majesty, power and authority, through Jesus Christ our Lord, before all ages, now and forevermore! Amen." —Jude 1:25, *NIV*

and appointed judge—just as we would honor the Father who sent him?[80]

When the Scriptures are examined carefully (apart from latter traditions), it becomes clear that Christians *do* have a sound basis for "worshiping" the Lord Jesus Christ—namely, *by the express will of his God and Father*. Jesus Christ is rightfully "glorified," "exalted," and given "worship" (*proskuneo*), but the ultimate end of such is the glorification of *his Father*, as the apostle Paul clearly communicated under divine inspiration. With God's happy approval and richest blessing, Jesus Christ remains the central object of the Christian's faith and affection; and it is no wonder, for he lived a life of uncompromising obedience to God even to the point of laying down his perfect life in sacrifice—"*this is why God has so highly exalted him.*" "Through Jesus, therefore, let us continually offer to God a sacrifice of praise—the fruit of lips that confess his name."[81]

> *"Come to him, a living stone, rejected by human beings but chosen and precious in the sight of God, and, like living stones, let yourselves be built into a spiritual house to be a holy priesthood to offer spiritual sacrifices acceptable to God through Jesus Christ."* —1 Peter 2:4-5, NAB

Colossians 2:9

> *"I want them to continue in good heart and in the unity of love, and so come to the full wealth of conviction which understanding brings, and grasp God's secret. That secret is Christ himself; in him lie hidden all God's treasures of wisdom and knowledge."*
> —Colossians 2:2-3, *New English Bible*

---

[80] Compare with Jesus' statement in John 13:20; a text showing how—in biblical thought—the way one responds to a messenger or agent is essentially equivalent to the way one would respond to the one who sent the messenger or agent forth: "Amen, amen, I say to you, whoever receives the one I send receives me, and whoever receives me receives the one who sent me."
[81] Hebrews 13:15, *NIV*

Paul's letter to the Colossians contains a very clear and significant reference to the divinity/godship of Jesus Christ. After focusing on Christ as the one in whom "lies hidden all the treasures of wisdom and knowledge," Paul warned the Colossians not to be taken in by the prevailing philosophies and traditions of men:

> **I say this in order that no one may delude you with beguiling speech. For though I am absent in body, yet I am with you in spirit, rejoicing to see your good order and the firmness of your faith in Christ. As therefore you received Christ Jesus the Lord, so live in him, rooted and built up in him and established in the faith, just as you were taught, abounding in thanksgiving. See to it that no one makes a prey of you by philosophy and empty deceit, according to human tradition, according to the elemental spirits of the universe, and not according to Christ.** *For in him the whole fullness of deity dwells bodily,* **and you have come to fullness of life in him, who is the head of all rule and authority.**[82]

A few of the older English translations say that in Christ dwells all the fullness of the "Godhead" (a somewhat archaic/outdated English word). The *Revised Standard Version* is an improvement for modern readers—the fullness of "deity"—representing a translation of the Greek *theotetos*, the abstract form of the noun *theos* (G/god). The word *theotetos* basically means, and is sometimes translated, "deity,"[83] "godship (or godhood)," "divine nature," "divinity," or, perhaps, even "godliness."[84] It is a term much like the English "kingship," representing "the power, status, or authority of a monarch." In

---

[82] Colossians 2:4-10, *RSV* (emphasis added).
[83] An English translation of Athanasius' writings suggests "*un*godliness" as a translation for *atheotetos*: "...on other days as well did the Lord heal 'all manner of sickness...' but they complained still according to their wont, and by calling Him Beelzebub, preferred the suspicion of Atheism [footnote: Or ungodliness, *atheotetos*], to a recantation of their own wickedness." — *Nicene and Post-Nicene Fathers, Athanasius, Selected Works and Letters*, Volume 4 (Peabody: Hendricksen, 2004), p. 151.
[84] In *A Greek English Lexicon* by Lidell and Scott (Oxford, 1968, p. 792), the classic lexicon of the Ancient Greek language, the meaning given is "divinity," "divine nature."

The Apostolic Testimony

other words, 'kingship' refers to the qualities[85] or attributes that make one king (the state of being king); or, as an English dictionary defines it specifically: "the dignity or rank or position of a king." Similarly, the concept of "godship" or "deity" in Greek really denotes "the dignity or rank or position of a god," or "the totality of attributes and qualities that make one a god."[86]

Today's English Version expresses the *RSV's* "whole fullness of deity" as "the full content of divine nature." The *Translator's Handbook* has the following remarks:

> *The full content of divine nature*: the word translated 'divine nature' (or 'deity' RSV) occurs only here in the NT...As in 1:19, Paul here emphasizes that all of God's nature is present in Christ, not diluted or dispersed among intermediary spiritual beings. This does not imply, of course, that there was no more 'divine nature' left in God, nor does it say that Christ is God.[87]

Jesus Christ, according to the language, possesses in himself the fullness of the qualities and attributes that make one a being of divine nature, the possessor of divine powers. All the fullness of the divine nature dwells in Christ *bodily*. But nothing in the apostle's letter indicates that the "fullness" (Gk. *pleroma*) of "divine nature" or "godhood" abides in Christ because he is "God the Son, the eternal, second person of the triune God." The Scriptures reveal, rather, that the fullness of Godship possessed by Christ abides in him because it *pleased God*—or that *God himself decided*—that this would be so. As the *New English Translation* renders Colossians 1:19: "For God was pleased to have all his fullness dwell in the Son." Or, as the *New American Standard Bible* translates: "For it was the *Father's* good pleasure

---

[85] Volume 3 of the *Theological Dictionary of the New Testament* by Kittel, page 119, observes: "Abstract nouns by their very nature focus on a quality."

[86] The Greek term *theotetos* does not demand the meaning of "deity" in the ultimate sense as "the Almighty (or absolute) Deity." It can refer to all the qualities that make one either *a* god or *the* God (just as in Greek the word *theos*, in and of itself, means 'god,' and not necessarily *the* God). And the English term "deity," as pointed out by Robert Hommel, "signifies all that makes God, God (or a god, a god)..." —Dr.J.Beduhn and R.Hommel: *A Discussion upon the translation of John 1:1c* (Christian Apologetics Research Ministry; Jan/Feb, 2002). However, whether the word is understood as "all the qualities that make one God" or "all the qualities that make one *a* god," what Paul states in 1:19 suggests that Christ possesses these qualities, not because he is the second member of a Trinity, but based on the decision of God to endow him with such.

[87] *A Handbook on Paul's Letters to the Colossians and to Philemon*, by Robert G. Bratcher and Eugene A. Nida (UBS, New York, 1977), p. 54 (words in italics originally underlined).

for all the fullness to dwell in Him..."

Regarding Paul's statement in Colossians 1:19, the *Translator's Handbook* observes:

> The meaning of what follows is disputed. The Greek may mean: God decided to have his fullness dwell in Christ, or God's fullness decided to dwell in Christ, depending on whether the neuter phrase *pan to pleroma* ['all the fullness'] is construed as an accusative, the object of the verb, or as nominative, the subject of the verb...It seems better to take 'all the fullness' as object, and God as the (unexpressed) subject of the sentence: 'it was God's choice/decision/pleasure (for the verb *eudokeo* compare 1 Cor 1.21, Gal 1.15; compare the noun *eudokia* in Eph 1.5, 9; Phil 2.13) to have all the fullness dwell in him.'...'It was God's will and plan. For it was by God's own decision may be expressed more simply as 'For God himself decided.'[88]

The *English Standard Version* renders the verse (1:19) in a slightly different way: "**For in him all the fullness of God was pleased to dwell...**" (Compare: 'the Father...dwells in me', John 14:10, *ESV*).

Here is an example that illustrates the importance of not drawing interpretive conclusions apart from the biblical contexts. One might argue, as a Trinitarian, that since in Christ dwells "all the fullness of God," that must mean that Christ is "God the Son" or "God in the flesh." However, in another letter written by Paul to the Christians at Ephesus, Paul expressed his desire that they too would be possessors of the same fullness. He wrote:

> **For this reason I bow my knees before the Father, from whom every family in heaven and on earth is named, that according to the riches of his glory he may grant you to be strengthened with might through his Spirit in the inner man, and that Christ may dwell in your hearts through faith; that you, being rooted and grounded in love, may have power to comprehend with all the saints what is the breadth and length and height and depth, and to know the love of Christ**

---

[88] Nida, *A Handbook on Paul's Letters*, p. 27 (words in italics originally underlined).

which surpasses knowledge, *that you may be filled with all the fullness of God.* [89]

With respect to Colossians 1:19 specifically, it was further pointed out in the *Tyndale Commentaries*: "There is no word for 'God' in the original of verse 19, but the grammatical subject ('fullness') must be a circumlocution [meaning, 'a roundabout expression' or 'an indirect way of expressing something'] of 'God in all his fullness' (see 2:9)."[90] This is why the *New International Version* translates it: "For God was pleased to have all his fullness dwell in him." *Jerusalem Bible*: "because God wanted all perfection to be found in him." *King James Version*: "For it pleased *the Father* that in him should all fullness dwell." *The Anchor Bible* (along with the words that follow): "For it was the will of God to let in [Christ] dwell all the fullness, and to reconcile through Him with him all things by creating peace through his blood of the cross, through Him, be it that, which is on earth, be it that, which is in the heavens."[91]

While some Trinitarian apologists like James White have attempted to deny or call into question the likelihood that Colossians 1:19 and 2:9 are referring to the same "fullness"[92] (both use the same word *pleroma*), it is difficult to understand what other sort of fullness Paul could have been referring to. Both occur in the same letter; both expressions form part of a unified or intimately-associated series of points being made by the same author.[93] Even Dr. Robert Reymond acknowledged the relationship between the two references: "I postponed the discussion of the phrase in 1:19, 'all the fullness,' to this point, because Paul uses the phrase in 2:9 with even greater clarity of meaning and *the phrase almost certainly means the same thing in both contexts*. In Colossians 1:19, Paul wrote: 'In him [God] willed all the fullness to dwell.' Here in 2:9 Paul says virtually

---

[89] Ephesians 3:14-19, *RSV*
[90] *The Tyndale New Testament Commentaries*, N. T. Wright, Colossians & Philemon, p. 75.
[91] *Anchor Bible*, p. 194.
[92] White, *The Forgotten Trinity*, p. 207.
[93] In his scholarly work, *The Theology of Paul the Apostle* (p. 205), James Dunn writes: "The point [of Colossians 1:19] is strengthened by its repetition in 2:9: 'in him [as usual, Christ] dwells all the fullness of the deity in bodily form.' Two of the key words are repeated from 1.19 — 'fullness (*plērōma*)' and 'dwells (*katoikeō*).' There is no reason why either should be given a different reference from that in 1.19."

The Apostolic Testimony

the same thing, but he specifies the nature of the 'fullness' and the manner in which the 'fullness' dwells in Jesus."[94]

In his commentary on Colossians, Gordon Clark translated the verse: "because [God] pleased that all the pleroma should dwell in him..."; and he went on to observe:

> The subject of the verb *pleased* is not in the text. An English speaking person is likely to supply the word *God* as the dative: it pleased God that...But the analogy of I Corinthians 1:21 strongly indicates that the noun *God* should be nominative: God pleased that the whole pleroma ['fullness'] should dwell in him. This verse, short as it is, gives the reason for Christ's pre-eminence...This verse gives another reason that supports the interpretation proposed for the previous verse. The reason Christ is (not will become) pre-eminent is that God pleased to have the whole pleroma ['fullness'] dwell in him...Although Meyer makes a telling point that the fullness of the Godhead cannot be the meaning here because Christ's Godhead is not the result of the Father's choice or good pleasure, but is inherently essential to Christ's person, it is hard to see what else it could mean.[95]

Interestingly, Clark refers to Meyer's objection to this interpretation because, according to both Clark's and Meyer's view,—that is, more specifically, their commitment to the doctrine of the Trinity—'Christ's godhead/deity is not the result of the Father's choice or good pleasure, but is inherently essential to Christ's person.' In other words, according to the tenets of Trinitarianism, the fullness of Godship (deity) possessed by Christ is a fullness he has always possessed. He has, according to the doctrine, *eternally* been a possessor or partaker of the essence of deity as "God-the-eternal-Son." It is, however, unnecessary to harmonize the Scriptures with post-biblical creedal formulations. What the apostle himself said about Christ in Colossians 1:19 satisfactorily provides us with the necessary information in terms of understanding why and how it is that Christ possesses in himself the fullness of deity or

---

[94] Reymond, *A New Systematic Theology of the Christian Faith*, p. 252 (emphasis added).
[95] *Colossians, Another Commentary on an Inexhaustible Message* (Jefferson: Trinity Foundation, 1979), p. 49.

The Apostolic Testimony

godship. It was, as *Today's English Version* expresses it, "**by God's own decision**..." C. B. Williams translated it: "It is so because it was the divine choice that all the divine fullness should dwell in Him..." *The Twentieth Century New Testament* renders it: "For it pleased the Father that in him the divine nature in all its fullness should dwell..." The *Amplified Bible* attempts to expand on the meaning: "For it pleased [the Father] that all the divine fullness—the sum total of the divine perfection, powers and attributes—should dwell in Him permanently..."

Other Bible commentators of a Trinitarian background have already discerned the same rather obvious connection. In the *Tyndale Commentaries*, N. T. Wright wrote: "*in Christ all the fullness of the Deity lives in bodily form*. This is probably to be taken simply as an expansion of 1:19; the tense is past there, present here, but in both the referent is the same..."[96] The renowned Greek scholar A. T. Robertson agreed:

> *For it was the good pleasure of the Father* (*hoti eudokesen*). No word in the Greek for 'the Father,' though the verb calls for either *ho theos* ['God'] or *ho pater* ['the Father'] as the subject. This verb *eudokeo* is common in the N.T. for God's will and pleasure (Matthew 3:17; 1 Corinthians 10:5). *All the fullness* (*pan to pleroma*). The same idea as in 2:9 *pan to pleroma tes theotetos* (all the fulness of the Godhead).[97]

Although some apologists have sought to deny the relationship between Colossians 1:19 and 2:9,—that both refer to the same "fullness"—as evangelical Gordon Clark pointed out, "it is hard to see what else it could mean."[98]

With regard to another expression found in the same verse, it has been common for Trinitarian expositors to insist that Colossians 2:9 is referring to the "incarnation of God the Son."

---

[96] *The Tyndale New Testament Commentaries*, N. T. Wright, Colossians & Philemon, p. 103.

[97] *Word Pictures in the New Testament, Volume IV, The Epistles of Paul*, p. 480. The footnote in the *NET* (p. 628) likewise says: "The noun 'God' does not appear in the Greek text, but since God is the one who reconciles the world to himself (cf. 2 Cor 5:19), he is clearly the subject of ευδοκησεν (*eudokesen*)."

[98] Other translations have: "It pleased God to make absolute fullness reside in him" (*New American Bible*, 1970); "because it pleased *God to have* the totality live in Christ" (*Simple English Bible*); "Because God wanted all fullness to be found in him" (*NJB*); "For it was the good pleasure *of the Father* that in him should all the fullness dwell" (*RV* 1881); "For it pleased God that all his perfection should dwell in Christ" (*New Testament in Plain English*).

That is to say, Jesus Christ is God ('deity') in a body of flesh. However, on this point, it may be instructive to note that the term "body" (Gk: *soma*), from which comes the word "bodily" (Gk: *somatikos*) in Colossians 2:9, is also used in Colossians 2:17: "for those things ['matters of food and drink...festival or new moon or Sabbath.' v. 16] are a shadow of the things to come, but the *reality* (*soma*) [the *solid reality*, NEB][99] belongs to Christ." This is why it was even noted in the *Tyndale Commentaries*: "The word translated 'in bodily form' [*NIV* rendering] can also mean 'actually' or 'in solid reality...'"[100] *The Interpreter's Bible* similarly notes: "Bodily (*somatikos*) may be taken to mean 'incarnate' [in the flesh] (Lightfoot); but it is not so understood by the ancient fathers, and it is probably better to interpret it as meaning 'genuinely' (i.e., not figuratively; so Cyril), or 'in a body,' 'as a corpus, not as *disject membra*,' in contrast with the distribution of divine attributes among the *stoicheia* ['elementary things/principles' (of the world) v. 8]."[101] *The Abingdon Bible Commentary* interprets the meaning as: "The totality of divine attributes is present as a whole in one 'Body' or *concrete individual personality*."[102]

The fact that the fullness of the divine nature dwells in Christ "bodily" does not necessarily mean or imply a *fleshly* body. If Paul was referring to Christ's literal 'body,' it is more likely that he was referring to the glorified (post-resurrection), immortal, heavenly/spiritual body now possessed by the Lord Jesus in his exalted status at the right hand of God.[103] Although

---

[99] The *NET* footnote states: "The term body here, when used in contrast to shadow (*skia*) indicates the opposite meaning, i.e., the reality or substance itself." The *ESV* translates: "the *substance* belongs to Christ."

[100] *The Tyndale New Testament Commentaries*, N. T. Wright, Colossians & Philemon, p. 103. In one of his most famous scholarly works, N. T. Wright noted: "Though it is dangerous to generalize in so widespread and pluriform a language as Koine Greek, it is generally true that adjectives formed with ending -*ikos* have ethical or functional meanings rather than referring to the material or substance of which something is composed (ftnt., Adjectives of 'material' tend to form in –*inos* (Moulton 1980-76, 2.359); those which end in -*ikos* indicate that what something is 'like', giving an ethical or dynamic relation as opposed to a material one (Moulton 2.378, quoting Plummer on 1 Cor. 3.1)." —*The Resurrection of the Son of God* (Minneapolis: Fortress Press, 2003), p. 351.

[101] *The Interpreter's Bible*, Volume 11, p. 193.

[102] *Abingdon Bible Commentary*, p. 1257.

[103] In his letter to the Philippians, Paul said that the Lord Jesus Christ would "change our lowly body to conform with his glorified body by the power that enables him also to bring all things into subjection to himself." —Philippians 3:21, *NAB*

some have objected to the idea of a "spiritual body," referring to it as an "oxymoron,"[104] the reality of such is biblically verifiable.[105] In the fifteenth chapter of his letter to the Corinthians, Paul wrote about the future resurrection from the dead in this way:

> **But someone may say, 'How are the dead raised? With what kind of body will they come back?' You fool! What you sow is not brought to life unless it dies. And what you sow is not the body that is to be but a bare kernel of wheat, perhaps, or of some other kind; but God gives it a body as he chooses, and to each of the seeds its own body.**

After discussing varying sorts of bodies (heavenly and earthly), Paul went on to say,

> **So also is the resurrection of the dead. It is sown corruptible; it is raised incorruptible. It is sown dishonorable; it is raised glorious. It is sown weak; it is raised powerful. It is sown a natural [or, 'soulish'] body;** *it is raised a spiritual body. If there is a natural body, there is also a spiritual one.* **So, too, it is written, 'The first man, Adam, became a living [soul],' the last Adam** *a life-giving spirit.* **But the spiritual was not first; rather the natural and then the spiritual. The first man was from the earth, earthly; the second man, from heaven. As was the earthly one, so also are the earthly, and as is the heavenly one, so also are the heavenly. Just as we have borne the image of the earthly one, we shall also bear the image of the heavenly one.**[106]

In summary, then, it can be pointed out, the fact that Jesus Christ has "all authority in heaven and on earth," that he is seated next to the Father in "the heavenly places," that he has the name that is above every name, that all things have been—or

---

[104] Like 'hot ice,' or a 'squared circle.'
[105] Unless we understand the sense of "spiritual body" (*soma pneumatikon*) in the sense argued for by N. T. Wright in his *The Resurrection of the Son of God*. Wright argues that Paul's intended meaning for "spiritual body" is not that of a body *composed* of spirit, but of "a body animated by the Spirit" of God. This is in contrast to the "natural body" (*NASB*) or "soulish body" (*Concordant Literal NT*) "characterized [by Wright] as 'ordinary human life'…" (pp. 347-356)
[106] 1 Corinthians 15:42-49, *NAB* (emphasis added).

ultimately will be—subjected underneath his feet, and that he truly possesses within himself "all the fullness of deity," the Godship necessary to have the entire universe in subjection, and to reconcile all things to God—these are all properties, powers, positions and attributes that properly fall under the category of that which God has been pleased to confer upon his Son.

The following translations represent various examples of how translators have attempted to express the thought of Colossians 2:9:

"The totality of divinity lives embodied in Christ."[107]
—*The International English Bible translation*
"For the full content of divine nature lives in Christ"
—*Today's English Version*
"Because in him resides all the fulfillment of the divine."
—*A Translation by Richard Lattimore*
"For it is in him that all the fullness of God's nature lives embodied." —*The New Testament, An American Translation*
"The fullness of divine nature lives in Christ's bodily form."
—*New Simplified Bible Translation*
"For it is in Christ that the fullness of God's nature dwells embodied." —*The New Testament in Modern Speech, Weymouth*
"Because in Him resides bodily every perfection of the Divinity."
—*The Holy Bible in Modern English, Ferrar Fenton*
"For in Christ the whole perfection of God's nature dwells bodily"
—*The New Testament in Plain English, Charles Kingsley Williams*

Hebrews 1:3

One of the striking features of Trinitarian theology is the way proponents have argued for the most extraordinary and unnatural expositions of Scripture. This is done, often, for the purpose of extracting a meaning that accords with received conceptions of Christ, even when the plain sense of a particular text seems to be in direct conflict with traditionally prescribed doctrines. What follows represents a case in point.

According to the orthodox Trinitarian formula, Jesus, the

---

[107] The statement might also be rendered: "For in him the fullness of divine nature [or 'godship'] dwells embodied."

Son, is said to be one who eternally "shares" the same "essence," "substance" or "being" as the Father; to use the classic theological terminology, "consubstantial" ('of the same being').

As already noted, Trinitarians believe that Jesus and the Father constitute two distinct "persons," yet, mysteriously, the two "persons" nevertheless constitute the same, or share the same, "being," the one being that is "God." As also previously discussed, the doctrine of the Trinity says that the *one* being of God is actually shared by a total of *three* distinguishable "persons," namely the Father, the Son, and the Holy Spirit—*One* God, *three* persons.

Apparently, the only text in Scripture that does tell us something very specific about God's *being* (the *reality* of who or what God is)—in connection with the Father-Son relationship—is found in Hebrews 1:3. Here, the writer was inspired to describe the Son of God in very lofty terms: "*In the past, God spoke to our forefathers on many occasions and in different ways through the prophets, but in the last of these days he has spoken to us through a Son, whom he appointed heir of all things and through whom he made the ages.*" In verse three, the author says of the Son:

He is the reflection/outshining of [God's] glory and the exact representation (*charakter*) **of his very being** (*hupastasis*)[108]

Of the word *charakter*, Bible translator C. B. Williams remarks that the "Grk. word means exact imprint; so the Son is the *perfect representation of* God's being."[109] Another commentary notes that the word refers to "an impression such as

---

[108] The *KJV* translates the verse, "the express image of his *person*." But the *NIV* is an improvement: "the exact representation of his *being*." J. N. Darby points out in the footnote to his translation that the Greek word used here refers: "clearly [to] 'substance,' 'essential being,' not 'person.'" Another reference work similarly states: "The Greek word translated 'nature' [*NASB*] (*hypostasis*) is also significant to note, since it denotes here the 'substantial nature, essence, actual being' of God, which the Son is thus said to reproduce exactly." —*A Biblical Theology of the New Testament* (DTS Faculty), p. 373. However, the English *nature* is probably a better translation of the Greek *phusis*, as in 2 Peter 1:4, where it is said that Christians would become "partakers of the divine nature (*theias koinōnoi phuseōs*)." Divine "nature" (*phusis*) is, according to Scripture, something Christians will partake in. Yet God's "being" (*hupastasis*) is something unique to, and owned by, God, and of which his Son is said to be the "exact reproduction" of.
[109] *New Testament* by C.B. Williams (footnote).

The Apostolic Testimony

a seal leaves on wax, *an exact reproduction of the original.*"[110] *Strong's Dictionary* defines *charakter* as "a graver (the tool or the person), i.e. (by implication) engraving, the figure stamped, i.e. *an exact copy* or [figuratively] representation)." *Thayer's Lexicon* says of *charakter*: "the exact expression (the image) of any person or thing, marked likeness, *precise reproduction* in every respect (cf. facsimile).''[111]

A. T. Robertson pointed out in his *Word Pictures in the New Testament*: "*Charakter* is an old word from *charasso*, to cut, to scratch, to mark. It first was the agent (note ending = *ter*) or tool that did the marking, then the mark or impress made, *the exact reproduction*, a meaning clearly expressed by *charagma* (Acts 17:29; Rev. 13:16f.)...The word occurs in the inscriptions for 'person' as well as for 'exact reproduction' of a person. The word *hupostasis* for the being or essence of God..."[112] The well-known Methodist commentator, Adam Clarke, also explained the meaning of both words: "The 'hypostasis' of God is that which is essential to Him as God; and the 'character' or *image* is that by which all the likeness of the original becomes manifest, and is *a perfect facsimile of the whole*. It is a metaphor taken from sealing, the die or seal leaving the full impression of its every part on the wax to which it is applied."[113]

The Son, according to the sacred text, is a perfect "copy" of the very "being"[114] of God. Thus the verse has been accurately translated: "he is the reflection of his glory and **the perfect representation** (*C. B. Williams*), "**the exact representation**" (*New International Version*), "**the exact likeness**" (*Today's English Version*), "**an exact copy**" (*New Century Version*), "**the**

---

[110] *The One Volume Bible Commentary*, J. R. Dummelow, p. 1016 (emphasis added).
[111] Emphasis added. The footnote to Hebrews 1:3 in the *Jerusalem Bible* refers to it as a "replica." A couple of translations even have: "the reflection of his glory and the *facsimile* of his essence." —*Modern Literal Version of the New Testament*; "The Son shows the glory of God. He is *a perfect copy* of God's nature." —*Holy Bible, Easy-to-Read-Version, 2001.*
[112] Robertson, *Word Pictures in the New Testament, Volume V*, p. 336 (emphasis added).
[113] *Adam Clarke's Commentary, One Volume Edition* (Grand Rapids: Baker, 1967) p. 1248.
[114] "God's *hypostasis* is his essential being, 'the reality of God'...The patristic distinction between three *hypostasis* and one *ousia* in God is irrelevant, since *hypostasis* is in fact used here with a meaning closer to that which *ousia/substance* acquired in later christological discussion. All the stress in this passage falls on Christ's unity with God, a traditional truth of which the readers probably needed to be reminded. For both author and readers, it probably went without saying that Jesus was distinguishable from God." —*The New International Greek Testament Commentary, The Epistle to the Hebrews, A Commentary on the Greek Text* by Paul Ellingworth (Grand Rapids: Eerdmans/Paternoster Press, 1995), p. 90.

The Apostolic Testimony

perfect copy" (*Jerusalem Bible/Beck*) of [God's] being."

Although not fully or correctly coming to terms with the real implication of his observations, Wayne Grudem was correct when he noted: "This Son, says the writer, 'reflects the glory of God and bears the very stamp [lit., is the 'exact duplicate,' Gk. *Character*] of his nature...Jesus is the exact duplicate of the 'nature' (or being, Gk. *hypostasis*) of God..."[115]

A Biblical Theology of the New Testament (page 373), produced by faculty members of Dallas Theological Seminary, claimed that this text, as Trinitarian doctrine dictates, reveals that Jesus is "sharing the very essence of God (v. 3c)."[116] In the *New Testament Commentary* by Hendriksen and Kistemaker, the very same argument was made. Although their point regarding the meaning of the word is factual, the subsequent commentary supposedly based on it represents a bizarre and surprising lapse in logic: "The word translated as 'exact representation' refers to minted coins that bear the image of a sovereign or president. It refers to a precise reproduction of the original. The Son, then, is completely the same in being as the Father."[117]

That is to say, the commentary correctly acknowledges that *charakter* refers to a 'precise reproduction of the original'— bearing in mind that, according to the text, the 'original' the Son is a "precise reproduction" of is the very "being" of "God." But the commentary goes on to reason that the Son, then, is "*completely the same in being as the Father*"—an extremely puzzling statement; because although their point was to explain

---

[115] *Systematic Theology*, p. 547. It was noted in another respected commentary that *charakter* "is 'the exact reproduction,' as a statue of a person; literally, the stamp or clear-cut impression made by a seal, *the very facsimile of the original*...The idea of *character* as a replica is further illustrated by the Bereschith rabba, 52. 3 (on Gn 21:2): 'hence we learn that he (Isaac) was the splendour of his (father's) face, as like as possible to him.'" —*The International Critical and Exegetical Commentary on the Epistle to the Hebrews*, James Moffatt D.D., (Edinburgh: T. & T. Clark, 1975) pp. 6, 7 (emphasis added).

[116] The argumentation is typical. A. Berkeley Mickelsen, Ph.D. also wrote, in his introductory outline-survey of the book of Hebrews in the *Revised Standard Version* (1962): "He shares the essence of deity and radiates the glory of deity...(1.1-3)." (p. 1204). Evangelical apologist Edward Doulcour likewise claimed: "Hebrews 1:3...teaches clearly that Jesus is of the same *substance* or *nature* as God the Father...The JWs, as well as the Mormons, say that Jesus is not the same *substance* or *nature* as God the Father, however the author of Hebrews expressively contradicts that idea...Jesus is of the *same substance* or nature as God the Father, as stated in Hebrews, however they are clearly distinct Persons." —*The Deity of Jesus Christ, Hebrews 1:3*: Department of Christian Defense (website).

[117] *New Testament Commentary, Thessalonians, the Pastorals, and Hebrews*, William Hendriksen and Simon J. Kistemaker (Baker Academic, Grand Rapids, 1984) p. 30 (emphasis added).

the meaning of the text based on the significance of the term (*charakter*), the conclusion offered simply contradicts the actual meaning of the term and the most natural implication of the language. That is, if the Son is a 'precise reproduction' of the Father's 'being,' then the Son being "completely the same in being as his Father" is precisely what he is not. If the Son is the *charakter* (exact representation) of the Father's being, then he is not one and the same being as the Father (the 'original')—a point that hardly needs to be made or further elaborated upon.

Strangely, Trinitarians somehow try to argue that "exact representation" of God's "being" means, or is somehow harmonious with, "sharing the same being," i.e., "consubstantial" (the Nicene formula). Of course, contrary to what Trinitarian apologists claim, the author of Hebrews neither states nor implies that the Son was or is a "partaker" of God's being.[118] In fact, it is quite clear from this one text alone that God the Father is the owner of his own being, since the Son is said to be a "representation" of *his* being. Or, to put it another way, in the interests of clarity, the Son is a "perfect representation" of a being *other than himself*, namely, that of God. And we can be sure that Jehovah God, the Most High, is no way a "copy" or "representation" of anyone else's being, nor could he properly be described as such. There is, however, one who is fittingly described as a copy of *his* being—God's unique and beloved Son, the Lord Jesus Christ.[119]

The question that should be asked today is: Why is it that whenever the writers of Scripture spoke deliberately about God's Son in the most distinctive and exalted ways (as in Hebrews 1:3) did they not "teach" what Trinitarianism teaches? If the Trinitarian concept is authentically true and biblical, then it

---

[118] It should really go without saying that if someone or something is a "copy" of something else, it is *not* that something else. To illustrate this conceptually, imagine that an artist sculptured a detailed statue or created a mold of the President's face. That statue or mold would obviously not *be* the President's face (the original) or a part of (or 'partaker' in) the President's face; but it could be properly said that the statue is an *exact copy*, *a replica*, or a *perfect representation* of it (regardless of the scale or correspondence in size). Similarly, in this passage, the Son is not described—in harmony with orthodoxy—as a *sharer* in the original being of God; but rather, as a "perfect representation" or an "exact copy" of it. Aside from theological bias or loyalty to an already-established creed, it is unclear why and how anyone would attempt to suggest that a "representation" of something is not distinct from that which it represents.

[119] This was a point made by Greg Stafford in a public debate that took place in December 2004.

follows that the most *significant*, most *outstanding* and most *distinctive* attribute of the Son of God is that he is, mysteriously, and amazingly, an "eternal partaker" of the Father's being—the one being of God. When the author of Hebrews was inspired to speak plainly about God's "being" and Christ's relationship to it, why did he not speak about such an extraordinary and amazing fact? Why did the author of Hebrews teach that the Son is a "copy" of God's being if he believed that God's being and the Son's being were *the same* being? Where is the consistency and where is the harmony? Or, it may be asked, if that is what the writer believed, what was the point in him saying something *other than* what he believed and wished for his readers to accept?[120]

The final question that arises: Why would advocates of the Trinity doctrine—particularly, those who profess to adhere to the 'Bible alone'—maintain that Jesus is the same being as God the Father when Hebrews 1:3 communicates something different, and when there is no Scripture in the Bible that says Jesus is the same being as his Father? Why would the theological notion (and language necessary to the formulation) that the Son mysteriously "shares the being" of God the Father take precedence over the clearly-articulated scriptural teaching and specific language that the Son is the "exact representation of God's being"?[121]

---

[120] Why, for example, did the author of Hebrews not say of the Son: "He is the reflection/outshining of the Father's glory, and an eternal partaker of the Father's essence," if that is what he believed? What apologists of Trinitarian dogma are ultimately suggesting is that, for some inexplicable reason, the author of Hebrews indicated that Jesus Christ is the exact 'copy/representation' of *his own* being—a nonsensical implication. Yet this is the inescapable outcome of the Trinitarian dogma. To say that the Son is the 'exact representation' of the Father's being would not fit, or harmonize, or make logical sense in Trinitarianism, simply because, according to Trinitarian doctrine, the Father's being *is* the Son's being.

[121] Some apologists have responded by arguing that if the Son is an *exact* representation of God's being, he must be *eternal* because God's being is eternal and therefore Jesus is God. White claims: "The Son has *eternally* been the *exact representation* of the Father's being," something the Scripture itself doesn't say. However, even if one were to accept the paradoxical notion that a *reproduction* of someone or something else possesses the same age as the original, one would still have to conclude that there are *two, distinct, eternal beings* (not simply 'persons' in the Trinitarian sense). However, the Trinity teaches that the Father and Son, although distinct as "persons," constitute *one* being. So whether eternal (in the sense of not having a beginning) or not, the author of Hebrews clearly has two beings in view (God's 'being' and a 'Son' who is a 'precise reproduction' of it), a fact which, logically speaking, is automatically at variance with Trinitarian doctrine. But it can in fact be fairly and logically argued that a "copy/reproduction," by definition, is something that came into existence at some point subsequent to the original. Actually, a point like this does not really need to be "argued."

The Apostolic Testimony

Since no straightforward or convincing answer has been offered by the apologists, we can safely conclude that the concept presented by Hebrews 1:3 is not a reflection of the traditional Trinitarian concept; simply because "exact representation/perfect copy of God's being"—what the Bible says—is not the same as "the *same* being," "*sharing* the same being," or "*of* the same being"—the classical Trinitarian formula. Traditional theology does not teach that Jesus Christ is the exact reproduction of God's being. It teaches, rather, that Jesus Christ is one "person" out of three who shares in the one being that is God in the ultimate sense. Therefore, the original first-century description of God's Son at Hebrews 1:3 does not harmonize with the *homoousious* ('of identical substance/being') formula of the fourth-century Nicene creed.

Those who seek to promote and defend the theological proposition that Jesus is literally Almighty God or "God-the eternal-Son" will, when discussing this particular text, find themselves in the strange and precarious position of trying to explain how God the Almighty could be described in Scripture as a "copy/representation of God's being," and in the equally unenviable position of trying to convince others that Jesus could be a representation of God's being while, at the same time, remain a "partaker" of God's being (the original).[122] It is only when one holds tenaciously to traditionally-prescribed post-biblical concepts that such a great deal of effort and specialized, out-of-the-ordinary methods of argumentation are required to uphold them. If, however, Christians were to simply think in the terms that the Bible itself presents to us, the concept of the Son as "consubstantial" with the Father, and the idea that one's very prospect of salvation is contingent upon acceptance of this, would never even come to mind; because all the Scripture has to say specifically about the Divine "being" is that the Son is a "copy/reproduction" of it. *That* is the scriptural teaching on this

---

[122] Again, it might be worthwhile to ask ourselves: If the apostles wanted Christians to believe that the Father and Son constituted one being, why didn't they just say so? Why did the writers of Scripture communicate in such a way that would lead us to believe, not that the Son is a part or "person" of (or sharer in) God's being, but a "perfect representation" of it? We should also remember that, if Jesus is a "copy" or "reproduction" of something (whatever that something is), he is *not* the original. That is what a copy/reproduction, by definition, is—and, by definition, a "copy" cannot be the original, or it is not a "copy"!

point. In the end, that is all that really needs to be said. The Scripture has already said it.

We should also be careful to note that in this text (the preceding verse), Jesus is not identified as "God," but he *is* said to be the one *through* whom "God" has spoken and the one *through* (literally '*in*') whom God created the ages/worlds ('all orders of existence,' *NEB*).[123] A.T. Robertson was correct to point out that the "Son as Heir is also the Intermediate Agent (*dia*) in the work of creation as we have it in Col. 1:16f. and John 1:3"[124]—a point that remains true regardless of what we take the 'creation' in these texts to have reference to.

With regard to the term often translated into English as "being" or "essence" (sometimes as 'nature'), it was confirmed by one source: "Etymologically, the word imports the lying or being placed underneath: and this is put in common usage, for 1. *substratum* or *foundation—fundamentum*"; and "this last seems to be the best meaning in our place: His *essential being*, His *substance*."[125] This is why we can be sure that whatever the underlying, substantial reality of what God truly is (God's very being), God's Son, Christ Jesus, is a perfect "reproduction" of that. He is, in fact, the Father's *Son*. That is, after all, essentially what a Son is, or supposed to be. How appropriate and how fitting it is that he is described the way Scripture describes him.

Hebrews 1:8

"But about the Son [God] says, 'Your throne, O God, will last forever and ever.'" —New International Version

Hebrews 1:8 is one of the few places in the Christian Scriptures where Jesus is, in all likelihood, rightfully honored with the title *theos* ('God'). In verse seven, the author quotes a Scripture from the Hebrew text of Psalm 104:4 where God spoke

---

[123] "It is noticeable that this writer uses the word for 'ages' (*aiones*) and not the usual word for worlds (*kosmoi*) when speaking about God's creative act. The reason is that the word for 'ages' is more comprehensive, including within it the periods of time through which the created order exists." —*The Tyndale New Testament Commentaries, The Letter to the Hebrews*, by Donald Guthrie (Grand Rapids: Eerdmans, 1998), p. 65.

[124] *Word Pictures in the New Testament, Volume V*, p. 335.

[125] *The Greek Testament* by Henry Alford, D. D., with revision by Everett F. Harrison. Th.D., P.hd, Volume IV, Hebrews-Revelation, (Chicago: Moody Press, 1958), p. 8.

The Apostolic Testimony

with reference to the angels:

> **And of the angels He says, 'who makes His angels winds, And His ministers a flame of fire.'**

Then, another Hebrew Scripture (Psalm 45:6-7) is quoted, bringing into focus a contrast between God's Son and the angels:

> **But of the Son *He says*, 'Your throne, O God, is forever and ever, and the righteous scepter is the scepter of Your kingdom. 'You have loved righteousness and hated lawlessness; Therefore God, Your God, has anointed You with the oil of gladness above Your companions.'**[126]

First, it is worth noting—for information purposes—that not all translators have opted (with complete certainty) for a reading that applies the title "God" to Christ at Hebrews 1:8. For example, the *NRSV*, although translating the verse as "your throne O God" in the main text, so that Christ is called "God," the marginal footnote alerts readers to the fact that the verse may be translated, with reference to Christ, "*God is your throne...*" Other versions have: "*Your throne is God for an age of ages.*"[127]

"God is your throne" is a translation that takes the phrase in Hebrews 1:8 as nominative, the case in Greek used for the subject of a given clause. Most English translators, however, have taken the phrase as a vocative, the case used for addressing a person. Additionally, the phrase *ho theos* normally means "God" (literally: 'the God') but can also mean "O God," as it likely does in a few cases in the Christian Scriptures.[128] These are some of the basic reasons why the verse is often considered ambiguous in terms of translation, and sheds light on why Bible translations have different wordings.

In his zeal to defend the orthodox conception of God as expressed by the Trinity, Wayne Grudem made this comment in the footnote to his discussion on this verse in his *Systematic Theology*: "The suggested translation of Heb. 1:8 in the RSV

---

[126] Hebrews 1:7-9, *NASB* (updated edition, marginal rendering 'Your' here placed in main text).
[127] *The Unvarnished New Testament* by Andy Gaus.
[128] Luke 18:11; 13, Hebrews 10:7

The Apostolic Testimony

margin, 'God is your throne forever and ever,' while possible grammatically, is completely inconsistent with the thinking of both Old and New Testaments: The mighty God who created everything and rules supreme over the universe would never be merely a 'throne' for someone else. The thought itself is dishonoring to God, and it should certainly not be considered as a possibly appropriate translation."[129]

However, Robert Bowman (a Trinitarian), although disagreeing with the translation in the *RSV* margin, noted that on "merely grammatical considerations, this translation ['God is your throne' or 'your throne is God'] is possible, and some biblical scholars have favored this rendering. According to such a reading, *the point of the statement is that God is the source of Jesus' authority.*"[130] Of course, contrary to Wayne Grudem, this is certainly a scripturally harmonious concept and anything but "dishonoring to God."

Although claiming that the translation would result in that which is "completely inconsistent with the thinking of both Old and New Testaments," other respected Trinitarian scholars have said otherwise. Bible scholar B. F. Westcott, who favored the translation "God is your throne," said the following in his commentary on the book of Hebrews:

> The LXX [Septuagint] admits of two renderings: *ho theos* can be taken as a vocative in both cases (*thy throne, O God,...therefore, O God, thy God...*) or it can be taken as the subject (or the predicate) in the first case (*God is Thy throne, or Thy throne is God...*), and in apposition to *ho theos sou* in the second case (*Therefore God, even Thy God...,*). The only important variation noted in the other Greek versions is that of Aquila, who gave the vocative [thee] in the first clause...and, as it appears also in the second...The presumption therefore is against the belief that *ho theos* is a vocative in the LXX. Thus on the whole it seems best to adopt in the first clause the rendering: *God is Thy throne* (or, *Thy throne is God*), that is 'Thy kingdom is founded upon God, the immovable Rock'; and to take *ho theos* as in apposition in the second clause.

---

[129] Grudem, *Systematic Theology*, p. 228.
[130] Robert Bowman, *Why You Should Believe in the Trinity*, p. 107 (emphasis added).

"The phrase 'God is Thy throne' is not indeed found elsewhere, but it is no way more strange than Ps. lxvi.3 [*Lord*] *be Thou to me a rock of habitation...Thou art my rock and my fortress.* Is.xxvi. (R.V.) *In the* LORD JEHOVAH *is an everlasting rock.* Ps. xc.1 *Lord, Thou hast been our dwelling place.* Ps. xci. 1 *He that dwelleth in the secret place of the Most high...*v. 2 *I will say of the Lord, He is my refuge and my fortress,* v.9; Deut.xxx111.27 *The eternal God is thy dwelling-place.*[131]

New Testament scholar A.T. Robertson, commenting on whether *theos* in Hebrews 1:8 should be viewed as the nominative or vocative case, stated:

O God (*ho theos*). This quotation (the fifth) is from Psa. 45:7f. A Hebrew nuptial ode (*epithalamium*) for a king treated here as Messianic. It is not certain whether *ho theos* is here the vocative (address with the nominative form as in John 20:28 with the Messiah termed *theos* as is possible, John 1:18) or *ho theos* is nominative (subject or predicate) with *estin* (is) understood: 'God is thy throne' or 'Thy throne is God.' Either makes good sense.[132]

Although there are valid grammatical, contextual and scripturally harmonious reasons for accepting the translation ('your throne is God' or 'God is your throne'), Murray Harris came to a conclusion different from B. F. Westcott; arguing that one may affirm "with a high degree of confidence that in the LXX [*Septuagint*] text from which the author of Hebrews was quoting *ho theos* represents a vocatival *elohim*." Harris also noted that—in terms of translation—some "scholars are reluctant

---

[131] *The Epistle to the Hebrews, The Greek Text with Notes and Essays* (Grand Rapids: Eerdmans, reprinted 1977), pp. 25, 26. Murray Harris argues: "A distinction must be drawn, however, between affirming that God is a person's rock, fortress, refuge, or dwelling place and that he is a person's throne. As a 'rock of refuge...towering crag and stronghold' (Ps. 71:3 NEB) God provides secure protection, a 'safe retreat' (Ps. 91:2, 9), for his people. But whether 'throne' signifies dynasty, kingdom, or rule, the concepts of 'God' and 'throne' are too dissimilar to permit a comparable metaphor. That is, unlike these other affirmations, 'God is your throne' is elliptical and must mean 'God is the foundation of your throne.' In a similar way, 'your throne is God' must mean 'your throne is founded on (or, protected by) God,' for, whatever *thronos* [throne] may signify by metonymy, it does not belong to the category of the divine." —*Jesus as God*, pp. 212, 213 (Note: 'metonymy' is 'a figure of speech in which one word or phrase is substituted for another with which it is closely associated, as in the use of *Washington* for *the United States government* or of *the sword* for *military power*').
[132] *Word Pictures in the New Testament, Volume V*, p. 339.

The Apostolic Testimony

to express a preference as to whether *ho theos* is nominative or vocative in verse 8, declaring that both interpretations are admissible and make good sense. But the overwhelming majority of grammarians, commentators, authors of general studies, and English translations construe *ho theos* as vocative ('O God')."[133]

Although, evidently, one cannot know for certain which translation is the correct one (both are in terms of grammar), it is important to consider the implications of Jesus being addressed as "God" based on the more common and perhaps more likely reading.

The Trinitarian argument based on the translation of Hebrews 1:8—"your throne O God"—may be summarized as follows: God (the Father) is the speaker and he is calling Jesus *God*: "Your throne *O God*, is forever and ever." This means that God the Father, the first person of the Trinity, is calling the second person of the Trinity (the Son) "God," in effect, proclaiming (or giving strong indication of) the Son's role and eternal position within the Trinitarian Godhead. This is one of the most common depictions given for this verse by Trinitarian apologists.[134] But is the presentation really valid?

The first crucial fact to understand is that the author of Hebrews quoted from Psalm 45:6-7 which most agree originally applied to the *human king of Israel*, possibly king Solomon.[135] In the original Psalm, the king was given the title "God" (Heb: *elohim*), representing another example in Scripture where an individual who held a position of authority was appropriately

---

[133] *Jesus as God, The New Testament Use of Theos in Reference to Jesus*, p. 215.

[134] See: Morey, *The Trinity, Evidence and Issues*, pp. 347-350. At one point Morey tries to suggest that the article *ho* before *theos* in Hebrews 1:8 is significant in terms of depicting the Son as "true deity" (in the Trinitarian sense). However, if the term *theos* does apply to the Son in this verse, the significance of "*ho*" actually *changes* from a definite article to the vocative address "O," as in "O God." So if the common translation is correct, *ho* does not even function with the force of a definite article; so it is difficult to understand how Dr. Morey could have attempted to argue for, and lead his readers into accepting, the validity of such an erroneous point.

[135] It was noted in the *Anchor Bible*: "It would be difficult to deduce which Israelite or Jewish king was first addressed in this Psalm as God's anointed one when he was enthroned, but by the time of the author of Hebrews, Ps 45 was sacred scripture which described the power and authority of a king who had been anointed, and anointed ones were called messiahs. Thus when the author of Hebrews took the central figure of Ps 45 to be the Messiah, he expressed a commonly held opinion. He identified the central figure with Jesus, who, as a Son, was also a king, the anointed one and, according to the author, a mighty one who was victorious in battle, who would crush his enemies and ascend to God's throne in his exalted position at God's right hand, from which he would rule justly." —*The Anchor Bible, To the Hebrews, A New Translation with Introduction and Commentary* (New York: Doubleday, 1972), p. 21.

designated by the word or title "God," even though that individual was not actually *the God* in the highest sense. As already discussed, although today many are unaccustomed to the idea that a human ruler could be honored or ascribed with the title "God," in the Hebrew mind—based on the ancient Hebrew culture and writings—this was not something entirely unusual or unheard of; nor did such usage of the term represent a difficulty in terms of their faith in the *one* Most High God of Israel ('biblical monotheism'). As it was perceptively pointed out in the *Tyndale Commentaries*, "since in Hebrew thought the occupant of the throne of David was regarded as God's representative, it is in this sense that the king could be addressed as God."[136] In *The Interpreter's Bible* it was further noted: "Because the rule of the king is marked by the love of equity and righteousness, two results follow. First, the dynasty will be perpetuated. Your throne, O God: In the ancient world kings were commonly accorded divine titles as vicegerents ['holders of delegated authority'] of deity or as belonging to the superhuman class...The Hebrews were acquainted with this usage (cf. 2:7; 89:27; Isa. 9:6)."[137] The footnote in the Dallas-Theological Seminary-sponsored *New English Translation* makes the same point: "Ps 45:6 addresses the Davidic king as 'God' because he ruled and fought as God's *representative* on earth."[138]

Professor Marianne Thompson gives added insight that helps to reinforce the overall point:

> In some instances *theos* ['god' in Greek] or *elohim* ['God' or 'gods' in Hebrew] predicates *a God-given privilege or function of an individual, with the exact nature of that privilege or function determined from context*. In Psalm 45:7, *elohim* certainly refers to the king. Other passages seem to refer to the gods (*elohim*) of the heavenly council (Ps. 82:1, 6 [MT]) or to various sorts of human judgment (Exod. 21:6; 22:7-9). In these passages in Exodus, the Targums [Aramaic paraphrases of the Scriptures] read 'judges' for *elohim*, and later midrashim [Jewish

---
[136] *Tyndale New Testament Commentaries, The Letter to the Hebrews*, p. 76 (emphasis added).
[137] *The Interpreter's Bible*, Volume 4, p. 237. One dictionary defines a "vicegerent" as "a person appointed by a ruler or head of state to act as an administrative deputy."
[138] Commenting on Isaiah 9:6 (emphasis added).

commentaries on the OT compiled between A.D. 400 and 1200] offer variations such as 'the judgment seat of God.' When *elohim* refers to heavenly beings, the LXX typically renders it as 'angels' (*angeloi*, Ps. 96:7; Job 1:6) or 'sons of God' (*huioi theou*, Deut. 32:43).[139]

Not only is it important to appreciate the point that the human king of Israel was properly given the title "God," it should be noted that, in the following verse, the king is spoken of as having one who is God to him: "Therefore *God, Your God*, has anointed you with the oil of gladness above your companions." Thus the application of the term "God" (Heb: *elohim*; *theos* in Greek) toward the king of Israel is put into clearer perspective once one takes into account that the king is not "God" in the absolute, unqualified sense; because although, as king, he is fittingly called "God," it remains true that the God of Israel, the Most High, is God to the king.

Trinitarian Murray Harris, in his book, *Jesus as God*, gives an exegesis for the original reference (again, quoted by the author of Hebrews in verses 1:8-9 and applied to the Son), providing helpful confirmation for the same point. He makes the point that, "the king himself, however elevated his person or office, must never forget that Yahweh is his *elohim* [God]"; and that, "He [the writer of the Psalm] forestalls misunderstanding by indicating that the king is not *elohim* without qualification. Yahweh is the king's God."[140]

In order to properly understand the *sense* in which the term "God" would fittingly apply to Jesus Christ at Hebrews 1:8, we cannot overlook the fact that all of the elements present in Psalm 45 (originally applying to the king of Israel) also figure into the author of Hebrews' quotation; but this time, the passage is applied to the Son of God. If all the elements are the same, why would we come to any other conclusion than that the Godship possessed by the Lord Jesus Christ—like the king to whom the Scripture originally applied—is *qualified* by the fact

---

[139] Thompson, *The God of the Gospel of John*, p. 32.
[140] Harris, *Jesus as God*, pp. 199-202. Additionally, Harris notes that "on occasion *elohim* is used of the heavenly beings around Yahweh's throne" and identifies the following scriptures as cases where *elohim* is applied to others: angels: Ps. 8:6; 97:7; 138:1, judges: Ps. 82:1, 6; Ps. 58:2, John 10:34-36, and Moses: Exod. 7:1; cf 4:16."

The Apostolic Testimony

that there is one who is God to him; and that because the Son is said to have one who is God to him,—the God that is said to have 'anointed' him—this effectively prevents the readers from misunderstanding the sense in which he rightfully bears the *theos* description.[141]

A human king was appropriately called "God." But we can be sure that he was not, and was not considered to be, *the Almighty God*, because the very next verse reveals that he himself has a God. Is it unreasonable to think that the same would apply to Christ if the same fact is true of him? In other words, if the verse is translated correctly,[142] and Christ is designated "God" by the Father, our understanding of the Godship possessed by Christ will, of necessity, be governed by the fact that he is spoken of as the kind of "*theos*" that has one who is "*theos*" to or above him. The *only* way it would not is if we were to disregard the actual elements present within the citation. At the same time, it is necessary that we take into account the way the word "God" was used in the Scriptures when trying to figure out what this text means or any other text that may be said to apply the term "God" to Jesus Christ.

It is, in fact, *undeniable* that the Godship ascribed to Jesus (and the Israelite king to whom the text originally applied) is qualified by the fact that, even in his exalted 'God-status' (*theos*), the Lord Jesus still has one who is 'God' (*theos*) above him. Almighty God, however, does not have one who is God to or above him. That's what makes him the Almighty and Most

---

[141] One writer, who discerned the flaw in the traditional Trinitarian interpretation of this verse, wrote: "Observe, therefore, which is the point of our argument in this case, that, even when spoken of as God, there is the Supreme God over him, from whom he receives his anointing, and by whom he is raised above his equals…In reading [the writer of Hebrews' words] we perceive that the exaltation of Christ is greater than we can fully comprehend. But at the same time we perceive, with equal plainness, delegated authority and absolute dependence on the Father."
—*The Doctrine of the Double Nature of Christ*, p. 4.

[142] Harris was correct when he pointed out: "The God who addresses his Son as 'God' is also God to his Son, even his exalted Son. Whether *ho theos* in verse 9 is nominative or vocative, *ho theos sou* ['your God' lit., 'the God of you'] remains. In addition, the eternal sovereignty that Jesus now exercises was accorded him as a gracious gift of God (v. 8a)…Also, it was the Son's God who anointed him with the 'oil of gladness' (v. 9). This element of the subordination of Jesus to his Father, a characteristic of NT Christology, is much in evidence elsewhere in Hebrews. The Son was dependent on God for his appointment as heir of the universe (1:2) and to the office of high priest (3:2; 5:5, 10), for his 'introduction' into the world (1:6), for the preparation of his body (10:5), for his resurrection (13:20), and for his exaltation to his Father's right hand (1:13)."
—*Jesus as God*, p. 226.

High God. The same cannot be said of Jesus, however, for even in his honorific and authoritative condition as *theos* and as *kurios*, Jesus still has one who is God to him, contrary to the clearly-articulated principles of Trinitarian theology (compare Ephesians 1:17).[143]

Hebrews 1:10-12

The very next verse in Hebrews chapter one is similar to Hebrews 1:8-9 in the sense that a text from the Old Testament that originally applied to one individual was applied to Jesus Christ for a specific purpose. In this case, a text that originally applied to Jehovah God himself in the book of Psalms (102:25-27) is now applied to God's Son.

> **And, 'You founded the earth in the beginning, Lord, and the heavens are the works of your hands. They will perish, but you continue. And they will all grow old like a garment, and like a robe you will fold them up and like a garment they will be changed, but you are the same and your years will never run out.'**[144]

Most evangelical theologians argue that because this text originally applied to God and is now applied to Christ by the writer of Hebrews, this means (or provides additional confirmation) that Jesus Christ is one divine person within a consubstantial Trinitarian Deity. Perhaps even more importantly, in the viewpoint of Trinitarian apologists, the text says that "the

---

[143] As pointed out in a previous footnote, Trinitarians generally claim that the Father *is* the God of Jesus *only* as it applies to Jesus' "human" nature. Compare the statement made by Tsoukalas: "By virtue of His *humanity*, and in keeping with biblical Trinitarianism, Jesus may state that the Father is His God, and at the same time not deny that he is God *the Son.*" —*Knowing Christ in the Challenge of Heresies*; footnotes, page 84 (emphasis added). However, in Hebrews 1:8, Jesus is called "God" and Trinitarians typically argue that this would denote his "absolute" and "coequal" deity with the Father. Yet in the very next verse (in the context of his *Godship*), Jesus is spoken of as having one who is God to him. If it is true that the application of *theos* to Christ in this verse denotes "coequal" deity with the Father, how can he then be spoken of as one who has a God to or above him? Similarly, Trinitarians argue the when Jesus is called "Lord" in the Scriptures that this is a title conveying the notion of "absolute deity." For example, in *The Forgotten Trinity* (p. 128), Dr. White claims: "Both [titles 'God' in reference to the Father, and 'Lord' in reference to Christ] are titles of deity..." Yet White fails to take into consideration that the Father is described in Scripture as *"the God* of our *Lord* Jesus Christ" (Ephesians 1:17). How can "(absolute) deity" ('Lord') have one who is "God" to him?

[144] Hebrews 1:10-12, *New English Translation*

heavens are the works of [his] hands"—ascribing to the Son the work of creation—and that, unlike the heavens, the Son will "remain" and his "years will never run out"—implying, in the viewpoint of many Trinitarians, the "eternality" of the Son.

In his popular and widely-read work, *The Forgotten Trinity*, well-known apologist and public debater, James White, argued the following based upon these particular references:

> [This passage] is speaking of characteristics that are *unique to the one true God.'*...The fact that it is speaking of *unique characteristics* [according to White: 'creatorship,' 'immutability,' and 'eternality'] *of the true God* is likewise unarguable. Therefore, the fact that Hebrews applies such a passage to the Son tells us what the writer himself believed about the nature of Jesus Christ. *One simply could not meaningfully apply such a passage to a mere creature, no matter how highly exalted.* What does it mean that the writer to the Hebrews could take a passage that *is only applicable to Yahweh* and apply it to the Son of God, Jesus Christ? It means that they saw no problem in making such identification, because they believed that the Son was, indeed, the very incarnation of Yahweh.[145]

Dr. White not only believes this text proves that Jesus Christ is the Creator, God, but that what is described in this passage is "only applicable Yahweh," and that therefore the writer of Hebrews believed Jesus to be the very incarnation of God.

What is often overlooked in regard to this Old Testament scriptural application to the Son is the fact that the writer of Hebrews, in verse two, had already revealed that someone else created the worlds/ages; specifically, that "God" created the worlds/ages, and that he did so "in/through" or "by means of" the "Son." The point is, in the preceding part of the same chapter, the writer already described the Son's (intermediary) role with respect to the creation in view in very specific terms, and that that specific description cannot be rightfully divorced from our understanding of Hebrews 1:10-12. *God* is the creator

---

[145] White, *The Forgotten Trinity*, pp. 133-134.

The Apostolic Testimony

of the universe (if the term 'ages' can be understood that way at this point); but, as Donald Guthrie correctly points out in the *Tyndale Commentaries*, "Christ is the agent through whom [the universe (more lit., ages)] was made." Guthrie goes on to observe: "The statement that God created the world through the Son is staggering. There is no denying that God could have made the universe apart from his Son, but the New Testament is at pains to show that he did not do so."[146]

The comments made in *The Interpreter's Bible* are likewise helpful at this point. It was correctly noted that the author's quotation is taken from Psalm 102:25-27, and that "these verses originally expressed the creative power of God and his permanence as against the transient creation. The LXX [*Septuagint* translation], however, introduces the vocative *kurie*, 'Lord,' *which permits our author to apply the words to the Son.*"[147] F. F. Bruce's commentary on this text is also beneficial.

> The words in which the psalmist addresses God, however, are here applied to the Son, as clearly as the words of Ps. 45:6f. were applied to him in vv.8 and 9. *What justification can be pleaded for our author's applying them thus?* First, as he has already said in v. 2. It was *through* the Son that the universe was made. The angels were but worshipping spectators when the earth was founded (Job 38:7), but *the Son was the Father's agent in the work. He therefore could be understood as the one who is addressed in the words: Of old thou didst lay the foundation of the earth; And the heavens are the work of thy hands.* Moreover, in the Septuagint text the person to whom these words are spoken is addressed explicitly as 'Lord' ('Thou, Lord, in the beginning didst lay the foundation of the earth'): and it is God who addresses him as thus...But to whom (a Christian reader of the Septuagint might well ask) could God speak in words like

---

[146] *Tyndale New Testament Commentaries, The Letter to the Hebrews, An Introduction and Commentary*, p. 65. The internationally-respected Swiss theologian and Trinitarian, Emil Brünner, pointed out that "the Son is called simply and solely the mediator of the Creation...The title ['creator'] is given to the Father alone." And in a footnote Brünner observes: "The Psalm-quotation in Hebrews 1:10 should not be used as an argument against the explicit doctrine of 1:2." —*The Christian Doctrine of God, Dogmatics*, Vol. I, p. 232.

[147] *The Interpreter's Bible, Volume XI*, p. 607. It was also noted, "the writer is clear that one of the divine functions of the Son was that of being *the agent of Creation*. This quotation is a graphic way of stating the eternity of the Son's dominion" (emphasis added).

these? And whom would God himself address as 'Lord,' as the maker of earth and heaven? Our author knows one person only to whom such terms could be appropriate, and that is the Son of God.[148]

With respect to how the author of Hebrews could legitimately apply a text to Christ that originally applied to his Father's creative work, Donald Guthrie stated similarly:

> The next three verses create a problem because the passage cited from Psalm 102:25-27 contains no reference to the Son. In the Septuagint verses 1-22 are addressed to God, but verses 1-22 consist of the answer. The writer understands God to be the speaker here. *In his mind it was legitimate to transfer to the Son what applied to God*, since he has already drawn attention to the eternal character of his throne. The passage has many interesting features which are apt when applied to Jesus Christ. *The writer has already spoken of the Son's part in creation [v. 2] and in view of this the Psalm 102 passage is appropriate.*[149]

Although one might say that "one simply could not meaningfully apply such a passage to a mere creature, no matter how highly exalted," one could, in fact—as the author of Hebrews did—*meaningfully* apply such a passage to the one "through whom God created the universe [lit., 'ages,'] (*TEV*)"—Jesus Christ, God's unique Son.[150]

The following part of the Old Testament quotation is also significant to the discussion. The fact that the Son is spoken of—in contrast to the aging heavens—as one who would "continue [as] the same" and as one whose "years will never run

---

[148] *The Book of Hebrews, The New International Commentary on the New Testament*, Revised Edition (Grand Rapids: Eerdmans, 1990), pp. 62-63 (emphasis added).

[149] *Tyndale New Testament Commentaries, The Letter to the Hebrews*, pp. 77, 78 (emphasis and word notation on verse added).

[150] Actually, the entire description of the Son as the one "through whom God created the ages," along with the application of Psalm 102:25-27 to the Son, may not even have reference to the original creation depicted in the Genesis account; but rather, to the *new* creation, the new Messianic order effected by God through the Son. For the very Psalm from which the author of Hebrews quotes states: "Let this be recorded for *a generation to come*, so that *a people yet to be created* [*a people not yet born*, *NAB*] may praise the LORD." And in Hebrews 2:5, the author writes: "For it was not to angels that God subjected *the world to come*, *of which we are speaking*."

out" does indeed speak for the "immutability" of the Son. However, such "immutability" or "changelessness" does not demand, in and of itself, that the Son is 'without beginning,' and that he should therefore be thought of as an *eternal* member a triune God. Nor does any concept of a Trinity appear in this letter. The statement does demand, however, the meaning that the Son *will always exist* and that his years will never come to completion. In other words, the Son is *immortal*—not subject to decay or death.

In light of the overall context and points made by the author, such descriptions may constitute a further reflection (or expansion) on the fact that the Son's kingdom will remain in place forever (Heb. 1:8-9), in connection with his immortal and unchanging nature, especially so since the time of the Son's resurrection and exaltation to the right hand of God. One may even remember the prophetic words spoken to Mary by the heavenly messenger before Jesus' birth: "He will be great, and will be called the Son of the Most High; and the Lord God will give to him the throne of his father David, and *he will reign over the house of Jacob for ever; and of his kingdom there will be no end.*"[151] Likewise, the focus in Hebrews 1:10-12 is not on an eternal existence (past, present and future). There is, rather, an emphasis on Christ's *present* condition, at the same time, *looking forward* to the constancy and everlasting nature of Christ's person and glorious existence.

In the same letter, chapter 13, verse 8, the author says: "Jesus Christ is the same today, yesterday, and forever." Concerning this statement (which *does* have reference to past, present and future), John Calvin commented: "The apostle is speaking not of Christ as he is in eternity, but of our knowledge of him...He is not speaking of Christ's being but, so to say, of his quality, or of how he acts toward us."[152] Similarly, in Hebrews 1:10-12 (which contains in it no reference to past existence), there is nothing in the words themselves ('you continue,' 'you are the same and your years will never run out') that demand the meaning "eternity-into-the-past." The expressions used more

---

[151] Luke 1:32-33, *RSV*
[152] Quoted in Timothy George, *Theology of the Reformers* (Nashville: Broadman & Holman Publishers, 1998), p. 100 (*Commentaries*, p. 160).

likely serve to emphasize the incorruptible nature of the Son's immortal existence since his resurrection to life eternal, in light of the permanent, immutable and *superior* character of the Son's throne and related rulership as God's appointed Messianic King. As the apostle Paul said in another place: "We know that since Christ has been raised from the dead, *he is never going to die again*; death no longer has mastery over him. For the death he died, he died to sin once for all, but the life he lives, he lives to God."[153] And as it was wisely observed in the *Tyndale Commentaries*: "In applying the passage, the writer draws attention to a profound idea about the Son, i.e. his changelessness. The earth and heavens seem substantial enough, yet they will perish...This magnificent glimpse by the psalmist into the winding up of the present age is intended to lead to the climax: *But thou are the same.* In the face of the disintegration everywhere else, the unchangeable character of the Son stands out in unmistakable contrast."[154]

The themes of the Son's unchangeable character, and that of the Son's "immortal" or "incorruptible" life, are important features of the book of Hebrews in general; for such a never-ending life was necessary to the mediatorial function of Christ's perpetual heavenly priesthood ('you are a priest forever,' Hebrews 6:5). As discussed later in the letter to the Hebrews, in the time under the law covenant—based on their physical membership of that particular ancestry—only men from the tribe of Levi were appointed to the priestly duties associated with the tabernacle and, later, with the temple in Jerusalem. But the office of high priest held by God's Son is far superior; for he is, as the author of Hebrews points out, "one who has become a priest not on the basis of a regulation as to his ancestry but *on the basis of the power of an indestructible life.*"[155] This is why the author goes on to say:

---

[153] Romans 6:9, 10, *NET* (emphasis added).
[154] *The Letter to the Hebrews,* Donald Guthrie, pp. 77, 78 (emphasis added).
[155] Hebrews 7:16, *NIV*. Says Donald Guthrie: "Although our high priest died, and his death was essentially a part of his priestly office, yet he can still be described as *indestructible* ['*akatalytou*, literally incapable of being dissolved,'...]. Death could not hold him. His high-priestly office continues by virtue of his risen life. If for no other reason, this fact would set him immeasurably above all the priests of Aaron's line...Although Jesus, our high priest, died, his priesthood did not cease, neither was it passed on to others, because his death was not a final act. It was eclipsed by

The Apostolic Testimony

For it is declared: 'You are a priest forever, in the order of Melchizedek.' The former regulation is set aside because it was weak and useless (for the law made nothing perfect), and a better hope is introduced, by which we draw near to God. And it was not without an oath! Others became priests without any oath, but he became a priest with an oath when God said to him: 'The Lord has sworn and will not change his mind: 'You are a priest forever.' Because of this oath, Jesus has become the guarantee of a better covenant. Now there have been many of those priests, since death prevented them from continuing in office; but because Jesus lives forever, he has a permanent priesthood. Therefore he is able [now and always, *TEV*] to save completely those who come to God through him, because *he always lives* to intercede for them.[156]

John 12:41

> *"When Jesus had said these things, he departed and hid himself from them. Though he had done so many signs before them, they still did not believe in him, so that the word spoken by the prophet Isaiah might be fulfilled: 'Lord, who has believed what he heard from us, and to whom has the arm of the Lord been revealed' [Isaiah 53:1]? Therefore they could not believe. For again Isaiah said, 'He has blinded their eyes and hardened their heart, lest they see with their eyes, and understand with their heart, and turn, and I would heal them.' [Isaiah 6:10] Isaiah said these things because he saw his glory and spoke of him."* —John 12:36-41, ESV

Trinitarian apologists consider the statement in John 12:41 (*'Isaiah said these things because he saw [Jesus'] glory and spoke of him'*) to be one of the strongest proof-texts for the "deity" of Christ in the New Testament, understood in the

---

his resurrection (*he continues forever*), thus setting him apart from all other priests." —*Tyndale New Testament Commentaries*, pp. 163, 166.

[156] Hebrews 7:15-25, *NIV* (emphasis added). Unlike the priesthood service performed under the Mosaic Law covenant on behalf of the people of Israel, a new, heavenly, and far superior priestly mediation is now being performed on behalf of all exercising faith in the appointment of "a Son who has been made perfect for ever" (Hebrews 7:28, *RSV*).

The Apostolic Testimony

orthodox Trinitarian sense. Evangelical Arthur W. Pink, for example, described this verse as a "striking testimony to the absolute Deity of Christ."[157] In the early 1800s, the Methodist Adam Clarke wrote: "It appears evident, from this passage, that the glory which the prophet saw was the glory of Jehovah: John, therefore, is saying here that it was the glory of Jesus, showing that he considered Jesus to be Jehovah."[158] The contemporary pastor John MacArthur likewise argued, "Isaiah 6:10, which John had just quoted, referred to Isaiah's vision of God (cf. Isa. 6:1-5). That the apostle applied it to Jesus Christ clearly testifies to his Deity."[159] In agreement, another modern commentary explained the interpretation with even more specificity: "Isaiah had seen the Lord of glory, who is none other than Jesus himself—Jesus is God, yet he is also a distinct part of the mysterious Trinity, and he is also Jesus the Son."[160]

Since previous to John 12:41 (verses 39-40) John quoted from Isaiah 6:10, and nine verses earlier, in the same chapter, it is said that the prophet "saw the Lord/Jehovah sitting upon a throne, high and lifted up" (6:1-3), and that "the whole earth" was "full" of Jehovah's "glory" (the cry of the seraphim in 6:3), when John said that Isaiah "saw [Jesus'] glory" in 12:41, Trinitarians reason that John was intentionally making the point that Jesus Christ and Jehovah God are one and the same—with particular emphasis on the fact that in both texts (John 12:41; Isaiah 6:1-3) the terms "saw" and "glory" are present. That is, for Trinitarians, "Isaiah said these things because he saw his glory" means, essentially, *"Isaiah said these things because he saw Jesus' glory as Jehovah God in a pre-incarnate state in the temple vision of Isaiah 6:1-5."* Therefore, Jesus *is* Jehovah—understood as the second "person" of the alleged "triune" God.

Although the argument is widely accepted, many do not realize that when apologist James White, for example, makes the dogmatic claim that "the only way to define what 'glory' Isaiah saw was to refer to the glory of Isaiah 6:3," and that there is "none other whose glory we can connect with Isaiah's words,"

---

[157] *Exposition of the Gospel of John, Volume One* (Grand Rapids: Zondervan, 1945), p. 282.
[158] *Clarkes' Commentary, Matthew-Revelation* (Nashville: Abingdon Press, 1810), p. 614.
[159] *The MacArthur New Testament Commentary*, John 12-21 (Chicago: Moody, 2008), p. 53.
[160] *Life Application Bible Commentary* (Wheaton: Tyndale House Publishers, 2003), p. 263.

The Apostolic Testimony

he is wrong.[161] In fact, the future "glory" of the promised Messiah, Jesus, is clearly depicted in the writings of Isaiah, not only in the surrounding context of Isaiah 53:1 (also quoted by John in 12:38), but throughout the writings of Isaiah overall, from the beginning to the ending sections (4:2; 9:6-7; 11:1-10; 16:5; 32:1; 33:17; 42:1-4; 49:1-6; 52:13-15; 61:1-3).

The following will explain, point-by-point, why the Trinitarian argument is an interpretative error, based on the prevailing tendency to read post-biblical Trinitarian concepts into Scripture.

1. John said, "**Isaiah said these things [Isaiah 53:1; Isaiah 6:10] because he saw his [the Messiah's] glory and spoke of him**" (John 12:41).

In this case, John's statement is a clear reference to Jesus, the Messiah, not Jehovah God. In all the Messianic references found throughout the book of Isaiah, the prophet never identifies the Messiah *as* Jehovah but as "the branch of Jehovah" (4:2), as the one upon whom Jehovah's "spirit" would be "upon" and "rest" (11:2; 61:1), as one whose "delight shall be in the fear of Jehovah" (11:3), as Jehovah's "chosen one, in whom [Jehovah's] soul delights," as Jehovah's wise and exalted "servant" (42:1; 52:13), as one who, prophetically, "grew up before Jehovah like a young plant" (53:2), as the one on whom Jehovah would lay "the iniquity of us all" (53:6), as the one Jehovah would "crush" in accordance with his "will," and the one in whose hand "the will of Jehovah shall prosper" (53:10). And, in harmony with these and all other biblical texts, Jehovah himself is portrayed as the "God" *of* the Messiah, not as the Messiah himself (49:5).

In no case does the prophet confuse the identities of Jehovah and the Messiah (Jehovah's 'servant'); nor does the

---

[161] White, *The Forgotten Trinity* (Minneapolis: Bethany House, 1998), p. 137. Although ultimately supportive of James White and other Trinitarians in the interpretation of John 12:41, in contrast to White's unwarranted dogmatism on this point, C. H. Williams correctly pointed out: "The clause 'Isaiah said these things (*tauta*)' (12:41a), need not, in this respect, relate solely to the quotation drawn from Isa. 6:10, but can embrace both quotations. John's Christological application in 12:41 can then be explained as follows: the prophetic testimony presented by Isaiah (53:1; 6:10) reflects his vision of Jesus' earthly glory (12:41b: 'because he saw his glory'), which enabled him to speak as he did about Jesus' earthly mission and to predict the unbelief that Jesus would encounter during his earthly life (12:41c: 'and spoke about him'). —*Isaiah in the New Testament*, Edited by Steve Moyise and M. J. J. Menken (London: T&T Clark: 2005), pp. 112-113.

prophet ever somehow merge their distinct identities into one. This, of course, harmonizes with all biblical texts that consistently portray Jehovah and the Messiah as two distinct figures (Compare, for example, Psalm 110:1; Daniel 7:13; Micah 5:4; Acts 3:13; John 17:3). That is, once it is established that John 12:41 is a reference to Jesus, *the Messiah*, we automatically know, scripturally speaking, that John's statement in 12:41 is not a reference to Jehovah as portrayed in Isaiah 6:1-5, particularly in such a way that would identify the Messiah *as* Jehovah, simply because Jehovah and the Messiah are, in every relevant scriptural example, presented as two distinct figures, with one (the Messiah) being "sent" by the other (Jehovah), with one (Jehovah) who is "greater" than the other (the Messiah), and with one (Jehovah) as the "God" of the other (the Messiah).[162]

2. Although there is a reference to the "glory" that filled the dwelling place of Jehovah in Isaiah 6:1 (LXX),—"*...and the house was full of his glory*," with the seraphim announcing, "*the whole earth is full of [Jehovah's] glory*" (v. 3, LXX; MT)— Isaiah is, again, writing about his glorious vision of Jehovah God, not the Messiah.

3. Trinitarian James White asserts that the Isaiah 6 passage is "the primary reference" we should look to for our understanding of John 12:41. He argues: "John speaks of Isaiah 'seeing' 'glory.' In Isaiah 6:1 the very same term is used of 'seeing' the LORD, and the very term 'glory' Isaiah saw was to refer to the glory of Isaiah 6:3." Therefore, according to White, Jesus is "None other than the eternal God in human flesh, Yahweh.[163]

As mentioned, White's argument at this point is short-sighted and erroneous. In the Septuagint translation of Isaiah 52:13-15—part of the same context as Isaiah 53:1, also referenced by John as among the "things" Isaiah "said" because he "saw" the Messiah's "glory"—it can be properly said that Isaiah, in his role as a prophet and visionary, "saw" the future "glory" of the Messiah and "spoke about him," especially so given that there are two explicit references in the Septuagint to

---

[162] Isaiah 61:1; John 5:30; 13:16; 14:28; Micah 5:2; Mark. 15:34; John. 20:17; Romans 15:6; Ephesians 1:17; Hebrews 1:9.
[163] *The Forgotten Trinity*, pp. 137, 138.

the Messiah's future glorification (or exceedingly-glorified-state) and "glory" which would "not be honored by the sons of men," precisely what takes place in the peoples' unbelief as described in John 12:37-40. Isaiah 52:13-15 in the Septuagint reads:

> "Behold, my servant shall understand, and be exalted, and *glorified exceedingly*. As many shall be amazed at you, so shall your face be without glory from men, and *your glory shall not be honored by the sons of men*. Thus shall many nations wonder at him; and kings shall keep their mouths shut..."[164]

4. Since reference is made to "**these things**" (plural), John's statement should apparently be understood as follows: "Isaiah said these things—'*Lord, who has believed our report? And to whom has the arm of the Lord been revealed?*'(Isaiah 53:1), and '*He has blinded their eyes and he hardened their heart, so that they would not see with their eyes and perceive with their heart...*' (Isaiah 6:10)—because Isaiah saw the Messiah's glory and spoke of him."

But why did John say that the prophet said *these things* (Isaiah 53:1; 6:10) "**because**" he saw the Messiah's glory and spoke about him?

Evidently, Isaiah said "these things"—the "things" regarding the peoples' blindness, hardness of heart, lack of perception, and unbelief—because Isaiah "saw" the same "glory" of the Messiah that would, *due to blindness and hardness of heart*, "not be honored by the sons of men" (52:14, LXX); again, the very occurrence described in John 12:37-38. In other words, as the apostle John reports, though Jesus "had done so many signs before them"—a clear demonstration of his Messianic "glory"—the people still did not believe nor honor him as the Messiah sent by God; and all of this was foreseen by Isaiah and foretold in his writings.

That the "glory" of Jesus was made manifest through the powerful "signs" he performed is made clear in John 2:11, where the apostle reports: "**Jesus did this** [the changing of water into

---

[164] Note also that Isaiah 53:1—quoted by John in this context (John 12:38)—is more closely-connected to Isaiah 52:13 than Isaiah 6:10 is to Isaiah 6:1-3—a closer reference by 4 verses respectively, according to the present division of the English Bible.

The Apostolic Testimony

wine] **as the beginning of his *signs* in Cana in Galilee *and so revealed his glory*, and his disciples began to believe in him**" (John 2:11, *NAB*). In stark contrast to this, the apostle says of the Jews in John chapter 12:37: "**Though he had done so many signs before them, they still did not believe in him.**"

That is, again, in John chapter 12, the people still did not put faith in Jesus even though he had displayed powerful "signs" before them—"signs" that represented a clear manifestation of the Messiah's "glory." This clearly demonstrates that the "glory" John said Isaiah "saw" could have been the glory Jesus manifested in his signs but which "the sons of men" (the Jews of John chapter 12) did not honor since "they still did not believe in him" (Compare Isaiah 52:14, Septuagint). As it was rightly pointed out in the article *Isaiah in the Gospel of John* by C. H. Williams: "…those who rejected Jesus have failed to see the revelation of 'the arm of the Lord' in his signs. John 12:37-38 therefore emphasizes that most people did not believe in Jesus despite the one aspect of his ministry that was most likely to produce faith, his visible manifestations of power."[165]

5. Dr. White is in error when he argues that Isaiah 6—as opposed to Isaiah 52/53—should be viewed as the "primary reference" for John 12:41.While both texts should evidently be taken into account ('these things [53:1; 6:10]' Isaiah said…'), there are, in fact, more connections to be found between John 12 and Isaiah 52/53 than with the similar language-elements ('saw' and 'glory') between John 12:41 and Isaiah 6:1-5.[166]

As mentioned, in Isaiah chapter 6, no clear reference to the Messiah is ever made; only a vision of Jehovah God exalted in the house that was filled with Jehovah's "glory." In fact,

---

[165] *Isaiah in the New Testament*, p. 108.
[166] Greg Stafford noted that in Isaiah 52:13, "Jehovah uses a demonstrative particle 'Look!' or 'Behold!' (Hebrew: *hineh*) pointing to his 'servant' who will be 'elevated and exalted very much,' which translates three different Hebrew words (*rum* ['lift up,' or 'be exalted'], *nasa'* ['lift up,' or 'be exalted'], and *gavah* ['be high,' or 'exalted']). The LXX [Septuagint] translates the underlined portions of 52:13 as 'Look! My servant…will be lifted up [Greek: *hypsothesetai*] and glorified extremely [*doxasthesetai sphodra*].' *Sphodra* is a Greek adverb meaning 'extremely' or 'greatly,' and here it modifies the Greek verb *doxazo*, which in reference to the Messiah or Christ means to 'glorify.' Isaiah then proceeds to 'see' this 'extreme glory' in the manner in which the Christ would appear and the affect he would have on 'many nations.' John uses the same verb 'lifted up' or 'exalted' (*hypso'o*) in John 12:32 that is used here in Isaiah 52:13 (LXX), both in reference to the humanity and death of the Christ." —*Response to Dr. James White Part Two: "He Saw His Glory, and He Spoke About Him."*

nowhere in Isaiah's vision of Jehovah in the temple scene does the prophet go on to clearly "speak about" the Messiah.

In Isaiah 53, however, immediately after the statement *"Who has believed what he has heard from us? And to whom has the arm of Jehovah been revealed?"*, the prophet goes on specifically to "speak about" the Messiah from verse 2 all the way through verse 12, quite explicitly and in great detail. The entire chapter is, in fact, about the suffering "servant," the foretold Messiah who would "come up like a twig" and "like a root out of waterless land." According to the prophet, the servant would be "despised and rejected by men," "wounded for our transgressions," "crushed for our iniquities," pouring out "his soul to the very death." Yet, after being victorious over death, he would "divide the spoil with the strong," "bring a righteous standing to many," and make "intercession for the transgressors." This demonstrates that the one who "spoke about" such things—Isaiah—was among the prophets mentioned by the apostle Peter who, long ago, "foretold the *sufferings* of Christ and the *glories to follow*", and, particularly in Isaiah 52-53, "saw his glory and spoke of him" (1 Peter 1:11; John 12:41).

In support of this conclusion, D.A. Carson observed that, in John chapter 12, the apostle "may well be thinking of the Suffering Servant who was exalted…what makes it very likely is the dozen or so overtones of Isaiah 52:13-53:12 found within John 12 that show the Evangelist had the Servant Song in mind when he composed this chapter."[167]

In response to James White, Greg Stafford made the same basic point, only with further supporting evidence:

> There is nothing anywhere in John 12 about Jesus being 'Yahweh,' and certainly there is nothing in Isaiah 6:10 or in Isaiah 53:1, or in their quotation and use by John in John 12, that makes such a point. Dr. White simply embeds Isaiah 6:1 into John 12:37-41 when we only have Isaiah 6:10 and Isaiah 53:1 used by John, the latter of which is where Isaiah 'speaks about him' and in the former of which he (Isaiah) 'speaks about them' (the Jews).

---

[167] *The Pillar New Testament Commentary, The Gospel According to John* (Grand Rapids: Eerdmans, 1991), pp. 449-450.

The Apostolic Testimony

Throughout John 12 John 'speaks about him' in the same way that Isaiah did in Isaiah 52/53, by describing or narrating the description of Jesus' being 'lifted up' and 'glorified' through his death and suffering, which 'glory' Isaiah 'saw' and 'spoke about' from Isaiah 52:9 (possibly 52:7) through the end of Chapter 53, part of which is quoted by John in John 12:38...The teaching of John 12:41 is simple, straightforward, and otherwise clear. Isaiah saw the 'glory' of the Christ's humanity, suffering, and death for our sins while being dishonoured among men, which John develops throughout John 12 and specifically from verse 16 onward (see John 12:16, 23, 32-34, 37-41), using the same verbs (*doxazo, hypso'o, pistueo,* and *horao*) and the same substantive (*doxa*) as we find in the LXX of Isaiah 52:10, 13, 14, 15 and Isaiah 53:1, 2, and 4. John notes that, like the 'Suffering Servant' of Isaiah 52/53 (specifically 53:1 which he quotes in John 12:38), the crowd did not 'put faith in him [Jesus]' (John 12:36, 37 [where, again, in both texts and in verse 38 we find forms of *pistueo*]), which is exactly the same language Isaiah used when speaking of the Messiah: 'Jehovah, who has believed [LXX: *epistuese* (form of *pistueo*) our report? And to whom has the arm of Jehovah been revealed?'[168]

It was similarly noted in the *New International Biblical Commentary*: "John's Gospel has been using the same verbs, 'lifted up' (v. 32; cf. 3:14; 8:28) and 'glorified' (vv. 16, 23; cf. 11:4) in reference to Jesus and his approaching death; it is likely that his choice of these words presupposes (as do many other NT passages) the identification of Jesus with the suffering servant whose career is prophetically sketched in Isaiah 52:13-53:12."[169]

Another evangelical scholar explicitly contradicted the traditional Trinitarian apologetic approach to John 12:41, with good reason:

"The first passage cited is Isa. 53:1 LXX (cf. Rom. 10:16). In the original context, reference is made to the Servant of the Lord, who was rejected by the people but exalted by God (cf. Isa. 52:13-15). In John, the verse is applied to

---

[168] Isaiah 53:1; John 12:38. Stafford, *Response to Dr. James White Part Two: "He Saw His Glory, and He Spoke About Him."*
[169] *New International Biblical Commentary, John,* J. Ramsey Michaels, p. 222

The Apostolic Testimony

Jesus the Messiah, who is that promised Servant, and to the rejection of his message and signs ('arm of the Lord') by the Jews...In the wake of two Isaianic quotes in 12:38 and 12:40, the evangelist concludes that 'Isaiah saw Jesus' glory' (cf. 8:56). In light of the preceding quotation of Isa. 6:10, some say that the background for the present statement is the call narrative in Isaiah 6. Yet though *autou* (his) probably refers to Jesus, John does not actually say that Isaiah saw *Jesus*, but that he saw Jesus' glory. Hence, it is not necessary to conclude that the evangelist believed that Isaiah saw 'the pre-existent Christ' (Schnackenburg 1990: 2.416; cf. Talbert 1992: 180; D. B. Smith 1999: 244) or that he saw Jesus 'in some pre-incarnate fashion' (Carson 1991: 449). Rather, Isaiah foresaw that God was pleased with a suffering Servant who would be 'raised and lifted up and highly exalted' (52:13), yet who was 'pierced for our transgressions' and 'bore the sins of many' (53:5, 12)...Hence, Isaiah knew that God's glory would be revealed through a suffering Messiah—something deemed impossible by the crowds (John 12:34). Like Abraham, Isaiah saw Jesus' 'day' (cf. John 8:56, 58)."[170]

6. Indeed it is possible, and quite likely, that the Gospel writer said Isaiah "saw" the Messiah's glory in a similar sense that Jesus said "**Abraham rejoiced to see [the Messiah's] day, he saw it and was glad**" (John 8:56). That is, there doesn't seem to be any one text in Genesis where Abraham is explicitly portrayed as 'seeing' the Messiah's "day"[171]; so Jesus' statement probably embraces the overall sense in which Abraham looked

---

[170] *Baker Exegetical Commentary on the New Testament* (Baker Academic: Grand Rapids, 2004), pp. 390-392. It is worth noting that Andreas Köstenberger (Ph.D., Trinity Evangelical Divinity School), the commentator who contradicts White on this point, is not only Trinitarian but Professor of New Testament and Director of Ph.D/Th.M. studies at Southeastern Baptist Theological Seminary. He is also "a prolific author, distinguished evangelical scholar, and Editor of the *Journal of the Evangelical Theological Society*."

[171] On this point it was remarked in the *NIV Study Bible* (p. 1610): "Jesus probably was not referring to any one occasion but to Abraham's general joy in the fulfilling of the purposes of God in Christ, by which all nations on earth would receive blessing (Ge. 18:18). *he saw it.* In faith, from afar." Albert Barnes wrote: "To see here means to have a view or distinct conceptions of. It does not imply that Abraham *expected* that the Messiah would appear during his life, but that he might have a representation of, or a clear description and foresight of the times of the Messiah." Additionally, the footnote in the *MacArthur Study Bible* (p. 1600) observes: "Hebrews 11:3 indicates that Abraham saw Christ's day ('having seen them afar off'...). Abraham particularly saw in the continuing seed of Isaac the beginning of God's fulfilling the covenant (Gen. 12:1-3; 15:1-21; 17:1-8; cf. 22:8) that would culminate in Christ."

The Apostolic Testimony

forward—with the 'eyes' of *faith*—to the "day" of the Messiah with appropriate joy and gladness, based on God's promises to him. In the same basic sense, in John 12:41, John may very well have meant that Isaiah prophetically "saw" the future "glory" of the Messiah—as the Messiah is portrayed in Isaiah, yet, not only in one specific text, but throughout the prophetic writings overall (Isaiah 4:2[172]; 9:6-7; 11:1-10; 16:5; 32:1; 33:17[173]; 42:1-4; 49:1-6; 52:13, 14; 53:1-12; 61:1-3).

That is to say, Isaiah did not have to literally "see," with physical eyes, the Messiah's "glory" in order to match what John said about him in John 12:41, just as Abraham did not have to literally "see," with physical eyes, the "day" of the Messiah in order to make what Jesus said about Abraham true (John 8:56). Scripturally speaking, men like Abraham and Isaiah could often "see" in advance—through the prophetic gift, and with the 'eyes' of faith—the glories of future events associated with God's purposes based on God's revelation to them.[174]

7. If John is identifying Jesus directly and 'ontologically' as 'Jehovah' in John 12:41, no automatically-resulting 'Trinitarian' concept emerges. In fact, if taken in this way, the

---

[172] In fact, Isaiah 4:2 speaks of "the branch of Jehovah" which "shall be **beautiful** and **glorious**"—a well-established and widely-accepted reference to the Messiah. The Aramaic Targum of Isaiah even renders the text: "at that time shall the *Messiah* of the Lord be for joy and *glory*." The *MacArthur Study Bible* observes that the term "branch" used in this way is a "messianic title" that "occurs also in Jer. 23:5; 33:15; Zech. 3:8; 6:12." The *New John Gill Exposition of the Entire Bible* observes: "Christ is called 'the branch,' ...and it chiefly regards his descent from David, and when his family was very mean and low; and a branch being but a tender thing, it denotes Christ's state of humiliation on earth, when he grew up as a tender plant before the Lord, and was contemptible in the eyes of men...and yet this branch became 'beautiful,' being laden with the fruits of divine grace... and 'glorious,' being the branch made strong to do the work of the Lord, by his obedience and death; and especially he became glorious when raised from the dead, when he ascended up to heaven, and was exalted there at the right hand of God; and when his Gospel was spread and his kingdom increased in the Gentile world, as it did, both before and after the destruction of Jerusalem, the time here referred to; and which will he in a more glorious condition in the last days; and now he is glorious in the eyes of all that believe in him, and is glorified by them..."

[173] Isaiah 33:17 in the Septuagint even says, in an agreed upon reference to the Messiah, "You will *see* a king with *glory*" (Hebrew text: "*Your eyes will see the King in his beauty*." As it was observed in the *MacArthur Study Bible*: "The prophecy moves beyond Hezekiah in his sackcloth, oppressed by his enemy, to Messiah in His beauty. Seeing Him in glory is another reward for the righteous. The near-future deliverance from Sennacherib anticipates a more distant wonder when the Messiah will sit on His throne" (p. 1004).

[174] As one commentary points out: "That Isaiah actually saw the glory (*doxa*) of Jesus (v. 41) is an astounding assertion, but perhaps nor more so than that Abraham would rejoice to see Jesus' day (8:56)." —D. Moody Smith, *John, Abingdon New Testament Commentaries* (Nashville: Abingdon, 1999), p. 243.

The Apostolic Testimony

common Trinitarian argument is really more conducive to the doctrinal concept of "Modalism" which says that Jesus Christ *is* God the Father, only, in another "mode." Hebrews chapter one makes clear that Jehovah, the God of the "prophets"—a reference that includes Isaiah—was God *the Father*, since he was the 'God' who once spoke in the 'prophets' but in these 'last days' has spoken in his 'Son.' Thus, to identify Jesus as the one Isaiah saw on the throne—as "Jehovah of hosts"—would be to identify Jesus as *God the Father*; since, again, this was the same 'God (*ho theos*)' who spoke at one time through prophets like Isaiah but who, in the Christian era, spoke through a 'Son.'

8. Much like other Trinitarian "proof texts," John 12:41 does not explicitly say "Jesus is Jehovah" or anything that resembles such. As so often the case, the Trinitarian conclusion is based on an uncertain and highly-debatable interpretation that ultimately ignores or overlooks alternative evidence, not an explicit statement of faith with a meaning that cannot be denied. If the text were not debatable or ambiguous in the interest of Trinitarian doctrine, there would be no real dispute, no viable interpretative options, and no Evangelical-Trinitarian scholars themselves presenting sound alternative explanations.[175] What we find after close scrutiny, however, is the opposite. For example, in their handbook on translation, Barclay M. Newman and Eugene A. Nida commented: *"Because he saw Jesus' [Gk: 'his'] glory* could mean that Isaiah saw in his own day the pre-incarnate glory which Jesus had."* This is, of course, in line with the traditional Trinitarian claim. Yet the translators go on to say: "However, it is better to understand this clause as referring to Isaiah's prophetic vision of the glory that Jesus would have as the result of his death and resurrection. One may translate, therefore, 'he saw ahead of time the glory that Jesus would have later' or '…how wonderful Jesus would be.'"[176]

---

[175] Other evangelical commentators, in contrast to apologists like James White, have been careful enough to point out alternative understandings of the text: "Isaiah's seeing *Jesus' glory* (41) has occasioned comment. It can be taken to mean that Isaiah prophesied concerning Jesus' ministry, and in that sense 'saw' and 'spoke about' him." It is also proposed: "Alternatively, John may be thinking of the pre-incarnate Christ. (*cf.* so Paul in 1 Cor. 10:4), either as part of the divine glory in Isaiah 6:1f., or as foreshadowed in the sacrifice on the altar by which the prophet was cleansed (Is. 6:6-7)." —Bruce Mine, *The Message of John, Here is your King!, with Study Guide* (Downer Grove: Inter-Varsity, 1993), p. 194.

[176] *A Handbook on The Gospel of John* (New York: UBS Handbook Series, 1980), pp. 419-420.

In agreement, another commentator observed: "Even the coming of the death and resurrection of Jesus will not be enough for all to believe and this was foreseen by God. As John points out, Isaiah himself had a basic understanding of this astounding unfaith. Isaiah experienced unbelieving rejection in his own ministry, but even more he saw Jesus' glory [death/resurrection] and spoke about him."[177]

We can conclude, therefore, that the connection Trinitarians so frequently attempt to make between the words **"Isaiah said these things because he saw [Jesus'] glory..."** and the "**glory**" associated with the prophet's vision of Jehovah in the temple is neither certain nor necessary. There is, by far, more evidence supporting a connection between John's statement about the "glory" of the Messiah (a 'glory' made manifest in the Messiah's powerful 'signs') and the descriptions of Jehovah's "servant" occurring in Isaiah 52:10-53:12 and in the totality of the prophet's Messianic references; and, in this light, Isaiah could very well have seen the *future* "glory" of the Messiah in a similar way that Abraham "saw" the Messiah's *future* "day" (John 8:56).[178] There is no good reason to insist that the statement in John 12:41 should be restricted exclusively to Isaiah's vision of God in the temple that would imply a one-to-one "ontological" identification between Jesus Christ and Jehovah God himself, particularly in a post-biblical Trinitarian sense; nor should one, when endeavoring to makes sense of John's statement, overlook the fact that whenever the Messiah is spoken of in Isaiah's writings (and in the writings of all the Hebrew prophets), he is, in every case, clearly portrayed as a figure distinguishable from Jehovah God—a point that, with clear scriptural reason, should govern our understanding of the text

---

[177] *The College Press NIV Commentary, John*, Beuford H. Bryant & Mark S. Krause (College Press Publishing Co., 1998), p. 279 (words in brackets in the original).

[178] C. H. Williams, like James White, believes the glory mentioned in John 12:41 must refer to the glory of Jehovah God in Isaiah 6:1-5. But, unlike White, Williams acknowledges that there are in fact "sound arguments for explaining the remark 'he saw his glory' in terms of Isaiah's vision of the glory of the *earthly* Jesus. Isaiah was already understood in the first-century Jewish context as a visionary prophet and foreseer of the future. Writing in the second century BCE, Ben Sira (48:24-25, Hebrew Ms B) describes the prophet Isaiah as follows: 'By a spirit of strength he saw the future and comforted the mourners of Zion. He declared what shall be until eternity and hidden things before they come to pass.'" —*Isaiah in the New Testament* (*Isaiah in John's Gospel*), pp. 111-112 (emphasis added).

The Apostolic Testimony

from the beginning.[179]

The "Glory" of the Messiah in the Writings of Isaiah

What follows are examples from the book of Isaiah where the foretold Messiah is portrayed as "glorious," as having "glory," and in a most "glorified" state. These widely-recognized Messianic texts demonstrate that the statement in John 12:41 could not only be connected to the depiction of the "exalted" and exceedingly "glorified" "servant" of Jehovah in Isaiah 52:13-14, but can encompass the fullness of the revelation given by God to Isaiah concerning the promised Messiah as depicted in his writings.

In each Scripture that follows, the Messiah—called the "servant of Jehovah" and "Prince of Peace"—is clearly presented in an exceedingly honorable, exalted, and "glorious" light, even when the actual term "glory" is not present; and, in light of all these references, it can be truly said that Isaiah *"saw [the Messiah's] glory and spoke about him."*

> "In that day the branch of Jehovah shall be **beautiful** and **glorious**…" —Isaiah 4:2

> "…and his name shall be called: Wonderful Counselor, Mighty God, Everlasting Father, Prince of Peace ['and he is named Messenger of Great Counsel,' LXX]. Of the increase of his government and of peace there will be no end ['His sovereignty is great, and his peace has no boundary' LXX], on the throne of David and over his kingdom, to establish it and to uphold it with justice and with righteousness from this time forth and forevermore…" —Isaiah 9:6-7

---

[179] With reference to the "great fourth servant song of Isaiah 52:13-53:12," Eugene Merrill, OT professor at Dallas Theological Seminary, observed that "the servant there, in terms of the OT understanding alone, is totally distinct from God." —*An Exegetical Commentary, Haggai, Zechariah, Malachi* (Moody Press: Chicago, 1994) p. 320. On this point, consider Micah 5:4 which says of the Messiah: "And he shall stand, and shall feed his flock in the strength of Jehovah, in the majesty of *the name of Jehovah his God*…for now shall he be great unto the ends of the earth." It is obvious from this one expression alone that the Hebrew prophets presented Jehovah as the Messiah's God, not as the Messiah himself.

"There shall come forth a shoot from the stump of Jesse, and a branch from his roots shall bear fruit. And the spirit of Jehovah shall rest upon him, the spirit of wisdom and understanding, the spirit of counsel and might, the spirit of knowledge and the fear of Jehovah…and he shall strike the earth with the rod of his mouth, and with the breath of his lips he shall kill the wicked. Righteousness shall be the belt of his waist, and faithfulness the belt of his loins…In that day the root of Jesse, who shall stand as a signal for the peoples—of him shall the nations inquire, and **his resting place shall be glorious**." —Isaiah 11:1-5, 10

"…then a throne will be established in steadfast love, and on it will sit in faithfulness in the tent of David one who judges and seeks justice and is swift to do righteousness." —Isaiah 16:5

"Behold, a king will reign in righteousness, and princes will rule in justice." —Isaiah 32:1

"Your eyes will behold the king in his beauty; they will see a land that stretches afar ['**You will see a king with glory**, and your eyes will see a land from far away,' LXX]." —Isaiah 33:17

"Behold my servant, whom I uphold, my chosen, in whom my soul delights; I have put my spirit upon him; he will bring forth justice to the nations…he will faithfully bring forth justice. He will not grow faint or be discouraged ['He will blaze up and not be overwhelmed' LXX]; till he has established justice in the earth and the coastlands wait for his law." —Isaiah 42:1-4

"Since you are precious in my sight, since **you are honored and I love you**, I will give other men in your place and other peoples in exchange for your life." —Isaiah 43:4

"For I shall be glorious ['honored' ESV] **in the eyes of the** LORD ['I will be gathered and **glorified before the Lord**' LXX], And My God shall be My strength." (NKJV) —Isaiah 49:5

The Apostolic Testimony

"**I will make you as a light for the nations**, that my salvation may reach to the end of the earth. Thus says Jehovah, the Redeemer of Israel and his Holy One..." —Isaiah 49:6

"Behold, my servant shall act wisely; **he shall be high and lifted up, and shall be exalted** ['**He shall be exalted and glorified exceedingly...and your *glory* shall not be honored by the sons of men'** LXX]...kings shall shut their mouths because of him..." —Isaiah 52:13-15

"...he shall see his offspring; he shall prolong his days; the will of Jehovah shall prosper in his hand...by his knowledge shall the righteous one, my servant, make many to be accounted righteous... Therefore I will divide him a portion with the many, and he shall divide the spoil with the strong..." —Isaiah 53:10-12

"...[the Lord Jehovah] **he has clothed me with the garments of salvation; he has covered me with the robe of righteousness, as a bridegroom decks himself like a priest with a beautiful headdress, and as a bride adorns herself with her jewels**. For as the earth brings forth its sprouts, and as a garden causes what is sown in it to sprout up, so the Lord Jehovah will cause righteousness and praise to sprout up before all the nations." —Isaiah 61:1:1-3, 10-11

6

The "I am" statements of the Gospel of John

> *"It is all too easy to read the traditional interpretations we have received from others into the text of Scripture. Then we may unwittingly transfer the authority of Scripture to our traditional interpretations and invest them with a false, even an idolatrous, degree of certainty. Because traditions are reshaped as they are passed on, after a while we may drift far from God's Word while still insisting all our theological opinions are 'biblical' and therefore true...Many local Bible teachers and preachers have never been forced to confront alternative interpretations at full strength; and because they would lose a certain psychological security if they permitted their own questions, aroused by their own reading of Scripture, to come into full play, they are unlikely to throw over received traditions."*
> — D. A. Carson, *Exegetical Fallacies*, pp. 17, 19

One of the most popular and frequently advanced arguments for the Trinitarian doctrine of Christ relates to certain occurrences recorded in the Gospel of John where Jesus used the expression *"ego eimi"* ('I am' or 'I am *he*,' John 8:24, *KJV*).[1] Traditionally, Trinitarians have argued that on several occasions when Jesus made use of this one expression, he used it specifically for the purpose of identifying himself before his listeners as the very incarnation of Jehovah God. Typically, argumentation has revolved around connecting the phrase "I am"—made by Jesus—to the phrase made by Jehovah God in response to Moses' inquiry at Exodus 3:14 (according to several English translations, Jehovah said to Moses, 'I am that I am'; saying further, 'Thus you shall say to the sons of Israel, *I am* has sent me to you'). However, some of the more careful Trinitarian

---

[1] Actually, Jesus probably spoke Aramaic or Hebrew; *ego eimi* is the expression used by the Gospel writer to communicate what Jesus spoke in the original language(s) that he used.

The 'I am' statements of the Gospel of John

expositors—upon closer examination of the contextual and translational issues—have realized the difficulty in maintaining an alleged connection of this kind.[2] For this reason, most now emphasize what they perceive to be a connection between Jesus' statements and the words of Jehovah God found in certain sections of the book of Isaiah.[3]

Some apologists have gone as far as to insist that when Jesus said "I am," even with an immediately following predicate or identification (as in 'I am *the living bread...*'), that the specific words "I am" still bear a special significance in terms of Jesus' alleged claim to be the Almighty come in the flesh. They argue that when Jesus said, "I am the bread of life," or "I am the good shepherd," or "I am the light of the world," that we should see this as meaning, "I am *God*, the bread of life," or "I am *God*, the light of the world," and that this is what Jesus intended for his audience to understand. This is perhaps one of the most peculiar and extraordinary arguments that some evangelicals have attempted to advance in recent years. In this case, it is somehow forgotten that the phrase *ego eimi* commonly functions in the Greek language as a connecting verbal expression on the way to a simple self-identification.[4] Unfortunately, such arguments actually redirect the focus of attention from the actual identity brought out—"the light of the world"—to the connecting verbal phrase (technically called a 'copula')—"I am..."

Arguments of these kinds, which have become quite popular in many evangelical circles, are just as strange, and just as fallacious, as if an individual were to identify himself by saying, "I am the doctor," or "I am the teacher," and then argue that by using the words "I am" in the sentence that that individual was claiming to be God (or alluding to an expression

---

[2] For example, with respect to Jesus' use of *ego eimi* at John 8:58, Robert Bowman admits, "Jesus certainly does not say, in so many words, 'I am the 'I Am,' nor does he quote Exodus 3:14 in its entirety and apply it to himself." —*Jehovah's Witnesses, Jesus Christ, and the Gospel of John*, p. 124. Dr. Dennis Hutchison also said: "You're familiar with John 8:58. But a lot of people look at that and they think immediately back to the Old Testament in Exodus 3:14. But you know in Exodus, when the Greeks translated that last phrase '*I am that I am*,' the last '*I am*' which is really the title of God, they didn't use *ego eimi*. They used a different form of that word but not that form. And I don't think that that phrase goes back to that verse in Exodus. I think when Jesus used it he had Isaiah 41 to 52 in mind." —*Bible Faculty Series, Gospel and The Person of Jesus Christ*, The Master's College Chapel CD, Oct. 29, 2004.
[3] Primarily Isaiah 41:4; 43:10; 46:4.
[4] The same way the words "I am" would function in the English sentence, "I am the President."

made by God in the Hebrew Scriptures); when, in fact, the real and obvious point is that the speaker is identifying himself as "the doctor" or "the teacher." Obviously, and in the same way, attempting to derive some extraordinary significance from the phrase "I am" in a statement like "I am the light of the world" results in an altering of the speaker's true intention. The point made by Jesus was that he is "the light of the world," not that he is the so-called "I am," a notion that would result in a strange and unnecessary adulteration of Jesus' words. And, in light of the self-evident error of such reasoning, it may seem perplexing that such arguments are ever even brought to mind and taken into serious consideration, particularly by those familiar with the Scriptures and formally trained in the original Bible languages. Trinitarian Millard J. Erickson recognized the same fallacy:

> One consideration that has frequently been appealed to in evaluating the bearing of John's witness on the doctrine of the Trinity is the 'I' statements of Jesus: 'I am the Good Shepherd'; 'I am the way, the truth, and the life.' On this basis, the argument is constructed that these are references back to God's statement in Exodus 3, where he answered Moses' question about his name by saying, 'I am,' or 'I will be.' If this is the case, then all of these statements constitute claims to deity...In my judgment, this argument as a whole is invalid and should not be utilized. It fails to recognize distinctions among the four uses of the copula, 'to be.' This is confusing the 'is of predication' (or possibly the 'is of inclusion') for the 'is of existence.'[5]

There still are, however, several other occasions in the Gospel of John where Jesus used the phrase *ego eimi* that are regularly appealed to as arguments in favor of the Trinitarian faith. These arguments are felt to be even stronger because *ego eimi* is used by Jesus without an immediate predicate or identification following in the sentence; similar to certain expressions made by Jehovah God several times throughout the Hebrew Scriptures, particularly in the prophecies of Isaiah. For example, in Isaiah 43:10, according to the *King James Version*

---

[5] *God in Three Persons* (Grand Rapids: Baker Books, 1995), p. 209.

rendering, God said, "Ye are my witnesses, saith the LORD, and my servant whom I have chosen that ye may know and believe me, and understand that I *am* he (Greek Septuagint: *ego eimi*; original Hebrew: *ani hu*; meaning: 'I [*am*] he'), before me there was no God formed, neither shall there be after me."

Since the expression *ego eimi* is used by God in the *Septuagint* rendering of this text, many Trinitarians argue that when Jesus used the same (so-called 'predicate-less') phrase, he was intending to identify himself as God. Dr. Hutchison of the Master's College even said, "I think when Jesus said *I am he*, with that phrase, it was the strongest claim to deity that he made any place. I don't think he made any stronger claim to being God than using that phrase."[6]

With respect to one text in particular where the phrase occurs (John 4:26), Anglican scholar Peter Toon argued that "Jesus told the Samaritan woman (4:26), he is the 'I am' without any predicate—the 'I am,' *Ego eimi* = Yahweh of Exodus 3:14ff, and of Isaiah 41:4, and of 43:10 (see further John 6:20; 8, particularly vv. 24, 28, 58; 13:19; 18:5-8)."[7]

Pastor Phillip R. Johnson, a popular evangelical teacher, although not specifically mentioning Jesus' use of *ego eimi*, made a similar argument based on Jesus' words in John chapter four in a sermon at Grace Community Church in 2003. Yet prior to his argument, Johnson said that Jesus revealed himself as "Son of God" to the man he had healed in John chapter nine, claiming that "Son of God" is "an expression of his deity," so that Jesus revealed "himself to [the man he had healed] as God."[8] Johnson went on to claim:

"This is one of only two places in the *entire* New

---

[6] Hutchison, *Gospel and The Person of Jesus Christ*, Oct. 29, 2004 (Audio).
[7] *Our Triune God, A Biblical Portrayal of the Trinity* (Victor Books: 1996), p. 33. In agreement, Dr. Hutchison said, "Jesus says 'I am he the one who is speaking to you.' And some people say 'Oh Jesus is agreeing with her [the Samaritan woman].' No. Now again she's partially right but she's also wrong because she hasn't gone far enough. And Jesus goes back and he says to her, 'I'm making the claim that Yahweh made concerning myself. Far more than just a prophet like Moses. I am Yahweh Himself.' He is making a declaration of his deity." —*Gospel and The Person of Jesus Christ*, October 29, 2004 (Audio).
[8] John 9:35-37. Saying that Jesus was called "Son of God" in this account was either an oversight on Johnson's part or he may have been reading from a translation like the *KJV*. The better manuscripts show that Jesus actually identified himself as "the Son of man" (*NASB*) on this occasion, not "the Son of God" (John 9:35, *KJV*).

The 'I am' statements of the Gospel of John

Testament where Jesus just came out and declared his deity or his Messiahship. The other case is John four where he tells the Samaritan woman at the well who he really is. That's the only other place where Jesus just comes right out and says, 'I am God in the flesh,' or 'I am the Messiah.'...he was the Son of God, God in the flesh."[9]

As shown, because Jesus used the phrase "I am *he*" in response to the Samaritan woman at the well, Dr. Toon and other promoters of Trinitarian theology[10] argue that Jesus was identifying himself as "God in the flesh" ('the I am') on that occasion. However, in this example, a simple examination of the context will clearly demonstrate the real predicate or identity in question and the error of such a surprising line of argumentation.

During his conversation with the woman, after having spoken of the importance of worshiping the Father in spirit and truth, and how the Father is seeking for worshipers like these, John reports: "The woman said to him, 'I know that the Messiah is coming, the one called Christ; when he comes, he will tell us everything.' Jesus said to her, 'I am *he* (*ego eimi*) the one who is speaking to you.'"

In Greek *ego eimi* often appears without a specifically expressed identity or predicate because one is not always required, as the context itself makes clear the meaning intended. In each case readers are able to discern the implied predicate by taking account of the immediate context and by simply following the natural flow and obvious sequence of thought presented there. Often *ego eimi* can simply convey the sense, "It is I," "I am the one," or "It is me," as it probably does at John 6:20. In this particular instance, when the disciples were on a ship at sea, a great wind was blowing. Then, when the disciples saw Jesus miraculously walking on the water toward the ship, not

---

[9] Audio Tape: *The Blind Man and Pharisee*, John 9:13-34, Grace Community Church, 2003. One question worth asking is: Where does the Bible teach that "Son of God" means "God in the flesh"? Dr. Colin Brown, based on careful study of the term in the OT, observed: "...the title 'Son of God' is not in itself a designation of personal deity or an expression of metaphysical distinctions within the Godhead. Indeed to be 'Son of God' one has to be a being who is not God!" —As quoted in *Focus on the Kingdom* Newsletter, May, 2004 Volume 6 No. 8.

[10] It is not clear from this statement if Johnson believed that Jesus' specific use of *ego eimi* meant that he was claiming to be God, or, that identifying himself as the Messiah amounted to a claim to be God, so that to be Messiah is *equivalent* to being God in Johnson's view.

immediately recognizing him, they became afraid; but Jesus said to them, "It is I (*ego eimi*); be not afraid" (*KJV*). In other words, "It's me, *Jesus* (not 'a ghost'), don't be afraid."[11]

In John 9:9, the account of the blind man who was healed by Jesus, John reports (after the healing had taken place): "Therefore the neighbors, and those who previously saw him as a beggar, were saying, 'Is not this the one who used to sit and beg?' Others were saying, 'This is he,' still others were saying, 'No, but he is like him.' He kept saying, '*I am the one* ['I am *he*' KJV, 'I am the man' *RSV*]'" (*NASB*). In this case, the people did not believe or did not realize that the man who was now able to see was the man whom Jesus had just healed. When confusion was expressed among the people, the formerly blind man responded by saying "*ego eimi*," the same expression used by Jesus when he was speaking to the woman at the well in John 4:26, as well as on other occasions. However, even though *ego eimi* technically occurs without an expressed predicate, the man who had been healed by Jesus was obviously not "making a declaration of his deity." The context itself discloses the identity that was in question—"the one who used to sit and beg."

It really does not require much in-depth explanation, for it is not difficult to see, that when Jesus used the phrase *ego eimi* at John 4:26 he was affirming that he was in fact the *Messiah* whom the woman was in expectation of; for, contextually, such was the only identity in question. The phrase *ego eimi* in this case means "I am *he*," that is, 'I am the *Messiah* you are speaking of,' a rather simple and obvious point.[12]

In any case, Dr. James White, although acknowledging the clearly-expressed predicates in many of Jesus' statements where *ego eimi* occurs in the Christian Scriptures,[13] argues strongly that Jesus used the phrase in what he and other Trinitarians have described as an "absolute" sense, specifically for the purpose of claiming "deity" with all the associated implications of Trinitarian theology.

---

[11] Compare Mark 6:48-49; Matthew 14:25-26; John 6:19-20.
[12] The woman said she knew that the Messiah was coming; Jesus responds, "I am *he*, the one speaking to you...", and Jesus' response is characterized by Johnson by saying that *he came right out* and declared to be God in the flesh! Again, it is almost difficult to believe that anyone would ever make that kind of claim based on such words considered in context.
[13] Including John 6:35; 6:41; 6:51; 8:12; 8:18; 10:7; 10:9; 10:11; 10:14; 11:25; 14:6; 15:1; 15:5.

John 8:24, 28

> *"I told you that you would die in your sins, for unless you believe that I am he you will die in your sins."*

In his book on the Trinity, James White calls attention to a series of Scriptures (John 8:24, 28; 13:19; 18:5, 6, 8; 8:58) to support his claim regarding the "deity" of Jesus Christ based on the phrase *ego eimi*.[14] The first, John 8:23-29, is an account of Jesus speaking with men from the Jewish sect of the Pharisees:

> **He said to them, 'You are from below; I am from above. You are of this world; I am not of this world. I told you that you would die in your sins, for unless you believe that I am he (*ego eimi*) you will die in your sins.' So they said to him, 'Who are you?' Jesus said to them, 'Just what I have been telling you from the beginning. I have much to say about you and much to judge, but he who sent me is true, and I declare to the world what I have heard from him.' They did not understand that he had been speaking to them about the Father. So Jesus said to them, 'When you have lifted up the Son of Man, then you will know that I am he (*ego eimi*), and that I do nothing on my own authority, but speak just as the Father taught me. And he who sent me is with me. He has not left me alone, for I always do the things that are pleasing to him.' As he was saying these things, many believed in him.**[15]

Dr. White believes that here Jesus is saying, essentially, that "if you do not believe that *I am* (that is, I am *God*, or that I am the same one who used the phrase 'I am' in the book of Isaiah) you will die in your sins." As pervasive as this interpretive connection has become among the apologists, many are unaware that other evangelical scholars do not find in Jesus' words here any connection to the expressions made by God that would result in a one-to-one identification of the two.

It is also worthy to note that *The New International*

---

[14] Dr. White even considers these to be "solid texts" in support of his claim (Apologetics Blog Archives: 12/18/2006).
[15] John 8:23-30, *ESV*

Version—sponsored by the Christian Reformed Church and the National Association of Evangelicals—renders this passage in a way that very well may bring out the true sense of Jesus' words at this point: "**I told you that you would die in your sins: if you do not believe that *I am the one I claim to be*, you will indeed die in your sins.**"

Here, the translators realized that the phrase appearing in the text is *ego eimi* (lit., 'I am'), but they render it, "I am the one I claim to be." Apparently, the translators did not recognize any connection between Jesus' words and the words used by Jehovah God in the Hebrew Scriptures (at least they did not indicate this by their rendering); but rather, that Jesus was simply saying that, in order to avoid dying in their sins, his listeners must believe that he was the one he had been claiming to be; and one could rightly understand this as referring to the identity brought out in the immediate context ('son of man'), or throughout Jesus' public ministry up to that point, in light of the overall picture the Gospel of John presents to us—namely, that Jesus was in fact the foretold and long-awaited *Messiah* of Israel, the sent-forth Savior of the world.

In a similar but more specific way, the scholarly New Testament by C. B. Williams rendered the verse: "So I have told you that you would die under the curse of your sins, for unless you believe that I am the Christ (ftnt: Grk., *I am He*), you will die under the curse of your sins."

Here, Williams believed—based on either the immediate context of John chapter eight, or on the entirety of John's Gospel account—that Jesus meant that they must believe that he was "the Christ"; or, in other words, *the one he had been claiming and showing himself to be the entire time*. Because of this, Williams supplies the implied predicate in the translation for the benefit of the readers, while relegating the literal translation, "I am *he*," to the marginal footnotes. Notably, numerous conservative commentators have expressed agreement with William's viewpoint, having arrived independently at the same basic conclusion. Albert Barnes, a respected Protestant Bible scholar of the nineteenth century, in his widely-read and widely-appreciated commentary, stated simply, "*That I am he*. That I am the Messiah."[16] Similarly, in his one-volume-commentary, the Reverend J. R. Dumellow wrote with reference to this verse: "I am he] viz. the Messiah, and the Saviour. He alone can say, 'Thy sins be forgiven thee.'"[17] Even the renowned sixteenth-century reformer, John Calvin, had the same or similar understanding:

> *Except ye believe that I am.* For there is no other way for the lost to recover salvation than by flying to Christ. The emphasis is on the phrase *that I am.* We must understand by it all that the Scripture ascribes to the Messiah and all that it tells us to expect from Him…Some of the ancients have misapplied this to the divine essence of Christ. He is in fact speaking of His office towards us.[18]

A reading of the entire account will show how, in the first part of the chapter, Jesus declared, "I am *the light of the world*" (v. 12), and for that reason many commentators think it is reasonable to believe that when Jesus said "I am *he*" in verse 24, that this could be taken as a reference to himself as that "light" just spoken of. Although A. T. Robertson leaned toward the common Trinitarian explanation, he nevertheless took note of all the significant elements in the context and acknowledged that "Jesus can mean either 'that I am from above' (verse 23), 'that I am the one sent from the Father or the Messiah' (7:18, 28), 'that I am the Light of the World' (8:12) or 'that I am the Deliverer from the bondage of sin' (8:28, 31, 36)."[19] In his commentary, Arthur W. Pink offered a paraphrased expansion of what he thought Jesus meant when he said, "I am *he*" (John 8:24); that is: "I am essentially and absolutely that which I have declared

---

[16] *Barnes' Notes, Electronic Database.* Copyright (c) 1997 by Biblesoft. The note in Knox's translation states: 'It is myself you look for'; literally, 'It is myself', that is, 'I am the Christ', as in Mk. 13:6; but here the elliptical phrase is helped out by verse 21 above, where our Lord has told the Jews that after his death they will be looking for him, i.e. looking for a Messias to deliver them." —Knox, *The Holy Bible, A Translation from the Latin Vulgate in light of the Hebrew and Greek Originals* (New York: 1956), p. 96.

[17] *The One Volume Bible Commentary*, p. 789. With respect to this particular statement, several Roman Catholic scholars have drawn the same conclusion. As one example, the footnote to John 8:24 in *The Holy Bible, Saint Joseph, New Catholic Edition* reads, "I am he: i.e., the Messias."

[18] *Calvin's New Testament Commentaries, St. John, Part Two 11-21 and 1 John* (Grand Rapids: 1961), p. 216. This is not to suggest that Calvin denied the Trinity doctrine; on the contrary, Calvin was quite dogmatic about this subject. However, Calvin's comments do show that he did not try or have to insist on the same meaning from this specific text like other Trinitarian apologists have done. When Calvin states, "His office toward us," he is evidently referring to Jesus' *Messianic* office.

[19] Robertson, *Word Pictures of the New Testament, Volume V*, p. 146.

The 'I am' statements of the Gospel of John

myself to be. I have spoken of 'light': *I am* that Light. I have spoken of 'truth': *I am* that Truth. I am the very incarnation, personification, exemplification of them."[20]

In our attempt to understand the significance of *ego eimi* in this case, it is essential to note that when Jesus said, "unless you believe that I am *he* you will die in your sins," the Jews responded with the question, "who are you?" (v. 25) If Jesus actually meant, in effect, "I am God," or used the phrase "I am" with the exact same sense as did God in the book of Isaiah, and the Jews really understood him in this way, it would be very difficult to explain why, immediately after making this statement, they wanted to know who he was and what he meant by *ego eimi*. Notice also that after they asked Jesus who he was, Jesus said to them, **"Just what I have been telling you from the beginning."** It is appropriate then, in fact, critical, to ask: *Who had Jesus been telling the Jews he was from the beginning?* Of course, when the statements made about Jesus' identity in the Gospel of John are traced from the beginning onward until John 8:25 (the point where the Jews asked Jesus who he was), a very clear picture begins to emerge. In chapter one, Jesus was identified by John the Baptist as "the Lamb of God, who takes away the sin of the world" (1:29). In the same account, John saw and bore witness that this one was in fact "the Son of God" (1:34). In chapter two, Jesus spoke of the temple as "my Father's house," confirming that he himself believed God to be *his Father*, and that, by necessary implication, he was God's unique Son (2:16). Later, Jesus spoke of himself clearly as God's Son (5:25) and as the "the Son of Man" who had been "given authority to execute judgment" (5:27); the sent one from the Father (5:36, 37); the one whom the Scriptures bore witness to and the one who had the power to give men life (5:39); "the Son of Man" on whom "God the Father has set his seal" (6:27); the one whom God sent (6:29); "the bread of life" (6:35, 48); the one "who is from God" and who "has seen the Father" (6:46); "the

---

[20] *Exposition of the Gospel of John, Volume Two, John 8 to 15:6* (Grand Rapids: Zondervan, 1945), p. 35. Commenting on verse 25, Adam Clarke wrote, *"Who art thou?* This marks the indignation of the Pharisees—as if they had said: Who are Thou that takest upon Thee to deal out threatening in this manner against us? *Jesus saith unto them, Even the same that I said unto you from the beginning.* Rather, 'Just what I have already told you,' i.e., that 'I am the light of the world'—the Saviour of mankind.'" —*Adam Clarke's Commentary, One Volume-Edition*, p. 923.

living bread that came down from heaven" (6:51); the one who taught God's teachings and who spoke with God's authority (7:16, 17; implied); and the one in whom belief in would result in an outflow of rivers of living water from the heart (7:37). In verse 12 of the same account where the *ego eimi* statement occurs, Jesus told his listeners that he was "the light of the world," the one who was sent by the Father (8:16), and the one who was "from above" (8:23). And in the verses following 8:24, Jesus identified himself as "**a man who has told you the truth that I heard from God**" (8:40); as the one who "**came from God**," and that he came, not of his own accord, but that God sent him (8:42). And most significantly, in verse 53, the question was asked of him again: "*Who do you make yourself out to be?*" To which Jesus answered: "**It is my Father who glorifies me, of whom you say, 'He is our God'**" (v. 54)—all of which results in a clear, harmonious and unified testimony that Jesus was in fact claiming to be God's own Son, the Messiah; and, indeed, "*to him all the prophets bear witness that everyone who believes in him receives forgiveness of sins through his name.*"[21]

The footnote to John 8:24 in the *New English Translation* (produced by Trinitarian scholars) states: "In this context there is an implied predicate nominative ('he') following the 'I am' phrase. What Jesus' hearers had to acknowledge is that he was who he claimed to be, i.e., the Messiah (cf. 20:31). This view is also reflected in English translations like NIV ('if you do not believe that I am the one I claim to be'), NLT ('unless you believe that I am who I say I am'), and CEV ('if you don't have faith in me for who I am')."[22]

It is also possible, in view of Jesus' words in the verses following, that he was speaking particularly about his identity as the "son of man"—the figure in Daniel 7:13-14 who was given dominion over all nations. In verse 28 Jesus went on to say to the Jews: "When you have lifted up the Son of man, then you will know that I am *he* (*ego eimi*)"; the predicate "he" referring quite naturally to "Son of man." Since the question of Jesus' identity

---

[21] The apostle Peter, Acts 10:43, *ESV*
[22] *NET, New Testament* (Biblical Studies Press, 1998), p. 310. In the footnotes they acknowledge the argument that the occurrence of "I am" should be taken in an "absolute sense," referring to it simply as a different view.

The 'I am' statements of the Gospel of John

as "God" (or 'God the Son, the second person of the Trinity') does not appear in the context, there is no sound reason to ignore the identity that *does* appear. And as one seeks to determine the nature of the relationship between Jesus and God, as set forth in Scripture, it would be helpful to remember that Jesus went on to say, in the same context: *"...that I do nothing on my own authority but speak thus as the Father taught me. And he who sent me is with me; he has not left me alone, for I always do what is pleasing to him."*[23]

Whatever the case may be—in John 8:24, 28—whether Jesus, by saying 'I am *he*,' specifically meant, "the light of the world," the one "from above," "Son of man," the "Christ/Messiah,"[24] or all of these, there is no solid or convincing reason to believe that Jesus was identifying himself as "God in the flesh" at this point (especially when the Jewish response in v. 25 is taken into serious consideration); and J. C. Fenton was right in his commentary on verse 24: "This verse makes it clear that without faith in Jesus as the one sent by God to bring salvation, there is no possibility of eternal life."[25]

John 13:19

"I tell you this now, before it takes place, that when it does take place you may believe that I am he."

Jesus' use of the expression *ego eimi* in John 13:19 is also viewed by James White and other Trinitarian apologists as another example where Jesus spoke in a way that would result in identifying him as God, based on the way God spoke in the prophecies of Isaiah.

On the night before the Passover festival, John relates how Jesus had foretold his own betrayal by the disciple Judas Iscariot. After having humbly washed his own disciples' feet, Jesus said to them:

---

[23] John 8:28, 29, *RSV*
[24] Note also that the expressions, "light of the world," the one "from above" and "son of man" (see: Daniel 7:13, 14) undoubtedly carry with them definite *Messianic* connotations.
[25] *The New Clarendon Bible, The Gospel According to John, With introduction and commentary* by J. C. Fenton (Oxford At the Clarendon Press, 1970), p. 100.

The 'I am' statements of the Gospel of John

'You call me Teacher and Lord; and you are right, for so I am (*ego eimi*). If I then, your Lord and Teacher, have washed your feet, you also ought to wash one another's feet. For I have given you an example, that you also should do as I have done to you. Truly, truly, I say to you, a servant is not greater than his master; nor is he who is sent greater than he who sent him. If you know these things, blessed are you if you do them. I am not speaking of you all; I know whom I have chosen; it is that the scripture may be fulfilled, 'He who ate my bread has lifted his heel against me.' [a reference to David's Psalm 41:9] I tell you this now, before it takes place, that when it does take place you may believe that I am he (*ego eimi*). Truly, truly, I say to you, he who receives any one whom I send receives me; and he who receives me receives him who sent me.' When Jesus had thus spoken, he was troubled in spirit, and testified, 'Truly, truly, I say to you, one of you will betray me.'[26]

Dr. White points out that not only does Jesus use some of the same words used by Jehovah God in Isaiah 43:10, but, like Jehovah, Jesus also foretells a future event (with respect to Judas Iscariot's betrayal), and hence "the evidence is overwhelming that this connection is intended by John himself [the writer of the Gospel account]."[27] However, the producers of *The New English Translation* observed that "R. E. Brown [like Dr. White] argues for a nonpredicated *ego eimi* here, *but this is far from certain.*"[28] Again, in this case, C. B. Williams rendered the verse: "From now on I will tell you things before they take place, so that when they do take place, you may believe that I am the Christ (ftnt: Grk. *That I am He*)." In agreement, John Calvin wrote in his commentary: "Moreover, by this phrase, *ye may believe that I am*, He means that He is the promised Messiah."[29] A footnote found in one Catholic translation expounds even further on the implied predicate signaled by the Old Testament quotation in the

---

[26] John 13:13-21, *RSV*
[27] White, *The Forgotten Trinity*, p. 100.
[28] *New English Translation* footnotes (emphasis added).
[29] *Calvin's New Testament Commentaries, St. John, Part Two 11-21 and 1 John* (Grand Rapids: Eerdmans, 1961), p. 63.

The 'I am' statements of the Gospel of John

previous verse (v. 18): "Here, as there [John 8:24], the sense is plainly, 'that I am the Christ'; but it has to be inferred, here as there, from the context, and the context seems to imply that our Lord is the Christ inasmuch as he is the person in whom David's prophecy is fulfilled."[30]

The commentary not only concludes that Jesus was implying an identification of himself as the Christ or Messiah (as in John 8:24), but they also take note of the previous statement made by Jesus in which he alludes to Psalm 41 ('he will lift up his heal against me')[31] which would be fulfilled in him through the act of betrayal by Judas Iscariot that very night. The point made by the commentary is that when Jesus said, "**that when it does take place you may believe that I am *he*,**" he was identifying himself as the one spoken of prophetically (or typologically) by David[32] in the Hebrew Scripture Jesus had just quoted from; which, of course, would have carried along with it the necessary implication that Jesus was in fact the promised Messiah, foretold long ago in the sacred Hebrew Scriptures ('that the scripture may be fulfilled', 13:18). The noted nineteenth-century Bible scholar, John Peter Lange, likewise pointed out: "He intimates what He will tell them repeatedly, and gives His reason for so doing.—That I am he...has here more of explicitness than chap. 8:24...The very Person is meant to whom that passage in the Psalms typically points. When the treachery of Judas stalked forth in all its horridness, the disciples (whose faith might have been shaken by the success of that treachery, Meyer) stood in special need of comfort; this was afforded them

---

[30] *Monsignor Knox's Translation of the New Testament*, p. 103. In the *Tyndale Commentaries* the writer quotes approvingly of Knox's observation, having said previously, "*I am*. As in 8:24, no predicate is expressed, but the sense in both passages is 'I am what I claim to be, *viz*. the Christ'." —*The Gospel According to St. John, An Introduction and Commentary*, p. 161. Professor Jason BeDuhn has the same conclusion: "In John 13:19, Jesus says that he predicts what will happen so that when it does happen people will believe 'I am (he)' (*ego eimi*). Once again, the immediate context fills out the implied identification. In the previous verse, Jesus quotes Psalm 41:9, which speaks of betrayal. Jesus quite obviously is identifying himself as the subject of this Old Testament passage." —*Truth in Translation*, p. 109.

[31] The verse in the Hebrew Scripture reads: "Even my bosom friend in whom I trusted, who ate of my bread, has lifted his heel against me." —Psalm 41:9, *RSV*

[32] Of course, the statement in David's Psalm had an immediate application to his own life.

when they contemplated the fulfilled word and sentence of God."[33]

Another conservative scholar of the late nineteenth-century observed that the "most natural interpretation is that affixed to these words in 8:24. It would greatly strengthen the faith of the disciples in Jesus' Messiahship, soon to be so severely tested, to recur to the distinct terms in which he announced the circumstances of his betrayal and death."[34]

Charles John Ellicott—described in the preface to his commentary as 'an outstanding conservative scholar of the 18th century'—agreed: "Ye may believe that I am he.—Comp. Note on Chaps. viii. 24 and xiv. 29. The result of His henceforth declaring these things unto them before the events, will be that they will find confirmation of their faith in Him as the Messiah."[35]

Although Arthur Pink speaks of Jesus as "the great I am" in association with his commentary on this passage (implying an understanding similar to that of Dr. White and other Trinitarians), he nevertheless correctly acknowledges the significance of Jesus speaking about the fulfillment of Psalm 41:

> …instead of the apostles being stumbled by the apostasy of one of their number, it should strengthen their faith in every written word of God to know that the very Word had long before announced what they were on the eve of

---

[33] *Lange's Commentary on the Holy Scriptures, Critical, Doctrinal and Homiletical* (Grand Rapids: Zondervan, 1871), p. 411. Charles Ryrie (former Chairman of the Department of Systematic Theology at Dallas Theological Seminary) had the same observation in his Study Bible: "*I am He.* I.e., the one to whom Ps. 41:9 refers." —*The Ryrie Study Bible, New American Standard Version New Testament*, p. 189. A. T. Robertson wrote: "*That I am he (hoti ego eimi).* As Jesus has repeatedly claimed to be the Messiah (8:24, 58, etc.)."

[34] *A Commentary, Critical, Expository, and Practical, on the Gospel of John*, by John J. Owen, D. D. (New York: Leavitt & Allen, 1860), p. 319. One Catholic translation of the New Testament renders the verse (along with an accompanying footnote), "I tell you now before it comes to pass, so that when it does come to pass you may believe who I am." Footnote: That is, that I am the Messiah, the Son of God." —*The New Testament of Our Lord and Saviour Jesus Christ, Translated into English from the Original Greek* by The Very Rev. Francis Spencer (1937).

[35] *Ellicott's Commentary on the Whole Bible, A Verse by Verse Explanation, The Four Gospels, Volume VI* (Grand Rapids: Eerdmans, 1954), p. 500. In the *Fourfold Gospel* Commentary the authors offer a paraphrased version of this account that they believe accurately expresses the basic thrust of Jesus' statement: "Hitherto I have held my peace about him [Judas Iscariot], but henceforth I shall point out his course, that my foreknowledge of his actions may strengthen your faith in my Messiahship, and not leave you in that condition of hopelessness and despair... Do not let his treachery shake your confidence in me…" —*The Fourfold Gospel*, also known as a "*Harmony of the Four Gospels*," by J. W. McGarvey and Philip Y. Pendleton.

The 'I am' statements of the Gospel of John

witnessing. Moreover, their faith in Christ should be strengthened, too. By calling their attention to the fulfillment of Psalm 41 He showed them that He was the Person there marked out; that He was a true Prophet, announcing the certain accomplishment of David's prediction before it came to pass..."[36]

The well-known Lutheran R. C. H. Lenski commented on this passage with a slightly different understanding: "What the eleven are to believe is expressed by *ego eimi*, 'that I am,' leaving the predicate to be supplied. Many think that this predicate should be, 'that I am the Messiah.' Some revert to the Old Testament and make the predicate, 'the absolute personality on whom all depends,' i.e., the person who is really God himself." Lenski concludes: "But in 8:24 and 28, as in other instances where Jesus uses this expression minus the predicate, it is the context alone which fills the gap. Here it must be, 'that I am the one who tells you this in advance in order that you may believe.' This is quite enough."[37]

Like Jesus' words in John 8:24, there seems to be a few intimately-related possibilities in John 13:19 in terms of what the specific predicate implied could be, in view of the circumstances and specific issues involved. Bible students of diverse backgrounds and denominational affiliations have rightly recognized that Jesus was likely pointing to himself as the promised *Messiah* in close connection with the fulfillment of Psalm 41, which would only serve to strengthen the disciples' confidence in him and in God's prophetic word (and in Christ as God's prophet); or that *ego eimi*, in this case, can be understood simply in the sense that "I am *he*," that is, 'the one I have been claiming to be throughout my entire ministry thus far'—the "Messiah," the "Son of God."[38]

---

[36] *Exposition of the Gospel of John, Volume Two, John 8 to 15:6* (Grand Rapids: Zondervan, 1945), p. 322. It is not necessary to claim that since Jesus foretold a future event that he must be God. It could be properly said, however, as pointed out by Arthur Pink, that Jesus was acting as "a true Prophet [of God], announcing the certain accomplishment of David's prediction before it came to pass"; or even, that Jesus was simply exhibiting his own faith and confidence in the sure fulfillment of God's prophetic word with respect to the Messiah's destiny.

[37] *The Interpretation of St. John's Gospel* (Minneapolis: Augsburg, 1943), pp. 935-936.

[38] The respected Bible scholar, C. K. Barrett, accurately summed up the general situation in his commentary on the Gospel of John: "[Jesus] pronounces (*ego eimi*) not to identify himself with God in any exclusive and final sense, but to draw attention to himself as the one in whom God is

The 'I am' statements of the Gospel of John

John 18:5, 6, 8

"When he said to them, 'I am he,' they drew back and fell to the ground."

In John chapter 18, when Jesus used the same phrase (*ego eimi*), many apologists argue that Jesus was actually uttering the divine name of God and applying it to himself, and that the power of the utterance caused a band of soldiers to fall to the ground. Verses 1-8 read as follows:

> **When Jesus had spoken these words, he went forth with his disciples across the Kidron valley, where there was a garden, which he and his disciples entered. Now Judas, who betrayed him, also knew the place; for Jesus often met there with his disciples. So Judas, procuring a band of soldiers and some officers from the chief priests and the Pharisees, went there with lanterns and torches and weapons. Then Jesus, knowing all that was to befall him, came forward and said to them, 'Whom do you seek?' They answered him, 'Jesus of Nazareth.' Jesus said to them, 'I am he (*ego eimi*).' Judas, who betrayed him, was standing with them. When he said to them, 'I am he (*ego eimi*),' they drew back and fell to the ground. Again he asked them, 'Whom do you seek?' And they said, 'Jesus of Nazareth.' Jesus answered, 'I told you that I am he (*ego eimi*); so, if you seek me, let these men go.'**

Dr. White claimed: "Here in the garden, after having already laid a foundation as we'll see, we have, I think, one of the clearest references to the divine nature, the divine name, that is communicated to us by *ego eimi*." Dr. White also claimed: "Historically, Christians have understood that when Jesus made this self-identification, when he uses these words of himself, that this was a supernatural event, that it was the glory of his person,

---

encountered and known..." And on page 342: "*ego eimi* does not identify Jesus with God, but it does draw attention to him in the strongest possible terms. 'I am the one—the one you must look at, and listen to, if you would know God.' This open form of words is better than 'I am the Christ, the one who can save you' (Sanders; cf. Lindars), just because it is open. More satisfactory is Bultmann: 'He is everything he has claimed to be.'" —*The Gospel According to St. John, An Introduction with Commentary and Notes on the Greek Text*, Second Edition, (Philadelphia: The Westminster Press, 1978), pp. 98, 342.

The 'I am' statements of the Gospel of John

and it was the power of the name that caused these men to fall back upon the ground."[39] Contrary to Dr. White's apologetic claim, however, another Bible commentator said: "On 'I am' see on 6:35, 8:24. Here it need not mean more than 'I am Jesus of Nazareth, the man whom you seek'..."[40]

The footnote in the *NIV Study Bible* does not express any awareness of Jesus declaring himself to be God by pronouncing "the divine name." It simply says: "They came to arrest a meek peasant and instead were met in the dim light by a majestic person."[41] The producers of the *Interpreter's Bible* concluded: "The moral majesty of Jesus astonished the captors, who recoiled in amazement, and some fell to the ground."[42] Aware of the arguments akin to that of Dr. White's, Jason BeDuhn wrote: "In John 18, Jesus asks the soldiers whom they have come for. When they say they are looking for Jesus of Nazareth, Jesus answers 'I am (he)' (*ego eimi*). In other words, 'I am Jesus, the one you are looking for.' Now when he says this the first time, the soldiers fall back in shock. But there is no reason to think that Jesus has used some sort of verbal spell on them. There is nothing in the words of *ego eimi* themselves that have power; it is Jesus who has the power."[43]

Some commentators, although not arguing that Jesus was uttering the name of God, believe that what occurred represented a characteristic manifestation of Jesus' supernatural power (the power of God working through him), the true cause of the soldiers' falling—a powerful sign or miracle consistent with Jesus' walking on water, calming the sea during a storm, opening the eyes of the blind, and raising people from the dead. This also appears quite reasonable, given the context. Jesus may have wanted to demonstrate his power over the guards, showing that, in reality, they had no power to take him, and that he would only submit himself into their custody of his own accord, with view to

---

[39] James White, *The Dividing Line*, *"I AM" and the Jehovah's Witnesses*, September 11, 1999
[40] *Peake's Commentary on the Whole Bible*, p. 864.
[41] *NIV Study Bible*, p. 1628.
[42] *The Interpreter's Bible*, Vol. 8, p. 756.
[43] BeDuhn, *Truth in Translation*, p. 109.

the voluntary sacrifice he came into the world to give.[44] A well-known Protestant commentary expressed a view like this:

> As soon as he said unto them, I am He, they went backward—recoiled and fell to the ground—struck down by a power such as that which smote Saul of Tarsus and his companions to the earth (Acts 26:14). It was the glorious effulgence of the majesty of Christ which overpowered them. This, occuring before His surrender, would show His *power* over His enemies, and so the *freedom* with which He gave Himself up...[45]

The same possibility was acknowledged by another source, namely, that Christ's "divine power was exerted to prostrate them."[46] Heinrich Meyer wrote in his commentary, "...presumptively, the very falling to the ground, and the designating those who fell generally and without exception, thus including the rest of the Roman soldiers, justifies the ancient commentators...in regarding it as a *miraculous* result of the *power of Christ.* Christ wished, before His surrender, to make known His might over His foes, and thus show the voluntariness of His surrender. He *could* remain free, but He is *willing* to surrender Himself, because He knows His hour is come..."[47]

J. W. McGarvey, however, did not believe Jesus was manifesting miraculous power in this case. He wrote: "The older commentators regard the falling to the ground as a miracle, but modern scholars look upon it as a result of sudden fear. Jesus merely manifested his dignity and majesty, and the prostration followed as a natural result."[48] Leon Morris said it "is possible that those in front recoiled from Jesus' unexpected advance, so that they bumped those behind them, causing them to stumble and fall. C. B. Williams translates: 'they took a lurch backward and fell to the ground.' But clearly what concerns John is the

---

[44] In John 19:17, 18, Jesus said: "This is why the Father loves me, because I lay down my life in order to take it up again. No one takes it from me, but *I lay it down on my own.*" —*NAB* rendering. *NEB* has "I am laying it down of my own free will."
[45] *Commentary Critical and Explanatory on the Whole Bible* Jamieson Fausset Brown.
[46] *People's New Testament* (electronic edition)
[47] *Meyer's Commentary on the New Testament, Gospel of John* (New York: Funk & Wagnalls, 1884), pp. 479-480.
[48] *The Fourfold Gospel*, by J. W. McGarvey and Philip Y. Pendleton.

majesty of Jesus thus underlined."[49] According to one evangelical commentary: "It may be that the boldness and moral grandeur of Jesus made them shrink like creatures in the presence of a strong light."[50] Another scholarly source observed: "The words which follow, 'they fell to the ground,' then, imply no more than that the men who came to make the arrest (some of whom at least did not previously know Jesus even by sight) were so overcome by His moral ascendancy that they recoiled in fear...On a previous occasion ([John] 7:44) they had faltered and failed to do so. It may have been a similar shrinking which caused some now to recoil from their distasteful task, and in the confusion they, or some of the crowd, stumbled and fell."[51]

Although viewing Jesus' answer to the soldiers as a possible divine self-disclosure, the *International Critical Commentary* was right for calling attention to the fact that the soldiers likely knew about Jesus' unique power and authoritative presence in light of their failure to arrest him in John chapter seven. The account says that some "of them wanted to arrest him, but no one laid hands on him. The officers then went back to the chief priests and Pharisees, who said to them, 'Why did you not bring him?' The officers answered, 'No man ever spoke like this man!'"

This account is significant in terms of understanding the overall background and likely mental disposition of the guards on the night of Jesus' arrest. In the *Pillar New Testament Commentary*, D. A. Carson observed: "The Evangelist has already testified to the effect of Jesus' words on temple officials sent to arrest him ([John] 7:45-46); indeed, it is not at all unlikely that some of the same personnel are again involved. If they have been awed by Jesus before, if they have been dumbfounded by his teaching, his authority, his directness in the full light of day in the precincts of the temple where they most

---

[49] *The New International Commentary on the New Testament, The Gospel According to John, The English Text with Introduction, Exposition and Notes* by Leon Morris (Grand Rapids: Eerdmans, 1971), pp. 743-744.

[50] *The Evangelical Commentary, The Gospel According to John, Vol. IV*, George Allen Turner Ph. D., Professor of Biblical, Literature, Asbury Theological Seminary and Julius R. Mantey, Professor Emeritus, Northern Baptist Theological Seminary (Grand Rapids: Eerdmans), p. 353.

[51] *International Critical Commentary, A Critical and Exegetical Commentary on the Gospel According to St. John, Volume II*, by Archbishop J. H. Bernard, Edinburgh. Edited by the Rev. A. H. McNeile, D. D. (T & T. Clark, 1963), p. 586.

feel at home, it is not hard to believe that they are staggered by his open self-disclosure on a sloping mountainside in the middle of the night..."[52]

In light of the different viewpoints that have been advanced as plausible explanations for the soldiers' falling, it is still wise to keep in mind, as one writer noted: "Exactly what caused them to go backward and fall to the ground, *the scriptures do not say.*"[53] In the same way, Albert Barnes observed:

> *The cause of [the soldiers'] retiring in this manner is not mentioned.* Various things might have produced it. The frank, open, and fearless manner in which Jesus addressed them may have convinced them of his innocence, and deterred them from prosecuting their wicked attempt. His disclosure of himself was sudden and unexpected; and while they perhaps anticipated that he would make an effort to escape, they were amazed at his open and bold profession. Their consciences reproved them for their crimes, and probably the firm, decided, and yet mild manner in which Jesus addressed them, the expression of his unequalled power in knowing how to find the way to the consciences of men, made them feel that they were in the presence of more than mortal man. There is no proof that there was here any miraculous power, any mere physical force, and to suppose that there was greatly detracts from the moral sublimity of the scene.[54]

Whatever the precise truth of the matter turns out to be, on the night of the arrest, there is no reason to doubt that when

---

[52] *The Pillar New Testament Commentary, The Gospel According to John*, p. 578. After this observation, Carson says, "the more so if some of them hear the overtones of God's self-disclosure in the prophecy of Isaiah." However, Carson does not argue that this is the only possible explanation. He simply suggests that if it were true that Jesus had uttered the divine name that this would have been an *added* reason for the soldiers to have fallen.

[53] *Restoration Light Bible Study Services "I am" in John 8:58* (Last update: April 14, 2004) (emphasis added). In the same article, the author writes: "to say it was Jesus' use of some Greek words, supposedly having power to knock them down, is an assumption and pure speculation. However, since speculating, our theory regarding this is that they could have been taken aback and fell to ground as the result of a power our Lord exercised over them (which power he had received from the only true Supreme Being, his Father), a power by which he might have resisted them entirely had he been so disposed. What he did was sufficient to show them and his apostles that his surrender was not a necessity, but that the Father's will might be done."

[54] *Barnes' Notes, Electronic Database.* Copyright (c) 1997 by Biblesoft (emphasis added).

The 'I am' statements of the Gospel of John

Jesus said "I am *he*," that he was affirming his identity as "Jesus of Nazareth," as a simple reading of the text will bear out. Again, Jesus asked the soldiers: "'Whom do you seek?' They answered him, 'Jesus of Nazareth.' Jesus said to them, 'I am *he*.'" After the soldiers had fallen, the account goes on to read: "Again he asked them, 'Whom do you seek?' And they said, 'Jesus of Nazareth.' Jesus answered, 'I told you that I am *he*; so, if you seek me, let these men go.'"

As to the specific reason *why* the soldiers drew back and fell to the ground, it is difficult to say with certainty. However, in verse six, the text does not say "*because* (Gk: *hoti*) Jesus said 'I am *he*' the soldiers fell," as if the very words in and of themselves were the direct *cause* of the reaction. The Gospel simply says, "*As, then, He said to them*, "I am *he*," they dropped behind and fell on the ground."[55] In terms of the soldiers' fall, there is nothing explicitly causal said or implied when Jesus used the simple method of self-identification "I am *he*"; and if the utterance of the ordinary words "I am *he*" carried divine power, it is difficult to explain why there was no comparable reaction on the part of Jesus' listeners in the previous instances where he used the same expression, as in John 4:25, 26; 8:24, 28; 13:19.

Although Trinitarians have continued to argue that Jesus' overall usage of the expression *ego eimi* amounted to a claim to be God incarnate, they do not usually notice that in Mark 13:6 Jesus used the same expression,—speaking to his disciples about a future time—telling them: "Many shall come in my name, saying, I am *he* (*ego eimi*); and shall lead many astray."[56] Here Jesus made use of the same phrase that in other instances allegedly amounted to his claim to be God himself. But most, if not all, commentators realize that Jesus was not implying that in the future people would come on the basis of his name claiming to be Jehovah God (or the one who 'eternally exists,' as some take the expression to mean); but that in the future many would come in his name claiming themselves to be the "Christ/Messiah,"[57] or, perhaps, endeavor to draw people after

---

[55] *Concordant Literal New Testament. NASB*: "*So when He said to them*, "I am He, they drew back and fell to the ground."
[56] *ASV* rendering
[57] See *NIV Study Bible* and *NET* footnotes. *King James Version* has "I am *Christ*…"

The 'I am' statements of the Gospel of John

themselves, in effect, attempting to usurp the Messianic status rightfully and uniquely held by Jesus.

The footnote on this verse in the *MacArthur Study Bible* states: "'I am *He*.' Many false prophets will come forward claiming to be messiahs and deliverers, offering themselves as the solution to the world's problems. Some will even claim to be Christ Himself. The number of false christs will increase as the end nears (cf. [Matt.] 24:23, 24)."[58]

Not only are we able to consult a respected Bible scholar for helpful insight on this point, but the disciple Matthew himself independently confirms what Jesus had in mind by making what is implied in Mark explicit in his own account: "For many will come in my name, saying, '*I am the Christ*,' and they will lead many astray."[59] Here, we find yet further corroborating evidence that the "I am *he*" statements of Jesus recorded in the Gospels consistently revolve around what is undeniably one of the most critical and all-encompassing themes of the New Testament documents, that Jesus is the very one he claimed to be—the Christ of God.

At the end of his discussion, in the chapter titled "I Am He," Dr. White argues: "Jesus here gives us the content and object of saving faith—real faith is that which focuses on the real Jesus...The Jews standing about Him during this conversation [in John 8:24] most assuredly would not have denied that He was a man—but that was not sufficient for faith." Dr. White even claims: "Some had *only* recently proclaimed Him as *Messiah— but that was not sufficient for faith*."[60] Yet in his first letter the apostle John reminded the Christians: "*Whoever believes that Jesus is the Messiah is a child of God* (literally: "is born/begotten of God)"[61]—demonstrating, clearly, that in the eyes of the first-century Christians, acceptance of Jesus' Messiahship was the central and foundational article of the faith—so much that the belief itself was intimately involved with

---

[58] *The MacArthur Study Bible*, p. 1491.
[59] Matthew 24:5, *RSV*
[60] White, *The Forgotten Trinity*, p. 104 (emphasis added).
[61] 1 John 5:1, *TEV*. If it is true that the sense of the passage is "the one (already) begotten of God confesses that Jesus is the Christ," so that the *result* of being born of God is faith in Jesus as the Messiah (and not the other way around), the point would be the same. The result of being born of God would be the confession that Jesus is the Christ, not that he is the "I am."

one's being "born of God." According to Matthew's Gospel, Peter's confession of Jesus as the *Messiah*—given through direct revelation from God the Father—resulted in the Lord's immediate approval and blessing ('blessed are you Simon son of Jonah!'), showing that such a confession of faith actually was "sufficient" for *real* faith, in the "real Jesus."

Commenting further on the *ego eimi* statements, however, Dr. White correctly noted that these "statements were not made in a vacuum—they are placed in a book that is rich with meaning and purpose."[62] But if we pay close attention to the surrounding circumstances and expressions previously made by Jesus in the examples cited, we can see that whether he meant "Son of man," "Messiah," the one "from above," "the light of the world," or 'the one in whom Psalm 41:9 would have fulfillment,' each would render to Jesus his rightful honor and deserved dignity as God's anointed one;[63] in each case they would be in harmonious accord with their individual contexts; and each would perfectly reflect the *clearly-stated meaning and purpose* of the Gospel of John:

> **But these are written so that you may come to believe that Jesus is the Messiah, the Son of God, and that through believing you may have life in his name.**[64]

---

[62] White, *The Forgotten Trinity*, p. 104.

[63] B. B. Warfield (1851-1921) identified Jesus as "God's representative, endowed with all authority and endued with all miraculous powers." He also noted: "To [Mark] Jesus is primarily the Messiah, and the Messiah is primarily the agent of God in bringing in the new order of things. Undoubtedly Mark's fundamental thought of Jesus is that He is the man of God's appointment, with whom God is." Of the Gospels viewed together, Warfield observed: "If we are to take the designations employed in the Gospel narratives as our guide, therefore, we should say that the fundamental general fact which they suggest is that Jesus was esteemed by His first followers as the promised Messiah, and was looked upon with reverence and accorded supreme authority as such." —*The Lord of Glory, A Study of our Lord in the New Testament with Especial Reference to His Deity* (Birmingham: Solid Ground Christian Books, 2003), pp. 33, 34, 35, 4.

[64] John 20:31, *NRSV*. Dr. Macarthur noted that these "verses constitute the goal and purpose for which John wrote the gospel…" See *MacArthur Study Bible*, p. 1627. Dr. William Varner said: "The promise of a 'Coming One,' that one most often referred to by both Jews and Christians as the 'Messiah' is what, in my opinion, forms the center of the entire Biblical revelation." —*The Messiah, Revealed, Rejected, Received* (Bloomington: Author House, 2004), p. xi.

The 'I am' statements of the Gospel of John

John 8:58

"Most assuredly, I say to you, before Abraham was, I am."

During the course of a hostile confrontation with the Jewish leaders, Jesus said to them (as rendered in the *New King James Version*):

> '**Your father Abraham rejoiced to see My day, and he saw it and was glad.' Then the Jews said to him, 'You are not yet fifty years old, and you have seen Abraham?' Jesus said to them, 'Most assuredly, I say to you, before Abraham was, I AM** (*ego eimi*).' **Then they took up stones to throw at Him; but Jesus hid Himself and went out of the temple, going through the midst of them, and so passed by.**[65]

In response to their question about his relation to their ancestor Abraham, Jesus declared to the Jews, "before Abraham was I am (*ego eimi*)." It has become virtually a standard argument put forward by evangelical teachers that the words of Jesus in this case are a reference to (or even a direct quote from) Exodus 3:14 where, according to the *King James Version*, the LORD (Jehovah) said to Moses:

> '**I AM THAT I AM** (Hebrew: '*ehyeh asher ehyeh*')' **and he said, 'Thus shalt thou say unto the children of Israel, I AM hath sent me unto you.**'[66]

The conclusion drawn by scores of evangelical preachers and commentators is that Jesus, in his dialogue with the Jews, was claiming the title "I AM" for himself, and that this means Jesus was actually proclaiming himself to be Jehovah, the God who made himself known to Moses and the people of Israel. For example, in his popular *Systematic Theology*, Wayne Grudem argued:

> When Jesus told his Jewish opponents that Abraham had seen his (Christ's) day, they challenged him, 'You are not yet fifty years old, and have you seen Abraham?' (John 8:57). Here a sufficient response to prove Jesus' eternity

---
[65] John 8:58, *NKJV*
[66] Exodus 3:14-15, *KJV*

The 'I am' statements of the Gospel of John

would have been, 'Before Abraham was, I was.' But Jesus did not say this.[67] Instead, he made a much more startling assertion...Jesus combined two assertions whose sequence seemed to make no sense: 'Before something happened [Abraham was], something in the present happened [I am].' ...when he said, 'I am,' he was repeating the very words of God when he identified himself to Moses as '*I AM* WHO I AM' (Ex. 3:14). Jesus was claiming for himself the title 'I AM,' by which God designates himself as the eternal existing One...When the Jews heard this unusual, emphatic, solemn statement, they knew that he was claiming to be God. 'So they picked up stones to throw at him...'[68]

The above explanation has gained wide acceptance among many groups and denominations. In fact, nearly every popular evangelical commentary has argued for the same basic point. Of course, few, if any, point out the existence of Bible translations that render both John 8:58 and Exodus 3:14 in a different way—in a way that would make it difficult to discern or identify any connection between the words of God's Son in the Gospel of John and the words of God himself in the book of Exodus. Other translations, for example, attempt to convey the sense of Jesus' words at John 8:58 in this way: **"I tell you, I existed before Abraham was born!"**

Goodspeed's 1923 *American Translation* renders the sense of Jesus' words into English in a way that does not demand a concept of "eternal pre-existence" or a quotation of Exodus 3:14, but in a way suggesting that Jesus did in fact exist (in some unspecified form or sense) even before the days of his physical birth as a man—having existed "before" the birth and

---

[67] Grudem errors when he says that "a sufficient response to prove Jesus' eternity would have been, 'Before Abraham was, I was.'" If Jesus would have made such a statement, the most one could legitimately conclude is that Jesus claimed to have existed before Abraham. It would not be specific enough to mean or demand a concept of "eternal" existence. If it were true that Jesus had *always* existed, one would have to derive that idea from other parts of Scripture.

[68] Grudem, *Systematic Theology*, pp. 545-546. Similarly, the *MacArthur Study Bible* (p. 1601) states in a footnote: "Here Jesus declared himself to be Yahweh, i.e., the Lord of the OT. Basic to the expression are such passages as Ex. 3:14, Deut. 32:39; Is 41:4; 43:10 where God declared Himself to be the eternally pre-existent God who revealed Himself in the OT to the Jews." It is stated in another source: "In certain places (e.g., John 8:59) the Greek words for *I am* were capitalized, I AM. It is our conviction that in these places Jesus identified Himself as Jehovah (cf. Exod. 3:14-15)." —*Preface to the Interlinear Hebrew, Greek, English Bible*, J.P. Green Sr Green

The 'I am' statements of the Gospel of John

time of Abraham, the ancient forefather of the Jewish nation.[69] This appears to harmonize well with what is brought out in the introduction to the same Gospel, when the apostle John said that the very *"world came into existence through him"* (John 1:10); and how Paul likewise stated that "in ['the beloved Son'] were created all things in heaven and on earth, the visible and the invisible...all things were created through him and for him," and that, "He is *before all things*..." (Colossians 1:16).[70] In fact, a reasonable case based on these texts and others can be made that the Messiah existed in a glorious form of some kind "before the world was" (John 17:5)—either *literally* and *personally*, as the firstborn Son of God, as some believe, or, *ideally* and *prophetically*, as "the word (*logos*)" of God's Messianic promise, as others believe (John 1:1).

Whatever the case may be, these points also appear to harmonize well with the creation account in Genesis, where it is revealed that God made all things by his spoken word. That is, according to the ancient text, God *spoke* or *commanded* what came to be into existence (Genesis 1:3; compare Hebrews 11:3); and that Jesus Christ was, according to the Gospel of John, the very person in whom God's "word became flesh and dwelt among us" (John 1:14).

Contrary to the popular explanation of John 8:58, Jesus was not identifying himself as the so-called "I AM." But, grammatically, the words *ego eimi* ('I am/exist') do project through a period "before Abraham was," so that the existence of God's Son—or of God's *promise* to send him forth, according to some interpreters—would once again be spoken of as already being in occurrence before the Son was physically born as a man on the earth.

Although the words of Jesus are translated "I am" in its main text, the footnote to the *New American Standard Bible*

---

[69] To clarify, some would argue that even if the translation is correct, Jesus did not necessarily mean that he *literally* existed as a *person* before Abraham, but that he existed, prophetically, in the form of the *promise* and *purpose* of God to send the Messiah into the world. See Appendix for insight into this perspective.

[70] Yet some Christians believe and present evidence that the expressions made in the first chapters of Hebrews and Colossians about the "ages" and "all things" created through (*dia*) and in (*en*) the "Son" actually have reference to the new *Messianic* age/order, the new creation God brings into existence through Christ, not the creation depicted in the Genesis account. See: Deuble, *They never told me this in church!*, pp. 184-238.

(1963 & 1971 editions) for John 8:58 has: "**Or, "I have been**" as a legitimate alternative rendering. The following is a facsimile of John 8:58 as it appears in the *NASB* 1971 edition (see left side):

Heb. 11:13	saw it, and was glad."
57 ªJohn 1:19	57 ªThe Jews therefore said to Him, "You are not yet fifty years old, and have You seen Abraham?"
58 ¹Lit., *came into being* ²Or, *I have been* ªJohn 17:5, 24; 1:1	58 Jesus said to them, "Truly, truly, I say to you, before Abraham ¹was born, ²ªI AM."
59 ¹Lit., *was hidden* ²Some	59 Therefore they ªpicked up stones to throw at Him; but Jesus ¹ᵇhid Himself, ²and went out of the temple.

Renowned Greek scholar, the late Dr. Julius R. Mantey (coauthor of the *Manual Grammar of the Greek New Testament*), referred to the New Testament translation by C. B. Williams as "the most accurate and illuminating translation in the English language."[71] Williams rendered the verse:

> **Then Jesus said to them, 'I solemnly say to you, I existed before Abraham was born.'**[72]

In *A Translator's Handbook on the Gospel of John*, it was observed that in "many languages it is impossible to preserve the expression *I Am* in this type of context, for the present tense of the verb 'to be' would be meaningless. To make sense, one must say 'Before Abraham existed, I existed' or '…I have existed.'[73] Although the translators point out that "I am" would be meaningless in many languages, the same proves to be

---

[71] The fuller endorsement reads: "While teaching a post-graduate Greek class and spending the whole year studying translations of the New Testament, we became convinced that Williams' translation, considering all the factors, is the most accurate and illuminating translation in the English language. Having this conviction, I have no hesitation in commending it to all who desire to penetrate into the depths and riches of the glorious revelation of the New Testament." Mantey also noted: "it became increasingly apparent to all those making the study that Dr. Williams' translation possessed unusual and unparalleled merit, not only in the rendering of tenses but also in bringing out clearly and accurately the meaning of all the Greek words and ideas. Dr. Williams has succeeded in surpassing all other translators of the New Testament in bringing out the tense significance of the Greek verbs." —Department of New Testament Interpretation, Northern Baptist Theological Seminary Chicago, Illinois. Introduction to *The New Testament* by C. B. Williams (Chicago: Moody Press, 1963).

[72] William Loader observed, "In [John] 6:20, 8:25, 28 and 58 Jesus uses the absolute, 'ego eimi' (lit. 'I am'). In 8:25, 28 the context favours the meaning, 'I am what I claim to be', understood in terms of the revealer pattern (so: esp 8:28). In 6:20 Jesus is identifying himself: 'It is I (not a ghost or the like)' and in 8:58 the text need mean no more than I am and was in existence before Abraham, still a majestic claim but not an allusion to the divine name." —*The Christology of the Fourth Gospel, Structures and Issues*, p. 52.

[73] *Helps For Translators, A Translator's Handbook on the Gospel of John*, by Barclay M. Newman and Eugene A. Nida (United Bible Societies, 1972), p. 295 (underlining in original).

true—in terms of grammar—with respect to our own English language as well. This is probably one of the reasons other versions of the Bible have rendered the verse in a similar way:

> **'Truly, truly I tell you,' said Jesus, 'I have existed before Abraham was born.'**
> —*The Bible, A New Translation by James Moffatt*
> **Jesus said to them, 'I tell you the truth: I was alive before Abraham was born.'**
> —*The Simple English Bible*
> **'The absolute truth is that I was in existence before Abraham was ever born!'**
> —*The Living Bible*
> **Jesus answered, 'The truth is, I existed before Abraham was ever born!'**
> —*New Living Translation*
> **'Truly, truly I tell you, before Abraham was born, I have already been.'**
> —*The Unvarnished New Testament by Andy Gaus*
> **Jesus said, truly I tell you, 'From before Abraham was, I have been.'**
> —*The New Testament, by G. Rh. Noyes*
> **'I am telling you the truth: I was alive before Abraham was born!'**
> —*The International English Bible translation*
> **'I tell you for a positive fact, I existed before Abraham was born.'**
> —*The Original New Testament, Schonfield*

Jason BeDuhn helpfully elaborated on the grammatical reasons for such a translation:

> John 8:58 has two verbs, one ('am') in the present tense, and the other ('came to be') in the past (technically, the 'aorist') tense. In most sentences where we see a past tense verb and a present tense verb, we would assume that the action of the past verb is earlier in time than the action of the present verb ('John wrote the book that I am reading': 'wrote' happened before 'am reading'). This is true in most cases in Greek as well as in English. But in John 8:58 this is not the case, and we know it is not the case because the preposition *prin*, 'before,' coordinates the relationship between the two actions represented by

the verbs. This preposition tells us that the action of the verb in the present tense ('am') happened (or began to happen, or was already happening) 'before' the action of the verb in the past tense ('came to be')...It is ungrammatical English for something referred to with a present 'am' to occur earlier in time than something described with a past 'came to be.'...A quick glance at Smyth's *Greek Grammar* reveals that what we are dealing with in John 8:58 is a well-known Greek idiom. The pertinent entry is section 1885 on verb tenses, which states, 'The present, when accompanied by a definite or indefinite expression of past time, is used to express an action begun in the past and continued in the present. The 'progressive perfect' is often used in translation. Thus,...*I have been long* (and am still) *wondering.*' I think you can see immediately that his entry applies to John 8:58, where the present verb *eimi* is accompanied by an expression of past time, *prin Abraam genesthai* ['before Abraham came to be'].[74]

Another scholarly source offers a translation for Jesus' words at John 8:58 that might be considered the most literal rendition into English possible: "*I have been in existence since before Abraham was born.*"[75] Professor BeDuhn observed: "In John 8:58, since Jesus' existence is not completed past action, but ongoing, we must use some sort of imperfect verbal form to convey that: 'I have been (since) before Abraham came to be.' That's as close as we can get to what the Greek says in our own language if we pay attention to all parts of the sentence."

Grammarians have described this type of speech as "extension from the past" or "present of past action still in progress." John 14:9 is a closely-related example in the English Bible which reads: "Jesus said to him, '*Have I been* so long with you, and yet you have not come to know Me, Philip?'" (*NASB*) The Greek is literally: "So much time with you *I am* (*eimi*, present tense) and not you have known me..." But in the Greek

---

[74] *Truth in Translation*, pp. 104-111 (words in brackets added for clarification).
[75] K. L. McKay, *A New Syntax of the Verb in New Testament Greek, An Aspectual Approach* (New York: Peter Lang Publishing, Inc., 1994), p. 42. McKay identifies it as "Extension from Past"—'When used with an expression of either past time or extent of time with past implications...the present tense signals an activity begun in the past and continuing to present time'"; citing Luke 13:7; 15:29; John 14:9; Acts 27:33 and John 8:58 as examples.

it means the same as it is translated into English ('*have I been* so long with you...?') and must be translated this way for the English to be grammatically coherent and intelligible. As it was correctly noted by Dr. White: "There are many instances in historical narrative or conversation where the Greek will use a present tense verb that is best rendered in English by the perfect tense. John 15:27 would be a good example: 'because you have been with me from the beginning.' The verb is in the present tense, but the context makes it clear that it is in reference to both the past and the present."[76]

At John 8:58 the Greek literally reads, "before Abraham came to be I am." However, it is legitimately translated into English: "before Abraham came to be I have been [or 'I have been in existence (since) before Abraham came to be']." This is so because the preposition "before" (Gk: *prin*) accompanied by the completed expression of past time—"Abraham came to be"—functions, grammatically, and for the purpose of English translation, as an indication that the action—"I am"—took place, or was taking place, *before* Abraham was born, and continued into the present. In other words, in terms of grammar, the phrase "I am/exist" (*ego eimi*) embraces the entire period from "before-Abraham-came-to-be" to the present; that is, the present moment that Jesus was speaking and standing before the Jews. In English, this is best conveyed by the phrase "I have been," where the action or state of the verb encompasses the past but does not exclude the present.[77] The translators of the *Contemporary English Version* attempted to capture the sense by translating John 8:58: "I tell you for certain that even before Abraham was, I was, and I am." Similarly, only with a reversal of word order, one Roman Catholic translation rendered the statement: "I tell you the plain truth,' replied Jesus; 'I am here—and I was before

---

[76] White, *The Forgotten Trinity*, p. 97. Another respected commentator similarly pointed out: "*Eimi* is used to express a former condition which is continued in the present, as in 14:9, 15:27, Luke 15:29,...Jer. 1:5, Septuagint." —Dr. Augustus Tholuck, *Commentary on the Gospel of John* (Edinburgh: T & T Clark, 1859), p. 243.

[77] It was pointed out by one Bible student: "In the sentence *prin abraam genesthai ego eimi* the main clause is *ego eimi*; and we must note that it follows an adverbial phrase of past time—a fact which changes its meaning rather dramatically. Why? Because in Greek when an adverb of time is followed by a statement which denotes continuing action which began in the past, Greek uses the present tense where English ordinarily uses the perfect tense." —M. James Penton, *The "I AM" of John 8:58, The Christian Quest Magazine*, p. 59.

The 'I am' statements of the Gospel of John

Abraham!'"[78]

Most Trinitarian apologists, however, contend that the *only* way to account for the violent reaction on the part of the Jews is to conclude that Jesus must have been making a claim to "deity" by applying the "divine name ('I AM')" to himself, or that he was making the "blasphemous" claim—in the eyes of the Jews—of "eternal preexistence." Apparently, James White agrees with other evangelicals who say that "the response of the Jews would be rather strong if this was simply a claim of preexistence."[79]

Unfortunately, it is generally overlooked that the Jewish reaction came at the end and climax of an obviously increasing sense of hostility toward Jesus based on the previous words exchanged between them. In verse 21, Jesus bluntly told the self-righteous religious leaders that they would "*die in their sin.*" In verse 37, he told them forthrightly, "*You are of your father the devil, and your will is to do your father's desires.*" In verse 47, Jesus said, "the reason why you do not hear [my words] is that *you are not of God.*" In turn the Jews insulted Jesus by calling him "a Samaritan" and accusing him of being "possessed by a demon" (verse 48), clearly demonstrating their increasingly aggressive and hostile disposition up to that point. In verse 55 Jesus called them *liars*: "you do not know [the Father], I know him. If I said I did not, I would be *a liar like you*, but I do know him and keep his word." Then, Jesus began to speak in a manner that seemingly suggested he was already acquainted with Abraham (a manner that, in the eyes of the Jews, probably seemed strange and presumptuous), a man who had lived and died long ago. Jesus said that their father Abraham rejoiced to see his day, and, "he saw it and was glad." To this the Jews responded, "you are not yet fifty years old and you have seen Abraham?" When Jesus finally declared to the Jews: "**The truth is, I existed before Abraham** [the great Jewish patriarch] **was ever born!**" (*NLT*), this was "the straw that broke the camel's back" so to speak. And, in a decidedly agitated and impulsive response to Jesus' extraordinary claim, the Jews became

---

[78] *The New Testament, Rendered From the Original Greek*, Kleist and Lily. *The Aramaic Peshitta New Testament Translation* (by Janet Magiera) has: "Before Abraham was, I was."
[79] White, *The Forgotten Trinity*, p. 97.

enraged, so they tried to hurl stones at him in order to kill him, "but Jesus hid and went out into the temple."

Dr. White's claim is further weakened when it is remembered that, in Luke chapter 4:14-30, the people of the synagogue tried to kill Jesus by throwing him down the brow of the mountain for what might be considered an equal, if not much lesser, offense. On that occasion, Jesus evidently suggested that he was not going to perform any more healings among the people of the synagogue in his hometown of Nazareth; and that, as Albert Barnes noted, "he would direct his attention to others [including Gentiles], and not to them." Because of this, the crowd was enraged to the point that they attempted to take Jesus' life by throwing him down the mountain side—"but Jesus passed through the midst of them."

It was even pointed out by the distinguished New Testament professor Craig Blomberg: "The fact that the Jews immediately tried to stone [Jesus in John 8:59] does not mean they understood his statement as a direct equation of himself with God. Claiming that Abraham had seen his day (verse 56) itself bordered on blasphemy, and the Jews had already tried to kill him for much lesser 'crimes' such as healing on the Sabbath (Mk. 3:6) and speaking of God's love for the gentiles (Lk. 4:29)."[80]

Strangely, Dr. White claimed emphatically that "to translate [John 8:58 as 'I have been'] is to miss the entire context and content of what is being said!"[81] Such comments are baffling. To argue that if Jesus would have claimed to have existed before Abraham when the very question was, "you are not yet fifty years old and you have seen Abraham?" is "to miss the entire context and content of what is being said" is a nonsensical objection, a mere assertion without any support.[82] The translation "I have been" is not only grammatically legitimate, if not necessary, but makes logical sense and fits the context perfectly. For Jesus to have opposed and repeatedly denounced the Jewish

---

[80] Blomberg, *The Historical Reliability of the Gospels* (Leicester/Illinois: Inter-Varisty Press, 1987), pp. 164, 165.
[81] White, *The Forgotten Trinity*, p. 97.
[82] It is also strange that Dr. White suggests that the connection between John 8:58 and Exodus 3:14 is traced through the *ani hu/ego eimi* statements of Isaiah. If any connection existed there would be no need to "trace" it through other Scriptures; the connection would stand on its own.

leaders in the manner that he did, and to have finally, as a man in his thirties, claimed to have been in existence before the great and highly-honored father of their very nation (who had died about two thousand years prior to that time[83]), quite clearly and satisfactorily accounts for the violent reaction on the part of the Jewish leaders.[84] Professor BeDuhn observed:

> It is Jesus' claim to be superior to Abraham, and to have a superhuman longevity, not a claim to a divine self-designation, that enrages his audience...Jesus' argument in 8:58 is that he has seniority over Abraham, and so by the standards of Jewish society, he has greater authority than the patriarch. No one listening to Jesus, and no one reading John in his own time would have picked up on a divine self-identification in the mere expression 'I am,' which, if you think about it, is just about the most common pronoun-verb combination in any language.[85]

When the context and purpose of Jesus' response to the Jews is carefully considered, it reveals that there is no relationship between Exodus 3:14-15 and John 8:58 that can properly be used to demonstrate that Jesus was actually claiming or teaching that he was applying the name (or meaning of the name) of Jehovah God himself. Although this is the alleged connection put forward by most evangelical commentaries, some of the more learned Trinitarian scholars have actually made the very same point in recent times.

Some apologists, however, still try to maintain a connection between the two verses in spite of these points; because, in the Septuagint translation of Exodus 3:14, the phrase *ego eimi* appears as part of an expression made by God relative to his revealed name. According to the Septuagint, God said, "*ego eimi ho on*," which can be translated into English: "I am the

---

[83] Abraham was probably born about 350 years after the Noahic flood, in about 2081 B.C.E.
[84] For Jesus to have claimed to have been in existence before Abraham is also consistent with the statement made by John the Baptist (according to some renditions), who said of Jesus, "He comes after me, but he is greater than I am, because he existed before I was born" (*TEV*); "he existed before me" (*JB*); "he was before me" (*KJV*). Some, however, take the expression to mean that Christ is "before" John the Baptist in the sense that he is "superior" to him. The *Concordant Literal New Testament* has: "'He Who is coming after me, has come to be in front of me,' for He was first, before me..." (John 1:15).
[85] *Truth in Translation*, p. 11.

The 'I am' statements of the Gospel of John

being" or "I am the existing one." Yet, according to the Septuagint, God did not tell Moses that he willed to be known by the phrase "I am" (*ego eimi*), but, rather, as "the being/existing one" (*ho on*), as indicated by the following verse: "Thus shall you say to the children of Israel, *the being* (*ho on*) has sent me to you." In response to his Jewish opponents in John 8:58, Jesus did not say, "*ego eimi ho on*." He simply used the expression "*ego eimi*" as part of a declaration revealing that he had been in existence before Abraham came into existence and which would have also necessarily included Jesus' present existence at that particular point in time. In the Septuagint the phrase "*ego eimi*" is simply the verb that sets up the actual identity, "*ho on*"; it is not the identity itself.[86]

In its main text, the *English Standard Version* has the more common English translation of the Hebrew for Exodus 3:14. However, in the footnote, attention is called to the fact that the verse may be translated, "*I WILL BE WHAT I WILL BE*" (Heb: '*ehyeh asher ehyeh*'). Although the most common translation of Exodus 3:14 is "I am that I am," the following observation was made in *The International Standard Bible Encyclopedia*:

> I will be who/what I will be…is preferable because the verb *hayah* [to be] has a more dynamic sense of being—not pure existence, but becoming, happening, being present—and because the historical and theological context of these early chapters of Exodus shows that God is revealing to Moses, and subsequently to the whole people, not the inner nature of His being [or existence], but his active, redemptive intentions on their behalf. He 'will be' to them 'what His deeds will show Him 'to be.'…the imperfect '*ehyeh* is more accurately translated 'I will be what I will be,' a Semitic idiom meaning, 'I will be all that is necessary as the occasion will arise,' a familiar OT idea. (cf Is 7:4.9; Ps 23)[87]

Significantly, Trinitarian apologist Robert Bowman acknowledged, "it is true that the expression in Exodus 3:14 is

---

[86] F. F. Bruce observed: "If a direct reference had been intended to Ex. 3:14 in the present passage, one might have expected *ho on* rather than *ego eimi*." —*The Gospel of John*, p. 193.
[87] *The New International Standard Bible Encyclopedia*, Vol. II, pp. 507, 1254.

probably better translated 'I will be what I will be'..."[88] In another one of Bowman's works, it was noted that "most Hebraists now recognize [EHYEH] to mean literally 'I will be,' with the connotation of 'I shall prove to be.' Although many evangelical scholars have argued that 'I am' is correct, there would appear to be solid reasons for accepting the rendering 'I will be' or 'I will become.' This would make the meaning of EHYEH ASHER EHYEH to be 'I will be what I will be,' or some such equivalent."[89]

Accordingly, several modern translators have rendered Exodus 3:14-15 in the following ways:

> **And God said to Moses, *'I will be what I will be'*; and he said 'You are to say to the sons of Israel *'Will Be* has sent me to you.'** —*The Bible in Living English*[90]
> **And God said unto Moses,** *I will become whatsoever I please*, **And he said—Thus shalt thou say to the sons of Israel,** *I Will Become* **hath sent me unto you.**
> —*Rotherham's Emphasized Bible*
> **God said unto Moshe:** *EHYEH ASHER EHYEH/I will be-there howsoever I will be-there*. **And he said: Thus shall you say to the   Children of Israel:** *EHYEH/ I-Will-Be-There* **sends me to you.** —*The Five Books of Moses, The Shocken Bible, Volume I, Translated by Everett Fox*

It was noted by another scholarly source:

> There can be no doubt that *ehyeh* normally means 'I will be' rather than 'I am,' and is so translated elsewhere, usually in God's affirmation about himself, such as in verse 12 of this same chapter. 'But I will be with you...' However it also occurs with the same future significance in the ordinary conversation of Israelites, e.g.: 'If you bring me home again to fight with the Ammonites, and the LORD gives them over to me, *I will be* your head.' (Judges 11:9) The fuller expression *'ehyeh asher ehyeh,'*

---

[88] Bowman, *Why You Should Believe in the Trinity*, p. 99.
[89] Bowman, *Jehovah's Witnesses, Jesus Christ, and the Gospel of John*, (Grand Rapids: Baker, 1989), p. 125 (word in brackets added)
[90] Most modern Bible translations, while retaining the words "I am that I am" in the main text, include "I will be who/what I will be" as an alternative rendering in the marginal footnotes. For examples, see footnotes to Exodus 3:14 in the following versions: *ASV, RSV, NRSV, NIV, NEB, REB, AB, TEV, CEV, TLB, NLT*.

The 'I am' statements of the Gospel of John

> when literally translated, will therefore read 'I will be who (or what-*asher* can mean either) I *will* be'...*ehyeh asher ehyeh* means 'I will be (or, become) whatever I will (or, please, choose).' The related name *yahweh* is the causative form of *hayah*, 'to be' (*Illustrated Bible Dictionary*, pp 571-572); in its context here it may be translated 'He who causes to be (or become) what He chooses.'[91]

According to another source:

> Such a translation as 'I am what I am' appears to be ruled out completely by the fact that the [Hebrew] verbs here are imperfects. 'I am' is the normal translation of the Hebrew perfect, not an imperfect...The translation offered here relates this explanation of the name to covenants with the patriarchs. As such it was a basis of assurance concerning Yahweh's presence and support. This thought is made explicit in the verse that follows, and the proper name Yahweh, the memorial name, is made synonymous with the description 'I shall continue to be what I have always been.' This makes the description a restatement of Yahweh's faithfulness, an assurance that he will fulfill the covenants with Abraham, Isaac and Jacob."[92]

And it was observed in the *Anchor Bible*:

> If one could say 'I am that I am' in Hebrew at all, it would probably be through some such barbarous circumlocution as *'anoki hu' 'aser 'anoki hu'*. Likewise, if the meaning were 'I am *'ehye(h)*,' as the second half of the verse might suggest, we would expect *'anoki (hu') 'ehye(h)*. And if the intention were ' *'ehye(h)* is who I am' ...again assuming this could be conveyed in Hebrew at all, we should get something like *'ehye(h) 'aser 'anoki hu'*. We still have the option of rendering *'ehye(h) 'aser 'ehye(h)* as *eye(h)* is who I will be,' but this seems a strange way for the Deity to identify himself. I follow, therefore, the translation of Aquila and Theodotion: *esomai (hos) esomai* 'I will be who I will be'...Or, if the

---

[91] James H. Broughton, Peter J. Southgate, *The Trinity True or False?* 2nd Edition (Nottingham: 'The Dawn Book Supply', 2002), pp. 46-47.
[92] J. Washington Watts, Professor of OT, New Orleans Baptist Theological Seminary, 1930-1968. *A Distinctive Translation of Exodus With An Interpretative Outline*, pp. 140, 1 (1977).

intent is evasion, an attractive alternative is 'I may be who I may be'...Notice how gradually Yahweh approaches the explicit pronouncement of his name: 'I will be who I will be (*'eye[h] 'aser 'ehye[h]*)... 'I -will-be' (*'eye[h]*) has sent me to you...Only the last truly answers Moses' question.[93]

Although several Bible translations render the words of God in the Exodus passage as "I am that I am," the real sense of the Hebrew verb is better translated "I will be"; and if the significance associated with the divine name is "I will be (or 'become,' or 'prove to be')," it should be clearly seen that the whole point of the supposed connection of the "I am" statements of Exodus 3:14-15 and John 8:58 (which are cited as absolute proof that Jesus was claiming to be God) is, after all, non-existent. There is, therefore, no sound basis for attempting to match the inaccurate English translation "I am" of Exodus 3:14 with Jesus' words at John 8:58.

As already mentioned, during that same account in John chapter eight, in his confrontational encounter with the Jews, Jesus said,

> **'If I glorify myself, My glory is nothing; it is my Father who glorifies Me, of whom you say, 'He is our God.'**[94]

The Hebrew Scriptures clearly and emphatically identify YHWH (*Jehovah*) as the God that the Jews professed to worship. In John chapter eight, Jesus revealed, not that he himself was the God of the Jews, but that the God of the Jews was *his Father*.

Similarly, in the book of Acts,—a record of the events following the resurrection and ascension of Christ—the apostle Peter, while preaching in Solomon's portico, declared to the Jews:

> **"The God of Abraham and of Isaac and of Jacob, the God of our fathers, glorified his servant Jesus, whom you delivered up and denied in the presence of Pilate...whom God raised from the dead. To this we**

---
[93] *The Anchor Bible,* Exodus 1-18, *A New Translation with Introduction and Commentary* (New York: Doubleday, 1999), pp. 204-205.
[94] John 8:54-55, *NASB*

The 'I am' statements of the Gospel of John

are witnesses."[95]

On another occasion, Peter and the other apostles made their position clear when addressing the Jewish Supreme Court, the Sanhedrin, when they declared:

"Obedience to God comes before obedience to men; it was the God of our ancestors [*Jehovah*] who raised up Jesus, whom you executed by hanging on a tree. By his own right hand God has now raised him up to be leader and Savior, to give repentance and forgiveness of sins to Israel"[96]

In his solemn proclamation to the first-century Jewish community, the apostle Peter did not identify Jesus as "the God of our ancestors." To Peter, Jesus was God's "servant," making clear that Jesus was glorified *by* the God of their ancestors, and explicitly declaring that *God raised Jesus from the dead*, the God of the Jewish ancestors—*Jehovah*.

If the apostles thought it crucial to communicate to their Jewish kinsmen that Jesus *was the God of their ancestors*, and that the God of their ancestors actually made an appearance in the flesh in the man Jesus, one wonders how and why they would not have proclaimed such an extraordinary and religiously significant fact to them, either at this point or in the letters that they would write later to those who had faith in Jesus as the Messiah. Again, the question could be asked: In their divinely-directed proclamation of the gospel, why did the apostles speak to their Israelite brothers in such a way that they would have understood them to mean, not that Jesus was "God-in-the-flesh," but that Jesus was God's servant whom God himself had raised from the dead?

After his encounter with the disciple Philip in Acts chapter eight, the Ethiopian who was baptized by him came to understand that Isaiah's prophecy (chapter 53) had fulfillment in the man Jesus of Nazareth—that he was indeed the long-awaited *Messiah*, the chosen and anointed one of God. Without a doubt, Isaiah and the rest of the Hebrew Scriptures (Genesis—Malachi),

---

[95] Acts 3:13-15, *RSV*
[96] Acts 5:29-31, *New Jerusalem Bible* (Name in brackets added for clarification).

make clear that the one true God is Jehovah, while the Christian Scriptures (Matthew—Revelation) clearly identify Jesus as the Christ, God's Son. Approximately two thousand years ago men and women, for the first time, put their faith and hope in Jesus as the promised Messiah, with view to salvation. Today, Christians share that same hope. Through faith in Jesus as God's Messiah we find peace with God, the forgiveness of our sins, and the hope of eternal life.[97] Such is the promise of Scripture. The God of Israel ('the God of our Fathers') demonstrated the depth of his compassionate nature and unfailing love by sending his own Son into the world to be its Savior; and God's Son always delighted in carrying out his Father's perfect will, even to the point of laying down his perfect life as a "ransom for all."[98]

Although many apologists still teach that acceptance of Jesus as the Messiah is *not* sufficient for faith, John Locke (1632-1704)—seventeenth-century Enlightenment thinker and Bible student—argued otherwise based on Scripture in a well-known essay called *The Reasonableness of Christianity*:

> This was the great proposition that was then controverted, concerning Jesus of Nazareth, whether he was the Messiah or no? and the assent to that, was that which distinguished believers from unbelievers...This was the faith which distinguished them from apostates and unbelievers, and was sufficient to continue them in the rank of apostles: and it was upon the same proposition, 'that Jesus was the Messiah, the Son of the living God', owned by St. Peter, that Our Saviour said, he would build his Church, Matt. xvi. 16-18...And, if we gather what was to be believed by all nations, from what was preached unto them; we may certainly know what they were commanded to teach the nations, by what they actually did teach all nations. We may observe, that the preaching of the apostles everywhere in the Acts tended to this one point, to prove that Jesus was the Messiah...it will be objected by some, that to believe only that Jesus of Nazareth is the Messiah, is but an historical, and not a justifying, or saving faith. To which I answer, that I allow to the makers of systems and their followers, to invent and use what distinctions they please, and to call things by what names they

---

[97] Romans 6:23; 2 Corinthians 5:18-19; Ephesians 2:8
[98] John 3:16; 1 Timothy 2:5-6; 1 John 2:2; 4:9-10.

think fit. But I cannot allow to them, or to any man, an authority to make a religion for me, or to alter that which God hath revealed. And if they please to call the believing that which our Saviour and his apostles have declared it so to be, and taught no others which men should receive, and whereby they should be made believers unto eternal life; unless they can so far make bold with Our Saviour, for the sake of their beloved systems, as to say, that he forgot what he came into the world for; and that he and his apostles did not instruct people right in the way and mysteries of salvation. For that this is the sole doctrine pressed and required to be believed in the whole tenor of Our Saviour's and his apostles preaching, we have shewed through the whole history of the evangelists and the Acts. And I challenge them to shew, that there was any other doctrine, upon their assent to which, or disbelief of it, men were pronounced believers or unbelievers; and accordingly received into the Church of Christ, as members of his Body, as far as mere believing could make them so, or else kept out of it. This was the only gospel-article of faith which was preached to them. And if nothing else was preached everywhere, the apostle's argument will hold against any other articles of faith to be believed under the gospel, Rom. x. 14, 'How shall they believe that whereof they have not heard?' For to preach any other doctrines necessary to be believed, we do not find that anybody was sent…[However] It is not enough to believe him to be the Messiah, the Lord, without obeying him ['These two, faith and repentance, i.e. believing Jesus to be the Messiah,' Locke calls 'indispensable conditions of the new covenant']: For that these he speaks to here were believers, is evident from the parallel place, Matt. vii. 21-23, where it is thus recorded: 'Not everyone who says Lord, Lord, shall enter into the kingdom of heaven; but he that doeth the will of my Father, which is in heaven.' …I desire those who tell us, that God will not (nay, some go so far as to say, cannot accept) any, who do not believe every article of their particular creeds and systems, to consider, why God, out of his infinite mercy, cannot as well justify man now, for believing Jesus of Nazareth to be the promised Messiah, the King and Deliverer, as those heretofore, and who believed only that God would, according to his promise, in due time send the Messiah, to be King and Deliverer.[99]

---

[99] *The Reasonableness of Christianity, with A Discourse of Miracles and Part of A Third Letter Concerning Toleration* (Stanford University Press, 1958; originally published in 1695), pp. 32-

In this light we benefit from recognizing that Christianity's most valuable and most distinctive teachings are not necessarily arrived at by means of a complex process of theological reflection, or through the "art and science" of skilled and scholarly "exegesis"; but *more safely established* through the direct and plainly-set-forth pronouncements of the one God ('the Father'), delivered by his chosen and approved servants, including the ancient prophets of Israel, God's very own Son ('the Messiah'), and the Son's chosen apostles.[100] The overall character of Scripture is such that its true principles for life and faith can be universally understood in their essence and applied by those who seek God in sincerity and true humility. It is strange that men would seek so diligently to establish such significant doctrines (like the 'Trinity' and the 'incarnation' of 'God the Son') on so many questionable scriptural extractions and doubtful interpretive connections, rather than emphasizing the doctrines that are established through express teaching. Those who claim that their peculiar doctrinal formulations (*not* directly presented in the gospel proclamation) are "necessary" for salvation, have not only complicated the simplicity of the true Christian faith, but have overstepped the boundaries of the original gospel message.

34, 37, 43-45, 50, 55.

[100] This is not to deny the legitimate role and significance of biblical exposition, or the importance of careful and in-depth Bible study. The point is, in an example such as the doctrine of the Trinity, one will find that the majority, if not all, of the Scriptures used to support the concept rely on questionable scriptural interpretations and debatable scriptural applications, rather than direct scriptural presentation. In stark contrast, we do not need to "exegete" Scripture or vigorously "argue" from Scripture to know that the one God is the Father, that Jesus is the Messiah, that God raised Jesus from the dead, and that salvation comes through faith in Christ. These are among the most important teachings of Christianity. That is why they are *directly* presented to us in the Bible.

The 'I am' statements of the Gospel of John

"But since men are so solicitous about the true church, I would only ask them here by the way, if it be not more agreeable to the church of Christ to make the conditions of her communion consist in such things only, as the Holy Spirit has in the holy Scriptures declared, in express words, to be necessary to salvation? I ask, I say, whether this be not more agreeable to the church of Christ, than for men to impose their own inventions and interpretations upon others, as if they were of divine authority; and to establish by ecclesiastical laws, as absolutely necessary to the profession of Christianity such things as the holy Scriptures do either not mention, or at least not expressly command? Whosoever requires those things in order to ecclesiastical communion, which Christ does not require in order to life eternal, he may perhaps indeed constitute a society accommodated to his own opinion, and his own advantage; but how that can be called the church of Christ, which is established upon laws that are not his, and which excludes such persons from its communion as he will one day receive into the kingdom of heaven, I understand not."
—John Locke, *A Letter Concerning Toleration* (1689), p. 24

"Whether we are learned or unlearned, I believe we must guard against dogmatism[101] and judgmentalism, as indicative, not of wisdom and discernment, but of both smallness of mind and smallness of spirit and heart... In summary, then, even as I am convinced that the one true religion is Christianity itself, not some religious system claiming to exemplify it, I also believe the truth is found in the Scriptures, not in any particular set of interpretations that men have developed or may yet develop. That truth is not only in the words themselves but primarily in the revelation they bring to us of God and of his Son. We will almost inevitably differ in our understanding on some points but, if governed by God's Spirit, should have no great difficulty in agreeing on those teachings clearly and plainly stated."
—Raymond Franz, *In Search of Christian Freedom*, p. 711

---

[101] The word *dogma* "in Greek has the basic meaning of 'what seems to be right,' but has come to stand for a tenet or code of tenets approved by religious authority. 'Dogmatism' stands for positiveness in assertion of opinion especially when unwarranted or arrogant. If a teaching is clearly taught in Scripture it warrants our acceptance as right teaching, true doctrine, something we can affirm and hold to with confidence. When such foundation is questionable, however, insistence on the teaching constitutes dogmatism." —*In Search of Christian Freedom* (footnote).

The 'I am' statements of the Gospel of John

"I am he" in the book Isaiah

The principal texts in the book of Isaiah Trinitarians point to as the source or influence of Jesus' "I am *he*" statements are Isaiah 41:4; 43:10 and 46:4. In the original Hebrew text, the phrase *ani hu* (literally, 'I *am* he') is translated in the Septuagint as *ego eimi* ('I am *he*'), the same words used by Jesus and others in the New Testament. In the Hebrew the phrase does not contain an expressed verb but does contain the predicate pronoun "he" (*ani hu* is literally 'I he'; the verb 'am' is implied and necessary for proper English translation). The Greek phrase *ego eimi* is literally "I am" while the predicate "he" or "the one" is normally implied and also necessary for proper English translation.[1]

James White claims that the "use of *ani hu* by Isaiah is a euphemism for the very name of God himself."[2] Consequently, when Jesus used the phrase *ego eimi* (the Septuagint translation for *ani hu*) in the Gospel of John, he was applying "the divine name" to himself. Thus, by applying to himself God's own name (or the 'euphemism' for God's name), Jesus was claiming to be God. Isaiah 41:4 reads:

> **Be quiet before Me, O coasts; and let peoples renew their power. They come near; then they speak. Let us draw near together for judgment. Who raised up the righteous one from the east? He called him to His foot; He gives nations before him, and subdues kings; He gives *them* as dust *to* his sword, as driven stubble *to* his bow; He pursues them; he passes on in peace; he does not go *by* the way with his feet. Who has planned and done *it*, calling forth the generations from the beginning? I Jehovah *am* the first and the last; I *am* He** (Hebrew: *ani hu*; Greek Septuagint: *ego eimi*). **The coasts have seen and fear; the ends of the earth tremble; they have drawn near; yea they come.**[3]

Translators and Hebraists have reason to believe that, in this case, *ani hu* carries the sense "I am the same" or "I am the

---

[1] And, as mentioned, the context often fills in the implied identity, as in John 9:9.
[2] White, *The Forgotten Trinity*, p. 99.
[3] Isaiah 41:1-4, *The Interlinear Bible, Hebrew-Greek-English, A Literal Translation of the Bible, One Volume Edition*, Jay P. Green, Sr. General Editor and Translator.

same one." J. B. Rotherham rendered it: "I Yahweh [who am] First, And with them who are last *I am the Same!*" Similarly, James Moffatt translated it: "…'twas I the Eternal [Yahweh], I who am the first and *at the last the same*" (*A New Translation*, 1922). One commentator translated the verse: "I, Yahweh, am the first, and with the last *I am still he*," and made the following remarks:

> 'I, Yahweh, the first—and with the last, I, the same.' (This translation attempts to produce the fact that the clauses are noun clauses. A verbal sentence can never have the force of such a noun clause, where the predicate is a substantive. Nominal sentences are in general untranslatable.) Properly to understand this 'divine self prediction', we should remember the opening lines of Psalm 90. There, God's eternity is made a ground for putting absolute trust in him in face of man's appointed end. Here, when God says of himself 'the first…the last', this indicates the ground which makes possible an activity of his that embraces the totality of universal history. Because his activity preceded all the movements of history, and will also terminate them all, he is the one 'who calls the generations from the beginning' (v. 4a). These words are only comprehensible if it is realized that v. 4b is not to be taken as it would be in present day thought, as denoting essence. What is expressed here is not the permanence of an always existent divine being, but the contrast between God and history in its totality ('and with the last I am still he'). It is the expression of a divine eternity related to history, and not of one philosophically contrasted with it.[4]

Albert Barnes approved of a similar rendering in his commentary but differed from the above commentary in terms of the implied meaning:

> *And with the last.* The usual form in which this is expressed is simply 'the last' (Isa 44:6; 48:12). The idea here seems to be, 'and with the last, *I am the same*;' that is, I am unchanging and eternal. None will subsist after me; since with the last of all created objects I shall be the

---

[4] Westermann, *Isaiah 40-66, A Commentary* (Philadelphia: The Westminster Press, 1969), p. 65.

same that I was in the beginning. Nothing would survive God; or in other words, he would exist forever and ever. The argument here is, that to this unchanging and eternal God, who had thus raised up and directed Cyrus, and who had control over all nations, they might commit themselves with unwavering confidence, and be assured that he was able to protect and deliver them.[5]

In order to properly understand the significance of *ani hu/ego eimi* in this text (whether it is taken as 'I *am* he' or 'I *am* the same'), it is critical to keep in mind that previous to the "I *am* he" statement, two questions were asked by the God of Israel: "Who raised up the righteous one from the east?" and "Who has planned and done it, calling forth the generations from the beginning?" Immediately following the second question, the God of Israel proceeds with the answer: "I Jehovah am the first and the last; I *am* he," or perhaps, "I am the one" (*NET*; *New Century Version* has 'I, the Lord, am the one').[6] Here, *ani hu/ego eimi* functions simply, and plainly, as a means of self-identification; the predicate "he" evidently referring to "*Jehovah, the one calling forth the generations from the beginning.*"[7] Contrary to the argument made by some, the phrase "I *am* he" is not another way of expressing the divine name (or the significance of the name) itself.[8] The phrase simply functions, in this particular case, as an emphatic answer to the question asked by Jehovah himself. *He is* the one who "raised up the righteous one from the east." *He is* the one "who has planned and done it, calling forth the generations from the beginning."

The same point applies to Deuteronomy 32:39, where Jehovah says, "I, even I, am he (*ani hu*), and there is no god beside me; I kill and I make alive; I wound and I heal..."

This particular use of *ani hu* is, likewise, an emphatic

---

[5] *Notes on the Old Testament, Explanatory and Practical* by Albert Barnes, Edited by Robert Frew, D.D, Isaiah, Vol. II (Grand Rapids: Baker, 1956), p. 83 (emphasis added).
[6] *The Bible in Living English* by Steven T. Byington reads the same.
[7] In the *Septuagint* "*ego eimi* ('I am *he*')" appears to refer back to "*theos* ('God')" for the previous verse has "*ego theos* ('I *am* God').
[8] Nineteenth-century Bible scholar Joseph Alexander, however, advocated the translation "I am he," saying, "*ani hu* is explained by some of the older writers as meaning *I am God*; by the latest, I *am the same* (*i.e.* unchangeable); but the simplest construction is the common one, *I am he, i.e.* the being to whom the interrogation has respect, *I am he who has wrought and done it.*" — *Commentary On Isaiah* (Grand Rapids: Kregel Publications, 1953 edition), p. 120.

means of self-identification, meaning, "It is I," or "I am he," or "I am the one"—that is, I am the "he" or the "one" self-described in the context. In other words, "I am he," that is, 'the one who has no rival god besides me,' 'the one who kills and makes alive,' 'the one who wounds and heals.' '*I am the one who does these things...*"

Isaiah 43:10-13

Isaiah 43:10-13 is probably the most frequently cited as the source of Jesus' use of the phrase "I am *he*." Again, it is believed that since God used this expression long ago in the prophetic writings, Jesus made use of the same expression to identify himself as God before his listeners:

> **Let all the nations be assembled, and let the peoples be gathered. Who among them can declare this and cause us to hear former things? Let them give their witnesses, that they may be justified. Or let them hear and say, *It is* true. You are My witnesses, says Jehovah; and My servant whom I have chosen; that you may know and believe Me, and understand that I am He** (Hebrew: *ani hu*; Greek Septuagint: *ego eimi*). **Before Me there was no god formed; nor *shall any* be after Me. I, I *am* Jehovah; and there is no Savior besides Me. I declared, and I saved, and I proclaimed; and there is no strange *god* among you. And you are My witnesses, says Jehovah, and I *am* God. Yea, from this day I *am* He** (*ani hu/ego eimi*), **and no one delivers from My hand.**[9]

Here, again, the phrase *ani hu/ego eimi* is a simple method of self-identification, and may be rendered, that they may "know and believe in me and understand that *it is I*"[10] (*New American Bible*), or "that I am the one" (*Bible in Living English*); that is, that I am *Jehovah* (first occurrence of *ani hu/ego eimi*), and that I am *God* (second occurrence); as the fuller text reads in the *New Jerusalem Bible*: "You yourselves

---

[9] Isaiah 43:9-13, *The Interlinear Bible, Hebrew-Greek-English, A Literal Translation of the Bible, One Volume Edition*
[10] The *Anchor Bible* has the same rendering.

are my witnesses, declares Yahweh, and the servant whom I have chosen, so that you may know and believe me and understand that *it is I*. No god was formed before me, nor will be after me. I, I am Yahweh..." Or, as C. K. Barrett observed in his commentary: "In the Isaiah passages the meaning of the Hebrew is apparently 'I am (for ever) the same'..."[11] In the *Pillar New Testament Commentary*, D. A. Carson similarly argued, in part: "In Isaiah [43:10], the context demands that 'I am he' means 'I am the same', I am forever the same', and perhaps even 'I am Yahweh'..."[12] Accordingly, *The Bible, A New Translation* by James Moffatt has as a translation: "You are my trusty witnesses, the servants I have chosen, to own me, to believe me, to see that *I am ever the same*..." Knox's translation for verse 13 reads: "I am God, and what I was, I am..."—with a footnote that says, "Literally, 'I am he', as in verse 10, but here the predominant sense is perhaps *I am the same God who brought you out of Egypt*', cf. verses 16, 17."[13]

In his examination of this text, Claus Westermann observed the following with respect to the divine declaration, "*that you may know and believe Me, and understand that I am he...*"

> What then is here to be known and believed and understood? We are told in terse words that defy translation, but which may be approximately rendered as, 'that it is I.' If we made this into a main clause, it would run, '*I am he*'—*a cry used in a personal encounter, whose significance depends in each case on the circumstances.* In the circumstances in which the Israelites were placed at the time, the words meant exactly what is detailed in the clauses that follow. For them, God is now the one who is able to create a future out of the ruins of the past. And what they are to know, believe and understand is that he, and he alone, can do this. Therefore, what the prophet has

---

[11] *The Gospel According to St. John, An Introduction with Commentary and Notes on the Greek Text*, 2nd edition (Philadelphia: The Westminster Press, 1955; second edition 1978), p. 342.

[12] *The Pillar New Testament Commentary, The Gospel According to John* (Grand Rapids, Michigan/Cambridge, U.K, 1991), pp. 343, 344. Respecting the second occurrence of *ani hu*, the note in Barnes' commentary had: "Isa 43:13 [I am he] I am the same (Isa 43:10)." —*Electronic Database*. Copyright (c) 1997 by Biblesoft.

[13] *A Translation from the Latin Vulgate in light of the Hebrew and Greek Originals* (New York: 1956), p. 662 (emphasis added).

in mind is a fully personal knowledge of such as comes only from encounter. Such knowledge embraces belief: it is knowledge that believes, or belief that has knowledge. But whenever Israel knows that God is truly God, she may become his witness; for the one thing which she is to attest is that she has encountered the God who is truly God.[14]

Isaiah 46:4

In Isaiah 46, Jehovah spoke with reference to the Babylonian gods "'Bel' ('originally the god of Nippur, the father of the gods and the god of heaven, later coalesced with Marduk, the great god of Babylon; see Jeremiah 50:2') and 'Nebo' (son of the Babylonian god Marduk)"[15] in this way:

> **Bel has bowed; Nebo stoops; their idols are for the beast, and for the cattle; your things carried are loads; a burden for the weary. They stoop; they bow together; they are not able to deliver the burden; and their soul has gone into captivity. Listen to me, O house of Jacob, and all the remnant of the house of Israel; who are born from the belly, who are lifted from the womb: Even to old age I *am* He ['I am the same,' *NAB*] (Hebrew: *ani hu*; Greek Septuagint: *ego eimi*); and I will bear to gray hair; I made, and I will carry; and I will bear and deliver.**[16]

John Calvin commented: "*I am the same.* The Hebrew word *hu* is, in my opinion, very emphatic, though some interpreters render it simply by the demonstrative pronoun *He*; but it means that God is always 'the same' and like himself, not only in his essence, but with respect to us, so that we ourselves shall feel that he is the same."[17] Albert Barnes made similar remarks: "*And* even *to* your *old age, I* am *he.* Or rather, *I am the same.* I remain, unchangeably, with the same tenderness, the

---

[14] Westermann, *Isaiah 40-66, A Commentary*, p. 122.
[15] See: *The Interpreter's Bible, Volume 5*, p. 536.
[16] Isaiah 46:1-4, *The Interlinear Bible, Hebrew-Greek-English, A Literal Translation of the Bible*
[17] *Commentary on the Book of the Prophet Isaiah by John Calvin, Vol. III*, Translated from the original Latin, and collated with the latest French version, by the Rev. William Pringle (Grand Rapids: Baker, reprinted 1979), p. 438.

The 'I am' statements of the Gospel of John

same affection, the same care. In this the care of God for his people surpasses that of the most tender parent, and the most kind nourisher of the young."[18]

This is probably why the *New American Standard Bible* (Updated edition) does not translate the phrase simply as "I am he" but, "Even to your old age *I will be the same*, And even to your graying years I will bear you!" The *New American Bible* renders it: "Even to your old age *I am the same*, even when your hair is gray I will bear you; It is I who have done this, I who will continue, and I who will carry you to safety." The *Christian Community Bible* (*Catholic Pastoral Edition*) expresses it: "Even to your old age, *I am He who remains the same*, even when your hair turns gray."[19]

In none of the aforementioned texts of Isaiah does the phrase *ani hu/ego eimi* function as a "euphemism" for God's name. Every time the phrase occurs it is used as a means of self-identification (the identity clearly implied or expressed directly in the passage itself); or, possibly, as an indication that the subject—God—will remain "the same." In fact, there was nothing exceptional or implicitly divine in character about the phrase *ani hu*, as David used it in reference to himself at 1 Chronicles 21:17. The surrounding circumstances are the key to identifying the specific reference in each case. For Jehovah, "I am he (*ani hu/ego eimi*)" referred to the fact that he was the powerful God self-described in each context (or that he remained *the same one*); in David's case, *ani hu* ('I am the one', *NASB*; or 'It is I', *RSV*) referred to "the one who (had) sinned and done very wickedly..." For the man who had been cured by Jesus from blindness, "I am *he* (*ego eimi*)" referred to the fact that he was in fact the blind man who had been healed (John 9:9). When Peter used the words "I am (*ego eimi*)," it referred to "the one you are looking for" (Acts 10:21); and, for Jesus, "I am *he*" generally referred to the fact that he really was the long-awaited

---

[18] *Notes on the Old Testament*, by Albert Barnes, Isaiah, Vol. II, pp. 167, 168 (emphasis added).
[19] The following translations all read the same or similar: *Rotherham's Emphasized Bible*; *The Bible, A New Translation by James Moffatt*; *The Holy Bible, Saint Joseph New Catholic Edition*; *The Bible, An American Translation, under the editorship of J. M. Powis Smith*; *Douay Rheims Bible*; *Jerusalem Bible*; *New Jerusalem Bible*; *The Modern Language Bible, New Berkley Version in Modern English*; *The Bible in Basic English*.

Christ/Messiah or (Messianic) Son of man[20] ('that I am the one I claim to be' John 8:24, *NIV*). In each case where *ani hu/ego eimi* occurs, the identity of the speaker is different yet made manifest and/or discernable through a consideration of the unique context in which it was written.

---

[20] In *The Lord of Glory* (p. 31), Warfield quotes approvingly of the Roman Catholic scholar, F. Tillmann, who said: "The result of our investigation is in brief this: The designation 'the Son of Man' is a title of the Messiah just as truly as the designation 'Son of David,' 'the Anointed,' and the like."

7

"Trinity" in the Old Testament?

The vast majority of Bible scholars—both Trinitarian and non-Trinitarian—recognize that the traditional orthodox concept of the Trinity is not taught in the Hebrew portion of the sacred Scriptures, and was, consequently, unknown to the ancient Hebrews. Roman Catholic scholar John L. McKenzie observed that the "OT does not contain suggestions or foreshadowings of the trinity of persons such as Father, Son, Word, Spirit, etc."[1] Gerard S. Sloyan, another Catholic scholar, similarly pointed out: "It is a matter beyond all question that there was no knowledge of the Trinity in the Old Testament period…"[2] Jesuit Edmund J. Fortman said, "[The Old Testament] tells us nothing explicitly or by necessary implication of a Triune God who is Father, Son and Holy Spirit…There is no evidence that any sacred writer even suspected the existence of a [Trinity] within the Godhead…"[3] Evangelical theologian Donald Macleod agreed that "no group possessing only the Old Testament has ever come to a knowledge of the doctrine of the Trinity."[4]

---

[1] McKenzie, S.J., *Dictionary of the Bible*, p. 900.
[2] Sloyan, *The Three Persons in One God*, p. 7.
[3] *The Triune God, A Historical Study of the Doctrine of the Trinity* (Grand Rapids: Baker, 1972), p. xv.
[4] Macleod, *Shared Life*, p. 9. Yet strangely, and in direct contradiction to the vast majority of learned Trinitarian scholars, Dr. Robert Morey claimed, "the Old Testament writers *clearly* depict God as multi-personal…" —*The Trinity, Evidence and Issues*, p. 167 (emphasis added). This is all the more strange considering the fact that no one known in Jewish history ever spoke of God as "multi-personal."

Deuteronomy 6:4: The True Christian "Creed"—

"Hear, O Israel: Jehovah is our God, Jehovah is one."
—Deuteronomy 6:4, *ASV* (marginal rendering)

"Well said, Master. You are right in saying that God is one and beside him there is no other." —Mark 12:32, *NEB*

Jesus' reference to the *shema*[5] as part of the "greatest commandment"—the central Hebrew confession of faith—demonstrates the continuity and preservation of the faith of the God of Israel held in Christian teaching (Mark 12:28-31). In the Christian Scriptures, however, we find no authorization for the doctrinal elaboration: "God-is-one-being-in-three-persons" or "God-is-one-and-yet-three" or "three-in-one." The authentically Christian "creed" or "confession of faith" remains *exactly* the same as that which was held by God's ancient people, based on God's revelation to them. According to the Hebrew *and Christian Scriptures*, God is "one" (or 'one LORD/Jehovah')—without qualification. This is, in fact, the only "numerical formula" ascribed to God in the sacred Scriptures—the only one authorized by Jesus.[6]

The arrival of Jesus Christ and the establishment of his congregation did not in any way represent a departure from Israel's faith based on their sacred oracles; but, rather, the true fulfillment of prophetic expectation; a confirmation of the veracity of God's covenant promise respecting the Messiah who would deliver God's people into the coming age. The first followers of Christ continued worshiping the same God, who is "one," and they continued teaching the same principles of loving God and loving neighbor, already affirmed in the inspired Hebrew Scriptures.

Professor Macleod observed: "…if the Old Testament is emphatic about the unity of God, it appears to have little to say about the second aspect of the doctrine of the Trinity, namely, the idea of more-than-oneness in God…in the oneness of God there were the Father, the Son, and the Holy Spirit. There is

---

[5] Deuteronomy 6:4 is known to Jews as the "Shema," which means "listen" or "hear."
[6] Deuteronomy 6:4; Mark 12:29; Romans 3:30; Galatians 3:20; James 2:19 ; Zechariah 14 :9.

scarcely a hint of this in the Old Testament."[7]

Macleod's observation is almost correct. It would be more accurate to say that the Old (and New) Testament has *nothing* to say about what Macleod describes as the "more-than-oneness in God." Scripture, along with the founder of the Christian faith, only emphatically affirms God's "oneness." Yet, astonishingly, one of the most popularly advanced arguments in support of the Trinity from the Old Testament actually revolves around the scriptural teaching that God is "one." Some defenders of Trinitarian doctrine have argued that Deuteronomy 6:4 is actually a proof of God's "multi-personal" nature, or his alleged "more-than-oneness." It is reasoned that the word *echad* (one) is used in other Scriptures to denote a "compound unity." For example, some would say that when Moses sent men to spy out the land of Canaan, they cut down "one" (*echad*) cluster of grapes.[8] Since, in this case, the word "one" had reference to the "one cluster" (containing multiple grapes), this shows that the word *echad* carries with it the idea of "plurality-in-unity." Consequently, when Moses taught that God is "one" (*echad*, Deut. 6:4), the underlying concept was that God too was actually a plurality in unity, exactly what the doctrine of the Trinity teaches.

It would be difficult to improve upon, or communicate in a clearer way, Anthony Buzzard's observations with respect to this common though erroneous argument put forward by popular Trinitarian apologists:

> It is untrue to say that the Hebrew word *echad* (one) in Deuteronomy 6:4 points to 'compound unity.' A recent defense on the Trinity (Robert Morey, *The Trinity: Evidence and Issues* (World Publishing, 1996) argues that when 'one' modifies a collective noun like 'bunch' or 'herd,' a plurality is implied in *echad*. The argument is fallacious. The sense of plurality is derived from the collective noun (herd, etc.), not from the word 'one.' *Echad* in Hebrew is the numeral 'one.' 'Abraham was one (*echad*)' (Ezek. 33:24; 'only one man,' NIV). Isaiah 5:12 also describes Abraham as 'one' (*echad*; 'alone,' KJV; 'the only one,' NJB), where there is no possible misunderstanding about

---
[7] Macleod, *Shared Life*, pp. 9, 11.
[8] Numbers 13:23

the meaning of this simple word. *Echad* appears in translation as the numeral 'one,' 'only,' 'alone,' 'entire, undivided,' 'one single.' (*Theological Dictionary of the Old Testament* (Grand Rapids: Eerdmans, 1974), 1:194. The claim that 'one' really means 'compound oneness' is an example of argument by assertion without logical proof. Robert Morey holds that *echad* does not mean an absolute one but a compound one. The argument involves an easily detectable linguistic fallacy. *Echad* appears some 960 times in the Hebrew Bible and in no case does the word itself carry a hint of plurality. It strictly means 'one and not two or more.' *Echad* is a numerical adjective and naturally enough is sometimes found modifying a collective noun—one family, one herd, one bunch. But we should observe carefully that the sense of plurality resides in the compound noun and not in the word *echad* (one). Early in Genesis we learn that 'the two will become one flesh' (Gen. 2:24). The word 'one' here means precisely one and no more (one flesh and not two 'fleshes'!). One bunch of grapes is just that—one and not two bunches. Thus when God is said to be 'one Lord' (Deut. 6:4; Mark 12:29, NASV) He is a single Lord and no more…Our point can be confirmed in any lexicon of biblical Hebrew. The lexicon by Koehler and Baumgartner gives as the fundamental meaning of *echad*, 'one single.' (*Hebrew and Aramaic Lexicon of the Old Testament* (Leiden: E.J. Brill, 1967) When the spies returned with evidence of the fruitfulness of the Promised Land they carried 'a single (*echad*) cluster of grapes' (Num. 13:23, NRSV). *Echad* is often rendered 'a single,' or 'only one.' (See RSV, Exod. 10:19, 'a single locust'; Exod. 33:5, 'a single moment'; Deut. 19:15, 'a single witness,' etc.) Thus when it comes to the matter of Israel's creed, the text informs us (as do the multiple singular pronouns for God) that Israel's supreme Lord is 'one single Lord,' 'one Lord alone.' It has been necessary to belabor our point because the recent defense of the Trinity makes the astonishing assertion that *echad* always implies a 'compound unity.' The author then builds his case for a multi-personal God on what he thinks is a firm foundation in the Hebrew Bible. The linguistic fact is that *echad* never means 'compound one,' but strictly a 'single one.' The fact that 'many waters were gathered to one (*echad*) place' (Gen. 1:9) provides no data at all for a compound sense for one, much less for a plurality in the Godhead. (In Genesis 1, 2 alone, we have examples of 'one day,' 'one place,' 'one of his ribs,' 'one of us.'

'Trinity' in the Old Testament?

...Since the strange argument about a so-called 'plurality' in the word one is so widespread and has apparently been accepted uncritically, we add here the comments of a Trinitarian professor of theology who concedes that the popular argument from the word *echad* (one) is as frail as the argument from the word *elohim*. 'No case for a multi-personal God can be based on the fact that 'one' in Hebrew and English may sometimes modify a collective term: Even weaker [than the argument from *Elohim*] is the argument that the Hebrew word for 'one' (*echad*) used in the *Shema* ('Hear O Israel, the Lord our God is one Lord') refers to a unified one, not an absolute one. Hence, some Trinitarians have argued, the Old Testament has a view of a united Godhead. It is, of course, true that the meaning of the word may in some contexts denote a unified plurality (e.g. Gen. 2:24, 'they shall become one flesh'). But this really proves nothing. An examination of the Old Testament usage reveals that the word *echad* is as capable of various meanings as is our English word one. The context must determine whether a numerical or unified singularity is intended.' (Gregory Boyd, *Oneness Pentecostals and the Trinity* (Baker Book House, 1995), 47, 48...It has sometimes been argued that God would have been described as *yachid*, i.e. 'solitary, isolated, the only one,' if there were only one person in the Godhead. The use of *echad* ('one single'), however, is quite sufficient to indicate that the One Person comprises the Deity. *Yachid* is rare in biblical Hebrew. It carries in the Bible the meaning 'beloved,' 'only-begotten' or 'lonely' and would be inappropriate as a description for the Deity. (*Yachid* is in fact found as a description of the One God in the Pseudepigrapha.) There is another Hebrew word *bad*, 'alone, by oneself, isolated,' which does in fact describe the One God. Deuteronomy 4:35 states that 'there is no one else besides Him.' The absolute singularity of the One God is similarly emphasized when He is addressed: 'You are Jehovah alone' (Neh. 9:6), 'You are God alone, the God of all the Kingdoms of the earth' (2 Kings 19:15), 'You alone are God' (Ps. 86:10). The One God of Israel is a single person, unrivaled and in a class of His own. He is One, with all the mathematical simplicity implied by that word.[9]

---

[9] Buzzard & Hunting, *The Doctrine of the Trinity*, pp. 25-29. "Morey includes a footnote to p. 25 of the standard Lexicon of Biblical Hebrew for support. But the page he appeals to contains not a word of support for his theory that 'one' really means 'compound unity.' The lexicons rightly define 'one' as the cardinal number 'one.' Echad is the word for 'one' in counting. Imagine the

'Trinity' in the Old Testament?

Those who try to support the Trinity based on the word *echad* also do not seem to realize that, after Jesus affirmed the 'oneness' (not 'more-than-oneness') of God, the scripturally well-versed Jewish scribe said approvingly in response, "That is true, Teacher; you are right to say that he [*auto*] is one, and there is no one else besides him [*autou*]" (Mark, 12:32, *NET*). The language confirms that, in the mind of the biblically-trained Jew, the God who was truly "one" had always been rightly understood, not as a "what,"—the so-called "triune God" of Christendom's creeds—but as a "he"—the one whom Jesus and the New Testament writers called "Father."

Genesis 1:1

Another argument from the Old Testament that is sometimes made in an effort to support the doctrine of the Trinity is found in the book *God, Coming Face to Face with His Majesty*, by John MacArthur. On page 20, MacArthur makes the following claim:

> The Old Testament expresses the plurality of the Godhead in its opening words: 'In the beginning God' (Gen. 1:1). The Hebrew word translated God is *Elohim*. The plural suffix, *im*, presents a singular God who is expressed as plurality.[10]

Unfortunately, what MacArthur points to as a defense for what he calls the "plurality of the Godhead" is in error, and has already been rightly identified as an error by other Trinitarian theologians as early as nearly 500 years ago, at the time of Protestant Reformation in Europe. In his commentary on Genesis, John Calvin wrote:

> Moses uses *Elohim*, a noun of the plural number, from which it is used to infer that there are three persons in the Godhead. This proof, however, of so important a doctrine

---

chaos of communication if 'one' really means more than one. Ecclesiastes 4:9 speaks of two being better than one (echad). The use of 'one' in the sentence 'The two shall become one flesh' does not mean that 'one' is really plural. It means that two human beings in marriage become one (not two) things. The idea of plurality is not found in the word 'one' at all. It is found in the context: male and female human persons." —Buzzard, *Does Everyone Believe In The Trinity?*

[10] *GOD, Coming Face to Face with His Majesty* (Victor Books, 1993), p. 20.

'Trinity' in the Old Testament?

appears to me by no means solid. And therefore I will not insist on the word but rather warn my readers against violent interpretations of this kind...To me it is sufficient that the plural number signifies the powers of Deity, which he exerted in creating the world.[11]

The same basic points were made in *Smith's Bible Dictionary*, a more modern Bible reference work:

> The plural form of Elohim has given rise to much discussion. The fanciful idea that it referred to the *trinity of persons* in the Godhead hardly finds now a supporter among scholars. It is either what grammarians call *the plural of majesty*, or it denotes the *fullness* of divine strength, the *sum of the powers* displayed by God.[12]

One Trinitarian writer, who believed that the Trinity doctrine could be more "clearly and expressly established" from other parts of Scripture, nevertheless made the following admission regarding the term *elohim* used in Genesis:

> From the words 'God created' our commentators in general deduce the mystery of the most Holy Trinity: the noun, as they conceive, denoting the Trinity of persons and the verb the unity of Essence—Unity in Trinity and Trinity in Unity. The reason assigned for this inference is that the expression in the original signifies not 'Gods, they created,' but 'Gods *He* created.' The Hebrews however attribute this phraseology to an idiom of their language. For the plural words Elohim and Baalim (masters) are used of men and lords, in relation to *individuals*, as *adonim kasha* = lords (plural) oppressive

---

[11] John Calvin, *Commentary on Genesis* 1:1. Although it could not be said for all of Calvin's expositions of Scripture, according to one contemporary Protestant scholar, "Calvin refused to twist the Scriptures in order to bolster the doctrine of the Trinity. Well-worn proof texts for the Trinity, such as the plural form of God (*Elohim*) in Genesis 1 or the thrice-repeated adulation of the seraphim in Isaiah 6:3 or Jesus' statement, 'I and my Father are one' (John 10:30) Calvin regarded as weak and spurious proofs for such an important doctrine." —Timothy George, *Theology of the Reformers* (Nashville: Broadman & Holman Publishers, 1998), p. 200.

[12] *Smith's Bible Dictionary* (Nashville: Thomas Nelson, 1986; originally published between 1813-1893) p. 220. It was observed by one source: "That the language of the OT has entirely given up the idea of plurality...['Elohim'] (as applied to the God of Israel) is especially shown by the fact that it is almost invariably construed with a singular verbal predicate, and takes a singular adjectival attribute...['*Elohim*'] must rather be explained as an intensive plural, denoting greatness and majesty, being equal to The Great God." —Aaron Ember, *The American Journal of Semitic Languages and Literatures*, Vol. XXI, 1905, p. 208.

(singular), Isa 19:4 ['a harsh lord'], and elsewhere. I am loath indeed to countenance the Jews, unless when they have truth manifestly on their side. But from other passages of Scripture the doctrine of the Trinity can be more clearly and expressly established. And we must contend against our adversaries with stronger weapons than this [argument from *elohim*], if we would not, by ignorance of their language, expose ourselves to their ridicule. I agree with the Jews in referring the usage under notice to a Hebrew idiom, but conceive that the plural noun is ascribed to God, chiefly in order to express the fullness of His excellencies, by which He diffuses Himself throughout the universe and exerts His majesty and power which are immense and inexhaustible.[13]

In his book on the Trinity, apologist Robert Bowman, speaking in reference to a controversial booklet that disagreed with the Trinity, wrote: "I would agree with the booklet's argument that the plural form *elohim* for God in the Old Testament cannot be evidence of the Trinity..."[14]

The reason why the plural *elohim* when applied to Jehovah cannot be used as support for the Trinity doctrine is simple. *Elohim* literally means "*gods*," not a plurality of "persons" in a so-called "Godhead." Trinitarian theology does not teach that the Trinity constitutes more than one God, but a plurality of "persons" who share the one God's "essence." This is why it was pointed out by one source: "*Elohim* is used in the plural as a figure of speech to emphasize the greatness of God...If *Elohim* is not plural because of a figure of speech, then it must be taken literally as a plural, and be translated as Gods."[15] Anthony Buzzard elaborated more fully on these points:

> A study of the Hebrew word for God (*elohim*) lends no support to the persistent idea that 'God' in Genesis 1:1 includes both God, the Father as well as His Son and

---

[13] John Mercer, Professor of Hebrew, Royal College, Paris, d. 1572.
[14] *Why You Should Believe in the Trinity*, p. 49. One author observed: "Most Trinitarians do not rely on this idea for support anymore because of one obvious implication, that being it would then say there are plural of Gods within God, which Trinitarians nor non-Trinitarians believe...Those who believe the word *Elo'him* means God is made up of plural persons are ignoring how the word is used in the Bible." —Holt, *Jesus—God or the Son of God?*, p. 126.
[15] Carden, *One God—The Unfinished Reformation*, p. 203.

'Trinity' in the Old Testament?

Spirit. We should not miss the obvious difficulty of such an interpretation. If *elohim* implies more than one person in this text, how is one going to explain that the identical word, *elohim*, refers to Moses: And the Lord said to Moses, 'See I make you God [*elohim*] to Pharaoh, and Aaron your brother shall be your prophet' (Exod. 7:1) Surely no one would claim plurality for the one person Moses. The single pagan god Dagon is called *elohim* (God): 'The ark of the God [*elohim*] of Israel must not remain with us, for His hand is ever on us and on Dagon our god [*elohim*]' (1 Sam. 5:7). Similarly the word *elohim* is used to describe the god of the Amorites: 'Will you not possess what Chemosh your god [*elohim*] gives you to possess? (Judges 11:24)'...From the evidence we conclude that the Jews, in whose language the Old Testament is recorded, did not employ the word *elohim*, used of the true God, to mean more than one person. Those who attempt to read the Trinity or Binity into Genesis 1:26, or into the word *elohim*, are involved in a forced interpretation. *Elohim* is plural in form but singular in meaning. When it refers to the One God it is followed by a singular verb. No one before the twelfth century imagined that plurality in the Godhead was in anyway indicated by the Hebrew title for God. Many Trinitarians have themselves long since ceased to argue for the Trinity from Genesis 1:1 or Genesis 1:26.[16]

Another Old Testament scholar summarized the implications of the scriptural use of the word *elohim* and the argument sometimes made by apologists in an effort to support the Trinity:

> *Elohim* has a plural ending but very often and always when the One Supreme God is spoken of, a singular signification. Accordingly we sometimes find it joined to a verb, adjective or pronoun in the singular number on account of its singular signification and sometimes to one in the plural number on account of its plural termination. No mystery lies in this. And they who infer from this both the unity of God and a plurality of persons in the Godhead not only show themselves to be void of true

---

[16] *The Doctrine of the Trinity*, p. 24.

critical skill, but by producing and urging such weak and frivolous arguments in its defense do a manifest injury to the cause which they are so zealous to support and establish.[17]

On the back cover of an evangelical work called *"Correcting the Cults,"* recognized evangelical "experts" Norman Geisler and Ron Rhodes are said to "identify and respond to the misuse of Scripture by adherents of various religions seeking validation for their own particular doctrines."[18] It is clear, however, that many of the most distinguished evangelical scholars themselves have been engaging in the very same practice. The argument on behalf of the Trinity based on the Hebrew *elohim* is yet another verifiable "misuse of Scripture" by Trinitarian apologists "seeking validation for their own particular doctrines." This is proven, most significantly, not by those who disagree with traditional Trinitarian theology, but by respected Trinitarian scholars themselves.

Genesis 1:26

"Let us make man in our image..."

In the same work already mentioned, John MacArthur claimed that the "plurality of the Godhead is also evident in Creation, for God said, 'Let *Us* make man in Our image,

---

[17] Abraham Dawson, *A New Translation of the First Five Chapters of Genesis*, 1763. The comment about those who have inferred the plurality of God based on *elohim* "show themselves to be devoid of true critical skill" is harsh and not cited with the intention of offending or showing disrespect to Dr. MacArthur or any other scholar who has made this argument. No doubt, Pastor MacArthur has shown himself to be a possessor of "true critical skill" in many ways and in numerous aspects of Bible teaching. However, those (including MacArthur) who have pointed to *elohim* as evidence for the Trinity have undoubtedly failed to think critically through the argument they are trying to advance based on the language at this point. They have also failed to take note of the research and critical conclusions made by other Trinitarian scholars who have already recognized and called attention to the serious flaw in the reasoning employed.

[18] *Correcting the Cults, Expert Responses to Their Scripture Twisting* (Grand Rapids: Baker Books, 1997). On page 21 Geisler and Rhodes claim: "it should be noted that the New Testament clearly teaches that God is a Trinity (Matt. 3:16-17; 2 Cor. 13:14; 1 Pet. 1:2), and, although the doctrine of the Trinity is not fully developed in the Old Testament, it is foreshadowed (cf. Ps. 110:1; Prov. 30:4; Isa. 63:7, 9-11)." The reader is encouraged to look up each of the Scriptures cited. Not *one* of these examples—whether viewed independently or collectively in light of each other—"clearly teaches that God is a Trinity"; and in neither of the Old Testament passages referred to is the Trinity "foreshadowed."

'Trinity' in the Old Testament?

according to *Our* likeness' (1:26, emphasis added)."[19]

In the same way, and for the same purpose, Wayne Grudem wrote what follows in his popular *Systematic Theology*:

> The fact that God created two distinct persons as male and female, rather than just one man, is part of our being in the image of God because it can be seen to reflect to some degree the plurality of persons within the Trinity. In the verse prior to the one that tells of our creation as male and female, we see the first *explicit indication* of a plurality of persons within God: 'Then God said, 'Let *us* make man in *our* image, after our likeness...' (Gen 1:26)[20]

Webster's Third New International Dictionary defines "explicit" as that which is "characterized by full clear expression: being without vagueness or ambiguity: leaving nothing implied: UNEQUIVOCAL...unreserved and unambiguous in expression: speaking fully and clearly..." Obviously, Wayne Grudem overstates his case when he claims that the expression "Let *us* make man in *our* image" constitutes an "explicit indication" of multiple persons within God.

However, the verse *does* suggest that at least one other individual was present with God during the Genesis creation. One possibility that has been suggested is that God was addressing another who bore his own image (given that God said, 'Let us make man in *our image*'), the one who was described by Paul as the "image of the invisible God" (Colossians 1:15)—if, indeed, "this one was in the beginning *with* God" and had "glory *alongside* [God] before the world was" in a literal/personal sense (John 1:2; 17:5).

Second-century Christian writer Justin Martyr probably had this possibility in mind when he wrote: "'Let Us make,'—I shall quote again the words narrated by Moses himself, from which we can indisputably learn that [God] conversed with someone who was numerically distinct from Himself, and also a rational Being."[21] In the third century, Bible scholar Origen, in his *Contra Celsum*, argued:

---

[19] MacArthur, *GOD, Coming Face to Face with His Majesty*, p. 20.
[20] Grudem, *Systematic Theology*, p. 455 (emphasis added).
[21] *Ante Nicene Fathers*, Volume 1, chap. 62, p. 228.

'Trinity' in the Old Testament?

'However, even if the Son of God, 'the firstborn of all creation', seems to have become man recently, yet he is not in fact new on that account. For the divine scriptures know that he is the oldest of all created beings, and that it was to him that God said of the creation of man: 'Let us make man in our image and likeness.'[22]

Or, it is possible that there were other individual beings beside, with, or near to, God, those whom God was addressing, other than himself. Such certainly cannot be taken as "an *explicit* indication of a plurality of persons *within* God." An article in the *Eerdman's Bible Dictionary* has the following observation along with a suggestion as to the identity of those whom God could have been addressing:

> The doctrine of the trinity has been related to various aspects of the Old Testament revelation, the most important being possible indications of plurality within the Godhead and indications of the deity and distinctness of the Spirit of God and of the Messiah. The support of all these aspects of the Old Testament revelation for Christian doctrine of the trinity have been exaggerated, especially what have been taken as indications of plurality in the Godhead. The 'us' in 'Let us make man in our image' (Gen. 1:26; cf. 3:22; 11:6-7) refers to 'sons of God' or lesser 'gods' mentioned elsewhere (6:1-4; Job 1:6; Ps. 29:1), here viewed as a heavenly council centered around the one God (cf. Ps. 82:1). In later usage these probably would be called 'angels.'[23]

The Jewish Study Bible is apparently in agreement on this matter: "The plural construction (*Let us...*) most likely reflects a setting in the divine council (cf. 1 Kings 22.19-22; Isa. ch 6; Job chs 1-2)."[24] The footnotes in the *New English Translation* (sponsored by Dallas Theological Seminary) have a similar observation:

---

[22] *Translated With an Introduction & Notes by* Henry Chadwick (Cambridge, 1953), p. 294. Or see: *Ante-Nicene Fathers, Roberts-Donaldson*, Vol. IV (Grand Rapids: Eerdmans, 1979), p. 560.
[23] *The Eerdmans Bible Dictionary*, p. 1019. However, Justin Martyr apparently denied that this expression had reference to angels.
[24] Oxford University Press, 1999.

'Trinity' in the Old Testament?

The plural form of the verb has been the subject of much discussion through the years, and not surprisingly several suggestions have been put forward. Many Christian theologians interpret it as an early hint of plurality within the Godhead, but this view imposes later trinitarian concepts on the ancient text...In 2 Sam 24:14 David uses the plural as representative of all Israel, and in Isa 6:8 the Lord speaks on behalf of his heavenly court. In its ancient Israelite context the plural is most naturally understood as referring to God and his heavenly court (see 1 Kgs 22:19-22; Job 1:6-12; 2:1-6; Isa 6:1-8). (The most well-known members of this court are God's messengers, or angels. In Gen 3:5 the serpent may refer to this group as 'gods/divine beings.'...) If this is the case, God invites the heavenly court to participate in the creation of humankind (perhaps in the role of offering praise, see Job 38:7), but he himself is the one who does the actual creative work (v. 27). Of course, this view does assume that the members of the heavenly court possess the divine 'image' in some way. Since the image is closely associated with rulership, perhaps they share the divine image in that they, together with God and under his royal authority, are the executive authority over the world.[25]

The view that sees the "us" in Genesis 1:26 as a reference to angels may be supported by a similar expression used in Isaiah 6:8. In this case, Jehovah said, *"Whom shall I send, and who will go for us?"*—a statement made in a context where "seraphim"[26] were clearly present with God (Isaiah 6:1-7).

Whoever God was speaking to at the time of man's creation (and at other times when a similar expression was used) does not demand the existence of "multiple persons" within God and is certainly not an "explicit" indication of such. The identity of the individual (or individuals) to whom God was speaking in Genesis is not disclosed in the text and probably cannot be known with absolute certainty from a human perspective. Those

---

[25] The same essential point was made in the Trinitarian *NIV Study Bible*: "God speaks as the Creator-King, announcing his crowning work to the members of his heavenly court (see 3:22; 11:7; Isa 6:8; see also 1Ki 22:19-23; Job 15:8; Jer 23:18)." —*NIV Study Bible, 10th Anniversary Edition* (Grand Rapids: Zondervan, 1995), p. 7.

[26] "Seraphim" (described by Isaiah as having six wings) are evidently high-ranking angels that dwell in the heavenly realm with God.

who believe in the personal pre-human existence of God's Son think it reasonable to suppose that God was speaking to him ('the image of God' and the one 'through' whom the world came into existence; compare 2 Corinthians 4:4; John 1:10). Others believe that God was speaking to the angels of the heavenly realm, also described as God's sons in Scripture.[27]

Whatever the case may be, with respect to the statement "Let *us* make man in *our* image...", *The New Interpreter's Bible* reminds us: "Far from either slighting divine transcendence or concealing God within the divine assembly, it reveals and enhances the richness and complexity of the divine realm. God is not in heaven alone, but is engaged in a relationship of mutuality within the divine realm..."[28]

Isaiah 9:6

> *"Unto us a Son is given; And the government will be upon His shoulder. And His name will be called Wonderful, Counselor, Mighty God, Everlasting Father, Prince of Peace."*—Isaiah 9:6

Isaiah's well-known prophecy is often taken as evidence that Jesus Christ should be considered "God" in the "absolute" sense—as "God the Son, the second member of the Trinity." One student of Scripture, however, pointed out the following:

> Many Trinitarian friends use this as a proof-text that Jesus is 'God.' Yet, they overlook the obvious, namely, the Jewish audience who originally heard this message saw no problem with the future prince of peace being a 'Mighty God.' They did not conclude from such that he would have to be of the same 'substance' with the LORD Almighty [*NIV* rendering. *ASV* has 'Jehovah of hosts,' v. 7] whose will was going to accomplish it. Their monotheism did not necessitate that any person to whom divinity was ascribed share the divinity of the one true God. Their language permitted other beings to wear the designation 'god' without usurping the sovereignty of

---

[27] Job 1:6. Without question, the "sons of God" mentioned in the book of Job were angels. *NIV* even translates "angels" where the Hebrew has *beneh ha' elohim*, "sons of God" (more literally: 'sons of *the* God'); the same verse tells us that "Satan proceeded to enter right among them."
[28] Vol.1, p. 345.

'Trinity' in the Old Testament?

Jehovah God. Trinitarians create a false dilemma which in essence is a semantic anachronism.[29]

As pointed out, the fact that Jesus is called "Mighty God" does not, as often assumed, necessarily speak in favor of Trinitarian doctrine. Consider the point that in the very same verse Jesus is also called "everlasting Father." Yet Trinitarianism does not teach that Jesus is *the Father* (as in 'God the Father'). Here, Isaiah's prophecy presents us with another example of how words and titles can be used in different senses throughout Scripture. The term "Father" is a relative term and is used of others beside the heavenly Father. In John 8:39 the Jews told Jesus, "Our father is *Abraham*"; yet in verse 41 they claimed, "We were not born of fornication; we have one Father, even *God*." Here is another example confirming that there are different levels of fatherhood—just as the Scriptures show that there are various levels and different degrees of godhood or godship.[30] *God* is not only "Father" to the Jewish people, but in the ultimate sense, for he is the very one who brought all things into existence. Abraham is the (patriarchal) father of the Hebrew nation, and even, "the Father of all those having faith."[31] Both God and Abraham were considered 'fathers' to the Jewish people, but each was "Father" on a different level, in a different sense. In one of his letters to the early congregations, the apostle Paul said that he had become "a father" to the Corinthian Christians "in Christ Jesus through the gospel."[32] Even the devil is regarded as a father; he is, according to Jesus, not only father to the Jews who were trying to kill him, but "a liar and *the father* of lies."[33]

In the case of the Messiah, "the one who leads men to life,"[34] he may be appropriately called "everlasting father" based

---

[29] James Caputo, In reply to Re: The Trinity/Theory/Reality posted by Defender on Th- Jan 24- 8:50pm (*Channel C: International Biblical Discussion Forums*).
[30] John 10:34-37
[31] Romans 4:11
[32] 1 Corinthians 4:15. In the previous verse, Paul said, "I am writing you this not to shame you, but to admonish you as my beloved children."
[33] John 8:44, *NAB* (emphasis added).
[34] Acts 3:15, *TEV*. While preaching to the Jews, Peter described Jesus as *archegon tes zoes* ('chief leader of life') "whom God raised from the dead." The *New English Bible* has, "him who has led the way to life." *A Reader's Greek-English Lexicon of the New Testament* (Grand Rapids: Zondervan, 1975) defines *archegos* as, "leader, ruler, prince; originator." This is why some

on a number of legitimate reasons. The fact that the Messiah possesses in himself the power to impart spiritual life; the fact that he was consecrated to carry out what may be considered a "fatherly" role in the outworking of God's purposes; that he is the one who "fathers" God's purposes in relation to God's kingdom; along with the fact that he will continue to live throughout all of eternity;[35] or that he is, as the Latin Vulgate translates the Hebrew, "the Father of the future age."[36]

The fact that the Son's name would be called "Mighty God" does not demand that he is the *Almighty*,[37] for the same reason that being described with such an exalted description as "everlasting father" does not demand the meaning that he is *God the Father*. If one were to insist that the Messiah must be the Almighty God because he is described as "Mighty God" in Isaiah's writings, then, by the same logic, and with equal force, one could insist that the Messiah and God the Father must be the same person based on his being described as "everlasting father."[38] Such descriptions, however, can be viewed as honorific, Messianic titles that would be given to God's Son at some point in the future.

The *Daily Study Bible Series* on Isaiah elaborates on the titles given to the Messiah in 9:6: "'Mighty God' or rather

---

translations have 'prince' or 'author' of life. Yet according to one source: "*Archegos tes zoes* is not easy to translate. Basically, *archegos* means 'pathfinder, pioneer' and was used of patrons, founders and [self-titled] heroes." —*The Anchor Bible: The Acts of the Apostles, A New Translation with Introduction and Commentary* by Joseph A. Fitzmyer, p. 286.

[35] Commenting on the meaning of the Messianic titles given in Isaiah 9:6, *The New Oxford Annotated Bible observes* in a footnote: "*Government*, symbol of authority. *Mighty God*, divine in might. *Everlasting Father*, continuing fatherly love and care. *Prince of Peace*, the king who brings peace and prosperity."

[36] "*Pater futuri saeculi,*" The Latin Vulgate (425 C.E.). As mentioned, the fact that the Messiah is called "eternal father" may also have reference to his ability to impart life (compare John 5:21). In this same light, it is possible to understand that although Adam was the father of the human race (the first human being through whom all others were born), Jesus Christ is the "everlasting Father" (or 'Father of the future age') in the sense that he is the second or "last Adam," the Father of a new race of people that will inhabit God's kingdom in the age to come.

[37] The Messiah is never called "Almighty" in the Scriptures.

[38] This is, in fact, the reasoning employed by some groups. In *The Forgotten Trinity* (p. 206), James White notes: "This passage is at times misused in the attempt to make Jesus the Father." But Robert Morey points out correctly: "I am called 'Father' by my children. Does this mean that I am God the Father? Of course not. In the same way, just because Jesus is called 'Father' in Isaiah 9:6, this does not necessarily mean that He is God the Father. The name 'Father' can have numerous meanings" (*The Trinity, Evidence and Issues*, pp. 520, 521). Yet we could rightly extend on the reasoning as follows: "…just because the Messiah is called 'God' in Isaiah 9:6, this does not necessarily mean that he is God Almighty. The term 'God' can have numerous meanings (or applications), as the Scriptures make clear."

'Divine Warrior' represents him as an invincible champion of the oppressed; 'Everlasting Father' sees in him an unfailing source of protection and love."[39] The footnote for Isaiah 9:6 in the *New American Bible* states: "...this passage is used to refer to Christ. Upon his shoulder dominion rests: authority. Wonder-Counselor: remarkable for his wisdom and prudence. God-Hero: a warrior and a defender of his people, like God himself. Father-Forever: ever devoted to his people. Prince of Peace: his reign will be characterized by peace." *The NIV Study Bible*, under "Mighty God," states: "His divine power as a warrior is stressed." Of "Everlasting Father," it says: "He will be an enduring, compassionate provider and protector." According to another source: "The word designated for the expected Messiah in Isaiah 9:6 is *el gibbor* (from the root word, *geber*). It is usually translated 'Mighty God,' but more exactly it is 'Powerful Champion' or 'Godly Hero.'"[40] These observations were made likely because *The Oxford Hebrew Lexicon* defines "mighty god" as a "mighty hero or divine hero, as reflecting the divine majesty."[41]

Although "Mighty God" (or 'Powerful Divine One') is correct English translation, some translators have attempted to communicate the force of the Hebrew expression into English in the following ways:

> ...he is named **Wonder-Counselor, Divine Champion, Father Ever, Captain of Peace.** —*Bible in Living English*[42]

---

[39] John F. A. Sawyer, *The Daily Study Bible Series, Isaiah*, Volume 1, p. 100.

[40] Edwin Louis Cole, *Courage, Winning Life's Toughest Battles* (Tulsa: Harrison House: 1991), p. 159 (words in italics originally in all capitals).

[41] Driver and Briggs, *Hebrew and English Lexicon of the Old Testament* (Oxford at the Claredon Press, 1995), p. 42. John Schoenhieit pointed out: "The word *gibbor* means strong or mighty, and refers to someone who is bold or audacious, strong or valiant. The phrase '*el gibbor*' is used in the plural in Ezekiel 32:21 (ESV, NRSV, RSV), where it is translated 'mighty chiefs,' 'mighty leaders (NIV), 'strong among the mighty' (KJV), 'mightiest heroes' (NJB), and 'mighty warriors' (Moffatt)." He argues: "Given that generally an '*el*' is a ruler in some sense, and *gibbor* means strong or mighty, 'Mighty Ruler' would be a good choice for the translation of Isaiah 9:6, and that is exactly what the Jews were looking for in their Messiah." —*The Sower* (bi-monthly magazine) Mar/Apr 2006, by *Spirit & Truth Fellowship International*.

[42] According to another source: "Over this reestablished Davidic kingdom there will rule an ideal king, who is acclaimed as a 'wonderful counselor,' one whose counsel will be effective for his people's well being; a 'divine [i.e. hero] warrior'; a 'father [of his people] from of old'..." — *Interpreter's One-Volume Commentary*, p. 338. Similarly, the footnote for Isaiah 9:6 in the *MacArthur Study Bible* states: "Mighty God. As a powerful warrior, the Messiah will accomplish

...his title will be: **Wonderful Counsellor, Mighty Hero, Eternal Father, Prince of Peace.**
—*Revised English Bible*
...**he shall be called in purpose wonderful, in battle God-like, Father for all time, Prince of peace.**
—*New English Bible*
...**and this the title that he bears—'A wonder of a counselor, a divine hero, a father for all time, a peaceful prince!'** —*A New Translation, Moffat*

Isaiah 48:12-17

A portion of Isaiah 48 reads as follows in the *New American Standard Bible*:

> **Listen to Me, O Jacob, even Israel whom I called; I am He, I am the first, I am also the last. 'Surely My hand founded the earth, And My right hand spread out the heavens; When I call to them, they stand together. 'Assemble, all of you, and listen! Who among them has declared these things? The LORD loves him; he will carry out His good pleasure on Babylon, And His arm will be against the Chaldeans. 'I, even I, have spoken; indeed I have called him, I have brought him, and He will make his ways successful. 'Come near to Me, listen to this: From the first I have not spoken in secret, From the time it took place, I was there.** *And now the Lord GOD has sent Me, and His Spirit.*' **Thus says the LORD, your Redeemer, the Holy One of Israel, 'I am the LORD your God, who teaches you to profit, Who leads you in the way you should go'** (Emphasis added).

In his widely-read work, *The Trinity, Evidence and Issues*, Robert Morey contended:

> If the passage is interpreted in its natural and normal meaning, there are three persons in this passage who are all God! But how can God be sent by God unless there are several Persons within the Godhead? Since the Father

---

the military exploits mentioned in 9:3-5 (cf. 10:21; Det. 10:17; Neh. 9:32)."

sent the Son and the Spirit in Trinitarian theology, this is exactly the kind of passage we would expect to find...How can non-Trinitarians handle a passage like this? They can't. So they identify that the speaker is God and claim that is actually Isaiah who is speaking in either verse 16b or the whole of verse 16!

According to Morey, Isaiah could not have been the one speaking in verse 16b because there seems to be no break in Jehovah's speech in the Hebrew and English Bible. Morey concludes:

> This passage is clear proof that the authors of the Bible believed that God was multi-personal. A Trinitarian would not have the least hesitation to write to the text as it stands. But Unitarians, Arians, Modalists, and Muslims could never do so.[43]

From Morey's comments one would get the impression that "non-Trinitarians" try in vain to get around such a "clear proof" of the "multi-personality" of God. But Morey doesn't mention that many of the most respected scholars, reference works and commentaries have identified the speaker in verse 16 as the prophet Isaiah himself; yet none were "Unitarian," "Arian," "Modalist," or "Muslim," but *Trinitarian*. These commentators made this identification, of course, not in an attempt to deny Trinitarianism, but because of their honest evaluation of the text, in its historical context.

"Clear proof" that the authors of the Bible believed that God was "multi-personal"? John Calvin wrote:

> *And now Jehovah hath sent me.* Isaiah now begins to speak of himself, and applies this statement to the preceding doctrine, and testifies that God, who hath spoken from the beginning, now speaketh by him, and consequently that we ought to believe those things which God now speaketh by him, in the same manner as if he were visibly present.[44]

---

[43] *The Trinity, Evidence and Issues*, pp. 101, 102.
[44] *Calvin's Commentaries, Isaiah 33-66, Commentary on the Prophet Isaiah*, Vol. III, Translated from the Original Latin, and Collated with the latest French version, By the Rev. William Pringle (Grand Rapids: Baker Book House, 1979), p. 483.

'Trinity' in the Old Testament?

In reference to the argument for the Trinity based on this passage in Isaiah, Albert Barnes—described in the preface of his commentary as the "beloved pastor of the large and influential First Presbyterian Church of Philadelphia"—warned that "such forced and violent interpretations should be avoided," having observed:

> Many of the reformers, and others since their time, have supposed that this refers to the Messiah, and have endeavoured to derive a demonstration from this verse of the doctrine of the Trinity...But the evidence that this refers to the Messiah is too slight to lay the foundation for such an argument; and nothing is gained to the cause of truth by such forced interpretations...The remark of Calvin on this verse, and on this mode of interpretation, is full of good sense...The *scope* of the passage demands, as it seems to me, that it should be referred to the prophet himself. His object is, to state that he had not come at his own instance, or without being commissioned. He had been sent by God, and was attended by the Spirit of inspiration. He foretold events which the Spirit of God alone could make known to men. It is, therefore, a strong asseveration that his words demanded their attention, and that they had every ground of consolation, and every possible evidence that they would be rescued from their bondage. It is a full claim to Divine inspiration, and is one of the many assertions which are found in the Scriptures where the sacred writers claim to have been sent by God, and taught by his Spirit.[45]

Yet some expositors—although viewing verse 16 as a reference to the prophet Isaiah—do believe that the reference could include with it a broader or extended prophetic application toward the Messiah. John Wesley said: "From the time that I first spoke of it, I am or was there, to effect what I had foretold. *The Lord*—God by his Spirit. *Me*—The prophet *Isaiah*; who was a type of Christ, and so this may have a respect to him also."[46] In his Bible commentary Reverend Thomas Scott expressed himself

---

[45] *Notes on the Old Testament, Explanatory and Practical, by Albert Barnes, Isaiah Vol. II*, Edited by Robert Frew, D.D. (Grand Rapids: Baker Book House, 1956), pp. 192, 193.
[46] *John Wesley's Explanatory Notes on the Whole Bible*

'Trinity' in the Old Testament?

along similar lines:

> There is some appearance of difficulty in ascertaining the speaker in this verse: but if the prophet be supposed to speak, it must be as a type of the 'Elect 'Servant of JEHOVAH,' before predicted (*Note,* xlii. 1—4). From the opening of his ministry, Isaiah had publicly spoken of those things which were coming to pass, and events had accorded to his predictions; he had from the first been at hand to declare the will of the Lord: and now the Lord GOD and his Spirit had sent him to predict the captivity, and also the deliverance of the Jews from it; it behooved them to come near and attend to his words.[47]

Nothing in this passage suggests a meaning dogmatically advanced by Trinitarian apologists like Robert Morey. It is simply another example of a forced interpretation, an unfair and deceptive attempt to advance an Old Testament text as "a clear proof of the Trinity" which, in reality, is quite far from "clear proof." As with so many other examples already cited, the arguments commonly employed to promote the already-established doctrine of the Trinity are actually disproven by Trinitarian scholars themselves, who, although not consciously attempting to overturn traditional theological constructions, are nevertheless able to expound upon particular scriptural texts with fairness and objectivity, rather than, as Morey and other apologists do, superimpose meanings that are really not there.[48] Unfortunately, Robert Morey's dogmatism on the meaning of Isaiah 48 is not only unscholarly and irresponsible but unfair and

---

[47] *The Holy Bible Containing the Old and New Testaments according to the Authorized Version; With Explanatory Notes, Practical Observations, and Copious Marginal References,* Vol. IV.

[48] The notes in the *New English Translation,* along with several Roman Catholic sources, identify the speaker as "Cyrus, the Lord's 'ally' mentioned in vv. 14-15." See footnotes to: *Jerusalem Bible* (p. 1221) and the *Saint Joseph's Edition of the New American Bible* (p. 874). But the footnote in the Catholic translation by Monsignor Knox states: "It is presumably the prophet who speaks here in his own person." —*Knox, The Holy Bible footnote,* p. 667. According to another source, verse 16 is a "reference to either Isaiah or the servant of the Lord. The Spirit of the Lord comes upon the servant in 42:1 (see note there) and upon the Messianic prophet of 61:1 (see note there)." —*NIV Study Bible,* p. 1080. According to another Evangelical commentary: "By its verse division MT links this with what precedes, but NIV rightly perceives a disjunction from vv. 12-16a. There Yahweh spoke, and v. 16a pairs with v. 12 as a bracket round the subsection. The I of v. 16b is the prophet, who is now beginning the introduction to vv. 17-19 in an especially emphatic way, putting Yahweh's authority firmly behind the words that follow." —*The New International Biblical Commentary, Isaiah, Based on the New International Version,* by John Goldingay (Hendrickson Publishers, 2001), p. 279.

entirely misleading.

Zechariah 12:10

In Zechariah 12:10, Jehovah God is the speaker. The text appears in the *King James Version* as follows:

> **And I will pour upon the inhabitants of Jerusalem, the spirit of grace and of supplications: and they shall look upon *me* whom they have pierced, and shall mourn for him, as one mourneth for his only son...**

In his popular Study Bible, John MacArthur argues:

> Israel's repentance will come because they look to Jesus, the One whom they rejected and crucified (cf. Is. 53:5; John 19:37), in faith at the Second Advent (Rom. 11:25-27). When God says they pierced 'Me,' He is certainly affirming the incarnation of deity—*Jesus was God.*[49]

The Abingdon Commentary makes a different point regarding the translation of this verse: "So the outpouring of the divine *spirit* impels the people, high and low, to *supplicate* Jehovah's favor and forgiveness for some great crime in which they had all had a share (v. 14). Some noble representative of Jehovah had been martyred (*pierced*, v. 10: read *they shall look upon him*, not *me*), and they are now filled with shame and sorrow."[50]

The reason why several English translations have "him" instead of "me" is alluded to in the footnote in the *Companion Bible* by E. W. Bullinger, which states, "Western codices read 'Me'; but the Eastern read 'Him', with one early printed edition. Whom they have pierced. See John 19.34, 37. Rev. 1.7."[51]

It is clear that the New Testament writers believed that Zechariah's prophecy was fulfilled in Christ. But the apostle John made reference to the prophetic text in the following form:

> **For these things were done, that the scripture should be fulfilled, A bone of him shall not be broken. And**

---

[49] *MacArthur Study Bible*, p. 1354.
[50] *The Abingdon Bible Commentary*, p. 830.
[51] Page 1293.

again another scripture [Zechariah 12:10] **saith, They shall look on *him* whom they pierced."**[52]

However, in reference to the reading that appears in the traditional Masoretic Text, distinguished OT professor of Dallas Theological Seminary, Eugene Merrill, said the following in his commentary on Zechariah:

> There is no textual reason…for rejecting the reading, 'they will look to *Me*, the one they have pierced through.' The difficulty lies, therefore, in the hermeneutical and theological aspects of the question. As to the former, the passage clearly teaches that YHWH (the speaker throughout in the absence of clues to the contrary), having poured out the spirit of grace leading to the people's supplications, will be seen by them as having been pierced by them…At the outset, it must be affirmed that the OT witness knows nothing of a 'mortal God,' one who can be fatally wounded as in this passage. Even at its most anthropomorphic extreme there is nothing approaching what occurs here in a literal reading of the text. The great fourth servant song of Isaiah 52:13-53:12 is no exception, for the servant there, in terms of the OT understanding alone, is totally distinct from God…This leads one to conclude that the piercing here in Zechariah 12:10 is figurative or substitution. The first of these will be considered and then the other. First, YHWH has been pierced by His people in the sense that they have wounded His holiness and violated His righteousness…A second possibility is that YHWH was pierced in the sense that someone who represented Him was pierced. This allows the text to stand as is and to direct the focus on the persons represented by the 'Me' and the 'him.' YHWH is pierced, only indirectly of course, so the eyes of those who wounded Him are directed to the person who directly received the mortal blow. The problem with this interpretation is that it is impossible to identify this second party short of concluding that it is a messianic figure—to the Christian, Jesus Christ. While the NT witness, to be discussed below, makes this not only possible but necessary in the fullest sense, ordinary

---

[52] John 19:37, *KJV*

hermeneutics would insist that the figure have some relevance, if only typological, to the time and audience of the prophet himself. It seems best, then, to adopt the interpretation that it is YHWH who has been pierced, if only in a figurative way...As far as the messianic character of 12:10 is concerned, there can be no question of its being taken that way in early Jewish tradition, to say nothing of NT Christology. The gospel of John reports: 'Another scripture says, 'They will look on him whom they pierced;' (John 19:37). Though John appears to follow a non-Masoretic reading [That is, he reads 'on him' rather than 'on me' with MT. See Raymond E. Brown, the Gospel According to John (xii-xxi)...here, he is 'quoting' Zech. 12:10 in support of the prediction of Jesus' crucifixion.[53]

If the reading of the Masoretic text is authentic, as professor Merrill points out, it is likely that YHWH was spoken of as being pierced in a *figurative* or *representational* sense, especially since the reference to the pierced one shifts so suddenly from "**me**" ('they shall look upon *me* whom they have pierced') to "**him**" ('and they shall mourn for *him*').

A comparable example is found in the New Testament in reference to Mary, the mother of Jesus. When the infant Jesus was presented by his parents in the Jerusalem temple, a devout man named "Simeon blessed them and said to his mother Mary, 'Listen carefully: This child is destined to be the cause of the falling and rising of many in Israel and to be a sign that will be rejected. Indeed, as a result of him the thoughts of many hearts will be revealed—*and a sword will pierce your own soul as well!*"[54] In this case, Mary was spoken of as one whose soul would be pierced, not because she would be literally/physically stabbed or pierced through, but likely, because of the deep pain she would endure while watching her innocent son die a criminal's death. John MacArthur expressed agreement on this point: "This was undoubtedly a reference to the personal grief Mary would endure when she watched her own Son die in agony

---

[53] *An Exegetical Commentary, Haggai, Zechariah, Malachi,* p. 318-322 (emphasis added).
[54] Luke 2:33-35, *New English Translation*

'Trinity' in the Old Testament?

(John 19:25)."[55] According to the study notes in the *New English Translation*: "The language is figurative, picturing great pain. Though it refers in part to the cross, it really includes the pain all of Jesus' ministry will cause, including the next event in Luke 2:41-52 and extending to the opposition he faced throughout his ministry."

However, John's quotation of Zechariah's prophecy in his own account could suggest that he was in possession of what should be accepted as the original reading—"him" and not "me." On this point, F. F. Bruce's observations are worth considering:

> Zech. 12:10, which foretells a day of great mourning in Jerusalem and the surrounding territory when, as the Masoretic Hebrew text puts it, 'they shall look unto *me* whom they have pierced' (so R.V.). The passage is quoted once and echoed once in the New Testament, and in both places the pronoun is not 'me' but 'him'. This is not so significant in the place where the passage is merely echoed (Rev. 1:7, 'and every eye will see him, every one who pierced him'), for that is not an exact quotation. Here the predicted looking to the one who was pierced is interpreted of the Second Advent of Christ. But in John 19:37 the piercing is interpreted of the piercing of Christ's side with a soldier's lance after His death on the cross, and here Zech. 12:10 is expressly quoted: 'And again another scripture says, 'They shall look on *him* whom they have pierced'.' It is a reasonable inference that this is the form in which the Evangelist knew the passage, and indeed the reading 'him' instead of 'me' appears in a few Hebrew manuscripts. The R.S.V. thus has New Testament authority for its rendering of Zech. 12:10, 'And I will pour out on the house of David and the inhabitants of Jerusalem a spirit of compassion and supplication, so that, when *they look on him* whom they have pierced, they shall mourn for him, as one mourns for an only child, and weep bitterly over him, as one weeps over a first-born.' Why then is the R.S.V. criticized for conforming to the New Testament here? Because, if the reading 'me' be retained, the reference would be to the speaker, who is God, and in view of the application of the

---

[55] *MacArthur Study Bible*, p. 1516.

'Trinity' in the Old Testament?

passage in the New Testament, there are some who see here an anticipation of the Christian doctrine of our Lord's divine nature. The reading 'me' is certainly quite early, for it appears in the Septuagint (which otherwise misses the point of the passage); but the New Testament seems to attach no significance to Zech. 12:10 as providing evidence for the deity of Christ...And, whoever the pierced one is, the fact that he is referred to elsewhere in the verse in the third person ('they shall mourn for him...and weep bitterly over him') suggests that he is Yahweh's representative (probably the anointed king), in whose piercing Yahweh Himself is pierced.[56]

Consider the rendering in the following English Bible translations:

...when they look on the one whom they have pierced, they shall mourn for him, as one mourns for an only child —*New Revised Standard Version*[57]
...and they shall look on him whom they have thrust through, and they shall mourn for him as one mourns for an only son —*New American Bible*
They will look on the one whom they have pierced; they will mourn for him as for an only son

---

[56] *History of the Bible in English* (Lutterworth Press, 1979 third edition), pp. 199-200 (emphasis added). It was also observed in one scholarly source: "*yla* 'unto me' is often emended to *wyla* 'unto him.' S. R. Driver said that about fifty MSS support *wyla* 'unto him' (Driver 266). The context supports *wyla* [unto him]. The fifth word in MT beyond this one is *wylax* 'upon him.' John 19:37 and Rev 1:7 read 'upon him' whom they pierced.' However, Yahweh may be the speaker and may be saying that the people had pierced him metaphorically by their rebellion and ingratitude, or they pierced him when they attacked his representative (perhaps some unidentified martyr). The NEB keeps both pronouns and reads '...on me, on him whom they have pierced.'" —*Word Biblical Commentary*, Volume 32, *Micah-Malachi*, Ralph L. Smith (Waco: Word Books, 1984), p. 276. In *The Anchor Bible*, the translators preserved the reading of the Masoretic Text, but they render the verse as follows: "so that they will look to me *concerning* the one they have stabbed." *The New Interpreter's Bible* Vol. 7, p. 828 (Nashville: Abingdon Press, 1996) observes: "Both translation and interpretation of these verses are difficult. It is possible to read, 'they will look to me whom they have pierced,' meaning that David's house and Jerusalem had pierced Yahweh. But piercing [Heb.*daqar*] elsewhere in the O.T. always means physical violence and usually death (e.g., Num. 25:8; 1 Sam 31:4); it does so expressly in 13:3. The mourning described in vv. 10b-12 is mourning 'for him,' the one pierced or stabbed. It seems preferable to take the MT's object marker before the relative pronoun as indicating an accusative of respect, allowing one to translate 'concerning the one whom they pierced' (cf. LXX.)."

[57] *Gesenius' Hebrew Grammar* (pp. 444, 445, 446) states: "The relative Pronoun...(2) Not depending on a governing substantive, but itself expressing a substantial idea. Clauses introduced in this way may be called independent relative clauses. This use of ['*asher*'] is generally rendered in English by he who, he whom, &...In Z[echariah] 12:10 also, instead of the unintelligible ['*elai eth asher*', 'to me whom'], we should probably read ['*el asher*', 'to him whom'], and refer this passage to this class [of 'independent relative clauses']" (Oxford: at the Clarendon Press, 1909).

'Trinity' in the Old Testament?

—*Jerusalem Bible*

...and they shall look on him whom they have thrust through, and they shall mourn for him as one mourns for an only son —*The Holy Bible, Saint Joseph, New Catholic Edition*

...and they shall look upon Him whom they have pierced; they shall wail for Him as one wails for an only son —*The Modern Language Bible, New Berkley Version*

...and they shall look at him whom they have stabbed to death; and they shall mourn for him like the mourning for an only child —*An American Translation, Goodspeed*

They will look at the one whom they stabbed to death, and they will mourn for him like those who mourn for an only child. —*Today's English Version*

...will feel deep sorrow and pray when they see the one they pierced with a spear. They will mourn and weep for him, as parents weep over the death of their only child —*Contemporary English Version*

...and they shall look upon Him Whom they pierced, and mourn over Him, as if mourning over a loved one; and grieve over Him, as over the first-born!
—*The Holy Bible in Modern English, Ferrar Fenton*

Zechariah 14:4

> *"Then Yahweh will take the field; he will fight against these nations as he fights in the day of battle. On that day, his feet will rest on the Mount of Olives..."* – Zechariah 14:3-4, *Jerusalem Bible*

Trinitarians sometimes point to Zechariah chapter fourteen in an attempt to shore up biblical evidence for the "incarnation" of "God the Son."[58] Since the text says that God's "feet" will one day rest on the Mount of Olives, and because some believe that Jesus' feet will descend on that same mountain at his second coming, according to some apologists, the prophecy must be referring to God incarnated as a human being in the returned

---

[58] The text is likewise appealed to by "Modalists" to prove that Jesus is God the Father.

Messiah, Jesus. In a 2010 radio discussion, Dr. Michael Brown[59] argued:

> "...there are quite a number of texts that in the Old Testament, in the Hebrew Scriptures, speak directly about Yahweh—directly and explicitly about Yahweh—but then are directly applied to Jesus in the New Testament...Zechariah 14 says...'Yahweh shall go forth and fight against the nations that come up against Jerusalem...that day His feet shall rest upon the Mount of Olives (which is opposite to Jerusalem); so Yahweh's feet will literally rest upon the Mount of Olives, yet we know this is direct prophecy of the return of Jesus based on Acts chapter one where he ascends from the Mount of Olives and he himself, his feet will touch right there on the Mount of Olives...this is one of the most explicit [prophecies]...It's perfectly understandable if the Son himself bears the divine nature[60] and therefore his feet touching the ground equal Yahweh's feet touching the ground. If he's just a created being, it doesn't work...How do you explain this? Yahweh's feet will literally touch the Mount of Olives when he comes to fight on the final war against the nations that attack Jerusalem. Acts one tells us that that is Jesus whose feet will touch the Mount of Olives."[61]

Dr. Brown's comments capture the sentiments of many evangelicals. The question for our present purpose is: Is there a valid, biblically-based way to "explain" the text outside the framework of Trinitarian doctrine?

---

[59] According to the description on his website, Dr. Brown is "a published Old Testament and Semitic scholar, holding a Ph.D. in Near Eastern Languages and Literatures from New York University. He has served as a visiting or adjunct professor at Trinity Evangelical Divinity School, Fuller Theological Seminary, Denver Theological Seminary, the King's Seminary, and Regent University School."

[60] Biblically speaking, there is no problem in accepting that the Son of God "bears the divine nature." According to the apostle Peter, Christians themselves will also be "partakers of the divine nature" (2 Peter 1:4), but that does not make them the same "being" as God. That is at least one reason why Christians can safely accept the fact that Jesus has a "divine nature" without meaning that he is "consubstantial" with the Father, as Trinitarian theology dictates and as Dr. Brown is implying in this case.

[61] *Line of Fire, Revolutionary Radio with Dr. Michael Brown: Dr Brown Debates Kermit Zarley on the Deity of Jesus (Part One)* January 12, 2010. http://lineoffireadio.askdrbrown.org/

The first point that needs to be recognized is that Zechariah 14:4 is not exactly—as Dr. Brown suggests—"directly" or "explicitly" applied to Jesus in Acts chapter one or anywhere else in the New Testament. Zechariah 14:4 says that "**Yahweh**" will fight against the nations and that "**his feet will rest upon the Mount of Olives.**" In Acts chapter one, when Jesus was evidently on the same mountain mentioned in Zechariah's prophecy (compare Acts 1:12), his disciples were gazing into heaven as Jesus was taken up, and two unidentified men in white robes said: "**This Jesus, who was taken up from you into heaven, will come in the same way as you saw him go into heaven**" (Acts 1:11; the key text).

As a simple reading of Acts 1:11 reveals, Zechariah 14:4 is nowhere *clearly* applied to Jesus' 'coming.' And, in spite of what Dr. Brown argues, the text does not say that Jesus' "feet will touch" the Mount of Olives, since no reference to the "feet" of Jesus is actually made in connection with the Mount of Olives in this instance.

Even though Jesus will, according to the two men in white robes, "**come in the same way as [the apostles] saw him go into heaven**," that doesn't necessarily have to mean that Jesus will physically come back to the precise geographical location from where he ascended. That is, contrary to Dr. Brown's claim, although it may certainly be *possible*, we do not really "know" that Zechariah 14:4 is a "direct prophecy of the return of Jesus," simply because Acts 1:11 never says that it is; nor does it actually use the language of Zechariah's prophecy and apply it to Jesus.

Secondly, it is true that Zechariah states that Yahweh's "feet" will rest on the Mount of Olives. But, again, contrary to Dr. Brown's confident assertion, the text does not say that Yahweh's feet will "literally" rest upon the Mount of Olives, as if the Hebrew Scriptures taught that God has *literal* flesh-and-blood "feet" like a man. No such qualification ('literal') appears in the text. In fact, as most Bible students recognize, it is not entirely unusual for the Scriptures to describe God with symbolic language, metaphors, and in human-like terms, in spite of the fact that, in certain instances, he is not *literally* what he is described as, or *literally* has what he is said to possess.

'Trinity' in the Old Testament?

For example, in the very same book, it is said that Yahweh's "arrow" will go forth like lightning, and that he will "blow the trumpet" and "march forth in the whirlwinds of the south" (Zechariah 9:14). Are these statements to be taken *literally?* Will Yahweh send forth a *literal* "arrow" and *literally* blow sounds out of a tangible trumpet using fleshly lips? Or, is the prophet—as the other prophets often did—simply making use of *vivid language* and *dramatic imagery* to communicate the point that God will take decisive action as a warrior would in a battle against his enemies?

Similarly, when the prophet says that Yahweh's "feet"[62] will rest upon the Mount of Olives, it does not necessarily mean that Yahweh has (or will have) *literal, tangible* or *human* feet— just as most Bible students understand that Yahweh does not *literally* have physical (or human) "hair," a "head" (Daniel 7:9), "nostrils" (Exodus 15:8; Psalm 18:15), a "right hand" (Exodus 15:12) or a physical "arm" of flesh like a man (Psalm 89:13)— or, even, a "shadow" like a material object (Psalm 91:1), or "wings" like a bird (Psalm 17:8; 61:4). Other texts even speak of God as a "dwelling place," a "refuge," a "rock," a "fortress" (Psalm 91:9; 2 Samuel 2:22), a "sun," and as a "shield" (Psalm 84:11). In the very same book Yahweh is described as a "wall of fire" to Jerusalem (Zechariah 2:5). Is this *literally* the case?

In Zechariah 9:8 Yahweh says: "...for now I see with my own *eyes.*" Here, Yahweh has "eyes" with which to "see." Does this mean that God has literal eyeballs, with pupils, lenses, corneas, optic nerves, and retinas? In Zechariah 13:7 God said, "I will turn *my hand* against the little ones." Does God have a flesh-and-bone/human hand (Psalm 98:1), with fleshly fingers and fingernails? Is God literally a "sun," a "rock" or a "fortress"?

---

[62] *The JPS Bible commentary* on this verse states: "***He will set His feet*** God appears as a warrior in battle. The stark *anthropomorphism* recalls Amos 9:1, in which the prophet envisages the 'Lord standing by [or: on] the altar' prophesying doom. The divine manifestation for battle in Hab. 3:6 has God make the earth shake 'when He stands' and the nations tremble 'when He glances.'" —*The JPS Bible Commentary, Haftarot* (Philadelphia: The Jewish Publication Society, 2002), p. 401 (emphasis added). According to *Theopedia, An Encyclopedia of Biblical Christianity,* "Biblical anthropomorphism is when human characteristics are projected on God...The Bible has examples of God referring to himself in anthropomorphic terms and the biblical writers referring to God in anthropomorphic terms—the purpose being to describe God in terms more understandable to humans. Without anthropomorphism, since God is invisible and immaterial, we would not have a framework on which to understand Him."

'Trinity' in the Old Testament?

Or were these meant to be understood as *metaphors* and *figures of speech* designed to communicate truths about the strength of the Almighty's protective power? (Psalm 84:11).

Nahum 1:3 says that "the clouds are the dust of [Yahweh's] *feet*."[63] In this verse, like Zechariah 14:4, God has "feet." Will Dr. Brown and other Trinitarian apologists argue that this text was intended to be taken as some kind of allusion to the "incarnation" of "God the Son" (God in human flesh)? Or would they accept this simply as an example of *figurative language* intended to emphasize the point that God is *exalted* in sovereignty, power, and glory, even above the lofty clouds of heaven?

In Ezekiel 43:7, Yahweh similarly declared to the prophet: "Son of man, this is the place of my throne and the place of *the soles of my feet*, where I will dwell in the midst of the people of Israel forever." Is this some kind of reference to the Trinitarian "God-in-the-flesh" concept? Or is it a figure of speech?

Clearly, Dr. Brown's argument that the statement about God having "feet" in Zechariah 14:4 must be taken to mean that God will have literal/physical or human "feet," and hence proof of the Trinitarian "incarnation," is not only unjustifiably dogmatic, but simply ignores the presence of the figurative language that occurs in the same book (Zechariah 2:5; 9:8; 13:7) and frequently throughout the books of the Bible (See for example: Ezekiel 43:7; Nahum 1:3; Isaiah 5:25; 60:13. Also: Exodus 15:8, 12;2 Samuel 2:22; Daniel 7:9; Psalm 17:8; 18:15; 61:4; 84:11; 89:13; 91:1; 98:1).[64]

In reference to Zechariah 14:4 and God's "feet," the distinguished Bible commentator Charles John Ellicott (1819-

---

[63] Similarly, in Isaiah 60:13 Yahweh says—in association with the beauty of his sanctuary—"I shall make the place of *My feet* glorious" (*NASB*).

[64] John Calvin even recognized the non-literal nature of the language used in Zechariah 14: "[The prophet] continues the same subject, that God's power would be then conspicuous in putting enemies to flight. He indeed illustrates here his discourse by figurative expressions, as though he wished to bring the Jews to see the scene itself; for the object of the personification is no other but that the faithful might set God before them as it were in a visible form; and thus he confirms their faith, as indeed it was necessary… The Prophet then, in order to aid our weakness, adds a vivid representation, as though God stood before their eyes." —*Commentaries on the Twelve Minor Prophets, Now First Translated from the Original Latin, by the Rev. John Owen, Volume Fifth, Zechariah, Malachi*, Christian Classics Ethereal Library, Grand Rapids, MI.

1905) concurred: "The language is, of course, figurative."[65] *The Anchor Bible* commentary made a similar observation:

> The language with which this verse begins is simple enough, but the image is staggering in its anthropomorphic depiction of Yahweh as a giant astride the heights of Jerusalem. Perhaps it is because of this dramatic scenario that we are presented with Yahweh's 'feet' positioned on the Mount of Olives rather than with 'Yahweh will stand.' Still, the direct corporeality of Yahweh rather than the divine action of God in the human sphere is what commands the reader's attention there. God's intervention as a military figure is a frequent theme in the prophecies of Second Zechariah, yet this is the first instance in which such blatantly anthropomorphic language appears in the service of the military theme....the heart of the image is the military implication—the vanquishing of the enemy and the rescue of God's people. Indeed, because the whole of the imagery of the next subunit (vv 6-11) revolves around the motif of Jerusalem as the high mountain that connects the realm of God with that of humanity, it is no wonder that Yahweh's place at this nexus of heaven and earth comes graphically to the fore.[66]

The same essential point was made in *The College Press NIV Commentary*:

> Yahweh intervenes, fighting **in the day of battle against those nations** that threaten Jerusalem. The statement uses traditional military language for Yahweh's fighting on behalf of the city (cf. Judg 5:4; 2 Sam 5:24; 2 Chr 20:17; Isa 42:13); the background for the image here may be that of Yahweh's defeat of the Egyptians at the crossing of the Red Sea (Exod 14:13–14). The *anthropomorphism* concerning the **feet** of Yahweh (cf. Isa 60:13; Ezek 43:7) standing on the Mount of Olives obviously continues the notion of military victory evidenced in verse 3. The same Yahweh

---

[65] *Ellicott's Commentary on the Whole Bible, A Verse by Verse Explanation, Volume V-VI, Jeremiah—Malachi* (Grand Rapids: Zondervan, 1959), p. 591
[66] *The Anchor Bible, Zechariah 9—14, A New Translation with Introduction and Commentary, Volume 25C*, Carol L. Meyers and Eric M. Meyers (New York: Doubleday, 1993), pp. 418-419.

'Trinity' in the Old Testament?

who has promised to give the Hebrews every place in Canaan where their feet trod (Josh 1:3) now makes a clear claim of ownership of the land...The Mount of Olives is the last stop in the vicinity of Jerusalem for the glory of Yahweh on the way to Babylon (Ezek 11:23). Therefore, the depiction of Yahweh stepping on the mount signals his return to dwell in Jerusalem. Just as Ezekiel 43:7 portrays the temple as the place for the soles of Yahweh's feet and where Yahweh dwells, here the standing of Yahweh on the mount adjacent to the city boldly depicts Yahweh's presence in and for the city. Presumably under Yahweh's feet, the Mount of Olives **splits**.[67]

However, even if the future coming of Jesus *does* represent the fulfillment of Zechariah's prophecy (something the Scriptures don't seem to directly verify), and Jesus will descend to the precise location from which he ascended, then that very well may mean that the Son's "feet" resting on the Mount of Olives equates to Yahweh's "feet" doing the same. But this would be so, *biblically speaking*, not because Jesus is literally "Yahweh" or the "second person" of a "triune God," but because Jesus, the Messiah, always comes in his Father's name as God's sinless emissary or representative—even when he acts as judge (John 5:30; 8:16; 12:48-49; Romans 2:16; Acts 17:30-31; Revelation 19:15).

In response to this point about "representation" (or 'agency') in connection with Zechariah 14:4, Dr. Brown argued:

> *"If I say I will personally come and hand this to you. My hand will shake your hand. And then I send somebody else to do it, then that didn't happen."*

In other words, in Dr. Brown's view, if the Bible says that Yahweh's feet will rest on the Mount of Olives, and Jesus is the fulfiller of the prophecy according to the Acts 1:11, then we either have to deny the truthfulness of the prophecy or we have to accept Brown's view that Jesus is himself Yahweh "in the

---

[67] Ham, C., & Hahlen, M., *The College Press NIV Commentary: Minor Prophets, Nahum-Malachi* (Joplin: College Press, 2001), p. 480 (emphasis added).

flesh." Unfortunately, in this case, Dr. Brown simply presents his audience with a false dilemma, a common fallacy of Trinitarian "apologetics." That is, in his attempt to defend the "orthodox" position on God's "complex unity," Dr. Brown overlooks the fact that, throughout the Scriptures, and in a variety of ancient and modern cultural contexts, a representative or agent of someone else can often be regarded or referred to as the individual himself, even though he or she is not *literally* that individual (Jesus, of course, is clearly portrayed this way in his relation to God the Father: John 13:20; 14:7; 12:44; Hebrews 1:3), as it was pointed out in *The Encyclopedia of Jewish Religion*:

> The main point of the Jewish law of agency is expressed in the dictum, 'a person's agent is regarded as the person himself' (Ned. 72B; Kidd, 41b). Therefore any act committed by a duly appointed agent is regarded as having been committed by the principal...[68]

Craig Blomberg of Denver Seminary made a similar kind of observation that actually helps us to make sense of quite a few scriptural texts:

> Every language and culture has many conventional expressions which do not mean what they literally seem to say. One of these common to modern Western and Eastern cultures is the habit of speaking about someone acting for himself even when he uses an intermediary. A news reporter may state flatly, 'the President of the United States today said...' when in fact it was his press secretary who spoke on his behalf, yet no one accuses the commentator of inaccurate reporting. Similarly, Matthew and Mark can speak of Pilate scourging Jesus (Mk. 15:15; Mat. 27:26) even though no governor himself would ever have lifted the whip but would have left that task to his soldiers. This type of linguistic convention undoubtedly explains the differences between Matthew's and Luke's narratives of the Capernaum centurion (Mt. 8:5-13; Lk.

---

[68] R.J.A. Werblowsky, G. Wigoder (New York: Adams Books, 1986), p. 15. If that is indeed the case, it is easy to accept that the act of Jesus (Yahweh's 'agent') resting his feet upon the Mount of Olives can "be regarded as having been committed by the principal," since the "person's agent [Jesus] is regarded as the person [in this case, Yahweh] himself."

'Trinity' in the Old Testament?

7:1-10); in the former the centurion himself comes to Jesus, while in the latter he sends emissaries to summon the Lord. Luke's account is more literally accurate, but Matthew's way of phrasing it would have been considered no less acceptable."[69]

Was Matthew falsely reporting the facts when he said that the centurion himself came to Jesus (since the centurion actually sent 'elders of the Jews', Luke 7:3)? Do the Gospels of Matthew and Luke contradict one another on this point? Or was Matthew—in line with the scriptural and culturally-understood principle of representation (or 'agency')—rightfully saying that the centurion went to Jesus since the elders he sent were acting as his appointed agents?

The same kind of observation was made in another evangelical reference work:

> In the first century, it was understood that when a representative was sent to speak for his master, it was as if the master was speaking himself…Therefore, Matthew states that a centurion came entreating Jesus about his sick slave, when in fact the centurion sent others on his behalf. So, when Matthew declares that the centurion was speaking, this was true, even though he was (as Luke indicated) speaking through his *official representative*.[70]

The point is, if Jesus himself will rest his feet on the Mount of Olives when he comes again, we can very well accept this as the fulfillment of Zechariah 14:4, a prophecy that speaks about the feet of "Yahweh"—since, in the ancient world, "actions taken by one's emissaries could be considered one's own."[71] Scripturally, we can confirm that Jesus is God's apostle[72] and anointed one—"the exact representation of his being"—who righteously executes the judgments of the God in whose name he acts. That is why it would have been perfectly appropriate for the Scriptures to have revealed that the Messiah's arrival in

---

[69] Craig Blomberg, *The Historical Reliability of the Gospels*, p. 134.
[70] Norman Geisler and Thomas Howe, *When Critics Ask, A Popular Handbook On Bible Difficulties* (Wheaton Illinois: Victor Books 1992), p. 334 (emphasis added).
[71] Craig Blomberg in *Reasonable Faith, Christian Truth and Apologetics* by William Lane Craig (Wheaton: Crossway Books, 1994), p. 208.
[72] Hebrews 3:1. "The word apostle (Greek *apostolos*) is a common term for someone sent forth or sent out, as an emissary." –*Theopedia, An Encyclopedia of Biblical Christianity*

judgment equals Yahweh's arrival in judgment, without making the Messiah "consubstantial" with the Father.

Conclusion

What may also not be fully appreciated by those who argue for the Trinity (or the incarnation of 'God the Son') based on these Old Testament texts, is that to insist that the God of Zechariah (the God of the Old Testament prophets) was going to be *literally* pierced through (to death) in the classic "incarnational" sense—or, likewise, that God will have *literal* human feet that will rest upon the Mount of Olives—would be more supportive of the doctrine that says Jesus Christ *is* God the Father ('Modalism').

According to Hebrews chapter one, the God of "our fathers" (Jehovah) is the Father of Jesus Christ (vs. 1, 2), for he is the one who spoke in times past by means of the prophets, but has, in the last days, spoken by means of a *Son*. It follows that whenever Jehovah is spoken of (or is shown to be the one speaking) in the Hebrew writings, it always constitutes a reference to God the Father, not to the Son of God, and never to the alleged "triune God." If taken to its logical conclusion, to insist that Jehovah was the one *literally* pierced through (Zechariah 12:10), or that God will have *literal* human feet (Zechariah 14:4), would really lend itself to the notion that *God the Father* became a man and was even put to death—once again, something Trinitarianism does not teach and cannot accept.

Whenever Jehovah God is the subject in the Hebrew Scriptures, it is always a reference to God the Father alone. The point was made by evangelical scholar Murray J. Harris:

> To whom was the author of Hebrews referring when he said (1:1), 'At many times and in various ways *God* spoke to our forefathers through the prophets'? That it was not the Holy Spirit in any ultimate sense is evident from the fact that in neither the OT nor the NT is the Spirit called 'God' *express verbis*. And, in spite of the fact that the LXX equivalent of *YHWH*, viz., *kurios*, is regularly applied to Jesus in the NT so that it becomes less a title

than a proper name, it is not possible that *ho theos* in Heb. 1:1 denotes Jesus Christ, for the same sentence (in Greek) contains '(the God who spoke…) in these last days has spoken to us in a Son (*en huio*.' Since the author is emphasizing the continuity of the two phrases of divine speech (*ho theos lalesas…elalesen*), this reference to a Son shows that *ho theos* was understood to be 'God the Father.' Similarly, the differentiation made between *ho theos* as the one who speaks in both eras and *huios* as his final means of speaking shows that in the author's mind it was not the Triune God of Christian theology who spoke to the forefathers by the prophets. That is to say, for the author of Hebrews (as for all NT writers, one may suggest) 'the God of our Fathers,' Yahweh, was no other than 'the God and Father of our Lord Jesus Christ' (compare Acts 2:30 and 2:33; 3:13 and 3:18; 3:25 and 3:26; note also 5:30). Such a conclusion is entirely consistent with the regular NT usage of *ho theos*. It would be inappropriate for *elohim* or *YHWH* ever to refer to the Trinity in the OT when in the NT *theos* regularly refers to the Father alone and apparently never to the Trinity.[73]

Although some Trinitarian scholars now recognize the error in the various arguments put forth based on the Old Testament writings, most of the above arguments are still used today as a means to preserve and perpetuate acceptance of traditional Trinitarian concepts. But Roman Catholic Edmund J. Fortman was correct when he pointed out in his work *The Triune God, A Historical Study of the Doctrine of the Trinity*: "…the Old Testament writings about God neither express nor imply any idea of or belief in a plurality of persons within the one Godhead. Even to see in them suggestions or foreshadowings or 'veiled signs' of the trinity of persons, is to go beyond the words and intent of the sacred writers."

---

[73] Harris, *Jesus as God, The New Testament Use of Theos in Reference to Jesus*, p. 47.

8

─────The Holy Spirit─────

"Therefore, since we have been justified by faith, we have peace with God through our Lord Jesus Christ, through whom we have gained access (by faith) to this grace in which we stand, and we boast in hope of the glory of God. Not only that, but we even boast of our afflictions, knowing that affliction produces endurance, and endurance, proven character, and proven character, hope, and hope does not disappoint, because the love of God has been poured out into our hearts through the holy Spirit that has been given to us."
—Romans 5:1-5, *New American Bible*

Although the Scriptures do not appear to present a formal definition of the holy Spirit, some—based on their study of Scripture—have attempted to describe the Spirit in the ways that will follow. Many of the sources cited are Trinitarian and their comments were not intended to be taken as denials of the Trinitarian interpretation of the holy Spirit; but their comments are significant in terms of communicating what seems to be the natural and overall impression many have come to with respect to the nature and role of the holy Spirit—or, at least, certain aspects of the Spirit—as set forth in the Scriptures, in view of the Christian life.

The Holy Spirit

The first references discuss the basic meaning of the term "spirit" in Hebrew and in Greek. The basic meaning and background of the word itself should lend at least some degree of insight into an accurate understanding of the Spirit's respective role and nature.

According to one reference work, "The basic idea of *ruah* [Hebrew for 'spirit'] (Grk *pneuma*) is 'air in motion.'...The *ruah* 'spirit' of God (from God) is in my nostrils.' (Job 27.3)...*ruah* can exhibit a range of meaning. The 'breath' of God may be a strong wind. (Is 40.7)...His 'spirit' may indicate no more than active power..."[1] Similarly, another source pointed out: "The Greek word translated as 'spirit' is *pneuma*, the most basic meaning is 'wind,' the movement of air. Wind is a force that we can feel, but cannot see or even really touch."[2]

In accordance with the basic background and sense of the word/concept "spirit," it is worth noting that the biblical expression "holy spirit" (Gk: *pneuma hagion*) has also been translated "sacred breath," as in *The Unvarnished New Testament* by Andy Gaus. Traditionally, in Genesis 1:2, where the Spirit is first mentioned, the verse has been accurately rendered, "The Spirit of God hovered over the waters." Some Bible translations, however, render the phrase, "the breath of God" (*Holy Bible in Modern English*), "a mighty wind" (*NAB*), "a divine wind" (*NJB*), "*or* the power of God; *or* a wind from God; *or* an awesome wind" (*TEV* ftnt.) swept over the waters."

Regarding references to the Spirit in the Hebrew Scriptures,[3] it has been noted: "In the Old Testament, the Spirit of God is associated closely with creation, God's presence, divine guidance, divine inspiration and human life and creativity."[4] The *New Catholic Encyclopedia* states, "by extension [spirit] came to mean the breath as signifying life and thence spirit, mind, and life principle...it comes from God as a creative, life-giving force."[5] Millard J. Erickson also observed

---

[1] *Theological Workbook of the Old Testament*, Vol 2 (Chicago: Moody Press, 1980) pp. 836, 837.
[2] BeDuhn, *Truth in Translation*, p. 144.
[3] The actual phrase 'holy spirit' occurs only twice in the Old Testament; Psalm 51:11; Isaiah 63:11. The phrase appears 87 times in the New Testament.
[4] Butin, *The Trinity, Foundations of Faith*, p. 16.
[5] *New Catholic Encyclopedia*, Volume XIII (Washington: The Catholic University of America, 1967), p. 570 (citing Gn 1.2; 27, 41,38; Ex 31.3; 1Sam 16.13; Jgs 3.10; Nm 24.2; Is 42.1; 59.21).

The Holy Spirit

that in "the Old Testament, there had been belief in the 'Spirit of God.' The Spirit was not necessarily differentiated as a separate person from Jehovah; rather, the focus was on his manifestation, activity, and power."[6] C. F. D. Moule, a respected Anglican scholar, also observed: "In the Old Testament, 'spirit' is used chiefly to denote God's powerful action on and within persons, and especially members of his own people; or occasionally, it means simply the breath of life."[7] A similar understanding was expressed by the following Protestant source:

> The root meaning of the word *spirit* in the Old Testament is *wind* or *breath*—not a breeze, but the powerful, sweeping desert wind; not a quiet, steady breathing, but agitated, violent breathing. Hence in the Old Testament *spirit* comes to denote the vital energy, the power of God. God created by his Word (Psalm 148:5), but by his Spirit he vitalized what he created (Psalm 104:30)[8]

After having sinned against Jehovah, David poured out his heart in sorrowful repentance in what has come down to us as Psalm 51. His petition to Jehovah was expressed: "Hide your face from my sins, and blot out all my iniquities. Create in me a clean heart, O God, and put a new and right spirit within me. Do not cast me away from your presence, and do not take your holy spirit from me. Restore to me the joy of your salvation, and sustain in me a willing spirit."[9]

Of this reference—considered independently in its original context—Albert Barnes said, "It is not certain that David understood by the phrase '[your] Holy Spirit' precisely what is now denoted by it as referring to the third person of the Trinity. The language, as used by him, would denote some influence coming from God producing holiness, *as if* God breathed his own spirit, or self, into the soul."[10]

In another Old Testament text, Zechariah spoke

The same article observes: "Since God is the life-giver, life breath comes from Him and man lives as long as God's breath remains in him (Jb 27.3; Is 42.5; Za 12.1). When God withdraws His breath, man and all flesh return to the ground [Ps 145 (146). 5; Jb34.14; Eccl 12.7]."
[6] Erickson Ph.D., *God in Three Persons, A Contemporary Interpretation of the Trinity*, p. 34.
[7] *The Holy Spirit* (New York: Continuum International Publishing, 2000), p. 19.
[8] *Hard Questions* (Chapter by John A. Simpson *M.A*; InerVarsity Press, 1977), pp. 48, 50.
[9] Psalm 51:9-13 *NRSV*
[10] *Barnes' Notes on the Old Testament, Psalms, Volume 1*, p. 88.

The Holy Spirit

prophetically of a future outpouring of a certain kind of spirit. The utterance of God through the prophet was: "And on that day I will seek to destroy all the nations that come against Jerusalem. And I will pour out a spirit of compassion and supplication on the house of David and the inhabitants of Jerusalem..."[11] In reference to the prophecy, Eugene Merrill of Dallas Theological Seminary wrote: "It would be theologically premature to identify the spirit here with the third person of the Godhead. The term (*ruah*) in this case should be understood as a persuasion or conviction from YHWH that prompts a course of action."[12]

With regard to the New Testament context, other reference works have said that the Spirit is:

> The manifestation of divine presence and power perceptible especially in prophetic inspiration...The Spirit appears in some texts as the autonomous agent of prophecy (Acts 1:16; Heb 3:7); the vehicle of sanctification (Rom 8:4; Gal 5:16-25), and intercession (Rom 8:27); the sign of God's acceptance (Acts 15:8; Gal 3:2); and a guarantee of future salvation (Rom 5:3-5; 2 Cor 5:5). It is also, however, clearly designated as the Spirit of God (1 Cor 2:11-12; Rom 8:9-17), the Spirit sent by God that represents in some sense God's active and indwelling presence.[13]

Similarly, other students of the Bible—based on their understanding of several scriptural references—have come to view the Spirit as the means through which God's power and presence were experienced by his people on earth:

> The spirit is to Christians and the church what the cloud and fire were in the wilderness: the powerful personal presence of the living God, holy and not to be taken lightly, leading and guiding the often muddled and rebellious people to their inheritance.[14]

> The sense that God is present through his Spirit, expressed for example in Ps. 51:11, appears also in Ps.

---

[11] Zechariah 12:9-10, *NRSV*
[12] Merill, *An Exegetical Commentary, Haggai, Zechariah, Malachi*, p. 318.
[13] *The Anchor Bible Dictionary*, Volume 3, p. 260; Volume 2, p. 1055.
[14] N. T. Wright (reflecting on Ephesians 1:11-14 in his commentary on Bishop of Durham's book on the New Testament; quoted in *Focus on the Kingdom* Newsletter, editor Anthony Buzzard).

The Holy Spirit

143:10; Hg. 2:5; Zc. 4:6...It is important to realize that for the first Christians the Spirit was thought of in terms of divine power clearly manifest by its effects on the life of the recipient; the impact of the Spirit did not leave individual or onlooker in much doubt that a significant change had taken place in him by divine agency.[15]

'Holy Spirit' denotes supernatural power...This is nowhere more clearly evident than in Acts where the Spirit is presented as an almost tangible force, visible if not in itself, certainly in its effects...For the first Christians, the Spirit was most characteristically a divine power manifesting itself in inspired utterance...The Spirit was evidently experienced as a numinous power pervading the early community and giving its early leadership an aura of authority which could not be withstood. (Acts 5:1-10)...It is important to realize that for Paul too the Spirit is a divine power.[16]

Kittel's Theological Dictionary of the New Testament agrees that "God's Spirit expresses his inner nature and presence."[17]

According to a Christian who lived in the late second century: "[The Holy Spirit] which operates in the prophets, we assert to be an effluence of God, flowing from Him, and returning back again like a beam of the sun."[18]

With respect to the understanding of the Spirit in association with the latter ecumenical councils, Erickson observed: "Not only Nicea, however, was silent about the deity of the Holy Spirit. The Scripture itself, Gregory of Nazianzus had to concede, did not 'very or clearly or very often call him God in so many words, as it does for the Father and later the Son.'"[19] But it was correctly noted by evangelical Murray Harris

---

[15] *The New Bible Dictionary*, J. D. Douglas, pp. 1138-1139.
[16] *The Dictionary of New Testament Theology*, Vol 3.
[17] Gerhard Kittle and Gerhard Friedrich, *Theological Dictionary of the New Testament*, Abridged in one volume, p. 880. C. F. D. Moule likewise noted, "'Spirit' certainly can be used, and in certain circumstances is used, simply for divine presence or divine activity; and for this there are other terms that, in some contexts, would serve equally well." —*The Holy Spirit*, p. 5.
[18] Athenagoras, *Ante-Nicene Fathers*, Volume II, p. 133. *Random House Webster's College Dictionary* defines 'effluence' as "the action or process of flowing out...something that flows out; emanation." *Webster's Third New International Dictionary* further describes it as "something that flows out (as from a person or substance)—usu. used of something having an effect..."
[19] Gregory of Nazianzus, Orations, 31.12 (Quoted in: Erickson, *God in Three Persons*, p. 88)

The Holy Spirit

that "the NT *never* uses *ho theos* ['God'] of the Holy Spirit..."[20]

At times Bible students have expressed uncertainty regarding the nature of the holy Spirit. Church Historian Augustus Neander reflected on the viewpoints expressed in the time after the Council of Nicea: "The unity of the Christian consciousness of God had here so little permeated as yet the apprehension of the idea, that Gregory of Nazianzen could still say, in the year 380: 'Some of our theologians consider the Holy Spirit to be a certain mode of the divine agency (as, for instance, Lactantius had done in the preceding period); others, a creature of God; others, God himself. Others say, they do not know themselves which of the two opinions they ought to adopt, out of reverence for the holy scriptures, which have not clearly explained this point.' Hilary of Poitiers held it best to remain fast by the simple scripture doctrine concerning the Holy Spirit, which, as it seemed to him, furnished not materials for exact logical definitions of this doctrine."[21] Likewise, with respect to the latter creedal definitions, the perspective of one scholarly source was expressed in this way: "The New Testament treatment of the Spirit is difficult, ambiguous, and sometimes even oblique to the interests of later trinitarianism."[22]

Professor of systematic theology Donald Macleod (representing the classical Trinitarian view that sees the Spirit as a 'person' of the 'Godhead') noted: "If, however, the Son and Spirit are with the Father and in the fullest sense divine, they must have an equal place in our adoration. In the New Testament, actual references to worshipping the Spirit are rare, although we are warned not to grieve him (Ephesians 4:30)[23] and the consequences of offending him are made clear in the story of Ananias and Sapphira (Acts 5:1-11)."

Although Macleod says that worship of the Spirit is "rare" in the New Testament, an article in the *International*

---

[20] Harris, *Jesus as God*, p. 43 (emphasis added).
[21] *General History of the Christian Religion and Church*, Volume 4 (London: Printed by W. Clowes and Sons, 1851), p. 84.
[22] *International Standard Bible Encyclopedia*, Vol. 4, p. 916.
[23] Bible student Ron Frye argued: "To say that because the Spirit of God can be grieved and lied to, he must be a person is to ignore the flexibility of language used in the Scriptures as well as the context in which the statements are made." —*The Father/Son Relationship*, p. 73. If a person were to say "my spirit was grieved" over a given matter, few would conclude that the word "spirit" refers to a second/separate person within.

The Holy Spirit

Standard Bible Encyclopedia actually notes that "the Holy Spirit in the New Testament is *never* an object of worship or prayer."[24] In reference to prayer specifically, Anglican scholar Peter Toon also pointed out the fact that, "In the New Testament there is *no* example of prayer being offered directly to the Holy Spirit. This practice came later after the dogma of the Trinity had been clarified..."[25]

Trinitarian Millard Erickson likewise pointed out that "in the New Testament we do not have either texts commanding or texts describing worship of or prayer to the Holy Spirit. Geoffrey Wainwright says, 'So we may conclude that there is *no case* in which the Spirit figures as an object of worship in the New Testament writings.' Arthur Wainwright also agreed: 'There is no evidence in the New Testament that the Spirit was worshipped or received prayer.'" Erickson concludes: "It appears, then, that in the New Testament the Holy Spirit was not the recipient, but rather, the instrument, the enabler, of prayer. Prayer was done 'in the Spirit,' or 'by the Spirit,' rather than 'to the Spirit.' If, then, we can find in the New Testament neither instruction nor example of worship of the Holy Spirit, we need to ask at what point such practice did enter the church?"[26]

It is difficult to determine with certainty when several now common practices that did not occur (or were not encouraged) in New Testament times developed. However, we do know, as Toon points out, that the "full, ontological doctrine of the consubstantiality of the Holy Spirit with the Father and with the Son had to wait until the Nicene teaching of Jesus Christ had been appropriated by the church during the fourth century, and for the theological clarity of the teaching of the Cappadocian Fathers (Basil the Great, Gregory of Nazianzus, and Gregory of Nyssa) concerning the *Person* of the Holy Spirit to be

---

[24] *International Standard Bible Encyclopedia*, Vol. 4, p. 916 (emphasis added).
[25] Toon, *Our Triune God*, p. 226 (emphasis added).
[26] Erickson, *God in Three Persons*, p. 324; Quoting Wainwright, *Doxology*, pp. 92-93; Arthur W. Wainwright, *The Trinity in the New Testament* (London: SPCK, 1962), p. 228 (emphasis added). According to Moule: "It seems more precise, therefore, to adopt, as a summary of New Testament tendencies regarding the relation of Christ and Spirit, some such formula as 'God, present as Spirit through Jesus Christ'." For he notes elsewhere: "Constantly, the activities and presence of the Spirit are seen as a guarantee that God is at work through Jesus Christ, continuing and implementing Christ's mission until the final consummation." —*The Holy Spirit*, pp. 26, 36.

received."[27]

As generally acknowledged by Trinitarian scholars, the holy Spirit did not appear as an object of worship or prayer in the inspired Hebrew and Greek Scriptures. This practice came about after the books of the Bible were written and made official within the institutionalized "church" of later centuries. Regarding the first-century, biblical portrayal of the Spirit, however, the Jesuit Bible scholar John L. McKenzie attempted to give a description in his *Dictionary of the Bible*:

> The spirit is basically the divine and heavenly dynamic force; it is conceived as peculiarly existing in Jesus (and specifically in the risen Jesus), as pervading the body of Jesus which is the Church, and as apportioned to the members of the Church...The spirit is not obviously and explicitly conceived as a distinct personal being in Paul. The occasional personifications which he employs do not go beyond the personifications found in the OT and in Judaism.[28]

The fact that the Spirit is sometimes depicted as "teaching," "speaking," "interceding," "guiding," and "helping" in the Scriptures has influenced many theologians to conclude that the Spirit must be a distinct person like God the Father and Jesus Christ. But because the Spirit does not have a personal/proper name like the Father and Son, is never shown to be an object of worship or recipient of prayer, and never depicted or identified as a member of a "triune" God in Scripture, other Bible students believe that these are simply a few out of many examples where Scripture uses the common linguistic device of *personification*—that is, the practice of ascribing personal attributes, qualities, or characteristics, to subjects that are not actually or literally persons. This method of communication appears all throughout the Scriptures. C. F. D. Moule observed: "When the Spirit is the mode of God's presence in the hearts and minds of his people, then there is a good case for personal

---

[27] Toon, *Our Triune God*, p. 40 (emphasis added). With respect to the 4th century formulation, Toon pointed out: "...the Creed of the Council of Constantinople (381) declares that the Holy Spirit is to be worshipped and glorified with both the Father and with the Son."

[28] *Bible Dictionary*, pp. 883, 844. Here, McKenzie has in mind the Pauline conception specifically.

The Holy Spirit

language. But this still does not force upon us a third eternal 'Person' (in the technical sense) within the Unity [of God]."[29] The viewpoint of one Bible student was similarly expressed: "In the New Testament, the Holy Spirit comes to represent both the presence and activity of God and the continuing presence of Jesus Christ in the church and in our lives, not as a 3rd person."[30] According to another popular reference work: "The Spirit within seems indistinguishable from Christ within. The Spirit is 'the Spirit of his Son' (Gal. 4:6). Paul seems to understand the Spirit as the mode whereby the exalted Lord is present on earth with his people, rather than as a person distinct from Christ."[31]

Christian author Raymond Franz discussed the idea of personification in connection with the Spirit in more detail. He is quoted here at length:

> It is true that, as others point out, the holy Spirit is spoken of as speaking, teaching, guiding, being grieved, etc., etc. However, anyone who has read the Bible as a whole would realize that it is extremely common to *personify* objects and forces, pictorially describing them as acting AS IF they were persons, though they are not. Wilderness, dry land, desert are spoken of as being glad, rejoicing with joy and singing (Isaiah 35:1, 2), the earth and the mountains are called on to break forth in singing (Isaiah 49:13), the rivers clap their hands and the hills sing together for joy (Psalm 98: 7, 8), or, in an opposite way, the gates of Jerusalem lament and mourn, and the city sits ravaged upon the ground (Isaiah 3:26)...In the book of Proverbs *wisdom* is spoken of as if it were a woman and far more is said about personified wisdom than is said about personified holy Spirit. She is said not only to speak, but to *cry out*, to *raise her voice, exhorting* people, extending her *reproof* as she offers to 'pour out her thoughts to them, make known her words to them,' but they *reject* her, *ignore* her counsel, *despise* her reproof; she *laughs* at and *mocks* them when disaster comes. (Proverbs 1:20-30) She also *keeps* and *guards* persons, can be *loved* and *embraced*. (Proverbs 4:5, 6, 8,

---

[29] Moule, *The Holy Spirit*, p. 50.
[30] Posted December 04, 2003; 02:53; PM (excerpt) *Origins of the Trinity*.
[31] *The Eerdmans Bible Dictionary*, p. 1020.

The Holy Spirit

9) She has a mouth, lips, lives with prudence, attains knowledge, both loves and hates, has insight, strength, walks in paths of justice, gives wealth to persons, has a house with its gates and doors, where she slaughters animals, sets table, has daughters or servant girls, offers bread and wine. (Proverbs 8:1-21, 34; 9:1-6) Trinitarians often make up a list of things said about the holy Spirit which, they say, demonstrates its personality. The list about wisdom far, far exceeds such list…And it is clear that the style of speaking, of personifying, was as true in the time of the writing of the Christian Scriptures as it was in the time of the writing of the Hebrew Scriptures. Thus we read at Matthew 11:19; Luke 7:35 that 'wisdom is vindicated by *her deeds*,' is 'vindicated by all *her children*,' essentially the same type of language as found in Proverbs. Trinitarians make much of texts of the holy Spirit speaking and seem to ignore that, not only the Spirit, but *blood* and *water* are spoken of as *testifying* and *agreeing together*. (1 John 5:6, 7) At Romans 10:6 it states that 'the righteousness that comes from faith says,' and righteousness is not a person…So we may ask, how different is it to speak of the holy Spirit as 'guiding' and to speak of wisdom as 'reproving,' 'guarding' and 'keeping'? How different is it to speak of the holy Spirit as 'being grieved' and to speak of love as being 'patient,' 'enduring,' 'not quick to take offense or be irritable?' If one asks, how can something not a person be grieved, one must similarly ask how can something not a person (love) show patience, endure, refrain from being resentful or irritable? If the things said of the holy Spirit actually demonstrated its personality then, by the same token, the things said about wisdom and love would show that they are persons.[32]

Although ultimately viewing the Spirit as a distinct "person" (in line with 'orthodoxy') the *New Catholic Encyclopedia* acknowledges:

The OT clearly does not envisage God's spirit as a person…If it is sometimes represented as being distinct from God, it is because the breath of Yahweh acts

---

[32] From the essay: *What is the Holy Spirit?* by Commentary Press: Atlanta, GA.

The Holy Spirit

> exteriorly...The majority of NT texts reveal God's spirit as something, not someone; this is especially seen in the parallelism between the spirit and the power of God. When a quasi-personal activity is ascribed to God's spirit, e.g., speaking, hindering, desiring, dwelling (Acts 8.29; 16.7; Rom 8.9), one is not justified in concluding immediately that in these passages God's spirit is regarded as a Person; the same expressions are used also in regard to rhetorically personified things or abstract ideas (see Rom 8.6; 7.17)...In Acts, the use of the words 'Holy Spirit,' with or without an article, is rich and abundant. However, again, it is difficult to demonstrate personality from the texts...St. Paul uses the word *pneuma* 146 times. Sometimes it means man's natural spirit, but more often it signifies the divine sanctifying power...[33]

Generally speaking, the holy Spirit appears to function as an extension of God's presence and power—his invisible, dynamic, creative, enlightening, animating, transforming, empowering, and life-giving, breath—his very life-force.[34] In the book of Genesis, when men began to multiply on the face of the ground, "Jehovah said, My *spirit* shall not strive with man for ever, for that he also is flesh: yet shall his days be a hundred and twenty years."[35] The *Contemporary English Version* renders verse 3, "I won't let my *life-giving breath* remain in anyone forever. No one will live more than one hundred twenty years."

The Bible speaks of man possessing a spirit, which constitutes that invisible, animating principle or life-breath. This is probably why some references speak of the Spirit in some sense as God's personal life-breath, yet which he is able to project outwardly toward his people for the accomplishment of his will, in accordance with his holiness; a life-principle that, at the same time, powerfully reflects (and projects) the will,

---

[33] *The New Catholic Encyclopedia*, Volume XIII, pp. 574, 575.
[34] According to one Protestant source: "In the OT the spirit of the Lord (*ruah yhwh*: LXX, *to pneuma kyriou*) is generally an expression for God's power, the extension of himself whereby he carries out many deeds (e.g., 1 Kings 8:12; Judg. 14:6ff; 1 Sam. 11:6)...The OT does not contain an idea of a semi-independent divine entity, the Holy Spirit. Rather, we find special expressions of God's activity with and through men." —*Ellwell's Evangelical Dictionary* (Electronic Version).
[35] Genesis 6:3, *ASV*

The Holy Spirit

personality, character, and "heart" of God.[36] When the Spirit is present in a believer's mind and heart, it is as if God's very own sanctifying and life-producing principle dwells within. As Benjamin Warfield put it: "As the spirit of man is the seat of human life, the very life of man itself, so the Spirit of God is His very life-element."[37]

In his discussion on the revelation of the holy Spirit in the Old Testament, Edmund J. Fortman made very similar remarks in terms of associating the Spirit with "life," "power" and "creativity": "...just as the wind and the breath of life can transform earth and flesh, so the spirit of Yahweh can animate man's spirit and give him new knowledge and energy." Fortman also notes: "The spirit of Yahweh has many functions. It is a creative force and a spirit of judgment (Job 33.4; Is 4.4). It is Yahweh's saving power and His all-pervading presence (Zech 4.6; Ps 139.7). The spirit of Yahweh is a charismatic spirit imparted to judges, to kings, to the messianic king, to the servant of Yahweh (Jg 3.10; 1 Sam 11.6; Is 11:2). It renews man inwardly (Ezek 36.26). It is a prophetic spirit, and the true instruments of the spirit were the prophets. To Amos, Hosea, Isaiah, and Jeremiah the spirit brought God's word and gave light to understand it and strength to proclaim it. 'By His Spirit...He infiltrated hearts in order to transform them, to open them up to His word.'" And, lastly, Fortman observes: "The spirit of Yahweh was often described in personal terms. The spirit was grieved, guided men, instructed them, caused them to rest (Ps 143.10; Neh 9:20; Is 63:10, 14). But it seems quite clear that the Jews never regarded the spirit as a person, nor is there any solid evidence that any Old Testament writer held this view."[38]

Cyril C. Richardson expressed himself along similar lines when he said: "The primary notion of Spirit in the Bible is that of God's dynamic activity. The Spirit is his breath, hence his vitality or life. Since a body without breath is dead, breath was

---

[36] On page 9 of his book, Moule notes: "'Spirit' and 'heart' are frequently used in parallel clauses as virtual synonyms to denote human impulses or intentions. (Random examples are in Exod. 35.21 and Ezek. 18.31)."
[37] *The International Standard Bible Encyclopedia*, Volume 5, p. 3020.
[38] *The Triune God, A Historical Study of the Doctrine of the Trinity*, p. 6.

The Holy Spirit

viewed as the vitalizing element in man. At man's creation God breathed into Adam's nostrils the breath of life, and thus he became a living soul (Gen. 2:7). As applied to God, then, his breath is his vitality and the means by which he does things and expresses his creative potency."[39]

With reference to the Spirit in the New Testament, one Protestant source likewise asked: "What is meant by the Holy Spirit?" And in offering an answer: "Nothing less than *the life of God* indwelling and empowering, activating and transforming the people of God, as individuals and as the body of Christ."[40] The *New Catholic Encyclopedia* likewise observed: "The spirit then is the source of a new creation (Gal 5.16-26; Rom 8.1-4) and the fulfillment of the OT promise (Jer 31.31-34; Ez 36.36-39) of a new covenant written in man's heart. It is a life-giving reality as its source is the 'life-giving spirit' (1 Cor 15.45; cf. Jn 3.5; 6.63-64)."[41] Catholic John McKenzie expressed himself in a similar way, saying: "The spirit in the Christian is a principle of life and activity proper to the Christian."[42]

Notably, the way the Spirit is described by the above Trinitarian sources in these instances is virtually the same as one non-Trinitarian source described it, as "the very power, mind and *life essence* of God..."[43] New Testament professor Marianne Thompson observed:

> ...the Spirit is virtually by definition the life-giving force or power of God. Through the Spirit one is born from above to become a child of God (1:12-13; 3:3-5), for it is the Spirit that gives life (6:63) and that becomes a source of life within a believer (4:14; 7:38). The Spirit of Truth empowers true worship of God (4:23-24), and guides believers into all truth. Because 'truth' belongs solely and necessarily to 'the one true God' (17:3), the Spirit confers life insofar as and because through the Spirit believers are led from the realm of darkness and death to truth and life.

---

[39] *The Doctrine of the Trinity* (Nashville: Abingdon Press, MCMLVII), p. 45.
[40] John A. Simpson *M.A, Hard Questions*, p. 50 (emphasis added).
[41] *New Catholic Encyclopedia*, Volume XIII, p. 571.
[42] *McKenzie Bible Dictionary*, p. 844.
[43] *The Good News, A Magazine of Understanding* (United Church of God, March-April, 2005) p. 31 (emphasis added).

The Holy Spirit

To put it differently, God is the Father who is the source of life. Jesus, the Son of the Father, confers God's life but, even more, is God's life-giving Word embodied in the flesh for the life of the world. The Spirit of God is the power of life and the agency through which life is received.[44]

One source attempted to describe the Spirit by saying: "The title 'holy Spirit' describes the *mind of God*—His power or sanctifying influence."[45] Another said, "[The Spirit is] God's will in action...It is an invisible, powerful, creative force emanating from God."[46] According to another source: "This spirit is not independent and self-existent, but is 'the mind of Christ' within the believer, influencing, guiding, teaching, reminding and pointing the believer to follow his Lord and Savior...Yet because it carries the *personal* presence of Christ into the life of every believer, the use of Personification is highly appropriate.[47]

There are a few scriptural texts commonly used by evangelicals to support the idea that the Spirit itself is a person and member of a "triune" Deity. One of these texts was discussed by a Christian writer:

> In some trinitatian presentations the text at Acts 5:3, 4, is used to show that the holy Spirit is God. In Acts 5:3 Ananias and Sapphira are said to have lied 'to the holy Spirit' while in verse 4 they are said to have 'lied to God.' These sources simply ignore all the cases in the Bible where an agency is spoken of as if doing what the person directing matters himself actually does. The Scriptures speak of Solomon as building the temple, yet they clearly show that he himself did not build it, did none of actual work. But it was *his* project, done at *his* direction, and so it is attributed to *him*. Similarly to lie to God is also to lie to his spirit and vice versa. But that does not make them interchangeable. We read that 'God is light.' But we would not say 'Light is God.' (1 John 1:5) So, too, we read that 'God is love,' but that does not mean that 'Love is God.' (1 John 4:8) Exodus 3:2-6 states that 'an angel of

---

[44] Thompson, *The God of the Gospel of John*, p. 229.
[45] *Who is God?* p. 26 (*He Leadeth Me Publications*)
[46] Corey Kalgleth, *The Home Christian's Handbook*, Chapter 8, p. 1.
[47] Graeser, Lynn, Schoenheit, *One God One Lord*, p. 596.

The Holy Spirit

the Lord [Jehovah]' appeared to Moses in a burning bush. Yet in subsequent verses it states that *God* called to Moses out of the bush. Was the angel Jehovah or is Jehovah an angel? Or was the angel simply an agency used by Jehovah? Which? (Compare similarly Genesis 16:7, 10.)

In Matthew's account, Jesus is presented as saying to his accusers: 'If it is by the *Spirit of God* that I cast out demons, then the kingdom of God has come to you.' Luke renders the same expression as follows: 'If it is by the *finger of God* that I cast out the demons, then the kingdom of God has come to you.' (Luke 11:20) If the holy Spirit were indeed part of a triune God, co-equal with the Father, as taught in trinitarian theology, how could that Spirit possibly be designated simply as the 'finger' of God?

1 Corinthians 12:11 and Hebrew 2:4 are sometimes cited as showing the holy Spirit has 'will.' The expression 'his will' in Hebrews 2:4 clearly refers to the will of God, mentioned at the start of the verse. As for 1 Corinthians 12:11, we may compare the expression 'just as the Spirit chooses,' with Jesus' statement to Nicodemus that 'the wind blows where it chooses.' (John 3:8) We would not thereby understand the wind to be a person.[48]

Trinitarian Cyril C. Richardson asked: "Is the Spirit *personal* in the New Testament? This issue has long been debated and given various answers. The difficulty really lies in what we mean by 'personal.' Perhaps the matter is best put in terms like these: the Spirit is God's active approach to us. Where the Spirit operates, there God himself is at work. The Spirit is not a 'thing,' over against God, but a way of expressing God in his relation to us. A distinction, to be sure, is implied in that God's breath is not exactly identical with his being, any more than his finger or hand is. Just as we can distinguish our breath or word from ourselves—and yet it is by means of our breath or word that we as selves becomes selves in relation to others, so the symbolism of God's word or breath is used to indicate God's relation to us. Where the Spirit is given a personal quality such

---
[48] Franz, *What is the Holy Spirit?*

The Holy Spirit

as teaching, revealing, witnessing, interceding, creating, and so on, it is not as an entity distinct from God, but as God himself doing these things and yet not compromising his transcendence."[49]

Similarly, according to another source: "In some cases where the Holy Spirit is described in a personal activity, we should understand this as God using his Holy Spirit as the *power* or *agency* through which He acts. Consider, for example, that if a man's hand takes hold of a book and lifts it, this does not make the hand a separate person. The hand is merely the agency through which the man is acting."[50]

To reinforce the clarity of the point, consider, again, how in Matthew 12:28 Jesus said:

But if it is by the Spirit of God that I cast out demons, then the kingdom of God has come upon you.

Yet in Luke's account (11:20), the text reads:

But if it is by the finger of God that I cast out demons, then the kingdom of God has come upon you.

That is, the Scriptures themselves use the language "Spirit of God" and "finger of God" interchangeably. What does this figure of speech naturally communicate? Is a person's "finger" a second "person" within that person's "being"? No. Is a person's "finger" the person himself? Not really. A person's finger is simply an extension of the person himself, something that belongs to him, and that which a person uses to move things, make things happen, execute the person's will, and so forth. So it appears that, in a very similar sense, God's Spirit is a kind of powerful extension of his very self into the world.

Another point that may give insight into the nature of God's Spirit: In Luke 1:46-47, Mary said,

My soul magnifies the Lord, and my spirit rejoices in God my Savior.

---

[49] *The Doctrine of the Trinity* (New York: Abingdon Press, MCMLVIII), pp. 52-53.
[50] *The Good New Magazine*, p. 31.

The Holy Spirit

Here Mary speaks about how her "spirit rejoices." Was Mary talking about an additional, distinct 'person,' so that Mary's singular 'being' is made up of 'multiple persons,' like the Trinity? Clearly not. What reason, then, do we have for believing such about God when Scripture speaks about him having a "Spirit"?

When Mary said that her "spirit rejoices," most readers likely get the sense of the language immediately. In other words, Mary's "spirit," her inner-most self, the invisible, inner principle of life that animates her body—including mind, feeling and emotion—rejoices. The same basic point would appear to be true in reference to God and *his* Spirit. That is, biblically speaking, the holy Spirit does not have to be understood as another "person" (so that God's 'being' is somehow made up of multiple 'persons'), but the very principle of life that God himself is animated by, yet which God is able to project from himself, to empower and fill others with, so that they are filled with, and animated by, *his* life, *his* mind, *his* personality, *his* point of view, *his* love, *his* goodness, *his* holiness.

In the beginning of his discussion on the Spirit in his book on the Trinity, Peter Toon made the following point:

> Most of us have no difficulty at all in thinking of the Spirit of God, or the Holy Spirit, as the general presence of God in his world or as the specific presence of God within the church of Jesus Christ and in the hearts of believers. Thus we are able to appreciate the two general aspects of the Spirit of YHWH which we encounter in both the Old and New Testaments. First of all, the Spirit is like wind and fire, a power which invades a person from without causing him to be moved in a direction of God's choosing. We read that the Spirit of God 'drove' Jesus into the wilderness after his baptism in the river Jordan (Mark 1:12); and in Acts the coming of the promised Spirit is accompanied by wind and fire (Acts 2:1-4). In the second place, the Spirit is like a fluid or substance with which a person is filled or into which he is immersed so that he has life, gifts, or virtues from the Spirit. 'God anointed Jesus of Nazareth with the Holy Spirit and with power,' said Peter (Acts 10:38). 'Be filled with the Spirit' (Eph. 5:18) and 'drink of one Spirit' (1

The Holy Spirit

Cor. 12:13), writes Paul. From this perspective, it is quite natural to refer to the Spirit as 'it,' just as we refer to the wind or human breath with the pronoun as neuter. In fact, the Greek word *pnuema* is, in terms of grammar, neuter in gender (in contrast to *ruach* in Hebrew which is feminine gender and *spiritus* in Latin which is masculine gender). Therefore, we find the neuter pronoun used of the Spirit (e.g., 'It had not fallen on any of them,' Acts 8:16)...In terms of both Christ and the Spirit dwelling in the heart or soul, we can say that Christ is the indwelling content while the Spirit is the quickening cause of Christ's indwelling.[51]

Perplexingly, some Trinitarian apologists have criticized certain Bible translations for rendering the neuter pronoun for the holy Spirit as "it" rather than "he." This, however, is not only legitimate, but more accurate than those translations that consistently refer to the Spirit as "he." For example, the *New American Standard Bible* gives a less-than-accurate translation of Romans 8:16: "The spirit *himself* bears witness with our spirit..." The *New American Bible* and *Concordant Literal New Testament* are truer to the sense: "The Spirit *itself* bears witness with our spirit that we are children of God..." Greek scholar Jason BeDuhn explains:

> Greek nouns have something called 'gender.' That is, some nouns are 'masculine,' some are 'feminine,' and some are 'neuter.' Greek has three forms of pronoun to match these three kinds of nouns. The noun *hos* is used of people and things the name of which is a 'masculine' noun. The pronoun *he*, likewise, is used of people and things named with a 'feminine' noun. Finally, the pronoun *ho* is used of anything to which a 'neuter' noun corresponds. Now it turns out that both 'masculine' and 'feminine' Greek nouns can be used for impersonal things as well as persons. But 'neuter' nouns are used only for impersonal things, such as objects, animals, forces, abstract principles, and so on. The same holds true for 'masculine,' 'feminine,' and 'neuter' pronouns. Greek tends to use personal pronouns more than English does.

---

[51] *Our Triune God, A Biblical Portrayal of the Trinity*, pp. 165-167, 188

The Holy Spirit

Some things that would be handled with 'which' in English, because they are not persons, are referred to with the equivalent of 'who/whom' in Greek because the nouns that name them are either 'masculine' or 'feminine.' But even though the 'personal' category is larger in Greek than in English, the 'Holy Spirit' is referred to by a 'neuter' noun in Greek...It is a 'which,' not a 'who.' It is an 'it,' not a 'he.' This is a case, then, where the importance of the principle of following primary, ordinary, generally recognized meaning of the Greek when translating becomes clear. To take a word that everywhere else would be translated 'which' or 'that,' and arbitrarily change it to 'who' or 'whom' when it happens to be used of 'the holy spirit,' is a kind of special pleading. In other words, it is a biased way to translate. And because this arbitrary change cannot be justified linguistically, it is also inaccurate. In acts 5:32 it is said, 'We are witnesses of these things, and (so is) the holy spirit, which (*ho*) God has given to those who obey him.' The NW has 'which,' the NAB uses 'that.' Both are accurate renderings of the relative pronoun *ho*. But the KJV, NASB, NIV, NRSV, and AB all change the word to 'whom,' the TEV and LB to 'who,' guided in this choice solely by a theological bias about the nature and character of the 'Holy Spirit' that overrides accurate translation.[52]

John 14:16 in the *NASB* has Jesus saying to his disciples: "I will ask the Father, and He will give you another Helper, that *He* may be with you forever..." In this case the pronoun is properly translated "he" in agreement with the grammatical gender of "helper" or "*parakletos*" in Greek. But in 14:17, *NASB* reads, "...the Spirit of truth, *whom* the world cannot receive, because it does not see *Him* or know *Him*, but you know *Him* because *He* abides with you and will be in you." The *New American Bible* is an improvement in terms of translation at this point: "...the Spirit of truth, *which* the world cannot accept, because it neither sees nor knows *it*. But you know *it*, because *it* remains with you, and will be in you."

In John 14:26, where Jesus spoke again about the Spirit as the "advocate" or "helper" ('comforter,' *KJV*), the *NASB* uses

---

[52] BeDuhn, *Truth In Translation*, pp. 140-141.

The Holy Spirit

the personal pronoun: "*He* will teach you all things." The marginal note in the *New English Translation* has: "*Grk: that one* will teach you."⁵³ John 15:26 in *NASB* reads: "When the Helper comes, whom I will send (*Concordant Literal New Testament* has '*which* I shall be sending,') to you from the Father, that is the Spirit of truth who ('which,' *Concordant*) proceeds from the Father, He (*Grk* 'that one', *NET* ftnt.) will testify about Me..."

Jesus also said, according to John 16:7-8 (*NASB*): "I tell you the truth, it is to your advantage that I go away; for if I do not go away, the Helper will not come to you; but if I go, I will send *Him* (Gk: *auton*) to you." Here, also, the subject is spoken of as "he" (masculine-personal-pronoun) in agreement with the masculine *parakletos* ('helper'). However, what the Gospel writer wrote here simply accords with the requirements of Greek grammar—in matching the gender of the pronoun with the gender of the word or subject it has reference to, and has nothing to do with a distinctive theological concept relating to a "tri-unity" of persons. The text goes on, "And He, when He (*Grk* 'when that one', *NET* ftnt.) comes, will convict the world concerning sin and righteousness and judgment..." In John 16:13-14 (*NASB*) Jesus said to his disciples: "But when He (*Grk* 'That one.', *NET* ftnt.), the Spirit of truth, comes, *He* will guide you into all the truth; for *He* will not speak on *His* own initiative, but whatever *He* hears, *He* will speak; and *He* will disclose to you what is to come. "*He* will glorify Me, for *He* will take of Mine and will disclose it to you." In this case, the personal pronouns "he" in *NASB* are correct; but, again, "he" corresponds grammatically to the masculine *parakletos* and does not tell us whether or not "the Spirit of truth" is a "person" in the sense ascribed to the Spirit by the "theology" of post-biblical times.⁵⁴

---

⁵³ *New English Translation*, p. 341. Most Trinitarian apologists have pointed to the use of the masculine pronoun (*ekeinos*) in connection with the Spirit as evidence of "personhood." However, Daniel Wallace of Dallas Theological Seminary, although Trinitarian, observed: "contrary to the supposition that the proximity of *pneuma* to *ekeinos* in John 14:26 and 15:26 demonstrates the Spirit's personality, because the *pneuma* is appositional, it becomes irrelevant to the gender of the pronoun...The fact that *pneuma* and not *parakletos* is the appositive renders the philological argument in these two texts void." —"*Greek Grammar and the Personality of the Holy Spirit*", Bulletin for Biblical Research (Wallace-HS), 2003, p. 108.

⁵⁴ Daniel Wallace confirmed the point: "The fact is, in all of John's Gospel, the only time a masculine pronoun is used concerning [*pneuma*] is in relation to [*ho parakletos*]." —*Greek*

In harmony with these points, Daniel Wallace—one of the most respected Greek scholars in the evangelical world—agreed that the traditional arguments Trinitarians have used to defend their doctrine of the Holy Spirit based on gender usage have a "poor foundation." At the end of his study in the journal *Bulletin for Biblical Research*, Wallace concluded: "The grammatical basis for the Holy Spirit's personality is lacking in the NT, yet this is frequently, if not usually, the first line of defense of the doctrine by many evangelical writers. But if grammar cannot legitimately be used to support the Spirit's personality, then perhaps we need to reexamine the rest of our basis for this theological commitment." Wallace even acknowledged: "Evangelical defenses of various doctrines occasionally are poorly founded. We sometimes claim things to be true because we want them to be true, without doing the exhaustive spadework needed to support our conclusions. Regarding the personality of the Holy Spirit, the quick leap to exploit Greek Grammar in defense may actually work against a carefully nuanced pneumatology [doctrine of the 'Holy Spirit']."[55]

In her book *The God of the Gospel of John*, Marianne Thompson makes some general comments about the 'word' of God, the Spirit as the Paraclete ('helper'), and implications that can be drawn from how they are portrayed in Scripture:

> The Word can be construed, on the one hand, as the spoken expression of God's thought, and, on the other hand, as virtually distinct from God, much as the Torah or Philo's Logos is described. Jesus is the man the Word becomes, and in his earthly life he is known as the Son of the Father. So also the Spirit of God can be spoken of, on the one hand, as the very life-giving breath of God, and, on the other hand, as a distinct agent of God. While the Spirit is the means through which God gives life to the world, at a particular time the Spirit takes on a specific set of functions, and even a particular 'form,' as the

---

Grammar and the Personality of the Holy Spirit", Bulletin for Biblical Research (Wallace-HS), p. 111.
[55] *"Greek Grammar and the Personality of the Holy Spirit"*, Bulletin for Biblical Research (Wallace-HS), 2003, pp. 125, 122.

The Holy Spirit

Paraclete. The Paraclete is now with Jesus' followers as the Spirit of truth, a teacher, and the witness to the one who was truth and embodied truth. As the Word of God became incarnate, thus embodying God's glory, truth, and grace, so the life-giving Spirit of God becomes present as the Paraclete, bearing witness to the embodied grace of the Father in the Son and convicting those who do not believe of their unbelief, and so making the life-giving presence of the Father in the Son a concrete reality...As the Spirit of Truth, the Paraclete leads one to the proper response to Jesus and his words, thus enabling one to pass form sin and its judgment to life.[56]

In his conversation with his disciples, in light of Christ's allusion to his then soon-approaching death, resurrection and ascension to the Father, C. F. D. Moule observed:

When Christ is removed from sight, and his disciples have to come to terms with the transitoriness and limitations of his mortal life among them, they will be fortified and consoled by the permanent presence of the Spirit. In this sense, the Spirit takes the place of the visible presence of Jesus. In 1 John 2.1 Christ himself is called a Paraclete (definitely, in that context, an Advocate). The Spirit, then, is 'another Paraclete' (John 14.16)...What seems to be intended in the Fourth Gospel is not to deny a future consummation in terms of Christ as himself the climax and ultimate 'shape' of human destiny, but to designate the experience of the Spirit as the mode of Christ's continued presence with his people.[57]

In his letter to the Corinthians, Paul wrote: "For who among men knows the thoughts of a man except the spirit of the man which is in him? Even so the thoughts of God no one knows except the Spirit of God."[58]

---

[56] Thompson, *The God of the Gospel of John*, pp. 185, 186. Thompson (p. 182) also observes: "The disciples are assured that they will know and experience the ongoing presence of the Father in the Son through the agency of the Spirit. Even the language of the Spirit's origin and mission shows that, ultimately, the Spirit comes from the Father in order to bear witness to the Son, to call to mind Jesus' teaching, and to make the presence of Jesus real precisely because of his absence."
[57] Moule, *The Holy Spirit*, p. 37.
[58] 1 Corinthians 2:11, *NASB*. In his book on the Holy Spirit (p. 7), Moule points out: "English conventions often force a decision as to when to use a capital S for Spirit, indicating it as divine, and when to spell it with a small initial. Ancient Greek manuscripts did not make such a distinction."

The Holy Spirit

Here, the spirit of man "knows" the thoughts of man. But the spirit of man is not a distinct "person" of man's "being," so that each man is composed of multiple persons. Likewise, the Spirit of God "knows" the thoughts of God. Since a parallel is made between the spirit of man and the Spirit of God, it would seem very doubtful that Paul thought of the Spirit as one of three "persons" of God. With respect to the parallel made by the apostle in this passage, a significant observation was made by Moule:

> Here, in Cor. 2, Paul, following this analogy rather than his usual habit, dares to express the affinity between God's Spirit and something in man by using the single word *pneuma* for both. Like the psalmist, he seems to be conscious of a kinship between the divine and the human. He speaks of the Spirit of God and the spirit of man, and treats the two as analogous to one another...Paul seems to be giving an account of what happens when God reveals himself to human consciousness—when revelation occurs. In revelation, Paul seems to say, the divine Spirit touches (or even coincides or coalesces with?) man's spirit. God's self-consciousness, if one may venture the term, becomes man's self-consciousness, so that man is enabled to think God's thoughts after him...For the moment, comparison of Ps. 51 and 1 Cor. 2 has shown that Hebrew and Christian monotheism, for all its recognition of God's transcendence and majesty, tolerated—indeed, required—the recognition of an analogy between God's 'self-knowledge' and man's, between God's Spirit and man's spirit."[59]

Greg Stafford, in a personal correspondence based on Romans chapter eight, reasoned out the following point: "Just as man possesses a spirit, yet that spirit is not a separate person from man himself, so too, God, in whose image we are made, has a spirit and it is not necessary to view *His* spirit as a person separate from him. However, even if we did accept that the holy spirit is a separate spirit being from God, that does not support the Trinity. It would merely be another spirit being in God's

---
[59] Moule, *The Holy Spirit*, pp. 9-10.

service, for a special purpose."[60]

In a correspondence with another Bible scholar, Stafford noted that "'personal qualities' are frequently given to impersonal objects in the Bible. To give but one example, the 'anointing' from God is said to 'teach' in 1 John 2:27...The spirit is *of God*. It belongs to *Him*. The Son is *of God*. Where, though, do we read of the Father *of God?* The spirit is *of God* just as our spirit is of *man/woman*. It is a property of God's being, not one of three 'persons' within Him."[61] A similar observation was made by another source:

> What 'the spirit of God' is can be understood by comparing it to the 'spirit of man.' Many score times does the Bible speak of man's inner attributes or disposition of mind which may be vented by his breath such as in anger. This 'spirit' is not another person but part and parcel of the person himself. Thus, the 'spirit of God' is also that inner attribute of the Divine Mind which the Creator can project from Himself to accomplish His will. The two cannot be separated. Thus, if a person sin against the spirit of God it is the same as sinning against God. (Numbers 12:1-16; Acts 5:1-4)[62]

In John chapter seven, Jesus spoke about the Spirit metaphorically, as streams of flowing "water." He said: "He that puts faith in me, just as the Scripture has said, 'Out from his inmost part streams of living water will flow.' However he said this concerning the spirit which those who put faith in him were about to receive..."[63] In this way, the Spirit is likened unto water, because, similar to the Spirit, the substance of water is that which humans know to be pure, clean, penetrating, powerful, able to purify and cleanse, to give and sustain life. In his letter to the Corinthians, Paul also spoke figuratively of the Spirit as that which Christians have partaken of as if from a liquid substance: "For in the one Spirit we were all baptized into one body—Jews or Greeks, slaves or free—and we were all made to drink of one

---

[60] Correspondence 11/27/02 (words in italics originally in capitals).
[61] *A Second Reply to Robert Hommel Regarding Mantey's Letter to the WTB&TS By Greg Stafford* (words in italics originally in capitals).
[62] *Friends of the Nazarene* online Bible Commentary.
[63] John 7:38

Spirit."[64] And in his letter to the Christians at Ephesus, Paul admonished them: "do not get drunk on wine, in which lies debauchery, but be filled with the Spirit."[65]

Christians should not be given to drunkenness, placing themselves under the excessive influence or control of alcoholic beverage, but should be filled, influenced, governed, moved and motivated by God's Spirit, which can only lead them to produce good deeds that bring glory to God and Christ.

The Scriptures even seem to suggest that God's Spirit is that which can be imparted in varying portions or degrees. A part of the apostle Peter's statement on the day of Pentecost in the *Revised Standard Version* reads: "in the last days it shall be, God declares, that I will pour out my Spirit upon all flesh…in those days I will pour out my Spirit…" But the footnote in Weymouth's translation tells us: "Here, and in verse 18, lit. 'of' or 'from My Spirit'—a share or portion…" This is why the *New American Bible* has: "'It will come to pass in the last days,' God says, 'that I will pour out a portion of my spirit upon all flesh… Indeed, upon my servants and my handmaids I will pour out a portion of my spirit in those days, and they shall prophesy." In a similar way, the apostle John wrote in reference to Christians: "By this we know that we abide in [God] and he in us, because he has given us of his own Spirit ['the share of his own Spirit,' *PME*]."[66] However, John the Baptist spoke about the Spirit in association with God's Son in this way: "The one who comes from heaven [the Son] is above all. He testifies to what he has seen and heard, but no one accepts his testimony. The man who has accepted it has certified that God is truthful. For the one whom God has sent speaks the words of God, for God gives the

---

[64] 1 Corinthians 12:13, *NRSV*
[65] Ephesians 5:18, *NAB*. It was pointed out by one source: "The figurative speech in all these passages should be noted: spirit like water is a cleansing agent (1:33); spirit like breath is a vital element (20:22); spirit as teaching, guiding, defending, is a divine power (chs. 14-16). Unifying them all is surely the concept of a *Christlike power* that is finally in the control of God, the heavenly Father…The Gospel material is more readily aligned with ideas of supernatural powers than with the Christian doctrine of the Third person of the Blessed Trinity. —George Johnston, *The Spirit-Paraclete in the Gospel of John*, SNTSMS 12 (Cambridge: Cambridge University Press, 1970), pp. 31-32.
[66] 1 John 4:13, *RSV*

The Holy Spirit

Spirit without limit"—or, as the *NRSV* puts it, "for he gives the Spirit without measure."[67]

After the Messiah's ascension to the heavenly Father, the apostle Peter declared on the day of Pentecost: "God has raised this Jesus to life, and we are all witnesses of the fact. Exalted to the right hand of God, he has received from the Father the promised Holy Spirit and has poured out what you now see and hear."[68]

This outpouring of the Spirit on that day resulted in the extraordinary ability to speak in languages the Christian disciples did not already know, so that Luke reports: "And they were amazed and wondered, saying, 'Are not all these who are speaking Galileans? And how is it that we hear, each of us in his own native language? Parthians and Medes and Elamites and residents of Mesopotamia, Judea and Cappadocia, Pontus and Asia, Phrygia and Pamphylia, Egypt and the parts of Libya belonging to Cyrene, and visitors from Rome, both Jews and proselytes, Cretans and Arabians, we hear them telling in our own tongues the mighty works of God."[69]

On that day the Christians communicated "the mighty works of God," and through the Spirit they were empowered to boldly proclaim the good news about the kingdom of God and the name of Jesus Christ to their countrymen.

The Watchtower Society and Jehovah's Witnesses have attempted to officially define the holy Spirit as "God's active force." It has even become customary in their publications, when they mention the Spirit, to say "the holy spirit *or* God's active force."[70] But one Bible scholar observed:

> Given the connotations of the word 'force,' it is a very unfortunate description of The holy spirit. Scientifically speaking all different forces operating in the universe can be traced back to the four fundamental forces, the strong and weak forces of the atom, electro-magnetism and

---

[67] John 3:31-34, *NIV*
[68] Acts 2:32, *NIV*
[69] Acts 2:8-11, *RSV*
[70] For example, a modern article in the Watchtower magazine said: "Jesus inherited no imperfections because he did not have a human father. Jehovah's holy spirit, or active force, came upon Mary, and his power 'overshadowed' her, miraculously causing her to become pregnant. (Luke 1:34, 35)" —*The Watchtower*, September 15, 2005, p. 5 (underlining added).

The Holy Spirit

gravity. But these four primary forces have one thing in common: they are blind! They just work in one way according to the laws of nature. To use the words 'God's active force' as a description of The holy spirit, therefore leaves much to be desired...The holy spirit has scores of operations, but the most important is that it conveys some of God's personality to us, some of the personal warmth and love of God. A *blind* force cannot do that![71]

Others have also expressed dissatisfaction with defining the holy Spirit as simply an impersonal "force" or "power":

> ...to say that holy spirit is purely the power of God is not in itself an adequate description of that spirit...Paul speaks of 'the spirit of the man, which is in him,' but does not restrict God's spirit with the same wording. God's spirit is not confined to a particular location, but proceeds from Him for the accomplishment of His purposes... Generally speaking, it may be said that the holy spirit is a function or activity always identified with the mind of God...where holy spirit is within the believer, it renews the mind after the pattern of Christ, through the word of God.[72]

> The Spirit of God is certainly not just an abstract power. Since it is God in action, it is most personal. It is God's outreach. God's Spirit is His personality extended to creation...the divine influence.[73]

Cyril Richardson made an analogy based on a Scripture already mentioned:

> The most revealing verse about the nature of the Spirit in Paul is I Cor. 2:11. There he compares God's Spirit to the

---

[71] Furuli, *The Role of Theology and Bias in Bible Translation*, p. 277. Furuli is a Witness and believes that the words "[active force] are the best words we have." But it is nevertheless significant that as a Witness he still finds the common "Watchtower" definition unsatisfactory on some level. Another source observed: "The Holy Spirit is the Spirit of God...It comes *from* God and can function in any manner or form God decides to have it function. It is *alive*, just as his word is alive, and can judge, because it actively impacts the purpose for which it is given. (Heb. 4:12) As respects Christians, the implanting of God's Holy Spirit in their hearts is designed to lead and transform their personality into the image (likeness) of Christ. That goal and purpose can be resisted by an individual and in that way defeat the purpose or 'grieve' God's Spirit—obstruct or hinder its intended purposes." —Frye, *The Father/Son Relationship*, p. 73.
[72] *What is the Holy Spirit?* A Bible Study from Faith Builders Fellowship
[73] Anthony Buzzard, *The Doctrine of the Trinity*

spirit within man, and makes the analogy that as a man's spirit knows a man's thoughts within him, so God's Spirit comprehends God's thoughts. From this it is clear that he thinks of God's Spirit as a good deal more than his dynamic energy, or the means of his operation. It is not merely God's breath, but his self-awareness, his mind, his inner being. This may be the source or seat of God's vitality, but it is more. It is his self-consciousness, his very being, the center of his 'person,' as we might say. Just as a man's spirit is his ultimate reality, when he is stripped of all that is accidental to his being, so God's Spirit is his inner self.[74]

Although one might attempt to describe the holy Spirit based on evidence found in Scripture, as well as in light of one's personal, Christian experience, the very term itself appears to be self-explanatory; to put it simply, it is God's Spirit, the Spirit *of* God.[75] There is the spirit of the world,[76] the spirit of man, and various sorts of spirits. The holy Spirit is the Spirit of the purest and most powerful being in the universe—the very Spirit of God himself. Professor Marianne Thompson made the following observation about the Spirit in association with the Gospel accounts:

---

[74] Cyril C. Richardson, *The Doctrine of the Trinity*, p. 50. Here, by saying the Spirit is God's "very being," Richardson probably did not mean it in the sense that the Spirit is a person *of* the being of God. In another place he said, "God's breath is not exactly identical with his being, any more than his finger or hand is." (Note: references in Scripture to God's 'arm,' 'hand,' 'finger,' 'face,' 'eyes,' 'nostrils,' etc. do not demand that God is a *physical* being, or that these terms are to be taken *literally*. In John chapter four, Jesus said that God is a Spirit.)

[75] Because God is holy, it follows that his Spirit is holy (and reflective of his holiness). Perhaps the basic definitions for "spirit" in the English dictionary can also shed light on our understanding. Seen in this way the Spirit might be described as "a vital principle or animating force," "associated with the mind, will, and feelings," "a causative, activating, or essential principle," "animation and energy in action or expression," "the animating principle of life," "vital essence," "An attitude or principle that pervades thought, stirs one to action, etc.," a "dominant tendency or character," "The breath of life," "The animating or vital principle giving life," "the active essence of the Deity serving as an invisible and life-giving or inspiring power in motion," "temper or disposition of mind," "the activating or essential principle of something (as an emotion or frame of mind) influencing a person" "an inclination, impulse, or tendency of a special kind" a "vital power" that is "Holy," that is, "Belonging to, derived from, or associated with a divine power; sacred," "set apart" "consecrated" "having a spiritually pure quality" "refers to divine, that which has its sanctity directly from God."

[76] It was pointed out by one source: "1 Corinthians 2:12 directly opposes the 'spirit of the world' with 'the spirit which is of God.' As the 'spirit of the world' is not a person separate from 'the world,' nether is the 'spirit of God' a person separate from God. Each is an influence emanating from a source that produces certain attitudes, behaviors or 'fruit.'" —Graeser, Lynn, Schoenheit, *One God & One Lord*, p. 597.

There is no explicit argument for the unity of the Spirit and God or, for that matter, for the Spirit and Jesus, whereas these are common place with respect to Jesus and the Father. Missing are the notable affirmations of and prayers for unity, such as 'I and the Father are one' (10:30)...In other words, there is no need to build a case that the Father and the Spirit are one, for the Spirit is the Spirit of God and, hence, by definition, nature, and character, comes from God. There are no formulas of mutual indwelling that relate the Father and the Spirit in the Gospels. Indeed, there are not explanations of the divine origins or source of the Spirit, perhaps these are simply taken for granted. From where would the 'Holy Spirit' come but God?...If we note the extent to which the activity of God and the Spirit overlap, the frequent use of Spirit as the means through which God acts, and the consistent assumption that God is the source of the Spirit, then it seems that the Spirit is primarily the means or mode by which God acts in the world. This is the portrait that emerges from the portions of the Gospels outside the Farewell Discourses. The Spirit is depicted here as God's life-giving power granted to the Son, who in his word and work granted the Spirit of life to others.[77]

Not only is the Spirit portrayed as a life-giving force from God in the Scriptures, evidently, the Spirit functions as the agency through which the personal presence of God and Christ inhabits, or take up residence in, the hearts and minds of believers. In John chapter fourteen, Jesus said, "If a man loves me, he will keep my word, and my Father will love him, and we will come to him and make our home ['our dwelling,' *NAB*; 'our abode,' *NASB*] with him."[78] Undoubtedly, as a careful consideration of John fourteen (and the rest of Scripture) will bear out, the Spirit is the agency through which such 'indwelling' would take place. As the apostle John said in another place: "When we keep his commands we dwell in him and he dwells in us. And this is how we know that [God] dwells

---

[77] Marianne Thompson, *The God of the Gospel of John*, p. 184.
[78] John 14:23, *RSV*

The Holy Spirit

within us: we know it from the Spirit he has given us."[79] And in his letter to the Ephesians, when the apostle Paul wrote about "the mystery/sacred secret"—relating to the unity of both Jews and Gentiles in one community under Christ—he likened the sum parts of the entire Christian household to a temple edifice to be inhabited by God. Of Jesus Christ, "the foundation cornerstone," Paul said: "He is the one who holds the whole building together and makes it grow into a sacred temple dedicated to the Lord. In union with him you too are being built together with all the others into *a place where God lives through his Spirit*."[80]

Although God dwells in heaven, and his Son at his right hand, both are present with Christians through the mediation of the holy Spirit, which guides, teaches, influences and fortifies Christians toward righteous living and godliness, enabling them to have "the mind of Christ." In this way, God's Spirit truly is a "helper" or "comforter" (*KJV* rendering of *parakletos*), because it creates and nurtures within believers a profound sense of fellowship and intimacy with the heavenly Father and Son; at the same time enabling God's servants to carry out his will, at times empowering them to perform extraordinary and even miraculous deeds in God's name, in harmony with God's purpose.[81]

In John chapter three, Jesus told Nicodemus: "The wind blows where it wills, and you can hear the sound it makes, but you do not know where it comes from or where it goes; so it is with everyone who is born of the Spirit."[82] The evidence or "fruitage" of the Spirit (what the Spirit produces) in the life of a believer, or one "born of the Spirit," is "love, joy, peace,

---

[79] 1 John 4:24, *NEB*. When Paul expressed his desire, "that Christ may dwell in your hearts through faith," it is also likely that this is something that would be accomplished through the indwelling Spirit (Ephesians 3:17).

[80] Ephesians 2:21-22, *TEV*. Or as other translations express it: "a dwelling place of God in the Spirit" (*RSV*), "a house where God lives, in the Spirit" (*JB*), "a habitation of God through the Spirit" (*KJV*). Actually, there is no definite article ('the') in the Greek, so the clause can be rendered, "a place for God to inhabit by spirit," or "God's dwelling place, in spirit." On the "sacred secret" or "mystery," compare Ephesians 3:5-6.

[81] McKenzie similarly states: "the spirit is a divine dynamic force, the charismatic spirit of the OT, which moves the apostles to preach and witness Jesus and empowers them to feats of courage and eloquence which are entirely beyond the personal capacities of these men as they appear in the Gospels. The spirit is not restricted to charismatic leaders, but is given with the messianic fullness to the entire body of believers." —*McKenzie Dictionary of the Bible*, p. 843.

[82] John 3:8, *NAB*

The Holy Spirit

patience, kindness, self-control..."[83]—and, "where the Spirit of the Lord is, there is freedom."[84]

Although the Scriptures do not offer a concise "theological" definition of the Spirit, we can understand the role and significance of the Spirit better through its effects on the Christian life, the very fruitage produced by it. It was observed by C. F. D. Moule:

> Meanwhile, a more profound and far-reaching observation is that the Holy Spirit within us puts into action, and sometimes into words, what it means to be a Christian. The Spirit, that is to say, reproduces in Christians the relation of Christ as Son to Father. That means that the Spirit is a revolutionary force. The character of Christ is the character of renewed humanity—humanity turned away from self and back to God; and to be under the power of his Spirit causes just such a turning or revolution in each Christian's character. ...it is by the Spirit that Christians are enabled to have 'the mind of Christ', to have insight into God's mind, to think God's thoughts after him, and to know that they are members of his family...And all this means not merely knowing with the head, but knowing with the will and the affections. It is by the Spirit, therefore, that Christians are enabled to act as Christians and kill dead all that is contrary to God's will (Rom. 8.13), and that Christ's character begins to be formed in each Christian through the filial relation with God.[85]

One source endeavored to describe the results associated with a person being filled with, or indwelt by, the Spirit of God, based on the prophetic expression in the book of Ezekiel:

---

[83] "Now the works of the flesh are obvious: immorality, impurity, licentiousness, idolatry, sorcery, hatreds, rivalry, jealousy, outbursts of fury, acts of selfishness, dissensions, factions, occasions of envy, drinking bouts, orgies, and the like...In contrast, the fruit of the Spirit is love, joy, peace, patience, kindness, generosity, faithfulness, gentleness, self-control. Against such there is no law." —Galatians 5:19-25, *NAB*

[84] 2 Corinthians 3:17, *NAB*

[85] *The Holy Spirit*, pp. 29, 30. Similarly, Professor Thompson points out that in the Gospel of John, "the work of the Spirit has a corporate manifestation, in that the Spirit effects the life-giving transformation that makes people 'children of God' (1:12) who are 'born from above' to eternal life (3:3, 5-6). That transformation is described, in keeping with the life-giving function of the Spirit, in terms of 'new birth,' a graphic description of the life given by the Spirit." —*The God of the Gospel of John*, p. 170.

The Holy Spirit

During the Babylonian captivity, the word of [Jehovah] came to Ezekiel, saying, 'And I will sprinkle clean water upon you, and ye shall be clean: from all your filthiness, and from all your idols, will I cleanse you. A new heart also will I give you, and a new spirit will I put within you; and I will take away the stony heart out of your flesh, and I will give you a heart of flesh. And I will put my Spirit within you, and cause you to walk in my statutes, and ye shall keep my judgments, and do them.' —Ezek. 36:26-38 ...The spirit which God would put in His people would not be 'new' in the sense of an innovation. Rather, it would be His spirit, an holy spirit. 'I, [Jehovah], change not' (Mal. 3:6). But in man it would indeed be new, entirely different from the 'spirit' of the natural fleshly man (1 Cor. 2:14). A new heart and a new spirit would amount to nothing less than a radical change in the inward man, with a corresponding change in character. And because the new spirit would be holy spirit, the resulting new character would necessarily be like God's. They would walk in His statutes and keep His judgments not from any external constraint, but from the heart, because they and God would be of like mind. And His standards would be reflected in all their thinking.[86]

Although it does not seem necessary—scripturally speaking—to view the Spirit as a "person" per se (particularly in the latter Trinitarian sense), it also does not seem necessary to think of the Spirit as merely an "impersonal force," for it is the Spirit of a *personal* being; the outwardly-extending though invisible expression and influence of the inward, personal reality and heart of the living God. To possess the Spirit, it seems, is to possess the mind, the attitude, and the personality of Jesus Christ. It is even likely that most, so-called "orthodox" Christians—in practice and in general thought—do not relate to or consider the Spirit as a distinct "person" like the Father and Son. This is so not because of any conscious denial of the traditional Trinitarian model, but due to the basic and overall impression that the Bible itself gives.

---

[86] *What is the Holy Spirit?* A Bible Study from Faith Builders Fellowship.

The Holy Spirit

It should be kept in mind that the discussion presented here is by no means exhaustive. Nor were the descriptions of the Spirit offered as any kind of "dogmatic" formulation. It is hoped, however, that the material presented thus far will stimulate others into further study and deeper reflection, with the goal of allowing the *God-breathed* Scriptures themselves guide the thinking and mold the outlook on these and on all other matters of Christian faith.

Whether one believes the holy Spirit to be a "person" or not a person (but the very Spirit *of a Person*, and which does in fact communicate and reflect the *personality* and will of a person or persons—namely, God and his Son), the Scriptures leave no doubt that the Spirit is that which "God has given to those who obey him"[87]; that, with respect to believers, God has, "put his seal on us and given us his Spirit in our hearts as a guarantee," or "down payment" (*ESV* ftnt), "first installment" (*NAB*), "a pledge and foretaste of future blessing" (*Weymouth*)[88]; and that being filled with the Spirit carries with it that needed strengthening power and inner-conviction to live righteously, to love selflessly, and to draw near in fellowship to the one God continually.

> *"If the Spirit of the one who raised Jesus from the dead dwells in you, the one who raised Christ from the dead will give life to your mortal bodies also, through his Spirit that dwells in you. Consequently, brothers, we are not debtors to the flesh, to live according to the flesh. For if you live according to the flesh, you will die, but if by the spirit you put to death the deeds of the body, you will live. For [all] those who are led by the Spirit of God are children of God. For you did not receive a spirit of slavery to fall back into fear, but you received a spirit of adoption, through which we cry, 'Abba, Father!' The Spirit itself bears witness with our spirit that we are children of God, and if children, then heirs, heirs of God and joint heirs with Christ, if only we suffer with him so that we may also be glorified with him."*
> — Romans 8:11-17, *New American Bible*

---

[87] Acts 5:32, *NAB*
[88] 2 Corinthians 1:21-22, *ESV*. *The Living Bible* paraphrases: "He has put his brand upon us—his mark of ownership—and given us his Holy Spirit in our hearts as guarantee that we belong to him, and as the first installment of all that he is going to give us." Compare *NIV* and *TEV* renderings.

**********APPENDIX**********

Appendix

—*Thoughts on the name "Christian"*—

> *"I, then, a prisoner for the Lord, urge you to live in a manner worthy of the call you have received, with all humility and gentleness, with patience, bearing with one another through love, striving to preserve the unity of the spirit through the bond peace: one body and one Spirit, as you were also called to the one hope of your call; one Lord, one faith, one baptism; one God and Father of all, who is over all and through all and in all."*
> —The apostle Paul, Ephesians 4:1-7, NAB

A "Christian" is a person who has faith in Jesus of Nazareth as the promised "Christ" or "Messiah" (lit., the 'anointed one') and is by definition "a follower of Christ." *Vine's Expository Dictionary* states: "*christianos*—a word formed after the Roman style, signifying *an adherent of Jesus.*" According to another source, Christians are defined as "*those who belong to, or are devoted to Christ.*"[1]

The footnote in the *MacArthur Study Bible* says that the name Christian was originally a "term of derision meaning 'of the party of Christ.'" However, not all commentators or Bible translators agree that the name was originally given as a term of derision or contempt. On this point Bible scholar Albert Barnes wrote: "whether the disciples assumed it themselves, or whether it was given by divine intimation, has been a matter of debate. That it was given in derision is not probable, for in the name 'Christian' there was nothing dishonorable."[2]

According to another source: "The word is formed with the Latin suffix which designates 'follower or partisan of' (cf. 'Herodians' in Mark 3:6). There is no adequate reason to think

---
[1] *The Anchor Bible Dictionary*, Volume I, p. 925 (emphasis added).
[2] *Notes on the New Testament, Explanatory and Practical*, by Albert Barnes, Edited by Robert Frew D.D., Acts (Grand Rapids: Baker Book House, 1967), p. 185.

Appendix

that the term was used in derision. It simply means people who follow Christ."[3]

The first time the name appears in the Bible is in the book of Acts, which reads:

> **And it came to pass, that a whole year they assembled themselves with the church, and taught much people. And the disciples *were called*** (Gk: *chreematisai*) **Christians first in Antioch.**[4]

It was observed in one reference work:

> The name first given at Antioch to Christ's followers. In the New Testament it only occurs in 1 Pe. 4:16; Acts 11:26; 26:27-28. Their name among themselves was 'brethren,' 'disciples,' 'those of the way' (Acts 6:1,3; 9:2), 'saints' (Rom 1:7). The Jews, as they denied that Jesus is the Christ, would never originate the name 'Christians,' but called them 'Nazarenes' (Acts 24:5). The Gentiles confounded them with the Jews, and thought them to be a Jewish sect. But a new epoch arose in the church's development when, at Antioch, *idolatrous* Gentiles…were converted. Then the Gentiles needed a new name to designate people who were Jews, neither by birth nor religion. And the people of Antioch were famous for their readiness in giving names: Partisans of Christ, Christiani, as Caesariani, partisans of Caesar; a Latin name, as Antioch had become a Latin city. But the name ['Christian'] was *divinely ordered* (as *chrematizo* always expresses, 11: 26)."[5]

The standard lexical definition for *chrematizo* is "a divine response or revelation: 'answer of God,' 'to utter an oracle, i.e. divinely intimate; by implication, to constitute a firm for business, i.e. (generally) bear as a title: KJV—be called, be admonished (warned) of God, reveal, speak."[6] According to another source, the word signifies: "to give a response to those

---

[3] *The Wycliffe Bible Commentary* (Chicago: Moody Press, 1962), p. 1144.
[4] Acts 11:26, *King James Version*
[5] *Fausset's Bible Dictionary* (Grand Rapids: Zondervan, 1963), p. 126. It might be more accurate to say, "as chrematizo *almost* always expresses," or "*normally* expresses" in the New Testament.
[6] *Biblesoft's New Exhaustive Strong's Numbers and Concordance with Expanded Greek-Hebrew Dictionary*. Copyright (c) 1994, *Biblesoft and International Bible Translators*, Inc.

Appendix

consulting an oracle, to give a divine command or admonition, to teach from heaven, 'to be divinely commanded, admonished, instructed,' 'to be the mouthpiece of divine revelations, to promulgate the commands of God,' 'to assume or take to oneself a name from one's public business, to receive a name or title, to be called.'"[7]

The primary lexical meaning of the Greek verb used at Acts 11:26 has led some Bible students to conclude that the name was given to the followers of Christ by divine appointment. In his one-volume commentary, for example, Adam Clarke wrote the following:

> It is evident they had the name *Christians* from *Christ* their Master, as the Platonists and Pythagoreans had their name from their masters, Plato and Pythagoras. Now as these had their name from those great masters because they attended their teaching and credited their doctrines, so *the disciples were called Christians because they took Christ for their Teacher*, crediting His doctrines and following the rule of life laid down by Him. It has been a question, By whom was this name given to the disciples? Some think they assumed it; others, that the inhabitants of Antioch gave it to them; and others, that it was given by Saul and Barnabas. The word in our common text which we translate *were called* signifies, in the New Testament, to 'appoint, warn, or nominate,' by divine direction. In this sense the word is used in Matt. ii. 12; Luke ii. 26; and in the preceding chapter of this book, v. 22. If, therefore, the name was given by divine appointment, it is most likely that Saul and Barnabas were directed to give it; and that therefore the name Christian is from God, as well as that grace and holiness which are so essentially required and implied in the character. Before this time the Jewish converts were simply called, among themselves, *disciples*, i.e., *scholars*; *believers*, *saints*, the *church*, or *assembly*; and by their enemies, *Nazarenes*, *Galileans*, the *men of this way* or *sect*...They considered themselves as one family, and hence the appellation of brethren was frequent among them. A Christian, therefore, is the highest character which any human being can bear upon

---

[7] *Thayer's Greek Lexicon and Brown Driver & Briggs Hebrew Lexicon*, Copyright (c)1993

Appendix

the earth; and to receive it from God, as those appear to have done—how glorious the title!"[8]

Most Bible versions do not translate Acts 11:26 in a way showing that the name "Christian" was given by divine direction. The Greek word *chrematizo* can also simply mean "to call/name" (without implying divine influence), as it likely does at Romans 7:3: "She *shall be called [chreematísei]* an adulteress." Aware of this fact, Albert Barnes observed in his *Notes on the New Testament*: "It cannot be denied, however, that the most usual signification in the New Testament is that of a *divine monition, or communication*."[9]

For this reason, several modern English translations have rendered Acts 11:26 in the following ways:

The disciples also were *divinely called* first in Antioch Christians.
—*Young's Literal Translation of the Holy Bible*, 1898
The disciples were *divinely called* 'Christians' first at Antioch.
—*McCord's New Testament Translation of the Everlasting Gospel*
It was first in Antioch that the disciples were *by divine providence* ['*to style divinely*,' *Kingdom Interlinear Translation*] **called Christians.** —*New World Translation of the Holy Scriptures*
In Antioch, *God called* the followers *of Jesus* 'Christians' for the first time. —*The Simple English Bible New Testament*

In their well-known *Cyclopedia of Biblical, Theological, and Ecclesiastical Literature*, however, McClintock and Strong suggested that the name was neither given in derision nor by divine appointment:

> There is no reason to think with some that the name 'Christian' was given in absolute *derision*. When used by Agrippa (Acts xxvi, 28), there is no proof that it was a term of reproach...The early adoption of it by Christians themselves, and the manner in which they employ it are sufficient to dispel all idea of this nature (1 Pet. iv, 16). The only reproach connected with the name would be the

---

[8] Abridged from the original six-volume work by Ralph Earle, Th.D (Grand Rapids: Baker, 1967), p. 987 (underlining added).
[9] The view of Barnes was expressed in his commentary in this way: "I incline to the opinion, however, that it was given to them by the Gentiles who were there, simply as an appellation, without intending it as a name of reproach, and that it was readily assumed by the disciples as a name that would fitly designate them."

Appendix

inevitable one arising from the profession of faith implied in it. Neither is the view of others more probable, that it was a name imposed by divine appointment. The term *chrematizo* (translated 'called' in the passage first quoted), usually relied upon to sustain this view, has other significations than that of an oracular response, and is fairly capable of the meaning assigned to it in our version.[10]

Whether one is persuaded that the name Christian was given by divine appointment based on the Greek word used at Acts 11:26 (along with the view of certain translators), or believes the name was given in derision,—or given without any reference to derision or divine influence—the following commentary by J. W. McGarvey would seem to adequately summarize the standing of the name as it applies to God's people, in view of the overall scriptural testimony:

> There has been much dispute as to whether this new name was given by Barnabas and Saul under divine authority, or by the Gentiles of Antioch, or by the disciples themselves. It would serve no practical purpose to decide between the latter two suppositions, for, with, whichever party it originated, it was subsequently accepted by the disciples in general...The whole world had heard something of Christ, as the remarkable personage who was put to death under Pontius Pilate, though many had heard nothing of the early history of his Church. From this fact, when strangers came to Antioch, and heard the new party who were attracting so much attention there, called *Christians*, they at once recognized them as followers of that *Christ* of whom they had already heard. This explains the fact stated in the text, that 'the disciples were called *Christians first* in Antioch.' The fact that Luke here adopts it, and that both Paul and Peter afterward recognized it, gives it all the validity of inspired usage, and, therefore, all the weight of divine authority. That it is a New Testament name is undisputed, and this

---

[10] Volume II, p. 269; "our version" is probably a reference to the *King James* (1611) or *Revised Version* (1881).

Appendix

renders its divine authority indisputable.[11]

In spite of the scriptural evidence, it is well known that a considerable number of religious groups and religious leaders—at different times and in the midst of various circumstances—have expressed a degree of dissatisfaction with the simple name "Christian." They have, for essentially the same reasons, expressed the need for the adoption of a supplemental and distinctive religious label.

The following sources represent two very distinct religious groups. Although quite different with regard to their overall interpretation of the Christian faith, both appeal to a very similar line of reasoning with respect to their belief in the *necessity* of taking on a name other than, or in addition to, the one given to the followers of Christ in the Scriptures. The well-known Calvinist theologian, R. C. Sproul, after a brief discussion on the background and meaning of the term "evangelical,"[12] and speaking as an Evangelical/Protestant, made the following argument in his book *Getting the Gospel Right*:

> In the religious nomenclature of historic Christianity, however, there have been many who claim the term *Christian* who reject personal rebirth, or who reject the content of the evangel or gospel. *It has been necessary for people to adopt such language to distinguish themselves theologically* from those who claim the term *Christian* for themselves while denying these disputed elements of Christianity...This is why *it is naive in the extreme for people to declare, 'I am simply a Christian; I won't use any other labels.'* This ignores two thousand years of the

---

[11] McGarvey's *Original Commentary on Acts*. Garvey also notes: "This name, whether given by divine or human authority, was not designed as an exclusive appellation, seeing that the others were continued in use after its introduction. It merely took its proper place among other names, to answer its own special purpose."

[12] The term *evangelical* means "pertaining to, or characteristic of the gospel." Technically, an "evangelical" could be or simply mean *one who believes in the evangel* or *gospel/good news*. The label *evangelical*, however, taken in its narrow and traditional sense, refers to one of many subgroups of Christendom holding to its own set of unique interpretations, post-biblical creeds, extra-biblical dogmas and ecclesiastical traditions. As pointed out by Sproul: "In popular usage *evangelical* signifies a species of the genus *Christian*. Therefore we often hear the term *evangelical Christian*, in which *evangelical* designates a particular kind of Christian...the Reformers called themselves *Evangelicals* to distinguish themselves from Roman Catholics. In this regard the term *Evangelical* functioned as a synonym for *Protestant*." —*Getting the Gospel Right, The Tie That Binds Evangelicals Together* (Grand Rapids: Baker Books, 1999), pp. 32, 34.

Appendix

church's struggle to distinguish heresy from orthodoxy, true Christianity from false forms of or claims to Christian faith.[13]

Similarly, in a book written on the history of their religious organization, the writer of a 1993 Watchtower publication, under the subtitle *Need for a Distinctive Name*, made the following comments about the history behind the adoption of the name "Jehovah's Witnesses":

> In time, it became increasingly evident that in addition to the designation Christian, the congregation of Jehovah's servants *truly did need a distinctive name*. The meaning of the name Christian had become distorted in the public mind because people who claimed to be Christians often had little or no idea who Jesus Christ was, what he taught, and what they should be doing if they really were his true followers...as our brothers progressed in their understanding of God's Word, they clearly saw *the need to be separate from those religious systems that fraudulently claimed to be Christian*...in 1931 we adopted the truly distinctive name Jehovah's Witnesses. Author Chandler W. Sterling refers to this as 'the greatest stroke of genius' on the part of J. F. Rutherford, then president of the Watch Tower Society.[14]

In the paragraph that follows, the writer implied that it was more than a "stroke of genius" on the part of the Watchtower President, and that the selection of the name "Jehovah's Witnesses" was likely the result of "divine providence." R. C. Sproul, an evangelical, although not implying that the term "evangelical" was the name chosen by God, seems to suggest that those who consider themselves to be simply "Christian" are somehow mistaken, or perhaps not very well informed respecting the two thousand years or so that have now passed since the time of Christ and his apostles. In his view, there seems to be no room for those who—precisely due to their knowledge of history, the Bible, and the present religious circumstances—choose to identify themselves with none other

---
[13] Sproul, *Getting the Gospel Right*, p. 32 (emphasis added).
[14] *Jehovah's Witnesses, Proclaimers of God's Kingdom* (Brooklyn: WTBTS, 1993), pp. 150-152 (emphasis added).

Appendix

than that of their head, the Lord Jesus *Christ*. Arguing as an "evangelical," the impression left with the reader is that in order to avoid taking a position that is "naive in the extreme," one must identify with some post-biblical movement and adopt a label such as "Evangelical" or "Protestant," and subscribe to the doctrines held by Sproul and the brand of "evangelicalism" he advocates.[15] In a similar vein, the Watchtower seems to suggest that if Christ's followers chose not to take on any other name than the one given in Scripture, that they would somehow be ignoring "divine providence" and be guilty of disregarding the pronouncements given by God through his alleged "sole channel of communication," the Watchtower Bible & Tract Society.[16]

Yet the scriptural evidence reveals that those seeking to follow Christ today are under no obligation to identify themselves as a member of any post-biblical sect, movement, or religious denomination. Unfortunately, belonging to, or having formal membership in, any one of such movements often carries with it the implication and expectation that its members adhere to a certain set of doctrinal beliefs unique to that particular group, many of which beliefs developed after the first century and the completion of the inspired Christian Scriptures.

It has been estimated that, today, there are over 20,000 groups, sects, and denominations that would fall under the category of "Christian Religions"[17] (almost all claiming to base their beliefs on the Bible). Most groups have taken on an *official* and *distinctive* name which normally identifies or pertains to

---

[15] In a correspondence F. F. Bruce once observed: "People who adhere to belief in the Bible only (as they believe) often adhere in fact to a traditional school of interpretation of *sola scriptura*. Evangelical Protestants can be as much servants of tradition as Roman Catholics or Greek Orthodox, only they don't realize that it is tradition."—*Focus on the Kingdom Magazine* (correspondence, June 13th, 1981).

[16] Although the writer of the Watchtower publication implies that the selection of the official name "Jehovah's Witnesses" was the result of "divine providence" (something Scripture only applies to the term 'Christian,'—according to Acts 11:26, *NWT*), all that can be proven is that the name adopted was the result of the decision of one man, Judge Rutherford, the President of the Watchtower Society in 1931.

[17] *The World Christian Encyclopedia, Second Edition, A Comparative Survey of Churches and Religions in the Modern World* (Oxford University Press, 1981), p. vii. The Editor, David Barrett, noted: "It was expected that the task of compiling this resulting encyclopedia would take about three years; in the event, it has taken twelve years. The reason for this lengthy period was that all those originally involved, including the editor, seriously underestimated the immense size and complexity of the Christian world. The number of denominations was found to be four times as numerous as the estimate made in 1968." In the same preface Barrett speaks specifically about the "proliferation of 20,800 denominations".

Appendix

their founder, their claims of authority, their emphasis or priority in doctrine/practice, or their unique interpretations of Scripture that set them apart from other groups. In one way or another, the variety of denominational and sectarian labels that have been adopted, ultimately, contribute to the division that Jesus Christ did not want for his true followers, for he prayed that his disciples would be *one*, just as he and his Father are *one* (John 17:21).[18] In spite of what is sometimes argued, such peculiar denominational labels are unnecessary for Christians and only seem to reflect a partisan spirit that is not authorized or supported by Scripture (1 Corinthians 1:10).

Among the more general names or classifications that are essentially broad in their application include: "(Roman) Catholic," "Eastern-Greek Orthodox," "Anglican," "Protestant," "Reformed,"[19] "(Conservative) Evangelical" (a family of Protestant groups), "Liberal," "Fundamentalist," "Pentecostal," and even "Orthodox."[20] Other groups have taken on designations attributing special emphasis to the divine name like "Jehovah's Witnesses" and the "Sacred Name" movements like "Yahweh's New Covenant Assembly (YNCA)," and "Yahweh's Assembly

---

[18] This does not mean the Scriptures would support a *uniting* of all denominations regardless of belief systems. In many cases, there are very serious and involved differences respecting the doctrine and claims to authority among the various churches. Unity among Christians must be a unity based upon *truth*, the truth of the gospel as found in the holy Scriptures. The foundational truth that *should* and *does* unite all Christians relates to the true identity of Jesus of Nazareth; this involves, primarily, acceptance of, and faith in, Jesus as the "Christ" or "Messiah," "the Son of the living God" (Matthew 16:13-18; compare 1 John 4:15; 5:1; Ephesians 4:13-14).

[19] According to a respected scholar from the "Reformed" tradition: "All Reformed Christians recognize especially John Calvin as their father. But Calvin can be understood in different ways, and, as is the case in any family, his children feel different degrees of dependence upon him...Moreover, there is no one authoritative statement of faith to which all Reformed churches subscribe. There are many different statements. They all bear a common family resemblance, but they differ from each other in emphasis, in the spirit in which they are written, and sometimes in theological content...There is plenty of room in the Reformed family, in other words, for individual differences and freedom of movement...strictly speaking, 'Reformed' is a theological, not a denominational, title. It is a mistake to limit it to any one denomination." —Shirley C. Guthrie, *Christian Doctrine, Revised Edition*, pp. 16, 17.

[20] One author observed: "The term [orthodox] itself is a fine one, coming from the Greek words *ortho* and *doxa* meaning simply 'right teaching' [or, 'right opinion' or 'right honor']. Actually, it has come to stand for a set of beliefs that have been defined and established as a result of the various councils held in earlier centuries. Some of those beliefs are simply restatements of Scripture and are obviously 'right teaching.' Others are the result of interpretation, argumentation and debate, and have been pronounced 'orthodox' by men in authority. As one source puts it, 'orthodox Christianity is something purely descriptive—referring simply to the majority opinion'" (Dr. Bruce Shelley, *Church History in Plain Language*, p. 62.). —Franz, *In Search of Christian Freedom*, pp. 704-705.

Appendix

of Messiah." Some of the more "mainstream" denominational names include "Presbyterian," "Episcopalian," and "Congregationalist"—names that reflect preferred styles of church government. Others identify themselves as "Lutheran," "Wesleyan," "Calvinist,"[21] "Arminian," "Amish," and "Mennonite"—referring to the name of their leader, founder, or most notable upholder of their particular doctrine. Still others have been called or have called themselves "Apostolic," "Abrahamic," "Baptist" (some are even more particular, identifying themselves as *Independent* Baptists,' *Reformed* Baptists,' *Particular* Baptists,' and still others),[22] "Charismatic," "Christadelphian," "Christian-Scientist," "Covenanter," "Ebionite," "Four-Square," "Gnostic," "Holiness," "Maronite," "Methodist," "Millerite," "Moravian," "Mormon (Latter-Day Saints)," "Nestorian," "Nazarene," "Pietist," "Plymouth Brethren," "Puritan," "Quaker," "Russellite," "(Seventh-Day) Adventist," "Socinian," "(Unitarian) Universalist," and more…

This is not to suggest that any of the members of certain denominational or non-denominational movements are automatically not Christians, or that there are not persons among them who sincerely endeavor to devote their lives to God through Christ. There are certainly many who *are*, with their whole hearts, trying to follow the Lord while functioning within the framework of the existing institutions. Likewise, there is nothing *inherently* wrong with the majority of denominational names. Most religious bodies and denominations *do* adopt their respective names based upon important biblical terms and concepts. For example, the fact that God's people are commanded to be *baptized* is certainly true and scriptural (*Baptists*). Similarly, the first followers of Christ were

---

[21] Some identify themselves (or are identified by others as) "four-point Calvinists," "moderate Calvinists," and even, "hyper-Calvinists."

[22] As far back as 1960 it was observed: "There are nearly three hundred separate denominations in America today, including more than twenty five Baptist groups, some of which continue to fragmentize" (William Adams in his introduction to *Life in the Son* by Robert Shank). In 2002, Charles Kimball, an ordained Baptist minister, wrote: "The number of denominations is mind-boggling. Baptists alone, in the United States today, have more than eighty officially recognized groups. These range in size from the Southern Baptist Convention, the largest Protestant denomination in the country, numbering more than sixteen million, to the National Baptist and Progressive National Baptist Conventions to small communions like the Primitive, Free Will, and Seventh-day Baptists." —*When Religion Becomes Evil*, p. 218 (footnote).

Appendix

admonished to live in expectation of his *arrival* or *advent*[23] (*Adventists*). Likewise, Christians are most assuredly called to put their faith in and proclaim the *Evangel* or *Gospel* (*Evangelical*). It might also be said that there is a sense in which all Christians are opposed to and *protestors* of those who would seek to impose false doctrines, fraudulent claims of religious authority, and misrepresentations of the Christian faith (*Protestant*). And, without a doubt, every Christian would *bear witness* and *testify* to the fact that Jehovah (YHWH) is the only true God of the Bible and of creation (*Jehovah's Witnesses*). Yet, when considered in the pure light of the Christian Scriptures, it is clear that none of the above names enjoys explicit apostolic-scriptural approval—and, therefore, divine authorization—as does the name **Christian** (Acts 11:26; 1 Peter 4:16).

When the apostle Paul found that the Christians in Corinth were quarreling among themselves, manifesting a divisive spirit, as they were expressing loyalty and attributing special prominence to certain individuals (including the apostle himself), he said to them: "What I mean is this: One of you says, 'I follow Paul';[24] another, 'I follow Apollos'; another, 'I follow Cephas'; still another, 'I follow Christ.' Then, the apostle asked, "Is Christ divided? Was Paul crucified for you? Were you baptized into the name of Paul? I am thankful that I did not baptize any of you except Crispus and Gaius, so no one can say that you were baptized into my name."[25]

Similar to our own time, men in the days of the apostle were evidently, in some measure, professing loyalty to entities other than, or in addition to, Christ Jesus. *Christians*, however, cannot ultimately be loyal to or dependent upon any human or group of humans; nor do they need to feel pressured into conforming to the demands of a humanly-contrived religious denomination or ecclesiastical hierarchy. Christians throughout history have known only one Owner and Master, the Lord Jesus Christ; for "he is able [now and always, *TEV*] to save completely those who come to God through him, because he always lives to intercede for them" (Hebrews 7:25, *NIV*). The Lord Jesus *himself*

---

[23] Also translated, *coming* or *presence* (Gk: *parousia*).
[24] Lit., "I am of Paul...I am of Apollos..."
[25] 1 Corinthians 1:12-15, *NIV*

Appendix

is "the way, the truth, and the life" (John 14:6), the "one mediator between God and men" (1 Timothy 2:5), and "there is salvation in no one else, for there is no other name under heaven given among men by which we must be saved" (Acts 4:12, *RSV*; compare Ephesians 4:1-6).

The name "Christian" is the name given to and adopted by the followers of Christ in the holy Scriptures. It emphasizes the fact that God's people should be devoted and faithful to the true teachings of his Son Jesus, the Christ. This does not mean that everyone who claims to be Christian is truly a disciple of God's Son; nor does it ignore the fact that religious groups and individuals, throughout history, have gravely misrepresented his true spirit and teachings; and that they will, inevitably, continue to do so in the future.

One of the greatest benefits of the name is that, when rightly understood, it communicates the idea that God's people are followers and promoters of *Christ*—not an imperfect religious leader, denomination, or one particular segment of the "Christian" religions. It must be pointed out, of course, that merely taking on the name, in and of itself, proves nothing.[26] Rather, it is the kind of life that one lives that will ultimately demonstrate the reality of one's profession of the Christian faith (James 3:13, *NRSV*); for the apostle John wrote: "By this we may be sure that we are in [union with, *NAB*] him: he who says he abides in him ought to walk in the same way in which [Jesus Christ] walked" (1 John 2:5-6, *RSV*). And surely, as the apostle Paul wrote, "God's firm foundation stands, bearing this seal: '*The Lord knows those who are his*' and, 'Let everyone who names the name of the Lord depart from iniquity'" (2 Timothy, 2:19, *RSV*).

In the time that we live (as the situation was in the first century), we can be sure that God's people are under no obligation to profess or submit wholesale loyalty to the

---

[26] A Christian of the early second century is alleged to have written: "It is fitting, then, not only to be called Christians, but to be so in reality. For it is not the being called so, but the being really so, that renders a man blessed...Let us therefore prove ourselves worthy of that name which we have received ['therefore, having become His disciples, let us learn to live according to the principles of Christianity.' *Shorter Version*]." —*The Epistle of Ignatius to the Magnesians, Ante-Nicene Fathers*, pp. 61, 63.

doctrines, interpretations, creeds, or theological systems devised by religious men—whether they be of, or represented in, Martin Luther, John Calvin, James Arminius, Joseph Smith, Charles Russell, the Pope, or the Watchtower Society. God's people can still be exclusively devoted to the pure, unadulterated message that comes from God *himself* through his Son Jesus *Christ*, and are therefore *Christians*.

Some noteworthy sayings on being a Christian

"Then, the proconsul urging him, and saying, 'Swear, and I will set thee at liberty, reproach Christ'; 'Polycarp declared, 'Eighty and six years have I served Him, and He never did me any injury: how then can I blaspheme my King and my Saviour?'…And when the proconsul yet again pressed him, and said, 'Swear by the fortune of Caesar,' he answered, 'Since thou art vainly urgent that, as thou sayest, I should swear by the fortune of Caesar, and pretendest not to know who and what I am, hear me declare with boldness, I am a Christian.'" —Polycarp (prior to martyrdom), 2nd century.

"None of these things is hid from you, if ye perfectly possess that faith and love towards Christ Jesus which are the beginning and the end of life. For the beginning is faith, and the end is love. Now these two, being inseparably connected together, are of God, while all other things which are requisite for a holy life follow after them…The tree is made manifest by its fruit; so those that profess themselves to be Christians shall be recognised by their conduct. For there is not now a demand for mere profession, but that a man be found continuing in the power of faith to the end ['Those that profess themselves to be Christ's are known not only by what they say, but by what they practice.', *Longer Version*]." —Epistle of Ignatius to the Ephesians Chapter XIV. (Exhortations to Faith and Love) *Shorter Version*, 2nd century.

"St. Paul, in 1 Cor. 3, would not allow Christians to call themselves Pauline or Petrine, but Christian. How then should I, poor, foul carcass that I am, come to have men give to the children of Christ a name derived from my worthless name? No, no, my dear friends; let us abolish all party names, and call ourselves Christians after Him Whose doctrine we have." —Martin Luther (16th Century)

"The high and mighty of this world have begun to persecute and hate Christ's teaching under the presence of the name of Luther. They call all of Christ's teaching 'Lutheran,' no matter who on earth proclaims it…This is now my fate. I began to preach the Gospel of Christ in 1516, long before anyone in our region had ever heard of Luther…At any rate, Luther did not teach me anything…The papists none of the less burden me and others maliciously with such names and say, 'You be a Lutheran, for you preach the way Luther

Appendix

writes.' I answer them, 'I preach the way Paul writes. Why do you not also call me a follower of Paul? Indeed, I proclaim the word of Christ. Why do you not call me a Christian?'" —Huldrych Zwingli (16th century), quoted in De Lamar Jensen, *Reformation Europe, Age of Reform and Revolution*, p. 102.

"Would God that all party names and unscriptural phrases and forms which have divided the Christian world were forgotten, and that we, as humble, loving disciples, might sit down at the Master's feet, read His Holy Word, imbibe His Spirit and transcribe His life into our own…With regard to the name Christian, I would say, there is none like it; give it to me, and in life and in death I would glorify God in this name." —John Wesley (1703-1791), Quoted in C. C. Crawford, *Sermon Outlines on the Restoration Plea*, 2nd ed., p. 47

"Whosoever will list himself under the banner of Christ, must, in the first place, and above all things, make war upon his own lusts and vices. It is in vain for any man to usurp the name of Christian, without holiness of life, purity of manners, and benignity and meekness of spirit…If the Gospel and the apostles may be credited, no man can be a Christian without charity, and without that faith which works, not by force, but by love." —John Locke, *A Letter Concerning Toleration* (1689), pp. 13-14.

"Since you would know by what name I would be distinguished from others, I tell you I would be, and hope I am, a Christian; and choose, if God should count me worthy, to be called a Christian, a believer, or other such name which is approved by the Holy Ghost. And as for those factious (or sect) titles of Anabaptist, Presbyterian, Independent, and the like, I conclude that they came neither from Antioch nor from Jerusalem, but from Hell and Babylon, for they tend to divisions; you may know them by their fruits." —John Bunyan, *Pilgrim's Progress* (1678)

"It is, however, an honored name—the most honorable appellation that can be conferred on a mortal. It suggests at once to a Christian the name of his great Redeemer; the idea of our intimate relation to him; and the thought that we receive him as our chosen leader, the source of our blessings, the author of our salvation, the fountain of all our joys. It is the distinguishing name of all the redeemed. It is not that we belong to this or that denomination…it is not that they stand high in courts, and among the frivolous, the fashionable, and the rich, that true honor is conferred upon men. These are not the things that give distinction and specialty to the followers of the Redeemer. It is that they are 'Christians.' This is their special name; by this they are known; this at once suggests their character, their feelings, their doctrines, their hopes, their joys. This binds them all together—a name which rises above every other appellation; which unites in one the inhabitants of distant nations and tribes of men; which connects the extremes of society, and places them in most important respects on a common level; and which is a bond to unite in one family all those who love the Lord Jesus, though dwelling in different climes, speaking different languages, engaged in different pursuits in life, and

Appendix

occupying distant graves at death. He who lives according to the import of this name is the most blessed and eminent of mortals." —Albert Barnes (1798-1870), *Barnes Notes on the New Testament,* Commentary on Acts 11:26

"To be a Christian is precisely the same thing as to be a Disciple of Jesus Christ. A Disciple, to speak in general terms, is one who acknowledges any one as his teacher, and faithfully follows his instructions...To be a disciple of Jesus Christ two things are necessary: to receive him as an Instructor, and to obey him as a Master. (1.) To receive Christ as a teacher, to regard him as the instructor of our souls, at whose feet we are ready to sit as humble docile pupils, and receive without question whatever he may communicate respecting God, and his character, and divine purposes. He that is thus eager and willing to learn of Jesus as God's appointed Teacher, or which is the same thing, to take his religion from the New Testament, is so far a Christian. And he has perfect claim to the title, when (2.) he carries into practical effect those instructions, and faithfully conforms himself to them in heart, disposition, and conduct. This faith and confidence in him as a divine Teacher and obedience to him as a Saviour, constitute a Christian. Some, however, will step in here, and tell us that this is not sufficient. They will name a certain list of doctrines, which it is necessary to believe that Jesus taught, and declare that no one is a Christian, who does not hold a certain specified form and number of religious articles.—To such I answer, who told you so? Who has given you a right to say, that there is only one sect in all Christendom which contains true disciples? For in fact the assertion amounts to this:—just as if it were not more pleasing to our Lord, that one should come to him and learn of him with right dispositions and faithful endeavors, than that he should simply attain a correct set of abstract opinions. There is not a passage in the New Testament, which requires a completely unerring faith, before one can be numbered with the disciples of Christ. I can point to a multitude of passages which require a life without error; but I do not remember one which requires a faith without error.—On the contrary, I recollect we are told 'to receive the weak in faith,' and, what is more, to receive them without 'doubtful disputations' (Rom. 14:1). I recollect too, that while the twelve were always acknowledged by their living Master as his disciples, they had many great errors of faith, even in respect to the nature of his kingdom. But then they were humble, sincere, diligent, learners,—they listened to him and followed him, and placed all their confidence in him; and therefore, notwithstanding their errors, they were received by him.—It is plain, therefore, that no man is to be refused the Christian name solely on account of the supposed imperfection of his faith. They that have drawn up their articles, and declare that all who do not conform to them are not Christians, are trying men by a wrong standard,—a standard, which their Master himself, by his conduct to his disciples, has discountenanced...I have stated these two cases strongly, because it is easiest thus to test the principle. Upon such cases, and they are by no means imaginary, there can be no difference of opinion; and they prove, that it is perfectly absurd to pretend that any certain set of opinions, beyond an acknowledgment of the divine authority of Jesus Christ and his gospel, is

Appendix

essential to a Christian, or constitutes a Christian. They prove to us further,—that he is a genuine Disciple, who, having patiently and humbly learned of Jesus whatever he teaches, and cast himself on his gospel for salvation, faithfully cultivates his spirit, and forms his character according to that teaching and his example. This is a definition which cannot be set aside. This will hold good amidst all the opposition of zeal and bigotry. This, in all practical decisions ever has been and ever must be appealed to, by the sober common sense and unanimous judgment of the whole Christian world...How important, then, is it for us to avoid the error of making our private opinions the standard by which to judge the claims of our fellow men. It is not the right standard by which to try ourselves; much less by which to try others. We cannot go beyond their general characters; and if their characters, under a charitable construction, are agreeable to the upright and devout spirit of the gospel, it is to the last degree arrogant and criminal in us to deny them the Christian name. We may think their opinions erroneous, and say so, if we please; but to denounce them as not Christians, because it is our opinion that their opinions are erroneous—words cannot express the absurdity." —Henry Ware (1764–1845)

"It will be seen, therefore, that while we claim to be Christians only, we do not claim to be the only Christians. Our principles will not allow us to be anything else; and we strive to have others satisfied with being the same. Hence the charge so often made, that we arrogate to ourselves alone the name Christian, is false. We simply decline to be more than this, because God's people in the New Testament times were nothing more. To those who love the simplicity of apostolic Christianity this position will commend itself with great force." —F. G. Allen, *"Our Strength and Our Weakness,"* in *New Testament Christianity*, Vol. 2, ed., p. 245 (1926)

"My brethren are Christians only. They have joined nothing of any kind. They have accepted the Lord Jesus Christ and in Him they worship God and serve their fellows. In this position they are entirely free from any responsibility for the divisions that exist. There is no denominational wall around us. All Christians on earth, all who have believed and obeyed Christ, are our brethren...We are separated from all denominational believers by the walls which *they* have erected about themselves. They are separated from each other by these same walls. Our plea is for these walls to come down, for all who believe in Christ to be left free under God in their local congregations to study, understand and practice the word of God, without the intervention of denominational authority or consideration for denominational creeds or confessions." —Jesse P. Sewall, *"Undenominational Christianity,"* *Abilene Christian College Lectures of 1922-23* (Abilene, TX: Abilene Christian College, 1923), p. 140. Emphasis added.

"The name 'Christian' is a name broad enough and great enough to include every being in the wide, wide world who accepts and obeys the teaching of the Lord Jesus Christ...Simply because one is obedient to Christ and wears the name 'Christian' is no indication that he feels he has a copyright on that name. I would to God that every man who is a Christian would wear that name and no other to indicate his religion. One child of God does not need to be distinguished or separated from another child of God. God's children should be one in purpose, one in spirit, and one in life. They are not to be divided and contending over names as did the church at Corinth. Such division produced carnality, and carnality leads to death. I would like to be helpful in bringing all Christians to the point that they are willing to lose sight of human names and wear simply the name of Christ." —J. C. McQuiddy, "*The Name 'Christian',*" *Gospel Advocate* (Oct. 14, 1920): 1003-1004

"I have never been so egotistic to say that my brethren with whom I commune on the fist day of the week are the *only* Christians on this earth. I never said that in my life. I do make the claim that we are Christians *only*. But there is a vast difference between that expression and the one formerly made. But you ask what my objective is…I am trying to get all of God's people everywhere to stand together as a solid phalanx against the opposing forces now working to destroy the church of our Lord. I know that the cause of Christ needs its full strength. I know that in unity alone strength can exist, and I think it a calamity for those who claim to believe the Bible, to reverence Jehovah, and to wear the name of Christ at all, to stand thus divided, and thereby invite the enemy to a victory over our scattered forces." —N. B. Hardeman, *Hardeman's Tabernacle Sermons, Vol. 3* (Nashville: Gospel Advocate Co., 1928), p. 125

"We are strictly unsectarian, and consequently recognize no sectarian name, believing with Paul, (read 1 Cor. 3:1-4) that where one saith I am of Paul, and I am of Apollos, or I am a Baptist, or I am a Methodist, etc., it is an evidence of *carnality*, and consequently in opposition to the Spirit of Christ. Did Paul or Apollos die for us? If so, let us call ourselves theirs. Were we baptized into the Methodist, Presbyterian, Baptist, or other denominational churches? If so, we *are* members of it, and should be properly recognized by those names. But if we were baptized into the one body or church of which Jesus is the one and only Head, then we are *members* in particular of his body, and the only appropriate name would be his; Scripturally called 'Church of Christ,' 'Christians,' 'Church of the first born,' and such general names…We have no creed (fence) to bind us together or to keep others out of our company. The Bible is our only standard, and its teachings our only creed…We are in fellowship with all Christians in whom we can recognize the Spirit of Christ, and especially with those who recognize the Bible as their only standard. We do not require, therefore, that all shall see, just as we do in order to be called Christians; realizing that growth in both grace and knowledge is a gradual process…If all Christians were to thus free themselves of prescribed creeds, and study the Word of God without denominational bias, truth and knowledge and real Christian fellowship and unity, would result. The Spirit of the Head would pervade the unfettered members of the body, and sectarian pride would vanish…We always refuse to be called by any other name than that of our Head—Christians—continually claiming that there can be no division among those continually lead by his Spirit and example as made known through his

Appendix

Word." —Charles Russell (1882)

"More and more sensitive persons are coming to the conclusion that something is wrong with the entrenched and divided state of people who claim to follow the same Lord and profess the same hope of eternal life in him...We have come to the point where practically everyone who professes Christianity has to have another 'label' for identification purposes. In the contexts of our religious division, each of us feels compelled to tag himself with an identifying term in addition to *Christian* in order to be specific about the people he or she claims as a spiritual fellowship...Yet practically everyone will agree that the original, first-century followers of Jesus of Nazareth were simply and only *Christians*...All denominational bodies maintain their identities by means of divisive creeds, human names, particular organizational structures, and the like. All of them appeal to the Bible—but the appeal is to the Bible *plus* some additional confession, approved interpretation, or clergy-prepared catechism. It is not Scripture that keeps the members of these various denominations apart from other believers. It is human formulations of faith in addition to the Bible which divide and separate...By giving up human names, human creeds, and human institutions, one can embrace a simpler faith which requires nothing as a test of fellowship except those things in Scripture which relate to Christ and eternal life in him. Christ is the only creed; Scripture is the only standard for faith and practice; and no human being or clergy council can sit in judgment on one's personal faith...It is possible, then, for people to be Christians, *just Christians*, and to experience corporate life in local assemblies which are *churches* in the New Testament sense of that term. If you doubt that such a thing could happen, you have forgotten the first several pages of the book of Acts. It is exactly how the church in the first century began. Individuals responded to the preaching of the gospel of Christ and were baptized in the name of Jesus. They met in small groups—what we would call 'house churches' (cf. Rom. 16:4-5; Phile. 2) or small local assemblies—first in Jerusalem, then in Samaria and Antioch, Corinth and Ephesus...Surely the appreciation I feel for Luther, Wesley, and Cambell is something like that I felt for Apollos, Paul, and Cephas by Christians at Corinth. But God forbid that we form societies of 'Lutherans,' 'Wesleyans,' or 'Cambellites'! Instead, let us learn whatever we can from these—or any other godly persons—which can point us to Christ. Then let us wear Christ's name, proclaim the gospel to the lost, worship as the first-century church did, and serve our fellow human beings in the spirit of compassion our Lord demonstrated among men. Doing so will produce unity in Christ; failing to do so will perpetuate the divisions already in existence...There are sincere, knowledgeable, and devout Christians scattered among the various denominations. Yet they are separated from one another by creedal formulations, human names, and cumbersome organizational structures which have found their way into the stream of human history since the time of Christ and the apostles. Let such divisions end. Let's just be *Christians only* and stand together in shared devotion to our Savior and mutual submission to his authoritative will." —*I Just Want to Be a Christian*, by Rubel Shelly (1984, 1986), pp.11, 27, 13, 17, 158

Appendix

"The concerted attempt of the Calvinistic Baptists to equate Calvinism with Baptist Orthodoxy is not shared by their Presbyterian and Reformed 'cousins.' These two groups are basically the same in doctrine: the term *Reformed* emphasizing the doctrines of the Reformation and the term *Presbyterian* emphasizing their form of church government...So Calvinism is to be equated with Reformed theology—not just by mere acquiescence, but being a fully cognate term. The aforementioned D. James Kennedy relates why he is a Presbyterian: 'I am a Presbyterian because I believe that Presbyterianism is the purest form of Calvinism.' ...One cannot be a Presbyterian or Reformed without being a Calvinist, but one certainly can be a Baptist. A Calvinistic Baptist should be a misnomer, because, in the words of the Dutch Reformed Herman Hanko: 'A Baptist is only inconsistently a Calvinist'...beginning in the time of Edward, there arose a party in England who desired a more complete reformation, although it was not till later that they acquired the name *Puritans*...The label *Arminian* was now used by Puritans to impugn those who rejected Calvinism. Arminianism (opposition to Calvinism) was termed Pelagianism. But as usual, some did not go along with the contrived Calvinist-Arminian debate...Richard Montagu (1577-1641) asserted that 'he was neither an Arminian, nor a Calvinist, nor a Lutheran, but a Christian.'"
—Vance, *The Other Side of Calvinism,* pp. 26-28; 169

"I am convinced that any theology and any council—however much it is to be understood in terms of its time and the time preceding it—must, insofar as it claims to be Christian, ultimately be judged by the criterion of what is Christian. And the criterion of what is Christian—also according to the view of the councils and popes—is the original Christian message, the gospel, indeed the original figure of Christianity: the concrete, historical Jesus of Nazareth, who for Christians is the Messiah..." —Hans Küng, *The Catholic Church, A Short History*, p. 23

"...we find no admonition in the Greek Scriptures to identify and join the right 'association.' Why? Because early Christians were disciples or followers of a *person*! Each individual who became a Christian took on the responsibility to follow Jesus' teachings, not just to find and join the 'right organization.' Their discipleship of and relationship with Jesus was defined by changed attitudes and behavior, not membership in a particular group...*The first Christians focused their attention on following Jesus, living in a way that showed that they were submitting to God and that they appreciated what God had done for them through Jesus* instead of organizational structure, tradition, external rites, unique interpretations or novel explanations of Scripture passages... [The early Christians did not] focus their attention on the Father apart from his official representative, Jesus Christ. Since Jesus represented his Father perfectly, and was given all authority in heaven and earth, their focus on Jesus in no way detracted from his Father, for it was the Father's will that all honor the Son just as they honor the Father: 'He who does not honor the Son does not honor the Father, who sent him.' (John 5:23) Jesus had told them that they would be *his* witnesses to the most distant part of the earth. (Acts

Appendix

1:8) *That is why Jesus' followers were called Christians.* They were his servants, for Jesus said: 'My Father will honor the one who serves me.' — John 12:26...The Scriptures clearly teach that those who truly follow Jesus can be identified primarily by their godly behavior. This is not merely an appearance of godly acts driven by selfishness or the desire for personal prominence, but the genuine article, motivated by deep love for God, which results in obedience to his commands. These true Christians are where you find them. Jesus has been and will continue to be absolutely, completely successful in finding all of his sheep. Each one hears his voice, and he will not lose even one of them. (Jn 6:39; 10:14)" —Tom Cabeen, *Where is the Body of Christ?*

[Christ's] call is, 'Come to **me**.' not come to an organization or to a church or denomination. (Matthew 11:28)...Because of the traditional mentality that has been perpetuated over the centuries, many are not able to grant full acceptance to another person who is not identified as approved by their particular group standard. Therefore, their aim will always be to have others become members of their movement—denominational or non-denominational. Sadly, this sectarian spirit makes it difficult for them to accept as children of God persons who do not belong to their movement and often confines them to association that narrows their love and stunts their spiritual growth...Whatever form a sectarian spirit may take, it is spiritually detrimental and is one that all seeking to be loyal disciples of Jesus Christ must resist...Many people do rise above the extreme manifestation of the sectarian spirit but are still negatively impacted by theological views that developed after the first century. A conditioned doctrinal orientation may interfere with their being able to develop a heartfelt appreciation of Christ's role in leading them to the Father. (1 Peter 3:18)...A proper recognition of who we are can prevent elevating any individual or group of individuals, attributing to them the kind of teaching authority that belongs exclusively to Jesus Christ. No human has the right to claim preeminence, for Christ alone is 'the firstborn among many brothers.' (Romans 8:29, *NIV*)...Individually, we are fellow brothers, listening to our senior brother's teaching. While some of us may grasp his instruction a little better and, in turn, may be able to teach fellow believers by calling to their attention what he taught, we remain fellow learners. Any fellowship among members of the family of God's children should harmonize with Jesus' words: 'You are not to be called 'Rabbi,' for you have only one Master and you are all brothers. And do not call anyone on earth 'father,' for you have one Father, and he is in heaven. Nor are you to be called 'teacher,' for you have one Teacher, the Christ. The greatest among you will be your servant.'" — Matthew 23:8-12, *NIV*." (From the essays "*What Can I do?*" and "*The Importance of Having a Personal Relationship with God and His Son*" by Commentary Press)

"That not all who subsequently took the name 'Christian' truly were such is evident. Christ Jesus warned of apostasy in his parable of the wheat and the weeds. The apostle Paul, who was known as a 'Christian,' echoed that

Appendix

warning in his writings. In the Revelation, the apostle John laid bare the impure adulterated state already existing in some congregations in his day. It was clearly recognized that there would be false Christians, many of them. But neither Paul nor John nor any of the Bible writers indicated that a change of name would in any way remedy the situation. It was not by the adoption of some different name, a new label as it were, but by means of a *life course* that exemplified genuine Christianity and by means of *adherence to truth* as found in the teachings of God's Son and his apostles and disciples that the only meaningful distinction could be made. When the angels of God carry out the final part of the parabolic picture in effecting the harvest of the wheat from the weeds, labels in the form of denominational names surely will play no part...God's Son gave the assurance that he would have true followers, not just in the first century or in this twentieth century, but in all the centuries in between, for he said, 'I am with you *always, to the close of the age.*' Intermixed though they were among all the 'weeds' that were bound to come, he would know who these genuine disciples were, *not* because they belonged to some organization but because of what they *were*, as *persons*. Wherever they were, however indistinguishable from the human standpoint their being part of his congregation may have been, down through the centuries he has known them, not only collectively but *individually*, and led them as their Head, their Master...God's Word shows that it is not up to men—not even possible for men—to separate people out so as to say that they have now gathered all the 'wheat' into one neat enclosure. The Scriptures make clear that only when God's Son makes known his judgments will that identification become manifest." —Franz, *In Search of Christian Freedom*, pp. 491-492

"[Prior to disaffiliating from near life-long membership in one religious organization] The question is asked, Where then do I go? What do I become? I feel no need to 'go' anywhere. For I know the One who has the 'sayings of everlasting life.' (John 6:68) I appreciate the strengthening companionship of those I have with whom to associate (either personally or by correspondence) and hope that the future will add to my acquaintance with yet other sincere persons whose concern is for truth, not simply in doctrine, in words, but as a way of life. (1John 3:18)...I am simply trying, then, to be a Christian, a disciple of God's Son. I cannot see why anyone would want to be anything else. I cannot understand how anyone could hope to be anything more." —Franz, *Crisis of Conscience*, p. 406

"The name *Christian* embodies within itself, in a more generic form, all the obligations specifically expressed by the other names ['saint,' 'disciple,' 'brother,' 'child of God']. Being derived from the name of him who is 'head over all things for the Church,' whose name is above every name, it is a title of peculiar honor and glory. It calls upon the man who wears it to act a part in consonance with the historic memories which cluster around it, and encourages him with the reflection that he wears a high dignity even when despised and spit upon by the powers of earth. So thought Peter, when this name was most despised...Not to multiply words upon this point, it is

Appendix

sufficiently evident, from the above considerations, that parties and party names among Christians should be obliterated. If we say that it is *impossible* to obliterate them, we are simply saying that it is impossible to bring Christians back to the New Testament model—for, in the New Testament period, there were no such divisions, and therefore a restoration of that state of the Church would be the destruction of parties and party names. If this is impossible, it can only be from one cause, and that is, that men professing to take the word of God as their guide are so hypocritical in this profession, that they will, at all hazard, persevere in despising its authority in reference to a prominent item of duty. How shameful it is, that men will uphold parties and party names, which they know perfectly that a strict conformity to the New Testament would utterly destroy!...Those who love God must break loose at once, as individuals, from the bondage of party, and take a position where they may be upholders of no party, and wearers of no party name. All who act thus will find themselves planted together on the plain letter of the Scriptures, as their only rule of faith and practice." —McGarvey's *Commentary on Acts*

> *"If you are insulted because of the name of Christ, you are blessed, for the Spirit of glory and of God rests on you. If you suffer, it should not be as a murderer or a thief or any other kind of criminal, or even as a meddler. However, if you suffer as a Christian, do not be ashamed, but praise God that you bear that name."*
> —1 Peter 4:14-16, *New International Version*

Appendix

יהוה

"...I have remembered your name O Jehovah...."
—Psalm 119:55

In most English translations of the Bible, whenever the title 'LORD' or 'GOD' appears (all capital letters), it always denotes these four Hebrew characters (above, read from right to left),—transliterated into English as **YHWH** or **JHVH**—generally referred to by Bible scholars as the "Tetragrammaton," meaning "four letters." These four letters represent the unique and personal name of God, "**Jehovah**" (*American Standard Version*) or "**Yahweh**" (*Jerusalem Bible*). The name occurs nearly 7000 (6,828) times throughout the Hebrew Scriptures or Old Testament. As one Bible Dictionary points out:

> The God of Israel is called by His personal name more frequently than by all other titles combined; the name not only identified the person, it revealed his character.[27]

Many believe that in the Hebrew language the divine name was originally pronounced as "Yahweh," and it is rendered as such in several modern English translations.[28] However, it is more likely that the name was originally pronounced in a three syllable form, as "**Yeh·o·wah**"[29] or "**Yah·u·wah**," or some such variation. Yet it remains true to say that no one knows with certainty how the name of God was precisely pronounced when

---

[27] *McKenzie Dictionary of the Bible,* p. 316.
[28] George Buchanan observed: "Only from Theodoret's Greek spelling of the Samaritan use of the term is there any basis for the pronunciation 'Yahweh' or 'Jahveh.' This is hardly enough evidence to overpower all of the other exhibits. When the name was pronounced with three syllables, it was 'Yahowah' or 'Yahuwah.'" —*"Some Unfinished Business With the Dead Sea Scrolls," Revue De Qumran* 13.49-52 (1988), p. 416.
[29] See: George W. Buchanan, *"How God's Name Was Pronounced," Biblical Archaeology Review* 21.2 (March-April 1995); "Some *Unfinished Business With the Dead Sea Scrolls," Revue De Qumran* 13.49-52 (1988).

Appendix

it was originally revealed in antiquity.[30]

In *The Bible, An American Translation*, the editor made the following comments regarding the translation of the divine name in the English Bible:

> In this translation we have followed the orthodox Jewish tradition and substituted 'the Lord' for the name 'Yahweh' and the phrase 'the Lord God' for the phrase 'the Lord Yahweh.' In all cases where 'Lord' or 'God' represents an original 'Yahweh' small capitals are employed. Anyone, therefore, who desires to retain the flavor of the original text has but to read 'Yahweh' wherever he sees Lord or God.[31]

Everett Fox, translator of the *Shocken Bible*, explained his preferred method of translating the sacred name of the Almighty as follows:

> The reader will immediately notice that the personal name of the Biblical God appears in this volume as 'YHWH.' That is pretty standard scholarly practice, but it does not indicate how the name should be pronounced... While the visual effect of 'YHWH' may be jarring at first, it has the merit of approximating the situation of the Hebrew text as we now have it, and of leaving open the unresolved question of the pronunciation and meaning of God's name...Historically, Jewish and Christian translations of the Bible into English have tended to use 'Lord,' with some exceptions...Both old and new attempts to recover the 'correct' pronunciation of the Hebrew name have not succeeded; neither the sometimes-heard 'Jehovah' nor the standard scholarly 'Yahweh' can be conclusively proven.

Although it is suggested that "Jehovah"[32] and "Yahweh" cannot be legitimized by conclusive evidence, both forms *do* have the merit of preserving the four consonants of the Hebrew Tetragrammaton ('YHWH' or the Latinized 'JHVH'), and most

---

[30] Other suggested forms for the original pronunciation of the divine name include variations like: "Yehuwah," "Yahowah," and "Yahuweh."

[31] *Preface to the American Translation*, p. 15.

[32] The form "Jehovah," however, is not an attempt to recover the correct pronunciation of the Hebrew original; it is an anglicized (English) form of the Hebrew-language name, as is "Jesus" (pronounced originally in Hebrew as 'Yeshua' or 'Yehoshua,' or the like).

Appendix

English Bible translations that include the name of God use either of these two forms. Consequently, both forms are familiar to most English-speaking Bible students and generally make possible for easy and immediate identification.

Some theologians have taken issue against the English form "Jehovah," referring to it as a "hybrid" and as an "erroneous pronunciation." It has been pointed out that God's name could never have been pronounced that way, and that today, if we make use of it, the name should be consistently pronounced and translated as "Yahweh." The claim of Bible translators, however, has never been that God's name was *originally* pronounced as "Jehovah." *Jehovah* is simply the form that conforms to normal English usage with respect to Hebrew names in the Bible. For example, in Hebrew, the name "Isaiah" was probably pronounced originally as "*Yeshayahu.*" Similarly, the English "Jerusalem" was, in Hebrew, likely pronounced "*Yerushalaim.*" "Jesus" was pronounced "*Yeshua*" or "*Yehoshua*" (Greek: *I·e·sous*). Neither of these names represents the *original* Hebrew/Aramaic or Greek pronunciations. It is, in fact, perfectly normal and proper for names to take on different pronunciations when they are transferred into a different language, as is made evident from the New Testament writings themselves. In Hebrew, God's name was possibly pronounced "*Yeh·o·wah*"; in Spanish it is "*Jehová* (pronounced: 'he-o-vá')"; in standard, contemporary English we say "*Jehovah,*" in accordance with the name's already-recognized status as part of the English language.

The chart below helps to illustrate how the pronunciation of biblical names commonly changes when used in different languages:

Hebrew	Spanish	English
Yeshua	Jesús (*he·soos*)	Jesus
Yerushalayim	Jerusalén (*her·oo·sa·lén*)	Jerusalem
Yehowah	Jehová (*he·o·váh*)	Jehovah

Appendix

Steven Byington, translator of *The Bible in Living English* (1972), made the following remarks regarding the name and pronunciation:

> ...the spelling and the pronunciation are not highly important. What is highly important is to keep it clear that this is a personal name. There are several texts that cannot be properly understood if we translate this name by a common noun like 'Lord,' or, much worse, by a substantivized adjective [for example, 'the Eternal'].

The avoidance of pronouncing God's name by Jews of latter times likely resulted from a misunderstanding of one of the "Ten Words" or "Ten Commandments"—"Thou shall not take the name of the LORD [Jehovah] thy God in vain" (Exodus 20:7, *KJV*). As one source commented:

> Whenever [Jewish] readers came to the word YHWH, they read *adonai* ['lord'], lest they should 'blaspheme' God by pronouncing his name out loud. *Never did God Himself require them to takes such measures*, but that is how they interpreted Exodus 20:7...In order to ensure that they would not take his name in vain, they simply refused to speak His name at all. It is hard to imagine that God intended such an extreme position, considering the fact that his name occurs 6,823 [or 6,828] times in the Old Testament. Furthermore, God inspired a Psalmist to say that he would call on 'the name of [Jehovah]" in response to His goodness...[33]

The Concise Bible Dictionary based upon the *Illustrated Bible Treasury* states:

> The Jews out of reverence for the holy name, shrank from pronouncing it, and wherever it occurs in the Old Testament, read 'Adonai'; and this practice, which prevailed from at least the third century b.c., influenced the translators.

Commenting further on the suppression of the divine name, the introduction to *Rotherham's Emphasized Bible* has the

---

[33] Graiser, Lynn, Schoenheit, *One God & One Lord, Reconsidering the Cornerstone of the Christian Faith*, p. 326 (emphasis added).

following observation:

> ...it remains true to say, that in our public versions the one especial Name of God is suppressed, wholly concealed from the listening ear, almost as completely hidden from the hastening or uncritical eye...It is therefore the most natural presumption that the suppression of The Name has entailed on the reader, and especially upon the hearer, irreparable loss...The passages commonly cited as furnishing good reason for the suppression cannot mean what is attributed to them, since there is a wide distinction between not taking His Name in vain, and not taking His Name into our lips at all, even for prayer or praise. In a word, the motive is respected; but the reverence is regarded as misapplied—the reason is seen to be invalid.

Another example of what is commonly offered as a justification for why translators render God's name as "LORD" (rather than his actual name) is found in the opening pages of the *NASB* (1979). In its preface the translators state the following:

> In the Scriptures, the name of God is most significant and understandably so. It is inconceivable to think of spiritual matters without a proper designation for the Supreme Deity...There is yet another name which is particularly assigned to God as His special or proper name, that is, the four letters YHWH (Exodus 3:14 and Isaiah 42:8). This name has not been pronounced by the Jews because of reverence for the great sacredness of the divine name. Therefore, it was consistently pronounced and translated LORD.

It is certainly true that God's name is sacred and that his people are to treat his name with great reverence. But what is frequently overlooked by many is the fact that the above reasoning offered for substituting the divine name with the title 'LORD' is, in reality, an appeal to an extra-biblical Jewish tradition/superstition rather than an appeal based upon the actual Scriptures themselves. There is no evidence in the Bible indicating that God ever willed or purposed that his people follow such a practice, particularly when reading aloud from the Hebrew portion of the holy Scriptures, where the name occurs

Appendix

nearly 7000 times. It must be remembered that the Jews who initiated and followed the practice of substituting the name *Adonai* (Lord) and *Elohim* (God) for YHWH were not the same noteworthy and exemplary *biblical* men of faith like Abraham, Moses, or David; nor were they the God-appointed prophets of ancient Israel, like Elijah, Isaiah, Jeremiah, Daniel, and Ezekiel. The faithful men of the Bible, in fact, called upon God's name and exhorted others to do the same. The psalmist was inspired to write "[Oh give thanks unto Jehovah, **call upon his name**; (*ASV*)] make known among the nations what he has done. Sing to him, sing praise to him; tell of all his wonderful acts. **Glory in his holy name**" (Psalm 105:1-3, *NIV*). Solomon wrote, "**The name of Jehovah *is* a tower of strength**; the righteous runs into it, and is set on high [given protection, *NWT*]" (Proverbs 18:10, *LITV*). The *New Jerusalem Bible* has the words of God declared through the prophet rendered: "I am Yahweh, and there is no other God except me. Though you do not know me, I have armed you so that it may be known from east to west that there is no one except me. **I am Yahweh and there is no other**" (Isaiah 45:5-6, *NJB*; compare Matthew 6:9; John 12:28; 17:6).

Although the majority of English Bible translators were influenced by the long-held Jewish tradition of replacing God's name with *adonai* (LORD), there are several modern English translations that fortunately do not follow that practice. Concerning the rendering of the sacred name as Jehovah, the Preface to the *American Standard Version* (1901) states:

> The change first proposed in the Appendix—that which substitutes 'Jehovah' for 'Lord' and 'God' (printed in small capitals)—is one which will be unwelcome to many, because of the frequency and familiarity of the terms displaced. But the American Revisers, after careful consideration, were brought to the unanimous conviction that a *Jewish superstition*, which regards the Divine Name as too sacred to be uttered, ought no longer to dominate in the English or any other version of the Old Testament, as it fortunately does not in the numerous versions made by modern missionaries. This Memorial Name, explained in Ex.iii. 14, 15, and emphasized as such over and over in the original text of the Old

Appendix

Testament, designates God as the personal God, as the covenant God, the God of revelation, the Deliverer, the Friend of his people; not merely the abstractly 'Eternal One' of many French translations, but the ever living Helper of those who are in trouble. This personal name, with its wealth of sacred associations, is now restored to the place in the sacred text to which it has an unquestionable claim.[34]

An article in the *International Standard Bible Encyclopedia* (Vol. II, p. 1266) also pointed out:

> It is illogical, certainly, that the later Hebrews should have shrunk from its pronunciation, in view of the appropriateness of the name and of the OT insistence on the personality of God, who as a person has this name. ARV quite correctly adopts the transliteration 'Jehovah' to emphasize its significance and purpose as a personal name of God revealed.

The significance of God's memorial name was revealed to Moses at Exodus 3:14-15, in the account of the burning bush. Although several popular Bible translations render God's words, in his response to Moses' question about his identity, as "**I am that I am** (Hebrew: *'ehyeh asher ehyeh,'* KJV, NKJV, NASB)," several scholarly sources suggest the following:

> Some scholars, however, prefer to take the word as a future, 'I will be,' in which case the name expresses rather the faithfulness of God, the assurance that He will be with His people as their helper and deliverer. Others, again, take the word to be the causative form of the verb, in which case it will mean, 'He causes to be,' 'the Creator'[35]

> As is always the case in the ancient Near East, *this name is not simply a label for identification, but much more profoundly a revelation of the divine nature.* This means that the meaning of the four consonants YHWH as they appear in the Hebrew Ex.3:15, 6:3 must be seen as a heightening of the awareness of the nature of God as he

---

[34] Preface to the *American Standard Version*, p. 4 (emphasis added).
[35] *The One Volume Bible Commentary*, edited by J.R. Dummelow, p. 51.

Appendix

revealed himself to Moses. There is a contrast drawn in chapter three between the way God revealed himself to the Patriarchs and the way he will now reveal himself to Israel. Before, he was Elohim Shaddai (God Almighty), but now he will be YHWH. It is generally agreed that the divine name here used is a form of the verb *hayah,* 'to be' [better 'to become'], as the various renderings of the name would indicate. It has been rendered 'I will be that I will be' as an indication of God's sovereignty and immutability: or 'I am that I am' with a similar connotation: 'I cause to be what is,' an eye toward God as Creator. Since the revelation of the name of Moses is the opening gesture in the redemption of Israel, however, it is probable that the name contains in it some element of promise pertinent to that redemption. The translation of the name that probably comes closest to the intention of God at this point is 'I will be there,' *which constitutes a promise of the divine presence through all the events of the Exodus and beyond. Understood in this way, God's very name is a promise to his people.*[36]

What follows are other possible nuances of meaning associated with the divine name, as the following versions of the Bible would indicate at Exodus 3:14:

"I WILL BE WHAT I WILL BE."
—*New International Version* (marginal rendering)
"I WILL BE THAT I WILL BE"
—*American Standard Version* (marginal rendering)
"I Will Become whatsoever I please."
—*Rotherham's Emphasized Bible*
"I SHALL PROVE TO BE WHAT I SHALL PROVE TO BE."
—*New World Translation*
"I will be-there howsoever I will be-there."
—*The Shocken Bible*, Everett Fox

The following reference work explains:

In Exodus 3:14 Jehovah is explained as the equivalent to 'ehyeh,' which is a short form of 'ehyeh 'asher 'ehyeh, translated in RV 'I am that I am.'...the imperfect 'ehyeh is more accurately translated "I will be what I will be,' a

---

[36] *Today's Dictionary of the Bible*, pp. 330-331 (emphasis added).

Appendix

> Semetic Idiom meaning 'I will be all that is necessary as the occasion will arise,' a familiar OT idea (cf Is 7 4.9; Ps 23)..., *yahweh*, 'he will be.'...It is the *personal* name of God, as distinguished from such generic or essential names as *'El, 'Elohim, Shadday*, etc. Character knowledge of God as a person; and Jehovah is His name as a person...Then God said unto Moses, I AM THAT I AM...The optional reading in ARVm is much to be preferred: 'I WILL BE THAT I WILL BE,' indicating His covenant pledge to be with and for Israel in all the ages to follow.[37]

Vol. 2, page 507 of *The International Standard Bible Encyclopedia* also states the following regarding the commonly-offered translation "I am that I am":

> 'I will be who/what I will be'...is preferable because the verb *hayah* [to be] has a more dynamic sense of being—not pure existence, but becoming, happening, being present—and because the historical and theological context of these early chapters of Exodus shows that God is revealing to Moses, and subsequently to the whole people, not the inner nature of His being [or existence], but his active, redemptive intentions on their behalf. He 'will be' to them 'what' His deeds will show Him 'to be.'

"My strength and my song is Jah, and he is become my salvation..."
—Psalm 118:14

"**Jah**," in English, is the abbreviated and poetic form of Jehovah in the Bible (represented by the first half of the Tetragrammaton, Y/J and H respectively). The psalmist declared, "Sing unto God, sing praises to his name: extol him that rideth upon the heavens by his name **JAH**, and rejoice before him" (Psalm 68:4, *KJV*). The name Jah is almost always associated with more moving and emotional expressions, like poems or songs of praise and affection expressed for Jehovah. The prophet Isaiah wrote: "Lo, God is my salvation, I trust, and fear not, For my strength and my song is **Jah Jehovah**, And He is to me for

---

[37] *The International Standard Bible Encyclopedia*, Vol. II, pp. 1254-1267.

salvation" (Isaiah 12:2, *YLT*).[38] Expressions of praise to Jah are found throughout the Book of Psalms (fifty times total) and four times in the Book of Revelation: "**Hallelujah!** Salvation and glory and power belong to our God, for true and just are his judgments" (Revelation 19:1-2, *NIV*). The expression "**Hallelujah**" means "**Praise Jah**," literally, "**Praise ye Jah**" (Psalm 148:1, *YLT*) or "**Praise Jah you people!**" (Psalm 146:1, *NWT*). *Rotherham's Emphasized Bible* reads, '**Praise ye Yah**' [*Yah*weh] (Psalm 150:6). "Jah" is also part of the composition of many Hebrew words and names; for example: Elijah ('my God is Jah'), Abijah ('my father is Jah'), Jedidiah ('beloved of Jah'), Jesus ('salvation [or help] of Jah' or, 'Jah saves').

"Jehovah of Armies is his name, the Holy One of Israel."
—Isaiah 47:4

Throughout the Scriptures, God is called, in Hebrew: "**Yahweh Sabaoth**," English: "**Jehovah of hosts**" (*ASV*) or "**Jehovah of Armies**" (*BLE*), "**the LORD of hosts**" (*KJV*). God's prophet observed the seraphim crying, "Holy, holy, holy is Yahweh Sabaoth [Jehovah of Hosts]. His glory fills the whole earth" (Isaiah 6:3 *NJB*). This divine title, "Jehovah of hosts" may originally have been referring to the "hosts" or "armies" of Israel, as in Samuel 17:45, "but at an early date came to comprise all the heavenly powers (that is, the angelic armies or hosts of heaven), ready to carry out Jehovah's command."[39]

Regarding the occurrence of the divine name in the Christian Scriptures or New Testament, one Christian author made the following observation:

> As to the Bible books written in the first century, there is no extant Greek manuscript evidence that the name appeared in any passage (Matthew to Revelation).[40] Regarding the possibility that this was the case in the original text when quotations were made from the

---
[38] *Young's Literal Translation*
[39] See: *The New Bible Dictionary*, J.D. Douglas, p. 431.
[40] However, the shortened form of the divine name "Jah" *does* appear four times in the book of Revelation (19:1-6) in the expression "hallelujah."

Appendix

Hebrew text, George Howard (in a *Hebrew Gospel of Matthew*, 1995) writes: *"The occurrence of the Divine Name in Shem Tob's Matthew [contained in his treatise Even Bohan, a 14th-century polemic work designed to help Jews defend their faith] supports the conclusions I reached in an earlier study of the Tetragrammaton in the New Testament, basing my observations on the use of the Divine Name in the Septuagint and in the Dead Sea Scrolls. Some pre-Christian copies of the Septuagint, for example, contain the Divine Name written into the Greek text...In my previous study, I concluded that the New Testament writers, who had access to such copies of the Septuagint, may have preserved the Tetragrammaton in their biblical quotations from the Septuagint. Now Shem-Tob's Matthew testifies to the use of the Divine Name in the New Testament...[I]t is very unlikely that Shem-Tob inserted the Divine Name into his text. No Jewish polemist would have done that. Whatever the date of this text, it must have included the Divine Name from its inception. One final note regarding the Divine Name: Shem Tob's Matthew shows a very conservative attitude toward its usage. The author of this text was not a radical Christian, arbitrarily supplying the gospel with the Tetragrammaton. His attitude was one of awe and respect. In fact, his use of the Divine Name corresponds to the conservative practice found in the Septuagint and in the Dead Sea Scrolls."* [Note: Shem Tob's Matthew, however, does not use YHWH, but employs "the Name" once and an abbreviated form thereof 18 other times.]

Whatever conclusion as to the written text of the 'New Testament' writings that one may reach on the basis of such evidence, there is no reason to doubt that, when seeing his Father's name in the Scriptures, Jesus would have read what was recorded and would have done likewise when quoting from memory. It was, however, the close filial relationship that Jesus expressed in calling God his Father that enraged the unbelieving Jews. (John 5:17, 18) He repeatedly addressed God as Father and taught his disciples to do the same. (Matthew 6:9; John 14:1-17:26) Therefore, if the divine name did occur in the original Greek manuscripts of the 'New Testament,' this would understandably not have been frequent, the

Appendix

emphasis being on the sonship of Jesus' disciples.[41]

Knowing and calling upon Jehovah's name can contribute to a sense of trust and confidence in the Creator. It can fill believers with great comfort and hope, especially when the significance of the name is understood. That is, there is a far richer meaning involved when one comes to know, truthfully, the *person* represented by that name. The name itself can serve to remind the faithful that God "will always be there," and that he will fulfill every promise he has made to his people in the holy Scriptures—in effect, 'proving to be' what he has declared from the beginning. And even though the Most High God is identifiable as "YHWH," scripturally, it is entirely appropriate for Christians to think of, refer to, and address God in prayer as, **"Our Heavenly Father,"** as Jesus himself did and as he taught his disciples to do (Matthew 6:9, 26; compare Galatians 4:6); and it should never be overlooked that one of the most fitting and unmistakable ways to identify the true God now is by the *apostolic* (divinely authorized) designation found frequently throughout the inspired Christian writings. He is: **"The God and Father of our Lord Jesus Christ**...the Father of Mercies and God of all Comfort..." (Romans 15:6, 2 Corinthians 1:2, 11:31, Ephesians 1:3, 17)

> *"O righteous Father, even though the world does not know you, I know you, and these know that you have sent me. I made known to them your name,*[42] *and I will continue to make it known, that the love with which you have loved me may be in them, and I in them."*
> —Jesus Christ, John 17:25-26, *ESV*

"In the Scriptures there is the closest possible relationship between a person and his name, the two being practically equivalent, so that to remove the name is to extinguish the person (Numb. 27:4; Deut. 7:24). To forget God's name is to depart from Him."
—*Zondervan Pictorical Bible Dictionary*, p. 571 (1964)

---

[41] From the article: *What Can I Do?* by Commentary Press
[42] "I made known to them your name" does not simply mean "I have (merely) made your label for identification known." The "name" here must represent *who* God is and everything he stands for in relation to his people; as the *NIV* puts it, "I have made *you* known to them."

Appendix
en morphē theou

The following is from *Jesus is Lord, Christology Yesterday and Today* (Great Britain: Christian Focus Publications, 2000) pp. 22-24, by Donald Macleod.

Professor Macleod's discussion on the Greek term *"morphe"* (form) is yet another example of a prominent Trinitarian scholar whose objective research compelled him to correct the errors of other Trinitarian scholars who have wrongly attempted to produce proof for the "Trinity" in the New Testament. In this case, Macleod adequately demonstrates the faulty and still commonly-advanced argumentation of distinguished evangelical scholars J. B. Lightfoot (1828-1889) and B. B. Warfield (1851-1921):

> **The Christ-hymn of Philippians**
> In Philippians 2:6 Paul refers to Christ in a way which falls little short of calling him *God*. He speaks of him as being 'in the form of God' (*en morphē theou*). The passage is important not only in its own right, but because it is the key to one of the richest veins of New Testament Christology. In a well-known study, J.B. Lightfoot concluded that *morphē* was the specific character of essence of a thing. He based this conclusion on the use of the word in Plato, Aristotle and later philosophers such as Plutarch. In these writers, a firm distinction is drawn between *morphē* and *schēma*. *Schēma* is the changing, fleeting shape or appearance. *Morphē* is permanent. It is the abstract conception realised, the impress of the idea on the individual essence or object. B.B. Warfield agreed with Lightfoot: 'Form,' he wrote, 'is a term which expresses the sum of those characterizing qualities which make a thing the precise thing that it is...When our Lord is said to be 'in the form of God,' therefore, he is declared in the most express manner possible, to be all that God is, to possess the whole fullness of the attributes which make God God.'
>
> It is highly debatable, however, whether the usage of classical philosophy can be accepted as decisive for the New Testament. It belongs to a different period and a different culture. It is certainly very difficult, with regard to the New Testament, to maintain *morphē/schēma* distinction

Appendix

consistently. In Mark 16:12, for example, we are told that Christ appeared to his disciples in *another form*. Here *morphē* is clearly synonymous with *schema*. The Lord's *appearance* changed. Even some of the instances quoted by Lightfoot in support of his own case really point in the opposite direction: 'We are transformed (*metamorphoumetha*) into the same image' (2 Cor. 3:18); 'Be transformed (*metamorphousthe*) by the renewing of your mind' (Rom. 12:2). Surely the very point here is that *morphē* is not permanent. It may be changed (while essence still remains). The same is true of Jesus' Transfiguration (Matt. 17:2; Mark 9:2). His *morphē* was changed but his essence was not. To adapt Warfield's words, he did not cease to possess the sum total of those characteristics which made him exactly who and what he was.

The clue to the meaning of *morphē* is probably to be found not in the classical philosophers but in the Septuagint. This is the approach taken by, among others, R.P. Martin. In the Septuagint *morphē* is virtually synonymous with *eidos* and *homoioma*, the usual words for *appearance*. This can be seen from such passages as Job 4:16, Isaiah 44:13 and Daniel 3:19. Job 4:16, for example, reads: 'It (a spirit) stood still, but I could not discern its *appearance*. A *form* was before my eyes; there was silence, then I heard a voice' (RSV). The parallelism here makes clear that appearance and form (*homoioma* and *morphē*) are synonymous. *Morphē* is the appearance appropriate to God.

But how can this be, since God is invisible? What appearance or form can be appropriate to God? The answer can only be: 'his glory!' This is what, according to John, Isaiah saw (John 12:41; Isaiah 6:1). It is also what Christ had with the Father before the world was (John 17:5). When Paul speaks of Christ as being in the form of God he is claiming that Christ was no other than the glory (*doxa*) of God.

But this is not a matter of mere inference. It is supported by several direct lines of evidence. For one thing, *morphē* is closely related not only to *eidos* and *homoioma*, but also to *eikon* and *doxa*. In the Septuagint, *eikon*, *morphē* and *doxa* are used interchangeably to render the two Hebrew words *tselem* and *demuth*. For example, in Daniel 3:19, *tselem* is rendered by *morphē*; in Genesis 1:26, it is rendered by *eikon*. The synonymous Hebrew word *demuth* is usually rendered

Appendix

by *eikon*; but in Numbers 12:8 it is rendered by *doxa* and in Job 4:16 it is rendered by *morphe*. It is fair to conclude that the three words *eikon*, *morphē* and *doxa* are broadly synonymous; and that they were closely assocated with the Hebrew words *tselem* and *demuth*.

The effects of this can be clearly seen in the New Testament in various allusions to Genesis 1:27, 'God created man in his own image.' In 1 Corinthians 11:17, for example, Paul alludes to the passage in the words, 'man is the image and glory (*eikon kai doxa*) of God.' In 2 Corinthians 4:4, he speaks of 'the light of the gospel of the glory of Christ, who is the *image* (*eikon*) of God'. Yet two verses later he speaks of 'the knowledge of the *glory* (*doxa*) of God in the face of Jesus Christ.'

We are left, then, with three closely related concepts.

First, Christ is the *image* of God. The most emphatic statement of this is in Colossians 1:15: 'Christ who is the image of the invisible God.' In the immediate context, Paul is emphasizing the cosmic functions of Christ: he antedates creation; creation was made through him; he holds it together; it exists for him; all other existences (especially angelic principalities and powers) are totally dependent on him. But all this rests on something deeper: he is the image of God."

Appendix

The following essay is by Robert Hach (English professor at Miami Dade College and author of *Possession and Persuasion: The Rhetoric of the Christian Faith*), who believes—based on his understanding of the Scriptures—that the Messiah existed before his birth in Bethlehem, not *literally* or *personally*, but as the *purpose* and *promise* of God that would one day become embodied (or made 'flesh') in the man Jesus Christ. The statements made and viewpoints expressed will give some insight into the perspective (and scriptural basis appealed to by) those who believe the Messiah, as an actual person, came into existence as the "Son of God" at the virgin birth.

The Prophetic Pre-existence of the Messiah

By Robert Hach

The question of the so-called "pre-existence" of the Messiah is not settled by a biblically-informed rejection of the doctrine of the Trinity. That the Messiah existed before his birth is clear from many NT texts. In what sense, or form, he existed remains a question insofar as it continues to be a matter of debate among those who believe that Jesus is the Messiah, the Son of God, while refusing to embrace the extra-biblical identification of Jesus as the Trinitarian "God the Son." Regarding the "pre-existence" of the Messiah, the options can be termed *personal pre-existence*, that is, that prior to his birth, the Son existed in some other-than-human form, and *prophetic pre-existence* (the option for which I argue in this paper).

Undeniable, I think, is the fact that the very term *pre-existence* is a product of the post-apostolic debate that gave birth to Trinitarian theology. While it is possible to reject the Trinity as a non-biblical formulation and a post-apostolic invention while, at the same time, retaining the doctrine of the *personal pre-existence* of the Messiah, it is not possible to trace any term that might be translated as *pre-existence* back to apostolic times. The Athanasian-Arian debate that was decided at the Council of Nicea in 325 C.E. seems to have been the cradle out of which emerged the terminology of *pre-existence*, which only afterward became enshrined in Christian theology.

Appendix

The term that, in my view, serves as the biblical equivalent of *pre-existence* is *foreknowledge*. The NT claim that the Messiah "was foreknown before the foundation of the world but was made manifest in the last times" (1 Pet. 1:20) is sufficient, in my view, to explain every NT text in which the concept of *pre-existence* is found.

To say that God the Father *foreknew* the Son "before the foundation of the world" is to say that the Son existed in the purpose of the Father from "the beginning" in the form of "the word" (John 1:1, 'and the word was God' in the sense not that "the word" was part of God's being but that "the word" was, thereafter, the revelatory form which God used to mediate his presence and purpose to his people and to the world).

No textual necessity for interpreting "the word" (Greek, *ho logos*) as a person (or a Person) exists in the prologue of John's Gospel. (The Greek pronoun, *autos*, is susceptible to either the neuter ["it"] or the masculine ["he"] rendering, depending on what the context makes the more likely.) The NT writers uniformly use "the word" to refer to *the gospel*, that is, *the message spoken by and about Jesus*. For the NT writers, "the word" is the message about the fulfillment in Jesus the Messiah of the biblical God's purpose in Adam and promise to Abraham.

When "the word became flesh" (John 1:14), God's Adamic *purpose* and Abrahamic *promise* became God's Messianic *person*. That is to say, the Son existed in the form, first, of God's *purpose* and, then, of God's *promise* before he existed in the form of the *person* of Jesus.

The biblical concept of *foreknowledge* is not compatible with the concept of *personal pre-existence*. If the Son existed as a *person* from "the beginning," how was his existence a matter of God's *foreknowledge*? That God *foreknew* the Messiah would seem to preclude the possibility that God also *knew* him in some *pre-existent* other-than-human form. Rather than God having both *foreknown* the coming Messiah *and known the pre-existent Son* at the same time (though in presumably two radically different *personal* forms), God's *foreknowledge* and his *knowledge* of his Messiah-Son were one and the same. This is the case in the sense that, from a biblical standpoint, what (or whom) God *foreknew* is what God *knew as a foreordained*

Appendix

reality before it came to pass in human history. (This has nothing in common with Calvinistic predestination, which asserts that God has *foreknown* and *foreordained* all that has ever happened or will ever happen; by comparison, biblical predestination is confined to what God *purposed* in Adam and, subsequently, *promised* to Abraham and, therefore, has fulfilled and will fulfill in his Son and Messiah Jesus.)

God's *foreknowledge* of the Messiah, then, is the biblical alternative to the doctrine of *personal pre-existence*. Biblical *foreknowledge* is, in the terminology of *pre-existence*, best represented in terms of *prophetic pre-existence*. That is to say, the existence of the Messiah was, prior to his birth, a matter of *prophecy*. And, from a biblical standpoint, to believe that God had made a promise, conveyed by the words of the prophets (that is, in the form of *prophecy*), was to believe that what God had *promised* (and, therefore, previously *purposed*) had been an inevitable reality from the instant God *purposed* it. (The literary-rhetorical term for this figure of speech is *prolepsis*: to speak of a future event as a present reality; in the case of "the word," however, *prolepsis* becomes far more than a mere figure of speech in that it is a matter of God's righteousness—that is, faithfulness—that what he has promised will inevitably come to pass and, therefore, can be spoken of as a present reality.)

This is consistent with the NT definition of faith: "Now faith is the reality [Greek, *hupostasis*] of things hoped for, the evidence of things not seen" (Heb. 11:1). The existence of the Messiah was a *reality of faith*—a reality in the eyes of God, that is to say, a *prophetic* reality—from its "beginning" as "the word" (John 1:1). The Messiah's existence passed from a *reality of faith* ("the reality of things hoped for") to a *reality of fact* when "the word became flesh" (John 1:14) in the person of Jesus.

Nothing about this idea is alien to the biblical testimony; in fact, the idea of *foreknowledge-as-prophetic-pre-existence* is rooted in the Hebrew prophetic tradition. When God promised to make Abraham "the father of many nations" (Gen. 17:5), Paul pointed out that God spoke as if the promise had created a *present reality*—"as it is written, 'I have made [not 'will make'] you the father of many nations'"—and then calls God the one who "calls into existence the things that do not exist" (Rom.

Appendix

4:17). Literally rendered, Paul wrote that God *calls things not being as being*. Which is to say that what the biblical God spoke in the form of a *promise*—having already been *foreknown* and, therefore, *foreordained* (that is, *predestined*) according to his *purpose* (see Rom. 8:29)—was a *prophetic reality* long before the promise was fulfilled, from the instant that the promise was made. Accordingly, Abraham was "the father of many nations" *in faith*, that is, *prophetically*, long before he became so *in fact*. Likewise, the Son existed—and, further, was crucified and resurrected and exalted—*in faith*, that is, *prophetically*, long before he existed *in fact*, that is, *personally*.

Accordingly, when John's Jesus asks the Father to "glorify me in your own presence with the glory that I had with you before the world existed" (John 17:5), he speaks of "the glory" that God had *purposed* in "the beginning" to manifest in the crucifixion and resurrection of the Messiah. This is clear in that Jesus asks the Father to "glorify me . . . with the glory that I had with you": the very same "glory" that the Father and the Son shared "before the world existed" would now be manifested in Jesus' crucifixion and resurrection. Not a "glory" that was manifested *then* (to whom?) and another "glory" that would be manifested *now* in his crucifixion and resurrection. Rather, the Son asks the Father to "glorify" him now *in fact* and *in person* "with the glory that I had with you" *in faith* and *in prophecy* from "the beginning" (John 1:1). Which is to say that Jesus' prayer to the Father was a prayer *of faith*, arising out of what Jesus *believed* the Father to have *purposed* and *promised* regarding his Messiah.

Only if the Messiah is understood to have been (as he is invariably and consistently affirmed to have been by the NT writers) a fully human being—one whose person originated in his mother's womb—can his *proclamation of the word* and his *crucifixion by the world* be understood as the manifestation of his *faith in the promise of God*. Otherwise, when John's Jesus speaks of his "glory" with the Father, he speaks not out of his faith in "the word" (John 1:1; 3:31-34), through which God revealed his destiny to him, but out of a god-like memory of an extra-human *pre-existence*.

Appendix

(Noteworthy in this regard is the fact that precisely the same construction in the original language for "the faith of Abraham" [Rom. 4:16] appears in multiple Pauline texts regarding faith and Jesus: Rom. 3:22, 26; Gal. 2:16, 20; 3:22; Phil. 3:9. Each of these texts is best understood as contrasting "works of law" with the "faith of" Jesus as the condition of his followers' righteousness, just as "the faith of Abraham" [Rom. 4:16] rather than his works was the condition of Abraham's righteousness. The fact that English NT versions almost invariably render these texts in terms of "faith in" rather than the "faith of" Jesus may be indicative of their Trinitarian bias. A Trinitarian "God the Son" would have had no need for faith. Neither, however, would a Son who could recall a *pre-existence* as a god-like spirit being.)

The NT writers' insistence on Jesus' humanity, and their testimony to his faith in the promise of God, must call into question any interpretation of so-called *pre-existence* texts that would cast doubt on either his exclusive humanity or his faith. The concept of *personal pre-existence* requires that, prior to his conception (laying aside the question of how a *pre-existent* being could be said to have been *conceived*) and birth, the Son must have been *some-other-than-human-kind-of-being* who would not have fit into any biblical category of being—neither God nor human nor angel (at least according to Hebrews 1) nor nonhuman animal. Such a *god-like spirit being* that the Son is believed to have been prior to his birth (?) in the person of Jesus, if he existed, did not begin as a human being but somehow "morphed" into humanity in the process of transitioning through the womb of Mary. (The question here is not whether or not God *could have* created such a being but whether or not the NT writers are best understood as testifying that God did so.)

If this is the case, the NT writers seem to have seen no need to name or explain this unique kind of being. Instead, they were content to repeatedly claim and affirm that he was a fully human being. For the NT writers, the Messiah's uniqueness was not that he was a one-of-a-kind *other-than-human* being before he was human. To the contrary, for them, the uniqueness of the Messiah was that he was a one-of-a-kind *human being* (whose

Appendix

resurrection, according to the NT writers, makes him the prototype for the new humanity of the coming age).

That he was "the firstborn of all creation" (Col. 1:15) identifies Jesus not as a *pre-existent person* but as the one who was *purposed* from the beginning *to inherit* (according to Hebrew tradition, the right of the firstborn son) all things from the Father (see Matt. 28:18; Eph. 1:22; Phil. 2:9-11; etc.). That God created "all things . . . in [Greek, *en*, in other texts not usually rendered 'by'] him" and "through him and for him" (Col. 1:16) does not make him the co-Creator but, rather, means that "the word" that *purposed* and later *promised* his coming was the blueprint and the instrument and the rationale for God's creation (which, after all, agrees with the testimony of Genesis 1 that the biblical God *spoke* his creation into existence).

When Jesus was created in the womb of his mother by the power of God, "the word became flesh" (John 1:14) in that God's promise to send his Messiah to deliver God's people from sin and death through his proclamation of the kingdom, crucifixion for sins, resurrection from the dead, and exaltation to God's side (that is, "the word") was fulfilled (that is, "became flesh").

The biblical concept of *foreknowledge* establishes the *prophetic pre-existence* of the Son in the Adamic *purpose* and, subsequently, in the Abrahamic *promise* of God. Moreover, biblical *foreknowledge* provides a reasonable and sufficient biblical paradigm for interpreting each of the NT texts that are used by both Trinitarian and some non-Trinitarian believers to support the *personal pre-existence* of the Son. Given that this is the case, the burden of proof would seem to rest with those who insist that the Son existed as *some-other-than-human-kind-of-being* in heaven before he existed as a human being on earth.

Appendix

An Alternative Approach to John 1:1-14

The Essay that follows was written by Christian minister Greg Deuble, former member of the Churches of Christ and author of the book *They never told me this in church!, A call to read the Bible with new eyes* (Atlanta: Restoration Fellowship, 2006). The reasoning and argumentation presented represents an alternative, biblically-based approach for understanding John 1:1-14 to the one presented in the main body of this work.

(Used with permission)

John Chapter One

Let us observe first what John's Prologue does *not* say. John did not write, "In the beginning was *the Son* and *the Son* was with God and *the Son* was God." But our inherited tradition automatically makes our eyes run in that groove. One of the reasons we tend to read *into* it this meaning is the very fact that our translations have put a capital "W" for "Word." The capital W subconsciously dictates that we think John means a person when he speaks of "the Word." But for those not familiar with NT Greek rest assured that this is not the case. Every single letter in the earliest Greek manuscripts is capitalized. (These manuscripts are called uncials. Other manuscripts are written in all lower case.) So it is a matter of what the translator decides to do in his translation that will have a big bearing on how we will read it.

In NT Greek "the word" (*logos*) happens to be of the masculine gender. Therefore, its pronoun—"he" in our English translations—is a matter of interpretation, not translation. Did John write concerning "the word" that "he" was in the beginning with God? Or did he write concerning "the word" that "it" was in the beginning with God? As already stated, in NT Greek the *logos* or word is a masculine noun. It is OK in English to use "he" to refer back to this masculine noun if there is good contextual reason to do so. But is there good reason to make "the word" a "he" here?

In fact, there are many English translations since the KJV that refer to the *logos* as "it." Churches of Christ people will be no doubt surprised to learn that their esteemed Alexander Cambell translated John 1:1 as:

> In the beginning was the Word, and the Word was with God, and the Word was God. **This** was in the beginning with God. All things were made by **it**, and without **it** not a single creature was made. **In it** was life, and the life was the light of men. And the light shone in darkness; but the darkness admitted it not.

To read it this way means, of course, that "the word" is not a person. This is a very acceptable translation. Indeed, I will now show that it is in fact preferable for the following reasons.

Appendix

The word *logos* appears many, many more times in this very Gospel of John. And nowhere else do the translators capitalize it or use the masculine personal pronoun "he" to agree with it! They know the context will not stand for this. Take John 2:22 which reads, "When therefore he was risen from the dead, his disciples remembered that he said this; and they believed the Scripture, and **the word which** Jesus had spoken." "The word" here is clearly not Jesus the person himself, but rather his message. Another instance: John 4:37 translates *logos* as a "saying": "For in this case **the saying** is true." Another one: "The man believed **the word** that Jesus spoke to him" (John 4:50). And so on for the many other cases in this very Gospel.

The rest of the New Testament is the same. *Logos* is variously translated as "statement" (Luke 20:20), "question" (Matt. 21:24), "preaching" (1 Tim. 5:17), "command" (Gal. 5:14), "message" (Luke 4:32), "matter" (Acts 15:6), "reason" (Acts 10:29). So there is absolutely no reason to make John 1 say that "the word" is the person Jesus himself, unless of course the translators are wanting to make a point. *In all cases* logos *is an "it."*

There is even strong evidence to suggest that John himself reacted to those who were already misusing his Gospel to mean that Jesus was himself the Word who had personally preexisted the world. When he later wrote his introduction to 1 John he clearly made the point that *what* was in the beginning was not a "who." He put it this way: "**What** was from the beginning, **what** we have heard, **what** we have seen with our eyes, **what** we beheld and our hands handled, concerning **the word of life**..."

These arguments, significant as they are, begin to take on strong proportions when we consider the next vital piece of information. That is, the apostle John's background was in the Hebrew Scriptures. It is surely better exegesis to read the prologue to John's Gospel with his Hebrew background in mind. And if we go back to the OT we can easily discover the framework for John's understanding of "the word." In the Hebrew Bible "word" is *never* a *person.* "Word" always means "promise" or "decree" or "proposal" or "plan" or "message" or just plain "word." (See for example Gen. 31:37; Jud. 3:19; Dan. 9:25; Ps. 64:5-6; Is. 8:10.) In fact "the word" is used about 1450 times in the Hebrew Bible this way. Not once does it refer to a preexisting Son of God. Not once does it mean a person.

The Hebrews certainly understood God's word to be the equivalent of His personal presence and power. What is announced is as good as done (Gen. 1:3, 9, 11, etc.). He watches over His word to perform it and fulfill it (Jer. 1:12). God's word carries the guarantee that He will back it up with action (Is. 55:10-11). Not one word of His will fail. His word carries His power. His word is as His deed. God's word *is* God in His activity in Hebrew understanding. When "**the word of the LORD** came to Jonah" instructing him to go the city of Nineveh and preach there, Jonah "ran away **from the LORD**" (Jonah 1:1-3). Here the word of God, which is His revealed will, equals God Himself expressing Himself. When God told

Appendix

Jonah His plan or His will and Jonah disobeyed, to the Hebrew mind Jonah ran away from God *Himself.*

The writer of the Gospel of John must be allowed to use his native categories and thought-forms. We must respect his Hebrew background. At the time his Gospel was composed, the Aramaic commentaries on the Hebrew Scriptures known as the *targums* used the term *memra* (the word) to describe God's activity in the world. The *memra* (word):

> performs the same function as technical terms like "glory," "Holy Spirit" and "Shekinah" which emphasized the distinction between God's presence in the world and the incomprehensible reality of God itself. *Like the divine Wisdom, the "Word" symbolized God's original plan for creation.* When Paul and John speak about Jesus as though he had some kind of preexistent life, they were not suggesting that he was a second divine "person" in the latter Trinitarian sense. They were indicating that Jesus transcended temporal and individual modes of existence. Because the "power" and "wisdom" that he represented were activities that derived from God, he had in some way expressed "what was there from the beginning." *These ideas were comprehensible in a strictly Jewish context, though later Christians with a Greek background would interpret them differently.* (Karen Armstrong, *A History of God: From Abraham to the Present: The 4000-year Quest for God,* p. 106, emphasis added.)

The fact that John introduces "the word" of God to us in personified terms is very much in keeping with this Hebrew culture. For instance, John's prologue shows obvious parallels with Proverbs 8:22-30 where Wisdom is personified (but never hypostatized, never turned into a real person). Another example perhaps more in keeping with the imagery of John's is found in Psalm 147:15 where we read, "He [God] sends forth His command to the earth; His word runs very swiftly." Here the command/word of God is indeed personified, but not hypostatized.

Also worthy of note is that many commentators are of the opinion that John 1:1-14 is poetic in its literary style. And a basic rule of interpretation is that poetry contains metaphorical language which must not be over-literalized. Thus John's poetic introduction must be allowed to make use of figurative language in keeping with such personification. A personified *logos* is not a revolutionary idea to John! Roger Haight endorses this sentiment when he writes: "One thing is certain, the Prologue of John does not represent direct descriptive knowledge of a divine *entity or being* called Word, who descended and became a human being. To read **a metaphor** as literal speech is misrepresentation." [*Jesus Symbol of God,* p.257].

As eminent professor of NT, T.W. Manson beautifully summarizes;

> I very much doubt whether John thought of the *Logos* as a personality. The only personality on the scene is Jesus the son of Joseph from Nazareth. That personality embodies the *Logos* so completely that Jesus becomes a complete revelation of God. But

Appendix

in what sense are we using the word 'embodies'?... For John every word of Jesus is a word of the Lord." (*On Paul and John*, p.156).

In the light of this background it is far better to read John's prologue to mean that in the beginning God had a plan, a dream, a grand vision for the world, a reason by which He brought all things into being. This word or plan was expressive of who He is.

The Word was *with* God

There is good evidence in the Hebrew Scriptures that the prepositions "with" (*im* and *et*) often describe the relationship between a person and what is in his heart or mind. We have a common expression in English when we say, "What's *with* him?" or "What's the matter *with* her?" Something is going on *inside* somebody. Here are a few examples of this use of the Hebrew preposition "with."

"Im (with), alone = in one's consciousness, whether of knowledge, memory or purpose"

Num. 14:24: "He had another spirit with him" (operating in his mind).

1 Kings 11:11: "This is with you [Solomon]" (what you want).

1 Chron. 28:12: "The pattern of all that was in the spirit with him" (in his mind).

Job 10:13: "I know that this was with you" (hidden in your heart).

Job 23:10: "He knows the way which is with me" (the way of which I am conscious).

Job 23:14" "He performs the things which are appointed for me and many such things are with Him" (He has many such purposes).

Job 27:11: "That which is with the Almighty I will not conceal" (His purposes).

Ps. 50:11: "Wild beasts of the field are with Me" (known to Me, in My thought and care).

Ps. 73:23: "I am continually with You" (in your thoughts).

"Et: a dream or word of Yahweh is said to be *with* the prophet."

Gen. 40:14: "Keep me in mind when it goes well with you" (literally, "remember me with yourself"). The word was what God had in mind.

2Kings 3:12: "there is with him the word of the Lord" (2 John 2: truth is "with us"; Gal 2:5: truth "remains with [*pros*] you").

Isa. 59:12: "transgressions are with us" (in our consciousness). (Cp. John 17:5, the glory which Jesus had with God—present to God's mind, as His purpose.)

Jer. 23:28: "The prophet with whom there is a dream" (the prophet who has a dream).

Jer. 27:18: "If the word of the Lord is with them."

Job 14:5: "His days are determined. The number of his months is with you" (known to you).

Prov. 11:2: "Wisdom is with the humble."

Appendix

The Bible says "As a man thinks in his heart, so he is" (Prov. 23:7). God is no different. For before He created a thing He had this dream with Him. This word was fully expressive of Himself. And when He created the universe and the purpose of the ages He worked according to His master plan, His dream. As Peter says, **"by the word of God the heavens existed** long ago, and the earth was formed out of water and by water" (2 Pet. 3:5). A similar idea is expressed by John in Revelation 4:11: "for You did create all things, and because of your **will** they existed, and were created." This agrees with the OT. For example in Psalm 33:6, 9 we are told that "by the LORD's word the heavens were made." God spoke and it was done. He commanded and the world stood fast. There was divine power in God's spoken word. All of this is simply to say that the Greek word for *logos* is masculine in gender but is not referring to a personally preexisting Son of God. "The word" for John is an "it," not a "he." On one occasion Jesus is given the name "the Word of God" and this is in Revelation 19:13. This name has been given to him after his resurrection and ascension, but we will search in vain to find it before his birth.

It is not until we come to verse 14 of John's prologue that this *logos* becomes personal and becomes the Son of God, Jesus the human being. "And the word became flesh." The great plan that God had in His heart from before the creation at last is fulfilled. Be very clear that it does *not* say that *God* became flesh. Not at all. It says "the word" became flesh. God's master plan is now reality in the man Jesus. Jesus is the final and full expression of all that God's wisdom planned "in the beginning."

This is the conclusion also of the definitive study of the Incarnation *Christology in the Making*. Listen to James Dunn's finding:

> The conclusion which seems to emerge from our analysis thus far is that it is only with v. 14 that we can begin to speak of the *personal* Logos...Prior to v. 14...we are dealing with personifications rather than persons, personified actions of God rather than an individual divine being as such. The point is obscured by the fact that we have to translate the masculine Logos as "he" throughout the poem. But if we translate the masculine Logos as "God's utterance" instead, it would become clearer that the poem did not necessarily intend the Logos in v. 1-13 to be thought of as a personal divine being. In other words, the revolutionary significance of v. 14 may well be that it marks...*the transition from impersonal personification to actual person.* This indeed is the astounding nature of the poem's claim. If it had asserted simply that an individual divine being had become a man, that would have raised fewer eyebrows. It is the fact that the Logos poet has taken language of personification and has *identified* it with a particular person, *as* a particular person, that would be astonishing: the manifestation of God become a man! God's utterance not merely come through a particular individual,

Appendix

but actually become that one person, Jesus of Nazareth! (Dunn, *Christology in the Making,* p. 243.)

There are some NT Greek scholars who note that John was very specific in what he penned back in verse 1. He wrote "and the word was God." He did not write "and the word was *the God*." In other words these scholars take God (Greek *theos*) *here in the adjectival sense.* The word was expressive of God, had the character of God, was divine in its character. As Dunn definitively says, "Nowhere either in the Bible or in the extra-canonical literature of the Jews is the word of God a personal agent or on the way to become such." (*Ibid.,* p. 219) "The *logos* of the prologue becomes Jesus; Jesus was the *logos* become flesh, not the *logos* as such." (Kuschel, *Born Before All Time?* p. 382)

Appendix

Jesus Christ as "the First and the Last..."

Evangelicals very often point to Revelation 1:17 as an evidence that Jesus is God, the second person of the Trinity. Since God the Father describes himself as "the first and the last" in Isaiah 44:6, and Jesus likewise calls himself "the first and the last" in the book of Revelation, Jesus is, like the Father, God—multiple "persons," one being. But notice the difference in context and intent. In Isaiah, Jehovah said, "I am the First and the Last, and **beside me there is no God**." In Revelation 1:17-18, Jesus said: "I am the First and the Last, **and the living one; and I became dead, but, look! I am living forever and ever, and I have the keys of death and of Hades.**"

Unlike the reference in Isaiah, where the subject is identified as the only "God," Jesus is the one who "was dead" but now lives, and the one who holds the keys of death and Hades. In two out of the three instances where Jesus describes himself as "the First and the Last" in the book of Revelation, the statement is made in association with his death and subsequent resurrection. In Revelation 2:8, for example, Jesus is once again described as: "The First and the Last, **who became dead and came to life again.**" There is clearly a connection here.[43]

If "the First and the Last" in this case means, or ultimately implies, "God (Almighty), the Eternal One," in what way would it make sense for Jesus to say, in effect, "I am the Eternal God, *I died* but I came to life"? How strange and how unlikely—if not impossible—would it have been for God to have died or to have said that he died? Even many Trinitarians teach that "God," or the "divine nature/aspect of Christ," did *not* die, in any way. According to orthodox teaching, Jesus—a possessor of

---

[43] Perhaps, as Solomon Landers suggests, Jesus was "the first and the last" in the sense that "Jesus was *'the First'* human to be resurrected to immortal spirit life (Colossians 1:18 [Compare Acts 26:23; John 6:40]). Moreover, he is *'the Last'* to be so resurrected by God personally. All other resurrections will be by and under the authority of Jesus Christ (John 5:25-30). Thus, he becomes "the living one...living forever and ever." He enjoys immortality. In this, he is like his immortal Father, who is called "the living God" (Revelation 7:2; Psalm 42:2); for all others of humanity, Jesus himself is "the resurrection and the life" (John 11:25). God has *given him* the authority to resurrect the dead. That is why Jesus can say that he has the keys to unlock the gates for those bound by death and Hades (the grave)."

Appendix

"two natures"—died only in a sense that can be ascribed to his "human" nature. When Trinitarians use this text to support the belief that Jesus is God (Almighty), in effect they have Jesus meaning, "I am the first and the last (I am God), I (God) died but I came to life." Yet we know that God does not and cannot die, according to the Bible, classical orthodoxy, and logic itself. So Trinitarians would have to argue, ultimately, that Jesus is identifying himself as God by calling himself "the First and the Last" and, immediately after, switching to, or speaking out of, his "human nature," due to the fact that he died. This would clearly be a case of "playing-fast-and-loose" with Scripture: "I am God (immortal), and I am man (capable of dying), but I came to life." Can it *really* be maintained that this is what is going on between the lines, in the original, first-century context?

This is very similar to the situation in Hebrews 1:8 where Jesus is evidently called "God." Yet the context shows that he is the kind that has one who is "God" to or above him (*'therefore God, your God has anointed you'*). This shows, verifiably, that in the author's mind, Jesus' "Godship" was not "absolute" or unqualified, simply because Almighty God, or God in the "absolute" sense, could not have a God to or above him, as Jesus does. Trinitarians repeatedly argue and emphasize that the Father is Jesus' God *only* in the terms of his "humanity." In this case (Heb. 1:8), Trinitarians would have to say that in this one line, Jesus is called "God"—proving his "deity"—and, in the next line, he is spoken of as having a God—something that can only be said in reference to his "humanity"—and that the author of Hebrews is silently switching in and out of the categories of "deity" and "humanity." This would be, of course, an outstanding example of an anachronistic, unbiblical, and ultimately nonsensical notion placed on a text by Trinitarian apologists. The fact is, Jesus, just like the king of Israel to whom the original text applied to, can be called "God"; yet we know that he, like the king of Israel, was not thought of as Almighty God because there is a God above him—knowing, at the same time, that the Scriptures allow the term "God" to apply to God's authorized representatives.

The significance of the phrase "the First and the Last," applied to Christ in the Book of Revelation, was discussed by

Appendix

adjunct professor of Biblical Studies at Trinity Lutheran College, Jan Fekkes III, in a 1994 Essay: *Isaiah and Prophetic Traditions in the Book of Revelation, Visionary Antecedents and their Development, Journal for the Study of the New Testament, Supplemental Series 93*:

> It is unanimously agreed among commentators that the phrase ['the First and the Last'] has its source in the divine self-predication found in Isa. 44.6, 48.12 and 41.4, and that John did not adopt the LXX version, but works directly from the Hebrew...['I am the First and the Last and the Living One.'] These are the first words of Christ to John in the climax of the prophetic commission scene of 1.10-20...The first words of Christ (1.17-18) are thus placed in conscious relation the first words of God (1.8), and are together with 22.13 play an integral role in the authoritative framework of the book. Hartman is undoubtedly correct in concluding that the self-predication of 1.8 is an accreditation statement which lends divine authority to John's *words of prophecy.* The same judgment can be applied to 1.17-18. This double authorization is merely an outworking of the dualistic revelatory scheme already in Rev. 1.1-2...In what way, then, is Christ here the *First and the Last*? What is the basis of his authority? Among commentators, two views appear most prominent. One group understands the designation as an expression of Christ's eternity, which underlies his authority as the Lord of all history. The other group connects the title with the event of Christ's resurrection and subsequent enthronement, which authenticated his past existence, confirmed his divine authority, and established him as God's agent of salvation and judgment.
>
> The first [common Trinitarian] view is based on the assumption that all three double titles, whether applied to God or Christ, have exactly the same force. Yet this overlooks the fact that *first and last* is reserved for Christ alone. Not only is it associated with the resurrection explicitly in two of its three uses (1.17-18; 2.8), but John relates Christ's 'firstness' specifically to the resurrection when in 1.5 he calls him the 'firstborn from the dead'. In addition, he repeatedly gives evidence that Christ's victory over death is the basis of his authority over the church and the world. It appears then that the second view best accords with the immediate context and John's overall perspective.

Appendix

...Revelation 2.8 ['*These are the things that he says, 'the First and the Last,' who became dead and came to life*']. It is surely significant that John here does not merely take over the first and last designation from 1.17, but retains its connection with the resurrection. Christ's power over life and death, his authority over the first and last phases of human existence serves here a parenetic function, which is directed to the circumstances of the Smyrnean church. In the face of persecution and possible death, they are to gain strength from Christ's example and take comfort in his authority to bestow the crown of life and deliver them from the second death (2.10-11).

...Revelation 22.13 ['*I...the first and the last*']. This final application reinforces the premise that *first and last* is fundamentally a title of authority. It stands here in connection with the role of Christ as the eschatological judge, whose judgment encompasses both wrath and reward (2.2, 19; 3.1-2, 8, 15; 11.18; 14.13; 20.12-13). The basis for his authority is not included in this passage, but there can be no doubt that, as in 1.17-18 and 2.8, it is related to Christ's victory over death (cf. 2.26-27 with 5.5-7).

The collocation of all three titles in Rev. 22.13 does not necessarily justify their being homogenized into a single theological kernel. Whereas God is *beginning and end* in relation to creation (4.11; 21.6), Christ is *first and last* in relation to the church.[44]

---

[44] However, some would dispute that in Revelation 22:13 Christ is the speaker. Note: the words in brackets [ ] throughout this citation were added for clarification purposes.

Appendix

The Contextual Key to John 20:28
Unlocking the Meaning of Thomas' Confession
by Mark J. Rich

Copyright © 2010 by Mark J. Rich
All verses are from the NKJV unless otherwise noted

Introductory Remarks

There are many issues and biblical texts not covered in this study[1] that bear on the identity of Christ. This study is being presented, however, to draw attention to one of the most important texts about Jesus and to what may well be the *key* to its correct interpretation. As many of you know, Thomas' statement in John 20:28 is often cited as indisputable proof for the "absolute deity" of Christ. The level of certainty attached to this claim, however, is unjustified and can be attributed to the fact that his statement is seldom interpreted in light of its proper context. To be specific, John 20:28 is seldom viewed in the light of Jesus' grand revelation to Thomas (and to the other disciples) in John 14:9-10. I believe the relationship between these two climactic passages has been largely overlooked[2] and deserves serious attention from students of every theological camp.

The thoughts which follow represent my current understanding of Jesus' identity and of the way various passages fit together to form a harmonic whole. I readily admit, however, that there are passages concerning the Savior that still mystify and intrigue me, inspiring me not only to continue my studies but to remain open to adjusting my views as further light is received.[3] Consequently, though I offer this study for your careful reflection, and as a potential paradigm by which to analyze and synthesize many of the New Testament statements concerning Christ, I certainly do not mean for it to be taken as the "gospel truth." Each of us, when reading spiritual or theological material, needs to follow the inspired admonition: "Test everything carefully. Hold on to that which is good. Keep away from every form of evil." (1 Thess. 5:21-22) Or as

Appendix

everyday language would have it: "Chew what's good and spit out the bones."

The Passage We'll Be Studying

Before we begin our study of John 20:28, let's read the verse in its immediate context. Verse 19 takes place on the very same day that our Savior was raised from the dead.

> **19 Then, the same day at evening, being the first day of the week, when the doors were shut where the disciples were assembled, for fear of the Jews, Jesus came and stood in the midst, and said to them, "Peace be with you." 20 When He had said this, He showed them His hands and His side. Then the disciples were glad when they saw the Lord... 24 Now Thomas, called the Twin, one of the twelve, was not with them when Jesus came. 25 The other disciples therefore said to him, "We have seen the Lord." So he said to them, "Unless I see in His hands the print of the nails, and put my finger into the print of the nails, and put my hand into His side, I will not believe." 26 And after eight days His disciples were again inside, and Thomas with them. Jesus came, the doors being shut, and stood in the midst, and said, "Peace to you!" 27 Then He said to Thomas, "Reach your finger here, and look at My hands; and reach your hand here, and put it into My side. Do not be unbelieving, but believing." 28 And Thomas answered and said to Him, "My Lord and my God!" 29 Jesus said to him, "Thomas, because you have seen Me, you have believed. Blessed are those who have not seen and *yet* have believed." 30 And truly Jesus did many other signs in the presence of His disciples, which are not written in this book; 31 but these are written that you may believe that Jesus is the Christ, the Son of God, and that believing you may have life in His name.**

A Clear Ascription of Deity?

There are very few verses in Scripture that refer to Jesus as "God." The Greek word for "God" is *theos*, and in his article, "*Jesus as 'Theos' in the New Testament*," G. H. Boobyer observed:[4]

Appendix

There is [a] rarity of New Testament references to Jesus as "God" (*theos*). Some nine or ten passages occur in which Jesus is, or might be, alluded to as "God" (*theos*). Usually cited are John 1:1, 18; 20:28; Romans 9:5; 2 Thessalonians 1:12; 1 Timothy 3:16; Titus 2:13; Hebrews 1:8f.; 2 Peter 1:1 and 1 John 5:20. Two or three of these, however, are highly dubious, and, of the remainder, varying degrees of textual or exegetical uncertainty attach to all save one, which is Thomas's adoring acclaim of the risen Jesus in John 20:28 as "My Lord and my God!" Distinguishing this passage from the others, Vincent Taylor—a moderately conservative scholar on christological problems—speaks of it as "the one clear ascription of Deity to Christ"[5] in the New Testament.

As Boobyer has noted, all of the verses commonly pointed to as identifying Jesus as "God" are subject to debate in terms of their textual, translational, or interpretive certainty. But what about John 20:28? Is it really "the one clear ascription of Deity to Christ" in the Bible? This claim has been made by "a *moderately* conservative scholar on christological problems." And it goes without saying that *fundamentalist* Trinitarians have long considered verse 28 an impregnable proof for the deity of Christ. But we only discover how pervasive this type of thinking is when we find that even James D. G. Dunn, an eminent *critical* scholar, is convinced that Jesus was eventually designated *God*, "particularly in John 20:28".[6]

Despite this uniformity of opinion among conservatives and liberals alike, we still need to examine the passage in light of its biblical context to see if the opinion is justified. We want to discover what Thomas *truly* had in mind when he expressed, "My Lord and my God!"

Some Preliminary Observations

When we listen closely to John 20:28, it is obvious that Thomas wasn't speaking into thin air when he exclaimed, "My Lord and my God!" He wasn't saying "My God!" in the sense

Appendix

people often do when they're taken by total surprise. Nor was he offering praise to God in heaven. The passage clearly states that Thomas was expressing something directly *TO* Jesus. "Thomas answered and *said to Him...*"[7]

But what exactly was Thomas saying? Translated literally, the Greek reads: "The Lord of me and the God of me." We know from John's Gospel that Jesus' disciples, and even outsiders, addressed him as "Lord" out of respect for his authority, power, and wisdom. He wasn't called *Lord* because they thought he was *God*.[8] But in the climactic passage before us, Thomas perceived in Jesus not only his *Lord*, but also his *God*. So we must ask ourselves this question: In what sense did he see "God" in his risen Savior? Did he actually think of Jesus as *being* God—the God of heaven and earth—or did he have something different in mind?

The Confession's Strategic Location

In our attempt to understand John 20:28, one of the things we must carefully note is that Thomas' statement (or "confession of faith") comes at a critical stage in John's well-ordered Gospel. John is about to reveal—just *three* verses later—the entire purpose for which he wrote his Gospel. (v. 31) And thus, whatever it is that Thomas expresses in verse 28, it is unlikely that it either contradicts or *surpasses* what John is about to reveal in verse 31. And we may also assume, because of the careful structure of John's Gospel, that whatever Thomas was saying of Christ in verse 28, it doesn't contradict, but rather summarizes—or brings to a climax—what was revealed of Christ in earlier portions of the Gospel.

Having made these contextual observations, a question naturally arises. What exactly was it that John stated of Jesus when he summarized, in v. 31, his Master's true identity? John stated, as forthrightly as possible, that he wrote his Gospel "that you may believe that Jesus is the Christ, the Son of God, and that believing you may have life in His name." He didn't say that his goal was to inspire faith in Jesus being *God*. He could have easily said that if that's what he meant.[9] Instead, his stated purpose was that his readers might believe that Jesus was God's *SON*, the promised "Christ" or Messiah. It was *this* faith, and not

Appendix

faith in Jesus being *God*, that John said would result in his readers "hav[ing] life in His name."

Another question we should ask ourselves when attempting to understand Thomas' confession in v. 28 is this: Is it likely that Thomas invented, on the spur of the moment, an exalted identification of Christ that Jesus *himself* never expressed? Was Jesus simply left to endorse,[10] in verse 29, Thomas' grand revelation? Or is it more likely that Thomas was merely acknowledging or paraphrasing something that Jesus had already revealed about himself and that Thomas had finally "come around" to believe? In my opinion, the latter is far more likely and can be easily confirmed if we simply locate in John's Gospel an earlier statement of Jesus that was *similar* to Thomas' confession.

A Climactic Teaching of Our Lord

But where in John's Gospel had Jesus said anything that would have led Thomas to make the kind of statement he made? John's Gospel is full of the magnificent teachings of Jesus, and there is much that can be looked at in relationship to our passage. But the teaching of Jesus that seems *closest* to Thomas' statement—in terms of both time and subject matter—can be found in the 14th chapter of John. In verse 7 of that chapter, our Lord made the following statement *directly to Thomas!*

> **If you had known <u>Me</u>, you would have known <u>My Father also</u>; and from now on you know Him and <u>have seen Him</u>. —John 14:7**

In this wonderfully revealing, yet enigmatic statement, Jesus was telling Thomas that he had already come to know and behold the Father. He had already come to know and see God. At this stage of the conversation, of course, Thomas had no idea what Jesus meant by these words. Nor did Philip who was present with Thomas. So Philip continued the conversation by asking...

> **Lord, show us the Father, and it is sufficient for us. —John 14:8**

Appendix

In the very next verse, Jesus responded to Philip's request, enlarging upon what he had just said to Thomas. But before we consider his remarkable response, we need to remember something of great importance to our study. Thomas didn't walk away when Philip joined the conversation. Thomas was still present when Jesus answered Philip. The twelve disciples had gathered with Jesus for what has commonly been called "the last supper." And this particular segment of dinner conversation had been largely inspired by a question from Thomas. (John 14:5) Thus, he would have been keenly interested in the direction the conversation was taking. Though he and the other disciples understood little of what Jesus was saying at the time, the Master's self-disclosure in this critical dialogue provided the foundation stones—the conceptual basis—for Thomas' later confession. This will begin to be clearer as we now listen to Jesus' response to Philip's request, *"Lord, show us the Father."*

> **Have I been with you so long, and yet you have [still] not known Me, Philip? He who has seen *ME has* seen *THE FATHER*; so how can you say, "Show us the Father"? Do you not believe that I am in the Father, and the Father in Me? The words that I speak to you I do not speak on My own (authority); but <u>the FATHER</u> who <u>dwells in ME</u> does the works. —John 14:9-10**

Did you notice the disappointment in Jesus' opening question? "Have I been with you so long, and yet you have [still] not known Me?" Jesus' question should function as an *alert signal* to every reader of John's Gospel. It lets us know that what Jesus is about to express is *A CULMINATING REVELATION CONCERNING HIS TRUE SIGNIFICANCE AND IDENTITY*. Listen to his question again. "Have I been with you so long, and yet you have [still] not known Me?" Upon hearing this question, our ears, just as those of the original disciples, should be *wide open* to receive what Jesus is about to reveal. It is something he had hoped his disciples would have understood by now. Jesus had hoped that by this time—when preparing to "depart from this world" (13:1)—his disciples would have understood more than they did about his unique identity. He had hoped they would understand that the Father actually dwelled within him. (John 10:38) They

594

Appendix

didn't need to look far off into heaven to see God. He wanted them to understand that when they looked at him with true eyes of discernment, they were seeing more than just "the *Man*, Christ Jesus." (1 Tim. 2:5) They were also beholding the Father who dwelled *within* His Son.[11] In a word, they were seeing *God* as well as God's *Son* in the person of Jesus Christ.

In John 14:9-10, Jesus was simply enlarging upon what he had already stated to Thomas just two verses earlier. *"If you had known Me, you would have known My Father also; and from now on you know Him and have seen Him."* (v. 7) In verses 9 and 10 Jesus clarified: *"He who has seen Me HAS seen the Father. ...The Father who dwells in Me does the works."* Do you see how these remarks provided the basis for Thomas' insight, less than two weeks later,[12] when he identified in Jesus both his Lord and his God? Jesus, of course, had long been his "Lord." Thomas had walked with Jesus and talked with him for the last three years of his life. And now that Jesus had explained that his Father (*God*)[13] actually dwelled *within* him and that it was the *Father* (*God*) within him who had performed the miracles *through* him (John 14:9-10), Thomas had the foundation for understanding that in Jesus could be found both his Lord *AND* his God. This is what Thomas finally understood and affirmed in his famous confession, "The Lord of me *AND* the God of me!" He no longer had to look heavenward in hopes of seeing God. He could see the Father in the Son. He could see *God* ("the Father") in his *Lord*, Jesus Christ.

At the Risk of Repetition

At the risk of repeating myself, please let me express what I've already stated, but in a slightly different manner. I am doing this because John 14:9-10 is so *very* important and receives far less attention than it deserves. Jesus' opening question can be broken into two parts. Each contains *vital implications.* Here once again are his words.

Have I been with you so long, and yet you have [still] not known Me, Philip? —John 14:9

The first half of this question, *"Have I been with you so long,"* signals that what Jesus is about to reveal is of a

Appendix

culminating or *climactic* character. It is something he has been trying to communicate for a "long" time. The second half, *"and yet you have [still] not known Me,"* identifies the *content* or *subject* of Jesus' revelation. It concerns his *identity*. It concerns *"knowing"* him and appreciating who he really is. When Jesus continues in verses 9 and 10 to unfold the significance of who he is, he does not indicate that he was the "second Person of the Trinity" or "God the Son" as Trinitarians believe. He states that *"the FATHER"* dwelled within him and performed the mighty miracles. This revelation is of such significance that we cannot afford to ignore it when seeking to interpret Thomas' later confession in 20:28. We simply *must* allow Jesus' self-disclosure to govern our understanding of Thomas' later confession—a confession which Jesus *endorsed*. (20:29)

A Theme Echoed Elsewhere in Scripture

The truth taught by Jesus in this remarkable passage has been restated or reiterated in a variety of biblical texts. As we already learned from John 14:9-10, Jesus revealed that when a person truly "sees" him for who he is, they recognize that they have not only beheld the *Son* of the Father, but *the Father* who dwelled in His Son. A similar idea was expressed by Paul when he identified Jesus as "the *image* of the invisible God". (Col. 1:15, 2 Cor. 4:4) Though God is by nature an invisible Being, His character, heart, and power were made "visible" as He operated within and through the life of His Son, Jesus Christ. Thus, when Paul referred to Jesus as "the *image* of the invisible God," he wasn't saying that Jesus actually *was* God.[14] He was identifying Jesus as God's visible *manifestation*. (1 Tim. 3:16) Or as Paul stated elsewhere, "the glory of *God*" could be seen "in the face of Jesus Christ." (2 Cor. 4:6) In other words, there is more to behold of Jesus than the veil of his outward humanity.[15] One can also perceive the Father who dwelled in the Son. One can recognize that God's presence dwelled just behind the veil. This is why Thomas, in his moment of revelation, could see in his Master both "the Lord of me *AND* the God of me." (John 20:28, lit.) He finally understood—or he finally *believed*—what Jesus had revealed during their last supper together: "He who has

Appendix

seen Me [really] *HAS seen the Father,*" for "*the FATHER dwells in ME.*" (14:9-10)

We need to remind ourselves that earlier in John's Gospel, Jesus had pointed in a similar direction when he described his own body as a *temple*. (John 2:19-21) A temple, of course, is a place where *God* dwells.[16] The apostle Paul stated a similar concept when he wrote these remarkable words: "In [Christ] dwells all the fullness of the Godhead *bodily*,"[17] (Col. 2:9) for "it pleased the Father that in [Jesus] all the fullness should dwell." (Col. 1:19) This notion of God being pleased that "all" of His fullness should dwell in Jesus' body ties in with John's observation that Jesus had received God's spirit "*without measure*" or "*without limit.*" (John 3:34 NASB, NLT) The Father, by means of His spirit,[18] dwelled richly in Christ as in no man before. (Ps. 45:7) For this reason, Jesus was suitably called "*the Anointed One,*" "*the Messiah,*" or "*the Christ.*" These are identical titles[19] that refer to one who has received God's spirit. Others before Jesus had been anointed by God and were referred to as "Jehovah's anointed,"[20] but the *ultimate* expression of this blessed phenomenon was found in "Christ *(Anointed)* Jesus, our Lord." (Rom. 6:23, 1 Cor. 15:31, Eph. 3:11, Phil. 3:8, Col. 2:6, 1 Tim. 1:12, 2 Tim. 1:2.) Perhaps you're familiar with the following prophecy. It was quoted by Jesus as pertaining to himself. (Luke 4:18-21)

> **The Spirit of the Lord Jehovah[21] is upon Me, because Jehovah has anointed Me to preach good tidings to the poor. He has sent Me to heal the brokenhearted, to proclaim liberty to the captives, and the opening of the prison to those who are bound... —Isaiah 61:1**

A similar prophecy about Jesus was found earlier in the Book of Isaiah.

> **There shall come forth a Rod from the stem of Jesse, and a Branch shall grow out of his roots. The Spirit of Jehovah shall rest upon Him, the Spirit of wisdom and understanding, the Spirit of counsel and might, the Spirit of knowledge and of the fear of Jehovah.**
> **—Isaiah 11:1-2**

Appendix

Manifesting and *Being* God Are Two Different Things

We have learned from a variety of Scriptures how Jesus was able to reveal God to humanity in a rich, unprecedented manner. Paul described Jesus as "the image of the invisible God," for in Jesus' person, the otherwise *invisible* God was made "visible" to the spiritually discerning. It was for this reason that Thomas was able to perceive in his Master—when faith and understanding were quickened in him—not only "the *LORD* of me" but "the *GOD* of me" too. (John 20:28) He perceived in the risen Christ the same Lord he had known for several years prior to Jesus' death and resurrection. And thus, in John 20:28, he mentioned this familiar aspect of Jesus' identity first, saying *"The Lord of me..."* But now he also recognized in Jesus the very God who resided *within* his Lord and had manifested Himself so powerfully through Jesus' words and works. (John 14:10-11, 10:38) And thus, in the *second* part of his affirmation, Thomas boldly expressed to Jesus, *"...AND the God of me!"*

Consequently, Thomas' confession, though exceptionally meaningful, was not a confession that Jesus was God or "the second Person of the Trinity." To interpret it thus would be to understand it in the shadows of 4th century dogma rather than in the light of Jesus' own teachings. Thomas was simply giving his "amen" to what Jesus had earlier taught him. In a word, he was saying, "I finally get it! You really are who you said you are! I believe you're not only my Lord, but that God actually dwells within you, just like you said. By being raised from the dead, I can no longer question that your teachings are true!" And thus, when a person rightly "sees" or perceives the Son of God, they also see the Father who dwelled *within* him. (John 14:9-10) Or to express this as Paul did in his letter to Timothy, in Jesus the otherwise *invisible* God "was manifested in the flesh." (1 Tim. 3:16)

Thomas was not confessing that Jesus was God Almighty. Jesus was "the *SON* of God" as John emphasized just three verses later. (John 20:31) But because of this wonderful fact—because Jesus was God's precious *Son*—God was pleased that in him all of His fullness would reside. (Col. 1:19) It was for this reason that Jesus was able to reveal God to humanity! It was

Appendix

for this reason that Jesus could be called *Immanuel*, "God is with us." (Matt. 1:32) God's presence was *with* Christ and *in* Christ and revealed *through* Christ as never before at any time or in any man since. One needn't believe that Jesus is God Almighty to love him with all of their heart, or to "have life in His name." (John 20:31) It is enough that with Peter (Matt. 16:16) and John (John 20:31) we joyfully confess that Jesus is "the *Christ*, the *Son* of the living God," and that in him the Father—as well as the Son—can be wonderfully known and seen! (John 14:7, 9-10) No wonder the apostle John stated with joy: "He who acknowledges the Son has the Father also." (1 John 2:23)

Endnotes

[1] I am delighted to have my study included as an appendix in this book. To comply with space limitations, however, it was necessary to remove a number of footnotes that were part of the original study.

[2] Until recently, I was not aware that anyone had interpreted John 20:28 in light of John 14:9-10 as I have done in this study. In *The Restitution of Jesus Christ*, however, Kermit Zarley proposed a similar interpretation and mentioned that in 1726, Samuel Crellius had seen the same connection. According to Crellius, Thomas was simply recalling Jesus' words from 14:9-10 when in 20:28 he essentially said, "Behold I see my God, God the Father, who is in Christ my Lord."

[3] Many years ago, before having his young life snatched by an assassin's bullet, a dear friend shared this intriguing saying: "It's pride not to read by the light of another man's candle." He believed in the benefits of reading biblical commentaries and theological treatises. There's so much we can learn from the insights of others, especially if we are willing to temper our understanding of 1 John 2:27—*"you do not need that anyone teach you"*—with Ephesians 4:11—*"He Himself gave...pastors and teachers"*. Unfortunately, we often prevent ourselves from gaining new perspectives by refusing to read anything but literature from our own theological camp. We say we're protecting ourselves from being "led astray," but at the same time we're closing ourselves off to the possibility of learning new truth. What ever happened to the spirit of the Protestant Reformation, of being willing to have our theological views "reformed"? We praise men like Martin Luther for breaking with traditional theology when it deviated from biblical truth, yet so many in evangelical, fundamentalist circles today act as if there's nothing new to learn—as if all of our ducks are in perfect order.

[4] My quotation of Boobyer is from his article in vol. 50 of *Bulletin of the John Rylands Library*, p. 253. The bulletin was published by Aberdeen University Press and copyrighted in 1968 by The John Rylands Library.

[5] Taylor's remark, notes Boobyer, is from an article in *Expository Times* entitled *"Does the New Testament Call Jesus God?"* (lxxiii, No. 4, January 1962, p. 118)

[6] From p. 388 of Dunn's book, *The Christ and the Spirit*.

[7] The expression, "answered and said to him," is common in Scripture. It can have a variety of meanings. It can suggest, as in modern usage, that a question has been asked and that someone is about to answer it. (Mark 8:29) But it can also indicate that a person is about to continue a conversation without a question having been asked at all. The person may simply be reacting to a remark that was just made. (Mark 7:28) And sometimes the phrase merely signals that one is about to speak in reaction to an *event* that has just transpired without conversation having preceded at all. (Mark 14:48) In each case, however, it seems that the concluding phrase ("and said to *him*" or "to *them*") indicates that the person's remarks were addressed to a particular person or group of people. They were not merely expressed into thin air.

[8] Consider these examples from the Gospel of John. Did the "woman caught in adultery" (8:3) have a deep understanding of Jesus' identity and metaphysical nature? Who would claim that she

Appendix

thought him to be God incarnate? Yet she readily addressed him as "Lord." (8:11) And what about the man born blind (9:1) whom Jesus healed? In 9:35-36 he confessed to not even knowing that Jesus was "the Son of God" (NKJV) or "the Son of Man" (NIV)—let alone God incarnate—yet he readily addressed him as "Lord" (v. 36). And even while confessing to his ignorance about Christ, Thomas addressed Jesus as "Lord" in the very same verse. (14:5) And when Mary Magdalene thought that a mere gardener was speaking with her, she addressed him as "Lord" (20:15) using the same Greek word (*kyrios*) that she used of *Jesus* only two verses earlier! (v. 13) So to suggest that using *Kyrios* of Jesus implies belief in his deity is to stretch the evidence beyond reason. It is true that Jesus was referred to not only as "Lord" but as "*the* Lord," but this too should not lead to unwarranted conclusions. The definite article may well have been used to acknowledge his *unique* authority and worthiness to be distinguished from all other lords.

[9] If John's goal in his Gospel was to prove that Jesus was *God*, why didn't he say so in his closing identification of Jesus? (John 20:31) And if he believed Jesus to be God, why was he silent on such an important matter in each of his *epistles* as well? 1 Jn. 5:20 identifies Jesus as "the true God" only in *biased* translations. The grammar of the text doesn't require this identification, nor is it likely that John would have contradicted in his *epistle* what his *Gospel* had made so clear. In John 17:3, Jesus specifically identified the *Father*—not himself—as "the only true God."

We should also note that in 1 John 5:1, when identifying the essentials of saving faith, it was faith in Jesus as "the *Christ*," not as "God," that John specifically identified. And if additional evidence is necessary, we should also notice that in the very first verse of his *Book of Revelation*, John dramatically *distinguished* Jesus from "God," not identified the two. He reported that it was *"God"* who had given the revelation to Jesus. (Rev. 1:1) This simple designation is significant. John simply wrote "God." He felt no need to specify who this "God" was whom he identified as having given the revelation to Jesus. He didn't say "God the Father" or "God the Son" or "God the Holy Spirit" as Trinitarians would be prone to do. That's because John had no concept of a triune God. There was no need to identify which of three divine "Persons" had given the revelation. It was sufficient to say that "God" had given the revelation since John believed, as did Paul, that "there is no other God but one, ...the Father". (1 Cor. 8:4-6, Eph. 4:6)

This monotheistic thinking of John and of Jesus becomes even clearer when we turn to Rev. 1:6 and 3:12. If you read these verses in your Bible, you'll notice that Jesus isn't being depicted as God. He is being spoken of, or he speaks, as one who *has* a God and who thinks of God as being *his* God. I believe we should keep all of these observations in mind before jumping to the conclusion that John thought of Jesus as God Almighty and was seeking to prove this in his Gospel.

[10] In verse 29, Jesus endorsed Thomas' new-found faith. There is nothing to suggest otherwise. The only thing *negative* Jesus said in v. 29 was that people are "blessed" who arrive at the same faith Thomas did, but without having had the same advantage he had. When Jesus said to Thomas, "Because you have seen Me you have believed," he was implying that Thomas would have never believed had he not seen the wounds in his body.

[11] The Father, though invisible, was able to manifest Himself to the world through His Son in whom He richly dwelled by His spirit. By manifesting Himself through Jesus' powerful life and teachings, the very character, heart, and wisdom of God could be "seen" as never before.

[12] It was a bit less than two weeks after John 14:9-10 was spoken that Thomas made his famous "confession." Jesus' teaching in John 14:9-10 was spoken at "the last supper," the night before his crucifixion. Jesus was raised from the dead three days after his execution, and according to John 20:26, it was eight days after his resurrection and first appearance to his disciples that Thomas beheld Christ and made his confession.

[13] We must remember that for Jesus and his Jewish disciples, "the Father" was synonymous with "God". These strict monotheistic Jews had no conceptual filter to confuse them like Christendom has had since the 4th century Council of Nicaea. When Philip asked Jesus to show him "the Father," (Jn. 14:8) he was asking to see the only true God. (17:3) And when Jesus said that "the Father" dwelled within him and could be seen in him, the disciples understood Jesus to mean that *God* dwelled within him and could be seen in him. (14:9-10)

[14] Jesus had the fullness of God within him and manifested God to the world, but this does not necessarily imply that Jesus *was* God. It is true that Jesus was *"in"* the Father and the Father was

Appendix

"in" Jesus. (John 10:38) And it is also true that Jesus was *"one"* with his Father. (John 10:30) But these *actual* realities sound very similar, if not identical, to the *potential* realities Jesus sought for his own disciples. (John 17:11, 21, 22, and 6:56, 15:4) Thus, Trinitarian and Oneness believers would be wise not to use verses like John 10:30 and 10:38 to prove the deity of Christ.

[15] Jesus' humanity was more than a "veil" for the Deity within him. He was a genuine human being in whom the Father dwelled. But the concept of his humanity "veiling" the divinity within is a legitimate one. Again and again in the Gospels, we find people failing to discern the true significance of Christ despite the richness of God's manifestation through his marvelous words and works. (Matt. 13:54-57)

[16] It is certainly true that no earthly temple can contain the vastness of God. Nor does the Maker of all things need a temple to dwell in. (1 Kings 8:27, Acts 7:48, 17:24) But the Bible does say that "the glory of *YHWH* filled the temple" built by Solomon. (2 Chr. 7:1-3) In this manner, God was pleased to be thought of as "dwelling" in an earthly temple. (2 Chr. 36:15, Ps. 76:2). Even Jesus spoke of the Jerusalem temple as a place where God dwelled. (Matt. 23:21) And in the NT epistles, Paul revels in the fact that God has chosen to dwell in His very own *people*—in the *"temple"* of their physical "bodies"! (1 Cor. 3:16, 6:19, 2 Cor. 6:16)

[17] It is imperative, when seeking to gird ourselves with truth, that we jettison false notions about God's alleged plurality. When we think about God residing in Christ, we mustn't think of a *second* of "three divine Persons" or a *third* of "the triune Godhead" dwelling in Jesus. These are fourth century notions. When Paul spoke of God dwelling in Christ, he was thinking of only one God. "For us," wrote Paul, "there is [but] one God, the Father." (1 Cor. 8:6, Eph. 4:6) Or as Jesus so clearly instructed, it was "the Father" who dwelled within him. (John 14:9-10) Not once did our Savior say "the Son dwells in me." Not once. He was the begotten Son *conceived* by God (Luke 1:35) *in whom* the Father was "pleased" to dwell. (Col. 1:19)

[18] Mr. Rich's original paper had a somewhat lengthy endnote here explaining his understanding of God's spirit and its vital role throughout the Bible.

[19] Each of these titles has the same meaning. They differ only as to the language they're derived from. "The Christ" is based on the Greek word *Christos*. "The Messiah" is based on the Hebrew word *Mashiyach*. Each of them means "the Anointed One."

[20] See, for example, 1 Sam. 24:6, 2 Sam. 23:1, Num. 3:3 and Num. 11:29.

[21] I have substituted "the Lord *Jehovah*" for "the Lord *GOD*" and *"Jehovah"* for "the *LORD*" in the NKJV rendering of this text. *Jehovah* is God's personal name and neither "God" nor "the Lord" are suitable translations of His name.

Appendix

General Scripture Index

The following is a general index of Scripture citations. All Scripture citations appearing throughout the book are not listed.

Genesis 1:1.....**470-474**
Genesis 1:2....503
Genesis 1:26.....**474-478**
Genesis 1:27.....217
Genesis 3:15.....155
Genesis 4:4.....220
Genesis 15:2.....151
Genesis 24:12.....151

Exodus 3:14.....414, 447-451, 564-566, **571-576**
Exodus 3:14-15.....438
Exodus 4:15-16.....241
Exodus 7:1.....241
Exodus 14:31.....168
Exodus 19:5.....311
Exodus 20:3-5.....362
Exodus 23:20-21.....137

Deuteronomy 6:4.....74, **466-470**
Deuteronomy 18:18-19

Judges 3:9-15.....250

1 Samuel 29:8.....151

1 Chronicles 29:11.....265

Nehemiah 9:27.....252

Daniel 4:25.....137
Daniel 7:13-14.....249
Daniel 7:14.....44, 138

Obadiah 1:21.....250

Psalm 8:5.....41, 243, 246, 248
Psalm 45:6.....246, 248
Psalm 68:4.....566-567
Psalm 82:1.....242
Psalm 82:6.....241, 246, 294

Psalm 110:1.....**147-158**
Psalm 136:2.....245

Proverbs 8:22-31.....**222-226**
Proverbs 30:4-6.....92

Isaiah 4:2.....401, 411
Isaiah 6:10.....400
Isaiah 9:6.....239, **478-482**
Isaiah 9:6-7.....401, 411
Isaiah 11:1-10.....401
Isaiah 16:5.....401, 412
Isaiah 32:1.....401, 412
Isaiah 33:17.....401, 412
Isaiah 41:1-4.....**457-460**
Isaiah 42:1-4.....401, 412
Isaiah 42:8......166-167
Isaiah 43:10.....244-245
Isaiah 43:10-13.....**460-462**
Isaiah 43:11.....250
Isaiah 46:4.....**462-463**
Isaiah 48:12-17.....**482-486**
Isaiah 49:1-6.....401, 412
Isaiah 52:13.....167
Isaiah 52:13-15.....401, 413
Isaiah 53:12.....155
Isaiah 61:1-3.....401, 413
Isaiah 61:1:1-3.....392
Isaiah 61:10-11.....392

Micah 5:2.....232

Zechariah 12:10.....**486-491**
Zechariah 14:3-4.....**491-501**
Zechariah 14:8-9.....208
Zechariah 14:9.....74

Matthew 1:23.....**50**
Matthew 3:16-17.....101-102, 109
Matthew 3:17.....133, 167
Matthew 7:12.....83

Appendix

Matthew 12:10-12.....175
Matthew 12:28.....517
Matthew 16:13-17.....102-103
Matthew 17:2.....104
Matthew 17:5.....102
Matthew 22:41-45.....147
Matthew 22:41-46.....133
Matthew 22:43-44.....147-158
Matthew 24:36.....138-144
Matthew 28:18.....248, 295
Matthew 28:18-20.....46-61
Matthew 28:19.....137, 142

Mark 2:7....135
Mark 2:10.....135
Mark 10:17-18.....144-146
Mark 12:28-31.....466-470
Mark 12:28-34.....74
Mark 13:32.....139

Luke 1:30-36.....101
Luke 1:34, 35.....527
Luke 1:46-47.....517
Luke 2:40, 52.....76
Luke 10:22.....135
Luke 11:20.....517
Luke 14:7-11.....146
Luke 18:9-19.....146

John 1:1.....239, 256-283, 328-333, 574
John 1:1-3.....181
John 1:1-14.....579-584
John 1:3.....211-212
John 1:10.....210, 213
John 1:14.....209, 257, 366, 440
John 1:18.....216, 239, 283-287
John 3:8.....531
John 3:16.....2, 105, 453
John 3:31-34.....527
John 3:35.....138
John 4:19-24.....54
John 4:23-24.....194
John 4:26.....417-419
John 5:18.....173-176

John 5:19-30.....181
John 5:20-24.....173
John 5:21-27.....179
John 5:23.....368
John 5:24-27.....178
John 5:26.....182
John 5:30.....176-177
John 5:37-38.....102
John 6:28-29.....161
John 6:45-46.....216
John 6:48, 51.....180
John 6:57.....180, 182, 232
John 7:16-18.....125
John 7:38.....525
John 8:24.....414
John 8:24, 28.....420-425
John 8:31-32.....95
John 8:39-40.....95
John 8:42.....93, 96
John 8:42-43.....93
John 8:50, 54.....146-147
John 8:51-55.....96
John 8:54-55.....451
John 8:58.....438-453
John 10:22-38.....287-288
John 10:30.....287-296
John 10:36.....244
John 12:36-41.....399
John 12:41.....399-413
John 12:44-50.....125
John 13:19.....425-429
John 14:1.....161, 168
John 14:6.....168
John 14:9.....217, 443
John 14:16.....520
John 14:17.....58, 520
John 14:23.....530
John 14:23-24.....162
John 14:26.....520
John 14:27-29.....169
John 14:28.....264
John 15:6.....58
John 15:26.....521
John 16:7-8.....521

Appendix

John 16:13-14.....521
John 17:2.....138, 174, 248
John 17:3.....12, 14, 41, 162-164, 196
John 17:5.....139, 165-166, 171, 440, 576
John 17:9-19.....164
John 17:10-11.....290
John 17:17.....164
John 17:17-21.....165
John 17:20.....167
John 17:20-23.....167, 290
John 17:22-24.....167
John 17:25-26.....570
John 18:5-8.....430-437
John 20:22-23.....136-137
John 20:28.....239, 253-256, 327, 589-601

Acts 1:7.....144
Acts 2:8-11.....527
Acts 2:29-33.....135
Acts 2:32.....527
Acts 2:34.....154
Acts 2:36.....43, 156
Acts 3:13.....167
Acts 3:13-15.....451-452
Acts 4:24-30.....213
Acts 5:1-11.....507
Acts 5:3-4....515
Acts 5:29-31.....452
Acts 5:32.....534
Acts 10:23.....424
Acts 10:38.....76
Acts 10:42.....160
Acts 11:26.....536-541
Acts 13:23.....119, 250
Acts 17:24-31.....214
Acts 17:29.....179
Acts 20:27.....63
Acts 20:28.....296-301

Romans 1:1-4.....130-133
Romans 1:4.....113, 130

Romans 3:2.....70
Romans 3:30.....74
Romans 5:1-5.....502
Romans 5:10.....119
Romans 6:23.....453
Romans 8:3-4.....127-128
Romans 8:11-17.....534
Romans 8:16.....519
Romans 9:5.....119, 239, 301-309
Romans 10:7-11.....14
Romans 13:8-10.....83
Romans 15:4-6.....56-57

1 Corinthians 1:1-5.....89
1 Corinthians 2:11.....523
1 Corinthians 4:6.....80
1 Corinthians 8:5-6.....42-43
1 Corinthians 8:6.....77, 171, 196, 214, 239
1 Corinthians 9:7.....212
1 Corinthians 11:2-3.....184
1 Corinthians 12:13.....526
1 Corinthians 13:12-13.....287
1 Corinthians 15:3.....129
1 Corinthians 15:23-28.....186
1 Corinthians 15:27.....142, 367
1 Corinthians 15:28.....185-208

2 Corinthians 1:21-22.....534
2 Corinthians 4:4.....212, 240
2 Corinthians 4:6.....216
2 Corinthians 5:18-19.....453
2 Corinthians 11:31.....57
2 Corinthians 13:14.....53

Galatians 3:20.....74
Galatians 3:23.....70
Galatians 4:4.....252
Galatians 4:4-7.....128
Galatians 4:6.....510

Ephesians 1:3.....57
Ephesians 1:17.....79, 253, 393
Ephesians 1:22.....45, 138

Appendix

Ephesians 2:18.....58, 61
Ephesians 2:21-22.....531
Ephesians 3:5-6.....531
Ephesians 3:17.....531
Ephesians 4:1-7.....536
Ephesians 4:14.....88
Ephesians 4:30.....507
Ephesians 5:18.....526

Philippians 2:1-11.....334-361
Philippians 2:5-11.....146
Philippians 2:6.....570-572
Philippians 2:8-11.....167
Philippians 2:9-11.....57

Colossians 1:13-17.....215
Colossians 1:15.....209, 235
Colossians 1:15-19.....215-226
Colossians 1:16.....208, 211, 214
Colossians 1:19.....371-374
Colossians 2:4-10.....370
Colossians 2:9.....369-378

1 Thessalonians 5:21.....37

1 Timothy 2:5-6.....453
1 Timothy 2:5-7.....168

2 Timothy 3:14-17.....39, 235
2 Timothy 3:15-17.....118
2 Timothy 3:16-17.....30, 234

Titus 2:13.....119, 239, 309-319

Hebrews 1:2.....208, 210, 214
Hebrews 1:3.....221, 235, 378-385
Hebrews 1:4.....247
Hebrews 1:6.....362-368
Hebrews 1:8.....239, 385-393
Hebrews 1:8-9.....253
Hebrews 1:10-12.....393-399
Hebrews 2:7.....243
Hebrews 2:14-15.....252
Hebrews 6:13.....170
Hebrews 11:1.....575

James 2:19.....74
James 3:13.....145

1 Peter 4:14-16.....557

2 Peter 1:1.....239, 319-323
2 Peter 1:16-18.....104

1 John 1:1.....104
1 John 2:2.....453
1 John 3:1.....194
1 John 3:21-24.....108
1 John 4:2-3.....107
1 John 4:7-16.....105
1 John 4:8.....82
1 John 4:9.....83
1 John 4:9-10.....453
1 John 4:13.....526
1 John 4:14.....119, 251
1 John 4:15.....107
1 John 4:24.....531
1 John 5:4-5.....106
1 John 5:5.....94
1 John 5:9-13.....107
1 John 5:18.....228-231
1 John 5:19.....244
1 John 5:20.....323-326

Jude 1:3.....33

Revelation 1:1.....139
Revelation 1:17.....585-588
Revelation 2:27.....137-138
Revelation 3:2, 12.....249, 253
Revelation 3:9.....264
Revelation 3:14.....227
Revelation 19:1-6.....158
Revelation 19:1-6.....568

Appendix

About the Author

The author, Patrick Navas, is a Christian and Bible student from Los Angeles, California. He earned a Bachelor's degree in History in 2005 and a Master's degree in Education through the University of La Verne in 2010. Currently he teaches American History at the middle school level for the Los Angeles Unified School District, but would eventually like to teach comparative religious studies at the college level.

For questions or comments, email: **patrick_navas@yahoo.com**
Or write to: 26893 Bouquet Canyon Road, Suite C, #177
Santa Clarita, CA 91350

Printed in Great Britain
by Amazon